QUESTIONS THAT MATTER

AN INVITATION TO PHILOSOPHY

W9-BZJ-722

SIXTH EDITION

ED. L. MILLER
UNIVERSITY OF COLORADO

JON JENSEN
LUTHER COLLEGE

**McGraw-Hill
Higher Education**

Boston   Burr Ridge, IL   Dubuque, IA   New York   San Francisco   St. Louis
Bangkok   Bogotá   Caracas   Kuala Lumpur   Lisbon   London   Madrid   Mexico City
Milan   Montreal   New Delhi   Santiago   Seoul   Singapore   Sydney   Taipei   Toronto

The McGraw-Hill Companies

**McGraw-Hill
Higher Education**

Published by McGraw-Hill, an imprint of The McGraw-Hill Companies, Inc., 1221 Avenue of the Americas, New York, NY 10020. Copyright © 2009, 2004, 1996, 1992, 1987, 1984. All rights reserved. No part of this publication may be reproduced or distributed in any form or by any means, or stored in a database or retrieval system, without the prior written consent of The McGraw-Hill Companies, Inc., including, but not limited to, in any network or other electronic storage or transmission, or broadcast for distance learning.

1 2 3 4 5 6 7 8 9 0 DOC/DOC 0 9 8

ISBN: 978-0-07-338656-0
MHID: 0-07-338656-1

Editor-in-chief: *Michael Ryan*
Publisher: *Lisa Moore*
Marketing manager: *Pamela Cooper*
Production editor: *Paul Wells*
Art director: *Jeanne M. Schreiber*
Art manager: *Robin Mouat*
Design manager: *Cassandra Chu*
Cover designer: *Laurie Entringer*

Production supervisor: *Tandra Jorgensen*
Media project manager: *Thomas Brierly*
Production service: *Scratchgravel Publishing Services*
Photo research coordinator: *Brian Pecko*
Photo researcher: *Poyee Oster*
Composition: *10/12 Palatino by Aptara-India*
Printing: *45# New Era Matte by R.R. Donnelley & Sons*

Cover images: Elm leaf, © Royalty-Free/Corbis. Dried leaves, © Pixtal/age fotostock

Credits: *The credits section for this book begins on page C-1 and is considered an extension of the copyright page.*

Library of Congress Cataloging-in-Publication Data
Miller, Ed. L. (Ed. LeRoy), 1937–
 Questions that matter : an invitation to philosophy/Ed. L. Miller, Jon Jensen.—6th ed.
  p. cm.
 Includes index.
 ISBN-13: 978-0-07-338656-0 (alk. paper)
 ISBN-10: 0-07-338656-1 (alk. paper)
1. Philosophy—Introductions. I. Jensen, Jon, 1967– II. Title.
BD21.M46 2009
100—dc22
                                            2008002054

The Internet addresses listed in the text were accurate at the time of publication. The inclusion of a Web site does not indicate an endorsement by the authors or McGraw-Hill, and McGraw-Hill does not guarantee the accuracy of the information presented at these sites.

www.mhhe.com

For
the fair
Cynthia
—E. L. M.

and

For Rachel,
my light
in the darkness
—J. J.

About the Authors

D. L. MILLER holds a Ph.D. in Philosophy from the University of Southern California and a Doctorate of Theology from the University of Basel, Switzerland. Professor Miller's philosophical interests encompass both the history of philosophy and philosophical theology. In addition to numerous articles and reviews, his other books include *Believing in God, Philosophical and Religious Issues, God and Reason,* and *Salvation History in the Prologue of John.* He has taught at California Lutheran University, St. Olaf College, and, for the last thirty years, at the University of Colorado, Boulder. In addition to being a member of the philosophy faculty, he also teaches for the Religious Studies Department and is Director of the Theology Forum, A Center for Theological/Philosophical Discussion. He is a member of the American Academy of Religion, the Society of Christian Philosophers, and Studiorum Novi Testamenti Societas. He is listed in *The Directory of American Scholars* and *Contemporary Authors.* Professor Miller travels regularly to Europe, and his family regards Switzerland as its "second home." Spare time is often spent on the plains doing research on the Colorado Indian War, in the mountains skiing, or on his speedboat on Lake Dillon.

JON JENSEN received his Ph.D. in Philosophy from the University of Colorado, Boulder, where he was a student of Professor Miller. While his philosophical interests vary widely, his research and publications focus on environmental philosophy. Jensen has taught at the University of Colorado, Green Mountain College, and now at Luther College, his alma mater. In addition to teaching philosophy, he directs Luther's Environmental Studies program and enjoys canoeing, bicycling, backpacking, and gardening. Jensen lives on a small farm near the Upper Iowa River with his wife, Rachel, and two young daughters, Sylvia and Lily.

Contents

PART ONE
THE QUESTION OF REALITY

8
THE WAY OF REASON 183

9
THE WAY OF EXPERIENCE 205

10
THE PROBLEM OF CERTAINTY 231

Readings from:
Kant, *Critique of Pure Reason, Prolegomena to Any Future Metaphysics*

PART THREE
THE QUESTION OF GOD

11
GOD AND THE WORLD   247

Readings from:
St. Thomas Aquinas, *Summa Contra Gentiles, Summa Theologiae;*
Jastrow, *God and the Astronomers;* Paley, *Natural Theology;* Tennant,
Philosophical Theology; Dembski, "The Intelligent Design Movement";
Black Elk Speaks; Hume, *Dialogues Concerning Natural Religion;* Kant,
Critique of Pure Reason

12
GOD AND REASON   279

Readings from:
St. Anselm, *Proslogium;* Descartes, *Meditations on First Philosophy;*
Kant, *Critique of Pure Reason;* Malcolm, *Knowledge and Certainty;*
Lewis, *Mere Christianity;* Rashdall, *The Theory of Good and Evil;*
Pascal, *Pensées;* Russell and Copleston, "The Existence of God";
Weil, *Waiting for God;* Broad, *Religion, Philosophy, and Psychical
Research;* James, *The Varieties of Religious Experience;* Freud, *The Future
of an Illusion*

PART FOUR
THE QUESTION OF MORALITY

PART FIVE
THE QUESTION OF SOCIETY

Readings from:
MacIntyre, *After Virtue*; Rawls, *A Theory of Justice*; Marty, "Rawls and the Harried Mother"; Nozick, *Anarchy, State, and Utopia*; Sheffler, "Natural Rights, Equality, and the Minimal State"; Feinberg, *Social Philosophy*; Okin, *Justice, Gender, and the Family*

Preface

The publication of this sixth edition of *Questions That Matter* comes 24 years after its initial printing and over a quarter century since the manuscript was first completed. This provides a sort of landmark because for the first time the book is older than many of the students likely to be enrolled in a traditional introduction to philosophy course. Obviously much has changed in the world in the past twenty plus years, and the book has evolved in response to these changes. But the majority of the material has not changed. It is a hallmark of philosophy that most of the "questions that matter" are timeless and remain as pressing today as they were more than 2,000 years ago when Socrates and his contemporaries were debating the nature of existence. The attempt throughout the life of this textbook has been to sustain the timeless while adapting to changing times. Hopefully we have succeeded in this attempt.

While maintaining the basic structure and approach, two major changes mark this sixth edition. First, the book is shorter by three chapters than previous editions. We responded to feedback from teachers and reviewers that the text was simply too long for the one-semester introduction to philosophy courses in which it is used. Three chapters have been cut from this editon to make a leaner, more user-friendly text. In each case, some key elements of the old have been adapted into neighboring chapters, so the basic questions are not lost even as the treatment is condensed significantly. Although we recognize that anything cut from the fifth edition will be missed by some users, we have listened to feedback in deciding where to trim the text. We hope you will agree that the benefits of a slightly shorter text outweigh the loss of important material. The second major change comes in the final section of the book, "The Question of Society," which deals with issues in social and political philosophy. Here a new chapter on democracy and a reworking of the material on liberalism update this area of philosophy that changes the most because of its inherent ties to our society and the real world of politics. We have attempted to make this section more relevant to our contemporary world while remaining firmly committed to a historical approach to the subject matter.

In addition to these changes, we have, of course, made minor adjustments throughout in the interest of accuracy, readability, and updating. Some new sections have been added and the whole has been enhanced by some new boxed material. We have continued the ongoing attempt to do justice to recent philosophical developments, especially the philosophical role and contributions of women. Beyond these improvements the book remains basically unchanged—which we take to be a plus.

As stated in previous prefaces, the book is intended as an introductory text for students whose college experience may not include a subsequent course in philosophy. We have endeavored to make lucid a very difficult and often confusing subject and, at the same time, to do justice to its history and importance. We hope that the integrity of the subject has survived our efforts at simplification and abbreviation.

In the pursuit of this goal we have been mindful of the classroom setting: (a) *The instructor's task.* The best way of showing respect and concern for the goals and methods of the individual instructor is to provide a text that is not confining or burdensome. Instead, it provides instructors with a point of departure that will enhance and strengthen their personal approaches to the subject and their goals for their students. (b) *The student's task.* Most of the students using this text will have no background in philosophy and are likely to be baffled by their first encounter with the subject's language, distinctions, concepts, and the like. This first encounter is likely to be the student's best (and for many, only) opportunity to master a subject that really does pose the questions that matter. A student can be cheated of that mastery but can never avoid the questions. Thus we have been guided throughout by a concern to represent and discuss the issues in a coherent, readable, and stimulating style. Furthermore, we have attempted to organize the content so that the students will be able to appreciate for themselves that there really are coherence and direction amid the twists and turns. We have also been guided by a conviction that explanatory aids can be utilized to promote understanding in an often difficult subject.

Our attempts to present the material in a way that will most profit the student and the classroom are evident in the following:

- Major historical thinkers have been discussed, but not to the exclusion of contemporary contributions.
- Appropriate and extended selections from primary sources have been included, interspersed throughout the discussions, making it possible for students to read the major thinkers for themselves.
- Major fields in philosophy have been included, as well as the major issues and traditions in those fields.

- No topic or issue has been excluded on the grounds that it was too difficult.
- The book seeks to accommodate the instructor's creative use of the primary materials, thus allowing him or her to develop self-designed exchange with the students.
- Fields and issues have been chosen that are most likely to be relevant to the student's mastery of elementary philosophy.

Each part of the book represents a major topic in philosophy, though instructors are encouraged to consider these topics in whatever order they deem appropriate. Each chapter contains a discussion of the relevant issues, plus a variety of supplemental material. The discussion is presented in as logical and historical a manner as possible, showing connections, roots, and influences. The issues and positions are documented with frequent and usually copious quotations from philosophers, woven into the text. The rather generous margins contain running summaries of the adjoining section. These serve the student not only as an indexing device, but also as a method for quick review of the most important ideas. At those points where basic terms, concepts, or positions need to be explained, summarized, or emphasized, the section is interrupted with a boxed insert. Still other insertions contain relevant information—for example, biographical sketches. Illustrations have been included so as to provide, on occasion, visual relief and reinforcement. Each chapter concludes with a review section that includes a brief summary, a list of basic ideas, a self-test, questions for reflection and possible discussion, and an annotated bibliography ("For Further Reading") of works of varying levels geared to assist especially in research and writing projects.

An introduction precedes the whole. Here we explain the nature of philosophy and include various definitions and concepts, as well as a discussion of issues and problems involved in the philosophical enterprise itself and its relation to other fields. We have shortened the introductory discussion of logic and focused more on informal arguments and fallacies.

With respect to the broad outline of the book, we feel that the more or less standard way of organizing and presenting philosophical material is, after all, the best. The reader will find here a much more restrained approach than may be found in some texts, which verge on the flamboyant and far-flung, and at the same time an attempt to provide, nonetheless, a visually arresting format. Furthermore, the interest in treating (whenever possible) *historical* contexts, connections, and developments can only benefit both the study and the teaching of philosophy.

This book has grown out of many years of teaching beginning philosophy courses to innumerable students. We have tried to pay attention to what works and what doesn't in the attempt to confront, engage, and instruct.

Beyond that, we have been much helped at every stage by editors at McGraw-Hill, most recently, Mark Georgiev, and previously, Jon-David Hague,

Judy Cornwell, Cynthia Ward, Kaye Pace, and Anne Murphy, and by those who reviewed the material for the sixth edition:

Christopher Eubanks, University of Arkansas
Thompson M. Faller, University of Portland
Barbara Hands, University of North Carolina at Greensboro
Andrew G. Kampiziones, Francis Marion University
Edward N. Martin, Liberty University
Norah Martin, Unversity of Portland

Closer to home Professor Miller again thanks his colleagues at the University of Colorado, including Wes Morriston, Diane Mayer, John O. Nelson, Phyllis Kenevan, Carol Cleland, Chris Shields, and my philosopher-friend, Lee Speer, who made invaluable contributions regarding the basic concept of the book and has provided excellent counsel all along the way, and other philosopher-friends, Beth and Paul Losiewicz, Paul Keyser, Paul Saalbach, and Garry Deweese. With respect to manuscript preparation, much thanks goes to several assistants; Craig Hubbard, Dan Handschy, Michael Thompson, Paul Awald, John S. Meyer, Michael McCloskey, Damian Baumgardner, Richard P. Becker, Jeff Brower, Erik M. Hanson, Glenn F. Ashton, Greg Johnson, and Deborah Nutter.

Jon Jensen wishes to thank his philosophical mentors, those people who taught me what it means to think clearly and carefully about the most important questions. Though many people have been influential, I wish to thank especially John Moeller, Richard Ylvisaker, Claudia Mills, Dale Jamieson, Jim Nickel, Bill Throop, and, of course, Ed. Miller. For help with the fifth edition, I am grateful to Anthony Smith for his diligent work. On this sixth edition, Matt Simpson, my colleague next door, was invaluable. His keen philosophical eye prevented many an error and his guidance improved Part Five significantly. Finally, and most importantly, I thank my dearest Rachel, the light and love of my life, whose support and friendship make everything possible.

> "For us who have undertaken the toil of abbreviating, it is no light matter, but calls for sweat and loss of sleep."
>
> —II Macc. 2:26 (Revised Standard Version)

Ed. L. Miller
and
Jon Jensen

QUESTIONS THAT MATTER

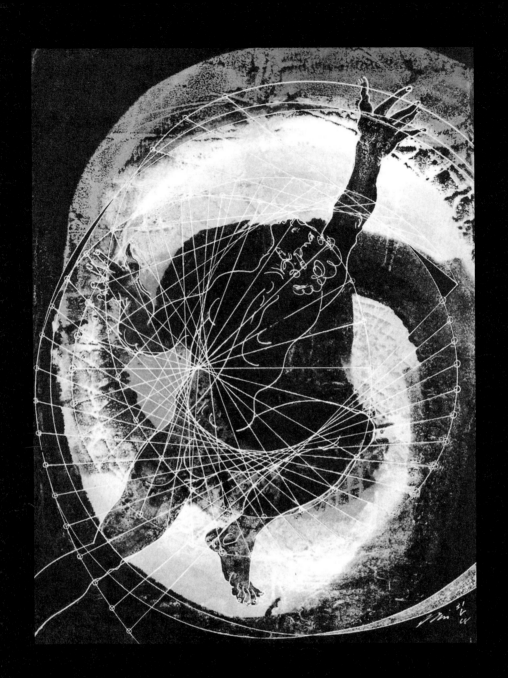

THE NATURE
OF PHILOSOPHY

"Philosophical reflection is not an activity indulged in only by specialists called philosophers who allegedly live in architectural monstrosities known as ivory towers. Just as each of us at times engages casually in horticulture or medicine or carpentry without special training, so practically all of us on certain occasions spontaneously occupy ourselves with philosophical questions.

"We may, for example, read in the newspapers of a child born hopelessly malformed and defective, but who, if operated upon at once, might nonetheless be kept alive. And we may read further that the physician in charge, realizing that the child's life could not be other than a grievous burden to himself, to his parents, and to society, refrained from operating and allowed the child to die. Then, in letters from the readers to the editors of newspapers all over the country, controversy rages about whether the physician's action was morally right or morally wrong. And even if we do not ourselves take active part in them, we too form opinions on the question.

"In such a controversy the participants do not merely state their moral appraisal of the physician's course. They also give reasons of one kind or another to support the validity of their judgment. And if these reasons are in turn challenged, each participant brings forth considerations he believes adequate to vindicate the validity of his reasons.

"The reasons, and the reasons for the reasons, that are thus appealed to as grounds for endorsing or condemning the physician's action, constitute a moral philosophy, or at least a fragment of one. And the mental activity of searching for those reasons, and of then so editing them as to purge them of the inconsistencies of exaggerations or errors that opponents were able to point out, constitute philosophizing, or philosophical reflection.

"In this example the issue is a moral one, and the philosophy constructed on the spur of the occasion by a participant is therefore, as far as it goes, a moral philosophy: that is, a theory of the nature of the difference between moral right and wrong, and the nature of the situations to which appraisal in terms of morality and immorality is congruous. But similar controversies, or indeed doubts within one person's mind, arise about issues of other kinds: about the merits of certain works of art, for example, or about educational issues, or about the sufficiency of the evidence offered as basis for a given assertion, and so on. The fragmentary philosophies similarly improvised on such occasions are then a philosophy of the art, a philosophy of education, or a philosophy of knowledge. And there can be no doubt that, on the occasions impelling us to engage in such reflection, a judgment shaped by the conclusions reached in that reflective manner is likely to be wiser than would be one made without it."

C. J. Ducasse, *The Key Reporter*, 23 (1958), p. 3.

CHAPTER 1

WHAT IS PHILOSOPHY?

nasmuch as this text seeks to introduce the reader to philosophy, it may seem appropriate to begin by defining the term. We will indeed try to define and characterize philosophy, but the reader should have no illusions that this is how one comes to understand it. The only way to understand what philosophy is about is to *participate* in it. This means to be confronted with philosophical questions, to use philosophical language, to become acquainted with differing philosophical positions and maneuvers, to read the philosophers themselves, and to grapple with the issues for oneself. Therefore it is not at the beginning but rather at the *end* of such a book as this that one might really understand something of philosophy. Nevertheless, we must begin somewhere, and it may be useful to have at least *some* idea of the subject before us, right at the start.

THE WORD ITSELF

Four ways of getting at the meaning and nature of philosophy may be proposed. *First*, let us look at the word itself. "Philosophy" comes from a Greek word that means "love of wisdom." It was first used by the ancient Greek thinker Pythagoras (about 600 B.C.), who likened philosophers—pursuers of wisdom—to spectators at ancient games:

Philosophy: The love of wisdom

> . . . when Leon the tyrant of Philius asked him who he was, he said, "A philosopher," and that he compared life to the Great Games, where some went to compete for the prize and others went with wares to sell, but the best as spectators; for

5

Pythagoras, the first to call himself a
"philosopher"

similarly, in life, some grow up with servile natures, greedy for fame and gain, but the philosopher seeks for truth.[1]

To be sure, something of the spirit and character of philosophy is suggested in this way by the very meaning of the word—but not much. We must know more about this "pursuit of wisdom."

THE FIELDS OF PHILOSOPHY

Let us then, *second,* approach the meaning of philosophy from a different standpoint—namely, from the standpoint of its several fields or areas of investigation. Not all lists of the fields of philosophy agree, but most of them would almost certainly include four: *metaphysics, epistemology, value-theory,* and *logic.* Some of these terms may seem to be taken from a foreign language, but they are not as difficult as they sound.

[1]Diogenes Laertius, *Lives of Eminent Philosophers,* VIII, 8, tr. R.D. Hicks (Cambridge, Mass.: Harvard University Press, 1925), II.

"Philosophy is like the measles. It must be caught from someone who is already infected. To learn to philosophize, you must try your luck arguing with a live philosopher."

Elmer Sprague, *What Is Philosophy?* (New York: Oxford University Press, 1961), p. 3.

As a philosophical concept, metaphysics originated in the first century B.C. when Andronicus, a scholar in Rhodes, was editing Aristotle's works. He found it difficult to classify one of these works and simply placed it *meta ta physika*, which in Greek meant "after the physical [works]." By a happy coincidence the *Metaphysics* of Aristotle did in fact concern primarily the "first principles" of things, the ultimate causes that lie after or beyond (*meta*) the physical (*physika*).

Metaphysics means, usually, the study or theory of reality. The question of metaphysics is, What is reality? What is real? This involves, of course, many related questions, such as, Is reality some kind of "thing"? Is it one or is it many? If it is one, then how is it related to the many things around us? Can ultimate reality be grasped by the five senses, or is it supernatural or transcendent? And so on. It should be mentioned that sometimes the word "metaphysics" is used in a narrower way to concern only *transcendent* reality—that is, reality that lies beyond the physical world and cannot therefore be grasped by means of the senses. Therefore supernaturalists do metaphysics in the first sense because they raise the question of reality, and they do metaphysics also in the narrower sense because they believe in supernatural or transcendent reality—say, God. On the other hand, materialists do metaphysics in the first sense because they too raise the question of reality, but their belief is not metaphysical in the narrower sense because they deny that anything is real except matter.

Metaphysics

Epistemology is the study or theory of knowledge. The question of epistemology is, What is knowledge? What does it mean "to know"? This too implies many other questions, such as, How is knowledge acquired? What, if anything, do the senses contribute to knowledge? What does reason contribute? Can we be really certain of anything? What is truth? Some philosophers think that the fields of metaphysics and epistemology are, in a way, the pillars of all the rest. Why would one say this? Are the questions, What is real? And how can I know it?, in some sense the most basic questions of all? Is it possible that how you answer these questions will determine your whole philosophical outlook?

Epistemology

Value-theory is, obviously, the study of value. The question here is, What is value? It should be noted that this question does not involve any particular sort of value, but value of *all* sorts—the value of tables, steaks, political ideologies, laws, actions. Most philosophers study value-theory in one of its subfields, where the focus is on a *particular* sort of value. *Ethics* is concerned with value as it applies to personal actions, decisions, and relations; it is concerned with *moral* value. Ethics raises questions such as, What is morally good? What is right? Are there any absolute or universal moral principles? Does the end ever justify the means? Am I my brother's keeper? Closely related to ethics is the study of *social* and *political* values, the values that determine the principles and institutions of our life together

Value-theory

Ethics

Aesthetics

in society and the state. Questions here include, What is justice? What is the basis of political authority? Which form of government is best? What rights do individuals possess? A third specific type of value-theory is *aesthetics*, which studies the values involved in art and our experience of beauty. It raises the questions, What is beauty? What is art? Are there any objective standards by which artistic works may be judged (or is beauty in the eye of the beholder)? Ethics, social/political philosophy, and aesthetics are all properly subfields of value-theory, but are more commonly studied than the question of value as such.

Logic

Logic is the study of the principles of reasoning. The question of logic is, What are the principles of right reasoning? We have saved logic for last, since traditionally it stands in a somewhat different relation to the philosopher than the other fields do. The other fields suggest something that is studied by the philosopher—reality, knowledge, value, and the like. Logic is a *tool* philosophers employ as they set about to investigate these issues. This was recognized already in antiquity. Aristotle was the first to formulate in a systematic way the principles of right reasoning, and the writings in which he did this (his "logical" writings) came to be called the *Organon*, which in Greek means "instrument" or "tool." This view of logic as a tool has, however, changed somewhat in recent years. With the rise of mathematical and symbolic logic, logic itself has become for many a proper *object* of philosophical study.

When we distinguish in this way the several fields of philosophy, we suggest something of the diversity of philosophical questions: the question of reality, the question of knowledge, the question of morality, and so on. But the questions posed by these various fields cannot, after all, be so neatly separated. In many ways these questions (and their answers) rise and fall together. Do not the questions of value-theory bear directly upon ethics, aesthetics, and metaphysics itself? Would not one's theory of reality (for example, one's affirmation or denial of God) probably hold implications for one's view of morality, knowledge, and reality? Would not the opinion that there is no certain knowledge whatsoever cast a certain light—or darkness— over all questions of reality, value, or anything else? In this way we must emphasize also the *unity* of philosophical questions.

The unity of
philosophical
questions

THE FIELDS OF PHILOSOPHY

- *Metaphysics:* The study of reality (sometimes also the study of transcendent reality).
- *Epistemology:* The study of knowledge.
- *Value-theory:* The study of value, including moral, aesthetic, social, and political values.
- *Logic:* The principles of right reasoning.

SECOND-ORDER INQUIRIES

An ordinary question, such as What is X?, is called a *first-order* question. A question about a first-order question is called a *second-order* question—for example, What is the meaning of the question, What is X? Second-order questions are also called *meta* questions, or "talk about talk." Sometimes whole studies can be oriented in the direction of second-order concerns. Thus *meta*ethics is talk about ethical talk. Philosophical areas such as philosophy of religion, philosophy of science, philosophy of law, and philosophy of education tend to be second-order inquiries. On the other hand, it is often difficult to separate talking about talk from the primary talking itself. Why would you raise a second-order issue unless you were interested in the primary issue in the first place?

In addition to the standard fields of philosophy some further areas should be mentioned—namely, where philosophical concern relates itself to other disciplines, the "philosophy of _____" category. Examples are the philosophy of religion, philosophy of science, philosophy of education, and philosophy of law. Here a particular discipline is viewed and treated *philosophically;* the philosopher is concerned with such issues as the nature of that discipline's subject matter, the adequacy of its methodology, the meaning and clarification of its concepts, its logical coherence, and its relation to and implications for other fields. In the "philosophy of _____" studies, it is sometimes difficult to separate the *primary* subject (religion, science, education, law) from the *secondary* questions raised by the philosopher (questions concerning methodology, concepts, logic relations). Nonetheless, it should be clear that the "philosophy of _____" studies are largely second-order studies—that is, studies *about* studies. If, for example, you ever take a course in the philosophy of science, you won't light any Bunsen burners, collect any specimens, or dissect any frogs. What you will do is think and talk *about* science. That is, you will analyze the meaning of science, scientific language and concepts, scientific procedures, conclusions, and implications.

The "philosophy of _____" areas

Second-order studies

It should be noted, though, that in actual usage the distinction between the fields of philosophy and the "philosophy of _____" areas is not hard and fast. Aesthetics, for example, could accurately be represented as the philosophy of art, whereas philosophy of religion would certainly raise, say, the metaphysical issue of God's existence and nature.

A RATIONAL, CRITICAL ENTERPRISE

In our *third* attempt to characterize philosophy we propose something more illuminating than giving the root meaning of the word and something less cumbersome than defining its several fields. And we come to the heart of the matter when we suggest that whatever else it may be, philosophy is a *rational* and *critical* enterprise.

Philosophy involves reason, criticism, examination, analysis

SOCRATES

S ocrates was born in Athens about 470 B.C. He must have come from a fairly well-to-do family (there is some evidence that his father was a stonecutter), since as a young man he was a fully armed hoplite (foot soldier) in the army. His appearance and character are notorious. He is said to have resembled a satyr (mythological creature, half human and half goat), we know that he had a

(*continued on next page*)

The word "rational" is important. Sometimes in philosophical discussion the words "rational," "rationalist," and "rationalism" are used with a rather technical meaning, as we shall see later. But here we intend these words in a more ordinary and loose sense. They have to do with *reason* and *reasonableness*. A rational argument, for example, is one that makes sense, is coherent, and is well founded. A rationalist is a person who is given to argument, investigation, and evaluation. And rationalism is the

RATIONALISM (THE LOOSE SENSE)

The view that affirms reason, with its interest in evidence, examination, and evaluation, as authoritative in all matters of belief and conduct.

pug nose, and the comic dramatist Aristophanes represented him as strutting like a waterfowl and rolling his eyes. We also know that he was a man of considerable physical endurance: He could spend long hours in meditation (once, a whole day and night) uninterrupted by the need for food; he once went barefoot on a wintry military expedition; and he could consume vast amounts of wine without becoming the least bit tipsy. More than once he distinguished himself for bravery during the Peloponnesian War, during which time he married Xanthippe, who according to tradition was one of the world's outstanding shrews. In Plato's *Symposium*, Socrates represents himself as having been instructed by Diotima, a prophetess-philosopher, who—if she actually existed—was an important thinker indeed.

In the *Apology* (Plato's account of Socrates' trial) Socrates relates the origin of his philosophical mission: Once a friend of Socrates asked the Delphic Oracle who the wisest of men was, to which the Oracle responded, "Socrates." Socrates himself was much perplexed by this answer and concluded that if indeed he was wisest it could only be because he was so aware of his *ignorance*. Much turned off by the Sophists, who seemed to him to be more interested in the appearance of truth than in truth itself (and even charged for their instruction), Socrates pursued abiding and fixed truth. In fact, Aristotle credits him with being the first to seek *definitions*, especially of moral ideas such as justice and piety. Socrates utilized *dialogue* as the method of this pursuit, confronting, interrogating, and wheedling his adversaries into clearer thinking.

Eventually, on the wrong side politically, he was tried and found guilty of trumped-up charges of teaching strange gods and corrupting the youth. He scorned the opportunity of escaping prison and willingly drank the poisonous hemlock. The year was 399 B.C.

Although universally regarded as the model of the philosophical spirit, and in some ways as the founder of Western philosophy, Socrates never published a word—and thus today would have been denied tenure at any major university.

position that affirms reason as one of the highest authorities—maybe even *the* highest authority—in matters of belief and conduct. There is, in all of this, a certain *critical* activity that must not be missed. In being a *rational* enterprise, philosophy seeks to eradicate from our perspectives every taint and vestige of ignorance, superstition, prejudice, blind acceptance of ideas, and any other form of irrationality. It challenges our ideas, analyzes them, and tests them in light of evidence and arguments. It presses us to coherent and valid expressions of our ideas.

The early Greek philosopher Socrates (ca. 470–399 B.C.) has always been regarded as a kind of *symbol* of philosophical activity, especially its rational and critical nature. It is no wonder. Socrates was constantly pressing himself and everyone else for clarity and answers. His method was to engage someone over the meaning of some term or idea, usually a moral concept, and then to cross-examine his opponent mercilessly until some progress or clarity was achieved. According to Plato's *Apology* (an account of Socrates'

Socrates: the symbol of philosophical activity

> "...it is owing to their wonder that men both now begin and at first began to philosophize; they wondered originally at the obvious difficulties, then advanced little by little and stated difficulties about the greater matters."
>
> —Aristotle

defense at his trial), Socrates likens himself to a gadfly that incessantly stings and disturbs and challenges the citizenry:

> If you put me to death, you will not easily find anyone to take my place. It is literally true, even if it sounds rather comical, that God has specially appointed me to this city, as though it were a large thoroughbred horse which because of its great size is inclined to be lazy and needs the stimulation of some stinging fly. It seems to me that God has attached me to this city to perform the office of such a fly, and all day long I never cease to settle here, there, and everywhere, rousing, persuading, reproving every one of you. You will not easily find another like me, gentlemen, and if you take my advice you will spare my life. I suspect, however, that before long you will awake from your drowsing, and in your annoyance you will take Anytus' advice and finish me off with a single slap, and then you will go on sleeping till the end of your days, unless God in his care for you sends someone to take my place....[2]

"The unexamined life is not worth living."

It is from this same context that perhaps the most famous line of all philosophical literature comes: "The unexamined life is not worth living":

> I tell you that to let no day pass without discussing goodness and all the other subjects about which you hear me talking and examining both myself and others is really the very best thing that a man can do, and that life without this sort of examination is not worth living....[3]

The limits of reason

As in Socrates, the accent in all philosophy clearly falls on reason and criticism. But can *everything* be reasoned? Must *every* proposition, idea, and belief be exposed to the searchlight of critical reflection? Some philosophers would answer with a loud Yes. Others would not be so optimistic, insisting that there are *limits* to the rational and critical enterprise. If true, then this in itself is an important fact about philosophy and must be reckoned with constantly. Many philosophers do in fact recognize that reality and our experience of it are, after all, bigger than philosophy: Not everything can be grasped intellectually; not everything can be reduced to an argument; not everything can be expressed in language. But what happens at the point where reason gives out? Do we simply draw a blank? Some would say that it is at this point that the *nonrational* too plays a role, and even an inevitable role. But it is important here that we do not confuse "nonrational"

Nonrational and irrational

[2]Plato, *Apology*, 30D–31A, in *The Last Days of Socrates*, tr. Hugh Tredennick (Harmondsworth: Penguin Classics, 1954.)

[3]Ibid., 38A.

NONRATIONAL AND IRRATIONAL

- A *nonrational* claim is one that is justified, if at all, through an appeal to something *other* than or *different* from reason. Authority, feeling, intuition, religious illumination, mystical experience, and the like are all nonrational justifications. Example: "I believe in heaven because of my faith in God."
- An *irrational* claim is *contrary* to reason. There are two forms of irrational claims.
  1. A claim that flies in the face of everything we would expect from history, experience, and nature.
     Example: "Herds of giraffes are currently roaming the White House." This is highly improbable and absurd, but it could conceivably be true.

  2. A claim that could not conceivably be true; it involves a self-contradiction and is therefore logically impossible.
     Example: "I have a collection of round squares."

with "irrational." That which is *ir*rational is incompatible with general experience or reason itself, whereas that which is *non*rational is simply different from and maybe even higher than experience or reason.

If we *do* believe in nonrational knowledge, what forms might it take? Certainly philosophers disagree among themselves about the possible significance of the claims of intuition in the sense of an immediate and direct apprehension of truth, mystical experience as a transcendent and ecstatic union with ultimate reality, various forms of religious and inner illumination, poetic visions or feelings, and the like. On the other hand, many would agree at least on the inevitable presence of *ultimate presuppositions* (also called basic assumptions, faith assertions, etc.) that are known with certainty as the foundations of all of our other ideas but that themselves cannot be proved. This view is known as *foundationalism.* Probably the most common defense of this view is the claim that from a purely logical standpoint not everything can be argued or there would never be an end to the arguing. A long time ago Aristotle pointed out that every argument finally rests on something that cannot be proved, and that it is the mark of an uneducated person not to realize that. There must be, as it were, a last outpost or final court of appeal. Do you believe with foundationalists that every philosophical system or position or argument necessarily rests at some point or other on some idea or ideas that are certain and basic and undemonstrable? If so, then you must believe that here, if no place else, the *non*rational too makes a contribution.

Foundationalism

A WORKING DEFINITION

Perhaps, *finally,* we may pose a working definition of philosophy, one that does some justice to what we have seen to be both its theme and its variations: *Philosophy is the attempt to think rationally and critically about the most important questions.*

Philosophy defined

The *theme* is that philosophy is a rational and critical activity. Philosophizing in all forms seeks to think and to think hard about something. But about what? Here we have the *variation*. There are quite differing ideas as to what philosophy should be rational and critical *about*. Still, even here philosophers have in common that they see themselves as addressing the really important questions, questions that are fundamental to everything.

PHILOSOPHY, RELIGION, AND SCIENCE

If this is what philosophy is, then how does it stand in relation to those two other great enterprises, *religion* and *science*?

What is religion?

As if we did not already have enough problems, "religion" is a slippery word indeed, as is evident from looking in any dictionary. But two things are clear. First, religion has to do with many of the same things philosophy has to do with: ultimate reality, the meaning of life, good and evil, immortality, human nature, and so on. In fact, religion usually involves *beliefs* about such things and beliefs that are worked out and adhered to in a fairly systematic and fixed manner, though perhaps not in as critical a manner as in philosophy. Second, in addition to this intellectual aspect of religion is a more important one, one that concerns not so much the thinking as the *willing* side of our being. What is really distinctive about religion is the *commitment* it involves.

It may be helpful to note that this latter aspect of religion is true to the very origin of the word: "Religion" comes from the Latin *religare*, which means "to bind one thing to another." The religious individual is someone who is personally *bound* to something. This something is usually understood to be God, and the worship of God and active participation in rituals, ceremonies, and proclamation are further evidence for the existential rather than intellectual character of religion. We might ask, however, whether the object of such commitment must be *God*. Perhaps the object of such commitment

Religion as ultimate concern

need only be something *ultimate*—as the German-American theologian Paul Tillich said, one's "ultimate concern." Could this something as easily be a political cause? the pursuit of pleasure? the acquisition of wealth? But then again, Tillich reminds us that some things may be perceived as being ultimate that really are not. Is it possible to be bound "religiously" to something that is not ultimate, to have an *idolatrous* faith, to be worshipping an idol instead of a real thing? Be that as it may, religion would appear to have mainly to do not so much with our intellects as with our decision, action, worship, and love—not so much with what we think as with what we do.

What is science?

Science brings us back to the *study* of something. In fact, our word "science" comes from the Latin *scientia*, which means simply "knowledge." It was in this sense of the word that it was held (and still is by some) that "theology is the queen of the sciences and philosophy is her hand-maid." For most people the word has lost this original meaning and is now used sometimes to refer to the *social* sciences (such as sociology, psychology, anthropology, etc.) but more often to the *natural* sciences (such as physics,

"Life without philosophy is inconceivable."

—Socrates

"Philosophy is a silent dialogue between the soul and itself."

—Plato

"All men by nature desire to know."

—Aristotle

biology, chemistry, astronomy, etc.). Almost always the words "science" and "scientist" are associated with such things as test tubes, dissections, microscopes, telescopes, periodic charts, nuclear fission chambers, and laboratories occupied by people wearing white jackets.

Taken in this usual sense, science is easily related to philosophy. *Like* philosophy science is the pursuit of knowledge: It is an intellectual activity and it *studies* something. *Unlike* philosophy, however, its focus is much more restricted. Specifically, it narrows its focus to the study of the *natural world alone*, whereas our experience of nature may be but one aspect of the total reality that interests philosophers. Likewise, the scientific *method* is more restricted than the philosopher's method may be. Inasmuch as scientists are interested in the world of nature, they naturally employ primarily the tools of *observation* and *experimentation*: the test tubes, dissections, microscopes, and telescopes mentioned above.

Science: the study of the natural world

A LITTLE LOGIC

But back to philosophy. We have seen that philosophers and careful thinkers strive to make their arguments, positions, and pronouncements *rational*—that is, well conceived, well evidenced, well stated, and persuasive. To ensure this goal philosophers pay attention to the philosophical discipline of *logic*, which we have already defined as the study of right reasoning. Not that there is any choice about it. The philosopher, and others who reason critically, can no more do without logic than the physicist can do without mathematics. It is the tool or, as someone has suggested, the "key" to philosophizing.

Logic: the key to philosophizing

From the traditional logic first formulated by Aristotle to the various forms of contemporary symbolic and mathematical logic (which seem to many like a foreign language), the science of logic has become a very complicated and sophisticated business. A real course in logic would have to take up many matters: the nature and uses of language, problems of definition, types of propositions, types of arguments, the construction and use of symbolic languages, probability theory, the nature of hypotheses and theories, and so on. We cannot do much here, but a beginner in philosophy should be introduced at least to some of the bare elements of logic, especially arguments and fallacies.

When you see the word "argument" you might think of disagreements or quarrels, often accompanied by shouting, clenched fists, tears, and the like. Well, an argument might or might not involve these things. Consider the following interchange:

> *A:* Capital punishment is immoral.
> *B:* No it isn't!
> *A:* Yes it is!
> *B:* Well, what do *you* know about it?!
> *A:* I know more about it than you do!
> *B:* Oh yeah? You're an idiot!

Argument: premises, conclusion...

There is plenty of disagreement and lots of noise here but no *argument*. An argument is an attempt to show that something is true by providing evidence for it. More technically, it is a group of statements in which one is said to follow from at least one other. The statement that follows from the others—that is, the "something to be shown"—is called the *conclusion;* the statements from which the conclusion follows—that is, the evidence—are called *premises.* Thus we have the argument

> It is immoral to kill persons.
> Capital punishment is the killing of persons.
>
> Therefore, capital punishment is immoral.

in which the first two statements are the premises of the argument and the third is the conclusion. Naturally, in an argument not just any old statements can serve as premises and conclusion, as in

> In fourteen hundred and ninety-two,
> Columbus sailed the ocean blue.
> Switzerland exports many cuckoo-clocks.
>
> Therefore, capital punishment is immoral.

...and inference

but there must be some *connection* between them. This connection, by which the conclusion is said "to follow" from the premises, is called an *inference,* or, more technically, an *entailment.*

In ordinary discourse, arguments may be presented in a variety of ways. Usually, though, there are certain words or expressions that introduce premises and other words that introduce conclusions. We list here just a few of them:

Premise signals: Since, because, for, as, inasmuch as, otherwise, in view of the fact that, for the reason that

Conclusion signals: Therefore, thus, accordingly, we may infer, which shows that, points to the conclusion that, as a result

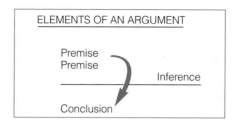

ELEMENTS OF AN ARGUMENT

Premise
Premise
Inference
_____
Conclusion

Can you separate the premises from the conclusion in the following argument?

> . . . for a producer to convince the institutions which finance movies that his film will be profitable, he has to line up a "bankable" star; and if he has a project for a political movie, the star is unlikely to sign on if he doesn't agree with the film's politics. Which means that the political movies the public is getting from Hollywood today represent, by and large, the political thinking of actors.[4]

What is the nature of the connection between premises and conclusion—the inference—that results in arguments? Here the important distinction between *deductive* and *inductive* arguments comes into play. It is sometimes said that deductive arguments reason from the whole to the part, or from the general to the specific, as in

Deductive and inductive arguments

All humans are mortal. — universal proposition
Socrates is a human.

Therefore, Socrates is mortal. — particular proposition

whereas inductive arguments reason from the part to the whole, or from the specific to the general, as in

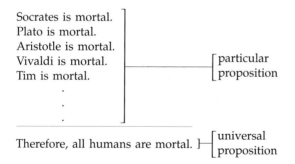

Socrates is mortal.
Plato is mortal.
Aristotle is mortal.
Vivaldi is mortal.
Tim is mortal.
  .
  .
  .

— particular proposition

Therefore, all humans are mortal. — universal proposition

While this is certainly true of *some* deductive and inductive arguments, it fails to express their real nature. What is more important, again, is the kind of connection that exists between premises and conclusion in deductive and

---

[4]Richard Grenier, "Jane Fonda & Other Political Thinkers," *Commentary*, June 1979.

Aristotle, credited as the first to formulate systematically the principles of reasoning. His "logical works" were eventually collected and issued under the title *Organon*.

inductive arguments. In a valid deductive argument the premises ensure, or *guarantee*, the conclusion: If the premises are true, the conclusion *must* be true also. It is a matter of *necessity*. In a good inductive argument, on the other hand, the premises *suggest* the conclusion ("to induce" means "to influence" or "to persuade"): If the premises are true, the conclusion is *probably* true. It is a matter of *probability*.

Let us consider deductive arguments a little further. What is this necessity we spoke of when we said that if the premises are true, the conclusion *must* be true? Why *must* the conclusion be true? Answer: By virtue of a relation of *entailment*, or logical implication, between terms or propositions in the premises: "To entail" means "to include" or "to involve." Thus deductive entailment has to do with the way in which a term or proposition may be included in another. And the way in which *this* may be done so as to result in a valid argument is specified by *valid argument forms*.

The syllogism

The most traditional and yet one of the most common forms of a deductive argument is the *syllogism*. This is a type of argument consisting of two premises and a conclusion ("syllogism" comes from a Greek word meaning "propositions considered together"). An example of a valid syllogism, or at least the *form* of one, is

All *X* are *Y*.
All *Y* are *Z*.

Therefore, all *X* are *Z*.

"A syllogism is a reasoning in which something different emerges with necessity from what has been laid down."

—Aristotle

A possible translation, or substitution for the symbols, might be

> All politicians are liars.
> All liars are despicable.
>
> Therefore, all politicians are despicable.

One of the most important things to appreciate here is that deductive validity has to do with *form,* and form *alone.* What makes an argument valid is that it conforms to a valid argument *form.* But there is a big difference between *validity* and *truth.* An argument may be absolutely valid even though every statement in it is false:

Truth, validity, and soundness

> All politicians are Communists.
> Babe Ruth is a politician.
>
> Therefore, Babe Ruth is a Communist.

It goes without saying that every proposition, including the conclusion, in an argument might be true, and the argument be invalid nonetheless:

> All U.S. presidents have been males.
> Abraham Lincoln was a male.
>
> Therefore, Abraham Lincoln was a U.S. president.

Obviously, what we are interested in is *both* validity and truth. We may call a deductive argument that is valid *and* whose premises are true a "sound" argument.

TRUTH, VALIDITY, AND SOUNDNESS

- *Valid* arguments display proper deductive *form.*
- *True* statements are possible in any argument regardless of form.
- *Sound* arguments have both *valid* form and *true* premises.

INDUCTIVE REASONING

It is hardly possible to give a better example of the essential nature of inductive reasoning than that provided by the master sleuth himself, Sherlock Holmes, whose "powers of deduction" were actually powers of *induction*. Look at the procedure and kinds of evidence he employs in *The Hound of the Baskervilles*:

"So far as I can follow you, then, Mr. Holmes," said Sir Henry Baskerville, "someone cut out this message with a scissors—"

"Nail-scissors," said Holmes. "You can see that it was a very short-bladed scissors, since the cutter had to take two snips over 'keep away.'"

"That is so. Someone, then, cut out the message with a pair of short-bladed scissors, pasted it with paste—"

"Gum," said Holmes.

"With gum on to the paper. But I want to know why the word 'moor' should have been written?"

"Because he could not find it in print. The other words were all simple and might be found in any issue, but 'moor' would be less common."

"Why, of course, that would explain it. Have you read anything else in this message, Mr. Holmes?"

"There are one or two indications, and yet the utmost pains have been taken to remove all clues. The address, you observe, is printed in rough characters. But the *Times* is a paper which is seldom found in any hands but those of the highly educated. We may take it, therefore, that the letter was composed by an educated man who wished to pose as an uneducated one, and his effort to conceal his own writing suggests that that writing might be known, or come to be known, by you. Again, you will observe that the words are not gummed on in an accurate line, but that some are much higher than others. 'Life,' for example, is quite out of its proper place. That may point to carelessness or it

(*continued on next page*)

Not necessity, but probability

We have seen above that in deductive arguments validity in the form results in a conclusion that follows as a matter of necessity. In the case of inductive arguments, however, there is no question of validity at all, and therefore no logical necessity in the conclusion can be expected. What *is* aimed at is truth in the premises and probability in the conclusion. It cannot be stressed too strongly that no inductive argument can deliver a conclusion that is demonstratively certain. The most that can be hoped for is a degree of probability, though the more supportive the premises, the more reasonable and the higher the probability of the conclusion. Thus, as with deductive arguments, not just any old premises will do. Here too there must be an inference between premises and conclusion, just as in deductive arguments. On the other hand, whereas in deductive arguments the inference is a strictly *logical* one resulting in a *necessary* conclusion, in inductive arguments the inference is a *supportive* one resulting in a *probable* conclusion.

may point to agitation and hurry upon the part of the cutter. On the whole I incline to the latter view, since the matter was evidently important, and it is unlikely that the composer of such a letter would be careless. If he were in a hurry it opens up the interesting question why he should be in a hurry, since any letter posted up to early morning would reach Sir Henry before he would leave his hotel. Did the composer fear an interruption—and from whom?"

"We are coming now rather into the region of guess work," said Dr. Mortimer.

"Say, rather, into the region where we balance probabilities and choose the most likely. It is the scientific use of the imagination, but we have always some material basis on which to start our speculations. Now, you would call it a guess, no doubt, but I am almost certain that this address has been written in an hotel."

"How in the world can you say that?"

"If you examine it carefully you will see that both the pen and the ink have given the writer trouble. The pen has spluttered twice in a single word, and has run dry three times in a short address, showing that there was very little ink in the bottle. Now, a private pen or ink-bottle is seldom allowed to be in such a state, and the combination of the two must be quite rare. But you know the hotel ink and the hotel pen, where it is rare to get anything else. Yes, I have very little hesitation in saying that could we examine the wastepaper baskets of the hotels round Charing Cross until we found the remains of the mutilated *Times* leader we could lay our hands straight upon the person who sent this singular message.*

This is an excellent illustration of what goes on in inductive arguments: moving from particular facts here, analogies there, common threads and connections everywhere, to a conclusion that is suggested by all of that evidence.

*A. Conan Doyle, *The Hound of the Baskervilles* (New York: McClure, Phillips & Co., 1902), pp. 46–48.

What is the connection, this "supportive inference," between premises and conclusion in an inductive argument that makes the conclusion at least reasonable and probable? We note here just two of the ways in which inductive arguments can take shape.

DEDUCTION AND INDUCTION

- *In a valid deductive argument:* If the premises are true, the conclusion must be true, by virtue of a logically necessary inference.

- *In a strong inductive argument:* If the premises are true, the conclusion is probably true, by virtue of a supportive inference.

The method of
generalization

The first and most obvious form of inductive reasoning is to *generalize* on the basis of particular instances. The simplest of this kind of argument is called *universal generalization* and has the form

Instance 1 of A is observed to be X.
Instance 2 of A is observed to be X.
Instance 3 of A is observed to be X.
Instance 4 of A is observed to be X.
Instance 5 of A is observed to be X.
.
.
.

Therefore, all A is X.

The method
of analogy

Quite different from the inductive methods of generalization is the method of *analogy*. This kind of reasoning can take many different forms, but its essential nature is indicated by

A is observed to be X and Y.
B is observed to be X and Y.
C is observed to be X and Y.
D is observed to be X and Y.
.
.
.

M is observed to be X.

Therefore, M is Y.

That is, if M is analogous, or similar, to A, B, C, D . . . in being X, it is probably also similar in being Y.

FALLACIES

Formal and informal
fallacies

Although logic covers many topics, understanding faulty reasoning or fallacies is one key component. Logical fallacies are often divided into two types: formal and informal. *Formal* fallacies are mistakes in reasoning that result from breaking some rule of validity: mistakes with respect to the *form* of an argument. A course in logic focuses primarily on deductive arguments and formal fallacies. *Informal* fallacies are quite different. They are mistakes that arise from carelessness with respect to the relevance of ideas or carelessness with respect to the clarity and consistency of our language. There are many such fallacies. We list here only some of the most common ones. Mastery of them will prevent many unnecessary blunders in philosophical discussion and, for that matter, any discussion whatsoever.

1. **Loaded language** is language with the sole purpose of swaying the emotions of the audience for or against an argument. Example: "It's

LOGICAL FALLACIES

- *Formal fallacies:* Mistakes in reasoning due to a failure in following the rules for the formal structure of valid arguments. These fallacies do not concern truth or falsity but validity.

- *Informal fallacies:* Mistakes in reasoning due to carelessness regarding relevance and clarity of language. These fallacies bear directly on issues of truth and falsity.

murder in cold blood. How could anyone say she has a right to have an abortion?"

2. **Equivocation** occurs when a word or expression changes its meaning in the course of an argument, sometimes referred to as a "weasel word." Example: "Everyone says she has good taste, so I would love to nibble her ear."

3. **Begging the question** occurs when the conclusion of an argument is already present, usually disguised, in one of its premises; also called circular reasoning. Example: "You can't expect eighteen-year-olds to vote intelligently because they are too young to have good judgment about the issues."

4. **Ad hominem** (appeal to the person) irrelevantly attacks the person making a claim rather than attacking the claim itself. Example: "You pro-choice people are selfless, godless, and immoral—probably Communists, too!"

5. **Straw man** inappropriately simplifies an opposing argument so that it becomes a cartoon or caricature of the true argument and is easy to refute. Example: "Now the anti-handgun fundamentalist will tell you that the mere presence of a loaded pistol means that Mr. Finnegan is going to get drunk and shoot Mrs. Finnegan. Or that the Finnegan grandchild will one day play with the pistol, it will go off, and there will be tragedy."

6. **"Person who"** is the fallacy of generalizing or drawing a conclusion from too little information. Also called a hasty induction, it often takes the form of "I knew a person who..." and then draws a conclusion based on one instance. Example: "Smoking does not cause cancer. My Uncle Joe smoked three packs of Camels every day for fifty-three years; then he died in an auto accident without even a trace of cancer."

7. **Ad populum** (appeal to the masses) seeks to stengthen a claim by an emotional appeal to the passions and prejudices of the listeners. Example: "Don't you think we all should get out early today?"

8. **Ad ignorantiam** (appeal to ignorance) affirms the truth of something on the basis of the lack of evidence to the contrary. Example: "The

FIND THE FALLACY!

Here are some examples of reasoning that involve informal fallacies. Can you identify them?

1. "I'm all for women having equal rights," said Bullfight Association president Paco Camino. "But I repeat, women shouldn't fight bulls because a bullfighter is and should be a man."

   San Francisco Chronicle, March 28, 1972

2. The Moral Majority's Rev. Jerry Falwell . . . claims that Jesus Christ favored the death penalty. On the Cross, Falwell says, He could have spoken up: "If ever there was a platform for our Lord to condemn capital punishment, that was it. He did not."

   Time, January 24, 1983

3. America is one of the few democracies to employ the death penalty, yet the death penalty has not been proved to deter criminals.

   Colorado Daily, May 24–27, 1991

4. Mysticism is one of the great forces of the world's history. For religion is nearly the most important thing in the world, and religion never remains for long altogether untouched by mysticism.

   John McTaggart and Ellis McTaggart,
   "Mysticism," *Philosophical Studies*, 1934

5. I also admit that there are people for whom even the reality of the external world . . . constitutes a grave problem. My answer is that I do not address them, but that I presuppose a minimum of reason in my readers.

   Paul Feyerabend, "Materialism and the Mind-Body
   Problem," *Review of Metaphysics,* 1963

(*continued on next page*)

superb quality of her character can be demonstrated by the fact that I've never heard a word spoken against her."

9. **Red herring** introduces an irrelevant or unimportant topic in order to divert attention from the main question. The term "red herring" comes from the practice of dragging a strong-smelling fish across the trail during fox hunts in order to confuse the hounds. Example: *Q:* "Should handguns be banned?" *A:* "Everybody talks about handgun accidents. But think of how many people are killed each year in auto accidents! Why don't we ban automobiles?"

10. **False dilemma** involves limiting the options considered to only two in a way that is unfair to the person facing the dilemma. This is the same as the failure to adequately consider alternatives. Example: "It seems to me that a person just can't win when it comes to what you eat. Either you eat meat and cause veal calves to be tortured or you starve to death on bread and water."

6. If elected, would you try to fool some of the people all of the time, all of the people some of the time or go for the big one: all of the people all of the time?

TV Guide cartoon

7. Pity the many teens who are influenced by atheism, humanism and secularism, who are swept along by vulgar dance and pornography and who party on drugs, tobacco and liquor. Sex is for marriage. Other ways breed heartache.

Letter to the Editor, *Time*, Dec. 30, 1985

8. LOTS of things are invisible, but we don't know how many because we can't SEE them.

"Dennis the Menace" cartoon

9. It's too bad that Mother Teresa cannot view other religions as being valid and as authentic as her own Roman Catholicism. Her holier-than-thou attitude toward Hinduism, Buddhism, Islam and Judaism smacks of bigotry and condescension.

Letter to the Editor, *Time*, Dec. 4, 1989

10. According to R. Grunberger, author of *A Social History of the Third Reich*, published in Britain, the Nazis used to send the following notice to German readers who let their subscriptions lapse: "Our paper certainly deserves the support of every German. We shall continue to forward copies of it to you, and hope that you will not want to expose yourself to unfortunate consequences in the case of cancellation."

Parade, May 9, 1971

11. As the loving mother of three happy children, I prefer the "silent scream" of the unwanted fetus to the reverberating cry of the unwanted child.

Letter to the Editor,
Time, April 15, 1985

PROFESSOR MILLER'S FOUR PRINCIPLES

It will be apparent soon enough that this book has a decidedly historical cast. To be sure, we want to pay attention to logic and current developments. But we want also to know about those thinkers, movements, and broad perspectives, strewn over 2,500 years, that have brought us where we are today and otherwise confront us with so many—yes—philosophical options. There are, however, pitfalls in the study of historical philosophy. As warnings against these pitfalls I have formulated Four Principles for the Study of the History of Philosophy. Heeding these principles may save you lots of misunderstanding and other troubles:

- The Clarification Principle
- The Deculturalization Principle
- The Modified Sergeant Friday Principle
- The Smartness Principle

ὁ δὲ ἀνεξέταστος βίος οὐ βιωτὸς ἀνθρώπῳ

"For man, the unexamined life is not worth living."

—Socrates

The *Clarification Principle* asserts that it is always easier to appreciate the clarity of an idea once the idea has been clarified. The point here is that we should not judge too harshly those who have not benefited from long years of critical reflection and consequent clarification of ideas. Some distinctions are hard to see until they are seen; then they are *easy* to see. Also, some claims are *obviously* true once the competing claims have been shown to be impossible; and so on.

According to the *Deculturalization Principle,* the real substance of philosophy should never be confused with the cultural elements necessarily involved in its expression. Any philosophy, in the attempt to express itself, must resort, for example, to a certain language. And is it a surprise that a philosophy may reflect a prevailing view of the physical universe, or draw upon standard ideas about the soul, or employ examples from conventional morality or images from popular religion? The important point is to recognize that these may be purely incidental to the real point, and not to throw out the baby with the bathwater. What is called for is, rather, a setting free of the real philosophy from these purely accidental features inevitably involved in its expression for a particular audience at a particular time and place.

The *Modified Sergeant Friday Principle* seeks to instill a healthy respect for the text—that is, what the philosopher actually wrote: "Just the text, ma'am, just the text."[5] It may, of course, sometimes be necessary or useful to speculate on what a philosopher might have said, should have said, or could have said, or to try to fill in some gaps or draw some inferences, but one must never lose sight of what is actually there in the text. That, in the end, is all we have.

Finally, the *Smartness Principle:* Always assume that the philosopher is smarter than you are. The danger here is that a philosopher may say something that seems to you to be silly, stupid, or absurd, so you give up on it, whereas if you had stayed with it you might have learned that, in the larger context or with further explanation, it wasn't stupid at all. It may, of course, turn out that you were right—"That really *was* dumb!"—but that too is something you may not be sure of if you throw in the towel too soon.

I don't pretend that these are the only principles relevant for the study of the history of philosophy, but I do claim that they're good ones and that they're suggestive of the sorts of concerns that make for solid study.

---

[5]For those readers who are too young to know, Sergeant Friday was the main character in the radio, and then TV, program *Dragnet*. He often responded to overly enthusiastic witnesses with a pointed "Just the facts, ma'am, just the facts."

FEMINIST PHILOSOPHY

It has often been observed that women are, by and large, conspicuous by their absence from the history of philosophy. It is true, for example, that in the massive *Encyclopedia of Philosophy* one searches in vain for women in philosophy, except for the most incidental references. Some have felt that there may be more going on here than meets the eye.

Feminist philosophers argue that a male bias has been at work in our philosophical tradition, resulting not only in excluding important contributions by women but even controlling some of our basic philosophical concepts. In the following extracts from an article in the *American Philosophical Association Newsletter on Feminism and Philosophy,* Alison Jaggar emphasizes the first, briefly develops "dualistic thinking" as an example of the second, and concludes that, if real, the male bias in philosophy betrays some of the ideals of philosophy itself.

The western philosophical tradition at first sight appears to be almost exclusively the creation of male minds. No woman is listed among the great names of philosophy, and those women whose names are mentioned in a philosophical context usually are presented as having made at best minor contributions. Harriet Taylor, for instance, is admitted to have helped J. S. Mill, but Mill's strong assertion that she was his main philosophical inspiration invariably is discounted. Other women in the history of philosophy fare even worse: Socrates' wife, Xanthippe, was a nag, seeking to divert her husband from his philosophical midwifery, while Queen Christina of Sweden was so immoderate in her demands that she caused Descartes' death by making him get up too early in the morning.

The apparent absence of women from the western tradition is far from entirely illusory. There is no doubt that women's opportunities to enter into philosophical discourse have been curtailed severely by lack of education and by other social constraints. Nevertheless, some feminists believe that a few women did manage to make a philosophical contribution, but that this contribution has been overlooked because of bias against work by women. . . .

One persistent theme in both French and Anglo-American feminist philosophy is a criticism of dualistic modes of conceptualization. Feminist philosophers frequently claim that the western tradition typically presents reality as structured by polar oppositions, pairs of entities or qualities that are defined in contrast to each other. Examples of such dichotomous categorizations include private/public, nature/culture, body/mind, particular/universal, concrete/abstract, object/subject, subjective/objective, emotion/reason. Feminists have asserted that these dichotomies evidence male bias at least in the sense that the first term in each pair historically has been associated with femininity and conceived as inferior to the second term, which is associated with masculinity. A considerable amount of feminist philosophy responds to these dualisms in various ways. Some feminists seek to free the dichotomies from their gendered associations; some retain the gendered connotations, but seek to invert the hierarchical ordering; others still claim that dualistic thinking itself is masculine and endeavor to rethink the distinctions in ways that will avoid the problems supposedly engendered by rigid dichotomies. . . .

(continued on next page)

Showing that claims of male bias in philosophy are possible does not establish, of course, that any such claims in fact can be substantiated. It may be that some claims can be substantiated and others cannot. The commitment to investigate male bias, however, springs from an impulse that is simultaneously philosophical and feminist. It is philosophical in so far as it seeks to understand the world in terms of categories and ideals that do not reflect and promote merely the interests of a few, and it is feminist in so far as it is inspired by a determination that women's achievements and capacities, concerns and interests, should receive full and fair appreciation and evaluation. If feminists are correct in even some of their claims, it is the western tradition rather than feminist philosophy that, perhaps unknowingly, has subordinated truth to politics and that therefore constitutes a highly sophisticated form of propaganda.*

Well, what about this? What do you make of the idea that concepts and ways of philosophizing might be male biased? Be that as it may, the traditionally male-dominated philosophical world is on notice. Feminist philosophy is achieving increased visibility and importance as is evident from the number of courses being offered on the topic of philosophy and women, the appearance of the *APA Newsletter on Feminism and Philosophy,* the publication (in progress) of a multivolume *A History of Women Philosophers,* the appearance of *Hypatia: A Journal of Feminist Philosophy,* and, of course, the increased numbers of women teaching philosophy and otherwise contributing to contemporary philosophical work. Can you imagine ways in which this may bear on the direction of future philosophizing?

*Alison Jaggar, "How Can Philosophy Be Feminist?," *American Philosophical Association Newsletter on Feminism and Philosophy,* April 1988, pp. 4, 6, 8.

OF BEARDS AND BREAD

A few final observations may be useful for understanding the nature of philosophy. For one thing, *Barba philosophum non facit,* "The beard does not the philosopher make."

In some sense we are *all* philosophers. We all think and reflect in our own critical way about the questions that matter most to us. Naturally, there are good philosophers and there are bad philosophers—some reason and reflect more critically than others, some are oblivious to the fallacies and mistakes in their reasoning, some are more coherent than others in their philosophical expression, some can give it more time than others, some are professionals while most are amateurs. But *everyone* asks the important

Is everyone
a philosopher
by nature?

"Those who wish to succeed must ask the right preliminary questions."

—Aristotle

questions and tries, however feebly, to formulate meaningful answers. Everyone participates, more or less, in the philosophical enterprise.

Some would even take philosophical awareness and activity as being constitutive of human nature; that is, philosophical activity is part of what it means to be a human being, or at least a full and healthy human being. Mind you, it is not just thinking that makes us philosophers, but thinking critically about the biggest things. Aristotle expressed it better than anyone in the very first words of his *Metaphysics:* "All men by nature desire to know."[6] And it is clear from what followed that he meant knowing about the biggest things, about the questions that really matter.

Another important point: *Philosophia panem non torrit*, "Philosophy bakes no bread." Sometimes this saying is intended to express the perception (often true enough) that there is little money in the philosophy business. More often, it is a way of expressing the apparent irrelevance or impracticality or *uselessness* of philosophy.

It has seemed to many that philosophical concerns are far removed from the everyday world of work, political parties, abortion, love, death, automobiles, euthanasia, radios, capital punishment, bank loans, and the draft. This impression is understandable. Questions about the eternity of the world, the nature of the highest good, whether tables and chairs continue to exist when we leave the room, whether a runner can pass through an infinite number of points in a finite amount of time, how the mind interacts with the body, and how many angels can dance on the head of a pin certainly appear abstract, academic, and remote from the real world. The impression is also very old. Plato tells that Thales, the first philosopher of the Western tradition, was once strolling along while gazing into the sky and making certain astronomical observations—and fell into a well. Ever since, people have poked fun at philosophers who seem to be so preoccupied with what is above their heads that they have little idea of what is at their feet.

But the idea that philosophers merely think about the world while others live in it obviously involves a misunderstanding of the real nature of philosophy. A moment's thought reveals that the questions that may seem to be the most remote are also the most important. What we think about our own selves, God, the physical universe, value, and the like—and, as we just insisted, we all *do* think about these things—determines how we actually live in the world, and what we think about things like abortion, politics, euthanasia, capital punishment, death, and the draft. Everything else in our practical lives is dictated in some way by our views about those "remote" things.[7] If you doubt this, a little reflection on your activities, commitments, aspirations, and decisions this very day will probably prove it.

Is philosophy
really useful?

Philosophical
issues as basic

---

[6]Aristotle, *Metaphysics,* 980a, tr. W. D. Ross, in *The Basic Works of Aristotle,* ed. Richard McKeon (New York: Random House, 1941).

[7]Sometimes the question How many angels can dance on the head of a pin? is cited jokingly as an example of the irrelevance of philosophical issues. But even this question (whether or not it was ever actually posed in this way) can be shown to involve an issue that, in its medieval and scholastic context, held important implications.

THE INEVITABILITY OF PHILOSOPHY

In his *A Preface to Philosophy*, Mark B. Woodhouse provides a nice set of examples of the inescapability of philosophical issues.*

1. A neurophysiologist, while establishing correlations between certain brain functions and the feeling of pain, begins to wonder whether the "mind" is distinct from the brain.

2. A nuclear physicist, having determined that matter is mostly empty space containing colorless energy transformations, begins to wonder to what extent the solid, extended, colored world we perceive corresponds to what actually exists, and which world is the more "real."

3. A behavioral psychologist, having increasing success in predicting human behavior, questions whether any human actions can be called "free."

4. Supreme Court justices, when framing a rule to distinguish obscene and nonobscene art works, are drawn into questions about the nature and function of art.

5. A theologian, in a losing battle with science over literal descriptions of the universe (or "reality"), is forced to redefine the whole purpose and scope of traditional theology.

6. An anthropologist, noting that all societies have some conception of a moral code, begins to wonder just what distinguishes a moral from a nonmoral point of view.

7. A linguist, in examining the various ways language shapes our view of the world, declares that there is no one "true reality" because all views of reality are conditioned and qualified by the language in which they are expressed.

8. A perennial skeptic, accustomed to demanding and not receiving absolute proof for every view encountered, declares that it is impossible to know anything.

9. A county commissioner, while developing new zoning ordinances, begins to wonder whether the *effect* or the *intent* (or both) of zoning laws makes them discriminatory.

10. An IRS director, in determining which (religious) organizations should be exempted from tax, is forced to define what counts as a "religion" or "religious group."

*Mark B. Woodhouse, *A Preface to Philosophy* (Belmont, CA: Wadsworth, 1980), pp. 25–26.

Or consider your view on some important or controversial issue, such as abortion or war. Do you not discover there are some fundamental philosophical principles or ideas at work? And why are you reading this book, anyway? In some sense, then, everyone is a philosopher, and philosophical questions are, in spite of their appearance, the most basic and most important of all.

SUMMARY

The best way to appreciate what philosophy is about is to *philosophize*. This book will enable you to actually confront basic philosophical issues and to engage many important philosophers on their own ground.

In the meantime, though, something important can be learned about philosophy through a consideration of the word itself (the "love of wisdom") and its several branches (metaphysics, epistemology, ethics, etc.). In an attempt to emphasize both the essence and the breadth of philosophical activity, we proposed a working definition: Philosophy is the attempt to think rationally and critically about the most important questions. One should always remember Socrates and his challenge, "The unexamined life is not worth living," as embodying the ultimate philosophical concern. On the other hand, it must be admitted that reason has its limits, and what role is to be played by the nonrational (say, ultimate presuppositions) is itself a good philosophical question.

Whatever else philosophers might be interested in, they are surely interested in coherent and persuasive reasoning. Laying down the rules and providing some techniques are the tasks of logic.

Still more relevant is the nature of *arguments*. If philosophers aren't good at arguing, what *are* they good at? A real argument is a carefully devised piece of reasoning involving premises (what is reasoned *from*), a conclusion (what is reasoned *to*), and an inference (the connection that yields the conclusion from the premises). But does the conclusion follow from the premises necessarily or probably? This is the difference between a valid *deductive* argument, where the conclusion is *guaranteed* by the premises, and an *inductive* argument, where the conclusion is *supported* by the premises.

Among the most important things to be learned from an introduction to logic are the informal fallacies. As opposed to *formal* fallacies, mistakes with respect to the formal structure of an argument, *informal* fallacies arise from inattention to the relevance or clarity of language.

Everyone is more or less engaged in the philosophical enterprise, and though philosophical issues may seem at times rather remote, a moment's reflection will reveal that they really are basic and, whether one realizes it or not, they deeply affect our daily lives. Let us, then, make the most of our philosophical impulses by beginning where we are and, by critical reflection, analysis, and clarification, progress if possible to someplace even better.

BASIC IDEAS

- The problem of understanding philosophy
- "Philosophy": the love of wisdom
- The fields of philosophy
    Metaphysics
    Epistemology
    Value-theory

Ethics
Aesthetics
Logic
- The unity of philosophical questions
- The nature of the "philosophy of _____" studies
- Second-order studies
- Rationalism (the loose sense)
- Socrates as a model of the philosophical spirit
- The limits of reason
- The nonrational and the irrational
- Foundationalism
- Philosophy: a working definition
- Philosophy and religion
- Philosophy and science
- Logic as the tool or key to philosophizing
- The nature and elements of an argument
- Deductive reasoning
- Logical entailment
- The syllogism
- The distinction between truth and validity
- Inductive reasoning
- The method of generalization
- Analogical reasoning
- The distinction between formal and informal fallacies
- Informal fallacies
- Professor Miller's Four Principles for the Study of the History of Philosophy
    Clarification Principle
    Deculturalization Principle
    Modified Sergeant Friday Principle
    Smartness Principle
- Philosophy as a universal enterprise
- The importance of philosophy

TEST YOURSELF

1. Why is Socrates regarded as a symbol of philosophizing?
2. Ethics and aesthetics can be construed as subfields of _____. Why?
3. Why is philosophy "rationalistic" (in the loose sense)?
4. What is the working definition of philosophy suggested in this chapter?
5. What are the two ways in which science differs from philosophy?
6. What is an argument?

7. What is the relation of premises and conclusion in a deductive argument? In an inductive argument?

8. What is the difference between a formal fallacy and an informal fallacy?

9. The Smartness Principle has most obviously to do with (a) respect for a philosopher, (b) the features of a culture that affect the expression of a philosophy, (c) the phenomenological approach to philosophy, (d) the nonneutral character of philosophical claims.

10. State exactly what is involved in *logical necessity*. Consider the statement "All barking dogs bark."

11. What kind of logician was Sherlock Holmes? Why?

QUESTIONS FOR REFLECTION

- In spite of their stress on the use of reason, some philosophers readily concede that reason has its limits. Do you believe that it is possible, nonetheless, to know something in a *non*rational way? Why do some even maintain that this is crucial to philosophizing itself? How might the appeal to the nontraditional be abused?

- Is the ideal of reasoning in a purely objective way (that is, uninfluenced by biases and the like) really possible? If not, then what? And what about the difference in intellectual "temperaments"? Is that good or bad? What's to be done about it?

- How might it be argued that the borderlines between philosophy and *all* other disciplines may often be very blurred? Why might philosophers look upon their own discipline as the biggest and best?

- Everyday talk is sometimes full of fallacies, especially informal fallacies. Can you spot and identify any in today's newspaper? You might pay special attention to the editorial pages and letters to the editor.

FOR FURTHER READING

John Arthur. *Studying Philosophy: A Guide for the Perplexed*. Second ed. Upper Saddle River, NJ: Prentice Hall, 2004. A study-centered guide to thriving in your first philosophy course.

A. J. Ayer. *The Central Questions of Philosophy*. London: Weidenfeld & Nicolson, 1973. A timeless introduction to the big questions of philosophy.

Simon Blackburn. *Think: A Compelling Introduction to Philosophy*. Oxford: Oxford University Press, 1999. A very engaging look at some central philosophical topics, including free will, ethics, and God.

Edward Craig (ed.). *The Shorter Routledge Encyclopedia of Philosophy*. London: Routledge, 2005. The "shorter" (one volume) version of this encyclopedia is still quite comprehensive.

Ted Honderich (ed.). *The Oxford Companion to Philosophy*. Oxford: Oxford University Press, 2005. Accessible entries on all the major thinkers and topics in philosophy that provide background and explanation.

D. Q. McInerny. *Being Logical: A Guide to Good Thinking*. New York: Random House, 2005. Short and accessible guide to applying logic to everyday life.

Thomas Nagel. *What Does It All Mean?: A Very Short Introduction to Philosophy*. New York: Oxford University Press, 1987. Very clear introductions to nine major philosophical questions in less than 100 pages.

Bertrand Russell. *The Problems of Philosophy*. Oxford: Oxford University Press, 1912. Classic introduction to philosophy that shows how the major questions are timeless.

Nigel Warburton. *Philosophy: The Basics*. Fourth ed. London: Routledge, 2004. Focuses on laying out contrasting arguments on major philosophical issues.

Anthony Weston. *A Rulebook for Arguments*. Third ed. Indianapolis: Hackett Publishing Co., 2000. Student-oriented introduction to informal logic and writing a philosophical essay.

Jamie Whyte. *Crimes Against Logic*. New York: McGraw-Hill, 2004. A witty book that exposes myriad logical flaws in contemporary society.

*In addition, see several relevant articles in *Routledge Encyclopedia of Philosophy*, ed. Edward Craig (London: Routledge, 1998): "Philosophy," "Philosophy of Law," "Philosophy of Religion," "Metaphysics," "Epistemology," etc.

Online resources:

Internet Encyclopedia of Philosophy, http://www.utm.edu/research/iep/
Stanford Encyclopedia of Philosophy, http://plato.stanford.edu/
Both of these sites provide alphabetical listings of major philosophers, theories, and topics with short descriptions and explanations.

A Dictionary of Philosophical Terms and Names, http://www.philosophypages .com/dy/
This is a concise guide to technical terms and personal names often encountered in the study of philosophy.

THE QUESTION OF REALITY

What is reality? What are things made of? What is ultimate? What is it that everything depends on for its existence? What is *really real*?

There are many ways of posing the question of reality. However you pose the question, you *do* have an answer—don't you? Your idea of reality may be only half-conscious (and it may be only half-baked), but you do have some answer of your own to the question: What is really real? The point is to have a *good* answer, an answer that is well conceived and well evidenced. Why is this so important?

Some philosophers would say that in some ways the metaphysical question, or the question of reality, is the basis of all the other questions that matter. Whether or not this is strictly true, no one would deny that the metaphysical question is at least a *basic* one. Doesn't what you believe about reality determine to some degree what you believe about all sorts of other things? If, for example, someone told you that he or she believes that all that exists is matter in motion, governed by fixed and unalterable laws, then couldn't you predict pretty much what that person thinks about some other important things? If, on the other hand, you were informed that he or she believes in a supernatural and absolute being, couldn't you immediately guess that his or her views on those matters would probably be quite different?

In this way, then, the question of reality is a fundamental one. How we answer it will determine in a big way our perspectives on many issues, as well as our perspective on the universe and our experience *generally.* Let us, then, have a care with respect to the question of reality.

CHAPTER 2

THE FIRST METAPHYSICIANS

Aristotle said that philosophy began (and always begins) with "wonder," and the Pre-Socratic philosophers (those philosophers who lived before Socrates) wondered mainly about *reality*. They asked the biggest question of all: What is reality? What is the essential nature of things? What is the *underlying* reality that is revealed in the many things about us? And how is this underlying, essential reality related to these many things? How are the many things about us *derived* from this underlying reality? This is the *problem of the One and the Many*. As one can see, it actually involves two questions:

- What is the ultimate reality (the One)?
- How is everything else (the Many) related to it?

It is important to appreciate this problem because philosophers grappled with it from the very beginning and still do.

THE PROBLEM OF THE ONE AND THE MANY

The problem of identifying the ultimate reality (the One) that underlies all things (the Many) and of explaining the relation between them or how the Many derives from the One.

THE FIRST THEORY OF REALITY

Thales, the first
philosopher

Western philosophy came to birth in about 600 B.C. More specifically, it was born in the city of Miletus on the western coast of Ionia (now Turkey) in the person of Thales, traditionally called the first philosopher. To the question What is ultimate reality? Thales seems to have answered, first, that reality is *one* thing. He and his followers in Miletus have therefore been called the Milesian monists. As a metaphysical theory, monism (literally, "one-ism") emphasizes in some way or other the *unity* of reality. Usually, it is the doctrine that everything is reducible to or is an expression of a single essence or nature.

The ideal of
simplicity

Why these earliest philosophers were bent on reducing all things to *one* reality is not easy to explain. Perhaps it was a carryover from the mythological period when everything was derived from the gods, who were themselves traced back through a genealogy of the gods to the divine Parents—and indeed Parent—of all. Be that as it may, the desire to reduce everything to *one* is not peculiar to these earliest philosophers. All of us take simplicity, economy, and unity as principles of explanation. In this way a scientific theory, for example, may be judged preferable to others by virtue of the fact that it encompasses and unifies the others.

Thales: Water is
reality

To the question What is ultimate reality? Thales answered, second, that it is *water*. Understandably, one might be amused at this view of ultimate reality. But it may not be as silly as it seems at first, and you could probably imagine why Thales said this. First, water is a necessity for all living things. Second, water, or moisture, seems to be present in most things. Third, water seems to be everywhere: It bubbles up out of the ground, it comes down from the sky, and it collects on windshields. Fourth, as we peer out over the vast expanses of the ocean, it might seem (as in fact is the case) that there is more of this "stuff" than anything else in the world. This may have been especially relevant for Thales, who lived on the edge of the Great Sea (the Mediterranean) and who inherited the belief that the world was surrounded by the great River Oceanus. Fifth, it should be noted that water, more obviously than other common substances, can exist in different forms; it exists usually in liquid form, but it can be frozen solid, and it can exist as a gas.

Aristotle on
Thales' claim

Aristotle gives us a brief account of the first philosopher's search for an underlying reality, and also some speculations of his own as to why Thales identified it with water.

MONISM

As a metaphysical term, monism (from the Greek *monos*, "one") is the belief that reality is in some sense *one*, usually one in essence or nature.

Thales, the first philosopher, believed that water is the underlying reality of all things.

Of the first philosophers, . . . most thought the principles which were of the nature of matter were the only principles of all things. That of which all things that are consist, the first from which they come to be, the last into which they are resolved (the substance remaining, but changing in its modifications), this they say is the element and this the principle of things, and therefore they think nothing is either generated or destroyed, since this sort of entity is always conserved, as we say Socrates neither comes to be absolutely when he comes to be beautiful or musical, nor ceases to be when he loses these characteristics, because the substratum, Socrates himself, remains. Just so they say nothing else comes to be or ceases to be; for there must be some entity—either one or more than one—from which all other things come to be, it being conserved.

Yet they do not all agree as to the number and the nature of these principles. Thales, the founder of this type of philosophy, says the principle is water (for which reason he declared that the earth rests on water), getting the notion perhaps from seeing that the nutrient of all things is moist, and that heat itself is generated from the moist and kept alive by it (and that from which they come to be is a principle of all things). He got his notion from this fact, and from the fact that the seeds of all things have a moist nature, and that water is the origin of the nature of moist things.[1]

In any event, this was the first metaphysical theory. Reality is *one,* and it is *water.* It was the first metaphysical theory, but it was hardly the last. Thales' successors had their own theories about ultimate reality.

---

[1]Aristotle, *Metaphysics,* 983b, tr. W. D. Ross, in *Basic Works of Aristotle,* ed. Richard McKeon (New York: Random House, 1941).

A GUIDE TO PRE-SOCRATIC PRONUNCIATION

Thales	Thā'-lēz
Anaximander	A-naks-i-man'-der
Anaximenes	An-aks-im'-e-nēz
Xenophanes	Ze-nof'-a-nēz
Heraclitus	Her-a-klī'-tus
Pythagoras	Pi-thag'-o-rus
Parmenides	Par-men'-i-dēz
Empedocles	Em-ped'-o-klēz
Anaxagoras	An-aks-ag'-o-ras
Leucippus	Loo-ki'-pus
Democritus	Di-mok'-ri-tus

THREE PRE-SOCRATIC TRADITIONS

The Ionians

We cannot go into detail on all the Pre-Socratic theories. We may, however, distinguish three broad traditions: the Ionian, the Italian, and the Pluralist. It was characteristic of the early philosophers living in Ionia to identify reality with some *sensible* substance—that is, with some substance we can see, touch, hear, and smell. Thales said *water.* Others in the Ionian tradition advanced other candidates. Anaximander, for example, proposed an *indeterminate* substance, perhaps a kind of mixture from which the sensible qualities (hot, cold, moist, dry) have been sorted out. Anaximenes proposed *air,* which, through thickening and thinning, produces the different things about us and holds all things together as a sort of life-principle. Xenophanes opted for both water and earth. Heraclitus stressed the fluctuating or ever-changing character of things and championed *fire* as the underlying reality, which, though continually transformed into and out of the other elements, always displays a divinely appointed balance and order.

The Italians

The thinkers in the Italian tradition, however, inclined in a different direction. Pythagoras and the Pythagoreans believed that everything is essentially *number.* It sounds strange, of course, to say that the underlying reality is number, and it is not perfectly clear, in fact, what Pythagoras and his followers meant by this. It *is* clear, though, that this idea points us away from the ordinary sensible elements in the physical world and in the direction of the non-sensible, or incorporeal, *structure* of things. Even more extreme in this regard were the philosophers from Elea. Parmenides, for example, insisted that only *being* is, and that being must be *one* and *immutable;* with this he denied utterly the reality of the sensible world along with all plurality and motion.

The Pluralists

The Pluralists, as may be guessed from the name, sought to identify reality with a plurality of substances while maintaining that each of these, at least, is a Being and thus one and immutable. Of the Pluralists, Empedocles was the first to posit the four traditional elements as principles of all

TWO PYTHAGOREAN VIEWS ON HOW THE WORLD BEGAN

Some say that the solid body is constructed from one point. For this point, by fluxion, creates the line, and the line, by fluxion, makes the plane, and this, by moving in depth, generates the three-dimensional body. But this position of the Pythagoreans differs from the earlier.*

The first principle of all things is the One. From the One came the Indefinite Dyad as material substance for the One, which is cause. From the One and the Indefinite Dyad came numbers; from numbers, points, lines; from plane figures, solid figures, sensible bodies, of which the elements are four: fire, water, earth, air. Changing and transforming themselves completely, there arises out of them a cosmos, animate, intelligent, spherical, surrounding the earth which is at the center and which itself is spherical and inhabited.[†]

Comment: The first of these accounts, with its image of a point flowing into a line, a line into a plane, etc., is the later and more sophisticated.

The point flows into a line;　　——————

the line flows into a square;

the square flows into a cube.

In the second account, the One, the ultimate reality, generates the "Indefinite Dyad" or "Two," which represents a sort of indeterminate matter out of which the One fashions numbers, the building blocks of the cosmos. In both accounts it is difficult to know where, if at all, the gulf between *incorporeal* and *corporeal* reality is bridged. It is often observed that this distinction did not even clearly exist at the time of the Pre-Socratics.

*From Sextus Empiricus, *Against the Mathematicians*, X, 281, tr. Ed. L. Miller.
[†]From Alexander Polyhistor, quoted in Diogenes Laertius, *Lives of Eminent Philosophers*, VIII, 25, tr. Ed. L. Miller.

things: *earth, air, fire,* and *water.* In addition he posited Love and Strife, which, respectively, draw the elements together and separate them in an endless cycle. A world, such as ours, results when the four elements are unified under the attraction of Love. Anaxagoras taught that all things are constituted by a mixture of an infinite number of infinitely divisible particles or *seeds* (each seed being dominated by a certain quality, and a given thing being determined by the kind of seeds that dominate it), but that pure *Mind* controls the whole. Leucippus and Democritus advocated the first atomic theory, explaining that everything arises mechanically out of a sort of coagulation of an infinite number of irreducible *atoms* (the Greek word *atomos* means, literally, "uncuttable" and therefore something irreducible).

SOME PRE-SOCRATIC PRONOUNCEMENTS*

"As our soul, being air, holds us together, so also spirit and air encompasses the whole world."

—Anaximenes

"You cannot step twice into the same river."

—Heraclitus

"It is necessary to say and think what *is*. For Being is, and Not-Being is not."

—Parmenides

"In everything there is a portion of everything else, except for Mind. And in some things there is Mind also."

—Anaxagoras

". . . the four roots of all things: Shining Zeus, life-bearing Hera, Aidoneus, and Nestis who with tears fills the springs of mortals· with water."

—Empedocles

"Nothing happens at random, but all things from reason and by necessity."

—Leucippus

*Tr. Ed. L. Miller

The historian of philosophy F. C. Copleston has provided a statement of the importance of the Pre-Socratics with respect to (1) their formulation and various resolutions of the problem of the One and the Many, (2) their more distinctive roles as the first cosmologists, the first to advance rational theories about the nature of the *kosmos* or world, and (3) their importance for the subsequent philosophies of Plato and Aristotle.

It is often said that Greek philosophy centres round the problem of the One and the Many. Already in the very earliest stages of Greek philosophy we find the notion of unity: things change into one another—therefore there must be some common substratum, some ultimate principle, some unity underlying diversity. Thales declares that water is that common principle, Anaximenes air, Heraclitus fire: they choose different principles, but they all three believe in one ultimate principle. But although the fact of change—what Aristotle called "substantial" change—may have suggested to the early Cosmologists the notion of an underlying unity in the universe, it would be a mistake to reduce this notion to a conclusion of physical science. As far as strict scientific proof goes, they had not sufficient data to warrant their assertion of unity, still less to warrant the assertion of any particular ultimate principle, whether water, fire or air. The fact is, that the early Cosmologists leapt beyond the data to the intuition of universal unity: they possessed what we might call the power of metaphysical intuition, and this constitutes their glory and their

COSMOS

Although the Pre-Socratics grappled in different ways with the problem of reality and change, they always maintained a respect for the world as *ordered* and *rational*. In fact, the Greek word for "world" was *kosmos,* which meant, originally, a "decoration" or "ornament," a thing of beauty. This overtone was eventually lost, but for the earliest philosophers *kosmos* could best be translated as "world-system."

claim to a place in the history of philosophy. If Thales had contented himself with saying that out of water earth is evolved, "we should," as Nietzsche observes, "only have a scientific hypothesis: a false one, though nevertheless difficult to refute." But Thales went beyond a mere scientific hypothesis: he reached out to a metaphysical doctrine, expressed in the metaphysical doctrine, that *Everything is One.*

Let me quote Nietzsche again, "Greek philosophy seems to begin with a preposterous fancy, with the proposition that *water* is the origin and mother-womb of all things. Is it really necessary to stop there and become serious? Yes, and for three reasons: Firstly, because the proposition does enunciate something about the origin of things; secondly, because it does so without figure and fable; thirdly and lastly, because in it is contained, although only in the chrysalis state, the idea—Everything is one. The first-mentioned reason leaves Thales still in the company of religious and superstitious people; the second, however, takes him out of this company and shows him to us as a natural philosopher; but by virtue of the third, Thales becomes the first Greek philosopher." This holds true of the other early Cosmologists; men like Anaximenes and Heraclitus also took wing and flew above and beyond what could be verified by mere empirical observation. At the same time they were not content with any mythological assumption, for they sought a real principle of unity, the ultimate substrate of change: what they asserted, they asserted in all seriousness. They had the notion of a world that was a whole, a system, of a world governed by law. Their assertions were dictated by reason or thought, not by mere imagination or mythology; and so they deserve to count as philosophers, the first philosophers of Europe.

But though the early Cosmologists were inspired by the idea of cosmic unity, they were faced by the fact of the Many, of multiplicity, of diversity, and they had to attempt the theoretical reconciliation of this evident plurality with the postulated unity—in other words, they had to account for the world as we know it. While Anaximenes, for example, had recourse to the principle of condensation and rarefaction, Parmenides, in the grip of his great theory that Being is one and changeless, roundly denied the facts of change and motion and multiplicity as illusions of the senses. Empedocles postulated four ultimate elements, out of which all things are built up under the action of Love and Strife, and Anaxagoras maintained the ultimate character of the atomic theory and the quantitative explanation of qualitative difference, thus doing justice to plurality, to the many, while tending to relinquish the earlier vision of unity, in spite of the fact that each atom represents the Parmenidean One.

We may say, therefore, that while the Pre-Socratics struggled with the problem of the One and the Many, they did not succeed in solving it. The Heraclitean philosophy contains, indeed, the profound notion of unity in diversity, but it is bound up with an over-assertion of Becoming and the difficulties consequent on the doctrine of Fire. The Pre-Socratics accordingly failed to solve the problem, and it was taken up again by Plato and Aristotle, who brought to bear on it their outstanding talent and genius.

. . . It should be clear that Pre-Socratic philosophy is not simply a pre-philosophic stage which can be discounted in a study of Greek thought—so that we should be justified in starting immediately with Socrates and Plato. The Pre-Socratic philosophy is *not* a pre-philosophic stage, but is the first stage of Greek philosophy: it may not be pure and unmixed philosophy, but it is philosophy, and it deserves to be studied for the sake of its own intrinsic interest as the first Greek attempt to attain a rational understanding of the world. Moreover, it is not a self-contained unit, shut off from succeeding philosophic thought in a watertight compartment; rather it is preparatory to the succeeding period, for in it we see problems raised which were to occupy the greatest of Greek philosophers. Greek thought develops, and though we can hardly over-estimate the native genius of men like Plato and Aristotle, it would be wrong to imagine that they were uninfluenced by the past. Plato was profoundly influenced by Pre-Socratic thought, by the Heraclitean, Eleatic and Pythagorean systems; Aristotle regarded his philosophy as the heir and crown of the past; and both thinkers took up philosophic problems from the hands of their predecessors, giving, it is true, original solutions, but at the same time tackling the problems in their historic setting.[2]

THE DISCOVERY OF FORM

It is true, in spite of their obscurity and fragmentary nature, that the speculations of the earliest philosophers are not only fascinating but also important. For here lie the roots of the first major philosophies. And in this respect yet another point must be made—namely, the progress of the Pre-Socratics toward "the discovery of form," as it is called by a noted historian of Greek philosophy, W. K. C. Guthrie:

The Egyptians had thought of geometry as a matter of individual rectangular or triangular fields. The Greek lifts it from the plane of the concrete and material and begins to think about rectangles and triangles themselves, which have the same properties whether they are embodied in fields of several acres or in pieces of wood or cloth a few inches long, or simply represented by lines drawn in the sand. In fact their material embodiment ceases to be of any importance, and we have made the discovery which above all others stands to the especial credit of the Greeks: the discovery of form. The Greek sense of form impresses itself on every manifestation of their activity, on literature and the graphic and plastic arts as much as on their philosophy. It marks the advance from percepts to concepts, from the individual examples perceived by sight or touch to the universal notion

---

[2]Frederick Copleston, *A History of Philosophy* (Baltimore: Newman Press, 1946–1974), I, pp. 76–80.

THE MOST FUNDAMENTAL QUESTION OF ALL: "WHY IS THERE ANYTHING?"

". . . each of us is grazed at least once, perhaps more than once, by the hidden power of this question, even if he is not aware of what is happening to him. The question looms in moments of great despair, when things tend to lose all their weight and all meaning becomes obscured. Perhaps it will strike but once like a muffled bell that rings into our life and gradually dies away. It is present in moments of rejoicing, when all the things around us are transfigured and seem to be there for the first time, as if it might be easier to think they are not than to understand that they are and are as they are. The question is upon us in bore-dom, when we are equally removed from despair and joy, and everything about us seems so hopelessly commonplace that we no longer care whether anything is or is not—and with this question "Why is there anything rather than nothing?" is evoked in a particular form.

"But this question may be asked expressly, or, unrecognized as a question, it may merely pass through our lives like a brief gust of wind; it may press hard upon us, or, under one pretext or another, we may thrust it away from us and silence it. In any case it is never the question that we ask first in point of time.

"But it is the first question in another sense—in regard to rank. This may be clarified in three ways. The question "Why is there anything rather than nothing?" is first in rank for us first because it is the most far reaching, second because it is the deepest, and finally because it is the most fundamental of all questions."

Martin Heidegger, *An Introduction to Metaphysics,* tr. Ralph Manheim (New Haven: Yale University Press, 1959), pp. 1–2 (with slight editing).

which we conceive in our minds—in sculpture no longer an individual man but the ideal of humanity; in geometry, no longer triangles but the nature of the triangularity and the consequences which logically and necessarily flow from being a triangle.[3]

But it remained for Socrates, Plato, and Aristotle to bring the discovery to full light and to draw out its full philosophical implications.

CHAPTER 2 IN REVIEW

SUMMARY

Something happened in about 600 B.C. that marked the beginning of our own philosophical tradition. The human intellect took a quantum leap in *critical* thinking. According to Aristotle, what sparked this leap was a new

---

[3]W. K. C. Guthrie, *A History of Greek Philosophy* (Cambridge: Cambridge University Press, 1962–1981), I, pp. 36–37.

and wide-eyed wonder at the world and a search for its underlying nature.

All of the early philosophers were guided by the Principle of Simplicity, and they sought to understand the world in terms of some *one* reality, or as few as possible. They differed, though, in the character and number of the underlying reality. The Ionian, Italian, and Pluralist traditions reflect the widely different courses taken by the Pre-Socratics. Always, however, it was the twofold problem of the One and the Many: (1) What is the underlying nature or reality of all things? and (2) How is the multiplicity of things around us derived from this reality, or how do we *get* from the One to the Many?

Already in the Pre-Socratics the idea of Form, or the ideal essence that is imperfectly represented in the Many, was emerging. As we will see in the next chapter, this was the dominating idea of Socrates, Plato, and Aristotle, and the whole continuing tradition stemming from these thinkers. We will also see that two Pre-Socratic philosophers—Heraclitus and Parmenides—exerted a special influence on the subsequent thinkers.

BASIC IDEAS

- The problem of the One and the Many
- Monism
- The ideal of simplicity in explanation
- The first theory of reality: water
- Three Pre-Socratic traditions
     The Ionians
     The Italians
     The Pluralists
- The emergence of form

TEST YOURSELF

1. The problem of the One and the Many is really *two* problems. What are they?
2. True or false: The Italian tradition was more abstract in its conception of reality than the Ionian tradition.
3. Give a few reasons Thales might have identified water as the ultimate reality.
4. What did the discovery of "Form" consist of?

QUESTIONS FOR REFLECTION

- Were the Pre-Socratics so odd in seeking a *simple* explanation for the nature of things? What is meant, exactly, by the claim that simplicity has *always* been a principle of explanation?

- It is always easy *when looking back* to judge an idea or theory as naive. What might be said *on behalf* of the earliest theories of reality as being well conceived, critical, and persuasive at the time?

FOR FURTHER READING

Jonathon Barnes. *The Presocratic Philosophers.* Revised ed. London: Routledge & Kegan Paul, 1982. A recent, full-scale, and authoritative investigation.

John Burnet. *Early Greek Philosophy.* Fourth ed. London: Macmillan, 1930. Old, standard treatment of the Pre-Socratic philosophers (selected fragments plus commentary) written from a positivistic perspective.

Frederick Copleston. *A History of Philosophy.* Baltimore: Newman Press, 1946–1974. I, Part I. Brief survey of the Pre-Socratics by a renowned historian of philosophy.

W. K. C. Guthrie. *A History of Greek Philosophy.* Cambridge: Cambridge University Press, 1962–1981. I and II. Two volumes of extensive accounts of the Pre-Socratics and commentary on relevant fragments, by a foremost historian of Greek philosophy.

Werner Jaeger. *The Theology of the Early Greek Philosophers.* Oxford: Clarendon Press, 1947. An old but enduring treatment of the Pre-Socratic thinkers, written (in opposition to Burnet) from a metaphysical, theological perspective.

G. S. Kirk, J. E. Raven, and M. Schofield. *The Presocratic Philosophers: A Critical History with a Selection of Texts.* Second ed. Cambridge: Cambridge University Press, 1984. The most up-to-date, comprehensive, and authoritative discussion, providing Greek text, English translation, and commentary on the most relevant Pre-Socratic fragments.

Alexander P. D. Mourelatos (ed.). *The Pre-Socratics: A Collection of Critical Essays.* Garden City, NY: Anchor Press, 1974. A hefty volume of scholarly essays on a variety of topics concerning Pre-Socratic philosophy.

Catherine Osborne. *Presocratic Philosophy: A Very Short Introduction.* New York: Oxford University Press, 2004. Intended for novices, this book introduces major Pre-Socratic thinkers and themes of the period.

*In addition, see the relevant articles ("Pre-Socratic Philosophy," "Heraclitus," etc.) in *Routledge Encyclopedia of Philosophy,* ed. Edward Craig (London: Routledge, 1998), and *Stanford Encyclopedia of Philosophy,* http://plato.stanford.edu.

THE IDEA OF FORM

Philosophy really came of age with Plato (427–347 B.C.). Here we encounter the first full-fledged philosophical *system*. By a philosophical system we mean a fundamental idea or theory that is worked out for all aspects of experience. Thus Plato's philosophy addresses everything from reality, to knowledge, to ethics, to art, to religion, to cosmology, and so on. So encompassing and magnificent is Plato's philosophy that Alfred North Whitehead called all subsequent philosophy a series of footnotes to it!

Plato, the first "systematic" philosopher

PLATO AND SOCRATES

Plato, who is sometimes called the finest writer of ancient Greece, expressed his philosophy in numerous "dialogues." In the earlier dialogues Plato develops the ideas of his teacher Socrates through portrayals of Socrates' discussions with his contemporaries, discussions that proceed by questions and answers. Socrates is usually represented as asking in one way or another, What is *X*? His respondent's answer is then subjected to a searching analysis that generates still more and better answers.

Platonic dialogues

A good example is the early dialogue *Euthyphro*. Here Socrates raises with Euthyphro the question "What is holiness?" The following excerpts show how Socrates deals with two of Euthyphro's answers. Notice the characteristic Socratic comment "Come, then, and let us scrutinize what we are saying," and the final bewilderment of the hapless Euthyphro, who complains that nothing seems to stay put. Incidentally, Socrates' question "Is

51

what is holy holy because the gods approve it, or do they approve it because it is holy?" is one of the most famous in the history of philosophy. If you agree with the first, then God's will seems to be arbitrary; if you agree with the second, then God's will seems to be determined by something beyond God himself.

SOCRATES: At present try to tell me more clearly what I asked you a little while ago, for, my friend, you were not explicit enough before when I put the question. What is holiness? . . .

EUTHYPHRO: Well, then, what is pleasing to the gods is holy, and what is not pleasing to them is unholy.

SOCRATES: Perfect, Euthyphro! Now you give me just the answer that I asked for. Meanwhile whether it is right I do not know, but obviously you will go on to prove your statement true.

EUTHYPHRO: Indeed, I will.

SOCRATES: Come, now, and let us scrutinize what we are saying. What is pleasing to the gods, and the man that pleases them, are holy; what is hateful to the gods, and the man they hate, unholy. But the holy and unholy are not the same; the holy is directly opposite to the unholy. Isn't it so?

EUTHYPHRO: It is.

SOCRATES: And the matter clearly was well stated.

EUTHYPHRO: I accept it, Socrates; that was stated.

SOCRATES: Was it not also stated, Euthyphro, that the gods revolt and differ with each other, and that hatreds come between them?

EUTHYPHRO: That was stated.

SOCRATES: Hatred and wrath, my friend—what kind of disagreement will produce them? Look at the matter thus. If you and I were to differ about numbers, on the question which of two was the greater, would a disagreement about that make us angry at each other, and make enemies of us? Should we not settle things by calculation, and so come to an agreement quickly on any point like that?

EUTHYPHRO: Yes, certainly.

SOCRATES: And similarly if we differed on a question of greater length or less, we would take a measurement and quickly put an end to the dispute?

EUTHYPHRO: Just that.

SOCRATES: And so, I fancy, we should have recourse to scales, and settle any question about a heavier or lighter weight?

EUTHYPHRO: Of course.

SOCRATES: What sort of thing, then, is it about which we differ, till, unable to arrive at a decision, we might get angry and be enemies to one another? Perhaps you have no answer ready, but listen to me. See if it is not the following—right and wrong, the noble and base, and good and bad. Are not these the things about which we differ, till, unable to arrive at a decision, we grow hostile, when we do grow hostile, to each other, you and I and everybody else?

EUTHYPHRO: Yes, Socrates, that is where we differ, on these subjects.

SOCRATES: What about the gods, then, Euthyphro? If, indeed, they have dissensions, must it not be on these subjects?

EUTHYPHRO: Quite necessarily.

SOCRATES: Accordingly, my noble Euthyphro, by your account some gods take one thing to be right, and others take another, and similarly with honorable and the base, and good and bad. They would hardly be at variance with each other, if they did not differ on these questions. Would they?

EUTHYPHRO: You are right.

SOCRATES: And what each one of them thinks noble, good, and just, is what he loves, and the opposite is what he hates?

EUTHYPHRO: Yes, certainly.

SOCRATES: But it is the same things, so you say, that some of them think right, and others wrong, and through disputing about these they are at variance, and make war on one another. Isn't it so?

EUTHYPHRO: It is.

SOCRATES: Accordingly, so it would seem, the same things will be hated by the gods and loved by them; the same things would alike displease and please them.

EUTHYPHRO: It would seem so.

SOCRATES: And so, according to this argument, the same things, Euthyphro, will be holy and unholy.

EUTHYPHRO: That may be.

SOCRATES: In that case, admirable friend, you have not answered what I asked you. I did not ask you to tell me what at once is holy and unholy, but it seems that what is pleasing to the gods is also hateful to them. . . .

Euthyphro then regroups his thoughts and advances another definition: Holiness is what is loved by all the gods.

SOCRATES: Then what are we to say about the holy, Euthyphro? According to your argument, is it not loved by all the gods?

EUTHYPHRO: Yes.

SOCRATES: Because it is holy, or for some other reason?

EUTHYPHRO: No, it is for that reason.

SOCRATES: And so it is because it is holy that it is loved; it is not holy because it is loved.

EUTHYPHRO: So it seems.

SOCRATES: On the other hand, it is beloved and pleasing to the gods just because they love it?

EUTHYPHRO: No doubt of that.

SOCRATES: So what is pleasing to the gods is not the same as what is holy, Euthyphro, nor, according to your statement, is the holy the same as what is pleasing to the gods. They are two different things.

EUTHYPHRO: How may that be, Socrates?

SOCRATES: Because we are agreed that the holy is loved because it is holy, and is not holy because it is loved. Isn't it so?

EUTHYPHRO: Yes.

SOCRATES: Whereas what is pleasing to the gods is pleasing to them just because they love it, such being its nature and its cause. Its being loved of the gods is not the reason of its being loved.

EUTHYPHRO: You are right.

SOCRATES: But suppose, dear Euthyphro, that what is pleasing to the gods and what is holy were not two separate things. In that case if holiness were loved because it was holy, then also what was pleasing to the gods would be loved because it pleased them. And, on the other hand, if what was pleasing to them pleased because they loved it, then also the holy would be holy because they loved it. But now you see that it is just the opposite, because the two are absolutely different from each other, for the one [what is pleasing to the gods] is loved because it is of a sort to be loved. Consequently, Euthyphro, it looks as if you had not given me my answer—as if when you were asked to tell the nature of the holy, you did not wish to explain the essence of it. You merely tell an attribute of it, namely, that it appertains to holiness to be loved by all the gods. What it is, as yet you have not said. So, if you please, do not conceal this from me. No, begin again. Say what the holy is, and never mind if gods do love it, nor if it has some other attribute; on that we shall not split. Come, speak out. Explain the nature of the holy and unholy.

EUTHYPHRO: Now, Socrates, I simply don't know how to tell you what I think. Somehow everything that we put forward keeps moving about us in a circle, and nothing will stay where we put it.[1]

In the dialogues, which were composed over many years, Plato gradually introduced his own (and more developed) ideas in place of those of the historical Socrates, though he continued to employ Socrates as the mouthpiece of these ideas. It is, of course, a problem to know where the real Socrates leaves off and Plato's own ideas begin. This is called the Socratic Problem. For the purpose of our discussion here we will not concern ourselves with this problem and will simply speak of the philosophy embodied in the dialogues as Plato's philosophy.

---

[1]Plato, *Euthyphro*, 6D, 7A–8B, 10D–11B, in *On the Trial and Death of Socrates*, tr. Lane Cooper (Ithaca, NY: Cornell University Press, 1941).

PLATONIC DIALOGUE

"Plato presented philosophy in an entirely spontaneous form, not as ponderous treatises but in dramatic dialogues between friends, in which Socrates figured as the presiding genius. He invented the form to make his concepts intelligible to the layman, and never was philosophy graced with more beauty; this first attempt to humanize knowledge was warm, personal, fresh, and frequently humorous, an intoxicating mixture of poetry and hard thought."

Felix Marti-Ibanez, *Tales of Philosophy* (New York: Potter, 1964), p. 31.

THE TWO WORLDS: APPEARANCE AND REALITY

Many philosophers have found it necessary to conceive of reality in two spheres or levels: what *appears* to be real, and what *is* real. Already in the beginning stages of the history of philosophy Plato introduced this two-layer view of reality. For Plato, too, it is the difference between Appearance and Reality, though he expressed it also by means of the terms *Becoming* and *Being*. With such talk Plato affirms his conviction that in addition to the ever-changing world around us (Becoming), there is another world, an eternal and unchanging reality (Being). Why would one believe in an *additional* world such as this?

The two-layer view of reality

Plato had many reasons for believing in a transcendent world—that is, a reality lying beyond space and time. We will limit ourselves to two of these reasons, but perhaps the two most important.

First, Plato's view of reality is a reaction to that of his predecessor, Protagoras. Protagoras, a Sophist[2] who was active in about 425 B.C., was responsible for one of the most famous lines ever uttered: "Man is the measure of all things." His meaning is clear from a more accurate and complete quotation:

A man is the measure of all things; of the things that are, that they are, and of the things that are not, that they are not.[3]

This means that the individual—each and every person—is the criterion unto himself or herself as to what exists and what doesn't. The thought was expanded, of course, to include truth and morality. Whatever you perceive as true or false *is* true or false, and whatever you think is good or bad *is* good or

Protagoras: "A man is the measure of all things"

---

[2]The Sophists (literally, "wise men") were the first to teach wisdom for a fee, something that irked Socrates. Actually, the Sophists may not have been as wise as they were clever with words, and they were accused of "making the stronger argument appear to be the weaker, and the weaker argument appear to be the stronger." But in the days of Athenian democracy, when an individual was required to defend himself in the law courts, the Sophists' "wisdom" was, understandably, much in demand!

[3]Protagoras, *Fragment 1,* tr. Ed. L. Miller.

bad. This is known as relativism or subjectivism because it makes the most important things *relative* to and dependent upon the individual (or community, society, etc.), or because it asserts that the subject (an individual, community, society, etc.) is the source and standard of being, truth, and goodness.

For Plato (and for most philosophers since) it was absurd to say that being, truth, and morality are "up for grabs" and can be or mean whatever an individual wishes! This would mean the immediate collapse of not only all serious talk about what's real and unreal, and what's true and false, but also all talk about moral responsibility, praise, blame, punishment, and so on. No, says Plato. Our understanding of being, truth, and goodness must—if it is to be really meaningful—be anchored in some *objective* (that is, it exists outside of our own minds), *independent* (it is not dependent on anything else for its existence), and *absolute* (it does not come or go or otherwise change) Reality. There must then exist above our minds and beyond this world another world, a world of Reality (Being).

Second, Plato's view of reality is a reaction to still another of his predecessors, the Pre-Socratic philosopher Heraclitus. Heraclitus went about saying things like, "The sun is new every day" and "We are and we are not." These are ways in which Heraclitus expressed his view—a very famous view—that everything is constantly changing, nothing stands still for a moment, the world and everything in it are in a ceaseless movement, activity, coming and going, ebbing and flowing. In fact, "All things flow" caught on as a Heraclitean slogan, and Heraclitus himself appears to have likened the fluctuating universe to a river: "You can't step twice into the same river." The idea is that by the time you have put a foot into the water, different water is flowing there.

What did this colorful and dynamic view of the world have to do with the development of Plato's conception of reality? Just as Protagoras' relativism, says Plato, leads to impossible conclusions, so does Heraclitus' doctrine of flux: If all reality is constantly changing, then all discourse is impossible, and the same is true for knowledge itself. Why is this? For the answer, read on.

Plato inherited from still another Pre-Socratic philosopher, Parmenides, the idea that genuine knowledge and discourse must be about what *is*, not what *is not*—after all, you can't think about, talk about, or have any knowledge of

TRANSCENDENT REALITY

. . . in philosophy usually means reality that transcends or lies beyond *space* and *time*. Thus God, as represented in classical theology, is a transcendent being, and true Reality, for Plato, is transcendent. Can you imagine a transcendent being in the sense of forming a mental image? The answer is No, for images are bound by spatiotemporal conditions, such as size, color, shape, motion, and the like. Can you *conceive* of a transcendent being? The answer is Yes, if by that you mean that you can have an idea or concept of that being. Thus you cannot *imagine* God, though you may have an *idea* of him.

HOW TO AVOID PAYING YOUR DEBTS

It appears that the playwright Epicharmus, a contemporary of Heraclitus, spoofed Heraclitus' doctrine of the ever-changing nature of things: You will have difficulty making me pay back money I borrowed from you because everything changes and I am no longer the one who borrowed it!

what *isn't*, can you? (The word "nothing" does not denote something, but rather the negation or absence of something.) Furthermore, what *is* (Being) must be *one* and *unchanging*. Do you see why Being must be one and unchanging? Do not multiplicity and change involve difference, absence, relativity, and degrees? And do not these in turn involve various sorts of nonbeing? Now since a thing cannot both be and not be (the Law of Non-Contradiction), it is *logically* impossible that what *is* could also be what *is not*. How then could that which *is* involve multiplicity and change? True Being is therefore one and unchanging. And only this can be an object of knowledge and discourse.

Now consider again Heraclitus' world of flux. What is it that you refer to when you comment on that table over there in the corner? "Why," you say, "just that table over there in the corner." But in the Heraclitean view there *is* no table over there in the corner: By the time you say "that table" it is no longer *that* table but has already become a *different* table. Likewise for everything in the Heraclitean world of flux. If then, says Plato, knowledge and talk about tables, chairs, dogs, cats, justice, and anything else are about anything *real*, it must be because there is more to reality than the sensible world of multiplicity and change. There must be a world of *Being* in addition to the world of *Becoming*.

In his dialogue *Timaeus*, Plato himself poses the distinction between the two worlds, the worlds of Being and Becoming, and the corresponding difference between knowledge and opinion, as clearly as one could hope for:

The implications of Heraclitean flux

> . . . we must make a distinction and ask, What is that which always is and has no becoming, and what is that which is always becoming and never is? That which is apprehended by intelligence and reason is always in the same state, but that which is conceived by opinion with the help of sensation and without reason is always in a process of becoming and perishing and never really is.[4]

Transcendent world
of BEING

Space-time
world of BECOMING

---

[4]Plato, *Timaeus*, 27D–28A, tr. Benjamin Jowett, in *Plato: The Collected Dialogues*.

The same distinction is strikingly posed in the *Republic,* where Plato clearly represents the world of Becoming as a "twilight" zone or "half-way region" between reality and unreality:

> . . . we have discovered that the many conventional notions of the mass of mankind about what is beautiful or honourable or just and so on are adrift in a sort of twilight between pure reality and pure unreality.
>
> We have.
>
> And we agreed earlier that, if any such object were discovered, it should be called the object of belief and not of knowledge. Fluctuating in that halfway region, it would be seized upon by the intermediate faculty.
>
> Yes.
>
> So when people have an eye for the multitude of beautiful things or of just actions or whatever it may be, but can neither behold Beauty or Justice itself nor follow a guide who would lead them to it, we shall say that all they have is beliefs, without any real knowledge of the objects of their belief.
>
> That follows.
>
> But what of those who contemplate the realities themselves as they are for ever in the same unchanging state? Shall we not say that they have, not mere belief, but knowledge?
>
> That too follows.
>
> And, further, that their affection goes out to the objects of knowledge, whereas the others set their affections on the objects of belief; for it was they, you remember, who had a passion for the spectacle of beautiful colours and sounds, but would not hear of Beauty itself being a real thing.
>
> I remember.
>
> So we may fairly call them lovers of belief rather than of wisdom—not philosophical, in fact, but philodoxical. Will they be seriously annoyed by that description?
>
> Not if they will listen to my advice. No one ought to take offence at the truth.
>
> The name of philosopher, then, will be reserved for those whose affections are set, in every case, on the reality.
>
> By all means.[5]

THE THEORY OF THE FORMS

Grasping the distinction between the two worlds is the first step toward an understanding of Plato's theory of reality. The next step is to grasp that for Plato the transcendent world, the world of Being, is populated by realities called Forms, which are the causes of the particular things that exist beneath them, like tables, chairs, dogs, cats, circles, human beings, instances of beauty, examples of justice, and so on for every different kind of thing there is.

We are ready, then, to consider Plato's *theory of the Forms*—at least that is what it is usually called. It is also sometimes called the *theory of Ideas.* But here we must be on guard not to confuse *these* Ideas (capital *I*) with

---

[5]Plato, *The Republic,* 479D–480A, tr. Francis MacDonald Cornford (New York: Oxford University Press, 1941).

PLATO

Plato was born in Athens in 427 B.C. According to one tradition he was originally named Aristocles but came to be called Plato (from the Greek *platus,* "wide") because of his broad shoulders. He came from an aristocratic family and no doubt received a very cultured education. He was at first bent on a career in politics, but was soon captivated by Socrates and his philosophy, and the fate of Socrates at the hands of the Athenian democracy (he was present at Socrates' trial) further sealed Plato's revulsion at such politics. From Socrates Plato learned to fix his attention not on the fluctuating objects of sense experience, but on the fixed and abiding *essence* of things as the only possible objects of true knowledge.

When he was about 40, Plato visited Italy, possibly to engage the Pythagoreans there and to see the volcanoes. In Italy he became friends with Dion, the brother-in-law of Dionysus I, tyrant of Syracuse. Dionysus I, however, disliked Plato and had him sold as a slave. He was recognized by an acquaintance, who ransomed him and had him sent back to Athens. There, in 388 B.C., he founded his school, the Academy, sometimes called the first European university. At the Academy Plato produced many elegant dialogues and lectured on many different topics (the lectures are lost), including rhetoric, biology, mathematics, astronomy, and, of course, philosophy—the pursuit of the highest reality and truth. Plato was intensely interested in political philosophy, and it was his desire to experiment with his ideal of the Philosopher-King that led him to return to Syracuse, where Dionysus I had been succeeded by his nephew, Dionysus II. Intrigues within the court spoiled Plato's philosophical education of Dionysus II, and the project was a failure.

Plato presided over the Academy until his death in 347 B.C. In the meantime, however, a pupil had matriculated at the Academy by the name of Aristotle.

Plato is universally regarded as one of the finest writers of Greek literature. His numerous and polished dialogues include the *Apology, Euthyphro, Phaedo, Phaedrus, Meno, Republic, Symposium, Theaetetus, Sophist, Timaeus, Statesman,* and *Laws.*

Forms of Ideas

the ideas (lowercase *i*) that exist merely in our minds. We will see that while our ideas have no existence apart from our minds, the Platonic Ideas exist objectively and absolutely: They would exist even if everything else were to disappear. In any case, it is useful to employ capital *F* and *I* to remind us of the unique status of the Platonic Forms and Ideas.

Why the word "Form"?

Why the word "Form"? It translates the Greek word *eidos*, which does, in fact, mean "form" in the ordinary, usual sense: shape, structure, appearance. As will shortly be seen, Plato certainly does *not* mean something visible. Still, it is easy to see why Plato took over this word for his own purpose. After all, a Platonic Form does have everything to do with what a thing *is*, and thus even with its physical structure, shape, or appearance. But if it helps, there are many expressions one could substitute for the word "Form": essence, nature, essential structure, object of a definition, and so on. Again, they all designate what a thing *is*, its "whatness."

It may be helpful, further, to outline the main features of Forms. They may be characterized as

Six features of Forms

- *Objective.* They exist "out there" as objects, independently of our minds or wills.
- *Transcendent.* Though they exist "out there," they do not exist in space and time; they lie, as it were, above or beyond space and time.
- *Eternal.* As transcendent realities they are not subject to time and therefore not subject to motion or change.
- *Intelligible.* As transcendent realities they cannot be grasped by the senses but only by the intellect.
- *Archetypal.* They are the models for every kind of thing that does or could exist.
- *Perfect.* They include absolutely and perfectly all the features of the things of which they are the models.

The theory of the Forms

Perhaps now we are ready for a more explicit statement of the theory of the Forms: It is the belief in a transcendent world of eternal and absolute beings, corresponding to every kind of thing that there is, and causing in particular things their essential nature.

More generally, for every particular and imperfect thing in the world of Becoming (a table, a chair, an instance of justice, an example of beauty, a circle) there is a corresponding reality that is its absolute and perfect essence or Form in the world of Being (Table, Chair, Justice, Beauty, Circle). The particular and imperfect thing, though imperfect, is what it is by virtue of its corresponding Form, which imparts to it, or causes in it, its essence or general nature. Because something has an essence or general nature it is an imperfect *something*. On the other hand, it is an *imperfect* something because, while it reflects being from above, it is invaded and contaminated by nonbeing from below: The changeless is set in motion, the one is multiplied into many, the absolute is relativized, the universal is particularized.

THE THEORY OF THE FORMS

... lies at the center of the whole Platonic philosophy. It portrays every changing, multiple, imperfect thing of a certain kind in the sensible world (a Many) as caused by an eternal and ideal essence, or Form, in the transcendent world (a One). It is Plato's resolution to the ancient problem of the One and the Many, which we encountered at the beginning of Chapter 2.

In view of all of this, the following passage from Plato's *Euthyphro* should make a lot of sense. Here Socrates has asked Euthyphro about the meaning of holiness. Euthyphro responded with examples of holiness.

SOCRATES: ... try to tell me more clearly what I asked you a little while ago, for, my friend, you were not explicit enough before when I put the question. What is holiness? You merely said that what you are now doing is a holy deed—namely, prosecuting your father on a charge of murder.

EUTHYPHRO: And, Socrates, I told the truth.

SOCRATES: Possibly. But, Euthyphro, there are many other things that you will say are holy.

EUTHYPHRO: Because they are.

SOCRATES: Well, bear in mind that what I asked of you was not to tell me one or two out of all the numerous actions that are holy; I wanted you to tell me what is the essential form of holiness which makes all holy actions holy. I believe you held that there is one ideal form by which unholy things are all unholy, and by which all holy things are holy. Do you remember that?

EUTHYPHRO: I do.

SOCRATES: Well then, show me what, precisely, this ideal is, so that, with my eye on it, and using it as a standard, I can say that any action done by you or anybody else is holy if it resembles this idea, or, if it does not, can deny that it is holy.[6]

This brief passage expresses or embodies many of the things we have just explained. Notice for example, (1) Plato's use of words or phrases like "essential form" and "ideal" for the essence in the world of Being; (2) the contrast between the *one* essence in the world of Being (in this case Holiness) and the *many* instances of it in the world of Becoming (numerous holy acts); (3) the way in which the Form is said to be the cause of its many sensible

---

[6]Plato, *Euthyphro*, 6C–E.

PLATO'S CONCEPTION OF FORMS AND THINGS

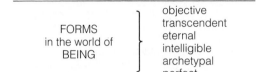

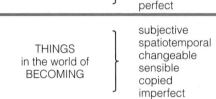

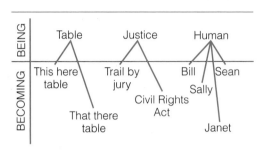

instances; (4) the Form referred to as a standard for judgment; and (5) the way in which the particular instance is said to resemble the model.

The relation of forms to particular things

This last point leads us further. We have said above that particular things have a nature or essence because they stand in some sort of relation to their Forms. But what, exactly, is this relation? How does the Form impart essence to the particular thing? This is a troublesome question, and Plato seems to have been bothered by it, though he never resolved it. Until now, we have been representing the Form as the model, and the sensible instance of the Form as a copy or imitation of it. This is the most common way of representing Plato's theory at this point. But Plato actually resorts to *two* explanations (really, *metaphors*) of how the Form gives essence to particular things. Sometimes, as in the above passage in the *Euthyphro,* he talks as if sensible things are *copies* or *imitations* of the Forms, and at other times he talks of a *participation* of the sensible thing in its Form. Thus a table is a table because it imperfectly reflects or is an imperfect copy of its pattern or model, the Form Tableness, or it is a table because it participates in the Form Tableness. The following passage from the *Phaedo* is useful not only because it makes explicit (though ambiguous) reference to a Form's relation to its sensible instances—he speaks of the Form's "presence in it or association with it"—but also because it shows that Plato did not concern himself with a rigorous explanation of this point:

> It seems to me that whatever else is beautiful apart from absolute beauty is beautiful because it partakes of that absolute beauty, and for no other reason. Do you accept this kind of causality?

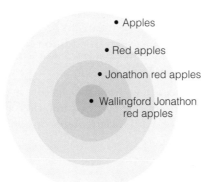

- Apples

- Red apples

- Jonathon red apples

- Wallingford Jonathon
  red apples

Yes, I do.

Well, now, that is as far as my mind goes; I cannot understand these other ingenious theories of causation. If someone tells me that the reason why a given object is beautiful is that it has a gorgeous color or shape or any other such attribute, I disregard all these other explanations—I find them all confusing—and I cling simply and straightforwardly and no doubt foolishly to the explanation that the one thing that makes that object beautiful is the presence in it or association with it, in whatever way the relation comes about, of absolute beauty. I do not go so far as to insist upon the precise details—only upon the fact that it is by beauty that beautiful things are beautiful. This, I feel, is the safest answer for me or for anyone else to give, and I believe that while I hold fast to this I cannot fall; it is safe for me or for anyone else to answer that it is by beauty that beautiful things are beautiful. Don't you agree?[7]

We will see later that Plato's failure to be precise on the nature of the Form's relation to the particular is exactly what Aristotle seized as the Achilles' heel of Plato's whole theory.

Another important matter: Things can participate in more than one Form. This can happen in two ways. *First,* Forms themselves "blend" with one another, so that by imitating or participating in one Form, a thing may actually be sharing in many Forms. Is this not necessary, since the Forms of both *X* and *Y* may hold some essential feature in common? For example, if it is the essence of trees, dogs, cats, and humans to live, then however their Forms may otherwise differ, they must at least all blend with the Form Life; if apples, cherries, bananas, and oranges are all by nature sweet, then whatever else each of their Forms involves, they must all encompass Sweetness. Plato does not, however, believe that blending can go on forever as if we could just keep throwing in new ingredients to explain more and more specialized kinds of things. There must be a last, most specific definition in order to account for the ultimate difference of things.

The "blending" of Forms

---

[7]Plato, *Phaedo,* 100C–E, in *The Last Days of Socrates,* tr. Hugh Tredennick (Harmondsworth: Penguin Classics, 1954).

Accidental features

But what about a feature that is not properly part of a thing's essence? Ink does not have to be blue in order to be ink, does it? This brings us to the *second* way things can imitate or participate in more than one Form. The Form Ink involves whatever it means to be *ink*, including having color. Now if this happens to be blue, then in addition to imitating or participating in the essential Form of Ink, including color, this ink must also participate in the Form Blue. Ask yourself: Is a certain feature of a thing part of that thing's very essence? If so, then that feature is one of the Forms that blend to make up the Form of that thing. If not, then that thing participates in this particular feature or Form accidentally or "on its own," as it were.

DEGREES OF REALITY AND KNOWLEDGE

So far we have been speaking as if Plato distinguished between two layers or levels of reality: *Being* and *Becoming,* Forms and their sensible copies. But Plato's theory of reality is somewhat more complicated than that. Here his famous image of the Divided Line, from the *Republic,* is helpful—Plato must have known that a picture is worth a thousand words.

The Divided Line

. . . take a line divided into two unequal parts, one to represent the visible order, the other the intelligible; and divide each part again in the same proportion, symbolizing degrees of comparative clearness or obscurity. Then (A) one of the two sections in the visible world will stand for images. By images I mean first shadows, and then reflections in water or in close-grained, polished surfaces, and everything of that kind, if you understand.

Yes, I understand.

Let the second section (B) stand for the actual things of which the first are likenesses, the living creatures about us and all the works of nature or of human hands.

So be it.

Will you also take the proportion in which the visible world has been divided as corresponding to degrees of reality and truth, so that the likeness shall stand to the original in the same ratio as the sphere of appearances and belief to the sphere of knowledge?

Certainly.

Now consider how we are to divide the part which stands for the intelligible world. There are two sections. In the first (C) the mind uses as images those actual things which themselves had images in the visible world; and it is compelled to pursue its inquiry by starting from assumptions and travelling, not up to a principle, but down to a conclusion. In the second (D) the mind moves in the other direction, from an assumption up towards a principle which is not hypothetical; and it makes no use of the images employed in the other section, but only of Forms, and conducts its inquiry solely by their means.

I don't quite understand what you mean.

Then we will try again; what I have just said will help you to understand. (C) You know, of course, how students of subjects like geometry and arithmetic begin by postulating odd and even numbers, or the various figures and the three kinds of angle, and other such data in each subject. These data they take as known;

and, having adopted them as assumptions, they do not feel called upon to give any account of them to themselves or to anyone else, but treat them as self-evident. Then, starting from these assumptions, they go on until they arrive, by a series of consistent steps, at all the conclusions they set out to investigate.

Yes, I know that.

You also know how they make use of visible figures and discourse about them, though what they really have in mind is the originals of which these figures are images: they are not reasoning, for instance, about this particular square and diagonal which they have drawn, but about *the* Square and *the* Diagonal; and so in all cases. The diagrams they draw and the models they make are actual things, which may have their shadows or images in water; but now they serve in their turn as images, while the student is seeking to behold those realities which only thought can apprehend.

True.

This, then, is the class of things that I spoke of as intelligible, but with two qualifications: first, that the mind, in studying them, is compelled to employ assumptions, and, because it cannot rise above these, does not travel upwards to a first principle; and second, that it uses as images those actual things which have images of their own in the section below them and which, in comparison with those shadows and reflections, are reputed to be more palpable and valued accordingly.

I understand: you mean the subject-matter of geometry and of the kindred arts.

(D) Then by the second section of the intelligible world you may understand me to mean all that unaided reasoning apprehends by the power of dialectic, when it treats its assumptions, not as first principles, but as *hypotheses* in the literal sense, things "laid down" like a flight of steps up which it may mount all the way to something that is not hypothetical, the first principle of all; and having grasped this, may turn back and, holding on to the consequences which depend upon it, descend at last to a conclusion, never making use of any sensible object, but only of Forms, moving through Forms from one to another, and ending with Forms.

I understand, he said, though not perfectly; for the procedure you describe sounds like an enormous undertaking. But I see that you mean to distinguish the field of intelligible reality studied by dialectic as having a greater certainty and truth than the subject-matter of the "arts," as they are called, which treat their assumptions as first principles. The students of these arts are, it is true, compelled to exercise thought in contemplating objects which the senses cannot perceive; but because they start from assumptions without going back to a first principle, you do not regard them as gaining true understanding about those objects, although the objects themselves, when connected with a first principle, are intelligible. And I think you would call the state of mind of the students of geometry and other such arts, not intelligence, but thinking, as being something between intelligence and mere acceptance of appearances.

You have understood me quite well enough, I replied. And now you may take, as corresponding to the four sections, these four states of mind: *intelligence* for the highest, *thinking* for the second, *belief* for the third, and for the last *imagining*. These you may arrange as the terms in a proportion, assigning to each a degree of clearness and certainty corresponding to the measure in which their objects possess truth and reality.

I understand and agree with you. I will arrange them as you say.[8]

---

[8]Plato, *The Republic,* 509D–511E.

There is no end to what could be said about Plato's philosophy on the basis of the Line. Here we will summarize the most important points.

To begin with, note that the Line is not divided into equal parts but *unequal* parts, and likewise the bottom and top segments of the Line are divided in the same ratio. This is Plato's way of suggesting that as we proceed from the bottom to the top of the Line we attain greater and greater degrees of reality and certainty. The first and major division of the Line represents, obviously, the distinction between the world of Being and the world of Becoming. By now we are certainly familiar with this distinction. But now each of the resulting lines, below and above, is in turn divided. This results in a sort of ladder of reality (on the metaphysical side of the Line) and a ladder of knowledge (on the epistemological side). The ladder of reality extends from mere images of sensible things (reflections in pools of water, photographs, paintings, memories, etc.) to the sensible things themselves (actual tables, chairs, humans, instances of justice or beauty, etc.), to the Forms that these sensible things copy. If the Form or essence includes a specific and concrete physical embodiment (Table, Circle, Human), then the Form is a "lower Form"; if the Form has no specific and concrete physical embodiment (Justice, Beauty), then it is a "higher Form." Corresponding to this ladder of reality is the ladder of knowledge. This extends from mere imagination (which grasps images) to perception (which grasps actual sensible things) to reason (which is a rational and deductive way of grasping the lower Forms) to understanding (which grasps the higher Forms in a direct and intuitive way).

PLATO'S DIVIDED LINE

Metaphysics	Epistemology
Higher Forms	Understanding
BEING	*KNOWLEDGE*
Mathematical forms	Reason
Sensible objects	Perception
BECOMING	*OPINION*
Images	Imagination

But there is more. It turns out that there is something above even the Forms themselves, something we must situate at the very top of the Line. In the *Republic* Plato calls it the "essential Form of the Good." Why must we believe in something even above the Forms, a sort of Form of the Forms? The answer is this: Just as the many images—say, in a pool of water—must derive their relative being from some one thing above them, like an actual table, and actual tables must derive their relative being from some one thing above *them*, the Form Table, so must the Forms (both lower and higher) derive *their* being from a source that is above *them*: the Form of the Good. And just as it is above all realities and is their ultimate source, so it is above all knowledge and is its ultimate source. Of course, in order to be the *source* of being and knowledge, it itself cannot be *a* being or *a* thing known. That is why Plato says of the Good that it is *beyond being and knowledge*.

The Good: Form
of the Forms

In a well-known analogy, Plato likens the essential Form of Goodness to the sun. The Good is to the intelligible world, or the world of Being, as the sun is to the visible world, or the world of Becoming:

> First we must come to an understanding. Let me remind you of the distinction we drew earlier and have often drawn on other occasions, between the multiplicity of things that we call good or beautiful or whatever it may be and, on the other hand, Goodness itself or Beauty itself and so on. Corresponding to each of these sets of many things, we postulate a single Form or real essence, as we call it.
>
> Yes, that is so.
>
> Further, the many things, we say, can be seen, but are not objects of rational thought; whereas the Forms are objects of thought, but invisible.
>
> Yes, certainly.
>
> And we see things with our eyesight, just as we hear sounds with our ears and, to speak generally, perceive any sensible things with our sense-faculties.
>
> Of course.
>
> Have you noticed, then, that the artificer who designed the senses has been exceptionally lavish of his materials in making the eyes able to see and their objects visible?
>
> That never occurred to me.
>
> Well, look at it in this way. Hearing and sound do not stand in need of any third thing, without which the ear will not hear nor sound be heard; and I think the same is true of most, not to say all, of the other senses. Can you think of one that does require anything of the sort?
>
> No, I cannot.
>
> But there is this need in the case of sight and its objects. You may have the power of vision in your eyes and try to use it, and colour may be there in the objects; but sight will see nothing and the colours will remain invisible in the absence of a third thing peculiarly constituted to serve this very purpose.
>
> By which you mean—?
>
> Naturally I mean what you call light; and if light is a thing of value, the sense of sight and the power of being visible are linked together by a very precious bond, such as unites no other sense with its object.

The Analogy
of the Sun

No one could say that light is not a precious thing.

And of all the divinities in the skies is there one whose light, above all the rest, is responsible for making our eyes see perfectly and making objects perfectly visible?

There can be no two opinions: of course you mean the Sun.

And how is sight related to this deity? Neither sight nor the eye which contains it is the Sun, but of all the sense-organs it is the most sun-like; and further, the power it possesses is dispensed by the Sun, like a stream flooding the eye. And again, the Sun is not vision, but it is the cause of vision and also is seen by the vision it causes.

Yes.

It was the Sun, then, that I meant when I spoke of that offspring which the Good has created in the visible world, to stand there in the same relation to vision and visible things as that which the Good itself bears in the intelligible world to intelligence and to intelligible objects.

How is that? You must explain further.

You know what happens when the colours of things are no longer irradiated by the daylight, but only by the fainter luminaries of the night: when you look at them, the eyes are dim and seem almost blind, as if there were no unclouded vision in them. But when you look at things on which the Sun is shining, the same eyes see distinctly and it becomes evident that they do contain the power of vision.

Certainly.

Apply this comparison, then, to the soul. When its gaze is fixed upon an object irradiated by truth and reality, the soul gains understanding and knowledge and is manifestly in possession of intelligence. But when it looks towards that twilight world of things that come into existence and pass away, its sight is dim and it has only opinions and beliefs which shift to and fro, and now it seems like a thing that has no intelligence.

That is true.

This, then, which gives to the objects of knowledge their truth and to him who knows them his power of knowing, is the Form or essential nature of Goodness. It is the cause of knowledge and truth; and so, while you may think of it as an object of knowledge, you will do well to regard it as something beyond truth and knowledge and, precious as these both are, of still higher worth. And, just as in our analogy light and vision were to be thought of as like the Sun, but not identical with it, so here both knowledge and truth are to be regarded as like the Good, but to identify either with the Good is wrong. The Good must hold a yet higher place of honour.

You are giving it a position of extraordinary splendour, if it is the source of knowledge and truth and itself surpasses them in worth. You surely cannot mean that it is pleasure.

Heaven forbid, I exclaimed. But I want to follow up our analogy still further. You will agree that the Sun not only makes the things we see visible, but also brings them into existence and gives them growth and nourishment; yet he is not the same thing as existence. And so with the objects of knowledge: these derive from the Good not only their power of being known, but their very being and reality; and Goodness is not the same thing as being, but even beyond being, surpassing it in dignity and power.[9]

---

[9]Plato, *The Republic*, 507A–509B.

It may be useful to spell out exactly the various elements in the analogy: The sun is analogous to the Form of the Good; the visible world is analogous to the intelligible world (the world of Forms); Light is analogous to Truth; the objects of sight are analogous to the objects of knowledge (the Forms); and sight is analogous to knowledge. Or perhaps a more visual summary will help.[10]

SUN		GOOD
in		in
VISIBLE WORLD		INTELLIGIBLE WORLD
by its	Analogous	by its
LIGHT	to	TRUTH
cause of		cause of
SIGHT		KNOWLEDGE
and existence of objects of sight		and existence of objects of knowledge (Forms)

The two main points of the analogy are: *First,* just as the sun lights up the world and makes physical objects visible to our eyes, so does the Good illuminate intelligible objects (Forms) and render them knowable by the mind. *Second,* and closely related, just as the sun actually causes things in the world to exist and sustains them—without the light of the sun, the world would wither away—so does the Good cause in the Forms their very being and truth.

In Plato's theory of reality, the Good is, then, the ultimate principle of reality and truth. Any degree or instance of being, truth, unity, harmony, beauty, or intelligibility found anywhere, either in the world of Becoming or in the world of Being, is traceable finally to the Good. This is, some would say, the closest thing in Plato to traditional conceptions of God, both Western and Eastern.

The Good is also the ultimate object of the soul's progress. And now we are ready for the Allegory of the Cave, one of the most famous passages in all literature. In this allegory Plato asks us to picture men imprisoned in an underground cavern who mistake the shadowy figures and echoes reflected on the wall facing them for reality. But how deluded they are! It is only by forcing them (and that is what it would take to dislodge them from their comfortable and familiar setting) out of the cave and into the upper world that, though temporarily dazzled and blinded by the true light, they would eventually recognize their former delusion. But read it for yourself.

---

[10]The chart is based on R. C. Cross and A. D. Woosley, *Plato's Republic: A Philosophical Commentary* (London: Macmillan, 1966), pp. 202, 231.

The Allegory
of the Cave

. . . here is a parable to illustrate the degrees in which our nature may be enlightened or unenlightened. Imagine the condition of men living in a sort of cavernous chamber underground, with an entrance open to the light and a long passage all down the cave. Here they have been from childhood, chained by the leg and also by the neck, so that they cannot move and can see only what is in front of them, because the chains will not let them turn their heads. At some distance higher up is the light of a fire burning behind them; and between the prisoners and the fire is a track with a parapet built along it, like the screen at a puppet-show, which hides the performers while they show their puppets over the top.

I see, said he.

Now behind this parapet imagine persons carrying along various artificial objects, including figures of men and animals in wood or stone or other materials, which project above the parapet. Naturally, some of these persons will be talking, others silent.

It is a strange picture, he said, and a strange sort of prisoners.

Like ourselves, I replied; for in the first place prisoners so confined would have seen nothing of themselves or of any other, except the shadows thrown by the fire-light on the wall of the Cave facing them, would they?

Not if all their lives they had been prevented from moving their heads.

And they would have seen as little of the objects carried past.

Of course.

Now, if they could talk to one another, would they not suppose that their words referred only to those passing shadows which they saw?

Necessarily.

And suppose their prison had an echo from the wall facing them? When one of the people crossing behind them spoke, they could only suppose that the sound came from the shadow passing before their eyes.

No doubt.

In every way, then, such prisoners would recognize as reality nothing but the shadows of those artificial objects.

Inevitably.

Now consider what would happen if their release from the chains and the healing of their unwisdom should come about in this way. Suppose one of them were set free and forced suddenly to stand up, turn his head, and walk with eyes lifted to the light; all these movements would be painful, and he would be too dazzled to make out the objects whose shadows he had been used to seeing. What do you think he would say, if someone told him that what he had formerly seen was meaningless illusion, but now, being somewhat nearer to reality and turned towards more real objects, he was getting a truer view? Suppose further that he were shown the various objects being carried by and were made to say, in reply to questions, what each of them was. Would he not be perplexed and believe the objects now shown him to be not so real as what he formerly saw?

Yes, not nearly so real.

And if he were forced to look at the fire-light itself, would not his eyes ache, so that he would try to escape and turn back to the things which he could see distinctly, convinced that they really were clearer than these other objects now being shown to him?

Yes.

And suppose someone were to drag him away forcibly up the steep and rugged ascent and not let him go until he had hauled him out into the sunlight, would he not suffer pain and vexation at such treatment, and, when he had come out into

Plato's Allegory of the Cave is one of the most famous passages in all literature. This artist's rendering of Plato's cave may be helpful as you read the story.

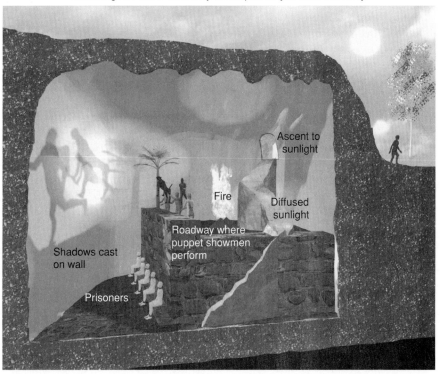

the light, find his eyes so full of its radiance that he could not see a single one of the things that he was now told were real?

Certainly he would not see them all at once.

He would need, then, to grow accustomed before he could see things in that upper world. At first it would be easiest to make out shadows, and then the images of men and things reflected in water, and later on the things themselves. After that, it would be easier to watch the heavenly bodies and the sky itself by night, looking at the light of the moon and stars rather than the Sun and the Sun's light in the daytime.

Yes, surely.

Last of all, he would be able to look at the Sun and contemplate its nature, not as it appears when reflected in water or any alien medium, but as it is in itself in its own domain.

No doubt.

And now he would begin to draw the conclusion that it is the Sun that produces the seasons and the course of the year and controls everything in the visible world, and moreover is in a way the cause of all that he and his companions used to see.

Clearly he would come at last to that conclusion.[11]

The point of the story should be obvious. We, like the prisoners in the cave, are deluded about reality. We mistake the unreal for the real, and only

[11]Plato, *The Republic*, 514A–516C.

with the greatest difficulty can we be turned, and indeed we might have to be *forced*, in the direction of truth and reality. But we *must* be turned in that direction, and we *must* ascend into the upper regions of truth and reality. Why? Because rationality is the essence of humanity. Thus our nature is fulfilled in the contemplation and knowledge of reality. And this means happiness or well-being. Even in this life, as much as possible we must be liberated and detached from the darkness of the sensible world of Becoming and opinion and live as much as possible in the enjoyment of Being and knowledge. At death, however, the soul will be freed forever from the distractions and imperfections of Becoming and can enjoy absolutely and without interruption the knowledge of Being. That is why, says Plato, the real philosopher—lover of wisdom—looks forward to death.

ARISTOTLE'S CRITICISM OF PLATO

As Plato was a student of Socrates and developed his ideas, so Aristotle was the student of Plato and developed *his* ideas. Less charitably, Aristotle ruthlessly criticized his master's theory of the Forms and propounded a quite different one.

Toward the beginning of his *Metaphysics*, Aristotle provides his own summary of the Socratic-Platonic theory:

Aristotle on Plato

> . . . [Plato], having in his youth first become familiar with Cratylus[12] and with the Heraclitean doctrines (that all sensible things are ever in a state of flux and there is no knowledge about them), these views he held even in later years. Socrates, however, was busying himself about ethical matters and neglecting the world of nature as a whole but seeking the universal in these ethical matters, and fixed thought for the first time on definitions; Plato accepted his teaching, but held that the problem applied not to sensible things but to entities of another kind— for this reason, that the common definition could not be a definition of any sensible thing, as they were always changing. Things of this other sort, then, he called Ideas, and sensible things, he said, were all named after these, and in virtue of a relation of these; for the many existed by participation in the Ideas that have the same name as they.[13]

Later Aristotle criticizes this view with a long string of objections; in fact, some have counted twenty-five or more. Not all of Aristotle's objections are as important as others, as when he twits Plato for creating an additional world of things, as if we did not already have enough to explain!

More important is Aristotle's so-called Third-Man Argument. It goes like this. In order to explain the similarity between (1) a first man and (2) a second man, we must posit (3) a third man, the Ideal Man or Form. But then

---

[12]Cratylus was a follower of Heraclitus but pushed the teaching of his master even further, for he said that one could not step into the same river even *once!*

[13]Aristotle, *Metaphysics*, 987a–b, tr. W. D. Ross, in *Basic Works of Aristotle*, ed. Richard McKeon (New York: Random House, 1941).

there will have to be a similarity between (1) the first two men and (2) the third man posited, the Form of Man. How do we now explain this similarity? We must again posit (3) a third and "higher" man. But then there will be a similarity between (1) all the previous men and (2) *this* third man. How do we explain *this* similarity? According to Aristotle, the process of positing a "third man" will have to go on forever, but in that case, the original similarity is never explained. Is this a fair argument against Plato? Some have countered that the argument will work only if you think the original third man, the Form of Man, is itself actually a *man* and possessing the features particular men possess. Would Plato agree to this? Is the Form of Man *itself* two-legged and rational? This is a difficult question, and much ink has been spilt trying to explain just how Plato viewed the Forms in this respect. Be that as it may, this is still not Aristotle's main objection to Plato.

The Third-Man
Argument

The main problem, for Aristotle, is the problem of the *chōrismos*, a Greek word that means "separation." Aristotle correctly represents Plato as having placed the ultimate causes of things (the Forms) in a transcendent world and thus *separated* from the things they are supposed to be the causes of. But this gives rise immediately to two very big questions, as Aristotle shows in the following:

> Above all one might discuss the question what on earth the Forms contribute to sensible things, either to those that are eternal or to those that come into being and cease to be. For they cause neither movement nor any change in them. But again they help in no wise either towards the knowledge of the other things (for they are not even the substance of these, else they would have been in them), or towards their being, if they are not in the particulars which share in them; though if they were, they might be thought to be causes, as white causes whiteness in a white object by entering into its composition. . . .
>
> But, further, all other things cannot come from the Forms in any of the usual senses of "from." And to say that they are patterns and the other things share in them is to use empty words and poetical metaphors. . . .
>
> Again, it would seem impossible that the substance and that of which it is the substance should exist apart; how therefore, could the Ideas, being the substances of things, exist apart? In the *Phaedo* the case is stated in this way—that the Forms are causes both of being and of becoming; yet when the Forms exist, still the things that share in them do not come into being, unless there is something to originate movement.[14]

The Problem
of the *chōrismos*

One question Aristotle poses is: How can the Forms be the causes of the natures or "whatnesses" of things without being *in* those things? His answer: They can't. *Another* question Aristotle poses is: How do Plato's transcendent and unchanging Forms account for the most evident fact about the things around us—namely, their coming into being and their motion and change? His answer: They don't. In sum, the *chōrismos*, or separation, between the Forms and particular sensible things, like a great gulf fixed, makes it impossible for the Forms to *do* anything for those things at the most

---

[14]Ibid., 991a–b.

critical points. That is bad enough. What is worse, when Plato attempts to explain how the Forms are related to sensible things, he provides no really rigorous philosophical explanation but resorts to "empty words and poetical metaphors" such as *participation* and *imitation*.

In fairness to Plato, it should be noted that many of Aristotle's specific criticisms (for example, the Third-Man Argument) were anticipated and discussed by Plato himself. More generally, in the *Timaeus* Plato did account for motion and change in the world, and as for his attempt to bridge the two worlds with "empty words and poetical metaphors," we saw in an earlier passage from the *Phaedo* that Plato freely granted the difficulty of language at this point.

ARISTOTLE'S VIEW OF FORM

One must not conclude from the above that Aristotle rejected Plato's theory of reality for a radically different one. Aristotle too believed absolutely in Forms. As with Plato, so with Aristotle: Only by means of Forms, the objective essences of things, can we account for the order around us, both in nature and in morality, and only because of Forms is knowledge of anything possible. The *difference* lies in their views of how the Forms are related to particular things.

It should be clear from the above quotation that Aristotle rejected Plato's idea of *transcendent* Forms in favor of an idea of *immanent* Forms—that is, a view of Forms as existing *within* particular sensible things. He overcomes Plato's unbridgeable chasm between Forms and sensible things by asserting that Forms can be causes of things only if they are *in* those things. But understand: There is no abstract "tableness" out there any more than there is any unimaginable formless matter or formless "stuff." What *is* out there are particular *tables*—this table, that table, and other tables. The Form or essence Table exists only as individualized or particularized (that is, turned into a concrete, particular thing) by some wood, glue, and varnish. And likewise with everything. The Form (which accounts for the essence or whatness of a thing) combined with matter (which gives that essence a concrete and particular expression) is what is *real*. As one slogan puts it, "No form without matter, and no matter without form." For those who prefer a more technical expression, this view or idea is called *hylomorphic composition* (from the Greek *hylē*, "matter," and *morphē*, "form"): Everything in the natural world

Aristotle: Forms must be in things

"No form without matter, no matter without form"

HYLOMORPHIC COMPOSITION

Although Aristotle himself never used this expression, it was eventually coined to represent the Aristotelian emphasis on the necessary twofold composition, material and formal, of everything in the natural world.

Plato and Aristotle, from "The School of Athens" (detail) by Raphael. In this representation, Plato and Aristotle are distinguishable from one another in several respects. How many of them can you identify?

is composed of both form and matter; there can be no instances of unformed matter or "unmattered" form.

Thus it is with everything in the *natural* world. With respect to God, the situation is quite different. The matter in a thing provides for its changeability and movement, since matter is the potential in a thing to change or become something different. Think of a table. It can be chopped into bits, burned into ashes, or dismantled and turned into a chair, only because there is *wood* there. But there can be no matter, or potential for change and motion, in God, who is the Unmoved Mover. God, the immutable source of all motion, must himself be utterly devoid of matter. He is Pure Form.

God: Pure Form

All of this so far may sound rather technical and bland. But the whole show is considerably enlivened when the *teleological* side of this theory of reality is stressed. And it should be stressed because it is a major feature of the Aristotelian perspective.

"Teleology" comes from the Greek word *telos*, "end" or "goal," and means the study of, or the belief in, principles that give rise to the order and purpose that pervade all reality. (We will see momentarily that these principles

Teleology

are otherwise called "final causes.") The conviction that reality is infused and governed by teleological principles is not new with Aristotle, though he thought it was. It is an obvious feature of the Platonic philosophy too, and it is clearly discernible in some of the Pre-Socratics. Still, it received with Aristotle perhaps the strongest expression in the whole history of philosophy. For Aristotle, there is, so to say, both an "inside" and an "outside" story. The inside story concerns the way in which anything, say, an acorn, is propelled naturally, by the form within, into a full-fledged, giant oak tree. What is immanent, then, is more than a static form—it includes a power that develops the thing into its full reality. As for the outside story: The oak tree is nourished by the nutrients in the ground, is dependent on the change of seasons, and otherwise stands in a complex relation to the rest of nature—using it for its own purposes, maintaining its own structure in the face of perturbances, and producing more acorns. The whole of nature is, in fact, a network of intimately related things, conspiring, as it were, upon the production of the efficient, harmonious, beautiful, and value-laden universe that confronts our sense at every turn.

Aristotle vs. Plato on art

The real difference between Plato's idea of *transcendent* Forms and Aristotle's idea of *immanent* Forms shows up very vividly in their discussions of art. In the last parts of the *Republic,* Plato argued that art is "thrice removed" from reality: A painting is an imperfect representation or copy of a man who himself is an imperfect copy of the real thing, Man; likewise a drama imperfectly represents people and things that are themselves imperfect copies of their Forms. For these reasons Plato advocated banishing the arts—at least the *representative* arts—from the ideal society. Aristotle, with his view of immanent Forms, draws exactly the opposite conclusion. It is because the essence and ideal of things are embodied *in* those things that the artistic representation brings us *closer* to reality. As Aristotle says in a helpful passage in his *Poetics,* what the artist does is represent things in their *universality,* to use Aristotle's term, and that is why the artist's work is more philosophical than, say, the historian's work, which represents things merely in their *particularity.*

> . . . the poet's function is to describe, not the thing that has happened, but a kind of thing that might happen, i.e. what is possible as being probable or necessary. The distinction between historian and poet is not in the one writing prose and the other verse—you might put the work of Herodotus into verse, and it would still be a species of history; it consists really in this, that the one describes the thing that has been, and the other a kind of thing that might be. Hence poetry is something more philosophic and of graver import than history, since its statements are of the nature rather of universals, whereas those of history are singulars. By a universal statement I mean one as to what such or such a kind of man will probably or necessarily say or do—which is the aim of poetry, though it affixes proper names to the characters; by a singular statement, one as to what, say, Alcibiades did or had done to him.[15]

---

[15] Aristotle, *Poetics,* 1451a–b, tr. Ingram Bywater, in *Basic Works of Aristotle.*

Two final points: First, although we have dwelt upon form and matter, according to Aristotle there are actually *four* principles, or "causes," that are necessarily involved in the constitution or explanation of a thing:

- Material cause
- Formal cause
- Efficient cause
- Final cause

Aristotle's Four Causes

The *material cause* is the matter, or "stuff," something is made out of; the *formal cause* is its essence, or whatness; the *efficient* or *moving cause* is what brings the thing into being; and the *final cause* is the end, or purpose, of the thing. Can you identify the four causes of, say, a table? It may be noticed that the last three causes are closely related, and Aristotle himself suggests that they may be lumped together under the formal cause, leaving with us the general twofold distinction: material cause/formal cause. Thus the key terms in the constitution and explanation of things are matter and form. Second, Aristotle stressed even more strongly than Plato the difference between "substantial" Forms and "accidental" Forms. Fido *necessarily* involves the Form Dog; it is of Fido's very nature or substance to be a dog. But it is only an accident that Fido involves the forms Shaggy, Brown, and Short-legged; it is not part of Fido's essence that he possesses these features—he might or might not, and still be a *dog*.

Substantial and accidental Forms

AFTER PLATO AND ARISTOTLE

Aristotle provides, thus, a criticism of Plato's theory of reality. But his own theory, after all, is not really all that different. For both Plato and Aristotle the true reality of something is identified with its Form. And this general view, often called *realism*, was propagated throughout subsequent centuries, mainly through the Christian thinkers St. Augustine (d. 430), who taught more or less the Platonic version, and St. Thomas Aquinas (d. 1275), who taught more or less the Aristotelian version.

Realism

Obviously, this kind of philosophy is radically different from all those approaches that reject Form as sort of philosophically superstitious. It was, in fact, against this very idea that William of Ockham (d. 1349?) formulated the principle known as Ockham's Razor, in an attempt to cut away all unnecessary principles and realities: *Entia non sunt multiplicanda praeter necessitatem*, "Entities are not to be multiplied without necessity." The resulting view was known as *nominalism* (from the Latin *nomen*, "name"), the view that Forms or universals (such as Animal, Whiteness, etc.) have no external or independent existence, but are merely names or words by which we group together things that possess similar features.

Ockham's Razor

Nominalism

Nominalism will perhaps appear to you as a very simple and clean approach: away with all that silly and needless talk about substantial forms,

"I can see the horse, Plato, but not horseness."

—Antisthenes

accidental forms, metaphysical causes, and the like! On the other hand, we must not forget about the problems that spawned the belief in Forms in the first place: Without objective Forms, or essences, how, for example, are real knowledge, rational discourse, and moral judgment possible?

Conceptualism

Or perhaps you would like a compromise. A third option is *conceptualism*. This is a philosophical halfway house between realism and nominalism inasmuch as it holds that there *are* universals but they are *mind-made*. Cat-ness, for example, has no existence outside the mind, but it certainly does exist within the mind—a mental entity—and is employed for the sake of meaningful thought and discourse about reality.

It should not be thought that the realist-nominalist debate is just an antiquated piece in the Museum of Philosophical Ideas. The issue yet exercises contemporary thinkers. A good example is Willard V. Quine, one of the most influential English-speaking philosophers of the twentieth century, who relates

What is mathematics about?

the issue to mathematics. What is mathematics about? Is it about *anything*? There are three possible answers. First, you can say, as *logicism* does, that mathematics is about mind-independent objects, and this would commit you to a belief in something like Platonic or Aristotelian Forms, or realism. Second, you can say, with *formalism,* that mathematics isn't about anything, really; it is a formal game similar to chess where the pieces have no significance apart from the board, other pieces, the rules, and so on; and this would be to take a nominalist view. Third, there is an intermediate position, *intuitionism,* according to which mathematics is about mental constructs, and this, of course, corresponds to conceptualism. Quine himself (at least the later Quine) is the sort of philosopher who, in trying to answer the question of what exists, tries as much as possible to keep both feet in the physical world and appeals to the fewest abstract entities required to do the job. Nonetheless, he finds himself having to appeal to abstract or mind-independent entities, and thus he turns out to be a kind of mathematical Platonist.

Be that as it may, in the following extract from "On What There Is," Quine states how the very old problem of universals is alive and well ("ontology" is the theory of what is, and a "bound variable" is a formal logician's equivalent to a pronoun).

Classical mathematics . . . is up to its neck in commitments to an ontology of abstract entities. Thus it is that the great mediaeval controversy over universals has flared up anew in the modern philosophy of mathematics. The issue is clearer now than of old, because we now have a more explicit standard whereby to decide what ontology a given theory or form of discourse is committed to: a theory is committed to those and only those entities to which the bound variables of the theory must be capable of referring in order that the affirmations made in the theory be true.

REALISM, NOMINALISM, CONCEPTUALISM

- *Realism:* The doctrine that Forms, or essences, possess objective reality.
- *Nominalism:* The doctrine that Forms, or universals, are merely universal names by which we group together things that possess similar features.
- *Conceptualism:* The doctrine that universals are mental constructs, and as such really exist in the mind.

Because this standard of ontological presupposition did not emerge clearly in the philosophical tradition, the modern philosophical mathematicians have not on the whole recognized that they were debating the same old problem of universals in a newly clarified form. But the fundamental cleavages among modern points of view on foundations of mathematics do come down pretty explicitly to disagreements as to the range of entities to which the bound variables should be permitted to refer.

The three main mediaeval points of view regarding universals are designated by historians as *realism, conceptualism,* and *nominalism.* Essentially these same three doctrines reappear in twentieth-century surveys of the philosophy of mathematics under the new names *logicism, intuitionism,* and *formalism.*[16]

CHAPTER 3 IN REVIEW

SUMMARY

"Form" is one of the most important words in the history of philosophy. In fact, when the first full-blown philosophies came on the scene, those of Plato and Aristotle, they were built almost entirely around this concept.

In an important sense, the idea of Form is an answer to many philosophies, such as those of Heraclitus (as Plato understood him) and Protagoras, that dissolve everything into a flux of relativity. According to Plato and other Form-philosophers, we must believe in an objective basis for the things existing around us, for knowledge and for value judgments. This basis is the Form, or essence, which constitutes the real *being* of a thing. As being, the Form must be one, immutable, ideal, transcendent, and the like, and this being is imperfectly represented in particular, sensible things by "participation" or "imitation." Plato conceives all reality as a ladder or scale and, corresponding to this, knowledge too (the image of the Divided Line). But the basic distinction is between the sensible world of Becoming and the transcendent or intelligible world of Being, with the essential Form of

---

[16]Willard Van Orman Quine, "On What There Is," in *From a Logical Point of View: Nine Logico-Philosophical Essays,* second ed., rev. (Cambridge, MA: Harvard University Press, 1980), pp. 13f.

Goodness ranging over all (the Analogy of the Sun). The practical point is to make our way, as much as possible in this life, into the higher realm of the intelligible and to enjoy the illumination of reality and truth (the Allegory of the Cave).

Aristotle belongs to this philosophical tradition too, but represents an important variation. He criticized Plato's theory of the Forms in several ways, but mainly because of the gap it leaves between the Forms and the things they are the Forms *of:* the problem of the *chōrismos.* Instead, Aristotle insisted that although we must believe in the Forms or objective essences of things, they cannot be separated from those things. This is Aristotle's doctrine of *immanent* (rather than transcendent) Forms: The Forms must be *in* things. His conception of matter as potentiality and therefore providing for change, and his doctrine of the Four Causes, are also important features of his thought.

In subsequent centuries the realist metaphysics of Plato and Aristotle received Christian reinterpretations and restatements, most notably at the hands of St. Augustine and St. Thomas Aquinas. On the other hand, it was also *attacked* by nominalist philosophers, such as Ockham, for whom the Forms were merely general or universal terms that lump similar things into classes. The debate between realism (Forms have objective reality), nominalism (Forms are universal terms), and conceptualism (Forms are mental entities) is a fundamental and continuing one.

BASIC IDEAS

- "Systematic" philosophy
- The nature of a Platonic dialogue
- The Socratic Problem
- The problem with Protagorean subjectivism
- The problem with Heraclitean flux
- The distinction between the worlds of Becoming and Being
- The meaning of "Form"
- Six features of Platonic Forms; they are:
    Objective
    Transcendent
    Eternal
    Intelligible
    Archetypal
    Perfect
- Platonic metaphors for the Form's relation to the particular
    Imitation
    Participation
- Two ways in which something can share in more than one Form
- The Divided Line: Degrees of reality and knowledge
- The Good as the Form of Forms

- The Analogy of the Sun
- The Allegory of the Cave
- Aristotle's main criticism of Plato's theory: The problem of the *chōrismos*, "separation"
- Aristotle's conception of immanent Forms
- Hylomorphic composition
- Aristotelian teleology
- Aristotle's Four Causes
    Material
    Formal
    Efficient
    Final
- Substantial and accidental Forms
- Ockham's Razor
- Realism, nominalism, and conceptualism
- Quine: a mathematical Platonist

TEST YOURSELF

1. True or false: Plato believed that "a man is the measure of all things."
2. According to Plato, the sun is to the _____ as the Good is to the _____.
3. What did Heraclitus and Parmenides contribute to Plato's theory of the Forms?
4. How does Quine figure in this chapter?
5. True or false: Aristotle's efficient cause is the agent through which something comes into being.
6. What is the point of the Allegory of the Cave?
7. Aristotle believed not in transcendent Forms but in _____ Forms.
8. Plato taught that Forms are related to particular things by means of (a) the final cause, (b) participation, (c) hylomorphic composition, (d) imitation.
9. True or false: Aristotle was a nominalist.
10. Plato's and Aristotle's theories of reality were preserved, in a Christian version, by_____ and _____, respectively.

QUESTIONS FOR REFLECTION

- Plato's philosophy is sometimes called a rather "poetic" one. What does this mean? Is it good or bad? What is to be made of the fact that Plato anticipated Aristotle's criticisms but did not regard them as decisive?
- If one rejects every philosophy of Forms, such as that of Plato or Aristotle, what then? What about the problems that sparked such philosophies in the first place?

- Is it necessary to accept, say, Plato's philosophy in its entirety and detail in order to be a "Platonist"? Is it possible to distinguish the central and essential idea of a philosophy from the particular, relative, and even mistaken trappings in which it was originally expressed? What is the *perspective* that characterizes any Platonic philosophy?

FOR FURTHER READING

Julia Annas. *An Introduction to Plato's Republic.* Oxford: Clarendon Press, 1981. Chs. 8–10. An up-to-date discussion of Plato's theory of knowledge, theory of the Forms, and the Sun, Line, and the Cave.

Frederick Copleston. *A History of Philosophy.* Baltimore: Newman Press, 1946–1974. I, Parts 3 and 4. Readable and indispensable accounts of both Plato's and Aristotle's theories of reality and their relation to one another by an esteemed historian of philosophy.

G. M. A. Grube. *Plato's Thought.* London: Methuen, 1935. Ch. 1. A long and excellent chapter titled "The Theory of the Forms" in an old but useful work.

G. E. R. Lloyd. *Aristotle: The Growth and Structure of His Thought.* Cambridge: Cambridge University Press, 1968. A classic work that describes Aristotle's intellectual development as well as major themes in his work.

William J. Prior. *Unity and Development in Plato's Metaphysics.* LaSalle, IL: Open Court, 1985. A recent scholarly analysis of texts, showing the continuity and progress of Plato's metaphysical ideas throughout the most relevant of his dialogues.

David Ross. *Aristotle.* Fifth ed. London: Methuen, 1949. Ch. 6. Discussion of Aristotle's doctrines of substance, matter, form, and other topics from an old but still standard work on Aristotle.

A. E. Taylor. *Plato: The Man and His Work.* London: Methuen, 1926. A standard work that provides an overview of Plato's philosophy and brief, running commentaries on his dialogues.

Gregory Vlastos (ed.). *Plato: A Collection of Critical Essays,* I. Garden City, NY: Anchor Books, 1971. Scholarly and sometimes technical discussions by Plato specialists on a variety of metaphysical and epistemological issues in Plato's philosophy.

Nicholas White. *A Companion to Plato's Republic.* Indianapolis: Hackett Publishing Co., 1979.

*In addition, see the relevant articles ("Plato," "Aristotle," "Universals," etc.) in *Routledge Encyclopedia of Philosophy,* ed. Edward Craig (London: Routledge, 1998), and *Stanford Encyclopedia of Philosophy,* http://plato.stanford.edu.

CHAPTER 4

MIND AND MATTER

I f you were to meet someone on the street and ask what he or she thinks reality is, you might get a response something like this:

Well, I know that I have a mind (or soul, or whatever you want to call it), and I know that in addition to my mind—and presumably other minds too—there is a world of material things like my own body, and tables and chairs, and all the other things "out there." And, well, I guess there is a real difference between mind and matter such that my mind might exist even apart from matter.

This view of reality, *mind-matter dualism*, is a very common one, held by many who have never heard its name or have never even heard of metaphysics. It is called a dualism because it reduces everything to two basic realities—in this case, mind and matter. As a genuine philosophical position, however, it is considerably more complex than the opinion expressed

A common theory of reality

DUALISM

The metaphysical view that all things are reducible to two different realities.

---

by our friend on the street. For its most forceful expression we turn to the French thinker René Descartes[1] (1596–1650).

DESCARTES: THE FATHER OF MODERN PHILOSOPHY

In addition to being a mathematician and scientist (he invented analytic geometry and made numerous contributions to physics), Descartes was a philosopher and has been called, in fact, the father of modern philosophy. Everything changed with Descartes, and nearly all modern philosophies may be traced back, in one way or another, to his.

In a sense, modern philosophy originated in a dream, or a series of dreams, in which a new approach to knowledge was revealed to Descartes. It is not known exactly what "came" to Descartes in these dreams, but it appears that it had something to do with the unity of all branches of knowledge and perhaps the method of achieving this unity. In his *Discourse on Method,* Descartes tells of his disillusionment with traditional philosophy:

> . . . seeing that it has been cultivated for many centuries by the best minds that have ever lived, and that nevertheless no single thing is to be found in it which is not subject of dispute, and in consequence which is not dubious, I had not enough presumption to hope to fare better there than other men had done. And also, considering how many conflicting opinions there may be regarding the self-same matter, all supported by learned people, while there can never be more than one which is true, I esteemed as well-nigh false all that only went as far as being probable.[2]

On the other hand, he was much struck by the certainty of mathematical procedures:

> Most of all was I delighted with mathematics because of the certainty of its demonstration and the evidence of its reasoning.[3]

Descartes'
"geometrical
method"

He determined that if philosophy too was to be successful, it must annex to itself something like a "geometrical method" so that its starting points and conclusions might be as certain as those of geometry.

It will be best to consider Descartes' conception of philosophical knowledge in Part Two, "The Question of Knowledge." Here it should be enough to say only that Descartes turned his back on the doubtful truths delivered through the senses, and turned rather to what could be known with certainty through *reason alone*—an "inside-out" philosopher rather than an "outside-in" philosopher. In the intellect he found, as in geometry, two fundamental, foolproof operations: *intuition* and *deduction*. Through intuition

Intuition and
deduction

---

[1]Pronounced *Day-cart'*.

[2]René Descartes, *Discourse on Method,* in *The Philosophical Works of Descartes,* tr. Elizabeth S. Haldane and G. R. T. Ross (Cambridge: Cambridge University Press, 1911), I, 85–86.

[3]Ibid., I, 85.

Title page of the English translation of the
Discourse on Method

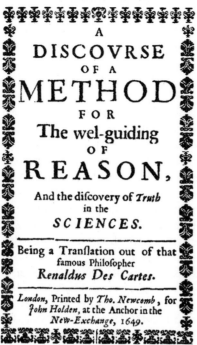

A
DISCOVRSE
OF A
METHOD
FOR
The wel-guiding
OF
REASON,
And the difcovery of *Truth*
in the
SCIENCES.

Being a Tranflation out of that
famous Philofopher
Renaldus Des Cartes.

London, Printed by *Tho. Newcomb*, for
John Holden, at the Anchor in the
New-Exchange, 1649.

he could know certain basic and undoubtable truths, and through deduction he could draw from these basic truths still further truths. Through both of them together he believed that he could construct a whole philosophy.

Armed with his geometrical method, Descartes set out to formulate a new and certain and definitive philosophy. The best expressions of this philosophy may be found in Descartes' *Discourse on Method* (especially Part Four) and his *Meditations on First Philosophy.* It may be helpful to anticipate a bit by saying that Descartes' philosophy unfolds in three major stages: first, the knowledge of the *mind;* second, the knowledge of *God;* and third, the knowledge of *matter.*

"WHAT CAN I KNOW FOR CERTAIN?"

We have already noted that Descartes was disillusioned with earlier philosophies because of their contradictions and muddledness. This distress was genuine (one may even detect an element of personal crisis in it) and probably reflected certain recent upheavals in the medieval view of the world. We can imagine him peering out his window and exclaiming, "If I cannot be certain that the sun moves across the sky (a major debate of the time because of Copernicus)—something I can see with my own eyes—then of what *can* I be certain?" Descartes thus resolved, first, to doubt anything and everything that was doubtable, in hopes of discovering something, even one thing, that was not doubtable, something certain, something unshakable, some indubitable truth that might serve as a secure foundation of his philosophy. In this respect, Descartes likened himself to the ancient Archimedes, who said in relation to his newly discovered principle of the fulcrum, "Give me a place to stand, and I will move the world!" Descartes said, in effect, "Give me just one certain truth, and I will build upon it an entire philosophy!"

Systematic doubt

Thus Descartes embarked on his process of *systematic doubt*—that is, the process of doubting everything that can be doubted to see if there is anything that *cannot* be doubted. Since our senses sometimes deceive us, Descartes supposed that perhaps the world of sense experience was not at all as it seems to be. Since people make the simplest mistakes in reasoning, he rejected as false all the demonstrations he had previously accepted. Noticing the similarities between waking life and dreams, he even ventured that nothing was more real than dreams. And noticing that two plus three equals five even when dreaming, he went so far as to devise the hypothesis of an "evil genius" bent upon constantly deceiving Descartes even about mathematical truths. Descartes documents his progress in the *Meditations:*

> I shall proceed by setting aside all that in which the least doubt could be supposed to exist—just as if I had discovered that it was absolutely false; and I shall ever follow in this road until I have met with something which is certain, or at least, if I can do nothing else, until I have learned for certain that there is nothing in the world that is certain. Archimedes, in order that he might draw the terrestrial globe out of its place, and transport it elsewhere, demanded only that one point should be fixed and immoveable; in the same way I shall have the right to conceive high hopes if I am happy enough to discover one thing only which is certain and indubitable.
>
> I suppose, then, that all the things that I see are false; I persuade myself that nothing has ever existed of all that my fallacious memory represents to me. I consider that I possess no senses; I imagine that body, figure, extension, movement and place are but the fictions of my mind. What, then, can be esteemed as true? Perhaps nothing at all, unless that there is nothing in the world that is certain.[4]

THE INTUITION OF MIND

Cogito ergo sum: "I think, therefore I am."

In this way Descartes sought to erase, as it were, everything from the chalkboard of human knowledge. Finally, he found himself exactly opposite to the naive realist who thinks that things are exactly as they appear. Descartes could doubt *everything*—except for one thing. In all of this doubting and erasing, one thing finally presented itself as *undoubtable* and *unerasable*. As he expressed it in the famous line from the *Principles of Philosophy: Cogito ergo sum,* "I think, therefore I am." After all, if I am mistaken about this, then there is no "I" to be mistaken!

---

[4]Descartes, *Meditations on First Philosophy,* in *The Philosophical Works of Descartes,* I, 149.

DESCARTES' METHOD OF DOUBT

As a way to find a new foundation for knowledge, Descartes set out to system-atically doubt everything. He found, however, that he couldn't doubt his own existence. Why? To doubt my existence presupposes my existence. In short, to doubt requires a doubter. Doubting is a form of thinking, and to think I must exist. Therefore, Descartes' famous conclusion: "I think, therefore I am."

. . . whilst I thus wished to think all things false, it was absolutely essential that the "I" who thought this should be somewhat, and remarking that this truth "I think, therefore I am" was so certain and so assured that all the most extravagant sup-positions brought forward by the sceptics were incapable of shaking it, I came to the conclusion that I could receive it without scruple as the first principle of the Philosophy for which I was seeking.[5]

Here, then, is rock-bottom certitude, unshakable even by the most radical doubt, a place for Descartes to stand as he sought to build a philosophy.

"I think, therefore I am." But *what* am I? What *is* mind? What *is* soul? What *is* my spirit? (Descartes uses all of these terms interchangeably.) Descartes' answer in the *Discourse:* It is "a substance the whole essence or nature of which is to think,"[6] or for short, a *thinking substance.* But here we must make our terms clear. We have a good idea what Descartes means by "thinking"; it means all the intellectual operations, such as affirming, deny-ing, imagining, doubting, reflecting, inferring, and the like. We may have more trouble with the word "substance." Some readers may find themselves almost hopelessly afflicted with the idea that substance means some con-crete, physical thing. But the word itself (from the Latin *substantia*) means, literally, "that which stands under" or "that which upholds" something. To use Descartes' own example, consider a ball of wax. It may be hard or soft and have a certain color, odor, and texture, and these may change from time to time, but then there is the wax *itself,* the substance of these qualities. Can you imagine texture or shape existing without something that *is* textured and shaped? Can you imagine thinking without something that *does* the thinking? Just as in grammar there could be no predicate without a subject, so in the world of sensible things there could be no qualities without a material

Mind: a substance
the essence of which
is to think

[5]Descartes, *Discourse on Method,* I, 101.
[6]Ibid.

COGITO ERGO SUM

"I think, therefore I am." Descartes' famous conclusion to his doubting.

RENÉ DESCARTES

René Descartes was born in Touraine, France, in 1596. His mother died in giving him birth, and from her he appears to have inherited a frail constitution. At eight years old he was enrolled in the Jesuit school at La Flèche, where his poor health won for him certain privileges, including sleeping late, a habit that Descartes cherished throughout his life. At La Flèche, he displayed the inclination for mathematics and geometry that later exerted such an influence over his whole philosophy.

(*continued on next page*)

substance, and in the intellectual world no thinking activities without a mental substance. But it is not just that there is no thinking apart from mind—mind *is* thinking, a thinking substance. It *may* affirm, deny, doubt, reflect, imagine, infer, and so on, but it *must* think.

In the *Meditations,* Descartes provides a summary of this first stage of his reasoning: (1) It is certain that I exist, and (2) I am a mind or thinking substance.

> . . . I was persuaded that there was nothing in all the world, that there was no heaven, no earth, that there were no minds, nor any bodies: was I not then likewise persuaded that I did not exist? Not at all; of a surety I myself did exist since I persuaded myself of something [or merely because I thought of something]. But there is some deceiver or other, very powerful and very cunning, who ever employs his ingenuity in deceiving me. Then without doubt I exist also if he deceives me, and let him deceive me as much as he will, he can never cause me to be nothing so long as I think that I am something. So that after having reflected well and carefully examined

At 16, Descartes left La Flèche and journeyed to Paris, where, provided by his father with a valet and money, he especially enjoyed gambling. (His friends attributed his gambling successes to the fact that he bet according to his unusual knowledge of mathematics rather than to chance.) In Paris, he made the acquaintance of the celebrated mathematician Mydorge. A certain restlessness and eagerness to learn from "the book of the world," as he put it, caused Descartes, in 1617, to go to Holland, where he enlisted as a volunteer without pay in the army of Prince Maurice of Nassau. He was not much of a soldier, though it was during this stint that he discovered analytic geometry, thus ensuring his niche in the history of mathematics. In 1619, the Thirty Years War broke out, and Descartes joined the Catholic forces and found himself eventually in Prague. On November 10, 1619, Descartes had his famous three dreams in which a way of unifying all knowledge was revealed to him. Tired of soldiering, he returned to Paris (which he found too hectic), and then, in 1628, he went to the Netherlands, where his serious philosophical and scientific activity and writing got under way, as well as other things: Here he had a mistress who bore him a daughter. It was during this period that Descartes published his major philosophical works, though, noting the fate of Galileo, he suspended the publication of a book on cosmology.

In time he was repeatedly entreated by Queen Christina of Sweden (a robust and masculine woman) to tutor her in his philosophy. Because of his physical condition he hesitated, but eventually accepted the invitation in 1649. Upon his arrival he learned to his horror that the queen insisted on receiving philosophy lessons at five o'clock in the morning! This first winter was especially severe, and Descartes quickly caught pneumonia and died. To the end of his life he professed the Catholic faith. He is buried in Ste. Geneviève du Mont in Paris.

Some of Descartes' more important works are *Rules for the Direction of the Mind*, *Discourse on Method*, *Meditations on First Philosophy*, *Optics*, *Geometry*, *Meteorology*, and *Principles of Philosophy*.

all things, we must come to the definite conclusion that this proposition: I am, I exist, is necessarily true each time that I pronounce it, or that I mentally conceive it. . . .

But what am I, now that I suppose that there is a certain genius which is extremely powerful, and, if I may say so, malicious, who employs all his powers in deceiving me? Can I affirm that I possess the least of all those things which . . . pertain to the nature of body? I pause to consider, I revolve all these things in my mind, and I find none of which I can say that it pertains to me. It would be tedious to stop to enumerate them. Let us pass to the attributes of soul and see if there is any one which is in me. What of nutrition or walking. . .? But if it is so that I have no body it is also true that I can neither walk nor take nourishment. Another attribute is sensation. But one cannot tell without body, and besides I have thought I perceived many things during sleep that I recognized in my waking moments as not having been experienced at all. What of thinking? I find here that thought is an attribute that belongs to me; it alone cannot be separated from me. I am, I exist, that is certain. But how often? Just when I think; for it might possibly be the case if I ceased entirely to think, that I should likewise cease altogether to exist. I do not now admit anything which is not necessarily true: to speak accurately I am not more than a thing which thinks,

SUBSTANCE

"Substance" is popularly thought to be a *physical thing*. But the term was used by Descartes and subsequent thinkers in quite a different way, and with its original sense of "that which stands under" and thus "upholds" something (from the Latin *substantia*). For Descartes and others, mind is the substance that underlies mental activities, as matter is the substance underlying and upholding physical qualities.

that is to say a mind or a soul, or an understanding, or a reason, which are terms whose significance was formerly unknown to me. I am, however, a real thing and really exist; but what thing? I have answered: a thing which thinks.[7]

Thus we are led to the first of Descartes' three major metaphysical conclusions: *There is mind.*

But that is not the only important thing that has been learned. Through reflection on the character of this primary certainty—I exist—Descartes has discovered what he can take as the hallmark or criterion of *any* indubitable and certain idea: *clarity* and *distinctness.*

Clear and distinct
ideas as the
foundation of
further knowledge

After this I considered generally what in a proposition is requisite in order to be true and certain; for since I had just discovered one which I knew to be such, I thought that I ought also to know in what this certainty consisted. And having remarked that there was nothing at all in the statement "*I think, therefore I am*" which assures me of having thereby made a true assertion, excepting that I see very clearly that to think it is necessary to be, I came to the conclusion that I might assume, as a general rule, that the things which we conceive very clearly and distinctly are all true—remembering, however, that there is some difficulty in ascertaining which are those that we distinctly conceive.[8]

THE DEDUCTION OF GOD

On the basis of mind as a thinking substance, along with the criterion of clear and distinct ideas, Descartes leads us to a further consideration: God. He provides two proofs for the existence of God, both of them rooted in the thinking self, both of them employing clear and distinct premises, and both of them involving the idea of perfection.

Descartes'
Eidological
Argument for God

The first of these two proofs has no particular name, so we may propose for convenience the label Eidological Argument for God, from the Greek word for "idea." Descartes' reasoning is that God must exist in order to account for our *idea of perfection*. Descartes discovered in his mind the idea

---

[7]Descartes, *Meditations on First Philosophy*, I, 150, 151–152.

[8]Ibid., I, 101–102.

DESCARTES' EIDOLOGICAL PROOF FOR GOD

If I have an idea of perfection, then there must actually exist a perfect being
   as its cause.
I have an idea of perfection.

Therefore, there must actually exist a perfect being.

of a being more perfect than himself—after all, he doubted, and it is a greater
perfection to know than to doubt—but where did this idea of something
more perfect come from? Now it is absurd that this idea might have come
from nothing, for I have a clear and distinct notion that nothing comes from
nothing. Nor could it have come from myself, since it is no less absurd that
the more perfect should come from the less perfect than that something
should come from nothing. We are driven rationally to the only conclusion:
The idea of perfection has been placed in our minds by a perfect being. This
proof comes out best in the *Discourse:*

> Following upon this, and reflecting on the fact that I doubted, and that consequently
> my existence was not quite perfect (for I saw clearly that it was a greater perfec-
> tion to know than to doubt), I resolved to inquire whence I had learnt to think of
> anything more perfect than I myself was; and I recognised very clearly that this
> conception must proceed from some nature which was really more perfect. As to
> the thoughts which I had of many other things outside of me, like the heavens, the
> earth, light, heat, and a thousand others, I had not so much difficulty in knowing
> whence they came, because, remarking nothing in them which seemed to render
> them superior to me, I could believe that, if they were true, they were dependen-
> cies upon my nature, in so far as it possessed some perfection; and if they were
> not true, that I held them from nought, that is to say, that they were in me because
> I had something lacking in my nature. But this could not apply to the idea of a
> Being more perfect than my own, for to hold it from nought would be manifestly
> impossible, and because it is no less contradictory to say of the more perfect that
> it is what results from and depends on the less perfect, than to say that there is
> something which proceeds from nothing, it was equally impossible that I should
> hold it from myself. In this way it could but follow that it had been placed in me
> by a Nature which was really more perfect than mine could be, and which even
> had within itself all the perfections of which I could form any idea—that is to say,
> to put it in a word, which was God.[9]

It should be noted that this is a *causal* argument for God; that is, it argues
that God must exist as the only adequate cause of something—in this case,
the cause of the idea of perfection. We are reminded, though, how seriously
Descartes takes mind and ideas. Even an idea is some sort of reality or *thing*

---

[9]Descartes, *Discourse on Method,* I, 102.

(though obviously not a physical thing), and a thing the existence of which needs explaining no less than tables or chairs or worlds or galaxies.

Descartes' second proof for God is a version of the Ontological Argument. As with the first, this one too is stated in the *Discourse*, though it is developed further in the *Meditations*. And like the first, it begins with the idea of perfection or the idea of a most perfect being. Descartes observed that the very concept of God implies his real existence. For what does "God" mean? It means a being who is a supremely perfect being, and who therefore possesses the sum of all possible perfections. Thus, to name a few, God must be— omniscient (for that is a perfection), God must be omnibenevolent (for that is a perfection), and God must *exist* (for that *too* is a perfection). Is not real existence just as necessary to a supremely perfect being as any other of these perfections? Could God be the absolutely perfect being if he were not omnipotent? Could God be the absolutely perfect being if he did not even *exist*? Of course it does not follow from the fact that you cannot separate the idea of a mountain from the idea of a valley that there *are* any mountains or valleys. But that is because existence is not part of what it means to be a mountain or valley. But it *is* part of what it means to be God. On this reasoning, as soon as you get hold of the idea of God as a supremely perfect being, you get hold of a God who exists. When we come to Part Three, "The Question of God," we will have to consider the Ontological Argument more carefully, and there we will give Descartes' own statement of it. For now we simply let it stand, along with his first argument for God, as bringing us to Descartes' second main conclusion: *There is a God.*

THE DEDUCTION OF MATTER

On the basis of God, and some other clear and distinct ideas, Descartes leads us to a further consideration: the world of material objects.

According to Descartes, it is only through the belief in God that we may be assured of the existence of the external world and the things in it: tables, chairs, dogs, cats, the earth, stars, our own bodies, and so on. How does Descartes arrive at this thesis? Surely, says Descartes, we can doubt the existence of such things. Aside from the inevitable distortions and misrepresentations of our senses, is it not at least *possible* that we are now dreaming, and that the world "out there" is not at all as we perceive it, or even that it *is* not at all—period? Apart from God, it is possible. But *with* God, it is not possible. Why not? Because we have "a very great inclination to believe" that the material world exists and that God, a supremely perfect being and the author of all good, is by his divine nature incapable of creating in us false or misleading ideas. And even if he could, he *wouldn't*, since deception is clearly a moral defect, whereas God is the supremely perfect being—can you imagine God being a deceiver?

God, the guarantor
of clear and
distinct ideas

To be sure, many of our ideas may be confused, obscure, or false, but that is because they have become contaminated with nothingness, "from below," as it were, whereas as created and implanted in us by God, "from above," they cannot fail to be true. And, to be sure, many of our judgments are mistaken. But that is because of a misuse of our will (also given by God) whereby because of passion, prejudice, or haste, we affirm as true or deny as false an idea that is not clear and distinct. If you look at the sun and judge it to be about two feet across, your decision has overstepped the boundaries of your clear and distinct ideas, and that is your problem, not God's. Descartes summarizes:

How errors occur

> . . . as often as I so restrain my will within the limits of my knowledge that it forms no judgment except on matters which are clearly and distinctly represented to it by the understanding, I can never be deceived; for every clear and distinct conception is without doubt something, and hence cannot derive its origin from what is nought, but must of necessity have God as its author—God, I say, who being supremely perfect, cannot be the cause of any error; and consequently we must conclude that such a conception [or such a judgment] is true.[10]

Thus God is the guarantor of our knowledge:

> . . . so I very clearly recognise that the certainty and truth of all knowledge depends alone on the knowledge of the true God, in so much that, before I knew Him, I could not have a perfect knowledge of any other thing. And now that I know Him I have the means of acquiring a perfect knowledge of an infinitude of things, not only of those which relate to God Himself and other intellectual matters, but also of those which pertain to corporeal nature. . . .[11]

And we are now in a position to reintroduce into our picture of reality what Descartes originally found it necessary to exclude: the external world of material objects.

Do we not have a clear and distinct idea of an external world? A world of tables, chairs, dogs, cats, the earth, stars, and our own bodies existing outside our minds and independently of us? Is not the "externality" of such a world and such things clearly and distinctly evident from the passivity of our sense perceptions? That is, we do not wish or imagine or dream up this world. It is just *there,* imposing itself on us, independently of our wills. Furthermore, is it not evident that just as it was required in the world of mind to believe in a *substance* that upholds and supports the various intellectual activities, so also in the external world there must be a *substance* that upholds and supports the various physical qualities we experience—colors, tastes, shapes, and the like? We will call this substance *material* substance. And is it not evident that extension (to use Descartes' expression), or the ability to occupy space or possess dimensions (to use our own), is the very essence of material substance? We observed earlier that minds (or thinking substances) *may* deny, affirm, imagine, remember, and so on, but *think* they *must.* Likewise, we may say of material objects that they may be red, or blue, or rectangular, or hard, or sweet, and so on, but *extended* they *must* be. Of

Knowledge of the external world

Matter: a substance the essence of which is to be extended

[10]Descartes, *Meditations on First Philosophy,* I, 178.
[11]Ibid., I, 185.

course, says Descartes, the things "out there" may not be entirely as they are represented to us by our senses, but they must at least possess the geometrical features that we clearly and distinctly perceive (such as length, breadth, and depth).

How many of the ideas in the above paragraph can you find substantiated in the following paragraph from the *Meditations*?

I further find in myself faculties employing modes of thinking peculiar to themselves, to wit, the faculties of imagination and feeling, without which I can easily conceive myself clearly and distinctly as a complete being; while, on the other hand, they cannot be so conceived apart from me, that is without an intelligent substance in which they reside, for [in the notion we have of these faculties, or, to use the language of the Schools] in their formal concept, some kind of intellection is comprised, from which I infer that they are distinct from me as its modes are from a thing. I observe also in me some other faculties such as that of change of position, the assumption of different figures and such like, which cannot be conceived, any more than can the preceding, apart from some substance to which they are attached, and consequently cannot exist without it; but it is very clear that these faculties, if it be true that they exist, must be attached to some corporeal or extended substance, and not to an intelligent substance, since in the clear and distinct conception of these there is some sort of extension found to be present, but no intellection at all. There is certainly further in me a certain passive faculty of perception, that is, of receiving and recognising the ideas of sensible things, but this would be useless to me [and I could in no way avail myself of it], if there were not either in me or in some other thing another active faculty capable of forming and producing these ideas. But this active faculty cannot exist in me [inasmuch as I am a thing that thinks] seeing that it does not presuppose thought, and also that those ideas are often produced in me without my contributing in any way to the same, and often even against my will; it is thus necessarily the case that the faculty resides in some substance different from me in which all the reality which is objectively in the ideas that are produced by this faculty is formally or eminently contained, as I remarked before. And this substance is either a body, that is, a corporeal nature in which there is contained formally [and really] all that which is objectively [and by representation] in those ideas, or it is God Himself, or some other creature more noble than body in which that same is contained eminently. But, since God is no deceiver, it is very manifest that He does not communicate to me these ideas immediately and by Himself, nor yet by the intervention of some creature in which their reality is not formally, but only eminently, contained. For since He has given me no faculty to recognise that this is the case, but, on the other hand, a very great inclination to believe [that they are sent to me or] that they are conveyed to me by corporeal objects, I do not see how He could be defended from the accusation of deceit if these ideas were produced by causes other than corporeal objects. Hence we must allow that corporeal things exist. However, they are perhaps not exactly what we perceive by the senses, since this comprehension by the senses is in many instances very obscure and confused; but we must at least admit that all things which I conceive in them clearly and distinctly, that is to say, all things which, speaking generally, are comprehended in the object of pure mathematics, are truly to be recognised as external objects.[12]

---

[12]Ibid., I, 190–191.

Thus we have arrived at Descartes' third conclusion: *There is matter.* And we have progressed from our knowledge of mind to a knowledge of God, and from our knowledge of God to a knowledge of matter.

The essential movement in Descartes' philosophy and the three pivotal ideas may be represented by a simple diagram:

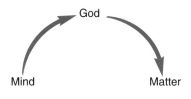

SOME OBJECTIONS

For all its importance and influence, Descartes' theory of reality has hardly escaped criticism. We may mention a few of these, first some lesser ones and then one very big one.

First of all, there is the question of Descartes' method. Few philosophers would align themselves with such a rigorous exclusion of sense experience as a legitimate means of acquiring knowledge; indeed many, quite opposite to Descartes, have admitted *only* sense experience as the source of knowledge, and with the result that they have arrived at quite different conclusions about reality. We will speak of this again in Part Two. Here it must suffice to say that there are more ways to begin a philosophy than with a *cogito.* And, speaking of the *cogito,* are we very sure that thinking requires a thinker? What would result if we simply denied the necessity of mental substance, or *any* substance? Why not let there be simply intellectual activities and physical qualities? We will see that some have in fact argued for just this view. Also, it has often been charged that Descartes has committed the informal fallacy of *Petitio Principii,* or circular reasoning. Upon his reflection on the *Cogito ergo sum,* Descartes is willing to accept any clear and distinct idea as indubitable; he uses such ideas in his proofs for God, but then insists that it is God who ensures the reliability of these clear and distinct ideas.

And regarding Descartes' proofs for God: In his first proof, some have stumbled over the notion that ideas are *things*, that they possess some sort of objective reality, and thus that they must be caused in a way similar to tables and chairs. And are we sure that the idea of God could not be devised without God actually existing? This, however, brings us to the Ontological Argument for God, and that will be best treated in Chapter 12.

THE MIND-BODY PROBLEM

Now we must address the really big problem posed by Descartes' philosophy. If we leave God aside and focus our attention on only the natural world (including ourselves as part of it), then Descartes' view of reality

THE MIND-BODY PROBLEM

If the mind and body are essentially different substances, then how can there be any causal connection between them?

may appropriately be called *dualistic:* There are *two* essentially different substances, mind and matter, that constitute the "stuff" of this world. This is, in fact, how Descartes' theory of reality is usually represented, and as such it poses one of the most vexing problems in the history of philosophy: *the mind-body problem.*

The mind-body problem simply stated is this: Once we define mind and matter as essentially different substances, which means that they can have nothing in common, no bridge between them, no causal connection, then *how do we get them back together again?* And we *must* get them back together again, for there clearly *is* some sort of connection between them. Obviously, our bodily states can affect our mental states. We are familiar with all sorts of ways in which physics and chemistry can affect the mind. Just think of the mental effects of caffeine, drugs, old age, the alteration of brain states, and the like, and if someone beats you over the head long enough, you will become *depressed*! On the other hand, it is also obvious that mental states can give rise to bodily states. Everyday events like willing myself to get up in the morning before I physically get out of bed demonstrate this. Or, have you ever felt physically ill because of some idea—like the prospect of failing a course? That the mind and body stand in a causal relation to each other appears to be a fact. The question is *how,* if they are absolutely different in nature from each other:

How can mind and body be causally connected?

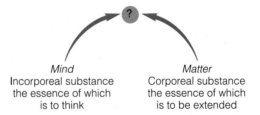

Mind
Incorporeal substance
the essence of which
is to think

Matter
Corporeal substance
the essence of which
is to be extended

So far we have represented the problem in terms of *causality.* But it may be represented in yet other ways. In the following, the contemporary philosopher John Searle suggests four aspects of our mental life that appear unconnectable (we might say) with the material world: (1) consciousness, (2) intentionality—but be careful, it does not mean what you may think, (3) subjectivity, and, of course, (4) causation.

There are four features of mental phenomena which have made them seem impossible to fit into our "scientific" conception of the world as made up of material things. . . .

The most important of these features is consciousness. I, at the moment of writing this, and you, at the moment of reading it, are both conscious. It is just a plain fact about the world that it contains such conscious mental states and events, but it is hard to see how mere physical systems could have consciousness. How could such a thing occur? How, for example, could this grey and white gook inside my skull be conscious?. . .

The second intractable feature of the mind is what philosophers and psychologists call "intentionality," the feature by which our mental states are directed at, or about, or refer to, or are of objects and states of affairs in the world other than themselves. . . . Now the question about intentionality is much like the question about consciousness. How can this stuff inside my head be *about* anything? How can it *refer* to anything?. . .

The third feature of the mind that seems difficult to accommodate within a scientific conception of reality is the subjectivity of mental states. This subjectivity is marked by such facts as that I can feel my pains, and you can't. I see the world from my point of view; you see it from your point of view. I am aware of myself and my internal mental states, as quite distinct from the selves and mental states of other people. . . .

Finally, there is a fourth problem, the problem of mental causation. We all suppose, as part of common sense, that our thoughts and feelings make a real difference to the way we behave, that they actually have some *causal* effect on the physical world. I decide, for example, to raise my arm and—lo and behold—my arm goes up. But if your thoughts and feelings are truly mental, how can they affect anything physical?. . . These four features, consciousness, intentionality, subjectivity, and mental causation are what make the mind-body problem seem so difficult. . . .[13]

But back to Descartes and the specifically *causal* issue involved in the mind-body problem. Descartes himself was not oblivious to the difficulty. The solution he proposed has been called *interactionism*. It is simply the view that there is, after all, some kind of interaction between the two essentially different substances.

Descartes' solution:
interactionism

Nature also teaches me by these sensations of pain, hunger, thirst, etc., that I am not only lodged in my body as a pilot in a vessel, but that I am very closely united to it, and so to speak so intermingled with it that I seem to compose with it one whole. For if that were not the case, when my body is hurt, I, who am merely a thinking thing, should not feel pain, for I should perceive this wound by the understanding only, just as the sailor perceives by sight when something is damaged in his vessel; and when my body has need of drink or food, I should clearly understand the fact without being warned of it by confused feelings of hunger and thirst. For all these sensations of hunger, thirst, pain, etc. are in truth none other than certain confused modes of thought which are produced by the union and apparent intermingling of mind and body.[14]

---

[13]John Searle, *Minds, Brains and Science* (Cambridge, MA: Harvard University Press, 1984), pp. 15–17.

[14]Descartes, *Meditations on First Philosophy*, I, p. 192.

Where does this "union" and "intermingling" of mind and body take place? Descartes' answer: the pineal gland, in the center of the brain. Apparently he thought that the pineal gland was a likely candidate for this honor because it is the most inward part of the brain and perhaps, too, because it appeared to Descartes to be the only thing in the body without a double or counterpart. (It is reported that Descartes would secure discarded carcasses from the local butcher for the purpose of dissection and examination.)

It has seemed to many that Descartes' solution was, of course, no solution at all. It only moved the question one step further back, and the question now becomes, *How* do mind and matter interact in the pineal gland? Nonetheless, interactionism as a solution to the mind-body problem is here to stay. After all, what constitutes a causal connection even between *like* substances is no easy matter. And who is to say outright what substances can or cannot do? Further, talk of an unbridgeable "gap" between mind and matter is strange inasmuch as mind is not conceived as spatial at all. On the other hand, mind *is* in space and time in *some* sense: Does not your mind exist right *here* and right *now*? At least in some way, then, mind and matter *do* occupy a common ground.

There have been other proposed solutions. Before mentioning two radical solutions, we shall mention three traditional ones. No sooner had Descartes presented the world with the mind-body problem than the French thinker

Occasionalism

Malebranche (1638–1715) proposed *occasionalism* as a solution: On the occasion of bodily stimuli or impressions, God creates the appropriate idea and response in the mind. The German philosopher Leibniz (1646–1716) pro-

Preestablished
harmony

posed a *preestablished harmony,* according to which bodily and physical states have been preordained by God to correspond at every point with appropriate mental states, like two clocks synchronized and set to ticking at the same time. The Dutch philosopher Spinoza (1632–1677) proposed what has been

The double-aspect
theory

called the *double-aspect theory.* In this view there is only one reality, unknown to us except through its attributes of mind and matter, two of the infinite number of aspects of this one reality.

The more radical
solution

There is, however, a much more radical approach to the mind-body problem. Like some forms of radical surgery, which cut out the disease by cutting out the organ, this approach cuts out the problem by cutting out one or the other of the substances. But which has to go? How you answer that may determine whether you go the way of *idealism* or the way of *materialism,* the topics of Chapters 5 and 6.

MIND: A SET OF DISPOSITIONS OR FUNCTIONS

In the meantime, however, we should consider looking at the issue in an entirely different way, involving some recent and analytic-style philosophizing. We mention here two important developments in philosophical psychology—critical thinking about mind and mental states—both of which nullify the mind-body problem. Notice we said "nullify" (not "solve"), for these approaches regard the mind-body problem itself, as traditionally

Diagrams from a work on physiology by Descartes showing the brain
and the pineal gland. Descartes believed this gland to be the locus
of the soul and its point of contact, or interaction, with the body.

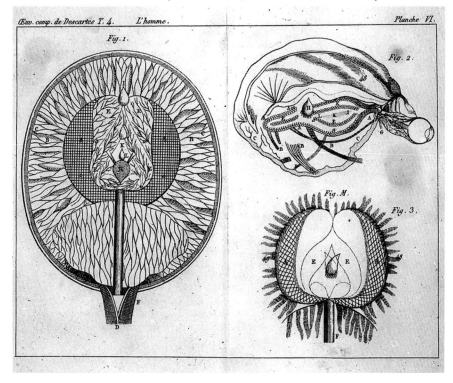

posed in "substance"-talk, to be misguided, or a pseudoproblem, or a mistaken and misleading way of representing the situation.

This is the view of the recent British philosopher Gilbert Ryle and a long
line of thinkers influenced by him. His 1949 book, *The Concept of Mind,* had
the effect of an exploding bombshell in the sphere of philosophical psychology. Ryle said that the mind-body problem, like so many philosophical
problems, is not a *real* problem, but results rather from *linguistic and conceptual confusion.* That is, it is a problem that results from our misunderstanding and misuse of *language* and *concepts.* He begins by sketching the
"official doctrine":

> There is a doctrine about the nature and place of minds which is so prevalent
> among theorists and even among laymen that it deserves to be described as the
> official theory. Most philosophers, psychologists and religious teachers subscribe,
> with minor reservations, to its main articles and, although they admit certain
> theoretical difficulties in it, they tend to assume that these can be overcome with-
> out serious modifications being made to the architecture of the theory. It will be
> argued here that the central principles of the doctrine are unsound and conflict
> with the whole body of what we know about minds when we are not speculat-
> ing about them.

Linguistic and
conceptual
confusion

PHILOSOPHERS: PEOPLE OF MANY FIELDS (SOMETIMES)

Many of the greatest philosophers have been geniuses in more than one field. Descartes is a good example. Besides his philosophical contributions, Descartes contributed many valuable mathematical and scientific insights, theories, and discoveries.

In addition to Descartes' invention of *analytic geometry* (the most important advance in mathematics since the Greeks), one scholar has summarized his achievements in *optics* as follows: the statement of the wave theory of light, the vector analysis of motion, the law of sines in refraction, the first theoretical account of farsightedness and nearsightedness, the first adequate account of space perception, the first adequate account of the theory of lenses, the first recognition of spherical aberration and of the method of correcting it, the determination of light-gathering power of a telescope, the principle of the iris diaphragm, the draw-tube, the telescopic finder, the use of illuminating equipment in conjunction with the microscope, and the parabolic mirror.

Likewise, his contributions to the field of *meteorology* may be summarized as the rejection of divine intervention as the explanation of events; the kinetic theory of heat and the concept of specific heat; the first outline of a scientific meteorology in his treatment of winds, clouds, and precipitation; a correct and accurate description and explanation of the primary, secondary, and reflection rainbows; a description of the division of white light into colors by a prism; and the apparatus of the slit spectroscope.*

*Cf. Laurence J. Lafleur, Introduction to *René Descartes: Discourse on Method*, 2d ed., tr. Laurence J. Lafleur (Indianapolis: Bobbs-Merrill, 1956), pp. xvii f.

The official doctrine, which hails chiefly from Descartes, is something like this. With the doubtful exceptions of idiots and infants in arms every human being has both a body and a mind. Some would prefer to say that every human being is both a body and a mind. His body and his mind are ordinarily harnessed together, but after the death of the body his mind may continue to exist and function.

Human bodies are in space and are subject to the mechanical laws which govern all other bodies in space. Bodily processes and states can be inspected by external observers. So a man's bodily life is as much a public affair as are the lives of animals and reptiles and even as the careers of trees, crystals and planets.

But minds are not in space, nor are their operations subject to mechanical laws. The workings of one mind are not witnessable by other observers; its career is private. Only I can take direct cognisance of the states and processes of my own mind. A person therefore lives through two collateral histories, one consisting of what happens in and to his body, the other consisting of what happens in and to his mind. The first is public, the second private. The events in the first history are events in the physical world, those in the second are events in the mental world.[15]

[15]Gilbert Ryle, *The Concept of Mind* (London: Hutchinson, 1949), pp. 11–12.

But what, exactly, is the confusion that Ryle sees in this "official doctrine"? Ryle said that Descartes and most people after him were guilty of a *category mistake,* as he called it. This is the mistake of treating a concept as if it belonged to one system or category of ideas when, in fact, it belongs to another. An example will help. Imagine yourself showing a visitor around the campus. Your friend asks you to point out the library, and you point at a building and say, "Over there." He then asks to see the student union, and you take him to another building. He then asks to be shown the humanities building, and you show it to him. Then he asks to see the *college.* But you are puzzled by this request because your friend appears to think that the college is something you can *see.* You might say to him: "What do you mean, 'Show me the college'? The college is not a building or a *thing,* it is an organization of various departments and faculties. You have confused the idea of a college with *things,* such as buildings." Ryle makes the application:

> I shall often speak of [the "official doctrine"] with deliberate abusiveness, as "the dogma of the Ghost in the Machine." . . . It is not merely an assemblage of particular mistakes. It is one big mistake and a mistake of a special kind. It is, namely, a category-mistake. It represents the facts of mental life as if they belonged to one logical type or category (or range of types or categories), when they actually belong to another. The dogma is therefore a philosopher's myth.[16]

Surely we have minds and these minds display mental characteristics. This is not what Ryle objects to. He objects to the "official doctrine" of the Ghost in the Machine, the representation of mind as a kind of great, nonphysical *blob.* Where did Descartes (and all the other proponents of the "official doctrine") go wrong? Right at the start, when he began thinking about the mental world in terms that were appropriate only for the physical world: "thing," "stuff," "attribute," "state," "process," "change," "cause," and "effect." It was, says Ryle, a colossal category mistake to employ *thing-*language in the attempt to throw light on the world of mind.

We cannot give here a full account of Ryle's more positive theory of mind. But is not mind more like a college than a building? Is it not, rather, a way of representing the organization, interrelationships, and activities of

---

[16]Ibid., p. 16.

CATEGORY MISTAKE

The mistake of employing a concept (e.g., mind) within a conceptual system to which it is inappropriate (substance, causality, etc.).

The category mistake

"In ordinary life . . . we seldom use the noun 'mind' or the adjective 'mental' at all. What we do is talk of people, of people calculating, conjuring, hoping, resolving, tasting, bluffing, fretting, and so on. Nor, in ordinary life, do we talk of 'matter' or of things being 'material.' What we do is to talk of steel, granite, and water; of wood, moss, and grain; of flesh, bone, and sinew. The umbrella-titles 'mind' and 'matter' obliterate the very differences that ought to interest us."

—Gilbert Ryle

Mind: a set of
dispositions

faculties—in this case *mental* faculties? Furthermore, and more important, would it not be truer to our actual evidence and experience to represent mental states as *dispositions*? As an "ordinary language analyst," Ryle asks us to pay attention to and to take our cue from the way in which we usually speak about such matters, and the way we usually speak betrays nothing at all of some private, concealed, sealed-off domain of mental processes, or any "ghost in the machine." What are we actually referring to when we speak of a person's thoughts, desires, convictions, moods, and inclinations? In our interpretation of such mental states do we not invariably include references to some relevant bodily and publicly accessible facts? What *is* a thought, desire, conviction, mood, or inclination apart from some accompanying physical states such as facial expressions, shrugs, weeping, speaking, gesturing, or other bodily and witnessable activity? Mental states would seem to have discernible meaning and real content only in relation to bodily states. And the task of the Rylean philosophers becomes, then, one of inquiring not into the spooky world of Cartesian minds, but into capacities, propensities, habits, and tendencies—in a word, dispositions—evident in what persons *do.*

One might be tempted to see here a form of materialism, but that would be a mistake. Ryle's point was not a metaphysical one involving the reduction of mind to matter, or mental states to bodily states, but rather an analytic-logical point: an attempt to clarify the logical status of the idea of mind, and to go from there—though certainly it can't be back to Descartes!

Functionalism

A second, related, and still more recent development is *functionalism*. It is, in fact, at present all the rage among those dealing with the philosophy of mind—which has become an ever-enlarging circle, including not only people from philosophy but also people from the fields of psychology, cybernetics, and linguistics, as well as many working in the areas of artificial intelligence and computational theory. All of this together is sometimes called cognitive science, which is the attempt to understand, from all relevant perspectives and on the basis of all possible data, the nature of knowing. We will encounter functionalism again, in Chapter 6 on materialism, though it is appropriate here to provide a sketch, especially since it is in some ways the current philosophical heir to Ryle's work.

It is not called "functionalism" for nothing. Again, our attention is shifted from traditional Cartesian substance-talk to a radically different way of talking about the mind: The mind and its various states are to be understood in terms of *function*. You do not give a definition of a coffeepot when you tell what it is made of (plastic, metal, rubber, etc.) but when you describe how it is put together and what it does (contains water, percolates, filters the water through a batch of ground coffee beans, etc.). Likewise, say the functionalists, when we address and assess the significance of mental states, it is not a question of what they are made of—that is irrelevant—but what they *do*. More specifically, the definition of a mental state, such as a belief, should delineate what it does, what role it plays, how it relates to and what contribution it makes to input, output, and other mental states—such language naturally suggests that mental states, in the functionalist view, may be likened to the program of a computer. Still better is the concise statement (plus example) by Paul M. Churchland, a major figure in the field of cognitive science:

> According to *functionalism*, the essential or defining feature of any type of mental state is the set of causal relations it bears to (1) environmental effects on the body, (2) other types of mental states, and (3) bodily behavior. Pain, for example, characteristically results from some bodily damage or trauma; it causes distress, annoyance, and practical reasoning aimed at relief; and it causes wincing, blanching, and nursing of the traumatized area. Any state that plays exactly that functional role is a pain, according to functionalism. Similarly, other types of mental states (sensations, fears, beliefs, and so on) are also defined by their unique causal roles in a complex economy of internal states mediating sensory inputs and behavioral outputs.[17]

But *why* functionalism? What consideration compels us to adopt this view? What problem does it solve? Here is where the issue is best considered in terms of Chapter 6, except to say that the total evidence from a variety of perspectives (such as those mentioned above) urges upon the functionalist a *nonreductivist* view of the mind that accommodates features that cannot be reduced to bodily states, behavior, or environment. Still leaving aside the metaphysical question as to the nature of mind, it is nonetheless surely not *these* things pure and simple.

Why functionalism?

CHAPTER 4 IN REVIEW

SUMMARY

Although the metaphysical theory known as mind-matter dualism has been widely held, it has nowhere received a more powerful expression than in Descartes, the father of modern philosophy.

[17]Paul M. Churchland, *Matter and Consciousness: A Contemporary Introduction to the Philosophy of Mind* (Cambridge, MA: MIT Press, 1984), p. 36.

Descartes unfolds a complete philosophy starting from reason alone (we will have more to say about his theory of knowledge in Part Two) and arrives, specifically, at a certain knowledge of the essentially different substances, mind ("a substance the essence of which is to think") and matter ("a substance the essence of which is to be extended"), with considerable help from his idea of God. He found that it was impossible to doubt the existence of the self—otherwise, the very activity of doubting would be impossible. Thus one of the best-known pronouncements in the history of philosophy: "I think, therefore I am." Armed with this fundamental certitude, Descartes then proceeded to demonstrate the existence of God from the presence in our minds of the idea of a perfect being (most notably, the Ontological Argument). On the basis of both our passivity to what must be external objects and the impossibility that God, the perfect being, should deceive us with respect to our faculty of clear and distinct ideas, we may also rest assured as to the existence and at least relative nature of the radically different world of material substances outside us. The main moves may be represented simply as: Mind → God → Matter.

However, any version of mind-matter dualism that portrays mind and matter as *essentially* different faces a tremendous problem: If they are so *different*, how can they relate to each other (as they obviously do) and therefore be in some necessary way the *same*? Traditionally, solutions were proposed in the form of interactionism, occasionalism, a preestablished harmony, and the double-aspect theory. More recently, however, it has been suggested that the whole problem stems from a mistaken concept of the mind. Ryle, for example, has argued that to view mind as if it were a substance underlying various activities is to import an inappropriate model: a category mistake.

BASIC IDEAS

- Dualism
- Descartes' method
- Two fundamental operations of the intellect
    Intuition
    Deduction
- Descartes' procedure of systematic doubt
- *Cogito ergo sum*
- Descartes' conception of mind
- Substance
- The nature and role of clear and distinct ideas
- Descartes' arguments for God
    Eidological Argument
    Ontological Argument
- God as the source of clear and distinct ideas
- How errors occur

- How we acquire knowledge of the external world
- Descartes' conception of matter
- Various objections to Descartes' philosophy
- The mind-body problem
- Some traditional solutions to the mind-body problem
    Interactionism
    Occasionalism
    Preestablished harmony
    Double-aspect theory
- Radical solutions to the mind-body problem: materialism and idealism
- The category mistake
- Mind as a set of dispositions
- Functionalism

TEST YOURSELF

1. Why is Descartes' method called a "geometrical" method?
2. In Descartes' view, mind is to doubting as matter is to (a) God, (b) color, (c) the pineal gland, (d) substance.
3. What is so important in Descartes' philosophy about *Cogito ergo sum*?
4. True or false: Descartes says that we have an immediate intuition of the external world.
5. What is Descartes' definition of mind? of matter?
6. True or false: Descartes' arguments for God are not based in any way on the sensible world.
7. According to Searle, what is the *four*fold problem in the mind-body problem?
8. Descartes' own solution to the mind-body problem is called _____.
9. What did Gilbert Ryle contribute to the discussion in this chapter?

QUESTIONS FOR REFLECTION

- At the beginning of the chapter it was asserted that mind-matter dualism is a very common metaphysical theory. Do you think so? Would you have answered the question of reality along these lines? What *would* have been your answer?
- It is sometimes observed that Descartes' way of viewing *mind* and its *activities* was too easily influenced by a prevailing way of talking about things in the external world in terms of *substance* and *qualities*. Would this in itself make Descartes' view of mind wrong? Might this be the origin of the category mistake that Ryle talks about?
- If you *do* maintain the mind-matter dualist position, what do *you* do about the mind-body problem?

FOR FURTHER READING

C. D. Broad. *The Mind and Its Place in Nature.* London: Routledge & Kegan Paul, 1925. Ch. 3. Treatment of "The Traditional Problem of Body and Mind" in an old but enduring work.

David J. Chalmers. *Philosophy of Mind: Classical and Contemporary Readings.* New York: Oxford University Press, 2002. A collection of important essays that cover major themes in philosophy of mind.

Frederick Copleston. *A History of Philosophy.* Baltimore: Newman Press, 1946–1974. IV, Chs. 3–5, 9, 11, 17. Chapters dealing with Descartes' dualistic theory of reality, his theory of interactionism, and the response of Leibniz and Spinoza, by a recognized historian of philosophy.

William Doney (ed.). *Descartes: A Collection of Critical Essays.* Garden City, NY: Anchor Books, 1967. Hefty essays by well-known philosophers on various aspects of Descartes' philosophy.

A. C. Ewing. *The Fundamental Questions of Philosophy.* New York: Collier, 1962. Ch. 6. Commonsensical discussion of "The Relation of Matter and Mind."

Owen J. Flanagan, Jr. *The Science of Mind.* Cambridge, MA: MIT Press, 1984. A thorough and critical discussion of the central issues in contemporary cognitive science, including dualism, introspection, functionalism, and so on.

Antony Flew (ed.). *Body, Mind, and Death.* New York: Macmillan, 1964. Selections from traditional and contemporary philosophers with a good introduction by a well-known philosopher of the analytic style.

Colin McGinn. *The Character of Mind: An Introduction to the Philosophy of Mind.* Second ed. New York: Oxford University Press, 1997. Provocative discussions of the nature of mind, including chapters on "Mind and Body" and "The Self."

John Searle. *Mind: A Brief Introduction.* New York: Oxford University Press, 2004. A lucidly written overview of the mind-body problem from a giant in the field.

Jerome A. Shaffer. *Philosophy of Mind.* Englewood Cliffs, NJ: Prentice-Hall, 1968. Chs. 3–4. Student-oriented treatments of consciousness, its relation to the body, the mind-body problem, dualism, and so on.

P. F. Strawson. *Individuals: An Essay in Descriptive Metaphysics.* Garden City, NY: Anchor Books, 1959. An influential work that, like Ryle, reflects the mind-body problem as a pseudoproblem, emphasizing the basic unity of the individual.

Richard Taylor. *Metaphysics.* Third ed. Englewood Cliffs, NJ: Prentice-Hall, 1983. Chs. 1–2. Student-oriented discussions on "Persons and Bodies" and "Interactionism."

*In addition, see the relevant articles ("Mind-Body Problem," "Descartes," etc.) in *Routledge Encyclopedia of Philosophy*, ed. Edward Craig (London: Routledge, 1998), and *Stanford Encyclopedia of Philosophy*, http://plato.stanford.edu.

IDEALISM

One way—a very radical way—of solving the mind-body problem is simply to deny the reality of matter. If all there is is mind, then there can hardly be a problem of relating it to something essentially different, for there *isn't* anything different. It is just a matter of doing away with one-half of Descartes' mind-matter dualism (matter) and exalting the other half (mind) as the *sole* reality.

A radical solution to the mind-body problem

WHAT IS IDEALISM?

To a beginner in philosophy it must sound remarkably strange to say that reality is *mind*. But this thesis is one of the most important in the history of philosophy and has had many advocates. In fact, there is a whole tradition in

From mind-matter dualism two radically different theories of reality may be hatched depending on which idea is suppressed. If the idea of matter is suppressed, then idealism may be hatched.

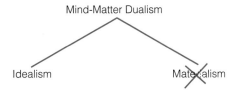

IDEALISM

The metaphysical theory that all things are constituted by mind and its ideas.

"Idealism": its
popular and
technical meanings

philosophy called *idealism*. As with so many other philosophical terms, this one too needs some explaining. By "idealism" we do not mean, as is often meant, a sort of utopianism or optimism about things. As used here, "idealism" is a metaphysical theory, a theory of reality, a theory about the ultimate nature of things. As a general definition we may say that idealism is the metaphysical view that mind (in some sense) is ultimate and that all things are thus reducible to mind and ideas. (If it helps, think of idealism as "idea-ism.")

Objective and
subjective idealism

As was said above, idealism has had many advocates. It has also had many variations. In the interest of simplicity, though, we will divide all idealists into two camps: the *objective* idealists and the *subjective* idealists. An objective idealist believes that all things are made out of mind and ideas, but that things exist nonetheless *objectively*—that is, "out there"— independently of our perceiving or knowing them; they would continue to exist even if we did not. A subjective idealist, on the other hand, believes that all things are made out of mind and ideas, but that these things have no existence apart from perception of them; they would cease to exist if all perceivers did. One way of getting a hold on this idea is to think again of Plato. Do you see that in a sense Plato was an objective idealist? He believed that reality was *intelligible* (that is, of the nature of ideas and apprehensible only by the mind) but also that it existed *outside* our minds. In this chapter it is not objective but *subjective* idealism that interests us. Surely it is one of the most fascinating views in the whole history of philosophy.

BERKELEY AND LOCKE

To many it will surely sound crazy to be told that things exist if and only if[1] they are *perceived*, that things cease to exist if they are not being at that moment experienced! We are all familiar with the question about whether a tree falling over on an uninhabited desert island would make any noise. But could we doubt that the tree itself and the whole island would disappear if no one were there to observe it? The Irish philosopher Bishop George Berkeley[2] (1685–1753) *did* doubt it. In fact, he was certain of it. And his arguments for it are not to be laughed off.

---

[1]Philosophers are fond of insisting on distinctions that would never occur to normal people. Thus philosophers often find it important to distinguish among "if," "only if," and "if, and only if." These terms do, in fact, have three quite different meanings. Think about these expressions until you see the differences.

[2]Pronounced *Barkly*.

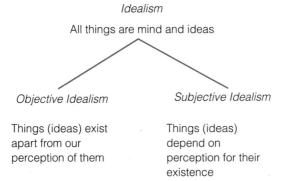

Idealism

All things are mind and ideas

Objective Idealism

Things (ideas) exist
apart from our
perception of them

Subjective Idealism

Things (ideas)
depend on
perception for their
existence

As with most other philosophies it is hardly possible to grasp Berkeley's theory of reality except against the background of what had gone before. Certainly Descartes lies in this background, but more important is the English philosopher John Locke (1632–1704), Berkeley's immediate predecessor. Here we must emphasize three features of Locke's philosophy, all of which had everything to do with Berkeley's radically new view.

First. Locke, like Descartes, believed in *substance.* This was conceived as an underlying *something* that upholds the physical qualities of sensible things (such as size, shape, color, position, sound, and movement), and a *something* that likewise underlies and upholds intellectual activities (such as thinking, willing, denying, and doubting). In the first case the something is *matter,* and in the second case it is *mind.* And since he believed that these are the only substances, at least in the natural world, Locke was, like Descartes, a *mind-matter dualist.*

Second. Locke expressed better than anyone else the view that has sometimes been called *epistemological dualism,* a view we will encounter again in Chapter 10. As you can guess from the label, it had to do with knowledge ("epistemological") and with two things ("dualism"). Specifically, it is the view that two main things are involved in the act of knowing: the knower and the known. But do not be misled here. While it is obvious that the thing that knows is the mind, the thing known is not the object "out there" in the external world such as a table. What is actually known must be something akin to the mind and *in* the mind. And what is in the mind and known by the mind is certainly not the table itself—that exists *out there*—but rather a mental representation or *idea* of the table: brown, rectangular, smooth, flat, and four-legged. What is important here is that according to Locke what the mind directly knows are ideas that themselves correspond to things in the external world.

Third. We mentioned above that Locke believed in matter as an underlying "something" that upholds the sensible qualities of a thing. Now what about these sensible qualities? Like many before him, Locke says that we must divide these qualities into two kinds: primary and secondary qualities. This will take a bit of explaining. A *primary quality* is a quality that exists independently of a perceiver; that is, it would exist even if no perceiver

Three features of Locke's philosophy:

(1) Two substances, mind and matter

(2) Ideas as the objects of knowledge

(3) Primary and secondary qualities

were present. Examples of primary qualities include size, position, shape, and movement. A *secondary quality* is a quality that depends for its existence on a perceiver; that is, it would cease to exist were no perceiver present. Examples of secondary qualities are color, sound, texture, and taste. Generally, we could say that primary qualities of things are *objective* (they exist in the object), whereas secondary qualities are *subjective* (they exist in the knowing or perceiving subject).

The basis for the distinction

The distinction between primary and secondary qualities is an important one and has figured recurringly in philosophical discussions. Why would one draw this distinction? What is the evidence for it? The evidence takes two forms. (1) Our perceptions, or ideas, of primary qualities *resemble* those qualities. For example, our perception or idea of triangularity resembles the shape of a triangle; our idea of motion resembles something in motion. But colors, sounds, and tastes do not resemble anything "out there": Red *is* the perception, loud *is* the perception, sweet *is* the perception. (2) Secondary qualities, unlike primary qualities, vary with perceivers and are therefore *relative*. What color is the beach ball? Well, it depends on whether you are color-blind, the way the sunlight and shadows are striking it, how far you are from it, and your sunglasses. Is the lemonade sweet enough for you? It depends on whether you have been sucking on a green persimmon. Was the thunderclap loud? It depends on how close you were and the condition of your ears. In the case of secondary qualities everything is *relative to* and thus *dependent on* the subject: the status of one's sense organs, one's perspective, one's position, and so on. No perceiver—no perception. Not so with primary qualities. Shape, motion, and extension, for example, are what they are irrespective of perceivers.

We are back to the tree falling over on a desert island. Do you see that it can make no sound and have no color or taste (secondary qualities), though it must have size, shape, and motion (primary qualities)? Of course, it depends on what you mean, for example, by "color" or "sound." Here these refer to *perceptions,* which exist in the perceiver, and not to color frequencies or sound waves, which exist in the external world. Note, however, that sound actually has both primary qualities (physical sound waves) and secondary qualities (a listener's perception of the sound).

PRIMARY AND SECONDARY QUALITIES

- *Primary qualities:* Those qualities of a thing that exist *independently* of a perceiver. They have *objective* existence. Examples: shape, size, position, and motion.

- *Secondary qualities:* Those qualities of a thing that *depend* for their existence on a perceiver. They have only *subjective* existence. Examples: color, sound, and taste.

What is the basis for this distinction? Why should one accept it?

Berkeley himself focused his theory of reality in a three-word Latin sentence: *Esse est percipi,* "To be is to be perceived." We just saw that Locke and others accepted this principle as applied to *secondary qualities* of things, but Berkeley means it *absolutely.* To be is to be perceived, period. *Everything* is dependent for its existence upon perception, and apart from a perceiving or knowing subject, *nothing* exists. In the absence of a perceiver, not only the tree's sound, color, taste, and other secondary qualities but also its sound *waves,* color *frequencies,* shape, motion, extension, coconuts, the sand, mountains, and the *entire island* cease to exist!

Berkeley summarizes his strange-sounding view:

> Wood, stone, fire, water, flesh, iron, and the like things which I name and discourse of are things that I know. And I should not have known them, but that I perceived them by my senses; and things perceived are immediately perceived; and things immediately perceived are ideas; and ideas cannot exist without the mind; their existence therefore consists in being perceived; when therefore they are actually perceived, there can be no doubt of their existence.[3]

Do you see the argument contained here? We may recast it as a simple syllogism:

Ideas exist only in minds.
All things are ideas.
_____

Therefore, all things exist only in minds.

You will note that this reasoning is perfectly valid; that is, if the premises are true, the conclusion must be true. The question is whether the premises *are* true.

Everything here depends on what Berkeley means by the word "idea." In fact, though, Berkeley means by "idea" what most everyone means, including probably you yourself and John Locke: the mental representation of something in the external world, say, a table, composed of all the qualities that make up that thing, such as brown, rectangular, smooth, flat, and four-legged. If so, then we can hardly object to Berkeley's first premise, *ideas exist only in minds.* It is, in fact, by its very conception; that is, it *must* be true by virtue of the very meaning of the terms involved. Well, what about the second premise? Must we accept that *all things are ideas*? With this claim Berkeley clearly rejects his predecessors' view that ideas represent or correspond to material objects in the external world: Those realities *are* ideas. Surely it is *this* premise that raises the real problems; in fact, we tend instinctively to reject it as fantastic and absurd.

Esse est percipi: "To be is to be perceived"

Summary of Berkeley's position

Berkeley's first premise

Berkeley's second premise

---

[3]George Berkeley, *Three Dialogues between Hylas and Philonous,* ed. Colin M. Turbayne (Indianapolis: Bobbs-Merrill, 1954), p. 76.

BISHOP GEORGE BERKELEY

George Berkeley was born in 1685 in the habitable part of the ruins of Dysert Castle, not far from Kilkenny, Ireland. He studied mathematics and classics at Trinity College, Dublin, where he was also instructed in the philosophies of Descartes and Locke. Berkeley conceived his subjective idealism when he was 22. Apparently its basic principles burst upon him in a sort of revelatory manner, not unlike Descartes' discovery of analytic geometry.

(*continued on next page*)

BERKELEY'S ARGUMENT

Ideas exist only in minds.
All things are ideas.

Therefore, all things exist only in minds.

We will see, though, that Berkeley himself regarded his subjective idealism as the most *commonsensical* view. He develops it in both his *Treatise Concerning the Principles of Human Knowledge* and *Three Dialogues between Hylus and Philonous.*

In 1707, Berkeley became a tutor at Trinity and later junior lecturer. About this time too he embarked upon his career as an Anglican churchman, being ordained as a deacon and then a priest. From this period comes his *Essay towards a New Theory of Vision* and his *Treatise Concerning the Principles of Human Knowledge.*

The year 1713 found Berkeley in London. The years following included writing (most notably, the *Dialogues*) and traveling. During this time he visited the French philosopher Malebranche, who may have suffered a premature death on account of Berkeley. The story goes that Malebranche, ill with pneumonia, argued with Berkeley so violently and loudly as to cause an inflammation of the lungs resulting in his death!

In 1720, Berkeley returned to Dublin. There he was awarded the BD and DD degrees by Trinity College and was made senior lecturer and university preacher. During this period he inherited a handsome sum and had a sort of vision of a better society. He obtained a charter from King George I and set out for Bermuda to found a college for educating the clergy and converting Indians. In September 1728 he set sail for the New World along with his bride. A navigational error brought them instead to Newport, Rhode Island. He remained there for two years, but the failure of promised funds to materialize made it impossible for him to realize his dream.

Back in Ireland, in 1734 Berkeley was made bishop of Cloyne in County Cork. Twenty years were now spent in episcopal duties. In poor health he moved in 1752 to be near his son, who had matriculated in Oxford. He suffered from gallstones and died suddenly in January 1753.

Berkeley conceived of his theory of reality, as contained in the *Principles* and the *Dialogues,* as the first part of a plan including, second, psychology and ethics, third, physics, and fourth, mathematics. He made headway only into the second, and even this was lost.

Berkeley's three most important works are *Essay towards a New Theory of Vision, Treatise Concerning the Principles of Human Knowledge*, and *Three Dialogues between Hylas and Philonous.*

FIVE PROOFS FOR SUBJECTIVE IDEALISM

Berkeley's often ingenious defense of his thesis may be reduced to five distinct lines of reasoning.[4]

First Proof: The Discontinuity of Dualism. The first argument brings us back to the mind-body problem and some comments we made at the beginning of this chapter. Berkeley inherited from Locke, who inherited it from Descartes, the view that all reality (at least in the natural world) is reducible to two essentially different substances, mind and matter. But, as we have now observed repeatedly, such a view of reality gives rise to the metaphysical problem of explaining how these two essentially different substances can

Can mind and matter be related?

---

[4]The following fivefold way of organizing Berkeley's arguments, as well as some of the terminology, is suggested by the useful outline in John Herman Randall, Jr., and Justus Buchler, *Philosophy: An Introduction* (New York: Barnes & Noble, 1942), pp. 210–212.

relate to each other. Obviously, Berkeley's idealism overcomes this problem by simply denying the existence of material substance: There is *one reality, mind and its ideas.*

Likewise, mind-matter dualism gave rise to an epistemological problem: How can mind know reality if reality is utterly unlike mind and its ideas? If the external world and the things in it are essentially unlike our ideas of them, how can our ideas represent or be *like* them? Again, with one stroke Berkeley cuts away the problem, for reality *is* ideas and is therefore of the same nature as mind. Closely related to this, Berkeley's idealism overcomes the skepticism, or doubt, about the external world implicit in epistemological dualism. In that view, how could we ever know that our ideas correctly represent or correspond to the external world? Are we not forever bound to our *ideas* of it? For Berkeley, such doubts could never arise because there *is* no difference between our ideas and reality. *Esse est percipi.*

Second Proof: Matter as a Meaningless Idea. A second argument directs our attention to the very idea of a material substance and asks whether it is even meaningful.

Is "matter" a meaningless word?

It could be asked, first, whether "matter" does not turn out to be an empty and meaningless word. Philosophers such as Descartes and Locke felt compelled to posit a substance underlying and upholding physical qualities, but what could they really say about it? In this respect, Locke likened himself to the Indian who was asked what held up the earth and answered that it was supported by a great elephant who stood on the back of an ancient tortoise. But when asked what held up the tortoise, he answered: "Something I know not what." This, in fact, was the best that Locke could say about the nature of material substance: "It is something I know not what." In this way, those who talk big about some underlying material substance in the end do not know what they are talking about!

But it is not just that they *don't* know what they're talking about—they *can't* know what they're talking about. For the very idea of matter is an *inconsistent* one. This is Berkeley's real point here. It is not even possible to

---

"Berkeley brought the manuscript of the *Dialogues* with him to London in January, 1713. Three years earlier he had published in Dublin *The Principles of Human Knowledge*. It had been most unfavorably received. In London, particularly, it had been immediately ridiculed. A physician argued that its author must be mad. A bishop pitied Berkeley for seeking notoriety by trying to start something new. A third critic said that Berkeley was not as far gone as another thinker who denied not only the existence of matter, but of persons. Many factors may have led to the failure of the *Principles*. To read it through required a great deal of intellectual effort. Moreover, the paradox that matter does not exist, which Berkeley advanced, was a bold one."

Turbayne, *Three Dialogues*, pp. vii–viii.

frame a meaningful *idea* of matter, because matter itself is devoid of any qualities (since it is said to *underlie* all qualities), and it is only by means of the qualities of something that we can have an idea of it, and we cannot know or talk about something we have no idea of. *Esse est percipi.*

Third Proof: The Unexperienced as Inconceivable. This point can be broadened. It is true not only in the case of matter, but in the case of *anything*, that it cannot be conceived except as experienced. If you doubt this, try to think of something that is not experienced. Can you? No. This is because the second you frame an idea of something (with its various qualities, such as red, circular, rough, loud, and bitter) you are thereby *experiencing* it. To say this in another way: You cannot think of something without thinking of its qualities, and to think of qualities is to perceive or experience them. *Esse est percipi.*

Can the unexperienced be thought?

Fourth Proof: The Inseparability of Primary and Secondary Qualities. In the fourth argument we return to the distinction between primary and secondary qualities.

It will be recalled that everyone accepts the subjectivity of secondary qualities. That is not the question. But consider now that primary qualities can no more be separated from secondary qualities than secondary qualities can be separated from primary qualities. They rise and fall together. The proof of this is simple. Try to conceive of primary qualities apart from secondary qualities. Try to think of a colorless shape. Imagine, for example, a beach ball. Of course it possesses a shape—it is round. And what color is it? Red, yellow, blue, alternating green and orange bands? Now in your imagination try to remove all color from the shape. It is impossible. Even a vague, dull gray is a color! And if some wiseacre announces that his beach ball is *transparent,* we would only ask him to tell us what are the colors of the things that he sees *through* the transparent sphere of the beach ball and thus fill the shape with colors. Similarly with other primary qualities. They cannot be conceived except as inseparably bound up with secondary qualities.

Can primary and secondary qualities be separated?

So what has this to do with *esse est percipi*? The answer is that since secondary qualities *are* accepted as subjective and requiring a perceiver, and since primary qualities must go the same way as secondary qualities, primary qualities *too* must be subjective. With respect, then, to *all* we can know about a table (its shape, texture, sound, weight, motion, color, etc.), *esse est percipi.*

Fifth Proof: The Relativity of All Qualities. The last argument also depends on the distinction between primary and secondary qualities. But whereas the previous argument reasoned that primary qualities must be subjective because secondary qualities are, here the argument is that primary qualities considered *in themselves* must be subjective.

We saw earlier that a decisive argument for the subjectivity of secondary qualities, or that they exist in the perceiver, is that they are *relative to perceivers.* This is the only way to account for the fact that colors, tastes, sounds, and the like vary with perceivers, or are perceived differently by different perceivers. But now Berkeley asks whether it is not the same with primary qualities. Are they not every bit as relative to perceivers?

Are primary qualities relative too?

We have a natural tendency to think that though colors, sounds, and tastes disappear with the perceiver, qualities like shape, size, and motion

BERKELEY'S FIVE PROOFS
FOR SUBJECTIVE IDEALISM

1. Discontinuity of dualism.

2. Matter as a meaningless idea.

3. Unexperienced as inconceivable.

4. Inseparability of primary and secondary qualities.

5. Relativity of all qualities.

Title page bearing the full title
of Berkeley's *Treatise*

A

TREATISE

Concerning the

PRINCIPLES

O F

Human Knowlege.

PART I.

Wherein the chief Caufes of Error and Difficulty in the *Sciences*, with the Grounds
of *Scepticifm*, *Atheifm*, and *Irreligion*, are
inquir'd into.

By *George Berkeley*, M. A. Fellow of
Trinity-College, Dublin.

DVBLIN:

Printed by AARON RHAMES, for JEREMY
PEPYAT, Bookfeller in *Skinner-Row*,1712.

continue even when unperceived. But take shape, for example. Is there really anything such as a perception of a rectangle? In fact, do two people ever perceive the same shape? Is not every shape relative to and dependent upon the perceiver's perspective? Consider a large rectangle drawn on a chalk-board or the rectangular surface of a table in the front of the room:

You *think* it's a rectangle. You *call* it a rectangle. But you do not actually *perceive* a rectangle. What do you perceive? Well, depending on your perspective, you may actually perceive this,

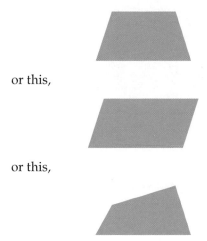

or this,

The relativity of
perception

or this,

or any one of an infinite number of other shapes, since there is an infinite number of viewpoints or perspectives. Even if you were to suspend yourself from the ceiling, centered directly over the surface of the table, you would perceive not a rectangle but something like this:

As for the other primary qualities, like size, position, and motion, just a moment's reflection should reveal that these too are relative to the perceiver, and that makes them *perceptions* or *ideas*. There is, then, no difference between primary and secondary qualities. *All* qualities are ideas in the mind of the perceiver. *Esse est percipi.*

This painting by M.C. Escher illustrates the relativity
of perception. What do you see in this picture?

HYLAS AND PHILONOUS

You will be able to appreciate some of the above points in the following
extracts from the *Three Dialogues between Hylas and Philonous.* Hylas (from the
Greek *hyle,* "matter") argues for the reality of material substance, whereas
Philonous (from *philos* and *nous*) is the "friend of mind" and thus represents
Berkeley's position.

PHILONOUS: You are still then of opinion that extension and figures are inherent in
external unthinking substances?

HYLAS: I am.

PHILONOUS: But what if the same arguments which are brought against secondary qualities will hold good against these also?

HYLAS: Why then I shall be obliged to think they too exist only in the mind.

PHILONOUS: Is it your opinion the very figure and extension which you perceive
by sense exist in the outward object or material substance?

HYLAS: It is.

PHILONOUS: Have all other animals as good grounds to think the same of the
figure and extension which they see and feel?

HYLAS: Without doubt, if they have any thought at all.

PHILONOUS: Answer me, Hylas. Think you the senses were bestowed upon all
animals for their preservation and well-being in life? Or were they given to men
alone for this end?

HYLAS: I make no question but they have the same use in all other animals.

PHILONOUS: If so, is it not necessary they should be enabled by them to perceive their own limbs and those bodies which are capable of harming them?

HYLAS: Certainly.

PHILONOUS: A mite therefore must be supposed to see his own foot, and things equal or even less than it, as bodies of some considerable dimension, though at the same time they appear to you scarce discernible or at best as so many visible points?

HYLAS: I cannot deny it.

PHILONOUS: And to creatures less than the mite they will seem yet larger?

HYLAS: They will.

PHILONOUS: Insomuch that what you can hardly discern will to another extremely minute animal appear as some huge mountain?

HYLAS: All this I grant.

PHILONOUS: Can one and the same thing be at the same time in itself of different dimensions?

HYLAS: That were absurd to imagine.

PHILONOUS: But from what you have laid down it follows that both the extension by you perceived and that perceived by the mite itself, as likewise all those perceived by lesser animals, are each of them the true extension of the mite's foot; that is to say, by your own principles you are led into an absurdity.

HYLAS: There seems to be some difficulty in the point.

PHILONOUS: Again, have you not acknowledged that no real inherent property of any object can be changed without some change in the thing itself?

HYLAS: I have.

PHILONOUS: But, as we approach to or recede from an object the visible extension varies, being at one distance ten or a hundred times greater than at another. Does it not therefore follow from hence likewise that it is not really inherent in the object?

HYLAS: I own I am at a loss what to think.

PHILONOUS: Your judgment will soon be determined if you will venture to think as freely concerning this quality as you have done concerning the rest. Was it not admitted as a good argument that neither heat nor cold was in the water because it seemed warm to one hand and cold to the other?

HYLAS: It was.

PHILONOUS: Is it not the very same reasoning to conclude there is no extension of figure in an object because to one eye it shall seem little, smooth, and round, when at the same time it appears to the other great, uneven, and angular?

HYLAS: The very same. . . .

PHILONOUS: "Material substratum" call you it? Pray, by which of your senses came you acquainted with that being?

HYLAS: It is not itself sensible; its modes and qualities only being perceived by the senses.

PHILONOUS: I presume then it was by reflection and reason you obtained the idea of it?

HYLAS: I do not pretend to any proper positive idea of it. However, I conclude it exists because qualities cannot be conceived to exist without a support.

PHILONOUS: It seems then you have only a relative notion of it, or that you conceive it not otherwise than by conceiving the relation it bears to sensible qualities?

HYLAS: Right.

PHILONOUS: Be pleased, therefore, to let me know wherein that relation consists.

HYLAS: Is it not sufficiently expressed in the term "substratum" or "substance"?

PHILONOUS: If so, the word "substratum" should import that it is spread under the sensible qualities or accidents?

HYLAS: True.

PHILONOUS: And consequently under extension?

HYLAS: I own it.

PHILONOUS: It is therefore somewhat in its own nature entirely distinct from extension?

HYLAS: I tell you extension is only a mode, and matter is something that supports modes. And is it not evident the thing supported is different from the thing supporting?

PHILONOUS: So that something distinct from, and exclusive of, extension is supposed to be the substratum of extension?

HYLAS: Just so.

PHILONOUS: Answer me, Hylas, can a thing be spread without extension, or is not the idea of extension necessarily included in spreading?

HYLAS: It is.

PHILONOUS: Whatsoever therefore you suppose spread under anything must have in itself an extension distinct from the extension of that thing under which it is spread?

HYLAS: It must.

PHILONOUS: Consequently, every corporeal substance being the substratum of extension must have in itself another extension by which it is qualified to be a substratum, and so on to infinity? And I ask whether this be not absurd in itself and repugnant to what you granted just now, to wit, that the substratum was something distinct from and exclusive of extension?

HYLAS: . . . The word "substratum" is used only to express in general the same thing with "substance."

PHILONOUS: Well then, let us examine the relation implied in the term "substance." Is it not that it stands under accidents?

HYLAS: The very same.

PHILONOUS: But that one thing may stand under or support another, must it not be extended?

HYLAS: It must.

PHILONOUS: Is not therefore this supposition liable to the same absurdity with the former?

HYLAS: You still take things in a strict literal sense; that is not fair, Philonous.

PHILONOUS: I am not for imposing any sense on your words; you are at liberty to explain them as you please. Only, I beseech you, make me understand something by them. You tell me matter supports or stands under accidents. How? Is it as your legs support your body?

HYLAS: No; that is the literal sense.

PHILONOUS: Pray let me know any sense, literal or not literal, that you understand it in.—How long must I wait for an answer, Hylas?

HYLAS: I declare I know not what to say. I once thought I understood well enough, what was meant by matter's supporting accidents. But now, the more I think on it, the less can I comprehend it; in short, I find that I know nothing of it.

PHILONOUS: It seems then you have no idea at all, neither relative nor positive, of matter; you know neither what it is in itself nor what relation it bears to accidents?

HYLAS: I acknowledge it.

PHILONOUS: And yet you asserted that you could not conceive how qualities or accidents should really exist without conceiving at the same time a material support of them?

HYLAS: I did.

PHILONOUS: That is to say, when you conceive the real existence of qualities, you do withal conceive something which you cannot conceive?

HYLAS: It was wrong I own. . . .

PHILONOUS: . . . if I understand you rightly, you say our ideas do not exist without the mind, but that they are copies, images, or representations of certain originals that do?

HYLAS: You take me right.

PHILONOUS: They are then like external things?

HYLAS: They are.

PHILONOUS: Have those things a stable and permanent nature, independent of our senses, or are they in a perpetual change, upon our producing any motions in our bodies, suspending, exerting, or altering our faculties or organs of sense?

HYLAS: Real things, it is plain, have a fixed and real nature, which remains the same notwithstanding any change in our senses or in the posture and motion of our bodies; which indeed may affect the ideas in our minds, but it were absurd to think they had the same effect on things existing without the mind.

PHILONOUS: How then is it possible that things perpetually fleeting and variable as our ideas should be copies or images of anything fixed and constant? Or, in other words, since all sensible qualities, as size, figure, color, etc., that is, our ideas, are continually changing upon every alteration in the distance, medium, or instruments of sensation—how can any determinate material objects be properly represented or painted forth by several distinct things each of which is so different from and unlike the rest? Or, if you say it resembles some one only of our ideas, how shall we be able to distinguish the true copy from all the false ones?

HYLAS: I profess, Philonous, I am at a loss. . . .

PHILONOUS: But neither is this all. Which are material objects in themselves—perceptible or imperceptible?

HYLAS: Properly and immediately nothing can be perceived but ideas. All material things, therefore, are in themselves insensible and to be perceived only by their ideas.

PHILONOUS: Ideas then are sensible, and their archetypes or originals insensible?

HYLAS: Right.

PHILONOUS: But how can that which is sensible be like that which is insensible? Can a real thing, in itself invisible, be like a color, or a real thing which is not audible be like a sound? In a word, can anything be like a sensation or idea, but another sensation or idea?

HYLAS: I must own, I think not.[5]

Along such lines as these, then, Berkeley defends his thesis that all things are ideas. What he says of a cherry he could say of *all* things: It is nothing more than a collection of perceptions:

PHILONOUS: . . . I see this cherry, I feel it, I taste it, and I am sure nothing cannot be seen or felt or tasted; it is therefore real. Take away the sensations of softness, moisture, redness, tartness, and you take away the cherry. Since it is not a being distinct from sensations, a cherry, I say, is nothing but a congeries of sensible impressions, or ideas perceived by various senses, which ideas are united into one thing (or have one name given them) by the mind because they are observed to attend each other. Thus, when the palate is affected with such a particular taste, the sight is affected with a red color, the touch with roundness, softness, etc. Hence, when I see and feel and taste in sundry certain manners, I am sure the cherry exists or is real, its reality being in my opinion nothing abstracted from those sensations. But if by the word "cherry" you mean an unknown nature distinct from all those sensible qualities, and by its "existence" something distinct from its being perceived, then, indeed I own neither you nor I, nor anyone else, can be sure it exists.[6]

What is the upshot of all this? Berkeley strains to get you to accept the *simplicity* of his claim. Consider the table again. What is it that you are considering? Well, the perceptions of brown, rectangularity, smooth surface, four-legged, at rest, five feet long, and the like. Why not just let the table *be* those things? Why insist on some mysterious, unknowable, and, indeed, incoherent notion of a material "something" beyond those perceptions? Why not allow the table to be just what it is perceived to be—namely, a bundle of different perceptions or *ideas*? Berkeley believed that such a view would immediately strike one as the most *commonsensical,* once the reasoning is followed and our built-in prejudices about "matter" are laid aside.

SOLIPSISM OR GOD?

Solipsism

It will appear to some readers that Berkeley must be a solipsist. Solipsism is the belief that only one thing exists, the solipsist himself. Everything else, including other people, exists only in his mind. One wonders, of course, what would happen if two solipsists were introduced to one another! It would be something like the gingham dog and the calico cat, who got into a fight and left only scraps of themselves behind since they ate each other up.

---

[5]Berkeley, *Three Dialogues between Hylas and Philonous*, pp. 28–30, 38–41, 47–48.
[6]Ibid., p. 97.

SOLIPSISM

Solipsism (from the Latin *solus*, "alone") is the belief in one reality, the solipsist himself, upon whose thought and perceptions all other things depend for their existence. It has been observed that if you ever meet a solipsist, you had better take good care of him, for when he goes we all go!

Berkeley certainly was *not* a solipsist. Like all other people in their right minds, Berkeley acknowledged the reality of things outside one's own mind. The simple and sole and sufficient evidence for the reality of things outside ourselves is the *passivity of perception*. Leaving our imagination out of it (by which in an instant we can create castles and fortunes) it is obvious that our senses respond passively to things outside us. For example, when you enter a room you do not *conjure up* blackboards, chairs, people, and light fixtures, you do not *will* them into existence, you do not say, "Let there be blackboards...." *They are simply there.* What you wish or will or say has nothing to do with it. (We encountered this idea in Chapter 4.)

The passivity of perception

But, now, does not Berkeley have a tremendous problem on his hands? Has he not maintained two incompatible theses? He argues on the one hand that all things are ideas existing only in minds, but he argues also that things do in fact exist outside our minds. How can he possibly reconcile these two incompatible and mutually exclusive claims?

Two Incompatible claims

A clue to the answer lies in noting that Berkeley has not said that all things exist in *our* minds but only that they exist in *some* mind. A further clue lies in the full title of his *Dialogues: Three Dialogues between Hylas and Philonous, in Opposition to Skeptics and Atheists*. For those who still cannot guess the answer, the following verses (adapted from Ronald Knox's well-known limerick) will remove all doubt:

> There once was a young man who said, "God
> Must think it exceedingly odd
> To find that his tree
> Won't continue to be
> When there's no one about in the quad."

> "Dear Sir:
> Your astonishment's odd.
> For I am always about in the quad.
> And that's why my tree will continue to be
> Since observed by
>   Yours faithfully,
>   God."

"WE HAVE TO TAKE CARE OF PROFESSOR MONOPSYCHOS. HE'S A SOLIPSIST. IF HE GOES, WE ALL GO!"

God: the perceiver
of all things

In fact, Berkeley's entire reasoning is, in a sense, a gigantic proof for the existence of God. For only on the hypothesis of God as an infinite Mind that constantly perceives all things can we believe *both* that all things are ideas existing in mind, *and* that they continue to exist even when unperceived *by us*. Berkeley puts the matter thus:

PHILONOUS: . . . You indeed said the reality of sensible things consisted in an *absolute existence* out of the minds of spirits, or distinct from being perceived. And, pursuant to this notion of reality, you are obliged to deny sensible things any real existence; that is, according to your own definition, you profess yourself a skeptic. But I neither said nor thought the reality of sensible things was to be defined after that manner. To me it is evident, for the reasons you allow of, that sensible things cannot exist otherwise than in a mind or spirit. Whence I conclude, not that they have no real existence, but that, seeing they depend not on my thought and have an existence distinct from being perceived by me, *there must be some other mind wherein they exist.* As sure, therefore, as the sensible world really exists, so sure is there an infinite omnipresent Spirit, who contains and supports it.

HYLAS: What! this is no more than I and all Christians hold; nay, and all others, too, who believe there is a God and that He knows and comprehends all things.

PHILONOUS: Aye, but here lies the difference. Men commonly believe that all things are known or perceived by God, because they believe the being of a God; whereas I, on the other side, immediately and necessarily conclude the being of a God, because all sensible things must be perceived by him.

HYLAS: But so long as we all believe the same thing, what matter is it how we come by that belief?

PHILONOUS: But neither do we agree in the same opinion. For philosophers, though they acknowledge all corporeal beings to be perceived by God, yet they attribute to them an absolute subsistence distinct from their being perceived by any mind whatever, which I do not. Besides, is there no difference between saying, *there is a God, therefore He perceives all things,* and saying, *sensible things do really exist; and if they really exist, they are necessarily perceived by an infinite mind: therefore there is an infinite mind, or God?* This furnishes you with a direct and immediate demonstration, from a most evident principle, of the *being of a God.*[7]

Again, it may be helpful to formulate this part of Berkeley's philosophy as a simple argument:

> The sensible world exists if, and only if, it is perceived by a mind.
> The sensible world exists unperceived by human minds.
>
> Therefore, the sensible world must be perceived by a nonhuman mind.[8]

It should be noted that Berkeley's view of God and the world involves a quite different notion of creation than the usual one. In the popular view, God created the world (bang!) so many years ago. But in Berkeley's view, creation is something that goes on constantly. *At this moment,* as at every moment, God is creating and sustaining the world by his continuing perception of it. Most theologians have not shared Berkeley's view of *esse est percipi* with its peculiar implications for God's existence. But they have, usually, shared the idea that God's creation of the world is such that the world depends at every moment upon the creative act of God.

Berkeley's idea of creation

We have tried to show throughout this chapter why and how Berkeley denies the reality of material substance (or matter) and claims that there is only one kind of reality: mental substance (mind) and ideas. But now we are in a position to understand the full meaning of Berkeley's claim. *Esse est percipi* commits us to a belief in (1) sensible things as ideas, (2) minds that are finite and created mental substances and that might or might not perceive those sensible things, and (3) a Mind that is an infinite mental substance and that perceives all sensible things at all times and creates finite minds to perceive them, too. As with Descartes, we know our own finite minds through introspection and an immediate self-intuition. But peculiar to Berkeley is the belief that we know the infinite and absolute Mind as a necessary condition for the continued existence of sensible things unexperienced by finite minds.

SOME OBJECTIONS

In spite of Berkeley's insistence that his idealist theory of reality is really the most commonsensical, it has always struck most people as fantastic, to say the least. As was noted above, during his own lifetime Berkeley was thought by some to be mad, and nearly everyone since has had a built-in resistance to his theory. You yourself probably instinctively object: "This just can't be true!"

---

[7]Ibid., pp. 55–56.
[8]Cf. Turbayne, in ibid., p. xx.

Before we comment on possible criticisms of Berkeley, a word of caution. To what degree is the acceptance or rejection of a philosophical view a matter of *psychology*? William James said that the history of philosophy is "a clash of temperaments," which of course involves differing tastes, styles, inclinations, and desires. This is no doubt inevitable, and it may even be helpful to the philosophical enterprise. But, again, it is the job of the philosopher (which means you, too) not to confuse temperament with reason. And how much more must we be on guard against blind and uncritical *prejudice*! It is probably truer in the case of Berkeley's philosophy than most others that it runs almost exactly counter to our *deeply rooted biases* and *preconceived notions* concerning the way things must be. But this is hardly grounds for its rejection. If you do reject Berkeley's philosophy, make sure that it is, as much as possible, a *philosophical* rejection.

Even though Berkeley (especially in the third *Dialogue*) anticipated and treated nearly all objections to his view, they persist: Berkeley denies the reality of sensible things; he abuses the ordinary meanings of language; he destroys the distinction between real things and ideas of them; he makes God the author of immoral and evil acts; he fails to account for the nature of illusory ideas; he makes it impossible for more than one person to experience the same thing; and so on. Surely the most famous refutation of Berkeley—and geared especially to his appeal to common sense—was that of Samuel Johnson, who repeatedly kicked against a stone and, rebounding from the thuds, exclaimed: "I refute him *thus*!"

Many, or even most, objections of this kind misfire. They sometimes involve an inattentive reading of Berkeley, or a failure really to *listen* and to *hear* what Berkeley says. For example, no one who really understood Berkeley's theory could really believe that the hardness of a stone is a contradiction to it. Do you see this? And do you see how Berkeley would answer some of the other criticisms too? In evaluating criticisms of Berkeley's

theory we must above all keep in mind that Berkeley did not deny the *reality* of things, but their *materiality*. He insists over and over:

> The question . . . is not whether things have a *real* existence out of the mind of this or that person, but, whether they have an *absolute* existence, distinct from being perceived by God, and exterior to all minds.[9]

Still, three further lines of criticism may be mentioned.

First, what about imagining and conceiving? Does Berkeley do justice to this distinction? He says that you cannot conceive the unexperienced. But surely we can conceive many things that we cannot experience. For to conceive something is to define it without contradiction. Thus we can define infinity, a thousand-sided figure, and even God, though we cannot *picture* any of them. Such conceptualizations, or pure concepts, would seem to be absolutely necessary to our thinking and knowing, but they are excluded by Berkeley's "sensationalist" view of ideas. This in turn raises the question

---

[9]Ibid., pp. 81–82.

whether knowledge and ideas can so simply be equated with sensations. What if one simply began with a quite different view of knowledge—such as Plato's, or Descartes'?

Second, we can raise here an objection that we raised against Descartes. Berkeley, though he denied the reality of material substance, nevertheless continued to affirm the reality of *mental* substance. But why not simply dissolve mind itself into a bundle of ideas? We will see in Chapter 9 that this is exactly what the philosopher Hume did, taking some of Berkeley's arguments against the reality of matter and applying them also to mind.

Third, the objections posed by Ryle against Descartes' idea of mental substance may be raised here too. Is it even meaningful to talk about mind as if it were a sort of *blob* of something, or a *thing*? Would it be, again, a *category mistake* to view mind as a *substance* and having attributes, causing things, being in certain states, and so on? Would it be like confusing a building on the campus with the university?

As you may guess, though, the most radical rejection of any idealist philosophy turns it exactly on its head: It denies the reality of mind and exalts *matter* as the essential "stuff" of all things, and this brings us to Chapter 6.

CHAPTER 5 IN REVIEW

SUMMARY

Idealism is the monist view that all reality is, in some way or another, mind. The most striking version of idealism is subjective idealism, and the most influential subjective idealist was Berkeley.

Berkeley propounded what to most ears would seem to be a preposterous idea: *Esse est percipi*, "To be is to be perceived." According to this principle, nothing exists except as an object of perception or experience, and that means everything that exists is an idea in the mind and nothing exists outside mind. Berkeley defended this thesis with several considerations: (1) the impossibility of having ideas that are similar to realities that are essentially different from ideas; (2) the impossibility of framing any meaningful idea of material substance; (3) the impossibility of thinking of something that is unexperienced; (4) the impossibility of separating primary qualities from secondary qualities, which makes primary as well as secondary qualities subjective, or "idea-istic"; (5) the impossibility of absolutizing even primary qualities, which thus turn out to be as relative as secondary qualities.

However, Berkeley, no less than others, had to reckon with the *passivity* of our perceptions, which leads us to posit objects that are, after all, outside us and independent of us. He thus introduced God, an infinite Mind, who perceives all things at all times. This preserves the reality of the world external to us (passivity of perception) but internal to God (*esse est percipi*).

In spite of Berkeley's insistence that subjective idealism is the most commonsensical of philosophies, many objections are bound to be raised. One of these should *not* be that Berkeley has denied the *reality* of things; his concern is, rather, for the *nature* of things—specifically, the mental nature of things.

BASIC IDEAS

- Idealism (popular sense)
- Idealism (metaphysical sense)
  Objective idealism
  Subjective idealism
- Epistemological dualism
- Primary and secondary qualities
- *Esse est percipi*
- Berkeley's basic argument
- The discontinuity of dualism
- Matter as a meaningless idea
- The unexperienced as inconceivable
- The inseparability of primary and secondary qualities
- The relativity of all qualities
- Solipsism
- The passivity of perception
- The necessity of God as the perceiver of all things
- Berkeley's idea of creation
- The difference between psychologically and philosophically grounded criticisms

TEST YOURSELF

1. What is the difference between an objective idealist and a subjective idealist?
2. Who are Hylas and Philonous?
3. True or false: Colors, sounds, tastes, shapes, and sizes are, for *Berkeley*, all examples of subjective qualities.
4. What is the simple argument that expresses Berkeley's subjective idealism?
5. One of Berkeley's proofs for the subjectivity of everything perceived is based on the inseparability of _____ and ____.
6. Is Berkeley a monist? Why or why not?
7. Solipsism is the belief in (a) one God, (b) one mind, (c) material substance, (d) continual creation.
8. According to Berkeley, how big is a mite's foot?
9. According to Berkeley, the existence of an all-knowing God solves what very big problem?
10. True or false: Berkeley says that the concept of matter is empty and useless.

QUESTIONS FOR REFLECTION

- As a theory of reality Berkeley's subjective idealism certainly is a radical departure from the ordinary view of things. But what *practical* difference does it make? Can you think of any sphere of actual life and practice that would be much altered (if at all) by the adoption of this theory?

- In spite of its apparent radicalness, Berkeley views his theory of reality as the most *commonsensical*. How would you defend this claim in your own words? In the end, is it *really* commonsensical?

- As in Descartes' philosophy, God plays a central role in Berkeley's. What exactly is the role? Is it a more crucial role than in Descartes' philosophy? Could Berkeley's theory of reality be construed as a gigantic proof for the existence of God?

FOR FURTHER READING

Frederick Copleston. *A History of Philosophy.* Baltimore: Newman Press, 1946–1974. V, Chs. 12–13. Summary of Berkeley's metaphysical ideas by an eminent historian of philosophy.

A. C. Ewing. *The Fundamental Questions of Philosophy.* New York: Collier Books, 1962. Chs. 4–5. Brief discussions of the concepts of matter and mind, involving many points raised in our chapter.

A. C. Ewing. *Idealism: A Critical Survey.* Third ed. London: Methuen, reprint 1974. A most useful and complete treatment of the various forms and problems of idealism.

Robert Fogelin. *Routledge Philosophy Guidebook to Berkeley and the Principles of Human Knowledge.* London: Routledge, 2001. A very short introduction to the life and work of George Berkeley.

A. A. Luce. *Berkeley's Immaterialism.* New York: Russell & Russell, 1945. Commentary on Berkeley's *Treatise,* addressing all aspects of Berkeley's basic principles.

C. B. Martin and D. M. Armstrong (eds.). *Locke and Berkeley: A Collection of Critical Essays.* Garden City, NY: Anchor Books, 1968. Contains weighty articles by well-known philosophers on primary and secondary qualities of matter, Berkeley's relation to Locke, and so on.

G. E. Moore. *Philosophical Studies.* London: Routledge & Kegan Paul, 1922. Ch. 1. "The Refutation of Idealism," a classic essay and point of reference for the study of idealism.

G. J. Warnock. *Berkeley.* Baltimore: Penguin Books, 1953. A standard survey of Berkeley's whole philosophy, with special emphasis on his subjective idealism.

Kenneth P. Winkler. *Berkeley: An Interpretation.* New York: Oxford University Press, 1989. A contemporary and compelling defense of Berkeley's idealism.

Kenneth P. Winkler. *The Cambridge Companion to Berkeley.* Cambridge: Cambridge University Press, 2005. A collection of essays on Berkeley's thought by leading scholars.

*In addition, see the relevant articles ("Idealism," "Primary and Secondary Qualities," "Berkeley," etc.) in *Routledge Encyclopedia of Philosophy,* ed. Edward Craig (London: Routledge, 1998), and *Stanford Encyclopedia of Philosophy,* http://plato.stanford.edu.

CHAPTER 6

MATERIALISM

Materialism is actually a form of *naturalism*, and it might be best first to get an idea of this larger metaphysical perspective. All naturalisms share a repudiation of any supernatural or spiritual reality. The claim is: All that exists can, at least in principle, be investigated scientifically. And just as believers in the supernatural or the spiritual are often given to faith, dogma, intuition, authority, and the like, so naturalists are generally given to observation, experimentation, and healthy doses of skepticism.

But we must distinguish between a narrower and a wider naturalism, corresponding to a narrower and a wider view of nature itself. The narrower view defines nature as the physical world and may be called *materialism*. The wider naturalism, on the other hand, defines nature more broadly so as to include matter as only one of *many* dimensions or aspects of nature. In this chapter we will focus our attention on materialism.

WHAT IS MATERIALISM?

As with the word "idealism," the word "materialism" also has a popular and a more technical sense. In popular usage materialism means a preoccupation with earthly goods (such as money, ski chalets, and sailboats), and a materialist in this sense is one whose life revolves around the pursuit of such things. But here we intend "materialism" in its more technical and metaphysical sense: Matter with its motions and qualities is the ultimate reality of all

MATERIALISM

The metaphysical doctrine that matter with its motions and qualities is the ultimate reality of all things.

things. More generally, this means that everything in the universe—from subatomic particles, to tables, chairs, dogs, and cats, to thoughts, feelings, perceptions, and ideals—*everything* is reducible to matter with its motions and qualities, to physical states, to a position in space and time, to what can be quantified.

There are few forks on the philosophical road that are more unmistakable than the one where idealism and materialism veer off from each other. We saw in our last chapter that one radical solution to the mind-body problem is simply to do away with matter. The result is *idealism,* the view that there is only one reality, and that is mind and its ideas. Materialism takes exactly the opposite course and denies the reality of mind, or at least reduces it (along with everything else) to matter. As a radical solution to the mind-body problem materialism is certainly as effective as idealism, for it too overcomes entirely the old problem of relating two essentially different substances, for there *is* no other substance, only matter. In the same way that Descartes, with his mind-matter dualism, unwittingly spawned modern idealism, so did he spawn modern materialism. This is not to say that the only reason for adopting materialism is that it is a way of avoiding the mind-body problem. As with idealism, materialism too has still other advantages. Advantages aside, certainly as a theory of reality it is in some respects the starkest and the most hard-headed.

Materialism is actually a very old philosophy. Already among the Pre-Socratics, Democritus and Leucippus taught that all things, including the soul, are made of indivisible particles or atoms. This idea was adopted by the Greek philosopher Epicurus (about 300 B.C.). He concluded from the

Materialism as a radical solution to the mind-body problem

Materialism, an old philosophy

From mind-matter dualism two radically different theories of reality may be hatched, depending on which idea is suppressed. If the idea of mind is suppressed, then materialism may be hatched.

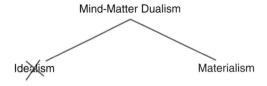

Mind-Matter Dualism

Idealism   Materialism

materialistic nature of the soul that upon death its parts disperse, and therefore there can be no life after death—so eat, drink, and be merry! After Epicurus, the Roman poet Lucretius (about 60 B.C.) wrote as if he himself were even then providing a materialistic (and atomistic) response to Descartes' mind-body problem:

Lucretius: an early
defender of
materialism

> I now declare that mind and soul are joined
>   together, and form one single entity,
>   but the head so to speak, that rules in all the body,
>   is counsel, mind, and intellect, as we say,
>   and this is placed midway within the breast.
> For here leap terror and panic, this spot feels
>   sweet joy; here, then, are intellect and mind.
> The rest of the soul, dispersed through all the body,
>   obeys the mind and moves to its command.
> For mind thinks its own thoughts, knows its own pleasures,
>   when nothing has stimulated soul or body.
> And as when injury attacks our head
>   or eye, they hurt, but we're not agonized
>   all over, thus the mind sometimes feels pain
>   or joy and strength, and when other parts of soul
>   in limb and joint have felt no novel impulse.
> But when the mind is deeply stirred by terror,
>   all through the body we see the soul affected;
>   we pale, and over all the body sweat
>   pours out, the tongue stumbles, voice goes awry,
>   eyes are befogged, ears ring, the knees give way,
>   yes, from sheer terror of mind we often see
>   men fall in a faint; thus readily we perceive
>   the union of soul and mind, for soul, when struck
>   by mind, in turn strikes body and makes it move.
> This argument also proves that soul and mind
>   are physical things. Clearly, they move our limbs,
>   arouse the body from sleep, change our expression,
>   and guide and govern the man in all his being.
> Yet without touch, we see, such things can't happen,
>   nor touch without matter; must we not then admit
>   the soul and mind in act are physical things?
> Besides, we see that in our bodies, soul
>   and body act and react in sympathy.
> If a bristling spear has driven deep, exposing
>   sinew and bone, and yet not taking life,
>   still faintness follows and sweet swooning down
>   to earth, and there a sense of rocking motion,
>   sometimes with vaguely felt desire to rise.
> And so the soul must be a physical thing,

since physical weapon and wound can make it suffer.
I'll now proceed to argument and proof
   of what makes up the soul, and what its substance.
To begin, I say the soul is subtly built
   of infinitesimal atoms. You may see
   and learn that this is so from what's to come.
Nothing whatever, we see, can move as fast
   as the mind when it conceives and starts an action;
   thus nothing whose nature clearly lies within
   our range of vision moves faster than the mind.
But whatever is so mobile must be made
   of very round and very tiny atoms,
   so that the slightest impulse starts them moving.
Yes, just a touch makes water move and flow:
   it's made, you see, of small-sized shapes that roll.
But the nature of honey tends to be more stable;
   its fluid is thicker and less disposed to move.
For all the atoms of its substance cling
   more closely, being of particles less smooth,
   you see, and not so delicate or so round.
Take poppyseed: a gentle puff of air
   at the top will blow a tall heap helter-skelter,
   but not, on the other hand, a heap of stones
   or grain. According, then, as particles
   are smallest and smoothest, they will move with ease.
But on the other hand, as some are found
   rougher and heavier, so are they more stable.
Now since the soul has been revealed to be
   uncommonly mobile, we must grant it made
   of atoms very tiny, smooth, and round.
Take this to heart, good friend; in many ways
   you'll find it a useful, helpful thing to know.
This fact, too, tells the nature of the soul,
   how fine its fabric, and in how small a space
   it could be held, if it were all rolled up:
   when once the carefree peace of death has seized
   a man, and the substance of soul and mind has left him,
   from his whole body you'd see nothing lost
   in appearance or in weight; death leaves him all
   but the humid heat and sentience that mean life.
The entire soul, then, must consist of tiny
   atoms, strung out through sinews, vitals, veins,
   since, when it all has gone from all the body,
   the outer dimensions of body-parts remain
   unaltered, and not an ounce of weight is lost.
It's such as when bouquet of wine floats off,
   or breath of perfume is wafted to the winds,

or when from a substance flavor dies away;
to the eye, the physical thing appears no smaller
for all of that, and suffers no loss of weight.
Why? Because many minuscule atoms make
flavors and scents throughout the range of things.
Thus you may know the substance of the mind
and soul, I insist, is formed of most minute
atoms, for slipping away, it steals no weight.[1]

In the modern period, the seventeenth-century English philosopher Thomas Hobbes expressed the materialist thesis with a theistic twist: The notion of *spirit,* as opposed to *matter* or *body,* should be reserved for God alone.

A modern statement

From these Metaphysics, which are mingled with the Scripture to make School Divinity, we are told, there be in the world certain Essences separated from Bodies, which they call *Abstract Essences, and Substantial Forms:* For the Interpreting of which *Jargon,* there is need of somewhat more than ordinary attention in this place. Also I ask pardon of those that are not used to this kind of Discourse, for applying my self to those that are. The World (I mean not the Earth only, that denominates the Lovers of it *Worldly men,* but the *Universe,* that is, the whole mass of all things that are) is Corporeal, that is to say, Body; and hath the dimensions of Magnitude, namely, Length, Breadth, and Depth: also every part of Body, is likewise Body, and hath the like dimensions; and consequently every part of the Universe, is Body; and that which is not Body, is no part of the Universe: And because the Universe is All,

Thomas Hobbes, a modern materialist

[1]Lucretius, *The Nature of Things,* III, 136–230, tr. Frank O. Copley (New York: Norton, 1977).

that which is no part of it, is *Nothing;* and consequently *no where.* Nor does it follow from hence, that Spirits are *nothing:* for they have dimensions, and are therefore really *Bodies;* though that name in common Speech be given to such Bodies only, as are visible, or palpable; that is, that have some degree of Opacity: But for Spirits, they call them Incorporeal; which is a name of more honour, and may therefore with more piety be attributed to God himself; in whom we consider not what Attribute expresseth best his Nature, which is Incomprehensible; but what best expresseth our desire to honour Him.[2]

Such a view of reality has taken several forms. No doubt the harshest is *mechanistic materialism.*

MAN A MACHINE

Mechanistic materialism

The key to understanding mechanistic materialism lies in the word "mechanistic," which means "machinelike." According to this theory of reality, not only are all things reducible to matter and motion and locatable in space and time, but all things happen and have their particular features according to a finite number of fixed physical laws. That is to say, the world and everything in it is a *machine.*

Some roots of the mechanistic view

Mechanistic materialism really took shape as a philosophical position (and in some ways even as a philosophical movement) soon after Descartes. The thinkers advocating this idea were very much influenced by the "new science," and were especially captivated by Sir Isaac Newton's Three Laws of Motion, the basis of Newtonian mechanics. They were also influenced by Descartes himself, who believed that—at least with respect to the *matter* part of his dualism—the world is ordered by fixed laws, and that animals, like everything else in the external world, are mechanisms.

---

[2]Thomas Hobbes, *Leviathan,* ed. A. D. Lindsay (New York: Dutton, 1950), chap. 46 (slightly edited).

NEWTON'S THREE LAWS OF MOTION

1. A body remains at rest or in motion with a constant velocity unless acted on by an outside force.

2. The sum of the forces acting on a body is equal to the product of its mass and acceleration.

3. For every action there is an equal and opposite reaction.

How do these laws play into the hands of mechanistic materialism? Can you think of concrete examples?

mech • a • nism (mek'ə • niz'əm) *n.* **1.** The parts or arrangement of parts of a machine: the *mechanism* of a watch. **2.** Something similar to a machine in the arrangement and working of its parts: The human body is a magnificent *mechanism*. **3.** The process or technique by which something works or produces an action or effect: the complicated *mechanism* of democracy. **4.** The technique or the mechanical method of execution of an artist, writer, etc. **5.** A theory that all natural phenomena can be explained by the laws of chemistry and physics. **6.** *Psychol.* The mental processes, conscious or unconscious, by which certain actions or results are effected. Abbr. *mech.*
mech • a • nist (mek'ə • nist) *n.* **1.** A mechanician. **2.** A believer in mechanism (def. 5).—*adj.* Mechanistic.
mech • a • nis • tic (mek'ə • nis'tik) *adj.* **1.** Of, pertaining to, or of the nature of mechanics. **2.** Pertaining to or based on mechanism (def. 5).—**mech'a • nis'ti • cal • ly** *adv.*

It is important not to miss the full force of the claim that the universe is a machine. It is not just that all things (and everything *about* all things) are caused. We all believe that. It is, rather, that everything is caused in such a way that *it could not have been otherwise.* This pen, this desk, that paperclip in just that position, the smoke curling upward from this pipe, everything that

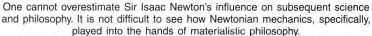

One cannot overestimate Sir Isaac Newton's influence on subsequent science and philosophy. It is not difficult to see how Newtonian mechanics, specifically, played into the hands of materialistic philosophy.

is and is going on in this room, in all rooms, in all the world, in all worlds—everything in the universe down to the minutest detail is, in this view, *exhaustively predetermined* by infinitely long and converging chains of blind, irrational antecedent causes. One of the most concise expressions of this mechanist point of view was provided by the French astronomer and mathematician Laplace:

> We ought then to regard the present state of the universe as the effect of its anterior state and as the cause of the one which is to follow. Given for one instant an intelligence which could comprehend all the forces by which nature is animated and the respective situation of the beings who compose it—an intelligence sufficiently vast to submit these data to analysis—it would embrace in the same formula the movements of the greatest bodies of the universe and those of the lightest atom; for it, nothing would be uncertain and the future, as the past, would be present to its eyes.[3]

That is, in the mechanistic view of things, if you could somehow know the exact status of every detail in the universe at one point as well as all the laws of nature, then you could know perfectly every detail in the universe at any point in the past or the future.

Even so, it is *still* possible that some may fail to note the full implications of the mechanistic claim. If *everything* in the universe is matter in motion and is governed by mechanistic laws, then so is man. And then so is his thinking, feeling, purposing, valuing, and willing. Man too, through and through, is a machine.

Is man a machine?

"Man a Machine" was in fact the title of a remarkable little volume published in 1748 by the French physician and agnostic La Mettrie. (He has been called "the scapegoat of eighteenth-century materialism.") Like many others before and after him, La Mettrie argued for a purely materialistic basis of human consciousness. Thoughts, sensations, and emotions are all a matter of organs, nerves, impulses, reflex movements, pumping blood, and the like. These in turn are physiological counterparts of springs, cogs, wheels, wire, and so on, so it all reduces to physics and chemistry. In such a view, as someone has said, the brain secretes thought in the same way that the liver secretes bile! A few passages from La Mettrie:

> Man is so complicated a machine that it is impossible to get a clear idea of the machine beforehand, and hence impossible to define it. . . .

[3]Pierre Simon de Laplace, *A Philosophical Essay on Probabilities,* tr. Frederick Wilson Truscott and Frederick Lincoln Emory (New York: Dover, 1951), p. 4.

MECHANISM

The view that conceives of the universe and everything in it as a machine—that is, something whose motions are completely determined by unalterable laws.

Title page of La Mettrie's *Man a Machine*. The verse by Voltaire: *Where is this reason, essence supreme, which so luminously is painted? Where is this spirit outliving us? It is born with our senses. And with the senses waxes and wanes. Alas, it too will die.*

L'HOMME

MACHINE.

Eſt-ce là ce Raion de l'Eſſence ſuprème,
Que l'on nous peint ſi lumineux?
Eſt-ce là cet Eſprit ſurvivant à nous même?
Il naît avec nos ſens, croit, s'affoiblit
comme eux.
Helas! il périra de même.

VOLTAIRE.

À LEYDE,
DE L'IMP. D'ELIE LUZAC, FILS.
MDCCXLVIII.

But since all the faculties of the soul depend to such a degree on the proper organization of the brain and of the whole body, that apparently they are but this organization itself, the soul is clearly an enlightened machine. . . .

The soul is therefore but an empty word, of which no one has any idea, and which an enlightened man should use only to signify the part in us that thinks. Given the least principle of motion, animated bodies will have all that is necessary for moving, feeling, thinking, repenting, or in a word for conducting themselves in the physical realm, and in the moral realm which depends upon it. . . .

Grant only that organized matter is endowed with a principle of motion, which alone differentiates it from the inorganic (and can one deny this in the face of the most incontestable observation?) and that among animals, as I have sufficiently proved, everything depends upon the diversity of this organization: these admissions suffice for guessing the riddle of substances and of man. It [thus] appears that there is but one [type of organization] in the universe, and that man is the most perfect [example]. . . .

Let us then conclude boldly that man is a machine, and that in the whole universe there is but a single substance differently modified. This is no hypothesis set forth by dint of a number of postulates and assumptions; it is not the work of prejudice, nor even of my reason alone; I should have disdained a guide which I think to be so untrustworthy, had not my senses, bearing a torch, so to speak, induced me to

MAN, A COMPUTER?

Especially with the rise of computer technology, the temptation to create man in the image of a computer has sometimes been irresistible.

"Each human being is a superbly constructed, astonishingly compact, self-ambulatory computer. . . ."

—Carl Sagan

follow reason by lighting the way themselves. Experience has thus spoken to me in behalf of reason; and in this way I have combined the two.

. . . Need I say that I refer to the empty and trivial notions, to the pitiable and trite arguments that will be urged (as long as the shadow of prejudice or of super-stition remains on earth) for the supposed incompatibility of two substances which meet and move each other unceasingly? Such is my system, or rather the truth, unless I am much deceived. It is short and simple. Dispute it now who will.[4]

Amid all the rest, do not fail to notice La Mettrie's concluding claim for his materialistic-mechanistic theory: "It is short and simple." Here again is the appeal to *simplicity* as a criterion of a better explanation that we with enconntered Ockham's Razor. In fact, it is often urged by materialists that the economy or simplicity of their theory decisively enhances its *explanatory power* over, say, dualistic theories.

THE NEW MATERIALISM

If you have the impression that the conception of man as a machine is just an idle piece displayed in the historical museum of philosophical ideas, your impression is quite wrong. It is true that the La Mettrie and pre-La Mettrie type of mechanism was based on the "billiard-ball" model of the universe (everything happens according to strict laws and direct or indirect physical contacts), and that the billiard-ball model is now "out." And even the classical Newtonian mechanics has now been succeeded by complicated things like *quantum mechanics* and Heisenberg's uncertainty principle, according to which there is no observable causal determinism at the level of atomic and subatomic particles. How this latter involves a "dematerialization" of matter is described by the scientist and philosopher N. R. Hanson:

The "dematerialization" of matter

Matter has been dematerialized, not just as a concept of the philosophically real, but now as an idea of modern physics. Matter can be analyzed down to the level

---

[4]Julien Offray de La Mettrie, *Man a Machine,* tr. Gertrude C. Bussey et al. (La Salle, IL: Open Court, 1912), pp. 18, 89, 140–141.

of fundamental particles. But at that depth the direction of the analysis changes, and this constitutes a major conceptual surprise in the history of science. The things which for Newton typified matter—e.g., an exactly determinable state, a point shape, absolute solidity—these are now the properties electrons do not, because theoretically they cannot, have. . . .

The dematerialization of matter . . . has rocked mechanics at its foundations. . . . The 20th century's dematerialization of matter has made it conceptually impossible to accept a Newtonian picture of the properties of matter and still do a consistent physics.[5]

Nonetheless, the materialistic perspective thrives. Consider, for example, the materialism of the Australian philosopher J. J. C. Smart. Under the sway of contemporary physics he rejects complete causal determinism but asserts, nevertheless, a purely physicalistic theory of mind. More specifically, he asserts what is called the Identity Thesis, which claims that mental states are nothing more (or less) than brain states. According to the Identity Thesis, our thoughts, feelings, emotions, dreams, and so on are all reducible to physical processes inside the brain. There are, according to Smart, no non-physical entities as he describes in the passage below:

The Identity Thesis

First of all let me try to explain what I mean by "materialism." I shall then go on to try to defend the doctrine. By "materialism" I mean the theory that there is nothing in the world over and above those entities which are postulated by physics (or, of course, those entities which will be postulated by future and more adequate physical theories). Thus I do not hold materialism to be wedded to the billiard-ball physics of the nineteenth century. The less visualizable particles of modern physics count as matter. Note that energy counts as matter for my purposes: indeed in modern physics energy and matter are not sharply distinguishable. Nor do I hold that materialism implies determinism. If physics is indeterministic on the micro-level, so must be the materialist's theory. I regard materialism as compatible with a wide range of conceptions of the nature of matter and energy. For example, if matter and energy consist of regions of special curvature of an absolute space-time, with "worm holes" and what not, this is still compatible with materialism: we can still argue that in the last resort the world is made up entirely of the ultimate entities of physics, namely space-time points.

. . . [M]y definition will in some respects be narrower than those of some who have called themselves "materialists." I wish to lay down that it is incompatible with materialism that there should be any irreducibly "emergent" laws or properties, say in biology or psychology. According to the view I propose to defend, there are no irreducible laws or properties in biology, any more than there are in electronics. Given the "natural history" of a superheterodyne (its wiring diagram), a physicist is able to explain, using only laws of physics, its mode of behavior and its properties (for example, the property of being able to receive such and such a radio station which broadcasts on 25 megacycles). Just as electronics gives the physical explanation of the workings of superheterodynes, etc., so biology gives (or approximates to giving) physical and chemical explanations of the workings of organisms or parts of organisms. The biologist needs natural history just as the engineer needs wiring diagrams, but neither needs nonphysical laws.

[5]N. R. Hanson, "The Dematerialization of Matter," in *The Concept of Matter*, ed. Ernan McMullen (Notre Dame, IN: University of Notre Dame Press, 1963), pp. 556–557.

It will now become clear why I define materialism in the way I have done above. I am concerned to deny that in the world there are nonphysical entities and nonphysical laws. In particular I wish to deny the doctrine of psychophysical dualism. (I also want to deny any theory of "emergent properties," since irreducibly nonphysical properties are just about as repugnant to me as are irreducibly nonphysical entities.)

Popular theologians sometimes argue against materialism by saying that "you can't put love in a test tube." Well you can't put a gravitational field in a test tube (except in some rather strained sense of these words), but there is nothing incompatible with materialism, as I have defined it, in the notion of a gravitational field.

Similarly, even though love may elude test tubes, it does not elude materialistic metaphysics, since it can be analyzed as a pattern of bodily behavior or, perhaps better, as the internal state of the human organism that accounts for this behavior. (A dualist who analyzes love as an internal state will perhaps say that it is a soul state, whereas the materialist will say that it is a brain state. It seems to me that much of our ordinary language about the mental is neither dualistic nor materialist but is neutral between the two. Thus, to say that a locution is not materialistic is not to say that it is immaterialistic.)

But what about consciousness? Can we interpret the having of an afterimage or of a painful sensation as something material, namely, a brain state or brain process? We seem to be immediately aware of pains and after-images, and we seem to be immediately aware of them as something different from a neurophysiological state or process. For example, the after-image may be green speckled with red, whereas the neurophysiologist looking into our brains would be unlikely to see something green speckled with red. However, if we object to materialism in this way we are victims of a confusion which U. T. Place has called "the phenomenological fallacy." To say that an image or sense datum is green is not to say that the conscious experience of having the image or sense datum is green. It is to say that it is the sort of experience we have when in normal conditions we look at a green apple, for example. Apples and unripe bananas can be green, but not the experiences of seeing them. An image or a sense datum can be green in a derivative sense, but this need not cause any worry, because, on the view I am defending, images and sense data are not constituents of the world, though the processes of having an image or a sense datum are actual processes in the world. The experience of having a green sense datum is not itself green; it is a process occurring in grey matter. The world contains plumbers, but does not contain the average plumber; it also contains the having of a sense datum, but does not contain the sense datum. . . .

It may be asked why I should demand of a tenable philosophy of mind that it should be compatible with materialism, in the sense in which I have defined it. One reason is as follows. How could a nonphysical property or entity suddenly arise in the course of animal evolution? A change in a gene is a change in a complex molecule which causes a change in the biochemistry of the cell. This may lead to changes in the shape or organization of the developing embryo. But what sort of

IDENTITY THESIS

Mental states = Brain states

chemical process could lead to the springing into existence of something nonphysical? No enzyme can catalyze the production of a spook! Perhaps it will be said that the nonphysical comes into existence as a by-product: that whenever there is a certain complex physical structure, then, by an irreducible extraphysical law, there is also a nonphysical entity. Such laws would be quite outside normal scientific conceptions and quite inexplicable: they would be, in Herbert Feigl's phrase, "nomological danglers." To say the very least, we can vastly simplify our cosmological outlook if we can defend a materialistic philosophy of mind.[6]

ARE THE MIND AND BODY IDENTICAL?

Two major criticisms of materialism center on (1) the claimed identity of mind and body and (2) the claimed universality of strict determinism. A little later, in our discussion of B. F. Skinner, we will address the second of these. For the moment, consider the first.

All forms of materialism involve a physicalistic interpretation of mind. In the case of Smart, we have just seen that this takes the form of the Identity Thesis, so-called because it views the mind (including thoughts, perceptions, emotions, etc.) as identical with brain states (nerve cells, electrical impulses, etc.):

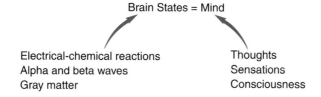

Brain States = Mind

Electrical-chemical reactions   Thoughts
Alpha and beta waves   Sensations
Gray matter   Consciousness

One of the most common objections to this view has already been anticipated by Smart. Are not the differences between mental states and brain states so great that no amount of empirical or scientific analysis can bridge them? For example, consider a surgeon who completes his last delicate and precise penetration into an innermost recess of the brain. What does he see there—*red* or *affection*? No. He sees more nerves, brain tissue, blood, cells, and so on. It's a serious question: Do the sensations of red, the idea of a table, the feeling of repulsion, and the desire for food sit right there in the brain alongside veins and synapses, waiting to be exposed?

Some are not satisfied that Smart and others have successfully laid this objection to rest. The American philosopher Richard Taylor presses the difference between mind and body by raising *logical* problems with identity-talk: I can be blamed, but can my *body* be blamed? I can be religious, but can my *body* be religious? My thoughts can be true or false, but can my *brain* be true or false?

Problems with the Identity Thesis

---

[6]J. J. C. Smart, "Materialism," *Journal of Philosophy*, 22 (October 1963), pp. 651–653, 660.

By "identity" the materialist must mean a strict and total identity of himself and his body, nothing less. Now to say of anything, X, and anything, Y, that X and Y are identical, or that they are really one and the same thing, one must be willing to assert of X anything whatever that he asserts of Y, and vice versa. This is simply a consequence of their identity, for if there is anything whatever that can be truly asserted of any object X, but cannot be truly asserted of some object Y, then it logically follows that X and Y are two different things, and not the same thing. In saying, for instance, that the British wartime prime minister and Winston Churchill are one and the same person, one commits himself to saying of either whatever he is willing to say of the other—such as, that he lived to a great age, smoked cigars, was a resolute leader, was born at Blenheim, and so on. If there were any statement whatever that was true of, say, Mr. Churchill, but not true of the wartime prime minister, then it would follow that Mr. Churchill was not the wartime prime minister, that we are here referring to two different men, and not one.

The questions can now be asked, then, whether there is anything true of me that is not true of my body, and vice versa. There are, of course, ever so many things that can be asserted indifferently of both me and my body without absurdity. For instance, we can say that I was born at such and such place and time, and it is not the least odd to say this of my body as well. Or we can say that my body now weighs exactly so many pounds, and it would be just as correct to give this as my weight; and so on.

But now consider more problematical assertions. It might, for instance, be true of me at a certain time that I am morally blameworthy or praiseworthy. Can we then say that my body or some part of it, such as my brain, is in exactly the same sense blameworthy or praiseworthy? Can moral predicates be applied without gross incongruity to any physical object at all? Or suppose I have some profound wish or desire, or some thought—the desire, say, to be in some foreign land at a given moment, or thoughts of the Homeric gods. It seems at least odd to assert that my body, or some part of it, wishes that it were elsewhere, or has thoughts of the gods. How, indeed, can any purely physical state of any purely physical object ever be a state that is *for* something, or *of* something, in the way that my desires and thoughts are such? And how, in particular, could a purely physical state be in this sense *for* or *of* something that is not real? Or again, suppose that I am religious, and can truly say that I love God and neighbor, for instance. Can I without absurdity say that my body or some part of it, such as my foot or brain, is religious, and loves God and neighbor? Or can one suppose that my being religious, or having such love, consists simply in my body's being in a certain state, or behaving in a certain way? If I claim the identity of myself with my body, I must say all these odd things; that is, I must be willing to assert of my body, or some part of it, everything I assert of myself. There is perhaps no logical absurdity or clear falsity in speaking thus of one's corporeal frame, but such assertions as these are at least strange, and it can be questioned whether, as applied to the body, they are even still meaningful.

The disparity between bodily and personal predicates becomes even more apparent, however, if we consider epistemological predicates, involved in statements about belief and knowledge. Thus, if I believe something—believe, for instance, that today is February 31—then I am in a certain state; the state, namely, of having a certain belief which is in this case necessarily a false one. Now how can a physical state of any physical object be identical with that? And how, in particular, can anything be a *false* physical state of an object? The physical states of things, it would seem, just *are*, and one cannot even think of anything that could ever distinguish one such state from another as being either true or false. A physiologist might give a complete physical description of a brain and nervous system at a particular time, but he could never distinguish some of those states as true and others as false, nor would he have any idea what to look for if he were asked to do this. At least, so it would certainly seem.[7]

An objection to the Identity Thesis has also been raised by the functionalists. We introduced functionalism at the end of Chapter 4, though we have put off until now an account of one of its major appeals. Functionalism is, quite simply, an alternative to the Identity Thesis, which it regards as utterly implausible. Why? The Identity Thesis insists on drawing straight lines, as it were, from specific mental states to specific brain states; it argues that all mental states of a given type—for example, being in pain—must be *identified* with a physical state of a certain type—for example, a C-fiber firing. But, the functionalist charges, could not many other physical systems be in pain without being in just the physical state we happen to be in when we are in pain? Through a well-known and imaginative device, Paul M. Churchland shows how this one-to-one correspondence of mental states to brain states need not hold.

Functionalism again

Imagine a being from another planet, says the functionalist, a being with an alien physiological constitution, a constitution based on the chemical element silicon, for example, instead of on the element carbon, as ours is. The chemistry and even the physical structure of the alien's brain would have to be systematically different from ours. But even so, that alien brain could well sustain a functional economy of internal states whose mutual *relations* parallel perfectly the mutual relations that define our own mental states. The alien may have an internal state that meets all the conditions for being a pain state, as outlined earlier. That state, considered from a purely physical point of view, would have a very different makeup from a human pain state, but it could nevertheless be identical to a human pain state from a purely functional point of view. And so for all of his functional states.

If the alien's functional economy of internal states were indeed *functionally isomorphic* with our own internal economy—if those states were causally connected to inputs, to one another, and to behavior in ways that parallel our own internal connections—then the alien would have pains, and desires, and hopes, and fears just as fully as we, despite the differences in the physical system that sustains or realizes those functional states. What is important for mentality is not the matter of which the creature is made, but the structure of the internal activities which that matter sustains.

If we can think of one alien constitution, we can think of many, and the point just made can also be made with an artificial system. Were we to create an electronic system—a computer of some kind—whose internal economy were functionally isomorphic with our own in all the relevant ways, then it too would be the subject of mental states.

What this illustrates is that there are almost certainly many more ways than one for nature, and perhaps even for man, to put together a thinking, feeling, perceiving creature. And this raises a problem for the identity theory, for it seems that there is

---

[7]Richard Taylor, *Metaphysics*, 2d ed. (Englewood Cliffs, NJ: Prentice-Hall, 1974), pp. 13–15.

no single type of physical state to which a given type of mental state must always correspond. Ironically, there are *too many* different kinds of physical systems that can realize the functional economy characteristic of conscious intelligence. . . . The prospects for universal identities, between types of mental states and types of brain states, are therefore slim.[8]

BEYOND FREEDOM AND DIGNITY: SKINNER

Probably the best recent example of one who asserts both a physicalistic view of mind and a pervasive causal determinism was not a philosopher but the behaviorist psychologist B. F. Skinner.

What is *behaviorism*? Generally, behaviorism is a school of psychology that emphasizes observable human behavior as the proper object of psychological study. Now here we have to draw a distinction. For there is a big difference between (1) the view that the description of observable behavior is the psychologist's task, which we may call descriptive or *soft* behaviorism, and (2) the view that observable behavior *is all there is*, which we may call *hard* behaviorism. Obviously, soft behaviorism is not our concern here inasmuch as it makes no claim at all about reality or human nature itself. Hard behaviorism, however, most certainly does involve a claim about reality—specifically a claim about the nature of human nature itself. This form of behaviorism is, therefore, at a certain level inseparable from a metaphysical perspective, and the perspective is a materialistic and mechanistic one. It is therefore appropriate to consider this form of behaviorism in a chapter on materialism, especially since, through Skinner's book *Beyond Freedom and Dignity*, it has enjoyed a renewed and far-reaching impact in recent years.

Behaviorism

The school of psychology that emphasizes observable behavior as the proper object of psychological study.

Soft Behaviorism	*Hard Behaviorism*
The form of behaviorism that limits itself to the description of observable behavior.	The form of behaviorism that extends itself beyond the task of describing behavior to the claim that there *is* nothing beyond behavior.

[8]Paul M. Churchland, *Matter and Consciousness: A Contemporary Introduction to the Philosophy of Mind* (Cambridge, MA: MIT Press, 1984), pp. 36f.

There can be no doubt about the physicalistic and mechanistic character of Skinner's appraisal of the human person. Though Skinner's physicalism, or reduction of the total person to physical states, underlies and pervades Skinner's work everywhere, it is nowhere really argued, at least not with any rigor. Rather, it is treated as an assumption that any enlightened twentieth-century person would surely embrace, in contrast to earlier and "prescientific" notions that uncritically employ ideas such as mind, transcendence, free will, and the like. Our interest in Skinner is not, therefore, so much with his defense of physicalism (because he gives none) but with what he does with it as the foundation of his proposed "technology of behavior," a program of psychological engineering, or manipulation of human nature in the interest of the improvement and progress of the species.

Almost all our major problems involve human behavior, and they cannot be solved by physical and biological technology alone. What is needed is a technology of behavior, but we have been slow to develop the science from which such a technology might be drawn. One difficulty is that almost all of what is called behavioral science continues to trace behavior to states of mind, feelings, traits of character, human nature, and so on. Physics and biology once followed similar practices and advanced only when they discarded them. The behavioral sciences have been slow to change partly because the explanatory entities often seem to be directly observed and partly because other kinds of explanations have been hard to find. The environment is obviously important, but its role has remained obscure. It does not push or pull, it *selects*, and this function is difficult to discover and analyze. The role of natural selection in evolution was formulated only a little more than a hundred years ago, and the selective role of the environment in shaping and maintaining the behavior of the individual is only beginning to be recognized and studied. As the interaction between organism and environment has come to be understood, however, effects once assigned to states of mind, feelings, and traits are beginning to be traced to accessible conditions, and a technology of behavior may therefore become available. It will not solve our problems, however, until it replaces traditional prescientific views, and these are strongly entrenched. Freedom and dignity illustrate the difficulty. They are the possessions of the autonomous man of traditional theory, and they are essential to practices in which a person is held responsible for his conduct and given credit for his achievements. A scientific analysis shifts both the responsibility and the achievement to the environment. It also raises questions concerning "values." Who will use a technology and to what ends? Until these issues are resolved, a technology of behavior will continue to be rejected, and with it possibly the only way to solve our problems. . . .

A child is born a member of the human species, with a genetic endowment showing many idiosyncratic features, and he begins at once to acquire a repertoire of behavior under the contingencies of reinforcement to which he is exposed as an individual. Most of these contingencies are arranged by other people. They are, in fact, what is called a culture, although the term is usually defined in other ways. Two eminent anthropologists have said, for example, that "the essential core of culture consists of traditional (i.e., historically derived and selected) ideas and especially their attached values." But those who observe cultures do not see ideas or values. They see how people live, how they raise their children, how they gather or cultivate food, what kinds of dwellings they live in, what they wear, what games they play, how they treat each other, how they govern themselves, and so on. These are the customs, the customary *behaviors,* of a people. To explain them we must turn to the contingencies which generate them.

Some contingencies are part of the physical environment, but they usually work in combination with social contingencies, and the latter are naturally emphasized by those who study cultures. The social contingencies, or the behaviors they generate, are the "ideas" of a culture; the reinforcers that appear in the contingencies are its "values."

A person is not only exposed to the contingencies that constitute a culture, he helps to maintain them, and to the extent that the contingencies induce him to do so the culture is self-perpetuating. The effective reinforcers are a matter of observation and cannot be disputed. What a given group of people calls good is a fact: it is what members of the group find reinforcing as the result of their genetic endowment and the natural and social contingencies to which they have been exposed. Each culture has its own set of goods, and what is good in one culture may not be good in another. To recognize this is to take the position of "cultural relativism." What is good for the Trobriand Islander is good for the Trobriand Islander, and that is that. Anthropologists have often emphasized relativism as a tolerant alternative to missionary zeal in converting all cultures to a single set of ethical, governmental, religious, or economic values. . . .

It is the nature of an experimental analysis of human behavior that it should strip away the functions previously assigned to autonomous man and transfer them one by one to the controlling environment. The analysis leaves less and less for autonomous man to do. But what about man himself? Is there not something about a person which is more than a living body? Unless something called a self survives, how can we speak of self-knowledge or self-control? To whom is the injunction "Know thyself" addressed?

It is an important part of the contingencies to which a young child is exposed that his own body is the only part of his environment which remains the same (*idem*) from moment to moment and day to day. We say that he discovers his *identity* as he learns to distinguish between his body and the rest of the world. He does this long before the community teaches him to call things by name and to distinguish "me" from "it" or "you."

A self is a repertoire of behavior appropriate to a given set of contingencies. A substantial part of the conditions to which a person is exposed may play a dominant role, and under other conditions a person may report, "I'm not myself today," or, "I couldn't have done what you said I did, because that's not like me." The identity conferred upon a self arises from the contingencies responsible for the behavior. Two or more repertoires generated by different sets of contingencies compose two or more selves. A person possesses one repertoire appropriate to his life with his friends and another appropriate to his life with his family, and a friend may find him a very different person if he sees him with his family or his family if they see him with his friends. The problem of identity arises when situations are intermingled,

". . . B. F. Skinner has profoundly changed the world—and for the better—even if much of the world does not know it. He is, it seems to me, a rare kind of prophet, one who is in possession of both facts and vision."

—John A. Weigel.

The late B. F. Skinner, the most influential
behaviorist, and advocate of a
"technology of behavior"

as when a person finds himself with both his family and his friends at the same time.

Self-knowledge and self-control imply two selves in this sense. The self-knower is almost always a product of social contingencies, but the self that is known may come from other sources. The controlling self (the conscience or superego) is of social origin, but the controlled self is more likely to be the product of genetic susceptibilities to reinforcement (the id, or the Old Adam). The controlling self generally represents the interests of others, the controlled self the interests of the individual.

The picture which emerges from a scientific analysis is not of a body with a person inside, but of a body which is a person in the sense that it displays a complex repertoire of behavior. The picture is, of course, unfamiliar. The man thus portrayed is a stranger, and from the traditional point of view he may not seem to be a man at all. "For at least one hundred years," said Joseph Wood Krutch, "we have been prejudiced in every theory, including economic determinism, mechanistic behaviorism, and relativism, that reduces the stature of man until he ceases to be man at all in any sense that the humanists of an earlier generation would recognize." Matson has argued that "the empirical behavioral scientist . . . denies, if only by implication, that a unique being, called Man, exists." "What is now under attack," said Maslow, "is the 'being' of man." C. S. Lewis put it quite bluntly: Man is being abolished.

There is clearly some difficulty in identifying the man to whom these expressions refer. Lewis cannot have meant the human species, for not only is it not being abolished, it is filling the earth. (As a result it may eventually abolish itself through disease, famine, pollution, or a nuclear holocaust, but that is not what Lewis meant.) Nor are individual men growing less effective or productive. We are told that what is threatened is "man *qua* man," or "man in his humanity," or "man as Thou not It," or "man as a person not a thing." These are not very helpful expressions, but they

REVEALING EXPRESSIONS FROM SKINNER

- "technology of behavior"
- explanation by "antecedent physical events"
- person as "a repertoire of behavior"
- values as "social contingencies"
- good and bad as "positive" and "negative" reinforcement
- "responsibility and achievement" of "the environment"
- "experimental analysis"
- "beyond freedom and dignity"

supply a clue. What is being abolished is autonomous man—the inner man, the homunculus, the possessing demon, the man defended by the literatures of freedom and dignity.

His abolition has long been overdue. Autonomous man is a device used to explain what we cannot explain in any other way. He has been constructed from our ignorance, and as our understanding increases, the very stuff of which he is composed vanishes. Science does not dehumanize man, it de-homunculizes him, and it must do so if it is to prevent the abolition of the human species. To man *qua* man we readily say good riddance. Only by dispossessing him can we turn to the real causes of human behavior. Only then can we turn from the inferred to the observed, from the miraculous to the natural, from the inaccessible to the manipulable.[9]

The above selections from Skinner emphasize several overlapping themes: the denial of free will and all human transcendence; a reinterpretation of values as being dependent on social contingencies or conditions; a purely physicalistic interpretation of all levels of human activity; the importance of the environment for the shaping of human nature. In sum, he argues for the abolition of man as traditionally conceived, and for a technology of human nature as conceived along "hard" behavioristic lines.

Is man a machine for Skinner? Although Skinner explicitly represents man as a "machine," in the following paragraph he appears to want to soften the blow.

Man is not made into a machine by analyzing his behavior in mechanical terms. Early theories of behavior, as we have seen, represented man as a push-pull automaton, close to the nineteenth-century notion of a machine, but progress has been made. Man is a machine in the sense that he is a complex system behaving in lawful ways, but the complexity is extraordinary. His capacity to adjust to contingencies of reinforcement will perhaps be eventually simulated by machines,

---

[9]B. F. Skinner, *Beyond Freedom and Dignity* (Indianapolis, IN: Hackett, 2002), pp. 24–25, 127–128, 198–201.

> Behaviorism is "a monumental triviality." It represents "question-begging on a heroic scale."
>
> —Arthur Koestler
>
> Behaviorism is guilty of "innate naivete, intellectual bankruptcy, and half-deliberate cruelty."
>
> —Peter Gay

but this has not yet been done, and the living system thus simulated will remain unique in other ways.[10]

Nevertheless, many think that Skinner's conception of human nature is essentially indistinguishable from the old-fashioned mechanistic one. Surely if there is any recurring theme in Skinner's work, it is the rejection of human autonomy and the invocation of a universal and strict causal determinism. And this brings us to the second major problem with materialism.

ARE ALL THINGS DETERMINED?

It should be apparent by now that while not every form of materialism embraces causal determinism (think of Smart), the two often do go hand in hand (as in Skinner). If all things are reducible to physical states, then all things must be causally determined. But for many philosophers causal determinism, especially as regards human activity, is extremely problematic.

It is important to recall an earlier point. The trouble is not over the principle of universal causality, pure and simple. Almost everyone believes that every event must have a cause; from nothing, nothing comes; or for everything that happens there must be a necessary (it couldn't happen without it) and sufficient (it can happen with it) condition. The problem arises with the further assertion that everything is causally *determined;* that is, for anything that happens, *it could not have happened otherwise.* To put it another way: There is a big difference (do you see it?) between saying (1) D could not occur without A, B, and C, and (2) Given A, B, and C, D *must* occur. It is, of course, this second claim, the principle of universal determination, that is so vexing.

In the first place, it is vexing from the standpoint of the belief in moral responsibility. If it is true that nothing can happen otherwise than it does, then this must apply also to our willing and choosing. And this means the denial of *free will.* On the other hand, is it not clear—so the argument goes—that morality presupposes free will? that *ought* implies *can*? Is it right to

Causality vs. determinism

Determinism and moral responsibility

---

[10]Ibid., p. 202.

CAUSALITY AND DETERMINISM

- *Principle of universal causality:* Everything that comes into being is caused.
- *Principle of universal determinism:* Everything that comes into being is caused in such a way that it could not have been otherwise.

assign praise and blame if one cannot choose and act *freely*? Is it not always relevant, when trying to establish blame or guilt or responsibility on the part of someone, to ascertain whether that person was forced, drugged, or suffering from some compulsion? Free will would seem to be a condition for moral respensibility.

More generally it may be asked whether the ideas of moral good and evil are even *meaningful* within the materialistic/determinist view of things. For in that view things just *are,* and they can't be otherwise. Whence, then, comes any *ought*? If you start with a morally neutral determined universe, how do you account for objective values or ideals or universally binding rights and wrongs? Or maybe something can come from nothing. Or maybe values aren't universal and objective, but, as Skinner says, they're just by-products of environment and accidental social conditions. But is this what you mean by genuine morality? (These questions will have to be considered again in Chapter 14.)

Determinism and intellection

In the second place, some think that determinism is downright incompatible with genuine *thinking,* using the word to cover a broad range of intellectual activities. Setting aside such intellectual experiences as intuition, flashes of insight, and creative imagination, which some think transcend the flux and flow of blind and mechanical causation, is not the determinist caught in a hopeless if not self-contradictory position? For we are told that all things are causally determined, could not be otherwise, and so on, and yet we are told also to think hard, to scrutinize, to evaluate, to analyze. But this puts the intellect in the position of *judging* things, which means that the intellect is different from, and higher than, those that it *judges*. That is, if your mind and intellectual processes themselves are but an example of physical and chemical processes, then how can your mind frame a theory *about* physics and chemistry? And what *is* truth?

But there may be worse. We are told by the determinist that all things are causally determined. But, then, that very statement too, as well as everything

"The problem is to induce people not to be good but to behave well."

—Skinner

But is it not good to behave well?

TWO MAJOR PROBLEMS FOR DETERMINISM

- Is moral experience compatible with universal causal determinism?
- Is cognitive experience compatible with universal causal determinism?

else the determinist maintains, *is itself causally determined*. As in the case of determining moral responsibility, does not intellectual responsibility mean freedom from constraints such as drug-inducement, compulsions, force, and the like?

Inevitably, someone will counter with the analogy of computers: Are not human minds supercomplex and glorified computers? The proper answer is, of course, that computers—even the most supercomplex—do so well only because they are programmed by something essentially different, a *non*computer—namely, a *human mind.*

It is all a question of *transcendence:* Do you believe that the categories of materialism and/or determinism are adequate to your total experience as a human being, especially your moral and intellectual experience? Or must there be some reality or dimension of human nature, however dimly perceived and understood, that stands outside and above matter, motion, and causal determination?

Transcendence?

CHAPTER 6 IN REVIEW

SUMMARY

The radical alternative to idealism is materialism, which entirely does away with mind (or mental substance) and affirms matter, with its motions and qualities, as the sole underlying reality of all things. This is a very old philosophical perspective with roots, as we have seen, even in the Pre-Socratic period.

An extreme form of materialism is mechanistic materialism, which imports the further principle that the motions in the universe are determined by fixed and unalterable laws: The universe and everything in it is a *machine*. But, then, so are human beings, as La Mettrie announced in his book *Man a Machine.* Of course, the image of a person as consisting of wheels, springs, cogs, and bolts is out of date, as the idea of matter itself has become considerably refined. Nonetheless, the physicalistic conception of mind persists, as in the Identity Thesis of Smart: Mental states are identical with brain states.

In recent times, something very much like mechanistic materialism has surfaced in conjunction with the behavioristic psychology of Skinner. We have called it "hard" behaviorism precisely because it assumes the truth of materialism as a theory of reality and a theory of human nature. Skinner's main purpose in *Beyond Freedom and Dignity* is to envision and advocate a "technology of human behavior," a manipulation of human behavior and transformation of values in accordance with the progress and ideals of the evolutionary process.

As materialism, and certainly *mechanistic* materialism, bears on human nature and life, it poses great problems. Specifically, if all things are exhaustively determined, and man is a machine, then what becomes of moral and cognitive experience? Many philosophers believe that moral responsibility and authentic thinking are immediately rendered impossible in the determinist view of things. This is to say nothing of the alleged self-refuting character of this thesis: If everything is causally determined, then so is this very claim, but then why pay any attention to it? And Taylor has pointed out some problems with the Identity Thesis.

In the end, the question becomes, Is it possible to live with the intellectual and practical implications that follow from the denial of *human transcendence*?

BASIC IDEAS

- Naturalism
- Materialism
- Materialism as a solution to the mind-body problem
- Mechanism
- The "dematerialization" of matter
- The Identity Thesis
- Objections to the Identity Thesis
- Behaviorism
    Soft behaviorism
    Hard behaviorism
- Technology of behavior
- Causality versus determinism
- Objections to causal determinism
- The question of transcendence

TEST YOURSELF

1. By what simple maneuver does materialism solve the mind-body problem?
2. True or false: Mechanism is compatible with both soft and hard behaviorism.
3. What thinker talks about a "technology of behavior"? What does he mean?
4. To many, complete causal determinism seems to be incompatible with _____ and _____.
5. How does the Roman poet Lucretius figure in the discussion in this chapter?
6. What fault does Taylor find with the Identity Thesis?

7. La Mettrie and Skinner hold in common that (a) human behavior is in theory entirely predictable, (b) moral decisions are not subject to causal determinism, (c) God is behind the mechanisms of nature.

8. True or false: Newton's Laws of Motion aided and abetted the mechanistic view of the world.

QUESTIONS FOR REFLECTION

• We will have occasion to look again at the problem of determinism in Chapter 14, but consider now: How serious a threat do you really think determinism is to morality and knowledge? How might materialists and/or determinists counter the charge that their position undermines morality and knowledge? And even if it does, so what? And just what does "transcendence" mean in this context, anyway? Is it a philosophically coherent and responsible concept?

• At the beginning of this chapter it was noted that some philosophers opt for a "wider naturalism," according to which both physical and mental reality should be subsumed under a higher nature, or regarded as dimensions of a single reality. Does this strike you as a plausible approach? Does it solve any problems? Does it create any new ones?

FOR FURTHER READING

John V. Canfield. *Purpose in Nature*. Englewood Cliffs, NJ: Prentice-Hall, 1966. Essays by various thinkers, including "Behavior, Purpose, and Teleology" and "Comments on a Mechanistic Conception of Purposefulness."

Hubert L. Dreyfus. *What Computers Can't Do: The Limits of Artificial Intelligence*. Revised ed. New York: Harper & Row, 1979. A critical account of work in artificial intelligence, arguing for the uniqueness of human cognition.

Gerald Dworkin (ed.). *Determinism, Free Will, and Moral Responsibility*. Englewood Cliffs, NJ: Prentice-Hall, 1970. Essays by several thinkers on the topics indicated in the title.

Owen J. Flanagan, Jr. *The Science of Mind*. Cambridge, MA: MIT Press, 1984. A thorough and critical discussion of the central issues in contemporary cognitive science, including behaviorism, Identity Theory, functionalism, and so on.

Antony Flew (ed.). *Body, Mind, and Death*. New York: Macmillan, 1964. Traditional and contemporary statements on mind and body, including some discussion of behaviorism and consciousness as brain processes.

Robert Kane. *A Contemporary Introduction to Free Will*. New York: Oxford University Press, 2005. An accessible introduction to issues in the free-will debate.

Robert Kane. *Free Will*, Blackwell Readings in Philosophy. Malden, MA: Blackwell, 2001. An anthology of landmark essays about free will and determinism.

John McLeish. *The Development of Modern Behavioral Psychology*. Calgary: Detselig, 1981. A complete account of the historical roots and continuing development and interaction of the several branches of behaviorism.

John O'Conner (ed.). *Modern Materialism: Readings on Mind-Body Identity.* New York: Harcourt, Brace & World, 1969. Essays by well-known thinkers on mind and brain processes, materialism in relation to the mind-body problem, mechanism, identity theories, and more.

David Rosenthal. *Materialism and the Mind-Body Problem.* Englewood Cliffs, NJ: Prentice-Hall, 1971. Good treatment of the mind-body problem and its contemporary solutions, including the materialistic.

Richard Taylor. *Metaphysics.* Third ed. Englewood Cliffs, NJ: Prentice-Hall, 1983. Chs. 3–5. Brief, student-oriented discussions on "The Mind as a Function of the Body," "Freedom and Determinism," and "Fate."

John A. Weigel. *B. F. Skinner.* Boston: Twayne, 1977. A brief and very useful volume that argues that Skinner is a "good and true prophet" whose ideas have been misunderstood and maligned.

*In addition, see the relevant articles ("Materialism," "Mechanism in Biology," "Naturalism," "Behaviorism," etc.) in *Routledge Encyclopedia of Philosophy,* ed. Edward Craig (London: Routledge, 1998), and *Stanford Encyclopedia of Philosphy,* http://plato.stanford.edu.

PART TWO

THE QUESTION OF KNOWLEDGE

In our introductory note to Part One we said that the question of reality may be in some ways the most basic question. But a similar claim could be made for the question of knowledge.

It is true that our answers to the question of reality will largely determine our answers to many other questions. But we cannot really answer any questions at all, not even the question of reality, until we have become clear on the still prior question of knowledge. Think about this until you see it: Judgments about reality, morality, art, society, religion, politics, science, or anything else presuppose judgments about knowledge itself—*whether* we can know, *how* we can know, and *what* we can know. Take, for example, your knowledge that "In fourteen hundred and ninety-two Columbus sailed the ocean blue." How did you arrive at this piece of knowledge? In your claim to "know" this there are surely contained already many implicit judgments about epistemological issues such as

- The limits of reason.
- The role of sense experience.
- The relevance of intuition.
- The assurances of historical investigation.
- The nature and criterion of truth.
- The nature and authority of "facts."
- The possibility of certainty.
- Degrees of certainty.

If such a welter of considerations is necessarily involved in such a harmless claim as "In fourteen hundred and ninety-two Columbus sailed the ocean blue," then how much more attention must we give the epistemological underpinnings of claims about reality, value, moral responsibility, society, and God?

CHAPTER **7**

SKEPTICISM

We may begin with *skepticism,* a fitting place inasmuch as it calls into question, in various ways and degrees, the very possibility of knowledge. The word "skepticism" comes from a Greek word that means "to reflect on," "consider," or "examine," so it is not surprising that it is usually associated with *doubting* or *suspending judgment.* A glance at the dictionary shows that, beyond being *doubters,* skeptics come in many varieties. We, however, wish to distinguish just three types or levels of skepticism.

The meaning of "skepticism"

VARIETIES OF SKEPTICISM

If a skeptic is someone who at one time or another had doubts or who suspends judgment about something, then all of us are skeptics. None of us can know everything, and you yourself would surely be skeptical about someone who claimed that he or she did. A dose of *commonsense* skepticism is indeed probably *healthy* for us. For one thing, it is a corrective to gullibility, superstition, and prejudice. All of us should rightfully be skeptical of the claim that a vast herd of giraffes is at this moment roaming the White House, or of certain promises made by politicians running for office. Skepticism is also an antidote to intellectual arrogance and presumption.

Commonsense skepticism

Clearly, skepticism in this form poses no problem—if anything it stimulates and enhances philosophical activity. But with *philosophical* skepticism

Philosophical skepticism

skep • tic (skep′tik) *n.* **1.** One who doubts, disbelieves, or disagrees with generally accepted conclusions in science, philosophy, etc. **2.** One who by nature doubts or questions what he or she hears, reads, etc. **3.** One who questions the fundamental doctrines of a religion, especially the Christian religion. **4.** *Sometimes cap.* An adherent of any philosophical school of skepticism. Also spelled *sceptic.* [<F *sceptique* <L *scepticus* or directly <LGk. *skeptikos* reflective < *skeptesthai* to consider]

—Syn. *Skeptic, freethinker, atheist, unbeliever,* and *agonistic* denote one who denies or doubts some prevailing religious or philosophical doctrine. *Skeptic* is a general term, and refers to a person who does not feel that the state of human knowledge, or the evidence available, is sufficient to establish the doctrine. A *freethinker* is one who refuses to accept a doctrine, especially a religious doctrine, simply on authority, and demands empiric proof. *Atheist* describes one who denies the existence of God; an *unbeliever* may also lack religious faith, but the word is more often applied to one whose faith is different from that of the speaker. An *agnostic* rejects a doctrine because he or she believes that human knowledge is, and always will be, incapable of determining its truth or falsity.

Skep • tic (skep′tik) *n.* In ancient Greek philosophy, a member of a school of skepticism, especially that of Pyrrho of Elis. [<SKEPTIC]

skep • ti • cal (skep′ti • kəl) *adj.* **1.** Doubting; questioning; disbelieving. **2.** Of, pertaining to, or characteristic of a skeptic or skepticism. Also spelled *sceptical.*—**skep′ti • cal • ly** *adv.*—**skepti • cal • ness** *n.*

skepti • cism (skəp′tə • siz′əm) *n.* **1.** A doubting or incredulous state of mind; disbelieving attitude. **2.** *Philos.* The doctrine that absolute knowledge is unattainable and that judgments must be continually questioned and doubted in order to attain approximate or relative certainty; opposed to *dogmatism.* Also spelled *scepticism.*—**Syn.** See DOUBT.

the plot thickens. By philosophical skepticism we do not mean any particular position or movement in philosophy, but the tendency of some philosophers to deny or doubt the more cherished philosophical claims. What are some of these claims? It depends, of course, on the particular philosopher, but at one time or another it has been denied or doubted that every event must have a cause, that God exists, that there are underlying substances, that the external world is as we perceive it to be, and the like. These issues, of course, are the really big ones in philosophy, and skepticism over such issues immediately marks out the boundaries of philosophical battlefields.

Absolute skepticism   Still more troublesome is what we might call *absolute* skepticism. What is denied or doubted here is the very possibility of knowledge itself. Believe it or not, there have been some thinkers (not many, but some) who have denied that we can know anything at all.

Surely the best example of this was Pyrrho of Elis (about 300 B.C.), who founded a school of philosophers who called themselves the *Skeptics*. Pyrrho appealed to the example of Socrates, who, in spite of his insistence on abiding truths, was always *asking questions*, and Plato, who, aside from his belief in the transcendent Forms, believed that our knowledge of the world about us was really only an *approximation* or *opinion*. A more legitimate source of Pyrrho's skepticism was the Sophists with their view that all knowledge is subjective and relative, and therefore that there is no *absolute* or *common* knowledge at all. Recall Protagoras: "A man is the measure of all things." And long before Pyrrho ever came on the scene, the Sophist Gorgias of Leontini (about 525 B.C.) expounded a skepticism about as absolute as could be imagined. His position—or nonposition—is expressed in his three theses: (1) nothing exists, (2) if something did exist, we could never know it, and (3) if we could know it, we could never express it.

Gorgias' three theses

Pyrrho and his followers taught that nothing whatsoever is certain, and therefore the wise man will suspend judgment on all matters or, at best, simply announce, "The matter *appears* to be thus and so." As with Protagoras, the evidence for the Skeptics that nothing whatsoever can be known with certainty amounts to an extended argument from the *relativity* of reason, sense perception, and custom. Just consider how different our thoughts

Nothing is certain

Pyrrho, the absolute skeptic, denied that we can know anything whatsoever.

"YOU MAY BE ABSOLUTELY SURE OF THIS, THAT NOTHING CAN BE KNOWN WITH CERTAINTY!"

and our sense perceptions can be about the *same things*! Did two people ever see the same rainbow? How does an onion taste? And if disagreements and contradictions rage over ordinary things "out there," like rainbows and onions, how much more do they rage over intellectual and moral percep-

The argument for skepticism

tions? The differences and contradictions stemming from our time, place, age, condition, perspective, sense faculties, intellectual faculties, social situations, inclinations, desires, purposes—all of these added up, for the Skeptics, to gigantic doubt and led to a suspension of judgment concerning *everything*.

Much of what we know about Pyrrho we know through the ancient philosophical biographer Diogenes Laertius. In the following from Diogenes' *Lives of Eminent Philosophers*, he states the radicalness of Pyrrhonic skepticism and then summarizes the famous *Ten Modes* (or "ways") leading to skepticism.

> The Skeptics . . . were constantly engaged in overthrowing the dogmas of all schools, but enunciated none themselves; and though they would go so far as to bring forward and expound the dogmas of the others, they themselves laid down nothing definitely, not even the laying down of nothing.

The Ten Modes of Doubt

I. Based on the Variety in Animals

The *first* mode relates to the differences between living creatures in respect of those things which give them pleasure or pain, or are useful or harmful to them. By this it is inferred that they do not receive the same impressions from the same things, with the result that such a conflict necessarily leads to suspension of judgment. . . . Some are distinguished in one way, some in another, and for this reason they differ in their senses also, hawks for instance being most keen-sighted, and dogs having a most acute sense of smell. It is natural that if the senses, e.g., eyes, of animals differ, so also will the impressions produced upon them. . . .

II. Based on the Differences in Human Beings

The *second* mode has reference to the natures and idiosyncrasies of men; for instance, Demophon, Alexander's butler, used to get warm in the shade and shiver in the sun. Andron of Argos is reported by Aristotle to have travelled across the waterless deserts of Libya without drinking. Moreover, one man fancies the profession of medicine, another farming, and another commerce; and the same ways of life are injurious to one man but beneficial to another; from which it follows that judgment must be suspended.

III. Based on the Different Structures of the Organs of Sense

The *third* mode depends on the differences between the sense-channels in different cases, for an apple gives the impression of being pale yellow in color to the sight, sweet in taste and fragrant in smell. An object of the same shape is made to appear different by differences in the mirrors reflecting it. Thus it follows that what appears is no more such and such a thing than something different.

IV. Based on the Circumstantial Conditions

The *fourth* mode is that due to differences of condition and to changes in general; for instance, health, illness, sleep, waking, joy, sorrow, youth, old age, courage, fear, want, fullness, hate, love, heat, cold, to say nothing of breathing freely and having the passages obstructed. The impressions received thus appear to vary according to the nature of the conditions. . . .

V. Based on the Disciplines and Customs and Laws, the Legendary Beliefs and the Dogmatic Convictions

The *fifth* mode is derived from customs, laws, belief in myths, compacts between nations and dogmatic assumptions. This class includes considerations with regard to things beautiful and ugly, true and false, good and bad, with regard to the gods, and with regard to the coming into being and the passing away of the world of phenomena. Obviously the same thing is regarded by some as just and by others as unjust, or as good by some and bad by others. . . . Different people believe in different gods; some in providence, others not. In burying their dead, the Egyptians embalm them; the Romans burn them; the Pœonians throw them into lakes. As to what is true, then, let suspension of judgment be our practice.

VI. Based on Intermixtures

The *sixth* mode relates to mixtures and participations, by virtue of which nothing appears pure in and by itself, but only in combination with air, light, moisture, solidity, heat, cold, movement, exhalations and other forces. For purple shows different tints in sunlight, moonlight, and lamplight; and our own complexion does not appear the same at noon and when the sun is low. Again, a rock which in air takes two men to lift is easily moved about in water, either because, being in reality heavy, it is lifted by the water or because, being light, it is made heavy by the air. Of its own inherent property we know nothing, any more than of the constituent oils in an ointment.

VII. Based on Positions and Intervals and Locations
The *seventh* mode has reference to distances, positions, places and the occupants of the places. In this mode things which are thought to be large appear small, square things round; flat things appear to have projections, straight things to be bent, and colorless colored. So the sun, on account of its distance, appears small, mountains when far away appear misty and smooth, but when near at hand rugged. Furthermore, the sun at its rising has a certain appearance, but has a dissimilar appearance when in mid-heaven, and the same body one appearance in a wood and another in open country. The image again varies according to the position of the object, and a dove's neck according to the way it is turned. Since, then, it is not possible to observe these things apart from places and positions, their real nature is unknowable.

VIII. Based on the Quantities and Formations of the Underlying Objects
The *eighth* mode is concerned with quantities and qualities of things, say heat or cold, swiftness or slowness, colorlessness or variety of colors. Thus wine taken in moderation strengthens the body, but too much of it is weakening; and so with food and other things.

IX. Based on the Frequency or Rarity of Occurrence
The *ninth* mode has to do with perpetuity, strangeness, or rarity. Thus earthquakes are no surprise to those among whom they constantly take place; nor is the sun, for it is seen every day.

X. Based on the Fact of Relativity
The *tenth* mode rests on inter-relation, e.g., between light and heavy, strong and weak, greater and less, up and down. Thus that which is on the right is not so by nature, but is so understood in virtue of its position with respect to something else; for, if that change its position, the thing is no longer on the right. Similarly father and brother are relative terms, day is relative to the sun, and all things relative to our mind. Thus relative terms are in and by themselves unknowable. These, then, are the ten modes of perplexity.[1]

IS ABSOLUTE SKEPTICISM A COHERENT POSITION?

Actually, there have been relatively few absolute skeptics. It is not hard to see why. Critics of this position have been quick to charge that it is impractical and impossible. It is *impractical* because, from the purely practical

---

[1]Diogenes Laertius, *Lives of Eminent Philosophers*, IX, 74, 79–88, tr. R. D. Hicks (Cambridge, MA: Harvard University Press, 1925), II. I have supplied the headings from the longer account of Sextus Empiricus.

SELF-REFUTING PROPOSITIONS

Propositions make claims, of course, about many things. When, however, a proposition is itself one of the things it makes a claim about, it sometimes turns out to be *self-refuting*. This means that if the proposition is taken seriously, then it backfires on itself—if it's true it must be false!

A well-known example of a self-refuting proposition is: "All generalizations are false." If all generalizations are false, then the claim itself, which is a generalization, must be false. Especially puzzling is the proposition

> The sentence in this box is false.

If it's false, then it must be true; if it's true, it must be false! Is the claim of the absolute skeptic, "We can be certain of absolutely nothing," another example of a self-refuting proposition?

standpoint of getting along in the world, no one in his or her right mind can actually live on such a premise. Our daily lives are pervaded by what we take to be (whether they actually are or not) assurances, certainties, and in a word, all kinds of *knowledge*. Why, for that matter, are you reading this book, studying philosophy, or studying *anything*, if not because you think that something can be learned, understood, *known*? And where, on the skeptical view, is there any place for responsible actions or serious commitments and decisions?

More specifically, according to the critics, all absolute skeptics founder sooner or later on the utter *impossibility* of their position. It is impossible for several reasons. First, must not even the staunchest skeptic admit that *some* things at least are certain? For example, that 2 + 2 = 4, and that whether or not our senses deceive us about the actual world, we are at least certain of the *impressions*? Second, does not the very assertion that we cannot know anything actually necessitate that we do know some things? For example, that we, who claim to know nothing, exist, and that the Law of Non-Contradiction, without which nothing—not even the skeptic's claim—can be asserted at all, is certain?

Finally, and still more decisive, is the charge that the absolute skeptics' assertion that they know nothing is strictly self-contradictory or *self-refuting*. For they maintain, *with the greatest assurance,* that we cannot maintain anything. Otherwise stated: If we cannot know anything, then how do we know *that*? You might think of it as a self-destructing proposition. Stated again: If absolute skepticism is *true*, then it must be *false*!

Pyrrho himself anticipated the similar criticism that his position implied its own falsehood. He retorted (as some skeptical-type readers will be tempted to retort) that he was not, in fact, even certain that he was not certain of anything. But, of course, that kind of talk could go on forever:

Is absolute skepticism impractical?

Is absolute skepticism even possible?

An infinite regress of ignorance

We cannot know anything.

We cannot know that we cannot know anything.

We cannot know that we cannot know that we cannot know anything.

.

.

Is it not necessary that there be at some point a *basis* for one's claims? We may, of course, argue over what counts as legitimate starting points—some have called them "properly basic beliefs"—but must we not have *some*? Did not Aristotle teach us a long time ago that an infinite regress of claims nullifies all of them?

One of the best-known refutations of skepticism comes from St. Augustine in the medieval period. He directs himself to the "Academicians," a school of skepticism in Augustine's day led by Carneades. Against these skeptics, Augustine argues for the certitude of logical truths, mathematical truths, the reality of the world, and one's own immediate perceptions. Which of these counterattacks can you identify in the following extract from Augustine's *Against the Academicians*?

You say that nothing can be apprehended in philosophy and, in order to spread your opinion far and wide, you make use of the disputes and contentions of philosophers and you think that these dissensions furnish arms for you against them. . . . I hold as certain either that there is or is not one world; and if there is not one, there are either a finite or an infinite number of worlds. Carneades would teach that that opinion resembles what is false. I likewise know that this world of ours has been so arranged either because of the nature of bodies or by some providence, and that it either always was and will be or that it began to exist and will by no means cease existing, or that it does not have its origin in time but will have an end, or that it has started to remain in existence and will remain but not forever, and I know innumerable physical phenomena of this type. For those disjunctions are true nor can anyone confuse them with any likeness to what is false. But take something for granted, says the Academician. I do not wish to do so; for that is to

THE GREEK SKEPTICS

"The Greek Skeptics are known to us only in fragments of their writings, particularly in references of them by their opponents. Pyrrho, the reputed founder of the school, composed no writings, perhaps esteeming silence the becoming attitude for a Skeptic. Yet Aenesidemus, nearly four hundred years later, wrote 'eight books' in summary of Pyrrho's alleged teachings. Pyrrho is a peg on which Skeptics generally hang their witty sayings, so that the word Pyrrhonism has come to be used almost interchangeably with excessive Skepticism."

Sterling P. Lamprecht, *Our Philosophical Traditions* (New York: Appleton-Century-Crofts, 1955), pp. 92–93.

say: abandon what you know; say what you do not know. But opinion is uncertain. Assuredly it is better that it be uncertain than that it be destroyed; it surely is clear; it certainly now can be called false or true. I say that I know this opinion. Prove to me that I do not know them, you who do not deny that such matters pertain to philosophy and who maintain that none of these things can be known; say that those disjunctive ideas are either false or have something in common with what is false from which they cannot altogether be distinguished.

Whence, he says, do you know that this world exists if the senses are untrustworthy? Your methods of reasoning have never been able to disprove the power of the senses in such a way as to convince us that nothing is seen and you certainly have never dared to try such a thing, but you have exerted yourself to persuade us urgently that (a thing) can be otherwise than it seems. And so I call this entire thing, whatever it is, which surrounds us and nourishes us, this object, I say, which appears before my eyes and which I perceive is made up of earth and sky, or what appears to be earth and sky, the world. If you say nothing is seen by me, I shall never err. For he is in error who rashly proves what seems to him. For you say that what is false can be seen by those perceiving it; you do not say that nothing is seen. Certainly every reason for arguing will be removed when it pleases you to settle the point, if we not only know nothing but if nothing is even seen by us. If, however, you deny that this object which appears to me is the world, you are making it a controversy in regard to a name since I said that I called it the world. . . .

It now remains for us to inquire whether the senses report the truth when they give information. Suppose that some Epicurean should say: "I have no complaint to make in regard to the senses; for it is unjust to demand more of them than they can give; moreover whatever the eyes can see they see in a reliable manner." Then is what they see in regard to an oar in the water true? It certainly is true. For when the reason is added for its appearing thus, if the oar dipped in the water seemed straight, I should rather blame my eyes for the false report. For they did not see what should have been seen when such causes arose. What need is there of many illustrations? This can also be said of the movement of towers, of the feathers of birds, of innumerable other things. "And yet I am deceived if I give my assent," someone says. Do not give assent any further than to the extent that you can persuade yourself that it appears true to you, and there is no deception. For I do not see how the Academician can refute him who says: "I know that this appears white to me, I know that my hearing is delighted with this, I know that this has an agreeable odor, I know that this tastes sweet to me, I know that this feels cold to me." Tell us rather whether the leaves of the wild olive trees, which the goat so persistently desires, are by their very nature bitter. O foolish man! Is not the goat more reasonable? I do not know how they seem to the goat, but they are bitter to me. What more do you ask for? But perhaps there is also some one to whom they do not taste bitter. Do you trouble yourself about this? Did I say they were bitter to everyone? I said they were bitter to me and I do not always maintain this. For what if for some reason or other a thing which now tastes sweet to a person should at another time seem bitter to him? I say this that, when a person tastes something, he can honestly swear that he knows it is sweet to his palate or the contrary, and that no trickery of the Greeks can dispossess him of that knowledge. For who would be so bold as to say to me when I am longing for something with great pleasure: Perhaps you do not taste it, but this is only a dream? Do I offer any opposition to him? But still that would give me pleasure even in my sleep. Therefore no likeness to what is false obscures that which I have said I know, and both the Epicurean and the Cyrenaics may say many other things in favor of the

"KNOWING" IS NOT A SIMPLE MATTER

When you claim to "know" something, is it perfectly clear what you are claiming? Actually, "to know" can mean many different things, and consequently there are many different types of knowledge.

Knowing or knowledge falls into at least three broad categories: (1) knowledge as personal acquaintance, as in the statement "I know Howard"; (2) knowledge as mastery of information or data, as in "I know German"; and (3) knowledge as involved in the claim that something or other is true (true-claims), as in "I know that in fourteen hundred and ninety-two Columbus sailed the ocean blue."

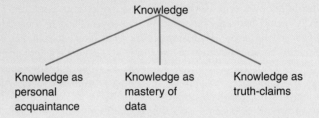

Epistemology, or the theory of knowledge, is concerned by and large (though not exclusively) with problems posed by knowledge as truth-claims.

senses against which I have heard that the Academicians have not said anything. But why should this concern me? If they so desire and if they can, let them even do away with the argument with my approbation. Whatever argument they raise against the senses has no weight against all philosophers. For there are those who admit that whatever the mind receives through a sense of the body, can beget opinion, but they deny (that it can beget) knowledge which, however, they wish to be confined to the intellect and to live in the mind, far removed from the senses. And perhaps that wise man whom we are seeking is in their number.[2]

Thus, at least, it has seemed to most philosophers: Whatever we may think of other forms of skepticism, absolute skepticism, or the denial of the very possibility of knowledge itself, must be rejected at the start. If so, the question becomes not *whether* we can know, but *what, how,* and *how much* we can know.

RORTY AND FRIENDS: HISTORICISM AND PLURALISM

Very different from the rather standard forms of skepticism mentioned above is the sort—not so bombastic, but very influential these days—that calls into question the very nature of the philosophical enterprise as traditionally

[2]St. Augustine, *Against the Academicians*, III, 23–26, tr. Sister Mary Patricia Garvey (Milwaukee, WI: Marquette University Press, 1957).

practiced. More specifically, this skepticism challenges the presumption of philosophy in conceiving itself to be a sort of umbrella discipline that sets the epistemological rules and agenda for other disciplines. This challenge presses for a much more restrained and modest role for the philosopher. The challenge has been delivered most forcefully by the contemporary philosopher Richard Rorty, aided and abetted by the contributions of other philosophers, such as Alasdair MacIntyre, Hans-Georg Gadamer, Jacques Derrida, Michel Foucault, Jürgen Habermas, and Paul Ricoeur.[3]

Actually, what we have here is a kind of philosophical version, or expression, of a more general movement called "postmodernism." This larger movement involves participants not only from philosophy "proper," but also from philosophy of science, religious studies, intellectual history, literary criticism, social theory, feminist criticism, and the like. What ties them all together in a sort of common cause may be summarized in four points: First is the wholistic manner in which they approach their agenda. Where others see and emphasize distinctions and dichotomies, these thinkers see connections and continuities—between subject and object, between theory and practice, between fact and value, between areas of study, between domains of culture. Second is their pragmatic insistence on the greater importance of the practical over the theoretical. As Marx said, "Philosophers have only interpreted the world in various ways; the point is to change it"; or as Nietzsche said, the ultimate test of a philosophy is whether one can live by it; or, as Dewey said, the measure of the overall value of a philosophy is whether it illuminates our ordinary life experiences and predicaments and makes our dealings with them more fruitful. Third, we have the insistence on the relativity of vocabularies to historical periods and traditions. Otherwise stated, this is the awareness and confession that our perspectives, doctrines, intuitions, sensibilities, vision, paradigms, and explanations are thoroughly conditioned by our *Sitz in Leben*, situation in life, or, more idiomatically, "where we're coming from." Finally, fourth is the rejection of the superscientific conception of facts as somehow neutral, uninterpreted, and simply given. Rather, everything in our experience is interpreted and "theory-laden" as soon as we experience it.

Postmodernism

But back to Rorty. In spite of his reputation as one who has said farewell to philosophy in general and epistemology in particular, he does indeed have a philosophy. Or at least a *meta*philosophy—that is, a philosophy *about* philosophy. That he is a participant in the movement we have just characterized is evident because his philosophy has been described as, historicist, and pluralist. Let's take a closer look at Rorty's *historicism* and *pluralism*.

Historicism insists on the necessity of putting fundamental distinctions, values, and starting points within the historical contexts in which they first appear, in order to understand what point or purpose they initially served and to see whether they might illuminate our own thought and life and alternatives. This is, obviously, a contextual approach. One important payoff

Rorty's historicism

---

[3]In the discussion that follows, I am greatly indebted to an unpublished paper by my colleague, Professor Robert Rogers, "Rorty and Friends."

for Rorty is the rejection of foundationalism, an idea mentioned already in Chapter 1 and exemplified in many places throughout this book. Foundationalism is the traditional attempt to find some ultimate ground or basis for knowledge, choice, action, and criticism that lies outside all that is merely contingent upon human practice, culture, and convention. Examples would include Platonic Forms, Aristotelian essences, God's revealed Word, Cartesian clear and distinct ideas, *a priori* truths, fundamental intuitions, and the like. The truth is, says Rorty, that such attempts to escape history and contingency to find some foundational, immutable point of departure merely raise to the level of the universal and necessary some practice, standard, or metaphor that happens to be dominant or suggestive at a particular time and place. To be historicist, then, is to be skeptical about any possibility of getting beyond the contingent and merely human. Traditional Philosophy—with a capital "P"—must be replaced by the much more modest enterprise of philosophy—with a lowercase "p." The latter, as Rorty says in quoting Wilfred Sellars, is "an attempt to see how things, in the broadest possible sense of the term, hang together, in the broadest possible sense of the term."[4]

Rorty's pluralism

Closely related to Rorty's historicism is his pluralism. As with his historicism, this is a metaphilosophical thesis. According to pluralism (in Rorty's sense), there is no neutral ground from which one might judge competing philosophical starting points. At the level of the most ultimate disagreements, there is no refutation of radical skepticism that does not beg the question; nor is there any neutral ground, acceptable to all parties, from which we might resolve the differences between the realist and the pragmatist, or the differences between the liberal and the totalitarian. Each of

Richard Rorty, advocate of
"edifying philosophy"

[4]Wilfred Sellars, *Science, Perception, and Reality* (London: Routledge, 1976), p. 19.

these competing positions is a genuine option; everything is up for grabs. Nor, of course, will there be any point, according to philosophical pluralists, in maintaining that nonetheless there is some truth here, whether or not one can establish that truth in a neutral way. Such a claim could only be that certain of these positions correctly represent the world, or human nature—the way it really is—whether or not we are able to *show* that it is that way, so what's the point? Any such appeal to representationalism—the view that the mind is a kind of mirror that captures and reflects what is "really out there"—has no real explanatory force.

So, what's left to do? Rorty's answer: Philosophy's job is to "keep the conversation going" and to "muddle through." To keep the conversation going is not merely to keep talking, of course, but to keep introducing new idioms, new metaphors, new readings of texts, and so on. In so doing, in practicing what Rorty calls "edifying philosophy," we attempt to keep philosophy and criticism from settling down into one language accepted as canonical, a fixed common framework for all philosophical inquiry. From Rorty's pluralistic point of view, it would be just as deplorable for philosophy to settle down within one generally accepted vocabulary, defined and sanctioned by the profession, as it would be—and at times has been—for the art of painting, say, to become confined within the approved canons of some religious—or governmentally—sponsored framework. No, what we have to do is play off certain basic commitments against others, trying to show the overall superiority of our own, but without the ability to appeal to principles and values accepted by all parties to the debate.

"Edifying philosophy"

Rorty's best-known book is called *Philosophy and the Mirror of Nature*. Its thesis is that the traditional image of the mind as able to reflect and represent accurately the reality "out there" is misguided and must be replaced by an image that does justice, for example, to the points made above. Some of these points are suggested in the following extract from Rorty's book, though the main point concerns the distinction between mainstream, constructive, "systematic" philosophy, centered in the traditional epistemology, and the peripheral, reactive, "edifying" philosophy that is suspicious of epistemology and exemplifies a very different and less pretentious approach—and a desire for "open space."

On the periphery of the history of modern philosophy, one finds figures who, without forming a "tradition," resemble each other in their distrust of the notion that man's essence is to be a knower of essences. Goethe, Kierkegaard, Santayana, William James, Dewey, the later Wittgenstein, the later Heidegger, are figures of this sort. They are often accused of relativism or cynicism. They are often dubious about progress, and especially about the latest claim that such-and-such a discipline has at last made the nature of human knowledge so clear that reason will now spread throughout the rest of human activity. These writers have kept alive the suggestion that, even when we have justified true belief about everything we want to know, we may have no more than conformity to the norms of the day. They have kept alive the historicist sense that this century's "superstition" was the last century's triumph of reason, as well as the relativist sense that the latest vocabulary, borrowed from the latest scientific achievement, may not express privileged representations of essences, but be just another of the potential infinity of vocabularies in which the world can be described.

The mainstream philosophers are the philosophers I shall call "systematic," and the peripheral ones are those I shall call "edifying." These peripheral, pragmatic philosophers are skeptical primarily *about systematic philosophy*, about the whole project of universal commensuration. In our time, Dewey, Wittgenstein, and Heidegger are the great edifying, peripheral, thinkers. All three make it as difficult as possible to take their thought as expressing views on traditional philosophical problems, or as making constructive proposals for philosophy as a cooperative and progressive discipline. They make fun of the classic picture of man, the picture which contains systematic philosophy, the search for universal commensuration in a final vocabulary. They hammer away at the holistic point that words take their meanings from other words rather than by virtue of their representative character, and the corollary that vocabularies acquire their privileges from the men who use them rather than from their transparency to the real.

. . . Great systematic philosophers are constructive and offer arguments. Great edifying philosophers are reactive and offer satires, parodies, aphorisms. They know their work loses its point when the period they were reacting against is over. They are *intentionally* peripheral. Great systematic philosophers, like great scientists, build for eternity. Great edifying philosophers destroy for the sake of their own generation. Systematic philosophers want to put their subject on the secure path of a science. Edifying philosophers want to keep space open for the sense of wonder which poets can sometimes cause—wonder that there is something new under the sun, something which is *not* an accurate representation of what was already there, something which (at least for the moment) cannot be explained and can barely be described.[5]

Rorty's "deconstruction" of philosophy has been criticized in various ways. We mention here three. First, there are many philosophers who share Rorty's historicist and antifoundationalist bent but who don't think that the consequences are all that great: The end of foundationalism would hardly mean the end of philosophic problems. Take, for example, the traditional problem of free will and determinism. The historicist-antifoundationalist might say that this problem can be formulated only within certain conceptual schemes, such as the modern period, when the concepts of causality and universal determinism became available, or in the Christian context, with its idea of divine foreknowledge. Likewise, according to this view, it is possible that at some point in the future the problem will no longer be demanding or even intelligible. But surely it does not follow from any of this that the problem is not a forceful and demanding one—an important and *real* one—for us, at our point in history, confronted as we are with the interpretation of *our* world and *our* experience, which is necessarily different from that of another age and culture.

The second criticism involves Rorty's rejection of necessary truths, or nonnegotiable, nonarguable, universally binding affirmations. Historicism and antifoundationalism may not themselves necessarily lead to a denial

---

[5]Richard Rorty, *Philosophy and the Mirror of Nature* (Princeton, NJ: Princeton University Press, 1979), pp. 367–370.

POSTMODERNISM: "STAR TREK, THE NEXT GENERATION"

"Modernity has been under attack since Friedrich Nietzsche (1844–1900) lobbed the first volley in the late nineteenth century. But the full-scale frontal assault did not begin until the 1970s. The immediate impulse for the dismantling of the Enlightenment project came from the rise of deconstruction as a literary theory, which influenced a new movement in philosophy.

"Deconstruction arose in response to a theory in literature called 'structuralism.' Structuralists theorized that cultures develop literary documents—texts—in an attempt to provide structures of meaning by which people can make sense out of the meaninglessness of their experience. Literature, therefore, provides categories with which we can organize and understand our experience of reality. Further, all societies and cultures possess a common, invariant structure.

"The deconstructionists (or poststructuralists) rejected the tenets of structuralism. Meaning is not inherent in a text itself, they argued, but emerges only as the interpreter enters into dialogue with the text. Consequently, the meaning of a text depends on the perspective of the one who enters into dialogue with it, so there are as many interpretations of a text as readers (or readings).

"Postmodern philosophers applied the theories of the literary deconstructionists to the world as a whole. Just as the meaning of a text depends on the reader, so also reality can be 'read' differently depending on the perspectives of the knowing selves that encounter it. This means that there is no one meaning of the world, no transcendent center to reality as a whole.

"On the basis of ideas such as these, the French philosopher Jacques Derrida called for the destruction of 'onto-theology' (the attempt to set forth ontological descriptions of reality) as well as the 'metaphysics of presence' (the idea that a transcendent something is present in reality). Because nothing transcendent inheres in reality, all that emerges in the knowing process is the perspective of the self who interprets reality.

"Michel Foucault added a moral twist to Derrida's call. Every interpretation is put forward by those in power, he theorized. Because 'knowledge' is always the result of the use of power, to name something is to exercise power and hence to do violence to what is named. Social institutions do violence by imposing their own understanding on the centerless flux of experience. Thus, in contrast to Bacon, who sought knowledge in order to gain power over nature, Foucault claimed that every assertion of knowledge is an act of power.

"Richard Rorty, in turn, jettisoned the classic conception of truth as either the mind or language mirroring nature. Truth is established neither by the correspondence of an assertion with objective reality nor by the internal coherence of the assertions themselves. Rorty argued that we should simply disband the search for truth and be content with interpretation. Hence, he proposed to replace classic 'systematic philosophy' with 'edifying philosophy,' which 'aims at continuing a conversation rather than at discovering truth.'

"The work of Derrida, Foucault, and Rorty reflects what seems to have become the central dictum of postmodern philosophy: 'All is difference.' This view sweeps

(continued on next page)

away the 'uni' of the 'universe' sought by the Enlightenment project, the quest for a unified grasp of objective reality. The world has no center, only differing viewpoints and perspectives. In fact, even the concept of 'world' presupposes an objective unity or a coherent whole that does not exist 'out there.' In the end, the postmodern world is merely an arena of dueling texts.

"Although philosophers such as Derrida, Foucault, and Rorty have been influential on university campuses, they are only a part of a larger shift in thinking reflected in Western culture. What unifies the otherwise diverse strands of postmodernism is the questioning of the central assumptions of Enlightenment epistemology.

"In the postmodern world, people are no longer convinced that knowledge is inherently good. In eschewing the Enlightenment myth of inevitable progress, postmodernism replaces the optimism of the last century with a gnawing pessimism. It is simply not the case that 'each and every day in each and every way we are getting better and better.' For the first time in many years, members of the emerging generation do not share the conviction of their parents that we will solve the enormous problems of the planet or that their economic situation will surpass that of their parents. They know that life on the earth is fragile, and the continued existence of humankind is dependent on a new attitude which replaces the image of conquest with cooperation.

"The new emphasis on wholism is related to the postmodern rejection of the second Enlightenment assumption, namely, that truth is certain and hence purely rational. The postmodern mind refuses to limit truth to its rational dimension and thus dethrones the human intellect as the arbiter of truth. Because truth is non-rational, there are other ways of knowing, including through the emotions and the intuition.

"Finally, the postmodern mind no longer accepts the Enlightenment belief that knowledge is objective. Knowledge cannot be merely objective, because the postmodern model of the world does not see the universe as mechanistic and dualistic, but historical, relational, and personal. The world is not simply an objective given that is 'out there,' waiting to be discovered and known. Instead it is relative, indeterminate, and participatory.

"In rejecting the modern assumption of the objectivity of knowledge, the postmodern mind likewise dismisses the Enlightenment ideal of the dispassionate, autonomous knower. Knowledge is not eternal and culturally neutral. Nor is it waiting to be discovered by scientists who bring their rational talents to the givenness of the world. Rather, knowledge is historically and culturally implicated, and consequently, our knowledge is always incomplete.

"The postmodern world view operates with a community-based understanding of truth. Not only the specific truths we accept, but even our understanding of truth, are a function of the community in which we participate. This basis in community, in turn, leads to a new conception of the relativity of truth. Not only is there no absolute truth; more significantly, truth is relative to the community in which we participate. With this in view, the postmodern thinker has given up the Enlightenment quest for the one, universal, supracultural, timeless truth. In its place, truth is what fits within a specific community; truth consists in the ground rules that facilitate the well-being of the community in which one participates.

(continued on next page)

"The postmodern perspective is reflected in the second 'Star Trek' series, 'The Next Generation.' The humans who make up the original Enterprise are now joined by humanoid life forms from other parts of the universe. This change represents the broader universality of postmodernity: humans are no longer the only advanced beings operative throughout the cosmos. More importantly, the understanding of the quest for knowledge has changed. Humankind is not capable of completing the mandate alone; nor does the burden of the quest fall to humans alone. Hence, the crew of the Enterprise symbolizes the 'new ecology' of humankind in partnership with the universe. Their mission is no longer 'to boldly go where no man has gone before,' but 'where no *one* has gone before.'

"In 'The Next Generation,' Data replaces Spock. In a sense, Data is Spock, the fully rational thinker capable of superhuman intellectual feats. Despite his seemingly perfect intellect, rather than being the transcendent human ideal Spock embodies, he is an android—a subhuman machine. His desire is not only to understand what it means to be human, but also to become human. However, he lacks certain necessary aspects of humanness, including a sense of humor, emotion, and the ability to dream (at least until he learns that his maker programmed dreaming into his circuitry).

"Although Data often provides valuable assistance in dealing with problems, he is only one of several who contribute to finding solutions. In addition to the master of rationality, the Enterprise crew includes persons skilled in the affective and intuitive dimensions of human life. Especially prominent is Counselor Troi, a woman gifted with the ability to perceive the hidden feelings of others.

"The new voyages of the Enterprise lead its varied crew into a postmodern universe. In this new world, time is no longer simply linear, appearance is not necessarily reality, and the rational is not always to be trusted. In contrast to the older series, which in typical modern fashion generally ignores questions of God and religious belief, the postmodern world of 'The Next Generation' also includes the supernatural, embodied in the strange character "Q." Yet its picture of the divine is not simply that of traditional Christian theology. Although possessing the classical attributes of divine power (such as omniscience), the godlike being 'Q' is morally ambiguous, displaying both benevolence and a bent toward cynicism and self-gratification."

Stanley J. Grenz, "Star Trek and the Next Generation: Postmodernism and the Future of Evangelical Theology," *CRUX* 30 (March 1994), pp. 24–32.

of the existence of necessary truths. What they insist on is a plurality of possible starting points for philosophy, a plurality of basic language games or conceptual schemes. Insofar as his historicism and antifoundationalism are concerned, Rorty might have freely granted a whole host of truths that are necessary truths. His particular version of pragmatism, for example, insists on a rather thoroughgoing wholism, within which there seems to be little place for necessary truths. Ironically, however, many of the points that Rorty himself insists on have at least the appearance of being, if true, then necessarily true.

Does Rorty himself invoke necessary truths?

Consider, for example, his claims that there is no neutral ground from which one might decide the issues between pragmatism and realism; that "there is no epistemological difference between truth about what ought to be and truth about what is"; that there is no single, right way to speak about nature; that we need to give up the idea that "intellectual or political progress is rational, in any sense of rational which is neutral between vocabularies"; and that "there is no noncircular theoretical backup for the belief that cruelty is horrible." Whether or not one agrees with these positions, one has to agree that they at least appear to be necessarily true, if true at all. Rorty's wholism, however, doesn't seem able to provide for such necessary truths. Furthermore, contrary to the character of his whole critique, not only does his philosophy contain a great many such statements, so central to his whole outlook, but many of them are clearly epistemological in nature. Nor are they all merely negative in form, as in his claim that new metaphors extend the realm of possibilities. In spite of Rorty's best efforts, then, the critic concludes that epistemology, of some sort, and maybe even a traditional sort, appears to be an important part of Rorty's own philosophy.

Is Rorty really a relativist?

Third, it is understandable that Rorty has been perceived and represented by many as a relativist. We have seen already that skepticism is fed by the relativity of reason, sense perception, and custom. In the case of Rorty and friends, however, the conclusion seems to be not only that we can have no absolute knowledge of anything but, at the same time, that we can have absolute knowledge of everything—*all* propositions must be *true*. As Alvin Plantinga says, this follows from Rorty's well-known definition, "Truth is what my peers will let me get away with saying."

> One widely popular version of relativism is Richard Rorty's notion that truth is what my peers will let me get away with saying. On this view what is true for me, naturally enough, might be false for you; *my* peers might let *me* get away with saying something that *your* peers won't let *you* get away with saying: for of course we may have different peers. (And even if we had the *same* peers, there is no reason why they would be obliged to let you and me get away with saying the same things.) Although this view is very much *au courant* and with-it in the contemporary intellectual world, it has consequences that are peculiar, not to say preposterous. For example, most of us think that the Chinese authorities did something monstrous in murdering those hundreds of young people in Tiananmen Square, and then compounded their wickedness by denying that they had done it. On Rorty's view, however, this is an uncharitable misunderstanding. What the authorities were really doing, in denying that they had murdered those students, was something wholly praiseworthy: they were trying to bring it about that the alleged massacre never happened. For they were trying to see to it that their peers would let them get away with saying that the massacre never happened; that is, they were trying to make it *true* that it never happened; and who can fault them for that? The same goes for those contemporary neo-Nazis who claim that there was no holocaust; from a Rortian view, they are only trying to see to it that such a terrible thing never happened; and what could be more commendable than that? This way of thinking has real possibilities for dealing with poverty

and disease: if only we let each other get away with saying that there isn't any poverty and disease—no cancer or AIDS, let's say—then it would be true that there isn't any; and if it were true that there isn't any, then of course there wouldn't *be* any. That seems vastly cheaper and less cumbersome than the conventional methods of fighting poverty and disease. At a more personal level, if you have done something wrong, it is not too late: lie about it, thus bringing it about that your peers will let you get away with saying that you didn't do it, then it will be true both that you didn't do it, and, as an added bonus, that you didn't even lie about it.[6]

Here Plantinga defends objective truth from the skepticism of Rorty and other postmodernists. But getting beyond skepticism is only the first step; then we must figure out the basis of knowledge, which is where we turn next.

CHAPTER 7 IN REVIEW

SUMMARY

Skepticism means a doubting or incredulous state of mind. It comes in many levels of intensity, and all of us are skeptical about something or other at one time or another. A dash of skepticism is surely healthy inasmuch as it serves as an antidote to gullibility. As with gullibility, however, overdoses of skepticism can be detrimental to one's philosophical health.

It is useful to distinguish between commonsense skepticism, philosophical skepticism, and absolute skepticism. The latter, which denies that we can know anything whatsoever, was exemplified in the ancient Pyrrho and his school. The arguments for skepticism are usually based on the relativity (or differences of opinion) in reason, sense perception, and custom. Amid such disagreements, what can one do but suspend judgment and abandon all hope of knowledge?

Not so fast, say those who charge that, at least, absolute skepticism is both impractical and impossible. It is impractical, they say, because no one can live a coherent life except on the assumption that some things can be *known*. It is impossible not only because we surely have certainty about such things as our own existence and impressions, but also because the absolute skeptics affirm with *complete conviction* their thesis that *nothing can be known* and are therefore hopelessly self-contradictory. Similar reasoning is employed by St. Augustine, whose attack on skepticism is perhaps one of the best known.

Richard Rorty represents the mood of postmodernism, and along with that, a broader kind of skepticism. Here, the traditional image of the mind as a reflector of reality is challenged in favor of the more modest image of

---

[6]Alvin Plantinga, "The Twin Pillars of Christian Scholarship," in *The Stob Lectures of Calvin College and Seminary,* 1989–1990 (Grand Rapids, MI: Calvin College: 1989) (pamphlet).

the mind as always struggling toward the truth, employing whatever suggestive tools it possesses, and conditioned by the culture of a particular time and place. In such a view, philosophy should both divest itself of grandiose illusions about its role among the disciplines and settle for a kind of "knowledge" that is much less knowledge in the traditional sense and much more in the nature of an ongoing conversation.

BASIC IDEAS

- The meaning of "skepticism"
- Three kinds of skepticism
    Commonsense skepticism
    Philosophical skepticism
    Absolute skepticism
- Pyrrho as an example of absolute skepticism
- Historical sources of Pyrrhonic skepticism
- The main argument for skepticism
- Pyrrho's *Ten Modes*
- Arguments against absolute skepticism
    Absolute skepticism as impractical
    Absolute skepticism as impossible
- Self-refuting propositions
- Augustine's refutations of skepticism
- General features of postmodernism
- Rorty's historicism
- Rorty's pluralism
- "Edifying philosophy"
- Three criticisms of Rorty

TEST YOURSELF

1. Why is a certain amount of ordinary skepticism a healthy sign?
2. The main argument for skepticism rests upon *relativity*. What does this mean? Give some examples from the *Ten Modes*.
3. Which of the following does not fit into Rorty's view: (a) wholism, (b) nonnegotiable, certain truths, (c) metaphilosophical ideas, or (d) historical relativity of truth?
4. True or false: Aristotle was a skeptic.
5. One philosopher who argued, against the Skeptics, that it is certain that the world either exists or does not exist was_____.
6. Why do some claim that absolute skepticism is self-refuting?
7. True or false: By "pluralism," Rorty means that there is no neutral ground on which we may evaluate various views.

- St. Augustine has been quoted here as a great opponent of skepticism. In another work, entitled *On the Advantages of Believing,* he argues that no practical or intellectual progress can be expected from one who is unwilling ever to accept certain claims on the authority of others. What do you think of this position? What might be said for it and against it?

- How do *you* come out on the question of skepticism? If you are persuaded by the arguments *against* skepticism, then what is the relevance, for epistemology, of the relativity of reason, perception, and custom?

FOR FURTHER READING

Julia Annas and Jonathan Barnes. *The Modes of Scepticism: Ancient Texts and Modern Interpretations.* Cambridge: Cambridge University Press, 1985. An "introduction to sceptical philosophy" by means of a historical survey of the Greek skeptics and chapters on each of the Ten Modes.

D. M. Armstrong. *Belief, Truth, and Knowledge.* Cambridge: Cambridge University Press, 1973. Ch. 11. A somewhat advanced discussion of "The Infinite Regress of Reasons," emphasizing the several possible responses to the problem.

A. J. Ayer. *The Problem of Knowledge.* London: Macmillan, 1958. Ch. 2. An instructive and readable account of "Skepticism and Certainty," concerned primarily with "philosophical skepticism," by the best-known logical positivist.

Christopher Butler. *Postmodernism: A Very Short Introduction.* New York: Oxford University Press, 2002. Accessible and fair-minded overview of postmodern thought.

Lawrence E. Cahoone. *From Modernism to Postmodernism: An Anthology.* Second ed. Malden, MA: Blackwell, 2002. A collection of landmark essays on the development of postmodern philosophy.

Frederick Copleston. *A History of Philosophy.* Baltimore: Newman Press, 1946–1974. II, Ch. 4. A brief but authoritative account of St. Augustine's theory of knowledge, including his attack against skepticism.

A. C. Ewing. *The Fundamental Questions of Philosophy.* New York: Collier Books, 1962. Ch. 1. An introductory chapter on the nature of philosophy, containing a short section on "Scepticism" that argues simply and forcefully against radical skepticism.

N. L. Gifford. *When in Rome: An Introduction to Relativism and Knowledge.* Albany, NY: State University of New York Press, 1983. A popular-level examination and refutation of epistemological relativism.

Alan R. Malachowski (ed.). *Reading Rorty: Critical Responses to "Philosophy and the Mirror of Nature" (and Beyond).* Oxford: Basil Blackwell, 2002.

Arne Naess. *Scepticism.* London: Routledge & Kegan Paul, 1968. Discussion of all aspects of skepticism, including a sympathetic chapter on specifically Pyrrhonic skepticism.

Michail A. Slote. *Reason and Scepticism.* London: George Allen & Unwin, 1970. A refutation of specifically epistemological skepticism.

Peter Unger. *Ignorance: A Case for Scepticism.* Oxford: Clarendon Press, 1975. A contemporary and sustained defense of a general form of skepticism, concluding with a chapter on "The Impossibility of Truth."

Michael Williams. *Groundless Belief: An Essay on the Possibility of Epistemology.* New Haven, CT: Yale University Press, 1977. Chs. 1 and 3. Considers "radical skepticism" and the problem of an infinite regress of justification in relation to contemporary epistemological issues.

*In addition, see the relevant articles ("Skepticism," "Sociology of Knowledge," etc.) in *Routledge Encyclopedia of Philosophy,* ed. Edward Craig (London: Routledge, 1998), and *Stanford Encyclopedia of Philosophy,* http://plato.stanford.edu.

THE WAY OF REASON

Where does knowledge come from? What is the basis of knowledge? The question of the origin of knowledge is one of the most important questions of philosophy. In fact, it is a *crucial* question. As we have said already in the introduction to Part Two, how you answer this question will have everything to do with the rest of your philosophy.

A crucial question: What is the basis of knowledge?

TWO MAIN THEORIES ABOUT THE BASIS OF KNOWLEDGE

Throughout the history of philosophy, thinkers have generally answered this question in two ways. On the one side, we have those philosophers who, in one way or another and in varying degrees, have emphasized *reason* as the source of knowledge ("inside-out" philosophers). On the other side, we have those philosophers who, in one way or another and in varying degrees, have emphasized *experience* as the source of knowledge ("outside-in" philosophers). The position stressing the role of the intellect or reason is called *rationalism*, and those holding to this position are called *rationalists* (from the Latin word *ratio*, "reason"). The position stressing the role of sense experience is called *empiricism*, and those holding this view are called *empiricists* (from the Greek *empeiria*, "experience").

Empiricism and rationalism

A special note is in order regarding the labels "rationalism" and "rationalist" because these terms, like so many other important terms, bear more than one meaning. Here again we must distinguish between a loose and a stricter sense of these terms. We have already encountered the loose sense of "rationalism" in the Introduction. There we said that rationalism is a dominating interest in reasoning, reflecting, criticizing, examining, and so on. This is what we meant when we defined philosophy as the attempt to provide, within limits, an essentially *rational* interpretation of reality as a whole, and when we characterized all philosophers as *rationalists*. Now, however, in the stricter or more technical sense of the word, rationalism is an *epistemological theory*, specifically a *theory about the basis of knowledge*. Note, then, that while a rationalist in the strict sense is necessarily a rationalist in the loose sense, it is not necessarily the case that a rationalist in the loose sense will be a rationalist in the strict sense—he or she may, rather, be an *empiricist*. As a term designating a theory about the basis of knowledge, rationalism is on a par with empiricism. Both empiricism and rationalism (in this technical sense) answer the question What is the basis of knowledge?, though in radically different ways.

REASON AS THE BASIS OF KNOWLEDGE

Rationalism: a more accurate definition

We will begin with rationalism. Above we said that rationalism emphasizes reason as the source of knowledge. This may now be refined somewhat: Rationalism is the belief that at least some knowledge about reality can be acquired through reason, independently of sense experience.

Knowledge about reality . . .

It is important here to stress, first, that the rationalist believes that *some* knowledge about reality can be acquired through reason alone. Few rationalists have ever insisted that sense experience plays absolutely no role whatsoever in the acquisition of knowledge. We will say more about this later, but for the moment just consider: Even if you are a strict rationalist, how do you know that swans are white? That in fourteen hundred and ninety-two Columbus sailed the ocean blue? Obviously there is much about the world that we could not possibly know apart from making observations, lighting Bunsen burners, taking field trips, and so on. The staunchest rationalists admit this. What they insist on is that at least *some* of the truths about reality (and usually the most important truths about reality) are known apart from sense experience.

. . . through reason

Second, we must stress that for rationalists reason is the source of at least some of our knowledge about *reality*. We do have, after all, knowledge that is *not* about reality. For example, we know that all barking dogs bark; that a triangle has three sides, that all bachelors are unmarried; and in short, that any statement of the form "A is A" is true. Such statements, as we will emphasize later, are absolutely and universally and necessarily true. But that is because they are true by definition—denying the statement involves a contradiction. As such they have no bearing on reality; they neither affirm nor deny the existence of anything; they must be true *no matter what*. Such truths do not depend upon sense experience; all you have to do is look at the proposition to see that it must be true. The rationalist, though, claims that at least some propositions that *are* about reality—that affirm or deny

HOW DO YOU KNOW WHEN YOU KNOW?

Epistemology is concerned primarily with the kind of knowledge involved in truth-claims—that is, when the truth or falsity of something is asserted.

But truth-claims come in many colors, and, therefore, so does this kind of knowledge. Consider, for example, the following claims. In each of them something is claimed to be "known," but the "knowing" in each is quite different from all the others.

- I know that in fourteen hundred and ninety-two Columbus sailed the ocean blue.
- I know that I exist.
- I know that God exists.
- I know that all swans are white.
- I know that this table exists.
- I know that my Redeemer liveth.
- I know that every event must have a cause.
- I know that you are suffering.
- I know that all barking dogs bark.
- I know that it will rain tomorrow.

Obviously, the kind of knowledge involved in a straightforward historical claim like "I know that in fourteen hundred and ninety-two Columbus sailed the ocean blue" is quite different from the kind of knowledge delivered through an introspective intuition, as in "I know that I exist." And both of these are quite different from the knowledge involved in the religious assertion "I know that my Redeemer liveth." And so on.

To see that these claims really involve quite different meanings of "know," just ask yourself in each case "how" that particular thing would be known—what sorts of considerations should be brought to bear, and so on.

the existence of something—may be known independently of sense experience, through reason alone.

Do you yourself possess any universal and certain knowledge about reality? Think of some possible examples:

- Every event must have a cause.
- It is morally wrong to kill people for the fun of it.
- All individuals are endowed with basic rights.

Can you derive such universal and certain knowledge from the limited, fluctuating, and relative evidence of sense experience? Where, then, does such knowledge come from?

As two classic examples of rationalism we may mention Plato and Descartes. We have, of course, already dealt with the *metaphysical* doctrines of these thinkers in Part One, where we discussed Plato's theory of the Forms

RATIONALISM (THE STRICT SENSE)

The theory that some knowledge about actual existing things is delivered by reason rather than sense experience.

and Descartes' mind-matter dualism. But now we consider the *epistemological* side of their philosophies.

THE RATIONALISM OF PLATO

Along with many other Greek philosophers, Plato believed that the *reason,* which distinguishes humans from the lower animals, comprises the essential nature of the human being. (The classical definition of man as "a rational animal" comes from these Greek philosophers.) Human good and happiness, therefore, lie in the activity and fulfillment of the rational faculty. That is, they lie in contemplation and *knowledge.* On the other hand, it will be recalled from our earlier discussion that Plato believed that the only proper object of knowledge, or the only thing that can *really* be known, is *Being.* This means that we can have no real knowledge of the world about us, the relative and fluctuating world of *Becoming.* Of this world we have only opinion, not knowledge.

Now, Plato has Socrates announce in the *Phaedo* that not only do real philosophers have no fear of death, but they actually desire and look forward to it. In fact, real philosophers view their lives as lifelong preparations for death. Why? Because as long as we are in *this* world we are held back from the attainment of real knowledge and therefore happiness. And why is this? For one thing, our bodies are a constant distraction from the higher pursuit of knowledge. The pursuit of knowledge does, after all, require some time and attention, but it seems that most of our time is taken up by the body: We must feed it, clothe it, cleanse it, and pay all sorts of attention to it. For another, and this is more important for the present point, as long as our souls are imprisoned in our bodies they have a natural tendency (if not necessity) to peer out, as it were, through the only windows of the prison, the five senses. As a result, our souls become contaminated by the distortions, illusions, and relativities of the sensible world.

Plato himself represents the twofold problem posed by the body as follows:

Now take the acquisition of knowledge. Is the body a hindrance or not, if one takes it into partnership to share an investigation? What I mean is this. Is there any certainty in human sight and hearing, or is it true, as the poets are always dinning into our ears, that we neither hear nor see anything accurately? Yet if these senses are not clear and accurate, the rest can hardly be so, because they are all inferior to the first two. Don't you agree?

*Why philosophers
desire death*

*Bodily hindrances
to knowledge*

Certainly.

Then when is it that the soul attains to truth? When it tries to investigate any-thing with the help of the body, it is obviously led astray.

Quite so.

Is it not in the course of reflection, if at all, that the soul gets a clear view of facts?

Yes.

Surely the soul can best reflect when it is free of all distractions such as hear-ing or sight or pain or pleasure of any kind—that is, when it ignores the body and becomes as far as possible independent, avoiding all physical contacts and associations as much as it can, in its search for reality.

That is so.

Then here too—in despising the body and avoiding it, and endeavoring to become independent—the philosopher's soul is ahead of all the rest.

It seems so.

Here are some more questions, Simmias. Do we recognize such a thing as absolute uprightness?

Indeed we do.

And absolute beauty and goodness too?

Of course.

Have you ever seen any of these things with your eyes?

Certainly not, said he.

Well, have you ever apprehended them with any other bodily sense? By "them" I mean not only absolute tallness or health or strength, but the real nature of any given thing—what it actually is. Is it through the body that we get the truest percep-tion of them? Isn't it true that in any inquiry you are likely to attain more nearly to knowledge of your object in proportion to the care and accuracy with which you have prepared yourself to understand that object in itself?

Certainly.

Don't you think that the person who is likely to succeed in this attempt most perfectly is the one who approaches each object, as far as possible, with the unaided intellect, without taking account of any sense of sight in his thinking, or dragging any other sense into his reckoning—the man who pursues the truth by applying his pure and unadulterated thought to the pure and unadulterated object, cutting himself off as much as possible from his eyes and ears and virtually all the rest of his body, as an impediment which by its presence prevents the soul from attaining to truth and clear thinking? Is not this the person, Simmias, who will reach the goal of reality, if anybody can?

What you say is absolutely true, Socrates, said Simmias.

All these considerations, said Socrates, must surely prompt serious philosophers to review the position in some such way as this. It looks as though this were a bypath leading to the right track. So long as we keep to the body and our soul is contami-nated with this imperfection, there is no chance of our ever attaining satisfactorily to our object, which we assert to be truth. In the first place, the body provides us with innumerable distractions in the pursuit of our necessary sustenance, and any diseases which attack us hinder our quest for reality. Besides, the body fills us with loves and desires and fears and all sorts of fancies and a great deal of nonsense, with the result that we literally never get an opportunity to think at all about anything. Wars and revolutions and battles are due simply and solely to the body and its desires. All wars are undertaken for the acquisition of wealth, and the reason why we have to acquire wealth is the body, because we are slaves in its service. That is why, on all these accounts, we have so little time for philosophy. Worst of all, if we do obtain any leisure from the body's claims and turn to some line of inquiry, the body intrudes once more into our investigations, interrupting, disturbing, distracting, and preventing us from getting a glimpse of the truth. We are in fact convinced that if we are ever to have pure knowledge of anything, we must get rid of the body and contemplate things by themselves with the soul by itself.[1]

O happy day, then, when the soul will finally be set free from the body by death! Only then will it come into the uninterrupted enjoyment of absolute knowledge of that other world, the world of truth and reality. In the meantime, we must minimize as much as possible the contaminations of the senses.

It seems, to judge from the argument, that the wisdom which we desire and upon which we profess to have set our hearts will be attainable only when we are dead, and not in our lifetime. If no pure knowledge is possible in the company of the body, then either it is totally impossible to acquire knowledge, or it is only possible after death, because it is only then that the soul will be separate and independent of the body. It seems that so long as we are alive, we shall continue closest to knowledge if we avoid as much as we can all contact and association with the body, except when they are absolutely necessary, and instead of allowing ourselves to become infected with its nature, purify ourselves from it until God himself gives us deliverance. In this way, by keeping ourselves uncontaminated by the follies of the body, we shall probably reach the company of others like ourselves and gain direct knowledge of all that is pure and uncontaminated—that is, presumably, of truth. For one who is not pure himself to attain to the realm of purity would no doubt be a breach of universal justice.[2]

Here then is a clearly rationalist view of knowledge. Sense experience is disdained as a hindrance to real knowledge. And true reality, by its very nature as transcendent and nonsensible, can be grasped adequately by the intellect alone.

But Plato's rationalism becomes clear in yet another way. Even in this world, knowledge—insofar as it is knowledge—is possible only because it is *innate*—that is, inborn. The theory of innate ideas is a popular one among rationalists. But it is important not to confuse innate ideas with *instinct*. Instinct is not a result of a cognitive activity; rather, it is the *subcognitive* and purely mechanistic behavior that enhances survival. Further, in none of its forms does the doctrine of innate ideas mean that the infant child is born into the world with its mind burgeoning with Einstein's theory of relativity. It usually means that fundamental ideas or principles are built right into the mind itself and require only to be developed and brought to maturity.

The theory
of innate ideas

---

[1]Plato, *Phaedo*, 65A–66E, in *The Last Days of Socrates*, tr. Hugh Tredennick (Harmondsworth: Penguin Classics, 1954).

[2]Ibid., 66E–67B.

In contrast to his friends, Socrates is glad at the prospect of his death,
for death is the liberation of the soul from the body, and this means the fulfillment
of his lifelong philosophical goal: knowledge.

Plato himself sought to prove the immortality of the soul, or, more accurately, the *preexistence* of the soul, on the grounds that we have in our minds certain ideas that we could not possibly have derived from sense experience alone. Such an idea is that of equality. Where, Plato asks, did we acquire this and similar ideas? Certainly not from the sensible world around us, for there is no instance of absolute equality to be found anywhere in this world. Of course the sensible world is full of things that are *more or less* equal, but you will search this world over, or any other world in space and time, and never come across an instance of *absolute* equality. We are back in the world of Heraclitus, where everything flows, and in Plato's world of Becoming, which is populated by imperfect copies or mere approximations to the true Realities, the eternal Forms.

Plato concludes that the only way to account for this knowledge is to believe that prior to its embodiment in this world, the soul was in the presence of the Forms, where it acquired knowledge of the Realities, including knowledge of Equality. This knowledge was lost or forgotten through the trauma of birth, though to some degree "recollected" subsequent to birth on the occasion of our experiences with more-or-less-equality—that is, Equality as it is encountered imperfectly in the sensible world. It is important to note that Plato's theory of knowledge as recollection, although it certainly emphasizes the innateness of our fundamental ideas, also accords some role to sense experience after all. At least in this life, no knowledge could be enjoyed at all were it not for the initial stimulation of the senses.

As a possible theory of innate knowledge, you might find Plato's doctrine of recollection a bit silly. On the other hand, one should always be cautious

Knowledge
as recollection

The role of sense
experience

in judging as silly the ideas of those who have exerted enormous influence on the way we ourselves think today. Plato's theory is both historically and philosophically interesting, and his own statement of it is worthy of close attention:

We admit, I suppose, that there is such a thing as equality—not the equality of stick to stick and stone to stone, and so on, but something beyond all that and distinct from it—absolute equality. Are we to admit this or not?

Yes indeed, said Simmias, most emphatically.

And do we know what it is?

Certainly.

Where did we get our knowledge? Was it not from the particular examples that we mentioned just now? Was it not from seeing equal sticks or stones or other equal objects that we got the notion of equality, although it is something quite distinct from them? Look at it in this way. Is it not true that equal stones and sticks sometimes, without changing in themselves, appear equal to one person and unequal to another?

Certainly.

Well, now, have you ever thought that things which were absolutely equal were unequal, or that equality was inequality?

No, never, Socrates.

Then these equal things are not the same as absolute equality.

Not in the least, as I see it, Socrates.

And yet it is these equal things that have suggested and conveyed to you your knowledge of absolute equality, although they are distinct from it?

Perfectly true.

Whether it is similar to them or dissimilar?

Certainly.

It makes no difference, said Socrates. So long as the sight of one thing suggests another to you, it must be a cause of recollection, whether the two things are alike or not.

Quite so.

Well, now, he said, what do we find in the case of the equal sticks and other things of which we were speaking just now? Do they seem to us to be equal in the sense of absolute equality, or do they fall short of it in so far as they only approximate to equality? Or don't they fall short at all?

They do, said Simmias, a long way.

Suppose that when you see something you say to yourself, This thing which I can see has a tendency to be like something else, but it falls short and cannot be really like it, only a poor imitation. Don't you agree with me that anyone who receives that impression must in fact have previous knowledge of that thing which he says that the other resembles, but inadequately?

Certainly he must.

Very well, then, is that our position with regard to equal things and absolute equality?

Exactly.

Then we must have had some previous knowledge of equality before the time when we first saw equal things and realized that they were striving after equality, but fell short of it.

That is so.

And at the same time we are agreed also upon this point, that we have not and could not have acquired this notion of equality except by sight or touch or one of the other senses. I am treating them as being all the same.

They are the same, Socrates, for the purpose of our argument.

So it must be through the senses that we obtained the notion that all sensible equals are striving after absolute equality but falling short of it. Is that correct?

Yes, it is.

So before we began to see and hear and use our other senses we must somewhere have acquired the knowledge that there is such a thing as absolute equality. Otherwise we could never have realized, by using it as a standard for comparison, that all equal objects of sense are desirous of being like it, but are only imperfect copies.

That is the logical conclusion, Socrates.

Did we not begin to see and hear and possess our other senses from the moment of birth?

Certainly.

But we admitted that we must have obtained our knowledge of equality before we obtained them.

Yes.

So we must have obtained it before birth.

So it seems.

Then if we obtained it before our birth, and possessed it when we were born, we had knowledge, both before and at the moment of birth, not only of equality and relative magnitudes, but of all absolute standards. Our present argument applies no more to equality than it does to absolute beauty, goodness, uprightness, holiness, and, as I maintain, all those characteristics which we designate in our discussions by the term "absolute." So we must have obtained knowledge of all these characteristics before our birth.

That is so.

And unless we invariably forget it after obtaining it we must always be born *knowing* and continue to *know* all through our lives, because "to know" means simply to retain the knowledge which one has acquired, and not to lose it. Is not what we call "forgetting" simply the loss of knowledge, Simmias?

Most certainly, Socrates.

And if it is true that we acquired our knowledge before our birth, and lost it at the moment of birth, but afterward, by the exercise of our senses upon sensible objects, recover the knowledge which we had once before, I suppose that what

INNATE IDEAS

Rationalists, who believe that we can have existential knowledge (knowledge of the actual existence or nonexistence of things) apart from sense experience, are surely obligated to account for this knowledge. One way is through a doctrine of *innate ideas*. "Innate" means "inborn"; thus theories of innate ideas are theories that teach that the mind in some way possesses at least fundamental ideas or intellectual structures from birth. The mind at birth is not a "blank tablet."

> "Most of all I was delighted with Mathematics because of the certainty of its demonstrations and the evidence of its reasoning."
>
> —Descartes

we call learning will be the recovery of our knowledge, and surely we should be right in calling this recollection.[3]

THE RATIONALISM OF DESCARTES

Another classic example of a rationalist philosopher is Descartes. As with Plato, we have already considered Descartes' theory of reality and thus have already been introduced to at least something of his theory of knowledge.

It will be recalled that Descartes was repelled by the contradictions he discovered among philosophers, but was attracted by the certainties he discovered in mathematics:

The model of mathematics

> Most of all was I delighted with Mathematics because of the certainty of its demonstrations and the evidence of its reasoning; but I did not yet understand its true use, and, believing that it was of service only in the mechanical arts, I was astonished that, seeing how firm and solid was its basis, no loftier edifice had been reared thereupon.[4]

This preoccupation with mathematics immediately betrays Descartes' rationalist bent. For the reason the truths of mathematics and the proofs of geometry are certain is that they are untainted by the tentativeness and fluctuations and relativities and illusions of sense experience. They are certain—*rationally* certain. Under the spell of mathematics, Descartes thus turned away from sense experience and toward *reason alone* as the source of philosophical certainty. And he conceived of a "geometrical method" for philosophy.

Descartes' "geometrical method" (again)

The essence of this new philosophical method may be found in Descartes' *Rules for the Direction of the Mind*. In Rule IV he stresses the absolute necessity of having a method and then explicitly defines it.

Rule IV. There is Need for a Method for Finding Out the Truth

So blind is the curiosity by which mortals are possessed, that they often conduct their minds along unexplored routes, having no reason to hope for success, but merely being willing to risk the experiment of finding whether the truth they seek lies there. As well might a man burning with an unintelligent desire to find treasure, continuously roam the streets, seeking to find something that a passer-by might have chanced to drop. This is the way in which most Chemists, many Geometricians, and Philosophers

---

[3]Ibid., 74A–75D.

[4]René Descartes, *Discourse on Method*, in *The Philosophical Works of Descartes*, tr. Elizabeth S. Haldane and G. R. T. Ross (Cambridge: Cambridge University Press, 1911), I, 85.

DESCARTES' RULES

In his *Rules for the Direction of the Mind,* Descartes presents a long list of rules that, if followed, ensure that the intellect will eventually grasp all that can be known. These rules are collapsed into four short paragraphs in the better-known *Discourse on Method:*

> The first of these was to accept nothing as true which I did not clearly recognise to be so: that is to say, carefully to avoid precipitation and prejudice in judgments, and to accept in them nothing more than what was presented to my mind so clearly and distinctly that I could have no occasion to doubt it.
>
> The second was to divide up each of the difficulties which I examined into as many parts as possible, and as seemed requisite in order that it might be resolved in the best manner possible.
>
> The third was to carry on my reflections in due order, commencing with objects that were the most simple and easy to understand, in order to rise little by little, or by degrees, to knowledge of the most complex, assuming an order, even if a fictitious one, among those which do not follow a natural sequence relatively to one another.
>
> The last was in all cases to make enumerations so complete and reviews so general that I should be certain of having omitted nothing.

Descartes' optimism about the practice of these rules, as well as the mathematical character of his method, is evident from the continuing comment:

> Those long chains of reasoning, simple and easy as they are, of which geometricians make use in order to arrive at the most difficult demonstrations, had caused me to imagine that all those things which fall under the cognizance of man might very likely be mutually related in the same fashion; and that, provided only that we abstain from receiving anything as true which is not so, and always retain the order which is necessary in order to deduce the one conclusion from the other, there can be nothing so remote that we cannot reach to it, nor so recondite that we cannot discover it.*

*Descartes, *Discourse on Method,* in *The Philosophical Works of Descartes,* I, 92.

not a few prosecute their studies. I do not deny that sometimes in these wanderings they are lucky enough to find something true. But I do not allow that this argues greater industry on their part, but only better luck. But however that may be, it were far better never to think of investigating truth at all, than to do so without a method. For it is very certain that unregulated inquiries and confused reflections of this kind only confound the natural light and blind our mental powers. . . . Moreover by a method I mean certain and simple rules, such that, if a man observe them accurately, he shall never assume what is false as true, and will never spend his mental efforts to no purpose, but will always gradually increase his knowledge and so arrive at a true understanding of all that does not surpass his powers.[5]

[5]Descartes, *Rules for the Direction of the Mind,* in *The Philosophical Works of Descartes,* I, 9.

WHAT ABOUT EMOTION?
A FEMINIST CRITIQUE OF RATIONALISM

Though not everyone is a rationalist like Plato and Descartes, all philosophers value reason. In fact, being rational—in the loose sense of relying on reason—was used in Chapter 1 as one of the defining features of philosophy. But what about emotion? What role do emotions play in the acquisition of knowledge? In the following excerpt, Alison Jaggar argues that, though ignored by most philosophers, emotions are essential to human life.

Western epistemology has tended to view emotion with suspicion and even hostility. This derogatory western attitude toward emotion, like the earlier western contempt for sensory observation, fails to recognize that emotion, like sensory perception, is necessary to human survival. Emotions prompt us to act appropriately, to approach some people and situations and to avoid others, to caress or cuddle, fight or flee. Without emotion, human life would be unthinkable. Moreover, emotions have an intrinsic as well as an instrumental value. Although not all emotions are enjoyable or even justifiable, life without any emotion would be life without any meaning.

Jaggar's critique of rationalism doesn't stop here, however. She goes on to argue that focusing exclusively on reason and devaluing emotion has been a tool for oppression of women and people of color.

Feminist theorists have pointed out that the western tradition has not seen everyone as equally emotional. Instead, reason has been associated with members of dominant political, social, and cultural groups and emotion with members of subordinate groups. Prominent among those subordinate groups in our society are people of color, except for supposedly "inscrutable orientals," and women.

Although the emotionality of women is a familiar cultural stereotype, its grounding is quite shaky. Women appear more emotional than men because

(*continued on next page*)

According to these last lines, anyone who follows Descartes' method would, in principle, be led to all possible knowledge. But what, more exactly, does this method consist in? Descartes reduces it, as we saw in Chapter 4, to two operations of the intellect: *intuition* and *deduction*. This, of course, is why Descartes' method has been called a "geometrical" method. As in geometry, it begins with fundamental and irreducible truths, and from these it deduces more truths. But now the notions of intuition and deduction require further comment.

Intuition

The word "intuition" is used in many ways, and we must be careful to distinguish it here from anything like "woman's intuition." In philosophy intuition means, usually, a direct and immediate knowledge of something. When we say that it is direct and immediate knowledge, we mean that it is not, like much of our other knowledge, *mediated*, or passed along through something else—say, through sense experience or through other ideas. An

they, along with some groups of people of color, are permitted and even required to express emotion more openly. In contemporary western culture, emotionally inexpressive women are suspect as not being real women, whereas men who express their emotions freely are suspected of being homosexual or in some other way deviant from the masculine ideal. Modern western men, in contrast with Shakespeare's heroes, for instance, are required to present a facade of coolness, lack of excitement, even boredom, to express emotion only rarely and then for relatively trivial events, such as sporting occasions, where expressed emotions are acknowledged to be dramatized and so are not taken entirely seriously. Thus, women in our society form the main group allowed or even expected to feel emotion. A woman may cry in the face of disaster, and a man of color may gesticulate, but a white man merely sets his jaw. . . .

Although there is no reason to suppose that the thoughts and actions of women are any more influenced by emotion than the thoughts and actions of men, the stereotypes of cool men and emotional women continue to flourish because they are confirmed by an uncritical daily experience. In these circumstances, where there is a differential assignment of reason and emotion, it is easy to see the ideological function of the myth of the dispassionate investigator. It functions, obviously, to bolster the epistemic authority of the currently dominant groups, composed largely of white men, and to discredit the observations and claims of the currently subordinate groups including, of course, the observations and claims of many people of color and women. The more forcefully and vehemently the latter groups express their observations and claims, the more emotional they appear and so the more easily they are discredited. The alleged epistemic authority of the dominant groups then justifies their political authority.*

*Alison Jaggar, "Love and Knowledge: Emotion in Feminist Epistemology," *Inquiry* 32, no. 2, 1989, pp. 151–176.

example of *mediated* knowledge is our knowledge that X is red, mediated or passed along through our sense experience of X and its color; or our knowledge that C is D, mediated or passed along through our prior understanding that if A is B then C is D, and A is B. In intuition, however, the truth or knowledge in question is grasped immediately by a direct awareness—it is *just there*. It is important to emphasize, though, that the intuitionist claims to know directly not only logical truths, as in "A is A," but truths about *reality*, as in our earlier examples: "Every event must have a cause"; "It is morally wrong to kill people for the fun of it"; and "All individuals are endowed with basic rights." As a theory about the basis of knowledge, intuitionism is the view that such truths may be known immediately and with certainty.

It is understandable why a doctrine of innate ideas has also been attributed to Descartes. Did he take, as it were, the Platonic Forms, place them in the mind, and then announce that we know them directly? Or does he

INTUITIONISM

The view that direct awareness of at least some fundamental ideas of reality as universally and necessarily true is either *the* basis of knowledge or one of its bases.

believe that what is innate is a sort of *disposition* of the mind, or a *structure* by which universal and necessary truth about reality can be developed? Of course the latter would better explain why infants do not appreciate Einstein. In any event, what is really important is that for Descartes *something* is innate, and intuition is the faculty of direct awareness by which knowledge is derived from the mind alone. Although Descartes made a big thing of intuition, many other philosophers too have appealed to intuition as an important and even necessary epistemological tool.

Deduction

But, Descartes continues, our knowledge is not limited to intuitions. For it is possible, says Descartes, to *deduce* further ideas and truths from our intuited ones. You already have an idea of deduction from our discussion of logic in Chapter 1. You will recall that it consists in the necessary inference of one statement from others; in valid deductive reasoning, if the premises are true, the conclusion *must* be true. It is, thus, by the faculty of deduction that from the original intuitions we are enabled to expand our knowledge indefinitely— but without any loss of certainty. In Chapter 4 on mind and matter we saw, in fact, how much Descartes deduced from his single intuition "I think."

In the following, again from the *Rules for the Direction of the Mind*, Descartes emphasizes and clarifies intuition and deduction as the basic tools of knowledge.

Rule III. In the Subjects We Propose to Investigate, Our Inquiries Should be Directed, Not to What Others Have Thought, Nor to What We Ourselves Conjecture, But to What We Can Clearly and Perspicuously Behold and with Certainty Deduce, for Knowledge is Not Won in Any Other Way.

. . . we shall here take note of all those mental operations by which we are able, wholly without fear of illusion, to arrive at the knowledge of things. Now I admit only two, viz. intuition and deduction.

By *intuition* I understand, not the fluctuating testimony of the senses, nor the misleading judgment that proceeds from the blundering constructions of imagination, but the conception which an unclouded and attentive mind gives us so readily and distinctly that we are wholly freed from doubt about that which we understand. Or, what comes to the same thing, *intuition* is the undoubting conception of an unclouded and attentive mind, and springs from the light of reason alone; it is more certain than deduction itself, in that it is simpler, though deduction, as we have noted above, cannot by us be erroneously conducted. Thus each individual can mentally have intuition of the fact that he exists, and that he thinks; that the triangle is bounded by three lines only, the sphere by a single superficies, and so on. Facts

DESCARTES' TWOFOLD BASIS OF KNOWLEDGE

- *Intuition:* The faculty by which truths are grasped immediately, without the intervention of sense experience or other ideas.
- *Deduction:* The faculty by which subsequent truths are known with necessity from intuited truths, or from intuited truths taken together with other deduced truths.

of such a kind are far more numerous than many people think, disdaining as they do to direct their attention upon such simple matters.

This evidence and certitude, however, which belongs to intuition, is required not only in the enunciation of propositions, but also in discursive reasoning of whatever sort. For example consider this consequence: 2 and 2 amount to the same as 3 and 1. Now we need to see intuitively not only that 2 and 2 make 4, and that likewise 3 and 1 make 4, but further that the third of the above statements is a necessary conclusion from these two.

Hence now we are in a position to raise the question as to why we have, besides intuition, given this supplementary method of knowing, viz. knowing by *deduction*, by which we understand all necessary inference from other facts that are known with certainty. This, however, we could not avoid, because many things are known with certainty, though not by themselves evident, but only deduced from true and known principles by the continuous and uninterrupted action of a mind that has a clear vision of each step in the process. It is in a similar way that we know that the last link in a long chain is connected with the first, even though we do not take in by means of one and the same act of vision all the intermediate links on which that connection depends, but only remember that we have taken them successively under review and that each single one is united to its neighbour, from the first even to the last. Hence we distinguish this mental intuition from deduction by the fact that into the conception of the latter there enters a certain movement or succession, into that of the former there does not. Further deduction does not require an immediately presented evidence such as intuition possesses; its certitude is rather conferred upon it in some way by memory. The upshot of the matter is that it is possible to say that those propositions indeed which are immediately deduced from first principles are known now by intuition, now by deduction, i.e. in a way that differs according to our point of view. But the first principles themselves are given by intuition alone, while, on the contrary, the remote conclusions are furnished only by deduction.

These two methods are the most certain routes to knowledge, and the mind should admit no others. All the rest should be rejected as suspect of error and dangerous. But this does not prevent us from believing matters that have been divinely revealed as being more certain than our surest knowledge, since belief in these things, as all faith in obscure matters, is an action not of our intelligence, but of our will. They should be heeded also since, if they have any basis in our understanding, they can and ought to be, more than all things else, discovered by one or other of the ways above-mentioned. . . . [6]

---

[6]Ibid., I, 5–8.

It is true that modern and contemporary philosophy has been dominated not by rationalist but, rather, by empiricist epistemology—this probably has not a little to do with the ascendancy of the physical sciences and the scientific method beginning in the sixteenth century—and that theories of innate ideas and the like are looked upon as quaint leftovers from our philosophical past. Everything was given a new twist, however, in the work of the linguist-philosopher Noam Chomsky of the Massachusetts Institute of Technology, and the philosophical world had to take note. How did Chomsky's work suddenly derail the empiricist approach that for so long controlled the philosophical scene? How has it resulted in an unexpected new lease on life for the rationalist?

The answer has to do with Chomsky's contributions to philosophical linguistics—philosophical analyses, problems, and implications of language. More specifically, his original contribution was called *transformational grammar,* which attempts to relate the "surface" structure of sentences, or what is actually heard, and the "deep" structure of the sentences, what is meant. This, however, has already become out of date and unfashionable, and has been superseded by Chomsky's newer and more comprehensive idea of *generative grammar,* which supplements the earlier ideas with talk about "principles and parameters" of language.

The word "principle" here signals the belief that there are certain *universal principles* inherent in all languages—that is, features of language that we are born with. We may call these principles "language universals." This claim may strike you as a sweeping generalization, but it appears to Chomskyites to be demonstrated conclusively by an in-depth analysis of, say, relative clauses and the referents of pronouns in English, as well as in a dozen or so of the other four thousand languages of the world. "Parameters" refers to what appears to be a *universal grammar* in the form of basic linguistic options that precede the learning of a language and are enacted or not in view of the demands of that particular language—you might think of them as hard-wire switches, built right into the mind, which are turned on or off at various points depending on the language being learned.

This is exceedingly difficult stuff, but what is important at the moment is this. The commonsensical model of language acquisition has always been an empirical one: A child acquires language through stimulus-response, conditioning, trial and error, and so on. But in this major development of contemporary philosophy of language, with Chomsky leading the way, it is argued that the phenomenon of language is impossible except on the postulation of *innate intellectual structures.* The implications for epistemology, and specifically for rationalism, are too obvious to miss, as Chomsky himself points out in *Aspects of the Theory of Syntax:*

Innate structures as conditions for language

> On the basis of the best information now available, it seems reasonable to suppose that a child cannot help constructing a particular kind of transformational grammar to account for the data presented to him, any more than he can control

Noam Chomsky, whose linguistic studies have proven
relevant for the doctrine of innate knowledge

his perception of solid objects or his attention to line and angle. Thus it may well
be that the general features of language structure reflect, not so much the course
of one's experience, but rather the general character of one's capacity to acquire
knowledge—in the traditional sense, one's innate ideas and innate principles.[7]

The position is spelled out further in the following, from his essay "Language and the Mind." Note especially his rejection of empiricist explanations of language acquisition, the recurring emphasis on innate structures as conditions for language, and, again, the relevance of this view of language for still other spheres of knowledge.

As far as language learning is concerned, it seems to me that a rather convincing
argument can be made for the view that certain principles intrinsic to the mind provide invariant structures that are a precondition for linguistic experience. . . .

The study of language, it seems to me, offers strong empirical evidence that
empiricists' theories of learning are quite inadequate. Serious efforts have been made
in recent years to develop principles of induction, generalization, and data analysis
that would account for knowledge of a language. These efforts have been a total
failure. The methods and principles fail not for any superficial reason such as lack
of time or data. They fail because they are intrinsically incapable of giving rise to
the system of rules that underlies the normal use of language. What evidence is now
available supports the view that all human languages share deep-seated properties
of organization and structure. These properties—these linguistic universals—can be

---

[7]Noam Chomsky, *Aspects of the Theory of Syntax* (Cambridge, MA: MIT Press, 1965), p. 59.

"What evidence is now available supports the view that all human languages share deep-seated properties of organization and structure. These properties—these linguistic universals—can be plausibly assumed to be an *innate mental endowment* rather than the result of learning."

—Chomsky

plausibly assumed to be an *innate mental endowment* rather than the result of learning. If this is true, then the study of language sheds light on certain long-standing issues in the theory of knowledge. Once again, I see little reason to doubt that what is true of language is true of other forms of human knowledge as well.

There is one further question that might be raised at this point. How does the human mind come to have the innate properties that underlie acquisition of knowledge? Here linguistic evidence obviously provides no information at all. The process by which the human mind has achieved its present state of complexity and its particular form of innate organization are a complete mystery, as much of a mystery as the analogous questions that can be asked about any other complex organism. It is perfectly safe to attribute this to evolution, so long as we bear in mind that there is no substance to this assertion—it amounts to nothing more than the belief that there is surely some naturalistic explanation for these phenomena.

There are, however, important aspects of the problem of language and mind that can be studied sensibly within the limitations of present understanding and technique. I think that, for the moment, the most productive investigations are those dealing with the nature of particular grammars and with the universal conditions met by all human languages. I have tried to suggest how one can move, in successive steps of increasing abstractness, from the study of percepts to the study of grammar to the study of universal grammar and the mechanisms of learning.

In this area of convergence of linguistics, psychology, and philosophy, we can look forward to much exciting work in the coming years.[8]

But there are problems. In spite of the allegedly scientific character of Chomsky's procedure, it appears at bottom to be founded on *intuitions*. For example, it is not clear to everyone, as it is to Chomsky, just what does and does not count as a "sentence" in English—making for great cocktail party fights and lifelong feuds! More generally, it is certainly relevant to pose two

Two questions   questions. First, how does the mind come to possess this structure in the first place? Chomsky answers, as you just saw, that it is a "complete mystery," and he doesn't see at the moment that any purely naturalistic explanation (he cites evolutionary development) is any better than any other. Another question, and certainly more epistemologically relevant: However it got there, what is the relation of this innate intellectual structure to *truth*? Are we driven to a view of knowledge as *arbitrarily* determined by a purely accidental endowment within the brain? Or can we believe in some sort of

[8]Noam Chomsky, "Language and the Mind," in *Readings in Psychology Today* (Del Mar, CA: C. R. M. Books, 1969), pp. 282, 286.

REVEALING PHRASES IN CHOMSKY

- "principles intrinsic to the mind"
- "deep-seated properties of organization and structure"
- "an innate mental endowment"

preestablished harmony whereby this intellectual endowment is made to correspond to reality? Are we driven to something like Plato's doctrine of the *preexistence of the soul*? Or perhaps our experienced reality is itself *determined* by our innate intellectual structures? Or maybe you can think of some other way out? Certainly the problem is an important one and worthy of serious discussion. In fact, it will crop up again in Chapter 10.

We have considered three rationalist conceptions of knowledge from three different periods. We do not raise here specific objections to these theories, because, in a way, the whole next chapter is itself a colossal challenge to them. Empiricism, with its doctrine that the mind is at birth a "blank tablet," rejects the very starting point of rationalism.

CHAPTER 8 IN REVIEW

SUMMARY

One of the most basic questions of epistemology, and therefore a basic question of all philosophizing, is What is the origin of knowledge? Philosophers have answered this question in two radically different ways. According to empiricism, all knowledge (at least "existential" knowledge, which informs us about existence) is derived from the five senses. Rationalism, on the other hand, teaches that at least some knowledge can be acquired apart from sense experience, through the intellect or reason alone.

In this chapter we have considered three ways in which rationalists have argued for their theories. We are already familiar with Plato's theory of reality (from Chapter 3), and we should recall that his image of the Divided Line represents as much a conception of knowledge as a conception of reality. The object of authentic knowledge is what *is*, as opposed to what is *becoming*. Such knowledge is hardly possible in this life, where the soul is imprisoned in the body, and where the body itself is a constant hindrance to the acquisition of knowledge. When the soul is liberated from the body at death, the soul comes into the possession of absolute knowledge. Until that time all we can do is cultivate as much as possible the innate truths that the mind is born with, but which, as they are "recollected," are invariably distorted by the world of Becoming, resulting in mere opinions, or *relative* knowledge.

Likewise, Descartes' theory of knowledge was anticipated in Chapter 4. Descartes, too, seeks to develop at least the foundation of his philosophy apart from the input of the senses. He saw in mathematics an especially good model for philosophical reasoning and adopted intuition and deduction as the principles of his philosophical method. He believed that, in principle, it would be possible to unfold a complete system of knowledge by the rigorous practicing of this method. As with Plato, it is important to see that with Descartes every attempt is made to exclude or minimize the illusory and deceitful intrusions of the senses.

Rationalist theories of knowledge are regarded by many as a bit naive and quaint. However, the critics have been given something of a jolt in recent years. The psycholinguistic research of Chomsky in particular has resurrected the theory of innate ideas. Specifically, his work has brought to light the presence of universal and innate intellectual structures that underlie all language and that explain the process of language acquisition better than the empirically oriented model of learning. Thus psycholinguistics (which is concerned with the connection between the mind and language) has emerged as an unexpected ally of the rationalist theory of knowledge.

BASIC IDEAS

- Empiricism
- Rationalism (strict sense)
- Plato: why philosophers desire death
- Two bodily hindrances to knowledge
- Innate ideas
- Knowledge of recollection
- Descartes' "geometrical method"
- Intuitionism
- Descartes' two operations of the mind
    Intuition
    Deduction
- The empirical theory of language acquisition
- Chomsky's generative grammar
    Principles
    Parameters

TEST YOURSELF

1. True or false: Plato taught that we bring our ideas into this world from a previous existence in an ideal world.   T
2. *Rules for the Direction of the Mind* was written by ___Descartes___ .
3. According to Plato, how does sense experience help us to "recollect" ideas?
4. True or false: By "intuition" Descartes meant a feeling or hunch about something.

5. The phrase "linguistic universals" is employed by _____. What does it mean?

6. True or false: To know something *immediately* is to know it through sense experience.

7. According to Plato, why is absolute knowledge impossible in this life?

8. Why was Descartes especially attracted to mathematics?

QUESTIONS FOR REFLECTION

- Does Plato's doctrine of recollection seem far-fetched or even bizarre? Even if it does, to what degree does it detract from his basic theory of knowledge? Is it itself basic? In evaluating philosophers' positions, is there a danger of throwing out the baby with the bathwater?

- Both Plato and Descartes decry the illusions and distortions of sense experience. Can you provide your own evidence and examples of this? Can you think of *any* sense representation that is not, as it were, "contaminated"? Is it possible to overdo this point? Or, with the rationalists, are we at some point driven to some "purer" faculty than sense perception?

- Think about these propositions: "Every event must have a cause"; "It is morally wrong to kill people for the fun of it"; "All individuals are endowed with basic rights." Would you say that you *know* or are *certain* of these claims? Are any of them *universally* true? What, if anything, does sense experience contribute to this knowledge?

FOR FURTHER READING

Robert R. Ammerman and Marcus G. Singer (eds.). *Belief, Knowledge, and Truth: Readings in the Theory of Knowledge.* New York: Scribners, 1970. A collection of traditional, recent, and important statements on all aspects of knowledge, including some encountered in our chapter (e.g., the *a priori*, intuition, etc.).

Bruce Aune. *Rationalism, Empiricism, and Pragmatism: An Introduction.* New York: Random House, 1970. Ch. 1. A discussion on "Descartes and Rationalism."

Roderick M. Chisholm. *Theory of Knowledge.* Third ed. Englewood Cliffs, NJ: Prentice-Hall, 1989. Ch. 5. A beginner's chapter on "The Truths of Reason," dealing briefly with the most important issues and problems concerning the rationalist view of knowledge.

Frederick Copleston. *A History of Philosophy.* Baltimore: Newman Press, 1946–1974. I, Ch. 19, and IV, Ch. 3. Authoritative accounts of Plato's and Descartes' theories of knowledge by a respected historian of philosophy.

Willis Doney (ed.). *Descartes: A Collection of Critical Essays.* Garden City, NY: Anchor Books, 1967. An anthology of advanced essays, including discussions of epistemological issues in Descartes.

A. C. Ewing. *The Fundamental Questions of Philosophy.* London. Routledge, Kegan & Paul, 1985. Ch. 2. A lucid chapter on "The 'A Priori' and the Empirical," which considers the nature and necessity of knowledge acquired apart from sense experience.

Anthony Kenny. *Descartes: A Study of His Philosophy*. New York: St. Augustine Press, 1993. Ch. 8. A brief and clearly presented chapter on Descartes' conception of "Reason and Intuition."

Paul K. Moser (ed.). *Empirical Knowledge: Readings in Contemporary Epistemology*. Second ed. Sowage, MD: Rowman & Littlefield, 1996. A student-oriented anthology of fifteen essays by prominent philosophers on issues and trends in contemporary epistemology.

A. Radford. *Transformational Syntax: A Student's Guide to Chomsky's Extended Standard Theory*. Cambridge: Cambridge University Press, 1988. A useful entrance into the obtuse and, for the beginner, seemingly inaccessible world of Chomsky's linguistic-epistemological theory.

Geoffrey Sampson. "Noam Chomsky and Generative Grammar." In *Schools of Linguistics*. Stanford, CA: Stanford University Press, 1980. A fairly simple overview with some criticisms of Chomsky's intuitions.

Tom Sorell. *Descartes: A Very Short Introduction*. New York: Oxford University Press, 2001. Intended for novices, this short and clear introduction situates Descartes' writings in the intellectual debates of his time.

Gregory Vlastos (ed.). *Plato: A Collection of Critical Essays*. Garden City, NY: Anchor Books, 1971. An anthology of advanced essays on Plato's metaphysics and epistemology, including a discussion on "Learning as Recollection."

Catherine Wilson. *Descartes'* Meditations: *An Introduction*, Cambridge Introductions to key Philosophical Texts. Cambridge: Cambridge University Press, 2003. A thorough examination of Descartes' most famous work by a leading scholar in the field.

*In addition, see the relevant articles ("Rationalism," "A Priori and A Posteriori," "Innate Ideas," etc.) in *Routledge Encyclopedia of Philosophy*, ed. Edward Craig (London: Routledge, 1998), and *Stanford Encyclopedia of Philosophy*, http://plato.stanford.edu.

THE WAY OF EXPERIENCE

W e turn next to the second general view of the basis of knowledge: *empiricism.* It was said earlier that empiricism is the view that emphasizes experience as the source of knowledge. We must now explain more carefully what we mean here by "experience."

WHAT IS EMPIRICISM?

There are many different sorts of experience, such as mystical experience, moral experience, aesthetic experience, lonely experience, and wild experience. But here we mean *sense* experience—that is, perceptions derived from the five senses: sight, sound, touch, taste, and smell. When empiricists say that experience is the basis of our knowledge, they mean sense experience, and therefore that the five senses are the foundation of all our knowledge.

Sense experience as the source of knowledge

As with rationalism, empiricism comes with varying emphases and in varying degrees. But as a general definition we may say that empiricism is the view that all knowledge of reality is derived from sense experience. This may be livened up somewhat by the empiricist metaphor of the *tabula rasa,* or "blank tablet." It is a shorthand way of expressing the empiricist denial that any ideas or even intellectual structure is inscribed on the mind from birth—the mind is at birth a *blank tablet,* devoid even of watermarks. The implication is, of course, that anything "written" on the tablet is written by the five senses.

Empiricism: the mind as a *tabula rasa*

EMPIRICISM

The theory that all knowledge of actual, existing things is delivered through the five senses.

CLASSICAL EMPIRICISM: ARISTOTLE AND ST. THOMAS

We will consider several forms of empiricism, beginning with the classical empiricism of Aristotle and St. Thomas. When we call the empiricism of Aristotle and St. Thomas *classical* empiricism, we not only reflect its Greek roots (Aristotle) but also distinguish it from various forms of empiricism in the modern period.

Plato vs. Aristotle

It will be recalled from Chapter 3 that Aristotle rejected Plato's theory of the Forms. This was because Plato had created a great gulf between the Forms and the particular things they were the Forms *of*. We saw that Aristotle countered that the Form must be *in* the thing of which it is the Form: The Form, or essence, of the table or chair must be right *there*, along with the matter of the table or chair, constituting it. He insisted on this for many reasons, and one of them was *epistemological:* How can the Form—that which is knowable about the table or chair—make the table or chair knowable if it is not *in* the table or chair? It is therefore no surprise that Aristotle, quite unlike Plato, believed that knowledge comes through our sense experience of particular things in the world—like tables or chairs. And he was one of the first to employ the empiricist comparison of the mind to a *tabula rasa*, or blank tablet.

The necessity of universal ideas

Let us close in on this a bit more. Like Plato, Aristotle believed that knowledge necessarily involves *general* or *universal* ideas—man, dog, table, chair, and the like. Think about this. Where would thinking, speaking, and knowing be without such concepts? Is it possible to think or say or know *anything* apart from such ideas? "Socrates is a man." "In fourteen hundred and ninety-two Columbus sailed the ocean blue." "This table is rectangular." Are not general concepts like man, ocean, table, rectangularity, and so on, necessary for thinking, speaking, and knowing? Now where do these ideas

"[The Platonic Forms] help in no wise . . . towards the knowledge of the other things (for they are not even the substance of these, else they would have been in them), or towards their being, if they are not *in* the particulars which share in them; though if they were they might be thought to be causes, as white causes whiteness in a white object by entering into its composition."

—Aristotle

come from? *Unlike* Plato, Aristotle answered that they come from our *experience* of *particular* men, tables, chairs, dogs, oceans, and so on.

The problem for such an approach is, of course, the same problem that bothered Plato: How do we arrive at *universal* ideas on the basis of our limited and fluctuating experience of *particular* things?

Aristotle's answer is that the universal and necessary elements of knowledge—the foundations of all subsequent reasoning—are built up in the mind through *induction.* This means, for Aristotle, that a wider and wider generalization is derived from repeated experiences of particular things until a *general* or *universal* concept is established in the mind: From the experience of the particular man Callias, the man Socrates, the man James, the man Tad, the man Bill . . . the intellect derives the general or universal idea of *man*—that is, *man as such.* From the experience of the particular dog Fido, the dog Lassie, the dog Rover, the dog Flip . . . the intellect derives the universal idea *dog.* And the universal ideas—man, dog, and innumerable other concepts derived from experience in the same manner—become the tools and building blocks of all reasoning. They then make it possible to say and know, "Socrates is a man," "In fourteen hundred and ninety-two Columbus sailed the ocean blue," and so on.

Aristotle likens the process by which the universal concepts are established in the intellect to a company of soldiers retreating in disarray until a first soldier halts and makes a stand, then a second, then a third, and finally the whole company is put in order and established:

> We conclude that these states of knowledge are neither innate in a determinate form, nor developed from other higher states of knowledge, but from sense-perception. It is like a rout in battle stopped by first one man making a stand and then another, until the original formation has been restored. The soul is so constituted as to be capable of this process.
>
> . . . When one of a number of logically indiscriminable particulars has made a stand, the earliest universal is present in the soul: for though the act of sense-perception is of the particular, its content is universal—is man, for example, not the man Callias. A fresh stand is made among these rudimentary universals, and the process does not cease until the indivisible concepts, the true universals, are established: e.g. such and such a species of animals is a step towards the genus animal, which by the same process is a step towards a further generalization.
>
> Thus it is clear that we must get to know the primary premisses by induction; for the method by which even sense-perception implants the universal is inductive.[1]

This conception of the origin of knowledge was passed from Aristotle to St. Thomas, the dominant Christian philosopher of the thirteenth century. It may be helpful to see how St. Thomas expresses the matter.

We saw that Aristotle taught that the mind is a blank tablet waiting to be written upon by the senses. St. Thomas expresses the same empiricist idea

---

[1] Aristotle, *Posterior Analytics,* 100a–100b, tr. G. R. G. Mure, in *Basic Works of Aristotle,* ed. Richard McKeon (New York: Random House, 1941).

with the words (everything sounds more profound in Latin) *Nihil in intellectu quod prius non fuerit in sensu,* "Nothing is in the intellect which was not first in the senses." For St. Thomas, as for Aristotle, the essences of things are locked inside the particular things of which they are the essences—individual human beings, animals, tables, chairs, dogs, and cats. The intellect, however, is able to liberate the essence in particular things and thus to "see" the universal idea of their common, essential nature: human, animal, table, chair, dog, and cat.

St. Thomas:
universal ideas
from experience
and abstraction

The intellectual faculty by which the essential or formal or universal element of particular things is unlocked and "seen" by the mind is called by St. Thomas *abstraction.* "To abstract" means to remove or separate something from something else. In this epistemological context, what is being abstracted is a common nature, and that from which it is being abstracted are the particular and varying instances of it. When we abstract the universal *human being* from Callias, Socrates, James, Sue, Bill, and Sally, their individual and peculiar features are left behind (Socrates is bald and snub-nosed; James is tall, blue-eyed, and hairy; Bill has a nose shaped like an eagle's beak and is short; etc.) and their *common* and *essential* nature is grasped: *human being.*

It remains to stress that for both Aristotle and St. Thomas we can say, think, or know anything only because of universal ideas derived from experience. It is only by such ideas and truths as man, animal, equality, red, that every event is caused, that the intellect can be guided amid the particularities, relativities, deceptions, and fluctuations of the sensible world. We begin, then, with the particular things we encounter in the sensible world. From these we derive universal concepts and principles. With our universal concepts and principles we are enabled to return to the sensible world and speak of it, think about it, and know it: "Socrates is a human being." These three stages of knowledge, according to Aristotle and St. Thomas, may be represented more vividly:

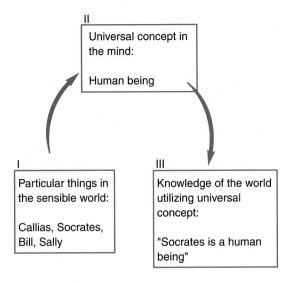

"What the mind thinks must be in it just as characters may be said to be on a writing-tablet on which as yet nothing actually stands written."

—Aristotle

"Nothing is in the intellect which was not first in the senses."

—St. Thomas

The following, from St. Thomas' *Summa Theologiae,* is brief but not easy. Try to see in it some of the above ideas at work, especially the movement: singular → universal → proposition. (In this quotation, "intelligible species" means the essence of a thing, and "phantasms" are the mental images of things.)

Our intellect cannot know the singular in material things directly and primarily. The reason for this is that the principle of singularity in material things is individual matter; whereas our intellect understands by abstracting the intelligible species from such matter. Now what is abstracted from individual matter is universal. Hence our intellect knows directly only universals. But indirectly, however, and as it were by a kind of reflexion, it can know the singular, because . . . even after abstracting the intelligible species, the intellect, in order to understand actually, needs to turn to the phantasms in which it understands the species. . . . Therefore it understands the universal directly through the intelligible species, and indirectly the singular represented by the phantasm. And thus it forms the proposition, "Socrates is a man."[2]

MODERN EMPIRICISM: LOCKE

It was the English philosopher John Locke (1632–1704) who laid the foundations of *modern* empiricism in his monumental *Essay Concerning Human Understanding,* published in 1690. Like Descartes, Locke was distressed over the muddles and uncertainties in metaphysics, theology, and moral philosophy. But unlike Descartes, who took the rationalistic method of geometry as his epistemological model, Locke took as his model the *experimental* methods of the new sciences, such as physics, astronomy, and medicine.

Locke begins on a negative note: a lengthy indictment of any theory of innate ideas. According to Locke, few philosophical theories are more firmly entrenched than the theory of innate ideas, which he characterizes as the belief that "there are in the understanding certain *innate principles;* some primary notions, *koinai ennoiai* [Greek: universal ideas], characters, as it were stamped upon the mind of man, which the soul receives in its very first

Locke's rejection of innate ideas

---

[2]St. Thomas Aquinas, *Summa Theologiae,* Pt. I, Qu. 86, Art. 1, in *Basic Writings of Saint Thomas Aquinas,* ed. Anton C. Pegis (Indianapolis, IN: Hackett, 1977), I.

being, and brings into the world with it."[3] He rejects the innateness of both "speculative" and "practical" principles, another way of saying "truths pertaining to reality and morality." In a word, Locke refutes the theory of innate ideas by charging that the arguments cited in support of it do not actually prove it, and that those who cite them do not pay sufficient attention to an altogether different and simpler explanation of the source of our ideas.

In the following excerpt he focuses on speculative principles, showing how innateness cannot be claimed even for the most certain of these, the Law of Identity and the Law of Non-Contradiction: Such principles are not universally agreed to, nor are they known by children, nor are they the products of reason. As with much of the quoted matter in this book, the following passages from Locke are classic statements and worthy of thoughtful scrutiny.

General Assent the Great Argument.

There is nothing more commonly taken for granted, than that there are certain principles, both *speculative* and *practical* (for they speak of both), universally agreed upon by all mankind; which therefore, they argue, must needs be the constant impressions which the soul of men receive in their first beings, and which they bring into the world with them, as necessarily and really as they do any of their inherent faculties.

Universal Consent Proves Nothing Innate.

This argument, drawn from universal consent, has this misfortune in it, that if it were true in matter of fact, that there were certain truths wherein all mankind agreed, it would not prove them innate, if there can be any other way shown, how men may come to that universal agreement in the things they do consent in; which I presume may be done.

"What Is, Is," and "It Is Impossible for the Same Thing to Be, and Not to Be," Not Universally Assented to.

But, which is worse, this argument of universal consent, which is made use of to prove innate principles, seems to me a demonstration that there are none such; because there are none to which all mankind give an universal assent. I shall begin with the speculative, and instance in those magnified principles of demonstration: "Whatsoever is, is," and "It is impossible for the same thing to be, and not to be," which, of all others, I think, have the most allowed title to innate. These have so settled a reputation of maxims universally received, that it will, no doubt, be thought strange if any one should seem to question it. But yet I take liberty to say, that these propositions are so far from having an universal assent, that there are a great part of mankind to whom they are not so much as known.

Not on the Mind, Naturally Imprinted, Because Not Known to Children, Idiots, Etc.

For, first, it is evident, that all children and idiots have not the least apprehension or thought of them: and the want of that is enough to destroy that universal assent,

---

[3]John Locke, *An Essay Concerning Human Understanding*, I, 2, 1, ed. A. S. Pringle-Pattison (London: Oxford University Press, 1924).

Title page of Locke's *Essay*. The influence of this
work on modern philosophy was monumental.

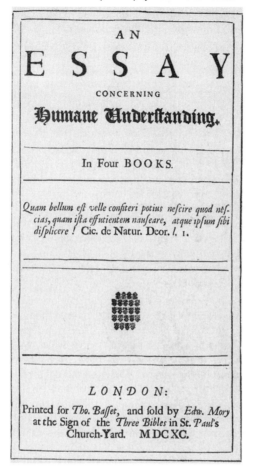

AN

E S S A Y

CONCERNING

Humane Underſtanding.

In Four BOOKS.

*Quam bellum eſt velle confiteri potius neſcire quod neſ-
cias, quam iſta effutientem nauſeare, atque ipſum ſibi
diſplicere !* Cic. de Natur. Deor. *l.* 1.

LONDON:

Printed for *Tho. Baſſet,* and ſold by *Edw. Mory*
at the Sign of the *Three Bibles* in St. *Paul's*
Church-Yard. M DC XC.

which must needs be the necessary concomitant of all innate truths: it seeming to me
near a contradiction to say, that there are truths imprinted on the soul which it perceives or understands not; imprinting, if it signify anything, being nothing else but the
making certain truths to be perceived. No proposition can be said to be in the mind
which it never yet knew, which it was never yet conscious of. . . . If truths can be
imprinted on the understanding without being perceived, I can see no difference there
can be between any truths the mind is capable of knowing in respect of their original:
they must all be innate, or all adventitious; in vain shall a man go about to distinguish
them. He therefore that talks of innate notions in the understanding, cannot (if he
intend thereby any distinct sort of truths) mean such truths to be in the understanding
as it never perceived, and is yet wholly ignorant of. For if these words "to be in the
understanding" have any propriety, they signify to be understood. If therefore these
two propositions: "Whatsoever is, is," and "It is impossible for the same thing to be,
and not to be," are by nature imprinted, children cannot be ignorant of them; infants,
and all that have souls, must necessarily have them in their understandings, know the
truth of them, and assent to it.

That Men Know Them When They Come to the Use of Reason, Answered.

To avoid this, it is usually answered, that all men know and *assent* to them, *when they come to the use of reason,* and this is enough to prove them innate. To apply this answer with any tolerable sense to our present purpose, it must signify one of these two things; either, that as soon as men come to the use of reason, these supposed native inscriptions come to be known and observed by them; or else, that the use and exercise of men's reasons assists them in the discovery of these principles, and certainly makes them known to them.

If Reason Discovered Them, That Would Not Prove Them Innate.

If they mean that by the *use of reason* men may discover these principles, and that this is sufficient to prove them innate, their way of arguing will stand thus: viz. That whatever truths reason can certainly discover to us, and make us firmly assent to, those are all naturally imprinted on the mind; and by this means there will be no difference between the maxims of the mathematicians and theorems they deduce from them: all must be equally allowed innate, they being all discoveries made by the use of reason, and truths that a rational creature may certainly come to know, if he apply his thoughts rightly that way.

It Is False That Reason Discovered Them.

But how can these men think the use of reason necessary to discover principles that are supposed innate, when reason (if we may believe them) is nothing else but the faculty of deducing unknown truths from principles or propositions that are already known? That certainly can never be thought innate which we have need of reason to discover, unless, as I have said, we will have all the certain truths that reason ever teaches us, to be innate. We may as well think the use of reason necessary to make our eyes discover visible objects, as that there should be need of reason, or the exercise thereof, to make the understanding see what is originally engraven in it. And I think those who give this answer will not be forward to affirm, that the knowledge of this maxim, "That it is impossible for the same thing to be, and not to be," is a deduction of our reason. For this would be to destroy that bounty of nature they seem so fond of, whilst they make the knowledge of those principles to depend on the labour of our thoughts. For all reasoning is search and casting about, and requires pains and application. And how can it with any tolerable sense be supposed, that what was imprinted by nature, as the foundation and guide of our reason, should need the use of reason to discover it?

Those who will take the pains to reflect with a little attention on the operations of the understanding, will find that this ready assent of the mind to some truths, depends not either on native inscription, or the use of reason, but on a faculty of the mind quite distinct from both of them, as we shall see hereafter.[4]

The source of ideas: experience

On the positive side, Locke is as explicit as one could hope for as to the actual origin of the ideas that undeniably exist in our minds: *experience.* But the next step is a little more subtle. For this experience takes two forms. First, there is what we might call the "external" experience by which objects in the external world, outside our minds, enter our minds through *sensation*—for

---

[4]Ibid., I, 2, 2–11.

example, hot, cold, red, yellow, hard, soft, sweet, and bitter. Second, there is the "internal" experience we have of the operations of our minds, or *reflection*—for example, thinking, willing, believing, doubting, affirming, denying, and comparing. Both of these are kinds of experience—reflection on what is going on inside no less than sensation of what is going on outside—and they are the two and only two means by which ideas become inscribed on the blank tablets of our minds. And just as the absence of ideas in infants is evidence against any doctrine of innate ideas, so the gradual development of ideas in children, corresponding to the development of their experience, is evidence for the empiricist doctrine that ideas originate in experience.

Two kinds
of experience:
sensation, reflection

Idea Is the Object of Thinking.

Every man being conscious to himself that he thinks, and that which his mind is applied about whilst thinking being the ideas that are there, it is past doubt that men have in their minds several ideas, such as are those expressed by the words, "whiteness, hardness, sweetness, thinking, motion, man, elephant, army, drunkenness," and others. It is in the first place then to be enquired, How he comes by them? I know it is a received doctrine, that men have native ideas and original characters stamped upon their minds in their very first being. This opinion I have at large examined already; and, I suppose, what I have said in the foregoing . . . will be much more easily admitted, when I have shown whence the understanding may get all the ideas it has, and by what ways and degrees they may come into the mind; for which I shall appeal to every one's own observation and experience.

All Ideas Come from Sensation or Reflection.

Let us then suppose the mind to be, as we say, white paper, void of all characters, without any ideas; how comes it to be furnished? Whence comes it by that vast store, which the busy and boundless fancy of man has painted on it with an almost endless variety? Whence has it all the materials of reason and knowledge? To this I answer, in one word, from EXPERIENCE; in that all our knowledge is founded, and from that it ultimately derives itself. Our observation, employed either about external sensible objects, or about the internal operations of our minds, perceived and reflected on by ourselves, is that which supplies our understandings with all the materials of thinking. These two are the fountains of knowledge, from whence all the ideas we have, or can naturally have, do spring.

The Objects of Sensation One Source of Ideas.

First, our senses, conversant about particular sensible objects, do convey into the mind several distinct perceptions of things, according to those various ways wherein those objects do affect them; and thus we come by those *ideas* we have of yellow, white, heat, cold, soft, hard, bitter, sweet, and all those which we call sensible qualities; which when I say the senses convey into the mind, I mean, they from external objects convey into the mind what produces there those perceptions. This great source of most of the ideas we have, depending wholly upon our senses, and derived by them to the understanding, I call, SENSATION.

The Operations of Our Minds the Other Source of Them.

Secondly, the other fountain, from which experience furnisheth the understanding with ideas, is the perception of the operations of our own minds within us, as it is employed about the ideas it has got; which operations when the soul comes to reflect on and consider, do furnish the understanding with another set of ideas which could not be had from things without: and such are perception, thinking, doubting, believing, reasoning, knowing, willing, and all the different actings of our own minds; which we being conscious of, and observing in ourselves, do from these receive into our understanding as distinct ideas, as we do from bodies affecting our senses. This source of ideas every man has wholly in himself: and though it be not sense, as having nothing to do with external objects, yet it is very like it, and might properly enough be called internal sense. But as I call the other Sensation, so I call this REFLECTION, the ideas it affords being such only as the mind gets by reflecting on its own operations within itself. By Reflection, then, in the following part of this discourse, I would be understood to mean that notice which the mind takes of its own operations, and the manner of them, by reason whereof there comes to be ideas of these operations in the understanding. These two, I say, viz., external material things as the objects of Sensation, and the operations of our own minds within as the objects of Reflection, are, to me, the only originals from whence all our ideas take their beginnings. The term *operations* here, I use in a large sense, as comprehending not barely the actions of the mind about its ideas, but some sort of passions arising sometimes from them, such as is the satisfaction or uneasiness arising from any thought.

All Our Ideas Are of the One or the Other of These.

The understanding seems to me not to have the least glimmering of any ideas which it doth not receive from one of these two. *External objects* furnish the mind with the ideas of sensible qualities, which are all those different perceptions they produce in us; and *the mind* furnishes the understanding with ideas of its own operations. These, when we have taken a full survey of them, and their several modes, combinations, and relations, we shall find to contain all our whole stock of ideas; and that we have nothing in our minds which did not come in one of these two ways. Let any one examine his own thoughts, and thoroughly search into his understanding, and then let him tell me, whether all the original ideas he has there, are any other than of the objects of his senses, or of the operations of his mind considered as objects of his reflection; and how great a mass of knowledge soever he imagines to be lodged there, he will, upon taking a strict view, see that he has not any idea in his mind but what one of these two have imprinted, though perhaps with infinite variety compounded and enlarged by the understanding, as we shall see hereafter.

Observable in Children.

He that attentively considers the state of a child at his first coming into the world, will have little reason to think him stored with plenty of ideas that are to be the matter of his future knowledge. It is by degrees he comes to be furnished with them: and though the ideas of obvious and familiar qualities imprint themselves before the memory begins to keep a register of time and order, yet it is often so late before some unusual qualities come in the way, that there are few men that cannot recollect the beginning of their acquaintance with them: and if it were worth while, no doubt a child might be so ordered as to have but a very few even of the ordinary ideas till he were grown up to a man. But all that are born into the world being surrounded with bodies that perpetually and diversely affect them, variety of ideas, whether care be taken about it or no, are imprinted on the minds of children. Light and colours are busy and at hand everywhere when the eye is but open; sounds and some tangible qualities fail not to solicit their proper senses, and force an entrance to the mind; but yet I think it will be granted easily, that if a child were kept in a place where he never saw any other but black and white till he were a man, he would have no more ideas of scarlet or green, than he that from his childhood never tasted an oyster or a pineapple has of those particular relishes.[5]

So far we have considered only the passive side of the mind, wherein it receives what Locke will now call the *simple* ideas contributed by sensation and reflection. It also has an active side, whereby it constructs *complex* ideas out of the simple ones, by means of combining, comparing, and abstracting.

The mind: both
passive and active

Uncompounded Appearances.

The better to understand the nature, manner, and extent of our knowledge, one thing is carefully to be observed concerning the ideas we have; and that is, that some of them are *simple,* and some *complex.*

Though the qualities that affect our senses are, in the things themselves, so united and blended that there is no separation, no distance between them; yet it is plain the ideas they produce in the mind enter by the senses simple and unmixed. For though the sight and touch often take in from the same object at the same time different ideas; as a man sees at once motion and colour, the hand feels softness and warmth in the same piece of wax; yet the simple ideas thus united in the same subject are as perfectly distinct as those that come in by different senses. The coldness and hardness which a man feels in a piece of ice being as distinct ideas in the mind as the smell and whiteness of a lily, or as the taste of sugar and smell of a rose; and there is nothing can be plainer to a man than the clear and distinct perception he has of those simple ideas; which, being each in itself uncompounded, contains in it nothing but one uniform appearance or conception in the mind, and is not distinguishable into different ideas.

The Mind Can Neither Make Nor Destroy Them.

These simple ideas, the materials of all our knowledge, are suggested and furnished to the mind only by those two ways above mentioned, viz., sensation and reflection. When the understanding is once stored with these simple ideas, it has the power to repeat, compare, and unite them, even to an almost infinite variety, and so can make at pleasure new complex ideas. But it is not in the power of the most exalted wit or enlarged understanding, by any quickness or variety of thought, to invent or frame one new simple idea in the mind, not taken in by the ways before mentioned; nor can any force of the understanding destroy those that are there. The dominion of man in this little world of his own understanding, being much-what the same as it is in the great world of visible things, wherein his power, however managed by art and skill, reaches no farther than to compound and divide the materials that are made to his hand, but can do nothing towards the making the least particle of new matter, or destroying one atom of what is already in being. The same inability will every one find in himself, who shall go about to fashion in his understanding any simple idea not received in by his senses from

---

[5]Ibid., II, 1, 1–6.

external objects, or by reflection from the operations of his own mind about them. I would have any one try to fancy any taste which had never affected his palate, or frame the idea of a scent he had never smelt: and when he can do this, I will also conclude, that a blind man hath ideas of colours, and a deaf man true distinct notions of sound. . . .

[Complex Ideas] Made by the Mind Out of Simple Ones.

We have hitherto considered those ideas, in the reception whereof the mind is only passive, which are those simple ones received from sensation and reflection before mentioned, whereof the mind cannot make one to itself, nor have any idea which does not wholly consist of them. [But as the mind is wholly passive in the reception of all its simple ideas, so it exerts several acts of its own, whereby out of its simple ideas, as the materials and foundations of the rest, the others are framed. The acts of the mind wherein it exerts its power over its simple ideas are chiefly these three: (1) Combining several simple ideas into one compound one; and thus all complex ideas are made. (2) The second is bringing two ideas, whether simple or complex, together, and setting them by one another, so as to take a view of them at once, without uniting them into one; by which it gets all its ideas of relations. (3) The third is separating them from all other ideas that accompany them in their real existence; this is called abstraction: and thus all its general ideas are made. This shows man's power and its way of operation to be much-what the same in the material and intellectual world. For, the materials in both being such as he has no power over, either to make or destroy, all that man can do is either to unite them together, or to set them by one another, or wholly separate them. I shall here begin with the first of these in the consideration of complex ideas, and come to the other two in their due places.] As simple ideas are observed to exist in several combinations united together, so the mind has a power to consider several of them united together as one idea; and that not only as they are united in external objects, but as itself has joined them. Ideas thus made up of several simple ones put together I call *complex;* such as are beauty, gratitude, a man, an army, the universe; which, though complicated of various simple ideas or complex ideas made up of simple ones, yet are, when the mind pleases, considered each by itself as one entire thing, and signified by one name.

Made Voluntarily.

In this faculty of repeating and joining together its ideas, the mind has great power in varying and multiplying the objects of its thoughts infinitely beyond what sensation or reflection furnished it with: but all this still confined to those simple ideas which it received from those two sources, and which are the ultimate materials of all its compositions. For simple ideas are all from things themselves; and of these the mind can have no more nor other than what are suggested to it. It can have no other ideas of sensible qualities than what come from without by the senses, nor any ideas of other kind of operations of thinking substance than what it finds in itself: but when it has once got these simple ideas, it is not confined barely to observation, and what offers itself from without; it can, by its own power, put together those ideas it has and make new complex ones which it never received so united.[6]

---

[6]Ibid., II, 2, 1–2; II, 12, 1–2.

The essential points in all of this may be summarized visually:

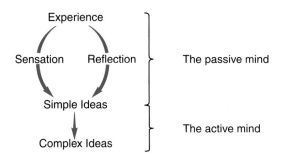

For Locke there are no innate ideas, of course, but there are innate faculties, powers of thinking, that work on simple ideas through combining, abstracting, and other processes to form complex ideas. Locke's theory of knowledge gets much more complicated, but this will suffice to show its empirical character and how it all gets off the ground.

Yet it is necessary to mention further features of Locke's theory. Perhaps more than anyone else, Locke emphasized what is sometimes called *epistemological dualism,* an idea that we encountered in our discussion of Berkeley's theory of reality. You will recall that this is the view that there are two factors involved in knowing: the mind, which does the knowing, and its ideas, which are known. That this is Locke's view is clear from repeated statements such as, ". . . the mind, in all its thoughts and reasonings, hath no other immediate object but its own ideas. . . ."[7] But, of course, there is a third factor—namely, the object in the external world that is known by means of ideas. That Locke blithely believed that our ideas *represent* those objects, and therefore really inform us about the external world, is clear from statements such as this:

*Epistemological
dualism*

> . . . simple ideas are not fictions of our fancies, but the natural and regular productions of things without us, really operating upon us; and so carry with them all the conformity which is intended, or which our state requires; for they represent to us things under those appearances which they are fitted to produce in us: whereby we are enabled to distinguish the sorts of particular substances, to discern the states they are in, and so to take them for our necessities, and apply them to our uses. And this conformity between our simple ideas and the existence of things is sufficient for real knowledge.[8]

Thus we have also what is sometimes called *representative perception,* the theory that our ideas correspond to and faithfully represent objects in the external world.

*Representative
perception*

So far so good. The trouble arises when we ask about this relation, or *correspondence,* of the perceived idea to anything "out there" in the external world. Any representative theory of knowledge, according to which the

[7]Ibid., IV, 1, 1.

[8]Ibid., IV, 4, 4.

THE EGOCENTRIC PREDICAMENT

Some philosophers claim that all we can know is our own ideas. But in this view we are trapped in the world of our own egos (or selves) and ideas. We could never get outside ourselves to verify whether ideas correspond to anything in the external world.

objects of the external world are represented to us by our ideas, immediately falls prey to the *egocentric predicament,* our hopeless inability to get outside our own minds and ideas. If all we can directly know is our own ideas (epistemological dualism), then how could we ever know whether our ideas correspond to anything, or even approximate anything, "out there" (representative theory of ideas)? Obviously, there is no standpoint from which we could look at an object in the external world and then look at our ideas in our minds, and announce: "Ah! They correspond. Our ideas really do represent things in the external world!" For in Locke's view, *all* we can perceive are *our own ideas.* That there *is* an external world we know from the passivity of our perceptions—our ideas simply *confront* us independently of our will. The question is: How do we know what it is *like*? Does this general theory end in a dismal skepticism about the things in the external world? How is the gap between the external world and our ideas of it to be overcome? This is a serious problem for anyone who holds both that all we can know is our own ideas and that our ideas represent the external world.

Berkeley was the immediate successor to Locke, and we saw in an earlier discussion how Berkeley solved this problem by means of his thoroughly idealist philosophy: We don't have to worry about any *correspondence* between ideas and things, because things *are* ideas; we don't have sensations *of* a table; the table *is* a sensation, or bundle of sensations, and there is no material substance, but only mental substance or mind. As before, this may strike you as an extreme position, but it is still not as extreme as what we are led to by the successor of Berkeley, David Hume.

RADICAL EMPIRICISM: HUME

The forms of empiricism that we have looked at so far might be called "mild" forms. In spite of their emphasis on sense experience, both Aristotle and St. Thomas believed that from experience we can nonetheless derive knowledge that is certain and universal, as with the principle of causality (every event must have a cause). Locke believed this also and, similar to Descartes, he believed that we can have a direct intuition of our own minds. Not so mild is the empiricism of the Scottish philosopher David Hume (1711–1776). It is, in fact, appropriately called *radical* empiricism.

It is important to follow the road from Locke to Berkeley to Hume: the three "British empiricists." Locke believed, as did Descartes, in two basic

David Hume, who carried British empiricism
to its skeptical conclusion

substances, mind and matter, though he confesses that while we have to believe in matter as something "out there" upholding the sensible qualities of things, we really cannot know what it is in itself; it is, Locke said, "something, I know not what." Berkeley followed Locke, but with his thoroughgoing idealist philosophy denied utterly the existence of matter, leaving only mind and its ideas. It remained for Hume to bring these ideas full circle to a kind of epistemological dead end.

Hume's understanding of how knowledge arises is similar to Locke's, but the terminology is somewhat different. All we have are *perceptions*. These, however, are to be divided between *impressions*, which are vivid or lively sensations, or the immediate data of experience, and *ideas*, which are sort of pale copies of impressions, and which provide the material for thinking. Hume goes on to distinguish between simple and complex perceptions (both impressions and ideas), but insists in any case on the priority of impressions over ideas: First, we have sensations, and then, second, we have ideas that are based on these sensations. The crucial point is that we have no ideas unless they are derived from impressions, and this brings us to the crunch. For in the derivation of all our ideas from sense data, Hume was much more rigorous or consistent or *radical* than either Locke or Berkeley. This radicalism shows up, first, in Hume's treatment of the idea of *substance*, both material substance in the external world and mental substance in the internal world.

It is natural to *believe* that there is Something, some mental substance, that underlies our intellectual activities: How can there be thinking and the like without something that *does* the thinking? Likewise, it is natural to *believe*

Perceptions =
impressions + ideas

Hume's analysis
of substance

Hume's "radical" empiricism is so-called because he applied the empiricist criterion of knowledge rigorously, consistently, and *exclusively.* Unlike previous empiricists, he allowed no rationalistic cracks or back doors: Our knowledge can extend absolutely no further than what is actually disclosed in sense experience.

that there is Something, some material substance, that underlies the sensible qualities in the external world: How can there be qualities without something that is *qualified?* But a "natural belief," as Hume calls it, for all its practical importance, is something very different from rational knowledge based on experience. Since we have no sense impressions whatsoever of substance, either external material substance or internal mental substance, we have no rational grounds at all for talk about matter or mind! Just as Berkeley dissolved Locke's material substance into a bundle of ideas (color, sound, taste), so Hume now dissolves Berkeley's mental substance, the "I," into a bundle of ideas. As Hume says, the dissolution of the one paves the way for the dissolution of the other. From *A Treatise of Human Nature:*

> Philosophers begin to be reconcil'd to the principle, *that we have no idea of external substance, distinct from the ideas of particular qualities.* This must pave the way for a like principle with regard to the mind, *that we have no notion of it, distinct from the particular perceptions.* . . .
>
> There are some philosophers, who imagine we are every moment intimately conscious of what we call our SELF; that we feel its existence and its continuance in existence; and are certain, beyond the evidence of a demonstration, both of its perfect identity and simplicity. The strongest sensation, the most violent passion, say they, instead of distracting us from this view, only fix it the more intensely, and make us consider their influence on *self* either by their pain or pleasure. To attempt a farther proof of this were to weaken its evidence; since no proof can be deriv'd from any fact, of which we are so intimately conscious; nor is there any thing, of which we can be certain, if we doubt of this.
>
> Unluckily all these positive assertions are contrary to that very experience, which is pleaded for them, nor have we any idea of *self,* after the manner it is here explain'd. For from what impression cou'd this idea be deriv'd? This question 'tis impossible to answer without a manifest contradiction and absurdity; and yet 'tis a question, which must necessarily be answer'd, if we wou'd have the idea of self pass for clear and intelligible. It must be some one impression, that gives rise to every real idea. But self or person is not any one impression, but that to which our several impressions and ideas are suppos'd to have a reference. If any impression gives rise to the idea of self, that impression must continue invariably the same, thro' the whole course of our lives; since self is suppos'd to exist after that manner. But there is no impression constant and invariable. Pain and pleasure, grief and joy, passions and sensations succeed each other, and never all exist at the same time. It cannot, therefore, be from any of these impressions, or from any other, that the idea of self is deriv'd; and consequently there is no such idea.
>
> But farther, what must become of all our particular perceptions upon this hypothesis? All these are different, and distinguishable, and separable from each other,

and may be separately consider'd, and may exist separately, and have no need of any thing to support their existence. After what manner, therefore, do they belong to self; and how are they connected with it? For my part, when I enter most intimately into what I call *myself*, I always stumble on some particular perception or other, of heat or cold, light or shade, love or hatred, pain or pleasure. I never can catch *myself* at any time without a perception, and never can observe any thing but the perception. When my perceptions are remov'd for any time, as by sound sleep; so long am I insensible of *myself*, and may truly be said not to exist. And were all my perceptions remov'd by death, and cou'd I neither think, nor feel, nor see, nor love, nor hate after the dissolution of my body, I shou'd be entirely annihilated, nor do I conceive what is farther requisite to make me a perfect non-entity. If any one upon serious and unprejudic'd reflexion, thinks he has a different notion of *himself*, I must confess I can reason no longer with him. All I can allow him is, that he may be in the right as well as I, and that we are essentially different in this particular. He may, perhaps, perceive something simple and continu'd, which he calls *himself*; tho' I am certain there is no such principle in me.

But setting aside some metaphysicians of this kind, I may venture to affirm of the rest of mankind, that they are nothing but a bundle or collection of different perceptions, which succeed each other with an inconceivable rapidity, and are in a perpetual flux and movement. Our eyes cannot turn in their sockets without varying our perceptions. Our thought is still more variable than our sight; and all our other senses and faculties contribute to this change; nor is there any single power of the soul, which remains unalterably the same, perhaps for one moment. The mind is a kind of theatre, where several perceptions successively make their appearance; pass, re-pass, glide away, and mingle in an infinite variety of postures and situations. There is properly no *simplicity* in it at one time, nor *identity* in different; whatever natural propension we may have to imagine that simplicity and identity. The comparison of the theatre must not mislead us. They are the successive perceptions only, that constitute the mind; nor have we the most distant notion of the place, where these scenes are represented, or of the materials, of which it is compos'd.[9]

What am I? I look within, in search of some enduring, stable reality—a self, an ego, an "I." But all I can come up with is a passing parade of perceptions. We have come a long way from Descartes', Locke's, and Berkeley's introspective intuition of mind, the mental substance!

But Hume is not through. The implications of his relentless and radical empiricism touch every aspect of philosophy. A second important example is the concept of *causality*. Again, do we not have a natural belief in a causal connection that binds things together in our experience? Is it not a universal and certain principle that every event must have a cause? Hume answers again: natural belief, Yes; rational knowledge, No. Look at your experience once more. What do you actually *perceive*? What are your *impressions*? Is it true that in a supposed causal relation, such as A causing B, we have a perception of A coming before B, and we have a perception of A standing next to B (or next to something that stands next to B), but none of this is sufficient to explain a real causal connection between A and B: A could be

Hume's analysis
of causality

[9]David Hume, *A Treatise of Human Nature*, ed. L. A. Selby-Bigge (London: Oxford University Press, 1888), pp. 251–253, 635.

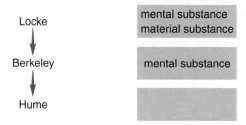

before B, and be next to B, but still not be the cause of B. What is required, in addition to temporal succession and spatial proximity, is a *necessary connection*. And *that* we *don't* perceive. It is a metaphysical figment without any rational justification whatsoever.

> The idea, then, of causation must be deriv'd from some *relation* among objects; and that relation we must now endeavour to discover. I find in the first place, that whatever objects are consider'd as causes or effects, are *contiguous;* and that nothing can operate in a time or place, which is ever so little remov'd from those of its existence. Tho' distant objects may sometimes seem productive of each other, they are commonly found upon examination to be link'd by a chain of causes, which are contiguous among themselves, and to the distant objects; and when in any particular instance we cannot discover this connexion, we still presume it to exist. We may therefore consider the relation of CONTIGUITY as essential to that of causation; at least may suppose it such, according to the general opinion, till we can find a more proper occasion to clear up this matter, by examining what objects are or are not susceptible of juxtaposition and conjunction.
>
> The second relation I shall observe as essential to causes and effects, is not so universally acknowledg'd, but is liable to some controversy. 'Tis that of PRIORITY of time in the cause before the effect. Some pretend that 'tis not absolutely necessary a cause shou'd precede its effect; but that any object or action, in the very first moment of its existence, may exert its productive quality, and give rise to another object or action, perfectly co-temporary with itself. But beside that experience in most instances seems to contradict his opinion, we may establish the relation of priority by a kind of inference or reasoning. 'Tis an establish'd maxim both in natural and moral philosophy, that an object, which exists for any time in its full perfection without producing another, is not its sole cause; but is assisted by some other principle, which pushes it from its state of inactivity, and makes it exert that energy, of which it was secretly possessed. Now if any cause may be perfectly co-temporary with its effect, 'tis certain, according to this maxim, that they must all of them be so; since any one of them, which retards its operation for a single moment, exerts not itself at that very individual time, in which it might have operated; and therefore is no proper cause. The consequence of this wou'd be no less than the destruction of that succession of causes, which we observe in the world; and indeed, the utter annihilation of time. For if one cause were co-temporary with its effect, and this effect with its effect, and so on, 'tis plain there wou'd be no such thing as succession, and all objects must be coexistent.
>
> If this argument appear satisfactory, 'tis well. If not, I beg the reader to allow me the same liberty, which I have us'd in the preceding case, of supposing it such. For he shall find, that the affair is of no great importance.

Having thus discover'd or suppos'd the two relations of *contiguity* and *succession* to be essential to causes and effects, I find I am stopt short, and can proceed no farther in considering any single instance of cause and effect. Motion in one body is regarded upon impulse as the cause of motion in another. When we consider these objects with the utmost attention, we find only that the one body approaches the other; and that the motion of it precedes that of the other, but without any sensible interval. 'Tis in vain to rack ourselves with *farther* thought and reflexion upon this subject. We can go no *farther* in considering this particular instance.

Shou'd any one leave this instance, and pretend to define a cause, by saying it is something productive of another, 'tis evident he wou'd say nothing. For what does he mean by *production*? Can he give any definition of it, that will not be the same with that of causation? If he can; I desire it may be produc'd. If he cannot; he here runs in a circle, and gives a synonimous term instead of a definition.

Shall we then rest contented with these two relations of contiguity and succession, as affording a complete idea of causation? By no means. An object may be contiguous and prior to another, without being consider'd as its cause. There is a NECESSARY CONNEXION to be taken into consideration; and that relation is of much greater importance, than any of the other two above-mention'd.

Here again I turn the object on all sides, in order to discover the nature of this necessary connexion, and find the impression, or impressions, from which its idea may be deriv'd. When I cast my eye on the *known qualities* of objects, I immediately discover that the relation of cause and effect depends not in the least on *them*. When I consider their *relations*, I can find none but those of contiguity and succession; which I have already regarded as imperfect and unsatisfactory.[10]

Hume's position is appropriately called *phenomenalism*. This is the view that all we can actually know is the phenomena or appearances (*phenomenon* means, literally, "an appearance") that are presented to us in our perceptions. For the time-honored view that substance (both material and mental) is a metaphysical entity and that causality is a metaphysical connection, the phenomenalist substitutes the view that they are no more than bundles of perceptions: colors, sounds, pains, pleasures, location, succession, and the like. These two pillars of traditional philosophizing now lay in dust before the chisel of Hume's phenomenalism.

Phenomenalism

If you find yourself thinking of Hume as a *skeptic*, you are right. Specifically, his is the sort of skepticism that denies that knowledge of metaphysical principles and relations is possible, or what we called in Chapter 7 "philosophical skepticism." Perhaps the best way of summarizing Hume's antimetaphysical skepticism is by means of his own derivation of all possible knowledge from two, and only two, sources: "relations of ideas" and "matters of fact." The following two paragraphs from Hume's *Enquiry Concerning Human Understanding* should be studied until the distinction is appreciated:

*"Relations of ideas"
and "matters of fact"*

All the objects of human reason or enquiry may naturally be divided into two kinds, to wit, *Relations of Ideas*, and *Matters of Fact*. Of the first kind are the sciences of Geometry, Algebra, and Arithmetic; and in short, every affirmation which is either intuitively or demonstratively certain. *That the square of the hypothenuse is equal to*

---

[10]Ibid., pp. 75–77 (slightly edited).

Hume's *Treatise of Human Nature* was first published in 1739. The disappointed Hume described it as having fallen "still-born from the press," so poor was the response to it. It was followed by the *Enquiry Concerning Human Understanding*.

A

T R E A T I S E

O F

Human Nature:

B E I N G

An ATTEMPT to introduce the experimental Method of Reaſoning

I N T O

MORAL SUBJECTS.

Rara temporum felicitas, ubi ſentire, quæ velis; & quæ
ſentias, dicere licet.　　　　　　TACIT.

BOOK I.

OF THE

U N D E R S T A N D I N G.

L O N D O N:
Printed for JOHN NOON, at the *White-Hart*, near
Mercer's-Chapel in *Cheapſide.*
MDCCXXXIX.

the square of the two sides, is a proposition which expresses a relation between these figures. *That three times five is equal to the half of thirty,* expresses a relation between these numbers. Propositions of this kind are discoverable by the mere operation of thought, without dependence on what is anywhere existent in the universe. Though there never were a circle or triangle in nature, the truths demonstrated by Euclid would for ever retain their certainty and evidence.

Matters of fact, which are the second objects of human reason, are not ascertained in the same manner; nor is our evidence of their truth, however great, of a like nature with the foregoing. The contrary of every matter of fact is still possible; because it can never imply a contradiction, and is conceived by the mind with the same facility and distinctness, as if ever so comfortable to reality. *That the sun will not rise to-morrow* is no less intelligible a proposition, and implies no more contradiction than the affirmation, *that it will rise.* We should in vain, therefore, attempt to demonstrate its falsehood. Were it demonstratively false, it would imply a contradiction, and could never be distinctly conceived by the mind.[11]

[11]David Hume, *An Enquiry Concerning Human Understanding,* in Hume's *Enquiries,* ed. L. A. Selby-Bigge, 2d ed. (Oxford: Clarendon Press, 1902), pp. 25–26.

PHENOMENALISM

The view that we have no rational knowledge beyond what is disclosed in the phenomena of perceptions. Mind, as far as it can be rationally known, is therefore merely a collection of perceptions.

Our knowledge is either based on *relations of ideas,* in which case it is certain but has no connection with reality, as with "three times five is equal to half of thirty," which, though absolutely certain, is absolutely certain independently of anything in the world of reality; *or* our knowledge is based on *matters of fact,* in which case it does inform us about the world of reality, as with "the sun will rise tomorrow," but can never be certain because it is derived from a limited and passing parade of perceptions. ("Relations of ideas" is a strange-sounding phrase. If it helps, draw the distinction between "matters of logic" and "matters of fact.")

This same skeptical and antimetaphysical distinction is restated in the celebrated outburst with which Hume concluded the *Enquiry:*

> When we run over libraries, persuaded of these principles, what havoc must we make? If we take in our hand any volume, of divinity or school metaphysics, for instance; let us ask, "Does it contain any abstract reasoning concerning quantity or number?" No. "Does it contain any experimental reasoning concerning matter of fact and existence?" No. Commit it then to the flames: for it can contain nothing but sophistry and illusion.[12]

It is difficult to overstate the depth of Hume's skepticism about knowledge. But note that he is only following empiricism to its logical conclusion. If *all knowledge* of reality must come from experience, then there are only two options. Either our ideas are certain but uninformative, or they are informative but never certain. And there we are stuck. But not for long.

---

[12]Ibid., p. 165.

HUME'S TWO BASES OF KNOWLEDGE

- *Relations of Ideas:* Ideas that simply by virtue of their meanings and relations are necessarily or *logically* true, but therefore irrelevant for the world of reality; for example, "The sum of the angles of a triangle equals 180 degrees."

- *Matters of Fact:* Ideas that bear upon and inform us about the world of reality, but that can never be certain because they are derived from specific experiences; for example, "Water freezes at 32 degrees Fahrenheit."

CHAPTER 9 IN REVIEW

SUMMARY

Empiricism is the epistemological claim that the mind at birth is a "blank tablet" and that all knowledge (exclusive of logical and mathematical knowledge) is derived ultimately from *sense experience*. In the previous chapter we considered three versions of rationalism, and in the present chapter we considered three versions of empiricism.

Classical empiricism has its origin in Greek philosophy and is most notably associated with Aristotle and, later, St. Thomas Aquinas. It will be recalled that Aristotle's is a Form-philosophy, wherein the object of knowledge is identified with the abiding essence of things. Unlike Plato, Aristotle believed that this essence is *in* particular things, and thus that it is with particular things that we must begin. From the particulars the mind is able to form a universal concept, which corresponds to the common essence in the particulars, and which guides knowledge and discourse amid the flux and multiplicity of the sensible world. St. Thomas introduced the intellectual faculty of abstraction, whereby the mind is enabled to lift the universal features from particulars, leaving behind in the particulars all that is not *essential* to them.

In some ways Locke is the giant of all empiricists, and certainly the one who set the empiricist agenda for the modern period. He began his famous *Essay Concerning Human Understanding* with a scathing rebuttal to the doctrine of innate ideas. In place of innate ideas Locke substitutes experience. This comes in two forms: sensation, our experience of external objects, and reflection, our experience of the internal workings of our minds. From sensation and reflection we form simple ideas, and from simple ideas the mind compounds complex ideas. In all of this the active and passive functions of the mind should be distinguished. Very important is Locke's epistemological or representative dualism, whereby our ideas are held to convey to us a likeness of the realities external to our minds: the perception of a tree, and the actual tree "out there." This, however, involves a great problem known as the egocentric predicament: If all we can know directly is our own ideas, how can we ever know whether they correspond to anything that is not an idea?

Locke believed in material and mental substance; Berkeley believed at least in mental substance; but Hume's *radical* empiricism pushes everything further. All we have are perceptions, divided into lively impressions and pale ideas; that's *all* we have. The time-honored concept of underlying but unperceived substance is, therefore, an unjustified figment, as is also the concept of causality, which, in its pre-Humean form, was thought to involve some unperceived metaphysical necessity. Hume's phenomenalism, which reduces knowledge to phenomena or appearances or "bundles of ideas," represents a serious skepticism: Either a proposition is a mere relation of ideas ("A is A"), which says nothing about reality itself, or it is a matter of fact ("Swans are white"), which can never be known with certitude because of the limitations of our perceptions.

BASIC IDEAS

- Empiricism
- *Tabula rasa*
- Universal concepts
- Intellectual abstraction
- Aristotle and St. Thomas: three stages of knowledge
- Locke's arguments against innate ideas
- Locke: experience, sensation, and reflection
- Simple and complex ideas
- The mind as passive and active
- Epistemological dualism, or the representative theory of knowledge
- The egocentric predicament
- Hume: perceptions, impressions, and ideas
- Hume's analysis of substance
- Hume's analysis of causality
- Phenomenalism
- Relations of ideas and matters of fact

TEST YOURSELF

1. True or false: Fido is an abstraction.
2. The impossibility of escaping the world of our own ideas is called _____.
3. Why does Hume have little time for talk about, say, "necessary connections" or substances?
4. Name a few of Locke's arguments against innate ideas.
5. Why, for St. Thomas, is the singular prior to the universal in one way, but the universal prior to the singular in another way?
6. What is the empiricist's attitude toward a claim such as "All barking dogs bark"?
7. What role does induction play in Aristotle's view of knowledge?
8. Who wrote *A Treatise of Human Nature*?
9. Why is Hume's empiricism called *radical* empiricism?
10. True or false: Locke, like Descartes, believed in mind or mental substance.

QUESTIONS FOR REFLECTION

- When considering thinkers who belong to the same traditions, such as the empiricist tradition, be able to identify what they hold in common and where they differ. Can you compare in this way the thinkers in this chapter?

- What do you yourself make of the egocentric predicament? Is it a genuine problem? If not, why not? If so, how do you propose to escape the skepticism inherent in it?
- What do you think about Hume's rejection of mind (as a mental substance) or causality (as a metaphysical connection)? Does it make any difference to your philosophical perspective? To your practical life?

FOR FURTHER READING

Robert R. Ammerman and Marcus G. Singer (eds.). *Belief, Knowledge, and Truth: Readings in the Theory of Knowledge.* New York: Scribners, 1970. A collection of traditional, recent, and important statements on all aspects of knowledge, including some encountered in our chapter.

Bruce Aune. *Rationalism, Empiricism, and Pragmatism: An Introduction.* New York: Random House, 1970. Chs. 2–3. Discussions oriented to beginners on "Hume and Empiricism" and "Contemporary Empiricism."

V. C. Chappel (ed.). *Hume: A Collection of Critical Essays.* Garden City, NY: Anchor Books, 1966. An anthology of advanced essays on Hume's philosophy, including issues considered in our chapter.

Frederick Copleston. *A History of Philosophy.* Baltimore: Newman Press, 1946–1974. I, Ch. 29; II, Ch. 38; V, Chs. 4–6 and 14–15. Authoritative accounts of the empiricist epistemologies of Aristotle, St. Thomas, Locke, and Hume, by a recognized historian of philosophy.

John Dunn. *Locke: A Very Short Introduction.* New York: Oxford University Press, 2003. The major historian of Locke provides a summary of his life and works.

A. C. Ewing. *The Fundamental Questions of Philosophy.* New York: Collier Books, 1962. Ch. 2. A beginner's discussion of the issue between rationalism and empiricism ("The 'A Priori' and the Empirical") by an intuitionist philosopher.

Antony Flew. *Hume's Philosophy of Belief: A Study of His First Inquiry.* London: Routledge & Kegan Paul, 1961. A standard treatment of the issues in Hume's *Enquiry,* including relations of ideas and matters of fact, the nature of empirical belief, the idea of necessary connection, and so on.

Etienne Gilson. *The Christian Philosophy of St. Thomas Aquinas,* tr. L. K. Shook. New York: Random House, 1956. Part II, Chs. 5–7. Technical treatments of St. Thomas's theory of knowledge, by a foremost Thomas authority.

E. J. Lowe. *Locke.* London: Routledge, 2005. Describes major problems in interpreting Locke's writing.

E. J. Lowe. *The Routledge Philosophy Guidebook to Locke on Human Understanding.* London: Routledge, 1995. A balanced and thorough introduction to Locke's theory of knowledge.

C. B. Martin and D. M. Armstrong (eds.). *Locke and Berkeley: A Collection of Critical Essays.* Garden City, NY: Anchor Books, 1968. An anthology that includes advanced discussions of some of Locke's positions encountered in our chapter.

Harold Morick (ed.). *Challenges to Empiricism.* Indianapolis: Hackett Publishing Co., 1980. Twelve contemporary thinkers criticize the fundamental empiricist thesis in relation to ontology, science, and linguistics.

Robert J. Swartz (ed.). *Perceiving, Sensing, and Knowing.* Garden City, NY: Anchor Books, 1965. A book of sometimes difficult readings from twentieth-century thinkers on perception and its role in the acquisition of knowledge.

*In addition, see the relevant articles ("Empiricism," "Phenomenalism," "Causation," "Aristotle," "Hume," etc.) in *Routledge Encyclopedia of Philosophy,* ed. Edward Craig (London: Routledge, 1998), and *Stanford Encyclopedia of Philosophy,* http://plato.stanford.edu.

THE PROBLEM OF CERTAINTY

We began this part of the book with a chapter on *doubt,* and it is fitting to conclude with a chapter on *certainty.* To see that certainty really does pose a problem, just ask yourself whether you are certain of any of the following propositions, and whether you are certain about them in different ways:

- 2 + 2 = 4.
- In fourteen hundred and ninety-two Columbus sailed the ocean blue.
- I exist.
- You exist.
- The sun will rise tomorrow.
- Right now I am perceiving this page.
- Barking dogs bark.
- Humans have evolved from lower animals.
- Every event must have a cause.

As you can see, the idea of certainty is not a simple one. In this chapter we will consider the problem in only one of its aspects, but, philosophically, a very basic one. Still more specifically, we will discuss one philosopher's attempt to account for certainty, especially in light of the preceding chapter. A warning: This may not be easy going, and the quoted material will be a good challenge.

KANT AND HUME

"I openly confess my recollection of David Hume was the very thing which many years ago first interrupted my dogmatic slumber and gave my investigations in the field of speculative philosophy a quite new direction."[1] Thus spoke the German philosopher Immanuel Kant[2] (1724–1804), who marks a turning point in modern epistemology.

Kant observed that there must be something radically wrong with the whole way of thinking that led finally to the phenomenalism and skepticism of Hume. For, Kant says, I *am* certain of some of the truths that Hume called "matters of fact." He cites, as an example from natural science, Newton's Third Law of Motion, that in all motion action and reaction must always be equal; and from metaphysics he cites the principle of causality, that every event must have a cause. For Kant it was not a question of *whether* we possess such knowledge but *how*. In his explanation of how propositions can be at once genuinely informative about reality *and* absolutely certain, Kant signals an altogether different approach to the problem, provides us with a sort of halfway point between rationalism and empiricism, and establishes himself as one of the greatest epistemologists of all time.

SOME IMPORTANT TERMINOLOGY

But, to begin at the beginning, it is necessary to study some terminology that Kant himself introduced into philosophical discussion.

A priori and *a posteriori* knowledge

First is the distinction between *a priori* knowledge and *a posteriori* knowledge. You can pretty much guess the meaning of these Latin terms just by looking at them. *A priori* knowledge is knowledge that comes before (prior to) sense experience and is therefore *independent* of sense experience. This, of course, is the emphasis of the rationalist. *A posteriori* knowledge is knowledge that comes after (posterior to) sense experience and is therefore *dependent* on sense experience. This is the empiricist emphasis.

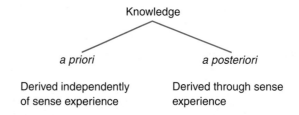

---

[1]Immanuel Kant, *Prolegomena to Any Future Metaphysics,* tr. Lewis W. Beck (Indianapolis: Bobbs-Merrill, 1950), p. 8.

[2]Rhymes with *font*.

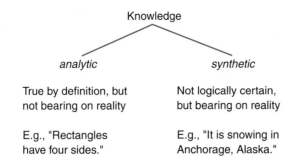

Second, we have the distinction between *analytic* and *synthetic* knowledge. Analytic knowledge is another way of expressing Hume's "relation of ideas." When this kind of knowledge is expressed in a proposition, the predicate is contained already in the subject. Examples are: "The sum of the angles of any triangle is 180 degrees"; "All bachelors are unmarried"; or any proposition where the predicate is contained already in the subject. Now all such knowledge or propositions "have to be true." For they are true by definition, or to say the same thing, they are *logically* true, and this means that you could not deny them without self-contradiction. (Such statements are sometimes called tautologies or redundancies.) Now no one questions the absolute truth of analytic propositions. Rationalists and empiricists alike agree that such propositions must be true no matter what. On the other hand, it is important to see that such truths do not really tell us anything about *reality.* They neither affirm nor deny the actual existence of anything. The proposition "All barking dogs bark" is necessarily true whether or not there are any dogs, or, for that matter, whether or not there is *anything.* A statement like "All barking dogs bark" only means "If there are any barking dogs, then they bark." The truth of these propositions is, then, *a priori* and utterly independent of sense experience and of the sensible world itself.

Synthetic knowledge, on the other hand, corresponds to Hume's "matters of fact." In synthetic propositions, the predicate *adds* something to the subject, and thus two ideas are "synthesized" in the proposition. Examples are: "Water freezes at 32 degrees Fahrenheit"; "Dogs bark"; and any proposition where the predicate amplifies the subject. In this way a synthetic proposition affirms or denies the existence of something (and is therefore sometimes called an "existential" proposition); it informs us about things; it really does tell us something about the actual universe.

IS THERE SYNTHETIC *A PRIORI* KNOWLEDGE?

Now we have just seen that everyone, rationalists and empiricists both, accepts the absolute truth of analytic propositions as *a priori* certain. It is also clear that few rationalists have ever insisted that sense experience plays absolutely no role *whatsoever* in the acquisition of synthetic knowledge. Just consider: Even if you are the staunchest rationalist, how do you know that swans are white? That in fourteen hundred and ninety-two Columbus sailed the ocean blue? Obviously there is much about the actual world that we could not possibly know except in an *a posteriori* way: making observations, lighting Bunsen burners, taking field trips, and the like. Everyone admits this.

It turns out then that both rationalists and empiricists accept analytic propositions as *a priori* certain, and that they both accept at least *some* synthetic propositions as *a posteriori* probable. The real question and the real issue between rationalists and empiricists is this: Can we possess any knowledge that is both *a priori* certain and synthetically informative? *Is there such a thing as synthetic* a priori *knowledge?* This is a crucial question, and how you answer it will make all the difference to your general philosophical perspective.

As we already have seen, Kant answered the question of synthetic *a priori* knowledge with a resounding Yes. But his explanation is hardly what traditional rationalists would have expected—or accepted. Kant turned the epistemological world upside down. In fact, he likened his contribution to the Copernican revolution, which, by radically shifting our viewpoint (the sun does not go around the earth, but the earth goes around the sun), resulted immediately in a superior explanation of the phenomena to be explained. Kant's "Copernican revolution" consisted, similarly, in the startling announcement that ideas such as substance and causality do not make their way into our minds through experience, but are "*a priori* categories of the understanding" that mold and shape and, in fact, *constitute* our experience. That is, substance and causality (along with ten additional categories) are *part* of what we *mean* by experience. Indeed, even space and time, in which substances standing in causal relations are enabled to appear at all, are contributed by our intellects. Space and time too, therefore, are *a priori* conditions of experience.

Kant's epistemology, then, was a complete reversal of previous theories. No longer do we form concepts based on our experience; rather, the concepts exist first and shape all of our experience.

In this way Kant redeems such principles as those of causality and substance from the skeptical clutches of Hume. As far as the world of appearance goes, "Every event must have a cause," for example, is a synthetic truth but also possesses *a priori* universality and necessity. We don't have any choice about it: We *have* to experience things as causally related because that

SYNTHETIC *A PRIORI*, A CRUCIAL QUESTION

One of the questions that divide philosophers into two different camps is the question of synthetic *a priori* knowledge: Is it possible to know synthetic propositions with *a priori* certainty? Are there any nonanalytic truths that are, nonetheless, universally and necessarily true?

KANT'S COPERNICAN REVOLUTION IN PHILOSOPHY

". . . the pure concepts of the understanding . . . do not derive from experience, but experience derives from them."

is one of the ways our minds *create* experience; if we're all wearing rose-colored glasses, everything must appear to be rose colored—to all of us. In the same way, for Kant, we all view the world through the mental categories of our understanding (such as causality), which shape how we see the world or experience it.

Kant's major work, the *Critique of Pure Reason,* was first published in 1781. In the following excerpts from the Introduction, Kant begins to explain in his own way the ideas we have already outlined. (1) He distinguishes between empirical or *a posteriori* knowledge derived from sense experience and pure or *a priori* knowledge, which is completely independent of experience, and he raises the question whether such pure knowledge exists; (2) he establishes the two identifying marks by which pure or *a priori* knowledge may be recognized and distinguished from empirical or *a posteriori* knowledge:

- Necessity
- Universality

(3) he distinguishes between analytic and synthetic propositions, and explains the nature of synthetic *a priori* knowledge both as being existentially informative and as bearing the marks of necessity and universality, something unaccountable for on the basis of experience.

Of the Difference Between Pure and Empirical Knowledge

That all our knowledge begins with experience there can be no doubt. For how should the faculty of knowledge be called into activity, if not by objects which affect our senses, and which either produce representations by themselves, or rouse the activity of our understanding to compare, to connect, or to separate them; and thus to convert the raw material of our sensuous impressions into a knowledge of objects, which we call experience? In respect of time, therefore, no knowledge within us is antecedent to experience, but all knowledge begins with it.

But although all our knowledge begins with experience, it does not follow that it arises from experience. For it is quite possible that even our empirical experience is a compound of that which we receive through impressions, and of that which our own faculty of knowledge (incited only by sensuous impressions), supplies from itself, a supplement which we do not distinguish from that raw material, until long practice has roused our attention and rendered us capable of separating one from the other.

It is therefore a question which deserves at least closer investigation, and cannot be disposed of at first sight, whether there exists a knowledge independent of experience, and even of all impressions of the senses? Such *knowledge* is called *a priori*, and distinguished from *empirical* knowledge, which has its sources *a posteriori*, that is, in experience.

We Are in Possession of Certain Cognitions *A Priori*, and Even the Ordinary Understanding Is Never Without Them

All depends here on a criterion, by which we may safely distinguish between pure and empirical knowledge. Now experience teaches us, no doubt, that something is so or so, but not that it cannot be different. *First,* then, if we have a proposition, which is thought, together with its necessity, we have a judgment *a priori;* and if, besides, it is not derived from any proposition, except such as is itself again considered as necessary, we have an absolutely *a priori* judgment. *Secondly,* experience never imparts to its judgments true or strict, but only assumed or relative universality (by means of induction), so that we ought always to say, so far as we have observed hitherto, there is no exception to this or that rule. If, therefore, a judgment is thought with strict universality, so that no exception is admitted as possible, it is not derived from experience, but valid absolutely *a priori*. . . . Necessity, therefore, and strict universality are safe criteria of knowledge *a priori,* and are inseparable one from the other. . . .

That these really exist in our knowledge such necessary, and in the strictest sense universal, and therefore pure judgments *a priori,* is easy to show. If we want a scientific example, we have only to look to any of the propositions of mathematics; if we want one from the sphere of the ordinary understanding, such a proposition as that each change must have a cause, will answer the purpose; nay, in the latter case, even the concept of cause contains so clearly the concept of the necessity of its connection with an effect, and of the strict universality of the rule, that it would be destroyed altogether if we attempted to derive it, as Hume does, from the frequent concomitancy of that which happens with that which precedes, and from a habit arising thence (therefore from a purely subjective necessity), of connecting representations. It is possible even, without having recourse to such examples in proof of the reality of pure propositions *a priori* within our knowledge, to prove their indispensability for the possibility of experience itself, thus proving it *a priori*. For whence should experience take its certainty, if all the rules which it follows were always again and again empirical, and therefore contingent and hardly fit to serve as first principles? For the present, however, we may be satisfied for having shown the pure employment of the faculty of our knowledge as a matter of fact, with the criteria of it.

Not only in judgments, however, but even in certain concepts, can we show their origin *a priori*. Take away, for example, from the concept of a body, as supplied by experience, everything that is empirical, one by one; such as colour, hardness or softness, weight, and even impenetrability, and there still remains the space which the body (now entirely vanished) occupied: that you cannot take away. And in the same manner, if you remove from your empirical concept of any object, corporeal or incorporeal, all properties which experience has taught you, you cannot take away from it that property by which you conceive it as a substance, or inherent in a substance (although such a concept contains more determinations than that of an object in general). Convinced, therefore, by the necessity with which that concept forces itself upon you, you will have to admit that it has its seat in your faculty of knowledge *a priori*. . . .

Of the Distinction Between Analytical and Synthetical Judgments

In all judgments in which there is a relation between subject and predicate (I speak of affirmative judgments only, the application to negative ones being easy), that relation can be of two kinds. Either the predicate B belongs to the subject A as something contained (though covertly) in the concept A; or B lies outside the sphere of the concept A, though somehow connected with it. In the former case I call the judgment analytical, in the latter synthetical. Analytical judgments (affirmative) are therefore those in which the connection of the predicate with the subject is conceived through identity, while others in which that connection is conceived without identity, may be called synthetical. The former might be called illustrating, the latter expanding judgments, because in the former nothing is added by the predicate to the concept of the subject, but the concept is only divided into its constituent concepts which were always conceived as existing within it, though confusedly; while the latter add to the concept of the subject a predicate not conceived as existing within it, and not to be extracted from it by any process of mere analysis. If I say, for instance, All bodies are extended, this is an analytical judgment. I need not go beyond the concept connected with the name of body, in order to find that extension is connected with it. I have only to analyze that concept and become conscious of the manifold elements always contained in it, in order to find that predicate. This is therefore an analytical judgment. But if I say, All bodies are heavy, the predicate is something quite different from what I think as the mere concept of body. The addition of such a predicate gives us a synthetical judgment. . . .

Empirical judgments, as such, are all synthetical; for it would be absurd to found an analytical judgment on experience, because, in order to form such a judgment, I need not at all step out of my concept, or appeal to the testimony of experience. That a body is extended, is a proposition perfectly certain *a priori*, and not an empirical judgment. For, before I call in experience, I am already in possession of all the conditions of my judgment in the concept of body itself. I have only to draw out from it, according to the principle of contradiction, the required predicate, and I thus become conscious, at the same time, of the necessity of the judgment, which experience could never teach me. But, though I do not include the predicate of gravity in the general concept of body, that concept, nevertheless, indicates an object of experience through one of its parts: so that I may add other parts also of the same experience, besides those which belonged to the former concept. I may, first, by an analytical process, realise the concept of body, through the predicates of extension, impermeability, form, etc., all of which are contained in it. Afterwards I expand my knowledge, and looking back to the experience from which my concept of body was abstracted, I find gravity always connected with the before-mentioned predicates, and therefore I add it synthetically to that concept as a predicate. It is, therefore, experience on which the possibility of the synthesis of the predicate of gravity with the concept of body is founded: because both concepts, though neither of them is contained in the other, belong to each other, though accidentally only, as parts of a whole, namely, of experience, which is itself a synthetical connection of intuitions.

In synthetical judgments *a priori*, however, that help is entirely wanting. If I want to go beyond the concept A in order to find another concept B connected with it, where is there anything on which I may rest and through which a synthesis might become possible, considering that I cannot have the advantage of looking about in the field of experience? Take the proposition that all which happens has its cause. In the concept of something that happens I no doubt conceive of something existing preceded by time, and from this certain analytical judgments may be deduced. But the concept of cause is entirely outside that concept, and indicates something different from that which happens, and is by no means contained in that representation. How can I venture then to predicate of that which happens something totally different from it, and to represent the concept of cause, though not contained in it, as belonging to it, and belonging to it by necessity? What is here the unknown *x*, on which the understanding may rest in order to find beyond the concept A a foreign predicate B, which nevertheless is believed to be connected with it? It cannot be experience, because the proposition that all which happens has its cause represents this second predicate as added to the subject not only with greater generality than experience can ever supply, but also with a character of necessity, and therefore purely *a priori,* and based on concepts. . . .[3]

Later in the *Critique*, Kant proposes *how* synthetic *a priori* knowledge is possible. Pay close attention to his insistence on the role of *a priori* concepts as conditions of experience and the epistemological consequences of this, as in the statement "If by them only it is possible to think any object of experience, it follows that they refer by necessity and *a priori* to all objects of experience." (By "intuition" Kant means the perception of objects as they are represented by the intellect.)

Two ways only are possible in which synthetical representations and their objects can agree, can refer to each other with necessity, and so to say meet each other. Either it is the object alone that makes the representation possible, or it is the representation alone that makes the object possible. In the former case their relation is empirical only, and the representation therefore never possible *a priori.* This applies to phenomena with reference to whatever in them belongs to sensation. In the latter case, though representation by itself (for we do not speak here of its causality by means of the will) cannot produce its object so far as its existence is concerned, nevertheless the representation determines the object *a priori,* if through it alone it is possible to know anything as an object. To know a thing as an object is possible only under two conditions. First, there must be intuition by which the object is given us, though as a phenomenon only, secondly, there must be a concept by which an object is thought as corresponding to that intuition. From what we have said before it is clear that the first condition, namely, that under which alone objects can be seen, exists, so far as the form of intuition is concerned, in the soul *a priori.* All phenomena therefore must conform to that formal condition of sensibility, because it is through it alone that they appear, that is, that they are given and empirically seen.

Now the question arises whether there are not also antecedent concepts *a priori,* forming conditions under which alone something can be, if not seen, yet thought as an object in general; for in that case all empirical knowledge of objects would necessarily conform to such concepts, it being impossible that anything should become an object of experience without them. All experience contains, besides the intuition of the senses by which something is given, a concept also of the object, which is given in intuition as a phenomenon. Such concepts of objects in general therefore must form conditions *a priori* of all knowledge produced by experience, and the objective validity of the categories, as being such concepts *a priori,* rests on this very fact that by them alone, so far as the form of thought is concerned, experience

---

[3]Immanuel Kant, *Critique of Pure Reason,* tr. F. Max Müller (Garden City, NY: Anchor Books, 1966), pp. 2–5, 7–9.

becomes possible. If by them only it is possible to think any object of experience, it follows that they refer by necessity and *a priori* to all objects of experience.

There is therefore a principle for the transcendental deduction of all concepts *a priori* which must guide the whole of our investigation, namely, that all must be recognised as conditions *a priori* of the possibility of experience, whether of intuition, which is found in it, or of thought. . . .[4]

Kant emphasizes that these innate concepts are essential for experience and are working prior to any sense experience. There can be no meaningful experiences without the concepts to filter, categorize, and even synthesize the raw material of the senses.

Kant goes on immediately to contrast his own theory of knowledge with that of his empiricist predecessors, Locke and Hume, and to show where they went wrong: *Locke* correctly recognized the existence of pure (necessary and universal) concepts but mistakenly sought them from sense experience and, at the same time, applied them *beyond* sense experience (for example, every event must have a cause, and God, a transcendent being, is the cause of the world); *Hume,* on the other hand, correctly saw that such concepts (necessary and universal) could not be derived from sense experience, and mistakenly denied that they are, after all, necessary and universal. Now, says Kant, neither Locke's "extravagance" nor Hume's "skepticism" squares with the epistemological facts (the givenness of synthetic *a priori* knowledge), whereas his own theory does account for the facts by steering a middle course between the false alternatives of his misguided predecessors.

Where Locke and
Hume went wrong

Locke, for want of this reflection, and because he met with pure concepts of the understanding in experience, derived them also from experience, and yet acted so *inconsistently* that he attempted to use them for knowledge which far exceeds all limits of experience. David Hume saw that, in order to be able to do this, these concepts ought to have their origin *a priori;* but as he could not explain how it was possible that the understanding should be constrained to think concepts, which by themselves are not united in the understanding, as necessarily united in the object, and never thought that possibly the understanding might itself, through these concepts, be the author of that experience in which its objects are found, he was driven by necessity to derive them from experience (namely, from a subjective necessity, produced by frequent association in experience, which at last is wrongly supposed to be *objective,* that is, from habit). He acted, however, very consistently, by declaring it to be impossible to go with these concepts, and with the principles arising from them, beyond the limits of experience. This empirical deduction, which was adopted by both philosophers, cannot be reconciled with the reality of our scientific knowledge *a priori,* namely, pure *mathematics* and *general natural science,* and is therefore refuted by facts. The former of these two celebrated men opened a wide door to *fantastic extravagance,* because reason, if it has once established such pretensions, can no longer be checked by vague praises of moderation; the other, thinking that he had once discovered so general an illusion of our faculty of knowledge, which had formerly been accepted as reason, gave himself over entirely to *scepticism.*[5]

[4]Ibid., pp. 72–73.
[5]Ibid., pp. 74–75.

"... although all our knowledge begins with experience, it does not follow that it arises from experience."

—Kant

THE LIMITS OF REASON

The noumenal and
phenomenal worlds

It is important to note, however, the high price that must be paid for synthetic *a priori* knowledge. One of the implications of Kant's analysis is that we can know nothing of reality as it is in itself (what Kant calls the *noumenal* world) but only as it appears to us through experience (he calls this the *phenomenal* world). The reason is clear: The *a priori* categories or concepts of the understanding are, as we have said, constitutive of our experience, and therefore they have no legitimate application *beyond* experience. Causality, for example, applies only to objects of possible experience. And when we try to apply such concepts beyond experience, what results is nonsense and absurdities.

This necessary limitation of the concepts of the understanding to the phenomenal world comes out well in the following from Kant's *Prolegomena to Any Future Metaphysics,* published in 1783 as a simplified version of the *Critique of Pure Reason.* (In these paragraphs, "intuition" again refers to what we normally might call perceptions, and the "Aesthetic" refers to a section of the *Critique.*)

Since the oldest days of philosophy, inquirers into pure reason have conceived, besides the things of sense, or appearances (*phenomena*), which make up the sensible world, certain beings of the understanding (*noumena*), which should constitute an intelligible world. And as appearance and illusion were by those men identified (a thing which we may well excuse in an undeveloped epoch), actuality was only conceded to the beings of the understanding.

And we indeed, rightly considering objects of sense as mere appearances, confess thereby that they are based upon a thing in itself, though we know not this thing as it is in itself but only know its appearances, namely, the way in which our senses are affected by this unknown something. The understanding, therefore, by assuming appearances, grants the existence of things in themselves also; and to this extent we may say that the representation of such things as are the basis of appearances, consequently of mere beings of the understanding, is not only admissible but unavoidable.

Our critical deduction by no means excludes things of that sort (*noumena*), but rather limits the principles of the Aesthetic to this, that they shall not extend to all things—as everything would then be turned into mere appearance—but that they shall hold good only of objects of possible experience. Hereby, then, beings of the understanding are granted, but with the inculcation of this rule which admits of no exception: that we neither know nor can know anything at all definite of these pure beings of the understanding, because our pure concepts of the understanding as well as our pure intuitions extend to nothing but objects of possible experience,

- *What we gain through Kant's theoretical reason: a priori* certainty and universality of fundamental concepts, such as causality and substance.
- *What we lose through Kant's theoretical reason:* the possibility of any theoretical knowledge of reality beyond objects of possible experience.

consequently to mere things of sense; and as soon as we leave this sphere, these concepts retain no meaning whatever.[6]

Thus, if we have gained *a priori* certainty and universality for synthetic knowledge, it has been at the cost of giving up any knowledge of reality beyond space and time. We will see in Chapter 11 that for Kant this included, naturally, God. Though seemingly a big loss, Kant actually saw this limitation on reason as good news, not bad. It is precisely the absence of knowledge of the noumenal world, including God and the divine, that makes room for faith. In his famous *Critique of Pure Reason*, Kant says it explicitly: "I have therefore found it necessary to deny *knowledge,* in order to make room for *faith*."[7] Kant believed that in addition to the "theoretical" reason, which is guided and limited by the *a priori* concepts of the understanding, there is open to us the "practical" reason, which builds on the entirely different foundation of *moral* experience, and which *does* give us, in a way, knowledge of God, freedom, and immortality. In Chapter 12, we will encounter Kant's Moral Argument for God.

The "theoretical" and the "practical" reason

CHAPTER 10 IN REVIEW
SUMMARY

In Chapter 9 we saw how the skeptical Hume brought traditional thinking about knowledge to a sort of dead end. This is precisely where Kant began.

Unlike Hume, Kant was certain of many truths of the sort Hume rejected—for example, that every event must have a cause. According to Kant, the universality and necessity that characterize such truths cannot be accounted for on empiricist, or *a posteriori*, grounds and require, rather, an *a priori* origin. On the other hand, such truths are not analytic, or empty redundancies, but synthetic, or existential. But how is synthetic *a priori* knowledge possible? Kant himself rightly regarded his answer as a revolution in epistemology, and even now one frequently encounters the expressions "pre-Kantian" and "post-Kantian" as demarcations of a watershed in the history of philosophy.

Kant distinguished between things as they are in themselves (the noumenal world) and things as they appear to us (the phenomenal world).

[6]Kant, *Prolegomena to Any Future Metaphysics*, pp. 61–62.
[7]Kant, *Critique of Pure Reason*, tr. Norman Kemp Smith (New York: St. Martin's Press, 1965).

Things-in-themselves are wholly unknown to us. Things-as-they-appear (that is, experience) are made possible first of all by the *a priori* conditions of space and time, and then by the *a priori* categories of the understanding, which further structure our experience into the world that we apprehend. It is crucial to see how Kant, with this reinterpretation of the origin and nature of knowledge, accounts for synthetic *a priori* knowledge. For example, *every* event *must* have a cause, because that is the only way in which our intellects work. On the other hand, this means that our "theoretical" reason, operating with substance, causality, and the like, has proper application only to objects of possible experience. And *this* means that we can have no theoretical knowledge of anything *beyond* experience. For such knowledge we must have recourse to an entirely different kind of reason, the "practical" reason, which begins not with experiential categories but with moral categories.

BASIC IDEAS

- Kant's rejection of Humean skepticism
- *A priori* and *a posteriori* knowledge
- Analytic and synthetic knowledge
- Synthetic *a priori* knowledge
- Kant's "Copernican revolution" in philosophy
- Space and time as *a priori* conditions of experience
- The categories of the understanding as conditions of experience
- The noumenal and phenomenal worlds
- The theoretical reason and the practical reason
- The limitations of theoretical reason

TEST YOURSELF

1. How did Hume awaken Kant out of his "dogmatic slumbers"?
2. Which of these is an analytic claim? (a) It is wrong to kill someone for the fun of it; (b) It is wrong to murder someone. Why?
3. True or false: Kant believed that "Every event must have a cause" is an example of a synthetic *a priori* proposition.
4. In what way was Kant's revolution in epistemology similar to Copernicus' revolution in astronomy?
5. True or false: In Kant's terminology, the "theoretical" reason is limited to objects of sense experience.
6. What is a "category of the understanding"? An obvious example is _____.
7. How did Kant account for synthetic *a priori* knowledge?

QUESTIONS FOR REFLECTION

- It would be a mistake to call Kant either a rationalist or an empiricist. Do you see why? On the other hand, he effected a sort of synthesis of the two. What is the rationalist element? What is the empiricist element?

- With his doctrine of the *a priori* conditions of experience, Kant sought to explain how we enjoy certitude of certain important claims. What are some of these claims? Are *you* certain of them? If not, are you a skeptic? If so, how do *you* account for the certainty?

FOR FURTHER READING

Henry E. Allison. *Kant's Transcendental Idealism: An Interpretation and Defense.* Revised edition. New Haven, CT: Yale University Press, 2004. A robust defense of Kant's theory of knowledge.

Frederick Copleston. *A History of Philosophy.* Baltimore: Newman Press, 1946–1974. VI, Chs. 11–12. An authoritative account of Kant's theory of knowledge, by a recognized historian of philosophy.

A. C. Ewing. *Idealism: A Critical Survey.* London: Methuen, 1934. Ch. 3. A good summary account of Kant's metaphysics and epistemology, including his solution to the problem of synthetic *a priori* knowledge.

A. C. Ewing. *A Short Commentary on Kant's Critique of Pure Reason.* Second ed. London: Methuen, 1950. A comprehensible commentary on an incomprehensible book, along with a highly instructive introduction.

Paul Guyer. *Kant,* The Routledge Philosophers. London: Routledge, 2006. Interpretation and analysis covering the full range of Kant's philosophical system.

Justus Hartnack. *Kant's Theory of Knowledge.* Tr. M. Holmes Hartshorne. New York: Harcourt, Brace & World, 1967. A highly useful and lucid summary of the *Critique of Pure Reason.*

H. A. Prichard. *Kant's Theory of Knowledge.* Oxford: Clarendon Press, 1909. An old but useful exposition of Kant's epistemology, with special reference to the *Critique of Pure Reason,* by an important twentieth-century philosopher.

Roger Scruton. *Kant: A Very Short Introduction.* New York: Oxford University Press, 2001. An accessible introduction to the philosophy of this challenging thinker.

W. H. Werkmeister. *Kant: The Architectonic and Development of His Philosophy.* La Salle, IL: Open Court, 1980. Ch. 5. A recent, learned, concentrated, and understandable treatment of Kant's theory of knowledge, by an esteemed Kant scholar.

Robert Paul Wolff. *Kant: A Collection of Critical Essays.* Garden City, NY: Anchor Books, 1967. An anthology of advanced discussions of various aspects of Kant's philosophy, including epistemological issues.

Allen W. Wood. *Kant,* Blackwell Great Minds. Malden, MA: Blackwell, 2004. A concise and insightful overview of Kant's life and work by a major scholar.

*In addition, see the relevant articles ("Certainty," "Synthetic and Analytic Statements," "Kant," etc.) in *Routledge Encyclopedia of Philosophy,* ed. Edward Craig (London: Routledge, 1998), and *Stanford Encyclopedia of Philosophy,* http://plato.stanford.edu.

PART THREE

THE QUESTION OF GOD

When Mark Twain was once traveling abroad he received news of a mistaken obituary back in the United States giving notice of his death. He sent back the message: "Reports of my death are greatly exaggerated." In the last century the German philosopher Friedrich Nietzsche boldly proclaimed, "God is dead." Again in the 1960s the proclamation was issued by the Death of God theologians. They were not the only ones (nor will they be the last) to give, in one way or another, notice of the demise of the deity, but many would insist that in every case the report has been greatly exaggerated. As the well-known piece of graffiti expresses it:

> GOD IS DEAD!
> —Nietzsche
>
> NIETZSCHE IS DEAD!
> —God

Certainly it is true that God is alive and well if the continuing interest in and discussion of God are any indication.

Still, some may sense a difference with the question of God. It has something to do with the fact that our society is such a melting pot of religious and anti-religious views. Even under "Churches" the yellow pages list, side by side, everything from Methodists, Baptists, Lutherans, and Catholics, to the Congregation of the Kindred Spirits, the Church of Good Science, and the Homosexual Church of the Universe. The difference also has to do with the sometimes passionate nature of belief or disbelief. How many times have we all heard it said

that friends should never talk about religion or politics lest they suddenly find themselves friends no longer? It is true that arguments over religion can become the most heated and can bring out the worst in all participants—atheists no less than believers. This is just to say that here, perhaps more than anywhere else, a special plea must be issued for identifying and laying aside (as best we can) prejudices, mental blind spots, and wishful thinking.

What we have called here "the question of God" actually includes much more than just God. The following are only some of the issues that are usually encompassed in what is known as "philosophy of religion" or, perhaps better, "philosophical theology":

- What does "God" mean?
- Can the existence of God be proven?
- What is the relation between God and morality?
- How does philosophical knowledge of God relate to divine revelation?
- What are the nature and relevance of religious faith?
- Does God care about the world?
- Are religious experiences relevant data for the existence of God?
- Can an all-powerful and all-loving God be reconciled with the evil in the world?
- Do we have immortal souls?
- What are the special features of religious language?

Obviously such issues overlap with metaphysical and epistemological issues. Nonetheless, there is here an identifiable core of connected issues. At the center lies the specific question of God, and radiating from that, all sorts of related questions. And a whole history of philosophy could be written around the question of God and related matters, which only shows that it must be one of the questions that matter.

CHAPTER **11**

GOD AND THE WORLD

It makes sense, of course, that the question of God's existence should come first in discussions concerning God and related matters. For, as St. Thomas Aquinas says near the beginning of his multivolumed *Summa Contra Gentiles,* if we don't first establish that he at least exists, then there is no point in going on:

> Now, among the inquiries that we must undertake concerning God in Himself, we must set down in the beginning that whereby His Existence is demonstrated, as the necessary foundation of the whole work. For, if we do not demonstrate that God exists, all consideration of divine things is necessarily suppressed.[1]

In this chapter and the next, we too will raise the question of God's existence, and we will consider some of the best-known arguments, pro and con.

NATURAL THEOLOGY

Before really getting into the arguments for God, the idea of *natural theology* must be introduced. First, what is *theology*? "Theology" comes from the Greek word *theos,* which means "God." Theology is therefore the study or

---

[1]St. Thomas Aquinas, *Summa Contra Gentiles,* I. 9, 5, tr. and ed. Anton C. Pegis (South Bend, IN: Notre Dame University Press, 1955), I.

What is
natural theology?

Humanity in search
of God, and God in
search of humanity

science or knowledge of God. What then is *natural* theology? Caution: It does *not* mean the study or science or knowledge of God through *nature*. It is true that some of the arguments for God are based on the physical world, but we will see too that many are not. Natural theology is the study or science or knowledge of God through the *natural intellect*. This means the intellect in its natural state, unaided by any special or supernatural input. It may be helpful to know that natural theology is sometimes known also by the less ambiguous labels *philosophical theology* and *rational theology*.

Natural theology is therefore to be distinguished from *revealed theology*, which means the knowledge of God through special revelation, such as the Bible, the Church, Moses, Christ, the Holy Spirit, and the like. If it is not overly simplistic, we may say that in natural theology people attempt through their own natural faculties to approach God, whereas in revealed theology God has in his own special way approached humanity:

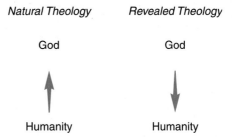

It is important to note, though, that those who accept both natural and revealed theology do not confuse what people do in natural theology with what God does in revealed theology. Natural theology, if successful, delivers some basic knowledge of God that may bear on people's philosophical life, such as knowledge of God's existence and perhaps something of his nature. But revealed theology, if true, delivers a knowledge that bears on human *salvation*. This was the point of the quip by Søren Kierkegaard (Danish philosopher of about 1850) that "to stand on one leg and prove God's existence is a very different thing from going on one's knees and thanking him," or from the exclamation of Tertullian (Church Father of about 200), "What has Athens to do with Jerusalem? What has the Academy to do with the Church?" or the distinction made by Blaise Pascal (French philosopher of about 1650) between "the God of the philosophers, and the God of Abraham, Isaac, and

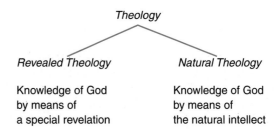

SOME DIFFERING CONCEPTIONS OF FAITH

Hebrews 11:1
"Faith is the substance of things hoped for, the evidence of things not seen."
(King James Version)

Random House Dictionary
"Confidence or trust in a person or thing."*

Søren Kierkegaard
"An objective uncertainty held fast in an appropriation-process of the most passionate inwardness."†

Paul Tillich
"Faith as the ultimate concern is an act of the total personality."‡

John Locke
"Faith...is the assent to any proposition, not...made out by the deductions of reason, but upon the credit of the proposer, as coming from God, in some extraordinary way of communication."§

St. Thomas
"...an act of the intellect assenting to the truth at the command of the will."‖

Blaise Pascal
"It is the heart which experiences God, and not the reason. This, then, is faith: God felt by the heart, not by reason."#

William James
"...our right to adopt a believing attitude in religious matters, in spite of the fact that our merely logical intellect may not have been coerced."**

A schoolboy
"Faith is believing what you know ain't true."

---

*Random House Dictionary of the English Language, College Edition (New York: Random House, 1968).
†Søren Kierkegaard, *Concluding Unscientific Postscript,* tr. David F. Swenson and Walter Lowrie (Princeton, NJ: Princeton University Press), p. 182.
‡Paul Tillich, *Dynamics of Faith* (San Francisco: Harper & Row, 1957), p. 4.
§John Locke, *An Essay Concerning Human Understanding,* ed. Alexander Campbell Fraser (New York: Dover, 1959) II, 416.
‖St. Thomas, *Summa Theologiae,* II–II, Qu. 4, Art. 5, in *Basic Writings of St. Thomas Aquinas,* ed. Anton C. Pegis (New York: Random House, 1945), II.
#Blaise Pascal, *Pensées,* tr. W. F. Trotter (London: Dent, 1908), no. 278.
**William James, *The Will to Believe and Other Essays* (New York: Longmans, Green & Co., 1896), p. 1.

Jacob." Indeed, a whole string of thinkers has repudiated as irrelevant if not misguided the philosophical or rational approach to God in favor of the approach through *faith.* (By the way, what *is* faith anyway?)

As usual, however, such a distinction as that between natural and revealed theology is not as neat and tidy as one might wish, and in the

IS BELIEF IN GOD "PROPERLY BASIC"?

Some recent philosophers (including Alvin Plantinga, William Alston, Nicholas Woltersdorff, and others) have introduced what they call "reformed epistemology" and have argued that belief in God is a "properly basic" belief—that is, a belief that may be accepted immediately, without evidence, as with "2 + 2 = 4," "The world has existed for longer than five minutes," "I had breakfast this morning," and "It is wrong to kill people for the fun of it." This of course does not mean that belief in God can be arbitrary or unjustified any more than any other properly basic beliefs, and this is where reformed epistemology comes in. These thinkers find in the sixteenth-century Protestant reformer John Calvin an account of a possible and appropriate ground for the properly basic belief in God:

> There is within the human mind, and indeed by natural instinct, an awareness of divinity....God himself has implanted in all men a certain understanding of his divine majesty....men one and all perceive that there is a God and that he is their maker.*

Belief in God may be embraced apart from rational evidence, and at the same time be justified as a natural disposition implanted in the soul by God himself.

*John Calvin, *Institutes of the Christian Religion,* tr. Ford Lewis Battles (Philadelphia: Westminster Press, 1960), I, 43–44.

actual history of philosophy and theology they have tended to blur into one another. This is not surprising in view of the fact that most philosophers who have propounded arguments for God's existence have already believed in divine revelation while at the same time believing that it is useful to demonstrate and understand through reason what they had already accepted through faith. Still, the distinction is an important and helpful one, and natural theology must be distinguished and understood. For, as we have seen, natural theology is itself a philosophical problem. Further, while some have rejected such (natural) knowledge of God, it has obviously not been rejected by those who have presented philosophical arguments for God's existence. Which brings us to...

THE COSMOLOGICAL ARGUMENT

A priori and
a posteriori
arguments

Many arguments for the existence of God have been formulated over the centuries. Here we will consider four of them, surely the most important: the Cosmological, Teleological, Ontological, and Moral Arguments for the existence of God. It is convenient, further, to divide these into two groups: The Cosmological and Teleological Arguments are *a posteriori*, and the

Title page of a Latin Bible printed in Basel, and bearing
the handwritten notations of Martin Luther, the great
sixteenth-century reformer, who took a very dim view
of *natural* theology, knowledge of God through reason.
Many who believe in *revealed* theology find the
revelation in sacred scriptures, such as the Bible.

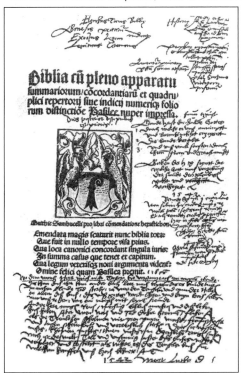

Ontological and Moral Arguments are *a priori.* From earlier encounters with
these expressions we know immediately that the first two arguments will
attempt to demonstrate the existence of God *by means of sense experience,*
whereas the second two arguments will attempt to demonstrate God *independently of sense experience*—that is, through reason alone. In this chapter
we will consider the *a posteriori* proofs.

The most familiar attempts to prove the existence of God are variations
of the *Cosmological Argument.* How many times have you heard something
like this: "There has to be a God, because, well, the universe couldn't just

The Cosmological
Argument stated

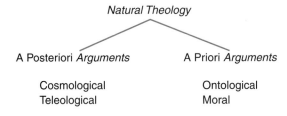

Natural Theology

A Posteriori *Arguments*   A Priori *Arguments*

Cosmological   Ontological
Teleological   Moral

happen. Do you think things just popped into being from *nowhere*? There must be a first cause of everything." This may not be the most sophisticated reasoning in the world, but it *is* a thumbnail expression of the Cosmological Argument. Why is this argument called "cosmological"? Because it is based on the *kosmos,* the Greek word for *world.* Of course, "world" means here not just the earth but the whole physical universe, or the sum total of space and time. It is also called, for short, the First-Cause Argument, since it attempts to show that there must be a first cause of the world.

The Cosmological Argument has been propounded by numerous thinkers and in various forms down through the ages, but most formulations of it involve the following reasoning:

1. Here is the world, or space and time.
2. It could not be the cause of itself.
3. It could not come from nothing.
4. It could not be an effect in an infinite series of causes and effects.
5. Therefore, it must be caused by something outside space and time, something uncaused and ultimate.

Stated in this way, it begins with the fact of the physical world and then by a process of elimination arrives at the only possible explanation for it: God, or the First Cause. But why cannot something be the cause of itself? Why cannot something come from nothing? Why cannot something be the final effect in an infinite series of causes and effects?

These are, indeed, difficult questions. They are addressed, or at least involved, in the most famous proofs for God ever formulated, the "Five Ways" of St. Thomas Aquinas. He presents them in his *Summa Theologiae:*

The "Five Ways" of St. Thomas

The existence of God can be proved in five ways.

The first and more manifest way is the argument from motion. It is certain, and evident to our senses, that in the world some things are in motion. Now whatever is moved is moved by another, for nothing can be moved except it is in potentiality to that towards which it is moved; whereas a thing moves inasmuch as it is in act. For motion is nothing else than the reduction of something from potentiality to actuality. But nothing can be reduced from potentiality to actuality, except by something in a state of actuality. Thus that which is actually hot, as fire, makes wood, which is potentially hot, to be actually hot, and thereby moves and changes it. Now it is not possible that the same thing should be at once in actuality and potentiality in the same respect, but only in different respects. For what is actually hot cannot simultaneously be potentially hot; but it is simultaneously potentially cold. It is therefore impossible that in the same respect and in the same way a thing should be both mover and moved, i.e., that it should move itself. Therefore, whatever is moved must be moved by another. If that by which it is moved be itself moved, then this also must needs be moved by another, and that by another again. But this cannot go on to infinity, because then there would be no first mover, and, consequently, no other mover, seeing that subsequent movers move only inasmuch as they are moved by the first mover; as the staff moves only because it is moved by the hand. Therefore it is necessary to arrive at a first mover, moved by no other; and this everyone understands to be God.

THE COSMOLOGICAL ARGUMENT

All Cosmological Arguments for God may be expressed as follows:

All contingent (or caused) being depends for its existence on some
  uncaused being.
The cosmos is a contingent being.

Therefore, the cosmos depends for its existence on some uncaused being.

As always, no conclusion in a deductive argument can be stronger than the
premises. What questions, doubts, or challenges might be raised against the
premises here? And does the "being" of the conclusion have to mean *God*?

The second way is from the nature of efficient cause. In the world of sensible
things we find there is an order of efficient causes. There is no case known (neither
is it, indeed, possible) in which a thing is found to be the efficient cause of itself;
for so it would be prior to itself, which is impossible. Now in efficient causes it is
not possible to go on to infinity, because in all efficient causes following in order,
the first is the cause of the intermediate cause, and the intermediate is the cause
of the ultimate cause, whether the intermediate cause be several, or one only.
Now to take away the cause is to take away the effect. Therefore, if there be no
first cause among efficient causes, there will be no ultimate, nor any intermediate,
cause. But if in efficient causes it is possible to go on to infinity, there will be no
first efficient cause, neither will there be an ultimate effect, nor any intermediate
efficient causes; all of which is plainly false. Therefore it is necessary to admit a
first efficient cause, to which everyone gives the name of God.

The third way is taken from possibility and necessity, and runs thus. We find
in nature things that are possible to be and not to be, since they are found to be
generated, and to be corrupted, and consequently, it is possible for them to be
and not to be. But it is impossible for all things which are, to be of this sort,[2] for
that which can not-be at some time is not. Therefore, if everything can not-be, then
at one time there was nothing in existence. Now if this were true, even now there
would be nothing in existence, because that which does not exist begins to exist
only through something already existing. Therefore, if at one time nothing was
in existence, it would have been impossible for anything to have begun to exist;
and thus even now nothing would be in existence—which is absurd. Therefore,
not all beings are merely possible, but there must exist something the existence
of which is necessary. But every necessary thing either has its necessity caused
by another, or not. Now it is impossible to go on to infinity in necessary things
which have their necessity caused by another, as has been already proved in
regard to efficient causes. Therefore we cannot but admit the existence of some
being having of itself its own necessity, and not receiving it from another, but
rather causing in others their necessity. This all men speak of as God.

The fourth way is taken from the gradation to be found in things. Among beings
there are some more and some less good, true, noble, and the like. But "more" and

---

[2]I have emended the translation in accordance with the best textual reading of this line: *Impossibile est autem omnia quae sunt, talia esse.*

ST. THOMAS AQUINAS

St. Thomas Aquinas was born at the end of 1224 or the beginning of 1225 in a castle near Naples. His aristocratic father was the count of Aquino. He received his earliest education in the Benedictine monastery of Monte Cassino, where he was placed by his parents when he was five, and at fourteen he went to the University of Naples. In Naples he was attracted to the Dominican

(*continued on next page*)

"less" are predicted of different things according as they resemble in their different ways something which is the maximum, as a thing is said to be hotter according as it more nearly resembles that which is hottest; so that there is something which is truest, something best, something noblest, and, consequently, something which is most being, for those things that are greatest in truth are greatest in being, as it is written in *Metaph*. ii. Now the maximum in any genus is the cause of all in that genus, as fire, which is the maximum of heat, is the cause of all hot things, as is said in the same book. Therefore there must also be something which is to all beings the cause of their being, goodness, and every other perfection; and this we call God.

The fifth way is taken from the governance of the world. We see that things which lack knowledge, such as natural bodies, act for an end, and this is evident from their acting always, or nearly always, in the same way, so as to obtain the best result. Hence it is plain that they achieve their end, not fortuitously, but designedly. Now whatever lacks knowledge cannot move towards an end, unless it is directed by some being endowed with knowledge and intelligence; as the

brothers and entered the Dominican Order. His family disapproved of this move, and Thomas' brothers kidnapped him during a journey to Bologna. His father, who was a military man and no doubt advocated the ideals of "breeding, leading, and bleeding," had Thomas imprisoned in a tower. He tried to draw Thomas back to sanity, even tempting him with a woman. But, faithful to his commitment, Thomas escaped after a year and traveled to Paris.

In Paris and then in Cologne, Thomas was the pupil of St. Albert the Great, whose interest in adapting the philosophy of Aristotle to Christianity was decisive for the direction of Thomas' own work. During this time Thomas was taunted as "the Dumb Ox" by his fellow students. (Thomas was exceedingly quiet and was immensely fat, with a frame not unlike a wine cask.) But Albert the Great announced: "You call our brother Thomas a dumb ox, do you? I tell you that someday the whole world will listen to his bellows." In 1252, Thomas returned to Paris, where he resumed his formal education at the university there, receiving his licentiate and his master's degree and lecturing as well.

In 1259, he returned to Italy, where he taught theology at the papal court in Rome and was commissioned by Pope Urban IV to compose the liturgy of the feast of Corpus Christi. During the years 1268–1272 he was once again lecturing in Paris. He was then sent to Naples to establish a Dominican *Studium Generale,* where he remained until 1274, when he was called by Pope Gregory X to participate in the Council of Lyons. It was on the journey to Lyons that Thomas died, on March 7, 1274.

There is a tradition that toward the end of his life Thomas enjoyed mystic experiences that made all he had previously written "seem as straw worthy to be burned." He became known as the Angelic Doctor and was canonized in 1323. In 1879 Pope Leo XIII proclaimed Thomism as the official philosophy of the Roman Catholic Church. St. Thomas bellowed loudly indeed.

St. Thomas was a prolific writer. In addition to many commentaries on the works of Aristotle, commentaries on biblical books, and works on specific philosophical and theological topics, he produced two of the most influential and majestic works of the entire history of philosophy: *Summa Theologiae* and *Summa Contra Gentiles.*

arrow is directed by the archer. Therefore some intelligent being exists by whom all natural things are directed to their end; and this being we call God.[3]

It should be noted what all of the Five Ways have in common. Each of them begins in an *a posteriori* way with the created world, and each of them presupposes the metaphysical principle *ex nihilo, nihil fit,* "from nothing, nothing comes." More specifically, St. Thomas shows in the Second Way why something cannot be the cause of itself (it would have to exist before it exists), and the impossibility of an infinite series of causes and effects is explicitly argued in the first three Ways. But here is a surprise. When St. Thomas argues against an infinite series of causes and effects, he is not

"First" Cause in
the sense of
ultimate cause

[3]St. Thomas Aquinas, *Summa Theologiae,* Pt. 1, Qu. 2, Art. 3, in *Basic Writings of Saint Thomas Aquinas,* ed. Anton C. Pegis (Indianapolis, IN: Hackett, 1997), I.

thinking of a *temporal* series, or one that *stretches infinitely backward in time*, but rather a *hierarchical* series, or one that *extends infinitely upward in being*. This is a crucial point for understanding St. Thomas' argument, and a picture may be worth a thousand words:

ULTIMATE CAUSE OF THE UNIVERSE

∞ . . . . . Y Y Y Y Y Y Y Y Y Y Y Y Y Y Y . Infinite temporal . . ∞ series

That is, every moment in the universe, even if the universe has always been here, is dependent for its existence, *at that moment,* upon an ultimate cause. Although he believed, on the basis of Genesis 1:1, that the world, and therefore time, had a beginning, for the sake of his proofs for God he grants that the world has always existed. After all, he reasons, if we can show that God must exist to account for a world that has always been here, how much more must he exist to account for a world that hasn't?

> The most efficacious way to prove that God exists is on the supposition that the world is eternal. Granted this supposition, that God exists is less manifest. For, if the world and motion have a first beginning, some cause must clearly be posited to account for this origin of the world and of motion.[4]

Although each of the Five Ways assumes the eternity of the world, this is most evident in the Third Way. There it is argued that not all things are merely possible, or can not-be, for that would mean that even now nothing would exist; for, given *enough time* all possible states, including the possible nonbeing of things, would come about, and such a state at some point in the *infinite* past must have by now come about; but from such a state of nothingness, nothing could possibly come (*ex nihilo, nihil fit*); but right now there *is* a world, and therefore it was wrong at the start to think that all things are merely possible; so there must be something necessary, and ultimately something necessary of itself. Stay with this until you see how this argument cannot possibly work except on the assumption that the world has always existed.

St. Thomas really thought of his Five Ways as variations on a single idea, which is the substance of all of them: We know from experience that the world is *contingent;* that is, it depends on something outside itself for its existence. And this would be true even if the world has always been here, for an infinite collection of contingent things is no less contingent than a finite one. But there must be some *unconditional, ultimate* being upon which the world depends; otherwise, it would have no *final* basis for existence.

There is, of course, a more obvious and more popular version of the argument. In philosophical circles this is sometimes called the *Kalam* Cosmological

---

[4]St. Thomas Aquinas, *Summa Contra Gentiles,* 1, 13, 30.

THE COSMOLOGICAL ARGUMENT: THOMISTIC FORM

Any form of the Cosmological Argument for God reasons, in one way or another, from the *contingency* of the world's being to the necessity of God's being. According to St. Thomas' version, no matter how long the world has existed—or even if it has always existed—it is *contingent*, or dependent, upon something else for its existence, and, finally, on Something that is *not* dependent. By its nature, this Something must be a transcendent (outside space and time) and ultimate being.

Argument (*kalam* is Arabic for "rational") because of its prominence in medieval Arabic philosophy, though it certainly has had its advocates in the Judeo-Christian tradition as well. Here, the infinite series of causes and effects *is* conceived as a temporal one stretching backward in time; it is denied that this series could be infinite, and it is concluded that God must exist as the "First" Cause—that is, the originator of this temporal series. We saw that even though St. Thomas accepted this as an article of faith (Genesis 1:1), from a purely philosophical standpoint he left the question open, and actually *argued* as if the world had no beginning. Others believe that it is philosophically *necessary* to believe in a beginning of the world. The reasoning goes like this. If the world *has* always existed, then an infinite number of years (or months, minutes, or whatever) has *already gone by*. But surely this is a self-contradictory claim. For an *infinite* series of years (or whatever) can never (by its very nature as being *infinite*) go by or be completed. How can one claim that prior to this moment (what lies in the future is irrelevant) the world has *passed through* an infinite number of years? Of course, you can *think* of an infinite number of years, but you can't *count* them; you can entertain the *idea* of an infinite series, but you can't actually *pass through* one and come out the other end. Or try this: If the universe has always existed, then it has taken *forever* to reach this point. But then it could never reach this point. But here we are! So it *didn't* take forever.

"First" Cause in the sense of original cause

Did the world have a temporal beginning?

THE COSMOLOGICAL ARGUMENT: POPULAR FORM

Whereas the Thomistic version of the Cosmological Argument is interested only in the *nature* of the world (as contingent), the more popular version is more interested in its *age*. According to this reasoning, it is impossible that the world has always existed, for that would mean that an infinite number of years (or whatever) has already gone by, but that is impossible because it is self-contradictory. Time must therefore have a beginning. And the cause of time must itself be Something transcendent (outside space and time) and ultimate.

According to the medieval picture of the universe, the earth is at the center, partly covered by water, surrounded by air and fire; then come the heavenly spheres, which carry round the moon, sun, and planets, followed by the *primum mobile,* the "first moved"; beyond this is "the Dwelling of God and all the Saints." Is St. Thomas' argument for God as the Unmoved Mover dependent on this picture of the universe?

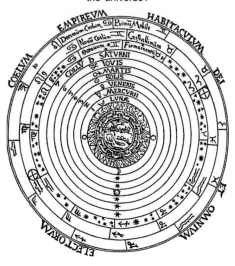

Cosmological evidence for the beginning?

It will be noted that this argument for the beginning of the world is purely rational or logical. Some have enlisted further and very different evidence from cosmology, the study of the origin and nature of the physical universe. You may be familiar with the theory of the "Big Bang." According to this theory, the present "expanding universe," or the recession of galaxies at unimaginable velocities, points to a moment, about fifteen billion years ago, when all the matter in the universe was condensed into something like a superdense atom, and exploded. Understandably, it is a temptation for some to identify this Big Bang with the origin of the universe. Others point to the Second Law of Thermodynamics: It is universally accepted that the energy in the universe is, at least on the large scale, irreversibly and evenly being distributed throughout—the universe is cooling down. But if the universe is running down, like a clock, must it not have once been wound up?

Thus Robert Jastrow, a well-known astronomer, on the implications of the Big Bang:

When an astronomer writes about God, his colleagues assume he is either over the hill or going bonkers. In my case it should be understood from the start that I am an agnostic in religious matters. However, I am fascinated by some strange developments going on in astronomy—partly because of their religious implications and partly because of the peculiar reactions of my colleagues.

The essence of the strange developments is that the Universe had, in some sense, a beginning—that it began at a certain moment in time, and under circumstances

"In the beginning God created the heavens and the earth."

—Genesis 1:1

that seem to make it impossible—not just now, but ever—to find out what force or forces brought the world into being at that moment. Was it, as the Bible says, that "Thou, Lord, in the beginning hast laid the foundations of the earth, and the heavens are the work of thine hands?" No scientist can answer that question; we can never tell whether the Prime Mover willed the world into being, or the creative agent was one of the familiar forces of physics; for the astronomical evidence proves that the Universe was created twenty billion years ago in a fiery explosion, and in the searing heat of that first moment, all the evidence needed for a scientific study of the cause of the great explosion was melted down and destroyed.

This is the crux of the new story of Genesis. It has been familiar for years as the "Big Bang" theory, and has shared the limelight with other theories, especially the Steady State cosmology; but adverse evidence has led to the abandonment of the Steady State theory by nearly everyone, leaving the Big Bang theory exposed as the only adequate explanation of the facts.

Implications of the Big Bang

The general scientific picture that leads to the Big Bang theory is well known. We have been aware for fifty years that we live in an expanding Universe, in which all the galaxies around us are moving apart from us and one another at enormous speeds. The Universe is blowing up before our eyes, as if we are witnessing the aftermath of a gigantic explosion. If we retrace the motions of the outward-moving galaxies backward in time, we find that they all come together, so to speak, fifteen or twenty billion years ago.

At that time all the matter in the Universe was packed into a dense mass, at temperatures of many trillions of degrees. The dazzling brilliance of the radiation in this dense, hot Universe must have been beyond description. The picture suggests the explosion of a cosmic hydrogen bomb. The instant in which the cosmic bomb exploded marked the birth of the Universe.

Now we see how the astronomical evidence leads to a biblical view of the origin of the world. The details differ, but the essential elements in the astronomical and biblical accounts of Genesis are the same: the chain of events leading to man commenced suddenly and sharply at a definite moment in time, in a flash of light and energy....

For the scientist who has lived by his faith in the power of reason, the story ends like a bad dream. He has scaled the mountains of ignorance; he is about to conquer the highest peak; as he pulls himself over the final rock, he is greeted by a band of theologians who have been sitting there for centuries.[5]

THE TELEOLOGICAL ARGUMENT

Closely related to the Cosmological Argument is the *Teleological Argument*. Obviously, this argument will have to do with *teleology* (from the Greek word *telos*: "purpose, design") and is called, for short, the Design Argument.

---

[5]Robert Jastrow, *God and the Astronomers* (New York: Warner Books, 1978), pp. 1–4, 115–116.

"God does not play dice with the universe."

—Einstein

The Teleological
Argument stated

This argument is closely associated with the Cosmological Argument, and it will be recalled that St. Thomas listed it as the Fifth Way, alongside the other four. As with the Cosmological Argument, the Teleological Argument is an *a posteriori* reasoning that employs the idea of causality. In this case God is posited as the only adequate explanation for the apparent order, purpose, unity, harmony, and beauty of the cosmos. It may go beyond the Cosmological Argument, however, in further identifying the ultimate cause as a *rational* cause: The rationality displayed in the cosmos must be the product of *mind*.

One of the best-known, though now out-of-date, statements of this argument is provided by the Anglican divine William Paley (1743–1805). In his famous *watch analogy*, Paley argued that the human eyeball demands an intelligent creator no less than a watch, and the reasoning should recall our discussion of inductive arguments by analogy in Chapter 1. From Paley's *Natural Theology*:

Paley's watch
analogy

> In crossing a heath, suppose I pitched my foot against a *stone* and were asked how the stone came to be there, I might possibly answer that for anything I knew to the contrary it had lain there forever, nor would it, perhaps, be very easy to show the absurdity of this answer. But suppose I had found a *watch* upon the ground, and it should be inquired how the watch happened to be in that place, I should hardly think of the answer which I had before given, that for anything I knew the watch might have always been there. Yet why should not this answer serve for the watch as well as for the stone; why is it not as admissible in the second case as in the first? For this reason, and for no other, namely, that when we come to inspect the watch, we perceive—what we could not discover in the stone—that its several parts are framed and put together for a purpose, e.g., that they are so formed and adjusted as to produce motion, and that motion so regulated as to point out the hour of the day; that if the different parts had been differently shaped from what they are, or placed after any other manner or in any other order than that in which they are placed, either no motion at all would have been carried on in the machine, or none which would have answered the use that is now served by it. To reckon up a few of the plainest of these parts and of their offices, all tending to one result: we see a cylindrical box containing a coiled elastic spring, which, by its endeavor to relax itself, turns round the box. We next observe a flexible chain—artificially wrought for the sake of flexure—communicating the action of the spring from the box to the fusee. We then find a series of wheels, the teeth of which catch in and apply to each other, conducting the motion from the fusee to the balance and from the balance to the pointer, and at the same time, by the size and shape of those wheels, so regulating that motion as to terminate in causing an index, by an equable and measured progression, to pass over a given space in a given time. We take notice that the wheels are made of brass, in order to keep them from rust; the springs of steel, no other metal being so elastic; that over the face of the watch there is placed a glass, a material employed in no other part of the work, but in the room of which,

In 1802 William Paley, an English clergyman, published his *Natural Theology*, in which he argued for God's existence on the basis of design in the cosmos. From this work comes the famous watch analogy: The world is to God as a watch is to a watchmaker.

if there had been any other than a transparent substance, the hour could not be seen without opening the case. This mechanism being observed—it requires indeed an examination of the instrument, and perhaps some previous knowledge of the subject, to perceive and understand it; but being once, as we have said, observed and understood—the inference we think is inevitable, that the watch must have had a maker—that there must have existed, at some time and at some place or other, an artificer or artificers who formed it for the purpose which we find it actually to answer, who completely comprehended its construction and designed its use....

Were there no example in the world of contrivance except that of the eye, it would be alone sufficient to support the conclusion which we draw from it, as to the necessity of an intelligent Creator. It could never be got rid of, because it could not be

ARGUMENTS BY ANALOGY

You may remember from our brief discussion of logic in Chapter 1 that analogies are commonly used in inductive arguments. Paley's Teleological Argument for God uses such an analogy, comparing the world to a watch and arguing that if we need a watchmaker, then surely we must also need a worldmaker. Can you think of other arguments by analogy?

In such an argument, one argues from an allegedly obvious example to a less clear one by comparing similar cases. When evaluating arguments by analogy, we must ask first about the strength of the analogy. Are the two cases relevantly similar? Or are there significant differences between them that weaken the argument? Apply these questions to Paley's analogy to evaluate the strength of the argument.

THE TELEOLOGICAL ARGUMENT

Most versions of the Teleological Argument are arguments from analogy and take some such form as

Watches, houses, ships, machines, and so on all exhibit design, and they are planned and produced by intelligent beings.
The universe exhibits design.

Therefore, the universe was planned and produced by an intelligent being.

accounted for by any other supposition which did not contradict all the principles we possess of knowledge—the principles according to which things do, as often as they can be brought to the test of experience, turn out to be true or false. Its coats and humors, constructed as the lenses of a telescope are constructed, for the refraction of rays of light to a point, which forms the proper action of the organ; the provision in its muscular tendons for turning its pupil to the object, similar to that which is given to the telescope by screws, and upon which power of direction in the eye the exercise of its office as an optical instrument depends; the further provision for its defense, for its constant lubricity and moisture, which we see in its socket and its lids, in its glands for the secretion of the matter of tears, its outlet or communication with the nose for carrying off the liquid after the eye is washed with it; these provisions compose altogether an apparatus, a system of parts, a preparation of means, so manifest in their design, so exquisite in their contrivance, so successful in their issue, so precious, and so infinitely beneficial in their use, as, in my opinion, to bear down all doubt that can be raised upon the subject. And what I wish, under the title of the present chapter, to observe is that, if other parts of nature were inaccessible to our inquiries, or even if other parts of nature presented nothing to our examination but disorder and confusion, the validity of this example would remain the same. If there were but one watch in the world, it would not be less certain that it had a maker. If we had never in our lives seen any but one single kind of hydraulic machine, yet if of that one kind we understood the mechanism and use, we should be as perfectly assured that it proceeded from the hand and thought and skill of a workman, as if we visited a museum of the arts and saw collected there twenty different kinds of machines for drawing water, or a thousand different kinds for other purposes. Of this point each machine is a proof independently of all the rest. So it is with the evidences of a divine agency. The proof is not a conclusion which lies at the end of a chain of reasoning, of which chain each instance of contrivance is only a link, and of which, if one link fail, the whole fails; but it is an argument separately supplied by every separate example. An error in stating an example affects only that example. The argument is cumulative in the fullest sense of that term. The eye proves it without the ear; the ear without the eye. The proof in each example is complete; for when the design of the part and the conduciveness of its structure to that design is shown, the mind may set itself at rest; no future consideration can detract anything from the force of the example.[6]

[6]William Paley, *Natural Theology: Selections*, ed. Frederick Ferré (New York: Bobbs-Merrill, 1963), pp. 3–4, 32–33.

THEISTIC EVOLUTION

The belief that God uses natural evolutionary processes to bring about his desired effect.

Paley's watch analogy is striking but considerably less powerful since 1859, the year in which Darwin published the *Origin of Species*. Paley, as well as almost everyone of his time, believed in a *special* creation of the universe and humans all at once, once upon a time, as a watchmaker makes a watch. Darwin, with his doctrine of the gradual and evolutionary development of humans over an untold number of years, dealt a serious blow to any Paleyan type of teleology. In the place of a God directly and immediately fashioning, say, the human eye, evolution substituted long and progressive sequences of natural causes and effects. It became possible to explain the human species, and everything about it, as well as much of the rest of the biological and physical universe, in purely naturalistic terms. To be sure, the name of Darwin is often associated with atheism, but this is a mistake. Darwin (whose sole earned academic degree was in theology) did not himself turn his theory of evolution against the existence of God but against only a certain view of *how* God created things, the Paleyan view.

The effect of Darwin

Charles Darwin published his *Origin of Species* in 1859 and his *Descent of Man* in 1871. His theory of evolution held revolutionary implications for many fields of thought—not the least of which was theology.

Indeed, though Darwin's theory of evolution dealt a blow to Paleyan teleology, it hardly dealt the deathblow to God. Enter *theistic evolution*. Is it not possible to reconcile evolution with a theistic interpretation of the world? Might not evolution itself be viewed as an instrument by which God has brought about, and is bringing about, his purpose in the cosmos? Many have answered Yes, including F. R. Tennant (1866–1957), one of the most persuasive of theistic evolutionists.

Tennant, who was himself a scientist before he was a philosopher and theologian, laid aside previous and, as he regarded them, dubious approaches to God, and set out in an "empirically-minded" and scientific way. He asks us whether it is not possible in this way to establish a "reasonable belief" in God that is as respectable as what any scientific theory can deliver. He asks us further whether the evidence does not cause us to set aside once and for all the *narrow* teleology of Paley and to adopt a *wider*, or *cosmic*, teleology. He asks us to shift our attention from specific instances of design to the *design of the whole*, and to appreciate natural processes and laws, including evolution, as "conspiring," as it were, upon the production of an intelligible universe, and upon humanity—the bearer of moral and aesthetic values—as its crowning glory.

The empirically-minded theologian adopts a different procedure. He asks how the world, inclusive of man, is to be explained. He would let the Actual world tell its own story and offer its own suggestions: not silence it while abstractive speculation, setting out with presuppositions possibly irrelevant to Actuality, weaves a system of thought which may prove to conflict with facts....

...[he] sets out from facts and inductions; its premises are as firmly established and as universally acknowledged as any of the stable generalisations of science. Here there is at least common ground, as distinct from private certitude, from which argumentation may proceed. Coercive demonstration being confessedly unattainable, it is to be inquired what kind of justification for reasonable belief natural theology can afford. And the first step is to set forth the facts and generalisations which collectively constitute our data or premises.

The forcibleness of Nature's suggestion that she is the outcome of intelligent design lies not in particular cases of adaptedness in the world, nor even in the multiplicity of them. It is conceivable that every such instance may individually admit of explanation in terms of proximate causes or, in the first instance, of explanation other than in terms of cosmic or "external" teleology. And if it also admits of teleological interpretation, that fact will not of itself constitute a rigorous certification of external design. The forcibleness of the world's appeal consists rather in the conspiration of innumerable causes to produce, by their united and reciprocal action, and to maintain, a general order of Nature. Narrower kinds of teleological argument, based on surveys of restricted spheres of fact, are much more precarious than that for which the name of "the wider teleology" may be appropriated in that the comprehensive design-argument is the outcome of synopsis or conspection of the knowable world.

...So long as organisms were believed to have originated, in their present forms and with all their specialised organs "ready made," the argument that adaptation of part to whole, of whole to environment, and of organ to function, implied design, was forcible. But its premiss became untenable when Darwin

PALEY'S REVENGE?
THE INTELLIGENT DESIGN MOVEMENT

For many people, Darwin's theory of evolution spelled the death of the teleological argument and particularly the special creation inherent in Paley's watch analogy. But a new movement called "Intelligent Design" is seeking to overturn Darwinism. In the excerpt below, William A. Dembski, one of the leading scholars of this movement, explains how the theory works:

> What then is Intelligent Design? Intelligent Design begins with the observation that intelligent causes can do things which undirected natural causes cannot. Undirected natural causes can place scrabble pieces on a board, but cannot arrange the pieces as meaningful words or sentences. To obtain a meaningful arrangement requires an intelligent cause. This intuition, that there is a fundamental distinction between undirected natural causes on the one hand and intelligent causes on the other, has underlain the design arguments of past centuries. . . .
>
> Within biology, Intelligent Design is a theory of biological origins and development. Its fundamental claim is that intelligent causes are necessary to explain the complex, information-rich structures of biology, and that these causes are *empirically detectable*.
>
> To say intelligent causes are empirically detectable is to say there exist well-defined methods that, on the basis of observational features of the world, are capable of reliably distinguishing intelligent causes from undirected natural causes. Many special sciences have already developed such methods for drawing this distinction—notably forensic science, cryptography, archeology, and the search for extraterrestrial intelligence (as in the movie *Contact*).
>
> Whenever these methods detect intelligent causation, the underlying entity they uncover is information. Intelligent Design properly formulated is a theory of information. Within such a theory, information becomes a reliable indicator of intelligent causation as well as a proper object for scientific investigation. Intelligent Design thereby becomes a theory for detecting and measuring information, explaining its origin, and tracing its flow. Intelligent Design is therefore not the study of intelligent causes per se, but of informational pathways induced by intelligent causes.
>
> As a result, Intelligent Design presupposes neither a creator nor miracles. Intelligent Design is theologically minimalist. It detects intelligence without speculating about the nature of the intelligence.*

*William A. Dembski, "The Intelligent Design Movement," *Cosmic Pursuit*, Spring 1998. http://www.leaderu.com/offices/dembski/docs/bd-idesign.html#

shewed that every organic structure had come to be what it now is through a long series of successive and gradual modifications. Gradualness of construction is in itself no proof of the absence of external design: it is not at this point that Darwinism delivered its alleged death-blow to teleology. The sting of Darwinism rather lay in the suggestion that proximate and "mechanical" causes

BLACK ELK ON THE ONENESS OF NATURE

One of the salient features of the Western religious tradition is its emphasis on the distinction between nature and the supernatural, and the human being's essential connection with the latter. This emphasis stands in stark contrast with other traditions. For example, Native American traditions stress humanity's unity with nature, as is evident in the following excerpt from *Black Elk Speaks*:

> My friend, I am going to tell you the story of my life, as you wish; and if it were only the story of my life I think I would not tell it....
>
> It is the story of all life that is holy and is good to tell, and of us two-leggeds sharing in it with the four-leggeds and the wings of the air and all green things; for these are children of one mother and their father is one Spirit....
>
> So I know that it is a good thing I am going to do; and because no good thing can be done by any man alone, I will first make an offering and send a voice to the Spirit of the World, that it may help me to be true. See, I fill this sacred pipe with the bark of the red willow; but before we smoke it, you must see how it is made and what it means. These four ribbons hanging here on the stem are the four quarters of the universe. The black one is for the west where the thunder beings live to send us rain; the white one for the north, whence comes the great white-cleansing wind; the red one for the east, whence springs the light and where the morning star lives to give men wisdom; the yellow for the south, whence come the summer and the power to grow.
>
> But these four spirits are only one Spirit after all, and this eagle feather here is for that One, which is like a father, and also it is for thoughts of men that should rise high as eagles do. Is not the sky a father and the earth a mother, and are not all living things with feet or wings or roots their children? And this hide upon the mouthpiece here, which should be bison hide, is for the earth, from whence we came and at whose breast we suck as babies all our lives, along with all the animals and birds and trees and grasses. And because it means all this, and more than any man can understand, the pipe is holy....

(*continued on next page*)

were sufficient to produce the adaptations from which the teleology of the eighteenth century had argued to God. Assignable proximate causes, whether mechanical or not, are sufficient to dispose of the particular kind of teleological proof supplied by Paley. But the fact of organic evolution, even when the maximum of instrumentality is accredited to what is figuratively called natural selection, is not incompatible with teleology on a grander scale: as exponents of Darwinism were perhaps the first to recognise and to proclaim. Subversive of Paley's argument, it does not invalidate his theistic conclusion, nor even his view that every organism and organ is an end as well as a means. Indeed the science of evolution was the primary source of the wider teleology current for the last half century, as well as the main incentive to the recovery of the closely connected doctrine of divine immanence. This kind of teleology does not set out from the particular adaptations in individual organisms or species

Now I light the pipe, and after I have offered it to the powers that are one Power, and sent forth a voice to them, we shall smoke together. Offering the mouthpiece first of all to the One above—so—I send a voice:

Hey hey! hey hey! hey hey! hey hey!

Grandfather, Great Spirit, you have been always, and before you no one has been. There is no other one to pray to but you. You yourself, everything that you see, everything has been made by you. The star nations all over the universe you have finished. The four quarters of the earth you have finished. The day, and in that day, everything you have finished. Grandfather, Great Spirit, lean close to the earth that you may hear the voice I send. You towards where the sun goes down, behold me; Thunder Beings, behold me! You where the White Giant lives in power, behold me! You where the sun shines continually, whence come the day-break star and the day, behold me! You where the summer lives, behold me! You in the depths of the heavens, an eagle of power, behold! And you, Mother Earth, the only Mother, you who have shown mercy to your children!

Hear me, four quarters of the world—a relative I am! Give me the strength to walk the soft earth, a relative to all that is! Give me the eyes to see and the strength to understand, that I may be like you. With your power only can I face the winds.

Great Spirit, Great Spirit, my Grandfather, all over the earth the faces of living things are all alike. With the tenderness have these come up out of the ground. Look upon these faces of children without number and with children in their arms, that they may face the winds and walk the good road to the day of quiet.

This is my prayer; hear me! The voice I have sent is weak, yet with earnestness I have sent it. Hear me!*

Black Elk Speaks: Being the Life Story of a Holy Man of the Oglala Sioux, as told through John G. Neihardt (Lincoln: University of Nebraska Press, 1961), pp. 1–6.

so much as from considerations as to the progressiveness of the evolutionary process and as to the organic realm as a whole....

In an exposition of the significance of the moral order for theistic philosophy, the first step is to point out that man belongs to Nature, and is an essential part of it, in such a sense that the world cannot be described or explained as a whole without taking him and his moral values into account. Prof. Pringle-Pattison, especially, has elaborated the doctrine that, as he expresses it, "man is organic to the world." What precisely this, or the similar phrase "man is the child of Nature," should mean, if either is to be more than a half-truth, needs to be made clear. In so far as man's soul, *i.e.* man as *noümenon,* or (in the language of spiritualistic pluralism) the dominant monad in the empirical self, is concerned, we are not authorised by known facts to regard man as organic to Nature, or as the child of Nature, in the sense that he is an emergent product of

NARROW VERSUS WIDER TELEOLOGY

- *Paley:* The world is full of particular instances of design—for example, the human eye. Each of these is an evidence for the direct creating and designing activity of God.

- *Tennant:* Particular instances of design, such as the human eye, can be adequately explained by natural causes, such as evolution. These natural causes, however, have produced a world that *as a whole* is an overwhelming evidence for the creating and designing activity of God.

cosmic evolution. We are rather forbidden by psychology to entertain any such notion. But, this proviso being observed—it must qualify all that is further said in the present connexion—we can affirm that man's body, with all its conditioning of his mentality, his sociality, knowledge and morality, is "of a piece" with Nature; and that, in so far as he is a phenomenal being, man is organic to Nature, or a product of the world. And this fact is as significant for our estimation of Nature as for our anthropology. If man is Nature's child, Nature is the wonderful mother of such a child. Any account of her which ignores the fact of her maternity is scientifically partial and philosophically insignificant. Her capacity to produce man must be reckoned among her potencies, explain it how we may. And man is no monstrous birth out of due time, no freak or sport. In respect of his body and the bodily conditioning of his mentality, man is like, and has genetic continuity with, Nature's humbler and earlier-born children. In the fulness of time Nature found self-utterance in a son possessed of the intelligent and moral status. Maybe she was pregnant with him from the beginning, and the world-ages are the period of her gestation. As to this anthropocentric view of the world-process, and its co-extensiveness with teleological interpretation, more will presently be said. But in the light of man's continuity with the rest of the world we can at once dismiss the view that Nature suddenly "stumbled" or "darkly blundered" on man, while "churning the universe with mindless motion." The world-process is a *praeparatio anthropologica*, whether designedly or not, and man is the culmination, up to the present stage of the knowable history of Nature, of a gradual ascent. We cannot explain man in terms of physical Nature; conceivably Nature may be found explicable—in another sense of the word—in terms of man, and can be called "the threshold of spirit." Judging the genealogical tree by its roots, naturalism once preached that Darwin had put an end to the assumption that man occupies an exceptional position on our planet; apparently implying that there is no difference of status between man and the primordial slime because stages between the two are traceable. But if we judge the tree by its fruits, Darwin may rather be said to have restored man to the position from which Copernicus seemed to have ousted him, in making it possible to read the humanising of Nature in the naturalising of man, and to regard man as not only the last term and the crown of Nature's long upward effort, but also as its end or goal.[7]

[7]F. R. Tennant, *Philosophical Theology* (Cambridge: Cambridge University Press, 1930), II, 78–79, 84, 100–102.

Both the Cosmological and the Teleological Arguments for God have been criticized in many ways. Here we can mention only a few of the objections.

Inevitably someone will ask: "If everything has to have a cause, then what caused God?" But this is to miss the point. It is not that every *thing* must have a cause, but that every *event*, or everything that *comes into being*, must have a cause. Now is God an event or something that comes into being? Of course not. How could he be, if he is the *cause* of events or things that come into being? It is hopeless confusion to try to think of God, who is by his nature transcendent and ultimate, as a being that comes into being or passes away. Similarly, some smart aleck might ask: "What was God doing before he created the world?" To this, one is tempted, with some ancients, to answer: "What was God doing before he created the world? Why, he was preparing hell for people who pry into divine mysteries!" More seriously, how can there be a "before" without creation? Apart from creation there *is* no time and therefore no "before." We must, in a word, take absolutely seriously the idea of God as a *transcendent* and *absolute* being.

What caused God?

Another objection questions whether the world even needs a cause. Just because everything in the universe is contingent, must the universe itself be contingent? The Cosmological and Teleological Arguments assume that the world needs an external explanation, but perhaps, critics argue, the world as a whole is not contingent and has always existed. Simply because the world we perceive is composed of entities that come into being does not necessarily mean that the whole is itself contingent. And isn't it possible that the apparent order in the universe is somehow innate, that matter is self-organizing? David Hume raises this possibility partially to illustrate the limits of our knowledge. Based on our experience, we simply don't know if the world requires an external cause, critics argue.

Even if the world has a cause, can we be certain that it is the God of the Bible, or even any god at all, that is this ultimate cause? St. Thomas ends each of his Five Ways with "this being we call God," but is that really what the argument shows? Critics point out that Aquinas argues for an uncaused first cause or designer but says nothing about the loving, personal God associated with Christianity. While establishing the need for a transcendent being is not to be underestimated, must theists take the next step to connect this first cause to the attributes of a particular deity?

Finally, we must raise what is probably the most troublesome feature of the Cosmological and Teleological Arguments for the existence of God. We have seen repeatedly that central to both of the arguments is the *principle of causality:* "From nothing, nothing comes," or "Every event must have a cause." But the concept of causality is far and away one of the most difficult in all philosophy. And this is especially true when it is applied to God's relation to the world.

We have already seen how both Hume and Kant in different ways destroyed the traditional concept of causality. Now we are in a better position to emphasize the implications for metaphysics, and specifically for discussions of God. In a way, Hume and Kant make the same criticism: *The concept of causality cannot be legitimately extended beyond the objects of possible sense experience, and therefore cannot be extended to God.* On the other hand, it is crucial to appreciate that Hume and Kant would interpret and justify this claim in radically different ways.

Hume. Aside from Hume's skepticism about causality as such (after all, we have no basis in experience for the claimed universality and necessity of the cause-effect relation) he raises a further question: Are we not limited by our experience to a small part of reality? What possible basis do we have for thinking that the causal relation holds for anything *beyond* our experience? Our idea of causality—insofar as we possess one—is based on our experience of causes (for example, carpenters) and effects (for example, houses) joined together over and over again right before our eyes. But surely God's creation of the world is hardly an object of possible experience, and is totally without analogy in the universe we know.

This is Hume's main and recurring point in the following passage from his *Dialogues Concerning Natural Religion,* in which, more or less, his own position is represented by Philo, who speaks the following:

> That all inferences, Cleanthes, concerning fact are founded on experience, and that all experimental reasonings are founded on the supposition that similar causes prove similar effects, and similar effects similar causes, I shall not at present much dispute with you. But observe, I entreat you, with what extreme caution all just reasoners proceed in the transferring of experiments to similar cases. Unless the cases be exactly similar, they repose no perfect confidence in applying their past observation to any particular phenomenon. Every alteration of circumstances occasions a doubt concerning the event; and it requires new experiments to prove certainly that the new circumstances are of no moment or importance. A change in bulk, situation, arrangement, age, disposition of the air, or surrounding bodies—any of these particulars may be attended with the most unexpected consequences. And unless the objects be quite familiar to us, it is the highest temerity to expect with assurance, after any of these changes, an event similar to that which before fell under our observation. The slow and deliberate steps of philosophers here, if anywhere, are distinguished from the precipitate march of the vulgar, who, hurried on by the smallest similitude, are incapable of all discernment or consideration.
>
> But can you think, Cleanthes, that your usual phlegm and philosophy have been preserved in so wide a step as you have taken when you compared to the universe houses, ships, furniture, machines, and, from their similarity in some circumstances, inferred a similarity in their causes? Thought, design, intelligence, such as we discover in men and other animals, is no more than one of the springs and principles of the universe, as well as heat or cold, attraction or repulsion, and a hundred others which fall under daily observation. It is an active cause by which some particular parts of nature, we find, produce alterations on other parts. But can a conclusion, with any propriety, be transferred from parts to the whole? Does not the great disproportion bar all comparison and inference? From observing the growth of a hair, can we learn anything concerning the generation of a man? Would the manner of a leaf's blowing, even though perfectly known, afford us any instruction concerning the vegetation of a tree?
>
> But allowing that we were to take the *operations* of one part of nature upon another for the foundation of our judgment concerning the *origin* of the whole

(which never can be admitted), yet why select so minute, so weak, so bounded a principle as the reason and design of animals is found to be upon this planet? What peculiar privilege has this little agitation of the brain which we call *thought,* that we must thus make it the model of the whole universe? Our partiality in our own favour does indeed present it on all occasions, but sound philosophy ought carefully to guard against so natural an illusion.

So far from admitting, continued Philo, that the operations of a part can afford us any just conclusion concerning the origin of the whole, I will not allow any one part to form a rule for another part if the latter be very remote from the former. Is there any reasonable ground to conclude that the inhabitants of other planets possess thought, intelligence, reason, or anything similar to these faculties in men? When nature has so extremely diversified her manner of operation in this small globe, can we imagine that she incessantly copies herself throughout so immense a universe? And if thought, as we may well suppose, be confined merely to this narrow corner and has even there so limited a sphere of action, with what propriety can we assign it for the original cause of all things? The narrow views of a peasant who makes his domestic economy the rule for the government of kingdoms is in comparison a pardonable sophism....

A very small part of this great system, during a very short time, is very imperfectly discovered to us; and do we thence pronounce decisively concerning the origin of the whole?

Admirable conclusion! Stone, wood, brick, iron, brass, have not, at this time, in this minute globe of earth, an order or arrangement without human art and contrivance; therefore, the universe could not originally attain its order and arrangement without something similar to human art. But is a part of nature a rule for another part very wide of the former? Is it a rule for the whole? Is a very small part a rule for the universe? Is nature in one situation a certain rule for nature in another situation vastly different from the former?

And can you blame me, Cleanthes, if I here imitate the prudent reserve of Simonides, who, according to the noted story, being asked by Hiero, *What God was?* desired a day to think of it, and then two days more; and after that manner continually prolonged the term, without ever bringing his definition or description? Could you even blame me if I had answered, at first, *that I did not know,* and was sensible that this subject lay vastly beyond the reach of my faculties? You might cry out sceptic and rallier, as much as you pleased; but, having found in so many other subjects much more familiar the imperfections and even contradictions of human reason, I never should expect any success from its feeble conjectures in a subject so sublime and so remote from the sphere of our observation. When two *species* of objects have always been observed to be conjoined together, I can *infer,* by custom, the existence of one wherever I see the existence of the other; and this I call an argument from experience. But how this argument can have place where the objects, as in the present case, are single, individual, without parallel or specific resemblance, may be difficult to explain. And will any man tell me with a serious countenance that an orderly universe must arise from some thought and art like the human because we have experience of it? To ascertain this reasoning it were requisite that we had experience of the origin of worlds; and it is not sufficient, surely, that we have seen ships and cities arise from human art and contrivance.[8]

---

[8]David Hume, *Dialogues Concerning Natural Religion,* ed. Henry D. Aiken (New York: Hafner, 1948), pp. 20–23.

DOES CAUSALITY APPLY TO GOD?

- *Hume:* No. Causality is limited to the sensible world because we know it only through sense experience. We have no grounds for applying it to a transcendent God.
- *Kant:* No. Causality is limited to the sensible world because it is *constitutive* of sense experience, it is part of what experience *means*. It therefore has no possible application to a transcendent God.

Do you see, then, just what Hume, the radical empiricist, would mean by the charge that the Cosmological and Teleological Arguments involve an unjustified application of the concept of causality to God?

Kant's criticism

Kant. But Kant would mean something very different. We saw earlier how Kant, contrary to Hume, *did* believe in "Every event must have a cause" as a certain and universal principle, but only because it is a way in which our minds necessarily grasp and *represent* reality. Do you recall the rose-colored glasses from our earlier discussion of Kant? We cannot help but experience things as standing in cause-effect relations, because causality is one of the ways in which our mind organizes or makes possible experience itself. But then, of course, causality can have no possible bearing on anything *outside* our sense experience, such as God.

In the following extract from the *Critique of Pure Reason,* Kant calls the Cosmological Argument a "transcendental illusion," and lists four lines of objection. The first of these concerns explicitly the proper, and limited, application of the principle of causality, though the limitation of the theoretical reason to objects of possible experience is a theme that otherwise recurs throughout.

> There are so many sophistical propositions in this cosmological argument, that it really seems as if speculative reason had spent all her dialectical skill in order to produce the greatest possible transcendental illusion....
>
> I said before that a whole nest of dialectical assumptions was hidden in that cosmological proof, and that transcendental criticism might easily detect and destroy it. I shall here enumerate them only, leaving it to the experience of the reader to follow up the fallacies and remove them.
>
> We find, first, the transcendental principle of inferring a cause for the accidental. This principle, that everything contingent must have a cause, is valid in the world of sense only, and has not even a meaning outside it. For the purely intellectual concept of the contingent cannot produce a synthetical proposition like that of causality, and the principle of causality has no meaning and no criterion of its use, except in the world of sense, while here it is meant to help us beyond the world of sense.
>
> Secondly. The inference of a first cause, based on the impossibility of an infinite ascending series of given causes in this world of sense, an inference which

the principles of the use of reason do not allow us to draw even in experience, while here we extend that principle beyond experience, whither that series can never be prolonged.

Thirdly. The false self-satisfaction of reason with regard to the completion of that series, brought about by removing in the end every kind of condition, without which, nevertheless, no concept of necessity is possible, and by then, when any definite concepts have become impossible, accepting this as a completion of our concept.

Fourthly. The mistaking the logical possibility of a concept of all united reality (without any internal contradiction) for the transcendental, which requires a principle for the practicability of such a synthesis, such principle however being applicable to the field of possible experience only, etc.[9]

As with Hume, Kant charges that the Cosmological and Teleological Arguments involve an illegitimate extension of the idea of causality to a sphere where it has no proper application. But Kant means something very different: It is not just that we have no basis for such an application of causality (Hume), but that causality could not *possibly* apply to God.

It must be seen that Hume's and Kant's criticisms of these theistic arguments follow from their respective views of knowledge. In both cases, it is important to appreciate this connection, and to appreciate, therefore, the importance of the starting point. And that takes us back to Chapters 9 and 10.

CHAPTER 11 IN REVIEW

SUMMARY

Some of the most interesting and instructive phenomena in the history of philosophy are the arguments for God's existence. Natural theology means knowledge of God acquired through our natural faculties of reason and/or experience. The best examples of this are the traditional arguments for the existence of God. We have considered two of these in this chapter:

- The Cosmological Argument
- The Teleological Argument

These are *a posteriori* arguments in that they attempt to demonstrate the existence of God on the basis of sense experience.

More specifically, the Cosmological Argument (First-Cause Argument) concludes that a transcendent and absolute being must exist as the only possible cause of the contingent universe. Actually there are two forms of this argument. If one grants that the world must have had a temporal beginning (as in the more common, or popular, version), then God is

---

[9]Immanuel Kant, *Critique of Pure Reason*, tr. F. Max Müller (Garden City, NY: Anchor Books, 1966), pp. 405–408.

posited as the first cause of the cosmos in the sense of its originator at a definite point in the past. If, on the other hand, one grants that the cosmos has always existed (as in the Thomistic version), then God is posited as the first cause of the cosmos in the sense of the ultimate being upon whom it depends at every moment in its (even infinite) existence. It is important to see that in either case, the world is regarded as *contingent* and therefore dependent upon something beyond itself, and finally upon something ultimate, for its existence.

The Teleological Argument (Design Argument) concludes that there must exist a transcendent and intelligent being as the only possible cause of the order and design in the universe. This argument also assumes two forms. In the older version of Paley, God is regarded as the direct cause of *specific* designs—say, the human eye. In the more recent version by Tennant, who was much influenced by the theory of evolution, God is responsible for the design of the *whole*, which he has achieved by long sequences of innumerable natural processes. This latter view involves theistic evolution, the idea that evolution itself is one of the natural processes instituted by God and employed as an instrument for his production of humanity and human values.

Numerous complaints have been filed against these arguments, but the most critical have to do with the concept of causality. Aside from the intrinsic problems with this concept (is it really a metaphysical certainty that "From nothing, nothing comes" or that "Every event must have a cause"?), some important philosophers (for example, Hume and Kant) have charged that whatever its application may be to the sensible world, it is certainly less clear how the concept of causality may relate to anything beyond the sensible world. According to Hume, we have no rational right to ascribe to some transcendent being the attributes and activities, such as *causal* activity, that we know only from our limited experience of the sensible world around us. According to Kant, it is not even *possible* that a concept of causality could be ascribed to God, since by its nature it is a principle of sense experience and therefore has no application beyond sense experience.

BASIC IDEAS

- Natural theology
- Revealed theology
- *A posteriori/a priori* arguments for God
- The Cosmological Argument
    Thomistic version
    Popular version
- St. Thomas' Five Ways
- Two meanings of "First" Cause
- Big Bang theory of the universe
- Second Law of Thermodynamics
- The Teleological Argument

- Teleology
- Paley's watch analogy
- Special creation versus evolution
- Theistic evolution
- Narrow versus wider teleology
- Miscellaneous objections to the *a posteriori* proofs
- Causality as the central problem
- Hume's criticism of divine causality
- Kant's criticism of divine causality

TEST YOURSELF

1. True or false: St. Thomas' argument for God presupposes a temporal beginning of the universe.
2. Knowledge of God by means of a special divine self-disclosure is called theology.
3. Why do both Hume and Kant reject the Cosmological Argument on the basis of their differing conceptions of causality?
4. How did Charles Darwin figure in the discussion in this chapter?
5. St. Thomas' Five Ways are all (a) *a posteriori,* (b) presented in his *Summa Theologiae,* (c) involved with the principle of causality, (d) based on the Bible.
6. Paley was a proponent of (a) wider teleology, (b) narrow teleology, (c) evolution, (d) theistic evolution.
7. Who was F. R. Tennant?
8. Some claim that there is *scientific* evidence for the temporal beginning of the cosmos. What is it?
9. True or false: Theistic evolution is the belief that God created the world and then abandoned it to its own course.
10. Paley claimed that ____ is to the ____ as a ____ is to a ____.

QUESTIONS FOR REFLECTION

- It is often observed that there is an essential difference between metaphysical and scientific reasoning. Do you agree with this? Can scientific theories, such as the Big Bang theory, hold any real relevance for metaphysical questions, such as the question of God? Can a scientific claim also be a metaphysical claim?
- It is sometimes said that St. Thomas' Five Ways are really five different expressions of the same argument. Do you see any truth in this? How might you defend it?
- For some people, the idea of "theistic evolution" is a contradiction in terms. But is evolution in itself necessarily atheistic? What does "evolution" mean? Does God work through nature in other respects? What,

suddenly, becomes so important about the interpretation of religious language, the use of symbols, and so on (think of the first chapters of the Bible)?

- If you were St. Thomas, would you feel devastated by either Hume's or Kant's attacks on your arguments for God? If not, why not?

FOR FURTHER READING

Donald R. Burrill (ed.). *The Cosmological Arguments.* Garden City, NY: Anchor Books, 1967. A useful collection of the standard statements both classical and contemporary, both positive and critical, on the Cosmological and Teleological Arguments.

William Lane Craig. *The Kalam Cosmological Argument.* New York: Barnes & Noble, 1977. A modern proposal of a medieval Arabic form of the Cosmological Argument (the "popular" version), and involving discussions of contemporary physics, mathematics, philosophy, and theology.

Brian Davies. *An Introduction to the Philosophy of Religion.* Third ed. New York: Oxford University Press, 2003. A critical and thoughtful examination of fundamental questions posed by religious belief, including arguments for the existence of God.

Lecomte du Noüys. *Human Destiny.* New York: Longmans, Green & Co., 1947. One of the best known of modern versions of the Teleological Argument, arguing from the infinitesimal odds against the chance occurrences required for the production of life.

Anthony Kenny. *Five Ways: St. Thomas Aquinas' Proofs of God's Existence.* London: Routledge & Kegan Paul, 1969. Commentary on the Five Ways of St. Thomas in an analytic style.

J. L. Mackie. *The Miracle of Theism: Arguments for and against the Existence of God.* Oxford: Clarendon Press, 1982. Chs. 5, 8. Heavy-duty treatments of the Cosmological and Teleological Arguments by an eminent contemporary philosopher, tying together traditional and recent moves.

Jacques Maritain. *Approaches to God.* San Francisco: Harper & Row, 1954. Readable chapters reflecting the Thomistic approach to God (especially Ch. 2) by a recent and esteemed Catholic thinker.

Hugo A. Meynell. *The Intelligible Universe: A Cosmological Argument.* New York: Barnes & Noble, 1982. A redevelopment of an earlier version of the Cosmological Argument, taking into account critical discussions of recent years.

Ed. L. Miller. *God and Reason: An Invitation to Philosophical Theology.* Second ed. Englewood Cliffs, NJ: Prentice-Hall, 1995. Chs. 1, 3–4. Introductory discussions of natural theology and the Cosmological and Teleological Arguments, reflecting standard historical and recent positions, pro and con.

Alvin Plantinga. *God, Freedom, and Evil.* Grand Rapids, MI: Eerdmans, 1974. Part 2, a–b. Brief and logically tight discussions and rejection of the Cosmological and Teleological Arguments by an influential contemporary philosopher of religion.

William L. Rowe. *The Cosmological Argument*. Princeton, NJ: Princeton University Press, 1975. A somewhat advanced discussion on all aspects of the subject, especially the principle of causality.

Jagjit Singh. *Great Ideas and Theories of Modern Cosmology*. New York: Dover, 1961. Ch. 16. Brief and mildly critical consideration of the cosmological-astronomical evidence for God.

Richard Swineburne. *The Existence of God*. Oxford: Clarendon Press, 1979. Chs. 7–8. Discussions in an analytic style, concluding that the Cosmological and Teleological Arguments hold no deductive validity though they do contribute inductive support.

Richard Taylor. *Metaphysics*. Third ed. Englewood Cliffs, NJ: Prentice-Hall, 1983. Ch. 10. Recent and readable treatments of the issues involved in the Cosmological and Teleological Arguments, reflecting a sympathetic approach.

*In addition, see the relevant articles ("Cosmological Argument," "Teleological Argument," etc.) In *Routledge Encyclopedia of Philosophy*, ed. Edward Craig (London: Routledge, 1998), and *Stanford Encyclopedia of Philosophy*, http://plato.stanford.edu.

GOD AND REASON

n Chapter 11 we looked at two arguments for God, both of them *a posteriori*—that is, based on sense experience. In this chapter we will consider two that are *a priori*—that is, based *not* on sense experience but on reason alone. Specifically, the first, the Ontological Argument, is based on the mere idea of God. The second, the Moral Argument, is based on the idea of moral law.

THE ONTOLOGICAL ARGUMENT

The *Ontological Argument* begins with the definition of God as the *greatest being possible*, or, if you prefer, as the most perfect being, the unlimited being, a being no greater than which is conceivable, and so on. It is important to see that it is not the linguistic symbol "God" that we are interested in, but rather the *idea* (of the greatest being possible) that most people, even atheists, mean by it. The simplest version of this argument then asks us: What is greater: to exist as a mere idea in the mind, or to exist in reality too? Obviously, so the argument goes, it is greater to exist objectively, in reality. (Wouldn't you rather have millions of real dollars than mental ones?) But, then, God must actually exist, because if he didn't, he would not be the greatest being possible. To say it another way: It is logically absurd to deny the existence of God, for you would be denying the existence of what *must* exist to be the thing you are talking about!

God, the greatest being, must exist

The first and most famous statement of the Ontological Argument was provided by St. Anselm (1033–1109) in his *Proslogium*. He takes as his definition of God "that than which nothing greater can be conceived," and concludes from this that God must, in fact, exist.

Truly There Is a God, Although the Fool Hath Said in His Heart, There Is No God

St. Anselm's version

And so, Lord, do thou, who dost give understanding to faith, give me, so far as thou knowest it to be profitable, to understand that thou art as we believe; and that thou art that which we believe. And, indeed, we believe that thou art a being than which nothing greater can be conceived. Or is there no such nature, since the fool hath said in his heart, there is no God? [Ps. 14:1]. But, at any rate, this very fool, when he hears of this being of which I speak—a being than which nothing greater can be conceived—understands what he hears, and what he understands is in his understanding; although he does not understand it to exist.

For, it is one thing for an object to be in the understanding, and another to understand that the object exists. When a painter first conceives of what he will afterwards perform, he has it in his understanding, but he does not yet understand it to be, because he has not yet performed it. But after he has made the painting, he both has it in his understanding, and he understands that it exists, because he has made it.

Hence, even the fool is convinced that something exists in the understanding, at least, than which nothing greater can be conceived. For, when he hears of this, he understands it. And whatever is understood, exists in the understanding. And assuredly that, than which nothing greater can be conceived, cannot exist in the understanding alone. For, suppose it exists in the understanding alone: then it can be conceived to exist in reality; which is greater.

Therefore, if that, than which nothing greater can be conceived, exists in the understanding alone, the very being, than which nothing greater can be conceived, is one, than which a greater can be conceived. But obviously this is impossible. Hence, there is no doubt that there exists a being, than which nothing greater can be conceived, and it exists both in the understanding and in reality.

God Cannot Be Conceived Not to Exist

And it assuredly exists so truly, that it cannot be conceived not to exist. For, it is possible to conceive of a being which cannot be conceived not to exist; and this is greater than one which can be conceived not to exist. Hence, if that, than which nothing greater can be conceived, can be conceived not to exist, it is not that, than which nothing greater can be conceived. But this is an irreconcilable contradiction. There is, then, so truly a being than which nothing greater can be conceived to exist, that it cannot even be conceived not to exist, and this being thou art, O Lord, our God.

So truly, therefore, doest thou exist, O Lord, my God, that thou canst not be conceived not to exist; and rightly. For, if a mind could conceive of a being better than thee, the creature would rise about the Creator; and this is most absurd. And, indeed, whatever else there is, except thee alone, can be conceived not to exist. To thee alone, therefore, it belongs to exist more truly than all other beings, and hence in a higher degree than all others. For, whatever else exists does not exist so truly, and hence in a less degree it belongs to it to exist. Why, then, has the

THE ONTOLOGICAL ARGUMENT

God is the greatest or most perfect being.
A being who exists is greater or more perfect than a being who does not exist.

Therefore, God must exist.

fool said in his heart, there is no God, since it is so evident, to a rational mind, that thou dost exist in the highest degree of all? Why, except that he is dull and a fool?[1]

Another statement is provided by Descartes, in his *Meditations*. He defines God as "the most perfect being," and concludes that as sum of *all* perfections, God must possess not only the attributes of omnipotence, omniscience, omnibenevolence, and so on, but also the attribute of existence.

...now, if just because I can draw the idea of something from my thought, it follows that all which I know clearly and distinctly as pertaining to this object does really belong to it, may I not derive from this an argument demonstrating the existence of God? It is certain that I no less find the idea of God, that is to say, the idea of a supremely perfect Being, in me, than that of any figure or number whatever it is; and I do not know any less clearly and distinctly that an [actual and] eternal existence pertains to this nature than I know that all that which I am able to demonstrate of some figure or number truly pertains to the nature of this figure or number, and therefore, although all that I concluded in the preceding Meditations were found to be false, the existence of God would pass with me as at least as certain as I have ever held the truths of mathematics (which concern only numbers and figures) to be.

Descartes' version

This indeed is not at first manifest, since it would seem to present some appearance of being a sophism. For being accustomed in all other things to make a distinction between existence and essence, I easily persuade myself that the existence can be separated from the essence of God, and that we can thus conceive God as not actually existing. But, nevertheless, when I think of it with more attention, I clearly see that existence can no more be separated from the essence of God than can its having its three angles equal to two right angles be separated from the essence of a [rectilinear] triangle, or the idea of a mountain from the idea of a valley; and so there is not any less repugnance to our conceiving a God (that is, a Being supremely perfect) to whom existence is lacking (that is to say, to whom a certain perfection is lacking), than to conceive of a mountain which has no valley.

But although I cannot really conceive of a God without existence any more than a mountain without a valley, still from the fact that I conceive of a mountain with

---

[1]St. Anselm, *Proslogium,* in *St. Anselm: Basic Writings,* tr. S. N. Deane (LaSalle, IL: Open Court, 1903), pp. 7–9.

a valley, it does not follow that there is such a mountain in the world; similarly although I conceive of God as possessing existence, it would seem that it does not follow that there is a God which exists; for my thought does not impose any necessity upon things, and just as I may imagine a winged horse, although no horse with wings exists, so I could perhaps attribute existence to God, although no God existed.

But a sophism is concealed in this objection; for from the fact that I cannot conceive a mountain without a valley, it does not follow that there is any mountain or any valley in existence, but only that the mountain and the valley, whether they exist or do not exist, cannot in any way be separated one from the other. While from the fact that I cannot conceive God without existence, it follows that existence is inseparable from Him, and hence that He really exists; not that my thought can bring this to pass, or impose any necessity on things, but, on the contrary, because the necessity which lies in the thing itself, i.e., the necessity of the existence of God determines me to think in this way. For it is not within my power to think of God without existence (that is of a supremely perfect Being devoid of a supreme perfection) though it is in my power to imagine a horse either with wings or without wings.[2]

In either St. Anselm's or Descartes' version of the Ontological Argument, the essential point is the same: It is impossible to think of God—or at least of the greatest being—without thinking of him as existing.

IS EXISTENCE A PREDICATE?

A misguided
criticism?

You probably have the uneasy feeling that the Ontological Argument is putting something over on you. If so, you are not alone. No sooner had St. Anselm shown why the atheist is a fool than a fellow monk, Gaunilo, wrote a rebuttal entitled *On Behalf of the Fool.* Among other things, Gaunilo asked how we could possibly derive the real existence of something from a mere idea of it. We might as well conclude from our idea of a lost, perfect, desert island (Gaunilo's example) that such an island actually exists! This is a very obvious criticism, but some think that it misses the point. Of course it does not follow from our idea of an island—even a perfect island—or a unicorn or a hundred dollars that these really exist, but that is because none of these is the *greatest* being, and therefore they do not *have* to exist in order to *be* that thing. The difference is between the greatest of a kind—Gaunilo's perfect island—and that than which nothing greater can be conceived—Anselm's definition of God. Only in the case of the *greatest* being, or the most perfect being in this latter sense, *must* it be said that it *must* exist. One more time: It is not part of the concept of a unicorn or other creature that it *exists,* but it is part of the idea of the *greatest* being:

---

[2]René Descartes, *Meditations on First Philosophy,* in *The Philosophical Works of Descartes,* tr. Elizabeth S. Haldane and G. R. T. Ross (Cambridge: Cambridge University Press, 1911), 1, 180–182.

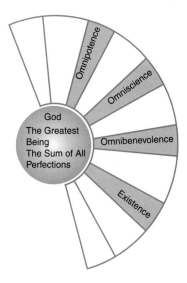

Or is it? Whereas the Ontological Argument clearly takes existence as a defining property, attribute, or *predicate* of God, many have charged that this is a mistake. In fact, the single most recurring attack against the Ontological Argument has consisted in the claim that existence is not a predicate.

Of course, existence is a predicate in a purely *grammatical* sense: In the sentence "God exists," "God" is the subject and "exists" is the predicate. But in a *logical* sense, existence is not a predicate in that it in no way adds anything, subtracts anything, or in any way modifies the concept of the subject. To see that this is so, in your imagination start building up the concept of a unicorn by supplying the appropriate predicates:

A unicorn is shaped like a horse.

A unicorn is white.

A unicorn has an ivory horn.

.

.

.

Every time you introduce a predicate, the subject becomes in some way changed and augmented. However, when we finally add,

A unicorn *exists.*

you see immediately that *nothing has been added whatsoever.* A unicorn that doesn't exist is no less a unicorn than one that does. Naturally, there is a difference between the nonexistent unicorn and the existent unicorn (try to ride the nonexistent one!), but the difference has nothing whatsoever to do with the *idea* or *concept* of the unicorn.

Kant was one of the first to press this attack on the Ontological Argument. In the following paragraphs from the *Critique of Pure Reason*, he attempts to show that the being or existence of God stands in a different relation to God than his regular attributes, such as omnipotence, and that, specifically, being or existence is not a predicate at all. (By an "identical judgment" Kant means an analytic judgment or a judgment of the form "A is A.")

If in an identical judgment I reject the predicate and retain the subject, there arises a contradiction, and hence, I say, that the former belongs to the latter necessarily. But if I reject the subject as well as the predicate, there is no contradiction, because there is nothing left that can be contradicted. To accept a triangle and yet to reject its three angles is contradictory, but there is no contradiction at all in admitting the nonexistence of the triangle and of its three angles. The same applies to the concept of an absolutely necessary Being. Remove its existence, and you remove the thing itself, with all its predicates, so that a contradiction becomes impossible. There is nothing external to which the contradiction could apply, because the thing is not meant to be externally necessary; nor is there anything internal that could be contradicted, for in removing the thing out of existence, you have removed at the same time all its internal qualities. If you say, God is almighty, that is a necessary judgment, because almightiness cannot be removed, if you accept a deity, that is, an infinite Being, with the concept of which that other concept is identical. But if you say, God is not, then neither his almightiness, nor any other of his predicates is given; they are all, together with the subject, removed out of existence, and therefore there is not the slightest contradiction in that sentence....

Being is evidently not a real predicate, or a concept of something that can be added to the concept of a thing. It is merely the admission of a thing, and of certain determinations in it. Logically, it is merely the copula of a judgment. The proposition, "God is almighty", contains two concepts, each having its object, namely, God and almightiness. The small word "is", is not an additional predicate, but only serves to put the predicate *in relation* to the subject. If, then, I take the subject (God) with all its predicates (including that of almightiness), and say "God is", or there is a God, I do not put a new predicate to the concept of God, but I only put the subject by itself, with all its predicates, in relation to my concept, as its object. Both must contain exactly the same kind of thing, and nothing can have been added to the concept, which expresses possibility only, but my thinking its object as simply given and saying, it is. And thus the real does not contain more than the possible. A hundred real dollars do not contain a penny more than a hundred possible dollars. For as the latter signify the concept, the former the object and its position by itself, it is clear that, in case the former contained more than the latter, my concept would not express the whole object, and would not therefore be its adequate concept. In my financial position no doubt there exists more by one hundred real dollars, than by their concept only (that is their possibility), because in reality the object is not only contained analytically in my concept, but is added to my concept (which is a determination of my state), synthetically; but the conceived hundred dollars are not in the least increased through the existence which is outside my concept.

By whatever and by however many predicates I may think a thing (even in completely determining it), nothing is really added to it, if I add that the thing exists. Otherwise, it would not be the same that exists, but something more than was contained in the concept, and I could not say that the exact object of my concept existed. . . .

Time and labour therefore are lost on the famous ontological (Cartesian) proof of the existence of a Supreme Being from more concepts; and a man might as well imagine that he could become richer in knowledge by mere ideas, as a merchant in capital, if, in order to improve his position, he were to add a few noughts to his cash account.[3]

That seemed, and still seems, to many to be a decisive refutation of the Ontological Argument. But this argument for God has a most inconvenient way of not staying dead, and it continues even yet to be a center of philosophical controversy.

One of the most pivotal of recent discussions is that of Norman Malcolm, who, in the early 1960s, published an essay entitled "Anselm's Ontological Arguments." Note the plural. Malcolm emphasized that we have in St. Anselm not one but *two* arguments. Look again at St. Anselm's formulation of his argument in *Proslogium*, Chapter 1, and his different formulation in Chapter 2 (both quoted above). The first formulation revolves around the notion that God is a greater being if he exists than if he does not: God's existence is one of his attributes, or predicates. But the second formulation revolves around the notion that God is a greater being if he cannot not-exist: *Necessary* existence is a divine predicate.

Anselm's *two* Ontological Arguments

With respect to the first of these, Malcolm agreed entirely with the Kantian criticism, which he restates and clarifies in his own way:

The doctrine that existence is a perfection is remarkably queer. It makes sense and is true to say that my future house will be a better one if it is insulated than if it is not insulated; but what could it mean to say that it will be a better house if it exists than if it does not? My future child will be a better man if he is honest than if he is not; but who would understand the saying that he will be a better man if he exists than if he does not? Or who understands the saying that if God exists He is more perfect than if He does not exist? One might say, with some intelligibility, that it would be better (for oneself or for mankind) if God exists than if He does not—but that is a different matter.

A king might desire that his next chancellor should have knowledge, wit, and resolution; but it is ludicrous to add that the king's desire is to have a chancellor who exists. Suppose that two royal councilors, A and B, were asked to draw up separately descriptions of the most perfect chancellor they could conceive, and that the descriptions they produced were identical except that A includes existence in his list of attributes of a perfect chancellor and B did not. (I do not mean that B put non-existence in his list.) One and the same person could satisfy both descriptions. More to the point, any person who satisfied A's description would *necessarily* satisfy B's description and *vice versa*! This is to say that A and B did not produce descriptions of necessary and desirable qualities in a chancellor. A only made a show of putting down a desirable quality that B had failed to include.

---

[3]Immanuel Kant, *Critique of Pure Reason,* tr. F. Max Müller (Garden City, NY: Anchor Books, 1966), pp. 399–403.

I believe that I am merely restating an observation that Kant made in attacking the notion that "existence" or "being" is a "real predicate."...Anselm's ontological proof of *Proslogion 2* is fallacious because it rests on the false doctrine that existence is a perfection (and therefore that "existence" is a "real predicate"). It would be desirable to have a rigorous refutation of the doctrine but I have not been able to provide one. I am compelled to leave the matter at the more or less intuitive level of Kant's observation.[4]

With respect to St. Anselm's second formulation, however, the situation is, says Malcolm, quite different. *Necessary* existence may, indeed, be properly construed as a predicate, and he formulates his own version of this form of the argument, which he thinks is absolutely sound.

Malcolm:
necessary existence
is a predicate

What Anselm has proved is that the notion of contingent existence or of contingent nonexistence cannot have any application to God. His existence must either be logically necessary or logically impossible. The only intelligible way of rejecting Anselm's claim that God's existence is necessary is to maintain that the concept of God, as a being a greater than which cannot be conceived, is self-contradictory or nonsensical. Supposing that this is false, Anselm is right to deduce God's necessary existence from his characterization of Him as a being a greater than which cannot be conceived.

Let me summarize the proof. If God, a being a greater than which cannot be conceived, does not exist then He cannot come into existence or have *happened* to come into existence, and in either case He would be a limited being, which by our conception of Him He is not. Since He cannot come into existence, if He does not exist His existence is impossible. If he does exist He cannot have come into existence (for the reasons given), nor can He cease to exist, for nothing could cause Him to cease to exist nor could it just happen that He ceased to exist. So if God exists His existence is necessary. Thus God's existence is either impossible or necessary. It can be the former only if the concept of such a being is self-contradictory or in some way logically absurd. Assuming that this is not so, it follows that He necessarily exists.[5]

---

[4]Norman Malcolm, "Anselm's Ontological Arguments," *The Philosophical Review*, Vol. LXIX, No. 1 (January 1960), in Norman Malcolm, *Knowledge and Certainty: Essays and Lectures* (Englewood Cliffs, NJ: Prentice-Hall, 1963), pp. 143–144.

[5]Ibid., pp. 149–150.

MALCOLM'S ONTOLOGICAL ARGUMENT

God is an unlimited being.
The existence of an unlimited being is either impossible or necessary.
The concept of an unlimited being is not self-contradictory, so such a being
  is not impossible.

Therefore such a being is necessary.

The above paragraphs deserve careful study, not only for the sake of the Ontological Argument but also for the sake of the instructive philosophical ideas and maneuvers involved. It is especially critical to see that the reasoning depends on what we might call the Consistency Principle: A logically consistent proposition could be true, but a self-contradictory proposition could not. Examples: The proposition, "A vast herd of giraffes is at the moment roaming through the White House" is, of course, an outrageous claim, but it is at least logically consistent and therefore *could* be true. But the proposition "There are barking dogs that do not bark when they are barking" is to be rejected at the start. It is impossible because it is logically incoherent. Be sure you understand how Malcolm arrives at the twofold conclusion that either God's existence is impossible or it is necessary, and how it can only be impossible if it is logically absurd—which, says Malcolm, it is not, leaving only the alternative that God exists, and exists necessarily.

The Consistency
Principle

THE MORAL ARGUMENT

Yet another argument for God must be considered. After the Ontological Argument you may have the feeling of being brought back down to earth, as this last argument bases itself on *experience* again. However, it is not sense experience but *moral* experience that is now in view. This means not our experience of empirical reality—such as tables and chairs and dogs and cats—but our experience of *moral* reality, our confrontation with *moral law*.

In a famous passage from his *Critique of Practical Reason*, Kant gives eloquent expression to our confrontation with, and the distinction between, the two worlds: the sensible world and the moral world.

> Two things fill the mind with ever new and increasing admiration and awe, the oftener and more steadily we reflect on them: the starry heavens above me and the moral law within me. I do not merely conjecture them and seek them as though obscured in darkness or in the transcendent region beyond my horizon: I see them before me, and I associate them directly with the consciousness of my own existence.[6]

And in spite of his rejection of the other arguments for God, Kant himself found it necessary to formulate a version of the *Moral Argument* for God.

As with the other arguments for God, there are several versions of the Moral Argument. But they all reduce to the same essential reasoning: They begin with the givenness of morality and conclude that there must be a Lawgiver that originates and stands behind moral law.

But what, exactly, is meant by "moral law"? It is important to distinguish between "moral laws" and "moral law." The former refers to our various and changing *perceptions* and *codifications* of morality, and the latter refers

*Sense experience
and moral
experience*

Moral laws versus
moral law

---

[6]Immanuel Kant, *Critique of Practical Reason*, tr. Lewis White Beck (Indianapolis: Bobbs-Merrill, 1956), p. 166.

C. S. Lewis, Oxford professor of medieval
English literature, is most widely known for his
rational and popular defenses of Christianity.

to morality *as it is in itself*. To be sure, some have argued that there are at least some universally recognized moral laws. Moral laws (in the plural) are not a matter of choice and chance, and they must be grounded in an adequate cause or source: a Lawgiver. This is the view of the late C. S. Lewis, a popular and effective defender of Christian ideas. From *Mere Christianity* (first published in 1943):

> I know that some people say the idea of a Law of Nature or decent behaviour known to all men is unsound, because different civilisations and different ages have had quite different moralities.
>
> But this is not true. There have been differences between their moralities, but these have never amounted to anything like a total difference. If anyone will take the trouble to compare the moral teaching of, say, the ancient Egyptians, Babylonians, Hindus, Chinese, Greeks, and Romans, what will really strike him will be how very like they are to each other and to our own. Some of the evidence for this I have put together in the appendix of another book called *The Abolition of Man;* but for our present purpose I need only ask the reader to think what a totally different morality would mean. Think of a country where people were admired for running away in battle, or where a man felt proud of doublecrossing all the people who had been kindest to him. You might just as well try to imagine a country where two and two made five. Men have differed as regards what people you ought to be unselfish to—whether it was only your own family, or your fellow countrymen, or everyone. But they have always agreed that you ought not to put yourself first. Selfishness has never been admired. Men have differed as to whether you should have one wife or four. But they have always agreed that you must not simply have any woman you liked.[7]

[7]C. S. Lewis, *Mere Christianity* (New York: Macmillan, 1976), p. 19.

Of course, some anthropologists and sociologists would have a field day with such claims, playing down cultural and moral similarities and playing up cultural relativities and differences. No matter. The point of departure for the Moral Argument is not so much the universality of moral laws (in the plural) as of the moral law (in the singular), not so much the universality of moral *conscience* as of moral *consciousness,* not so much that everyone has the same moral opinions but that everyone has *some* moral opinions, not that everyone thinks that certain things are right or wrong but that everyone thinks that *something* is right or wrong. We may disagree and be confused about moral laws, but we all acknowledge moral law. And we recognize it as being objective (existing independently of our own interests or wills) and absolute (universally binding). Don't we? Why spend so much time and energy in reviewing, testing, and purifying our moral laws? Isn't it because we think that to some degree and however imperfectly they can embody the absolute moral law?

This, then, is the first premise in the Moral Argument for the existence of God: There is an objective and absolute moral law. The next step is to argue that such a moral law cannot be, as it were, just floating about out there like something accidental or capricious. No, if it is really a morally binding law, then it must have a rational and abiding basis. And just as it is absurd to think of fluctuating and finite moral laws and ideals as existing apart from our own minds, so is it absurd to think of an *absolute* moral law as existing apart from an *absolute* mind. Think about this. Ideals and values, unlike tables, chairs, dogs, cats, and light fixtures, exist by their nature in *minds.* But what or whose mind is an adequate source for ideals and values? Bridget's mind? But her mind is constantly changing. How could it be the source of unchanging and universally binding ideals? Henry's mind? But we all know how fickle and limited his mind is. How could any finite and changeable human mind be the basis of the moral law? Thus, the second premise: An absolute moral law requires an absolute mind as its adequate foundation. And the conclusion is, by now, obvious: There must exist an absolute mind. It remains only to unpack the full meaning of "absolute mind." What could an "absolute" mind be, except one that is unchanging, eternal, transcendent, ultimate, and so on? And what could this be, except what most people call "God"?

From the moral law to an absolute mind

This version of the Moral Argument is summarized by the English theologian and philosopher Hastings Rashdall (1858–1924) in his book *The Theory of Good and Evil:*

> We say that the Moral Law has a real existence, that there is such a thing as an absolute Morality, that there is something absolutely true or false in ethical judgments, whether we or any number of human beings at any given time actually think so or not. Such a belief is distinctly implied in what we mean by Morality. The idea of such as unconditional, objectively valid, Moral Law or ideal undoubtedly exists as a psychological fact. The question before us is whether it is capable of theoretical justification. We must then face the question *where* such an ideal exists, and what manner of existence we are to attribute to it. Certainly it is to be found, wholly and completely, in no individual human consciousness. Men

MORAL LAWS AND MORAL LAW

- *Moral laws* are the particular, changing, and (to some degree) relative views that human beings formulate about morality. Our moral *conscience* reflects such views.

- *Moral law*, on the other hand, denotes the objective and absolute moral principles that are imperfectly expressed in moral laws. Our moral *consciousness* reflects the belief in morality itself, apart from our views of it.

actually think differently about moral questions, and there is no empirical reason for supposing that they will ever do otherwise. Where then and how does the moral ideal really exist? As regards matters of fact or physical law, we have no difficulty in satisfying ourselves that there is an objective reality which is what it is irrespectively of our beliefs or disbeliefs about it. For the man who supposes that objective reality resides in the things themselves, our ideas about them are objectively true or false so far as they correspond or fail to correspond with this real and independent archetype, though he might be puzzled to give a metaphysical account of the nature of this "correspondence" between experience and a Reality whose *esse* is something other than to be experienced. In the physical region the existence of divergent ideas does not throw doubt upon the existence of a reality independent of our ideas. But in the case of moral ideals it is otherwise. On materialistic or naturalistic assumptions the moral ideal can hardly be regarded as a real thing. Nor could it well be regarded as a property of any real thing: it can be no more than an aspiration, a product of the imagination, which may be useful to stimulate effort in directions in which we happen to want to move, but which cannot compel respect when we feel no desire to act in conformity with it. An absolute Moral Law or moral ideal cannot exist *in* material things. And it does not (we have seen) exist in the mind of this or that individual. Only if we believe in the existence of a Mind for which the true moral ideal is already in some sense real, a Mind which is the source of whatever is true in our own moral judgements, can we rationally think of the moral ideal as no less real than the world itself. Only so can we believe in an absolute standard of right and wrong, which is as independent of this or that man's actual ideas and actual desires as the facts of material nature. The belief in God, though not (like the belief in a real and an active self) a postulate of there being any such thing as Morality at all, is the logical presupposition of an "objective" or absolute Morality. A moral ideal can exist nowhere and nohow but in a mind; an absolute moral ideal can exist only in a Mind from which all Reality is derived. Our moral ideal can only claim objective validity in so far as it can rationally be regarded as the revelation of a moral ideal externally existing in the mind of God.

We may be able, perhaps, to give some meaning to Morality without the postulate of God, but not its true or full meaning. If the existence of God is not a postulate of all Morality, it is a postulate of a sound Morality; for it is essential to that belief which vaguely and implicitly underlies all moral beliefs, and which forms the very heart of Morality in its highest, more developed, more explicit forms. The truth that the moral ideal is what it is whether we like it or not is the most essential element in what the popular consciousness understands by "moral obligation." Moral obligation means moral objectivity. That *at least* seems to be implied in any legitimate use of the term: at least it implies the existence of an absolute, objective moral ideal. And such a belief we have seen imperatively to demand an explanation of the Universe which shall be idealistic or at least spiritualistic, which shall recognize the existence of a Mind whose thoughts are the standard of truth and falsehood alike in Morality and in respect of all other existence. In other words, objective Morality implies the belief in God. The belief in God, if not so obviously and primarily a postulate of Morality as the belief in a permanent spiritual and active self, is still a postulate of a Morality which shall be able to fully satisfy the demands of the moral consciousness. It may conveniently be called the secondary postulate of Morality.[8]

[8]Hastings Rashdall, *The Theory of Good and Evil* (Oxford: Clarendon Press, 1907), II, 211–213.

BEYOND REASON: PASCAL'S WAGER

Many religious people (including many philosophers) have rejected the idea that it is possible to provide rational proof for their belief in God. One of the most famous was the French philosopher Blaise Pascal. Pascal argued that we should gamble on God's existence even though we can't prove it. We must, Pascal claimed, make a choice, and the benefits of believing and being right are much greater than the cost of any other option. So why not "wager" that God exists? Consider Pascal's "argument":

> "Either God is or he is not." But to which view shall we be inclined? Reason cannot decide this question. Infinite chaos separates us. At the far end of this infinite distance a coin is being spun which will come down heads or tails. How will you wager? Reason cannot make you choose either, reason cannot prove either wrong.
>
> Do not then condemn as wrong those who have made a choice, for you know nothing about it. "No, but I will condemn them not for having made this particular choice, but any choice, for, although the one who calls heads and the other one are equally at fault, the fact is that they are both at fault: the right thing is not to wager at all."
>
> Yes, but you must wager. There is no choice, you are already committed. Which will you choose then? Let us see: since a choice must be made, let us see which offers you the least interest. You have two things to lose: the true and the good; and two things to stake: your reason and your will, your knowledge and your happiness; and your nature has two things to avoid: error and wretchedness. Since you must necessarily choose, your reason is no more affronted by choosing one rather than the other. That is one point cleared up. But your happiness? Let us weigh up the gain and the loss involved in calling heads that God exists. Let us assess the two cases: if you win you win everything, if you lose you lose nothing. Do not hesitate then: wager that he does exist."*

*Blaise Pascal, *Pensées*, tr. A.J. Krailsheimer (Baltimore and Harmondsworth: Penguin Books, 1966).

An important note: If you do, in fact, accept the reality of an objective and universally binding morality, but balk at the claimed implications of this for the existence of God, well, has not the Moral Argument accomplished its real objective anyway? For you would, then, believe in a transcendent, independent, and absolute reality—namely, the moral law. But does not that commit you, if not to God, at least to a definitely spiritualist and *sort* of theistic view of things? A view that posits, behind the fluctuating and relative world of experience and opinions, an invisible and eternal Reality that confronts us and demands rightness from us? And is this *so* different from God? Does it matter all that much what you *call* it?

IS THERE A MORAL LAW?

If anything is clear about the Moral Argument it is that it cannot possibly work except with the belief in objective and absolute morality. If one rejects this, well, the axe has been laid to the root of this tree.

Certainly there are those who do deny that morality is anything more than the perceptions, desires, inclinations, or tastes of the individual—an individual person, community, society, or whatever. The issue between moral absolutism (morality is independent of the individual) and moral relativism (morality is relative to the individual) is better treated in Chapter 14, "Challenges to Morality." Here we only summarize a few points.

The major evidence for relativism is the wide variety of differences and disagreements that do, in fact, exist from person to person and culture to culture. On the other hand, as Lewis asked, are the differences all that great? In any event, we have already distinguished between our varying opinions of morality and morality itself. Furthermore, even if some, or even most, of our ideas have been learned or culturally instilled, it hardly follows that they therefore should be rejected as false! Finally, if the relativist is right, how could one ever be morally mistaken? Would not every moral opinion have to be correct for the individual holding it? And whatever one *says* about moral relativism, can he or she *actually live* (praise, blame, argue, vote, crusade, judge, etc.) except on the belief that values are real and binding on everyone?

Is morality absolute or relative? Objective or subjective?

Moral relativism: pro and con

THE MORAL ARGUMENT

There is an absolute moral law.
An absolute moral law must have an absolute mind as its basis.

Therefore, there must be an absolute mind as the basis of the moral law.

How might one defend the two premises of this argument?

Such issues, pro and con, are clearly focused in the following selection from a lively debate originally broadcast over the BBC. The participants are two English philosophers: Bertrand Russell, who here defends the relativist position, and Fr. Frederick C. Copleston, who defends the absolutist position and its implications for the existence of God.

COPLESTON: ... what's your justification for distinguishing between good and bad or how do you view the distinction between them?

RUSSELL: I don't have any justification any more than I have when I distinguish between blue and yellow. What is my justification for distinguishing between blue and yellow? I can see they are different.

COPLESTON: Well, that is an excellent justification, I agree. You distinguish blue and yellow by seeing them, so you distinguish good and bad by what faculty?

RUSSELL: By my feelings.

COPLESTON: By your feelings. Well, that's what I was asking. You think that good and evil have reference simply to feeling?

RUSSELL: Well, why does one type of object look yellow and another look blue? I can more or less give an answer to that thanks to the physicists, and as to why I think one sort of thing good and another evil,

The English philosopher Bertrand Russell was very influential in a wide range of philosophical issues, and more activistic and outspoken than most. He was especially antireligious, and once wrote a book entitled *Why I Am Not a Christian.*

probably there is an answer of the same sort, but it hasn't been gone into the same way and I couldn't give it to you.

COPLESTON: Well, let's take the behavior of the Commandant of Belsen. That appears to you as undesirable and evil and to me too. To Adolf Hitler we suppose it appeared as something good and desirable. I suppose you'd have to admit that for Hitler it was good and for you it is evil.

RUSSELL: No, I shouldn't quite go so far as that. I mean, I think people can make mistakes in that as they can in other things. If you have jaundice you see things yellow that are not yellow. You're making a mistake.

COPLESTON: Yes, one can make mistakes, but can you make a mistake if it's simply a question of reference to a feeling or emotion? Surely Hitler would be the only possible judge of what appealed to his emotions.

RUSSELL: It would be quite right to say that it appealed to his emotions, but you can say various things about that among others, that if that sort of thing makes that sort of appeal to Hitler's emotions, then Hitler makes quite a different appeal to my emotions.

COPLESTON: Granted. But there's no objective criterion outside feeling then for condemning the conduct of the Commandant of Belsen, in your view?

RUSSELL: No more than there is for the color-blinded person who's in exactly the same state. Why do we intellectually condemn the color-blinded man? Isn't it because he's the minority?

COPLESTON: I would say because he is lacking in a thing which normally belongs to human nature.

RUSSELL: Yes, but if he were in the majority, we shouldn't say that....

COPLESTON: Well, do you think that the word "ought" simply has an emotional connotation?

RUSSELL: No, I don't think that, because you see, as I was saying a moment ago, one has to take account of the effects, and I think right conduct is that which would probably produce the greatest possible balance in intrinsic value of all the acts possible in the circumstances, and you've got to take account of the probable effects of your action in considering what is right.

COPLESTON: Well, I brought in moral obligation because I think that one can approach the question of God's existence in that way. The vast majority of the human race will make, and always have made, some distinction between right and wrong. The vast majority I think has some consciousness of an obligation in the moral sphere. It's my opinion that the perception of values and the consciousness of moral law and obligation are best explained through the hypothesis of a transcendent ground of value and of an author of the moral law. I do mean by "author of the moral law" an arbitrary author of the moral law. I think, in fact, that those modern atheists who have argued in the converse way "there is no God; therefore, there are no absolute values and no absolute law," are quite logical.

RUSSELL: I don't like the word "absolute." I don't think there is anything absolute whatever. The moral law, for example, is always changing. At one period in the development of the human race, almost everybody thought cannibalism was a duty.

COPLESTON: Well, I don't see that differences in particular moral judgments are any conclusive argument against the universality of the moral law. Let's assume for the moment that there are absolute moral values; even on that hypothesis it's only to be expected that different individuals and different groups should enjoy varying degrees of insight into those values.

RUSSELL: I'm inclined to think that "ought," the feeling that one has about "ought" is an echo of what has been told one by one's parents or one's nurses.

COPLESTON: Well, I wonder if you can explain away the idea of the "ought" merely in terms of nurses and parents. I really don't see how it can be conveyed to anybody in other terms than itself. It seems to me that if there is a moral order bearing upon the human conscience, that that moral order is unintelligible apart from the existence of God.

RUSSELL: Then you have to say one or other of two things. Either God only speaks to a very small percentage of mankind—which happens to include yourself—or He deliberately says things that are not true in talking to the consciences of savages. . . .

COPLESTON: It seems to me to be external customs and taboos and things of that sort which can most easily be explained simply through environment and education, but all that seems to me to belong to what I call the matter of the law, the content. The idea of the "ought" as such can never be conveyed to a man by the tribal chief or by anybody else, because there are no other terms in which it could be conveyed. It seems to me entirely—[Russell breaks in].

RUSSELL: But I don't see any reason to say that—I mean we all know about conditioned reflexes. We know that an animal, if punished habitually for a certain sort of act, after a time will refrain. I don't think the animal refrains from arguing within himself, "Master will be angry if I do this." He has a feeling that that's not the thing to do. That's what we can do with ourselves and nothing more.

COPLESTON: I see no reason to suppose that an animal has a consciousness of moral obligation; and we certainly don't regard an animal as morally responsible for his acts of disobedience. But a man has a consciousness of obligation and of moral values. I see no reason to suppose that one could condition all men as one can "condition" an animal, and I don't suppose you'd really want to do so even if one could. If "behaviorism" were true, there would be no objective moral distinction between the emperor Nero and St. Francis of Assisi. I can't help feeling, Lord

Russell, you know, that you regard the conduct of the Commandant of Belsen as morally reprehensible, and that you yourself would never under any circumstances act in that way, even if you thought, or had reason to think, that possibly the balance of the happiness of the human race might be increased through some people being treated in that abominable manner.

RUSSELL: No. I wouldn't imitate the conduct of a mad dog. The fact that I wouldn't do it doesn't really bear on this question we're discussing.

COPLESTON: No, but if you were making a utilitarian explanation of right and wrong in terms of consequences, it might be held, and I suppose some of the Nazis of the better type would have held that although it's lamentable to have to act in this way, yet the balance in the long run leads to greater happiness. I don't think you'd say that, would you? I think you'd say that that sort of action is wrong—and in itself, quite apart from whether the general balance of happiness is increased or not. Then if you're prepared to say that, then I think you must have some criterion of right and wrong, that is outside the criterion of feeling, at any rate. To me, that admission would ultimately result in the admission of an ultimate ground of value in God....[9]

Try to understand every move made by the participants. Does it help you make your own decision about the Moral Argument for God?

IS RELIGIOUS EXPERIENCE EVIDENCE FOR GOD?

Naturally, many will balk at arguments for the existence of God right from the start. Nor will they necessarily be atheists. Some of the critics will be themselves believers, objecting that somehow such proofs are irrelevant or inappropriate to the overpowering majesty of God. "No," they will say, "God is not known in this way. Just as he transcends the world and our reason, so is he known in a way that transcends our ordinary knowledge." It is just as silly to think that God can be captured by an argument as it is to think that he can be confined to Solomon's Temple: "Even heaven and the highest heaven cannot contain you, much less this house that I have built!" (I Kings 8:27). On the more human side, do not religious experiences come *first*, and the arguments and rationalizations *second*? The French contemplative philosopher Simone Weil[10] thought so:

When we are eating bread, and even when we have eaten it, we know that it is real. We can nevertheless raise doubts about the reality of the bread. Philosophers raise doubts about the reality of the world of the senses. Such doubts

---

[9]Bertrand Russell and F. C. Copleston, "The Existence of God: A Debate Between Bertrand Russell and Father F. C. Copleston," in Bertrand Russell, *Why I am not a Christian* (London: Allen & Unwin, 1967).

[10]Pronounced *vay*.

published in 1902), William James takes on precisely this accusation and, in turn, accuses it of simple-mindedly confusing the "facts of mental history" with "their spiritual significance." That is, what is important is not how person X got that way, but whether what he or she says is worthy, true, and so on. He asks, furthermore, why any other state of mind—for example, that of the skeptic or the atheist—should be exempt from the same trivializing explanation: What is good for the goose is good for the gander. Pay close attention to his indictment of "medical materialism":

Perhaps the commonest expression of this assumption that spiritual value is undone if lowly origin be asserted is seen in those comments which unsentimental people so often pass on their more sentimental acquaintances. Alfred believes in immortality so strongly because his temperament is so emotional. Fanny's extraordinary conscientiousness is merely a matter of overinstigated nerves. William's melancholy about the universe is due to bad digestion—probably his liver is torpid. Eliza's delight in her church is a symptom of her hysterical constitution. Peter would be less troubled about his soul if he would take more exercise in the open air, etc. A more fully developed example of the same kind of reasoning is the fashion, quite common nowadays among certain writers, of criticizing the religious emotions of showing a connection between them and the sexual life. Conversion is a crisis of puberty and adolescence. The macerations of saints, and the devotion of missionaries, are only instances of the parental instinct of self-sacrifice gone astray. For the hysterical nun, starving for natural life, Christ is but an imaginary substitute for a more earthly object of affection. And the like.

We are surely all familiar in a general way with this method of discrediting states of mind for which we have an antipathy. We all use it to some degree in criticizing persons whose states of mind we regard as overstrained. But when other people criticize our own more exalted soul-flights by calling them "nothing but" expressions of our organic disposition, we feel outraged and hurt, for we know that, whatever be our organism's peculiarities, our mental states have their substantive value as revelations of the living truth; and we wish that all this medical materialism could be made to hold its tongue.

Medical materialism seems indeed a good appellation for the two simple-minded systems of thought which we are considering. Medical materialism finishes up Saint Paul by calling his vision on the road to Damascus a discharging lesion of the occipital cortex, he being an epileptic. It snuffs out Saint Teresa as an hysteric, Saint Francis of Assisi as an hereditary degenerate, George Fox's discontent with the shams of his age, and his pining for spiritual veracity, it treats as a symptom of a disordered colon. Carlyle's organ-tones of misery it accounts for by a gastroduodenal catarrh. All such mental overtensions, it says, are, when you come to the bottom of the matter, mere affairs of diathesis (auto-intoxications most probably), due to the perverted action of various glands which physiology will yet discover.

And medical materialism then thinks that the spiritual authority of all such personages is successfully undermined.

Let us ourselves look at the matter in the largest possible way. Modern psychology, finding definite psycho-physical connections to hold good, assumes as a convenient hypothesis that the dependence of mental states upon bodily conditions must be thoroughgoing and complete. If we adopt the assumption, then of course what medical materialism insists on must be true in a general way, if not in every detail: Saint Paul certainly had once an epileptoid, if not an epileptic

William James' *Varieties of Religious Experience* is a classic of religious philosophy, and the chapters dealing with mysticism are perhaps the most frequently consulted discussions of the subject.

seizure; George Fox was an hereditary degenerate; Carlyle was undoubtedly auto-intoxicated by some organ or other, no matter which—and the rest. But now, I ask you, how can such an existential account of facts of mental history decide in one way or another upon their spiritual significance? According to the general postulate of psychology just referred to, there is not a single one of our states of mind, high or low, healthy or morbid, that has not some organic process as its condition. Scientific theories are organically conditioned just as much as religious emotions are; and if we only knew the facts intimately enough, we should doubtless see "the liver" determining the dicta of the sturdy atheist as decisively as it does those of the Methodist under conviction anxious about his soul. When it alters in one way the blood that percolates it, we get the Methodist, when in another way, we get the atheist form of mind. So of all our raptures and our drynesses, our longings and pantings, our questions and beliefs. They are equally organically founded, be they religious or of non-religious content.

To plead the organic causation of a religious state of mind, then, in refutation of its claim to possess superior spiritual value, is quite illogical and arbitrary, unless one has already worked out in advance some psycho-physical theory connecting spiritual values in general with determinate sorts of physiological change. Otherwise none of our thoughts and feelings, not even our scientific doctrines, not even our *dis*-beliefs, could retain any value as revelations of the truth, for every one of them without exception flows from the state of its possessor's body at the time....

In the natural sciences and industrial arts it never occurs to anyone to try to refute opinions by showing up their author's neurotic constitution. Opinions here are invariably tested by logic and by experiment, no matter what may be their author's neurological type. It should be no otherwise with religious opinions. Their value can only be ascertained by spiritual judgments directly passed upon them,

"MEDICAL MATERIALISM"

A term that William James contemptuously applies to the attempts to undermine the religious and spiritual significance of religious experiences by attributing them to disorders of a psychological or even physiological nature.

judgments based on our own immediate feeling primarily; and secondarily on what we can ascertain of their experiential relations to our moral needs and to the rest of what we hold as true.

Immediate luminousness, in short, *philosophical reasonableness,* and *moral helpfulness* are the only available criteria. Saint Teresa might have had the nervous system of the placidest cow, and it would not now save her theology, if the trial of the theology by these other tests should show it to be contemptible. And conversely if her theology can stand these other tests, it will make no difference how hysterical or nervously off her balance Saint Teresa may have been when she was with us here below.[13]

Surely James is right about the epistemological irrelevance of medical materialism's criticism of religious claims. On the other hand, that does not make those claims true. As he himself insists in the last two paragraphs above, those claims, like others, must satisfy some tests before they are accepted: They must be philosophically reasonable, and they must cohere with and advance the rest of our moral and intellectual life. And here is James' more positive contribution to the discussion. James was a major contributor to Pragmatism, a philosophy that stressed practicality, workability, usefulness, and consequences or results as the criteria of true beliefs. And he did, in fact, believe that the claims advanced by the world's great religious or theological personalities satisfy the test—at least when reduced to their common, universal essence. Following his indictment of medical materialism, the main part of the *Varieties of Religious Experience* is an extended consideration of the relevance and worthiness of various religious claims and perspectives, and at the end, he states clearly his positive assessment. In the following brief extract from his Postscript, James sets himself squarely against the prevailing "current" and votes in favor of a religious reality (by "piecemeal supernaturalism" James means a conception of the supernatural that envisions it as actually intruding into and affecting our world).

The pragmatic value of religion

...the current of thought in academic circles runs against me, and I feel like a man who must set his back against an open door quickly if he does not wish to see it closed and locked. In spite of its being so shocking to the reigning intellectual tastes, I believe that a candid consideration of piecemeal supernaturalism and a complete discussion of all its metaphysical bearings will show it to be the

[13]William James, *The Varieties of Religious Experience* (New York: Longmans, Green, and Co., 1902), pp. 10–18.

hypothesis by which the largest number of legitimate requirements are met. That of course would be a program for other books than this; what I now say sufficiently indicates to the philosophic reader the place where I belong.

If asked just where the differences in fact which are due to God's existence come in, I should have to say that in general I have no hypothesis to offer beyond what the phenomenon of "prayerful communion," especially when certain kinds of incursion from the subconscious region take part in it, immediately suggests. The appearance is that in this phenomenon something ideal, which in one sense is part of ourselves and in another sense is not ourselves, actually exerts an influence, raises our centre of personal energy, and produces regenerative effects unattainable in other ways. If, then, there be a wider world of being than that of our every-day consciousness, if in it there be forces whose effects on us are intermittent, if one facilitating condition of the effects be the openness of the "subliminal" door, we have the elements of a theory to which the phenomena of religious life lend plausibility. I am so impressed by the importance of these phenomena that I adopt the hypothesis which they so naturally suggest. At these places at least, I say, it would seem as though transmundane energies, God, if you will, produced immediate effects within the natural world to which the rest of our experience belongs.[14]

[14]Ibid., pp. 523–524.

IS RELIGION AN ILLUSION?

One of the most famous attacks on religion was that of Sigmund Freud, who explained it away as the result of various psychological needs and complexes. But it is often observed that his attack involved a gigantic informal fallacy. What was it?

…we turn our attention to the psychical origin of religious ideas. These, which are given out as teachings, are not precipitates of experience or end-results of thinking: they are illusions, fulfillments of the oldest, strongest and most urgent wishes of mankind. The secret of their strength lies in the strength of those wishes. As we already know, the terrifying impression of helplessness in childhood aroused the need for protection—for protection through love—which was provided by the father; and the recognition that this helplessness lasts throughout life made it necessary to cling to the existence of a father, but this time a more powerful one. Thus the benevolent rule of a divine Providence allays our fear of the dangers of life; the establishment of a moral world-order ensures the fulfillment of the demands of justice, which have so often remained unfulfilled in human civilization; and the prolongation of earthly existence in a future life provides the local and temporal framework in which these wish-fulfillments shall take place. Answers to the riddles that tempt the curiosity of man, such as how the universe began or what the relation is between body and mind, are developed in conformity with the underlying assumptions of this system.*

*Sigmund Freud. *The Future of an Illusion*, tr. W. D. Robson-Scott, rev. and ed. James Strachey (Garden City, NY: Anchor Books, 1964), pp. 47–48.

James aside, many are drawn at least to a more general conclusion: It is true that the world is full of kooks, liars, and deluded persons, and surely this should put us on guard against accepting, willy-nilly, every claim to direct experience with God. On the other hand, isn't it a bit nervy to scoff at such claims when they are made by some of the finest, most articulate, and most positively influential people the world has ever known?

CHAPTER 12 IN REVIEW

SUMMARY

In this chapter we have considered two further arguments for the existence of God:

- The Ontological Argument
- The Moral Argument

It is important to appreciate that whereas the other arguments began with the world, these attempt to demonstrate the existence of God through something given in the reason alone.

The Ontological Argument is an excellent example of completely *a priori* reasoning. Nowhere is there any reference to sense experience or the physical world. Rather, it attempts to show from a consideration of the *idea* of God (or most perfect being, unlimited being, etc.) that such a being, by virtue of being the *greatest*, must actually exist. Can such a being lack the attribute or perfection of existence any more than it can lack the attribute or perfection of omniscience, omnipotence, love, or justice? Or, as Descartes asks, can the existence of God (*that* he is) be separated from his essence (*what* he is) any more than a mountain can be separated from a valley?

But it is just with such talk of existence as an attribute or *predicate* that the Ontological Argument runs afoul of the most important objection. Kant observed that existence does *not*, in fact, actually add anything to the content of any concept; that is, existence is *not* a real predicate of anything, including the greatest thing. On the other hand, some, such as the contemporary philosopher Malcolm, have conceived a version of this proof that sidesteps the complaint that existence is not a predicate, and have formulated an Ontological Argument on the ground that *necessary* existence is a predicate, and that necessary existence is part of what "greatest being" must mean. Discussion of the Ontological Argument has raged for centuries and still rages. There is surely a lesson in this for those who think that this argument for God involves some simple-minded mistake.

The Moral Argument shifts our attention to our idea of moral law or, to say it differently, to our moral consciousness. If you believe in an objective and absolute morality, then how do you explain or justify it apart from an objective and absolute lawgiver? It is important to distinguish between believing in moral law and knowing what it is. The Moral Argument requires only the former. The relativity of moral opinions might not, therefore, be relevant here: I may be hopelessly confused about the content of the moral law but still be constrained to believe in it.

But, of course, that is the problem. Why should one believe in the first place in an objective and absolute morality? Some would answer, among other things, that the alternative—namely, ethical relativism or subjectivism—turns out on reflection to be philosophically indefensible (Is it not possible to be morally mistaken?) and certainly impossible to put into practice (Can one live apart from the practice of ideals and values?).

Knowledge of God by way of religious experience is, in contrast to the rational and argumentative approach, *non*rational or *supra*rational. And this means, for the proponent of religious experience, a directness and personalness about this knowledge.

Although the participant in religious experience will have no interest in skeptical attacks on its validity ("He who sees, sees, and he who does not see, does not see"), the directness and personalness (or subjectivity) of the experience are exactly what make for great difficulties in treating it as an evidence for God.

BASIC IDEAS

- The Ontological Argument
    St. Anselm's version (two forms)
    Descartes' version
- Existence as a predicate
- Kant's rejection of existence as a predicate
- Malcolm: necessary existence as a predicate
- The Consistency Principle
- The Moral Argument
- Distinction between moral conscience and moral consciousness (moral laws and the moral law)
- Moral objectivism (absolutism)/moral subjectivism (relativism)
- Subjectivism: reasons for and against
- The nonrational approach to God
- Religious experience as evidence for God: pro and con
- "Medical materialism"
- The pragmatic value of religion

TEST YOURSELF

1. Who said it? "I don't have any justification [for distinguishing between good and bad] any more than I have when I distinguish between blue and yellow."
2. Norman Malcolm (a) defended the Moral Argument against Bertrand Russell, (b) believed that necessary existence is a predicate of God, (c) was a

scholar of Renaissance and medieval literature, (d) argued that morality is purely relative.

3. Who extolled "the starry heavens above me and the moral law within me"?

4. True or false: "A vast herd of giraffes is at the moment roaming through the White House" is a logically consistent claim.

5. What, exactly, is the difference between moral laws and the moral law?

6. How does Hastings Rashdall figure in the discussion in this chapter?

7. Knowledge of God based on moral consciousness is (a) an instance of special revelation, (b) propounded by Bertrand Russell, (c) *a priori*, (d) refuted by Kant.

8. True or false: St. Anselm's and Descartes' versions of the Ontological Argument construe existence as a predicate or attribute of God.

9. What is the problem with religious experience as evidence for the reality of god?

QUESTIONS FOR REFLECTION

• Whether or not you accept the Ontological Argument, it is important to understand it. Specifically, can you reproduce *with understanding* Malcolm's version? Bearing in mind that Malcolm is not a fool, can you find any flaws in it?

• Do you see the distinction between believing in morality and knowing what it consists in? Do you think that *how many* people affirm a certain value or ideal is relevant? Who do you think was the victor in the Copleston-Russell debate on the Moral Argument? Why?

• In the last two chapters we have seen that while Kant rejected the *a posteriori* arguments, he himself formulated a version of the Moral Argument. Can you explain the epistemological basis of this? Do you recall from Chapter 10 Kant's distinction between the noumenal and phenomenal worlds? the limitations of the theoretical reason and the possibilities of the practical reason? What is the application here?

• What is your own honest evaluation of the claims of religious experience? Do the subjectivity and privacy of such experiences render them irrelevant as evidence for an unseen reality? Can you think of any consideration pro or con not mentioned in the text?

FOR FURTHER READING

Frederick Copleston. *A History of Philosophy.* Baltimore: Newman Press, 1946–1974. II, Ch. 15, and IV, Ch. 3. Accounts of St. Anselm's and Descartes' Ontological Proofs for the existence of God by a recognized historian of philosophy.

Brian Davies. *An Introduction to the Philosophy of Religion.* New York: Oxford University Press, 2003. Chs. 4, 7, and 10. Nontechnical, brief, but suggestive accounts of the Ontological Argument, religious experience, and the relation of morality and religion.

Charles Hartshorne. *Anselm's Discovery.* LaSalle, IL: Open Court, 1962. A reexamination of St. Anselm's Ontological Argument, by a contemporary and influential advocate of a form of this argument.

J. L. Mackie. *The Miracle of Theism: Arguments for and against the Existence of God.* Oxford: Clarendon Press, 1982. Chs. 3, 6, and 10. Readable though sometimes heavy discussions of the Ontological and Moral Arguments and religious experience, concluding with their rejection.

Ed. L. Miller. *God and Reason: An Invitation to Philosophical Theory.* Second ed. Englewood Cliffs, NJ: Prentice-Hall, 1995. Chs. 2, 5, and 6. Introductory discussions of the Ontological and Moral Arguments, representing points pro and con, as well as the role of religious experience.

H. P. Owen. *The Moral Arguments for Christian Theism.* London: George Allen & Unwin, 1965. An attempt to show that theism is reasonable if not demonstrable in light of morality, with special reference to the Christian tradition.

Alvin Plantinga. *God and Other Minds: A Study of the Rational Justification of Belief in God.* Ithaca, NY: Cornell University Press, 1967. Chs. 2–3. A critical and sometimes technical discussion of the Ontological Argument, including Malcolm's version.

Alvin Plantinga (ed.). *The Ontological Argument: From St. Anselm to Contemporary Philosophers.* Garden City, NY: Doubleday, 1965. A compendium of relevant statements on the Ontological Argument pro and con, with a brief but very useful introduction by Richard Taylor.

Richard Swinburne. *The Existence of God.* Oxford: Clarendon Press, 1979. Ch. 13. An excellent discussion of religious experience (five types) in terms of contemporary issues, concluding that it possesses "considerable evidential force."

*In addition, see the relevant articles ("Ontological Argument for the Existence of God," "Moral Arguments for the Existence of God," "Anselm, St." "Ethical Relativism," etc.) in *Routledge Encyclopedia of Philosophy,* ed. Edward Craig (London: Routledge, 1998), and *Stanford Encyclopedia of Philosophy,* http://plato.stanford.edu.

GOD AND EVIL

One might easily imagine that just as the theists are able to line up their evidence *for* the existence of God, say the traditional arguments, the atheists likewise are able to marshal a long list of arguments *against* the existence of God. But this is not quite the case. If you stop and reflect, you will probably agree that you have seldom heard anyone really propound an argument against the existence of God. What you probably *have* heard are many arguments *against* the arguments *for* the existence of God. That is, the atheist, unable to present any positive *dis*proof of God's existence, is usually content, or forced, to find flaws in the theist's position. There is, of course, one notable exception to this: *the argument against the existence of God on the basis of the evil in the world.* But this alone has wrought plenty of havoc for the theist.

Evil: the most notorious evidence against God

WHAT IS THE PROBLEM?

What is meant by "evil"? Two things. *First,* we have *natural* evil, or the evil that results from natural causes. This is otherwise known as the *evil of suffering*. Starvation, cancerous pain, physical deformity, disease—these and innumerable other sources of undeserved anguish are, rightfully, called *evils* in our world. *Second,* we have *moral* evil, the evil that results from personal depravity. Torture, murder, war, cheating, exploitation—these too, though very different from natural evils, are certainly evils. Either one or both of these types of evil figure in the "problem of evil."

Two kinds of evil

307

NATURAL EVIL AND MORAL EVIL

- *Natural evil:* The evil or suffering that springs from natural causes. Think of Hurricane Katrina, AIDS, the great San Francisco earthquake, the sinking of the *Titanic,* and so on.
- *Moral evil:* The evil that springs from the human will. Think of the Nazi death camps, genocide in Rwanda, tortured prisoners of war, and the like.

Theodicy

But what is the problem? The problem is how to reconcile the evil in the world with a God who is at once omnipotent (all-powerful) and omnibenevolent (all-loving). The problem is also called *theodicy,* which means, literally, "the justification of God." The idea here is, How can God, in the traditional sense of the word, be justified or vindicated in the face of all, or even any, of the evil in the world?

Hardly a more powerful statement of the problem may be found than in the outburst of the English philosopher John Stuart Mill, for whom the impossibility of reconciling God and evil played an important role in his rejection of Christianity:

> Not even on the most distorted and contracted theory of good which ever was framed by religious or philosophical fanaticism, can the government of Nature be made to resemble the work of a being at once good and omnipotent.[1]

A more extended statement may be cited from Hume's *Dialogues Concerning Natural Religion,* from which we have already noted the attack on God's causal ordering of the world. Note how both natural and moral evil figure in his "catalogue of woes."

> The whole earth, believe me, Philo, is cursed and polluted. A perpetual war is kindled amongst all living creatures. Necessity, hunger, want stimulate the strong and courageous; fear, anxiety, terror agitate the weak and infirm. The first entrance

---

[1]John Stuart Mill, *Three Essays on Religion* (New York: Henry Holt & Co., 1874), p. 38.

THEODICY

From two Greek words meaning, literally, "the justification of God," theodicy is the attempt to reconcile the traditional view of God with the evil in the world. How can God be vindicated in the face of evil?

into life gives anguish to the new-born infant and to its wretched parent; weakness, impotence, distress attend each stage of that life, and it is, at last finished in agony and horror.

Observe, too, says Philo, the curious artifices of nature in order to embitter the life of every living being. The stronger prey upon the weaker and keep them in perpetual terror and anxiety. The weaker, too, in their turn, often prey upon the stronger, and vex and molest them without relaxation. Consider that innumerable race of insects, which either are bred on the body of each animal or, flying about, infix their stings in him. These insects have others still less than themselves which torment them. And thus on each hand, before and behind, above and below, every animal is surrounded with enemies which incessantly seek his misery and destruction.

Man alone, said Demea, seems to be, in part, an exception to this rule. For by combination in society he can easily master lions, tigers, and bears, whose greater strength and agility naturally enable them to prey upon him.

On the contrary, it is here chiefly, cried Philo, that the uniform and equal maxims of nature are most apparent. Man, it is true, can, by combination, surmount all his *real* enemies, and become master of the whole animal creation; but does he not immediately raise up to himself *imaginary* enemies, the demons of his fancy, who haunt him with superstitious terrors and blast every enjoyment of life? His pleasure, as he imagines, becomes in their eyes a crime; his food and repose give them umbrage and offence; his very sleep and dreams furnish new materials to anxious fear; and even death, his refuge from every other ill, presents only the dread of endless and unnumberable woes. Nor does the wolf molest more the timid flock than superstition does the anxious breast of wretched mortals.

Besides, consider, Demea: This very society by which we surmount those wild beasts, our natural enemies, what new enemies does it not raise to us? What woe and misery does it not occasion? Man is the greatest enemy of man. Oppression, injustice, contempt, contumely, violence, sedition, war, calumny, treachery, fraud—by these they mutually torment each other, and they would soon dissolve that society which they had formed were it not for the dread of still greater ills which must attend their separation.

But though these external insults, said Demea, from animals, from men, from all the elements, which assault us form a frightful catalogue of woes, they are nothing in comparison of those which arise within ourselves, from the distempered condition of our mind and body. How many lie under the lingering torment of diseases? Hear the pathetic enumeration of the great poet.

> Intestine stone and ulcer, colic-pangs,
> Demoniac frenzy, moping melancholy,
> And moon-struck madness, pining atrophy,
> Marasmus, and wide-wasting pestilence.
> Dire was the tossing, deep the groans: *Despair*
> Tended the sick, busiest from couch to couch.
> And over them triumphant *Death* his dart
> Shook: but delay'd to strike, though oft invok'd
> With vows, as their chief good and final hope.

The disorders of the mind, continued Demea, though more secret, are not perhaps less dismal and vexatious. Remorse, shame, anguish, rage, disappointment, anxiety, fear, dejection, despair—who has ever passed through life without

THE SIMPLEST STATEMENT
OF THE PROBLEM OF EVIL

"Is he willing to prevent evil, but not able? then is he impotent. Is he able, but not willing? then is he malevolent. Is he both able and willing? whence then is evil?"

—Hume

cruel inroads from these tormentors? How many have scarcely ever felt any better sensations? Labour and poverty, so abhorred by everyone, are the certain lot of the far greater number; and those few privileged persons who enjoy ease and opulence never reach contentment or true felicity. All the goods of life united would not make a very happy man, but all the ills united would make a wretch indeed; and any one of them almost (and who can be free from every one?), nay, often the absence of one good (and who can possess all?) is sufficient to render life ineligible.

Were a stranger to drop on a sudden into this world, I would show him, as a specimen of its ills, an hospital full of diseases, a prison crowded with malefactors and debtors, a field of battle strewed with carcases, a fleet floundering in the ocean, a nation languishing under tyranny, famine, or pestilence. To turn the gay side of life to him and give him a notion of its pleasures—whither should I conduct him? To a ball, to an opera, to court? He might justly think that I was only showing him a diversity of distress and sorrow.

There is no evading such striking instances, said Philo, but by apologies which still further aggravate the charge. Why have all men, I ask, in all ages, complained incessantly of the miseries of life? . . .

And is it possible, Cleanthes, said Philo, that after all these reflections, and infinitely more which might be suggested, you can still persevere in your anthropomorphism, and assert the moral attributes of the Deity, his justice, benevolence, mercy, and rectitude, to be of the same nature with these virtues in human creatures? His power, we allow, is infinite; whatever he wills is executed; but neither man nor any other animal is happy; therefore, he does not will their happiness. His wisdom is infinite; he is never mistaken in choosing the means to any end; but the course of nature tends not to human or animal felicity; therefore, it is not established for that purpose. Through the whole compass of human knowledge there are no inferences more certain and infallible than these. In what respect, then, do his benevolence and mercy resemble the benevolence and mercy of men?

Epicurus' old questions are yet unanswered.

Is he willing to prevent evil, but not able? then is he impotent. Is he able, but not willing? then is he malevolent. Is he both able and willing? whence then is evil?[2]

Pay special attention to the concluding lines of the above quotation. These questions embody the best-known and simplest expression of the

[2]David Hume, *Dialogues Concerning Natural Religion,* ed. Henry D. Aiken (New York: Hafner, 1948), pp. 62–64.

problem of evil. Note also that it isn't simply some evil but the specific evils and the amount of evil that must be explained to address the problem.

SOME SOLUTIONS

The believer who seriously confronts this dilemma might appreciate the saying "There are many ways to skin a cat, but whatever way you choose, don't expect the cat to cooperate." That is, the problem is indeed a difficult one, and the believer should be cautioned against any glibness or overconfidence. There are no easy answers. Still, the bottom line is this: It is clear to most theists that neither God's omnipotence nor his omnibenevolence can be given up.

Or can they? Mill himself resorted to just this "radical surgery": Let us simply deny, flat out, that God is omnipotent. Mill states this rather startling thesis in his *Three Essays on Religion* (1874):

God is limited

It is not too much to say that every indication of Design in the Kosmos is so much evidence against the Omnipotence of the Designer. For what is meant by Design? Contrivance: the adaptation of means to an end. But the necessity for contrivance—the need of employing means—is a consequence of the limitation of power. Who would have recourse to means if to attain his end his mere word was sufficient? The very idea of means implies that the means have an efficacy which the direct action of the being who employs them has not. Otherwise they are not means, but an incumbrance. A man does not use machinery to move his arms. If he did, it could only be when paralysis had deprived him of the power of moving them by volition. But if the employment of contrivance is in itself a sign of limited power, how much more so is the careful and skilful choice of contrivances? Can any wisdom be shown in the selection of means, when the means have no efficacy but what is given them by the will of him who employs them, and when his will could have bestowed the same efficacy on any other means? Wisdom and contrivance are shown in overcoming difficulties, and there is no room for them in a Being for whom no difficulties exist. The evidences, therefore, of Natural Theology distinctly imply that the author of the Kosmos worked under limitations; that he was obliged to adapt himself to conditions independent of his will, and to attain his ends by such arrangements as those conditions admitted of.

And this hypothesis agrees with what we have seen to be the tendency of the evidences in another respect. We found that the appearances in Nature point indeed to an origin of the Kosmos, or order in Nature, and indicate that origin to be Design but do not point to any commencement, still less creation, of the two great active elements of the Universe, the passive element and the active element, Matter and Force. There is in Nature no reason whatever to suppose that either Matter or Force, or any of their properties, were made by the Being who was the author of the collocations by which the world is adapted to what we consider as its purposes; or that he has power to alter any of those properties. It is only when we consent to entertain this negative supposition that there arises a need for wisdom and contrivance in the order of the universe. The Deity had on this hypothesis to work out his ends by combining materials of a given nature and properties. Out of these materials he had to construct a world in which his designs should be carried into effect through given properties of Matter and Force, working together and fitting into one another. This did require skill and contrivance, and the means by which it is effected are often such as justly excite our wonder and admiration: but exactly because it requires wisdom, it implies limitation of power, or rather the two phrases express different sides of the same fact.[3]

The believer will find this thesis considerably more than "startling." Mill's statement involves an interesting piece of reasoning and is well worth digesting. But, some would say, the idea of a limited or *finite* God is as absurd as that of a malevolent or *evil* God. There must be another way.

We are stuck, then, with these two claims:

1. There is an omnipotent, omnibenevolent God.
2. There is evil.

That these two propositions seem to be incompatible is clear. But the first question to be asked is whether the incompatibility here is a *logical* incompatibility—that is to say, a logical contradiction. If the two propositions are *logically* incompatible, well, that is the end of the matter—one of them must be false. And since we can hardly deny the existence of evil, we must deny the existence of an omnipotent and omnibenevolent God. But *are* they logically incompatible? It would seem not. However difficult it may be to reconcile the two propositions, there is nothing in the concept of an omnipotent and omnibenevolent God that *logically* excludes there being evil in the world. If so, it is at least *possible* for both propositions to be true, and the traditional believer's job is to show how.

One of the most popular proposals is to involve the transcendence and inscrutability of God: God lies so far above us that it is impossible to understand his ways and purposes, and presumptuous even to try. Was this not God's own answer to the suffering Job?

God's ways are inscrutable

> Then the LORD answered Job
>   out of the whirlwind:
> "Who is this that darkens counsel
>   by words without
>   knowledge?
> Gird up your loins like a man,
>   I will question you, and you
>   shall declare to me.
>
> "Where were you when I laid the
>   foundation of the earth?
> Tell me, if you have
>   understanding.
> Who determined its
>   measurements—surely you
>   know!

---

[3]John Stuart Mill, *Three Essays on Religion*, pp. 176–178.

Or who stretched the line upon
  it?
On what were its bases sunk,
  or who laid its cornerstone
  when the morning stars sang
  together
  and all the heavenly beings
  shouted for joy?
"Or who shut in the sea with
  doors
  when it burst out from the
  womb?—
  when I made the clouds its
  garment,
  and thick darkness its swaddling
  band,
  and prescribed bounds for it,
  and set bars and doors,
  and said, 'Thus far shall you
  come, and no farther,
  and here shall your proud waves
  be stopped'?"

Job 38:1–11 (New Revised Standard Version)

And what does he say in *Isaiah*?

For my thoughts are not your
  thoughts,
  nor are your ways my ways,
  says the LORD.

For as the heavens are higher than
  the earth,
  so are my ways higher than
  your ways
  and my thoughts than your
  thoughts.

Isaiah 55:8–9 (NRSV)

But though this may be an appropriate and satisfying approach from a *religious* standpoint, from a *philosophical* standpoint it is a retreat, and issues a *carte blanche* for ignorance and uncritical reflection on the most urgent of issues.

Some other attempted resolutions may be mentioned. Closely related to the last is the emphasis on the goodness of the whole: If everything could be viewed from the divine standpoint, then it would immediately be appreciated how everything, even evil, actually contributes to the unity, harmony,

The goodness
of the whole

SOME SOLUTIONS TO THE PROBLEM OF EVIL

- God is not omnipotent after all.
- God's plan for the world is inscrutable.
- All things, including evil, actually contribute to the goodness of the whole.
- A perfect world is a logical impossibility.
- Evil is a necessary by-product of nature.

A perfect world is logically impossible

beauty, and, in a word, goodness of things considered as a *totality*. A quite different angle was proposed by Leibniz, who taught that it would in fact be *logically impossible* to have a world without evil: Anything created by God would have to be *less* than God just by virtue of being *dependent* on him, and this means immediately that it must be less than perfect, and *this* means immediately the presence of various sorts of imperfections. How could God create something that was perfect, and therefore independent, and therefore uncreated? It is *logically* impossible. Similar is the view of Tennant. In an earlier chapter we saw that he emphasized the presence of order in the world. But even Tennant saw that unfortunate and unhappy things are inevitable by-products of nature. It is impossible (*logically* impossible?) to have a physical cosmos, with its multiplicity, change, and natural processes, and not also have mishaps, accidents, disease, famines, and the like.

Evils as necessary by-products of nature

Some of these solutions to the problem of evil may strike you as more relevant than others, but each of them deserves, at least, to be understood and weighed. Two further views, however, must be considered somewhat more carefully: the privation theory of evil and the therapy theory of evil.

EVIL AS A PRIVATION OF GOODNESS

The first of these has a long tradition, but is most notably associated with the medieval Christian philosopher and theologian St. Augustine (354–430).

Evil is not a "thing"

It is our natural tendency to think of evil as some kind of thing, a "stuff," a substance, or a *blob*. However, Augustine and many others have argued, exactly counter to this grain, that evil is no *thing* at all. It is, rather, the absence or privation of something—namely, of being and goodness. And this is true both of natural evil and of moral evil. It is true that when God created the world and the human race he said, "It is good." But he did not mean—*could* not mean—that they were *absolutely* good or good in the same way that God is. How could they be? For then they would not be created things, but God himself.

St. Augustine was a Christian Platonist, though as a Christian he certainly disagreed with much of Plato's philosophy. But he did hold broadly to the Platonic idea that the world is necessarily a mixture, as it were, of being and nonbeing: It is becoming. And one of the hallmarks of the relative nonbeing in the world is its multiplicity and change—the *absence* of full being along with its unity and unchangeableness. But this multiplicity and change give rise to natural processes, and these in turn give rise to famines, disease, plagues, and the like, and these in turn give rise to suffering, which St. Augustine believed is visited on human beings as a just punishment for their sins. But, then, what about sin? Moral evil, or sin, likewise may be traced to an absence of goodness. It results when something goes wrong with the will; when it breaks down; when it falls short; when it fails to will the good; when it is derailed and turns aside from the good; when it is corrupted. As disease is the absence of health in the body, so sin is the absence of health in the will.

The basic idea here may not be easy to get hold of, but if you think about it enough it might come to you in a sort of intuitive flash. Perhaps Augustine's own statements will help. The general principle of evil as a privation of goodness is explained in the following extract from *The Enchiridion on Faith, Hope, and Love:*

What Is Called Evil in the Universe Is But the Absence of Good

. . . in the universe, even that which is called evil, when it is regulated and put in its own place, only enhances our admiration of the good; for we enjoy and value the good more when we compare it with the evil. For the Almighty God, who, as even the heathen acknowledge, has supreme power over all things, being Himself supremely good, would never permit the existence of anything evil among His works, if He were not so omnipotent and good that He can bring good even out of evil. For what is that which we call evil but the absence of good? In the bodies of animals, disease and wounds mean nothing but the absence of health; for when a cure is effected, that does not mean that the evils which were present—namely, the diseases and wounds—go away from the body and dwell elsewhere: they altogether cease to exist; for the wound or disease is not a substance, but a defect in the fleshly substance—the flesh itself being a substance, and therefore something good, of which those evils—that is, privations of the good which we call health—are accidents. Just in the same way, what are called vices in the soul are nothing but privations of natural good. And when they are cured, they are not transferred elsewhere: when they cease to exist in the healthy soul, they cannot exist anywhere else.

All Beings Were Made Good, But Not Being Made Perfectly Good, Are Liable to Corruption

All things that exist, therefore, seeing that the Creator of them all is supremely good, are themselves good. But because they are not, like their Creator, supremely and unchangeably good, their good may be diminished and increased. But for good to be diminished is an evil, although, however much it may be diminished, it is necessary, if the being is to continue, that some good should remain to constitute the being. For however small or of whatever kind the being may be, the good which makes it a being cannot be destroyed without destroying the

EVIL AS A PRIVATION OF GOODNESS

One of the most enduring solutions to the problem of evil is to interpret evil, both natural and moral, not as a positive substance but as the absence of being and goodness. The world and human souls are seen as created by the highest being (who is goodness) "from above," but at the same time as corruptible by nonbeing (or evil) "from below." God is, thus, responsible for the *isness* and *goodness* in the world, not the *nonbeing* and *evil*.

being itself. An uncorrupted nature is justly held in esteem. But if, still further, it be incorruptible, it is undoubtedly considered of still higher value. When it is corrupted, however, its corruption is an evil, because it is deprived of some sort of good. For if it be deprived of no good, it receives no injury; but it does receive injury, therefore it is deprived of good. Therefore, so long as a being is in process of corruption, there is in it some good of which it is being deprived; and if a part of the being should remain which cannot be corrupted, this will certainly be an incorruptible being, and accordingly the process of corruption will result in the manifestation of this great good. But if it does not cease to be corrupted, neither can it cease to possess good of which corruption may deprive it. But if it should be thoroughly and completely consumed by corruption, there will then be no good left, because there will be no being. Wherefore corruption can consume the good only by consuming the being. Every being, therefore, is a good; a great good, if it cannot be corrupted; a little good, if it can; but in any case, only the foolish or ignorant will deny that it is a good. And if it be wholly consumed by corruption, then the corruption itself must cease to exist, as there is no being left in which it can dwell.[4]

The principle is further explained and applied specifically to sin in the following from *On Free Choice of the Will:*

Because the will is moved when it turns from an immutable good to a changeable one, you may perhaps ask how this movement arises. For the movement itself is certainly evil, although the free will must be numbered among the goods, because without it no one can live rightly. Even if this movement, that is, the turning of the will from the Lord God, is without doubt a sin, we cannot say, can we, that God is the cause of sin? This movement will not be from God, but what then is its origin? If I should answer your question by saying that I do not know, you would perhaps be disappointed; yet that would be the truth, for that which is nothing cannot be known. Only hold to your faith, since no good thing comes to your perception, understanding, or thought which is not from God. Nothing of any kind can be discovered which is not from God. Wherever you see measure, number, and order, you cannot hesitate to attribute all these to God, their Maker. When you remove measure, number, and order, nothing at all remains. Even if the

---

[4]St. Augustine, *The Enchiridion on Faith, Hope, and Love,* tr. J. F. Shaw, ed. Henry Paolucci (Chicago: Henry Regnery, 1961), pp. 12–13.

ST. AUGUSTINE

The main writers of the early centuries of the Christian church are called the Church Fathers. The last and greatest of these was St. Augustine. He was born in a Roman province on the north coast of Africa in 354. His father was a pagan, and his mother, who wielded a great deal of influence over him, was a Christian: St. Monica. He did not particularly excel at his early studies, though eventually he became expert in rhetoric when he moved as a student in 370 to Carthage. The loose morals of the city, however, undermined the Christian morals of this impressionable young man, and he gradually fell away from Christianity. He took a mistress, by whom he had a son during his second year in Carthage.

(*continued on next page*)

During this time, Augustine rejected not only Christian morals but also Christian doctrines. He was especially troubled by the failure of Christianity to explain how a good God could be responsible for a world with so much evil in it. He turned to the materialistic ideas of Manichaeism, the doctrine that the world is dominated by two eternal and opposed principles, good and evil, light and darkness. In 383 Augustine traveled to Rome, where he opened his own school of rhetoric, but he had so much trouble getting his students to pay their tuition that he moved to Milan. This was decisive for Augustine. His commitment to Manichaeism was by this time wavering anyway, and his discovery of certain "Platonic writings" (probably the writings of the Neoplatonist Plotinus, who lived about A.D. 200) introduced him to an altogether different and superior idea of things: a spiritual and transcendent conception of God, and the view that evil is a privation of goodness. This discovery, along with the influence of the sermons of St. Ambrose, bishop of Milan, and Augustine's own study of the New Testament, set the stage for his conversion to Christianity in the summer of 386. On Holy Saturday, 387, he was baptized by St. Ambrose, and in the autumn of 388 he departed for Africa.

Back in Africa, Augustine was ordained as a priest by the bishop of Hippo, a seaport city about 150 miles west of Carthage, and he himself became bishop of that city in 396. During this period his literary output continued and included three of the most important theological and philosophical works ever written: the *Confessions* (the world's first autobiography), the *City of God* (the first philosophy of history), and *On the Trinity.* At the same time, he was combating the heresies of Manichaeism, Donatism (which claimed to be the only true church), and Pelagianism (which overemphasized the role of free will in man's salvation), and developing further his own philosophy of Christian Platonism. Augustine died on August 28, 430, as the Vandals laid siege to Hippo, and as he was reciting the Penitential Psalms.

In addition to being one of the world's greatest philosophers and theologians, Augustine was one of the world's great authors. Besides the *Confessions*, the *City of God*, and *On the Trinity*, he wrote innumerable commentaries on biblical books and a prodigious number of works on various topics and against various heresies.

beginning of some form were to remain, where you do not find order or measure or number (since wherever these exist, form is complete), you must remove even that very beginning of form which seems to be the artisan's raw material. If the completion of form is a good, there is some good even in the rudimentary beginning of form. Thus, if all good is completely removed, no vestige of reality persists; indeed, nothing remains. Every good is from God. There is nothing of any kind that is not from God. Therefore, since the movement of turning away from good, which we admit to be sin, is a defective movement and since, moreover, every defect comes from nothing, see where this movement belongs: you may be sure that it does not belong to God.

Yet since this defect is voluntary, it lies within our power. You must not be willing to fear this defect, for if you do not desire it, it will not exist. What greater security can there be than to live a life where what you do not will cannot happen to you? Since a man cannot rise of his own will as he fell by his own will, let us hold with firm faith the right hand of God, Jesus Christ our Lord, which is stretched out to us. Let us wait for Him with steadfast hope; let us love Him with burning love.[5]

Is it clear? While God, who is the highest being, is the cause of all lesser being, he is not, nor can he be, the cause of the relative nonbeing in the world, for nonbeing is nothing at all. The advocate of the evil-is-a-privation-of-goodness position might therefore exclaim: "Rather than blame God for the relative nonbeing present in the world, and least of all for the wickedness that people themselves freely introduce, praise him for the relative beauty, harmony, goodness, and being in the world which *he* has introduced!"

One very big caution is in order. In view of this talk about evil as a privation or absence of goodness, you may be tempted to think that the reality of evil is simply being denied. But that would be to miss an important point. Who in his or her right mind would care to deny the reality of evil? What is involved here is a question not about the *reality* of evil, but, rather, about the *nature* of evil. And though St. Augustine denied that evil is a substance and called it the absence of goodness, few have been more sensitive to its awful reality.

Evil: not a substance, but real nonetheless

THE FREE-WILL DEFENSE

You may have a nagging feeling that at least the moral evil in the world is not God's fault but rather is due to the free choices and acts of human beings. And you might suspect that moral evil is just the price that has to be paid if there is to be any genuine moral responsibility and human goodness in the world. All of this suggests, in fact, an important angle to the problem of God and evil, and raises at the same time a host of difficult questions:

• Why did God endow humans with free will, knowing they would abuse it?
• Is free will a condition for real humanhood?
• Does God's foreknowledge of what we will do mean that what we do is actually predetermined?
• Could God have made us free *and* unable to sin?

Some of these issues you will have to ponder or discuss on your own. Others, however, will have to be considered, along with that "important angle" mentioned above.

Note Augustine's reference, in the last passage quoted above, to the "voluntary" defection of human beings from the good. He is very emphatic on

---

[5]St. Augustine, *On Free Choice of the Will,* tr. Anna S. Benjamin and L. H. Hackstaff (Indianapolis: Library of Liberal Arts, 1964), pp. 83–84.

Free will as a
condition for
morality

the necessity of free will as a condition of morality and as the source of moral evil in the world. In another place in the same work he says explicitly that "no righteous act could be performed except by free choice of the will, and I asserted that God gave it for this reason."[6] Actually, Augustine means that God gave *Adam* and *Eve* free will. Adam and Eve misused (note again the negative tone) their free will, and sin thus made its entry into the world. Everyone after Adam and Eve has inherited the effects of the Fall, and this includes a loss of free will and a consequent "bondage of the will." Nonetheless, at least in the case of the first human beings, Adam and Eve, free will was a condition of authentic humanhood, though it also meant the possibility of sin. Leaving aside the difficult question of Adam and Eve's fall and its consequences for their descendants, this view is essentially what is nowadays called the *Free-Will Defense.*

The contemporary American philosopher Alvin Plantinga summarizes the idea:

> . . . among good states of affairs there are some that not even God can bring about without bringing about evil: those goods, namely, that *entail* or *include* evil states of affairs. The Free Will Defense can be looked upon as an effort to show that there may be a very different kind of good that God can't bring about without permitting evil. There are good states of affairs that don't include evil; they do not entail the existence of any evil whatever; nonetheless God Himself can't bring them about without permitting evil.

> So how does the Free Will Defense work? And what does the Free Will Defender mean when he says that people are or may be free? What is relevant to the Free Will Defense is the idea of *being free with respect to an action.* If a person is free with respect to a given action, then he is free to perform that action and free to refrain from performing it; not antecedent conditions and/or causal laws determine that he will perform the action, or that he won't. It is within his power, at the time in question, to take or perform the action and within his power to refrain from it. Freedom so conceived is not to be confused with unpredictability. You might be able to predict what you will do in a given situation even if you are free, in that situation, to do something else. If I know you well, I may be able to predict what action you will take in response to a certain set of conditions; it does not follow that you are not free with respect to that action. Secondly, I shall say that an action is *morally significant,* for a given person, if it would be wrong for him to perform the action but right to refrain or *vice versa.* Keeping a promise, for example, would ordinarily be morally significant for a person, as would refusing induction into the army. On the other hand, having Cheerios for breakfast (instead of Wheaties) would not normally be morally significant. Further, suppose we say that a person is *significantly free,* on a given occasion, if he is then free with respect to a morally significant action. And finally we must distinguish between *moral evil* and *natural evil.* The former is evil that results from free human activity; natural evil is any other kind of evil.

> Given these definitions and distinctions, we can make a preliminary statement of the Free Will Defense as follows. A world containing creatures who are significantly free (and freely perform more good than evil actions) is more valuable,

---

[6]Ibid., p. 78.

all else being equal, than a world containing no free creatures at all. Now God can create free creatures, but He can't *cause* or *determine* them to do only what is right. For if He does so, then they aren't significantly free after all; they do not do what is right *freely*. To create creatures capable of *moral good,* therefore, He must create creatures capable of moral evil; and He can't give these creatures the freedom to perform evil and at the same time prevent them from doing so. As it turned out, sadly enough, some of the free creatures God created went wrong in the exercise of their freedom; this is the source of moral evil. The fact that free creatures sometimes go wrong, however, counts neither against God's omnipotence nor against His goodness; for He could have forestalled the occurrence of moral evil only by removing the possibility of moral good.[7]

To this, however, an objection is frequently heard: But is there a real contradiction in the idea that God might have so constituted his creatures that they *always* choose the right? This is the point made by the late British philosopher J. L. Mackie:

If God has made men such that in their free choices they sometimes prefer what is good and sometimes what is evil, why could he not have made men such that they always freely choose the good? If there is no logical impossibility in a man's freely choosing the good on one, or on several occasions, there cannot be a logical impossibility in his freely choosing the good on every occasion. God was not, then, faced with a choice between making innocent automata and making beings who, in acting freely, would sometimes go wrong: there was open to him the obviously better possibility of making beings who would act freely but always go right. Clearly, his failure to avail himself of this possibility is inconsistent with his being both omnipotent and wholly good.[8]

Now, many who are "incompatibilists" (people who believe that genuine free will is logically incompatible with determinism) have an immediate intuition that there is something wrong with the idea that God can so

---

[7]Alvin Plantinga, *God, Freedom, and Evil* (Grand Rapids, MI: Wm. B. Eerdmans, 1977).

[8]J. L. Mackie, "Evil and Omnipotence," in *The Philosophy of Religion,* ed. Basil Mitchell (London: Oxford University Press, 1971), p. 92.

THE FREE-WILL DEFENSE

By means of the Free-Will Defense, many thinkers, ancient and modern, have undertaken to defend God from the charge that he is responsible for moral evil: In order for human beings to be truly capable of moral goodness, they must also be capable of moral evil; but this means that with respect to good and evil they must have genuine free choice; but this means the real possibility (or inevitability?) of the introduction of moral evil into the scheme of things.

WHAT EVEN GOD CANNOT DO

"Nothing which implies contradiction falls under the omnipotence of God."

—St. Thomas

constitute us that we always *freely* choose to do good. It is true that there is no logical contradiction in the proposition

1. All people always freely choose to do good.

But there is a contradiction in the proposition

2. God so constitutes all people that they always freely choose to do good.

because that entails 1, plus the proposition

3. No one can do otherwise than choose to do good.

which is incompatible with 1.

Similarly, Plantinga himself asks us to consider the Mackie-type claim that God can bring about a world in which everyone freely chooses to do good. Is this really a coherent idea? Virtually everyone has accepted that even an omnipotent Being must be bound by the laws of reason—it is a mark of God's *perfect* nature and *un*limited power that he is prevented from creating irrational things like four-sided triangles and dogs that don't bark while they're barking—in fact, these latter "things" can't be *things* at all, right? Now, Plantinga asks, how can *God* bring about a world in which all people freely choose to do good, a world that must, at least in part, be brought about by *someone else*—namely, those people he creates to freely bring it about?! It is, even for God, an impossible state of affairs. Thus the debate can become very sticky, and even more so if we take seriously God's omniscience. If God knows *everything* and stands outside of time, then does God know what I will "freely" choose to do tomorrow? If he does, then do I really have free will? Suffice it to say that free will is not as simple as it first appears.

EVIL AS THERAPY

Alongside the theory of evil as a privation of goodness we may mention another very important theory: evil as *therapy.* To call evil "therapeutic" may strike you as being not only a bit odd but also silly or trivializing. But you must bear in mind that "therapy" involves more than aches, pains, exercise, and massages. It means, literally, *healing:* a healing power applied to physical and psychological disabilities and disorders. Thus, to press the therapeutic character of evil as a way of solving the problem of evil is to argue that evil is the instrument by which God has determined to correct, purify, and instruct his creatures—in a word, *to bring them to spiritual health and maturity.*

This view, too, is both a very old and a very modern one. One of its most ardent advocates is the contemporary philosopher of religion John Hick. In his important book *Evil and the God of Love,* Hick enlists an early example of this approach in the ancient Christian writer Irenaeus[9] (130?–202?), bishop of Lyons. Irenaeus emphasized the *development* that goes on in human beings, as well as the whole human race, and the methods God has chosen to bring this development about. The experience of evil is a necessary part of this "soul-making" activity of God. From Irenaeus' *Against Heresies:*

> Man has received the knowledge of good and evil. It is good to obey God, and to believe in Him, and to keep His commandment, and this is the life of man; as not to obey God is evil, and this is his death. Since God, therefore, gave [to man] such mental power man knew both the good of obedience and the evil of disobedience, that the eye of the mind, receiving experience of both, may with judgment make choice of the better things; and that he may never become indolent or neglectful of God's command; and learning by experience that it is an evil thing which deprives him of life, that is, disobedience to God, may never attempt it at all, but that, knowing that what preserves his life, namely, obedience to God, is good, he may diligently keep it with all earnestness. Wherefore he has also had a twofold experience, possessing knowledge of both kinds, that with discipline he may make choice of the better things. But how, if he had no knowledge of the contrary, could he have had instruction in that which is good? For there is thus a surer and an undoubted comprehension of matters submitted to us than the mere surmise arising from an opinion regarding them. For just as the tongue receives experience of sweet and bitter by means of tasting, and the eye discriminates between black and white by means of vision, and the ear recognizes the distinctions of sound by hearing; so also does the mind, receiving through the experience of both the knowledge of what is good, become more tenacious of its preservation, by acting in obedience to God; in the first place, casting away, by means of repentance, disobedience, as being something disagreeable and nauseous; and afterwards coming to understand what it really is, that it is contrary to goodness and sweetness, so that the mind may never even attempt to taste disobedience to God. But if any one do shun the knowledge of both these kinds of things, and the twofold perception of knowledge, he unaware divests himself of the character of a human being.
>
> . . . If, then, thou are God's workmanship, await the hand of thy Maker which creates everything in due time; in due time as far as thou art concerned, whose creation is being carried out. Offer to Him thy heart in a soft and tractable state, and preserve the form in which the Creator has fashioned thee, having moisture

Evil: a means
of growth

---

[9]Pronounced *eye-ray-neé-us.*

John Hick, an advocate of a contemporary
Irenaean theodicy

in thyself, lest, by becoming hardened, thou lose the impressions of His fingers. But by preserving the framework thou shalt ascend to that which is perfect, for the moist clay which is in thee is hidden [there] by the workmanship of God. . . . If, then, thou shalt deliver up to Him what is thine, that is, faith towards Him and subjection, thou shalt receive his handiwork, and shalt be a perfect work of God.[10]

Hick provides a useful summary of the differences between the Irenaean and Augustinian theodicies, and stresses (he calls it a "significant fact") the antiquity of the Irenaean.

There is thus to be found in Irenaeus the outline of an approach to the problem of evil which stands in important respects in contrast to the Augustinian type of theodicy. Instead of the doctrine that man was created finitely perfect and then incomprehensibly destroyed his own perfection and plunged into sin and misery, Irenaeus suggests that man was created as an imperfect, immature creature who was to undergo moral development and growth and finally be brought to the perfection intended for him by his Maker. Instead of the fall of Adam being presented, as in the Augustinian tradition, as an utterly malignant and catastrophic event, completely disrupting God's plan, Irenaeus pictures it as something that occurred in the childhood of the race, an understandable lapse due to weakness and immaturity rather than an adult crime full of malice and pregnant with

---

[10]Irenaeus, *Against Heresies*, IV, 39, 1–2, tr. Alexander Roberts and James Donaldson, in *The Ante-Nicene Fathers*, I (Grand Rapids, MI: Eerdmans, 1979).

perpetual guilt. And instead of the Augustinian view of life's trials as a divine punishment for Adam's sin, Irenaeus sees our world of mingled good and evil as a divinely appointed environment for man's development towards the perfection that represents the fulfillment of God's good purpose for him.

Irenaeus was the first great Christian theologian to think at all systematically along these lines, and although he was far from working out a comprehensive theodicy his hints are sufficiently explicit to justify his name being associated with the approach that we are studying in this part. It is true that Irenaeus' name does not belong to this type of theodicy as clearly and indisputably as Augustine's name belongs to the predominant theodicy of Western Christendom; it is also true that within Irenaeus' own writings there are cross-currents and alternative suggestions that I have left aside here. Nevertheless, to speak of the Irenaean type of theodicy is both to name a tradition by its first great representative and at the same time to indicate the significant fact that this mode of responding to the problem of evil originated in the earliest and most ecumenical phase of Christian thought.[11]

It is not hard to see how *natural* evil, with its sufferings and hardships, may contribute to the development of a mature and virtuous soul, but what about *moral* evil? And how do the innocent victims of murder and torture fit into the picture? We are back to the Free-Will Defense. At this point Hick adopts the same sort of reasoning as Augustine: Free will is a condition of humanhood, and sin enters the world through human free will. And he provides his own response to the Mackie-type view that God could have so made humans that they would freely but always choose the right. Hick's position is that while there may be no contradiction in God so making his creatures that they always act freely but rightly, there *is* a contradiction in God so constituting his creatures that they freely respond to him in a loving, trusting, and faithful relationship. Why? Because such a relationship is *two-sided*, and if the freely proffered love, trust, or faith of the one party is, as it were, programmed by the other party, then for that party it could not possibly *be* a relationship of love, trust, or faith, at least not *authentic* love, trust, or faith, to use Hick's word. Free will and *independence* from the Creator are, in this way, marks of genuine humanity. But, of course, this makes for the possibility of disobedience, and that means *sin*.

Hick's argument for this version of the Free-Will Defense is especially effective because of his analogy involving posthypnotic suggestion.

Is it logically possible for God so to make men that they will freely respond to Himself in love and trust and faith?

I believe that the answer is no. The grounds for this answer may be presented by means of an analogy with posthypnotic suggestion, which Flew uses in this connection. A patient can, under hypnosis, be given a series of instructions, which he is to carry out after waking—say, to go at a certain time to a certain library and borrow a certain book—and he may at the same time be told that he will forget having received these instructions. On coming out of the hypnotic trance he

Back to the
Free-Will Defense

---

[11]John Hick, *Evil and the God of Love,* rev. ed. (San Francisco: Harper & Row, 1978), pp. 214–215.

will then be obediently unaware of what transpired in it, but will nevertheless at the prescribed time feel an imperious desire to go to the library and borrow the book, a desire that the ordinary resources of the educated intellect will find no difficulty in rationalizing. The patient will thus carry out the hypnotist's commands whilst seeming both to himself and to others to be doing so of his own free will and for his own sufficient reasons. In terms of the definition of a free act as one that is not externally compelled but flows from the character of the agent, the actions of one carrying out post-hypnotic suggestions are free actions and the patient is a free agent in his performance of them. Nevertheless, taking account of the wider situation, including the previous hypnotic trance, we must say the patient is not free as far as these particular actions are concerned *in relation to the hypnotist*. In relation to the hypnotist he is a kind of puppet or tool. And if the hypnotist's suggestion had been that the patient would agree with him about some controversial matter or, coming closer to an analogy with our relationship with God, trust the hypnotist, or love him, or devotedly serve him, there would be something inauthentic about the resulting trust, love, or service. They would be inauthentic in the sense that to the hypnotist, who knows that he has himself directly planted these personal attitudes by his professional techniques, there would be an all-important difference between the good opinion and trust and friendship of the patient and that of someone else whose mind has not been conditioned by hypnotic suggestion. He would regard and value the two attitudes in quite different ways. His patient's post-hypnotic friendship and trust would represent a purely technical achievement, whereas the friendship and trust of the other would represent a response to his own personal qualities and merits. The difference would be that between genuine and spurious personal attitudes—genuine and spurious, not in respect of their present observed and felt characters but in respect of the ways in which they have come about. For it is of the essential nature of "fiduciary" personal attitudes such as trust, respect, and affection to arise in a free being as an uncompelled response to the personal qualities of others. If trust, love, admiration, respect, affection, are produced by some kind of psychological manipulation which by-passes the conscious responsible centre of the personality, then they are not real trust and love, etc., but something else of an entirely differ-ent nature and quality which does not have at all the same value in the contexts of personal life and personal relationship. The authentic fiduciary attitudes are thus such that it is impossible—logically impossible—for them to be produced by miraculous manipulation: "it is logically impossible for God to obtain your love-unforced-by-anything-outside-you and yet himself force it.". . .

. . . It would not be logically possible for God so to make men that they could be guaranteed freely to respond to Himself in genuine trust and love. The nature of these personal attitudes precludes their being caused in such a way. Just as the patient's trust in, and devotion to, the hypnotist would lack for the latter the value of a freely given trust and devotion, so our human worship and obedience to God would lack for Him the value of a freely offered worship and obedience. We should, in relation to God, be mere puppets, precluded from entering into any truly personal relationship with Him.[12]

Thus Hick, renewing the therapy thinking of Irenaeus and pressing a new version of the Free-Will Defense, argues that this mortal existence, with

---

[12]Ibid., pp. 308–310.

its authentic freedoms and its disciplining and healing and maturing environment, is "a vale of soul-making." Some readers will of course respond with an incredulous outburst: "How naive can you be? This is obviously not a vale of soul-making but a vale of soul-*breaking*! Are we supposed to believe, to take just one example, that the Nazi death camps were divinely appointed means of spiritual progress?" And if it is answered that somehow the position holds true at least for the race as a whole, the second response will immediately be: "Small consolation for those *individuals* whose innocent lives were snuffed out in the gas chambers." Naturally, Hick's actual view is much richer than what we have been able to recount here, and naive it certainly is not. Nonetheless, the point is well taken. And it leads to the next section.

EVIL IS IRRATIONAL

We have now mentioned several attempts to reconcile evil with God. In spite of their differences, they all have in common at least a faith in the ability of reason to unravel to some degree the mystery of evil. They all say, in one way or another: "If only we think hard about the matter—draw the right distinctions, introduce the relevant concepts, and so on—we are able to see that the problem of good and evil is not as desperate as we thought." Not all are so optimistic. In fact, some abandon all hope of explaining evil and see it, rather, as the supreme evidence of the ultimate *irrationality* of human existence.

We are, of course, now in the presence of a radically different philosophical perspective. It is not only an atheistic one but also, in some sense, a *nihilistic* one. "Nihilism" means, literally, "nothingism" (from the Latin *nihil*, "nothing"). As a label, nihilism usually refers specifically to values and ideals and is the denial that they have any objective reality. It is understandable how, for such a perspective, evil is the most vivid expression of our finally hopeless situation.

If we take nihilism to mean the *utter* and *absolute* rejection of all value and meaning, then there have not been very many nihilists. And, if there ever was one, he or she should have just sat down and died. For even the barest pursuit of one's life is an affirmation of *some* value and meaning, isn't it? But with some philosophers the irrationalist or absurdist position takes a truly interesting turn. First, these philosophers are atheists or *humanists*. Humanism, as one could guess from the word, is the exaltation of humanity itself as the ultimate reality. Second, for these thinkers the problem of evil becomes one of reconciling evil not with God (there is no God) but, rather, with *man*—not theodicy, but, if you will, *anthropodicy*.

One way in which this may be done is suggested in certain strains of atheistic or humanistic existentialism. We will have more to say about existentialism in Chapter 14. For now, we just say that existentialism, which was renewed by the horrors of the world wars, generally rejects most

NIHILISM

The rejection of values as having any objective validity. Life is ultimately meaningless.

philosophizing as abstract and irrelevant, and emphasizes the concrete business of living authentically. The late French writer Albert Camus is a good example:

> Judging whether life is or is not worth living amounts to answering the fundamental question of philosophy. All the rest—whether or not the world has three dimensions, whether the mind has nine or twelve categories—come afterwards. These are games. . . . I have never seen anyone die for the ontological argument. . . . the meaning of life is the most urgent of questions.[13]

The defiance of evil

But what about evil, specifically? Camus, the atheist, says that we must *recognize* it in all its horror and irrationality, but we must not *accept* it. Human dignity lies precisely in our struggle against evil, in living in constant revolt against its reign. This comes out well in Camus' novel *The Plague*. In this novel the plague itself may be understood on several levels. But on the most basic level it represents evil, and at least one of the characters in the novel expresses vividly the absence of God and the necessity of defiance as the only meaningful response to evil.

> ". . . since the order of the world is shaped by death, mightn't it be better for God if we refuse to believe in Him and struggle with all our might against death, without raising our eyes toward heaven where He sits in silence."
> Tarrou nodded.
> "Yes. But your victories will never be lasting; that's all."
> Rieux's face darkened.
> "Yes, I know that. But it's no reason for giving up the struggle."
> "No reason, I agree. Only, I now can picture what this plague must mean for you."
> "Yes. A never ending defeat."
>
>   . . .
>
> "Who taught you all this, doctor?"
> The reply came promptly:
> "Suffering."[14]

---

[13]Albert Camus, *The Myth of Sisyphus and Other Essays,* tr. Justin O'Brien (New York: Vintage Books, 1955), pp. 3–4.

[14]Albert Camus, *The Plague,* tr. Stuart Gilbert (New York: Modern Library, 1948), pp. 117–118.

And in his *The Myth of Sisyphus and Other Essays,* Camus juxtaposes the two most extreme possible responses to the human condition: suicide, which is "giving in," and conscious revolt. It is already clear which path Camus urges us to follow.

Now I can broach the notion of suicide. It has already been felt what solution might be given. At this point the problem is reversed. It was previously a question of finding out whether or not life had to have a meaning to be lived. It now becomes clear, on the contrary, that it will be lived all the better if it has no meaning. Living an experience, a particular fate, is accepting it fully. Now, no one will live this fate, knowing it to be absurd, unless he does everything to keep before him that absurd brought to light by consciousness. Negating one of the terms of the opposition on which he lives amounts to escaping it. To abolish conscious revolt is to elude the problem. The theme of permanent revolution is thus carried into individual experience. Living is keeping the absurd alive. Keeping it alive is, above all, contemplating it. Unlike Eurydice, the absurd dies only when we turn away from it. One of the only coherent philosophical positions is thus revolt. It is a constant confrontation between man and his own obscurity. It is an insistence upon an impossible transparency. It challenges the world anew every second. Just as danger provided man the unique opportunity of seizing awareness, so metaphysical revolt extends awareness to the whole of experience. It is that constant presence of man in his own eyes. It is not aspiration, for it is devoid of hope. That revolt is the certainty of a crushing fate, without the resignation that ought to accompany it.

This is where it is seen to what a degree absurd experience is remote from suicide. It may be thought that suicide follows revolt—but wrongly. For it does not represent the logical outcome of revolt. It is just the contrary by the consent it presupposes. Suicide, like the leap, is acceptance at its extreme. Everything is over and man returns to his essential history. His future, his unique and dreadful future—he sees and rushes toward it. In its way, suicide settles the absurd. It engulfs the absurd in the same death. But I know that in order to keep alive, the absurd cannot be settled. It escapes suicide to the extent that it is simultaneously awareness and rejection of death. It is, at the extreme limit of the condemned man's last thought, that shoelace that despite everything he sees a few yards away, on the very brink of his dizzying fall. The contrary of suicide, in fact, is the man condemned to death.

That revolt gives life its value. Spread out over the whole length of a life, it restores its majesty to that life. To a man devoid of blinders, there is no finer sight than that of the intelligence at grips with a reality that transcends it. The sight of human pride is unequaled. No disparagement is of any use. That discipline that the mind imposes on itself, that will conjured up out of nothing, that face-to-face struggle have something exceptional about them. To impoverish that reality whose inhumanity constitutes man's majesty is tantamount to impoverishing him himself. I understand then why the doctrines that explain everything to me also debilitate me at the same time. They relieve me of the weight of my own life, and yet I must carry it alone. At this juncture, I cannot conceive that a skeptical metaphysics can be joined to an ethics of renunciation.

Consciousness and revolt, these rejections are the contrary of renunciation. Everything that is indomitable and passionate in a human heart quickens them, on the contrary, with its own life. It is essential to die unreconciled and not of one's own free will. Suicide is a repudiation. The absurd man can only drain everything

Through novels, plays, and essays, Albert Camus
addressed the futility of the human situation.

to the bitter end, and deplete himself. The absurd is his extreme tension, which he maintains constantly by solitary effort, for he knows that in that consciousness and in that day-to-day revolt he gives proof of his only truth, which is defiance. This is a first consequence.[15]

Such a stance is not without problems. Our discussion of the denial of moral law in Chapter 12 is relevant here, and our discussion in Chapter 14 will also be to the point. For the moment, we may reiterate: Any philosophy that rejects the objective reality of values will surely have a hard time when it turns right around and argues passionately for certain values. In the case of Camus, it might be asked: In a universe devoid of real values, what is it that justifies and gives value to the life of revolt? Why is the revolt itself a value? Of course Camus might just as easily respond, "There you go again with your academic questions! Don't you understand that in a world such as this it is not reasoning but *acting* that is called for?"

Be that as it may. With the emphasis on evil as the supreme evidence for the ultimate irrationality of the world, we appear to have come full circle: God may be dead, but the Devil is very much alive! And now the *theist* might attack:

Can there be real values in an irrational universe?

[15]Camus, *The Myth of Sisyphus*, pp. 39–41.

THE MYTH OF SISYPHUS

"The gods had condemned Sisyphus to ceaselessly rolling a rock to the top of a mountain, whence the stone would fall back of its own weight. They had thought with some reason that there is no more dreadful punishment than futile and hopeless labor.

". . . Sisyphus is the absurd hero. He is, as much through his passions as through his torture. His scorn of the gods, his hatred of death, and his passion for life won him that unspeakable penalty in which the whole being is exerted toward accomplishing nothing. This is the price that must be paid for the passions of this earth. Nothing is told us about Sisyphus in the underworld. Myths are made for the imagination to breathe life into them. As for this myth, one sees merely the whole effort of a body straining to raise the huge stone, to roll it and push it up a slope a hundred times over; one sees the face screwed up, the cheek tight against the stone, the shoulder bracing the clay-covered mass, the foot wedging it, the fresh start with arms outstretched, the wholly human security of two earth-clotted hands. At the very end of his long effort measured by skyless space and time without depth, the purpose is achieved. Then Sisyphus watches the stone rush down in a few moments toward that lower world whence he will have to push it up again toward the summit. He goes back down to the plain.

"It is during that return, that pause, that Sisyphus interests me. A face that toils so close to stones is already stone itself! I see that man going back down with a heavy yet measured step toward the torment of which he will never know the end. That hour like a breathing-space which returns as surely as his suffering, that is the hour of consciousness. At each of those moments when he leaves the heights and gradually sinks toward the lairs of the gods, he is superior to his fate. He is stronger than his rock.

"If this myth is tragic, that is because its hero is conscious. Where would his torture be, indeed, if at every step the hope of succeeding upheld him? The workman of today works every day in his life at the same tasks, and this fate is no less absurd. But it is tragic only at the rare moments when it becomes conscious. Sisyphus, proletarian of the gods, powerless and rebellious, knows the whole extent of his wretched condition: it is what he thinks of during his descent. The lucidity that was to constitute his torture at the same time crowns his victory. There is no fate that cannot be surmounted by scorn.

"If the descent is thus sometimes performed in sorrow, it can also take place in joy. This word is not too much. Again I fancy Sisyphus returning toward his rock, and the sorrow was in the beginning. When the images of earth cling too tightly to memory, when the call of happiness becomes too insistent, it happens that melancholy rises in man's heart: this is the rock's

(continued on next page)

THEIST: You atheists are always attacking us theists on the ground that we cannot show how evil in the world can be reconciled with an all-powerful, and all-loving God. You call it "the problem of evil."
ATHEIST: Right!

victory, this is the rock itself. The boundless grief is too heavy to bear. These are our nights of Gethsemane. But crushing truths perish from being acknowledged. Thus, Oedipus at the outset obeys fate without knowing it. But from the moment he knows, his tragedy begins. Yet at the same moment, blind and desperate, he realizes that the only bond linking him to the world is the cool hand of a girl. Then a tremendous remark rings out: "Despite so many ordeals, my advanced age and the nobility of my soul make me conclude that all is well." Sophocles' Oedipus, like Dostoevsky's Kirilov, thus gives the recipe for the absurd victory. Ancient wisdom confirms modern heroism.

"One does not discover the absurd without being tempted to write a manual of happiness. "What! by such narrow ways—?" There is but one world, however. Happiness and the absurd are two sons of the same earth. They are inseparable. It would be a mistake to say that happiness necessarily springs from the absurd discovery. It happens as well that the feeling of the absurd springs from happiness. "I conclude that all is well," says Oedipus, and the remark is sacred. It echoes in the wild and limited universe of man. It teaches that all is not, has not been, exhausted. It drives out of this world a god who had come into it with dissatisfaction and a preference for futile sufferings. It makes of fate a human matter, which must be settled among men.

"All Sisyphus' silent joy is contained therein. His fate belongs to him. His rock is his thing. Likewise, the absurd man, when he contemplates his torment, silences all the idols. In the universe suddenly restored to its silence, the myriad wondering little voices of the earth rise up. Unconscious, secret call, invitations form all the faces, they are the necessary reverse and price of victory. There is no sun without shadow, and it is essential to know the night. The absurd man says yes and his effort will henceforth be unceasing. If there is a personal fate, there is no higher destiny, or at least there is but one which he concludes is inevitable and despicable. For the rest, he knows himself to be the master of his days. At that subtle moment when man glances backward over his life, Sisyphus returning toward his rock, in that slight pivoting he contemplates that series of unrelated actions which becomes his fate, created by him, combined under his memory's eye and soon sealed by his death. Thus, convinced of the wholly human origin of all that is human, a blind man eager to see who knows that the night has no end, he is still on the go. The rock is still rolling.

"I leave Sisyphus at the foot of the mountain! One always finds one's burden again. But Sisyphus teaches the higher fidelity that negates the gods and raises rocks. He too concludes that all is well. This universe henceforth without a master seems to him neither sterile nor futile. Each atom of that stone, each mineral flake of that nightfilled mountain, in itself forms a world. The struggle itself toward the heights is enough to fill a man's heart. One must imagine Sisyphus happy."

Camus, *The Myth of Sisyphus*.

THEIST: But don't you have a similar problem? Why is it any more difficult to have evil *with* God than to have goodness *without* him? On your atheistic view, how can you account for all the goodwill, generosity, and self-sacrifice in the world? Call it "the problem of goodness."

ATHEIST: But all those good things come from *human beings*!

THEIST: Well, I doubt it. But even so, I will insist just as emphatically that sin *also* comes from humans.

ATHEIST: But if your God is all-powerful, he could have prevented men from sinning.

THEIST: I invoke the Free-Will Defense.

ATHEIST: Oh. But what about natural evil? Your Free-Will Defense will not explain *that*.

THEIST: You're right. But I have all sorts of other ideas about it—I'll tell you about them sometime. In the meantime, what's *your* explanation for natural evil? Isn't it as big a problem for you as for me? Give a little and take a little!

CHAPTER 13 IN REVIEW

SUMMARY

The presence in the world of evil, both natural and moral, is surely the biggest stumbling block to belief in an all-powerful and all-loving God.

Many attempts have been made on the theistic side to overcome this difficulty. We have considered several of them, but especially two. One of the most enduring is the view of evil as a privation, or absence, of good. Associated most notably with St. Augustine, this view emphasizes that God is responsible for the creation of *things*, not *no-things*. But evil is a no-thing; it is the absence of being and goodness. It cannot therefore be attributed to God. Natural evil has its origin in the (necessary) relative non-being of the natural world, and moral evil has its root in the relative nonbeing of the will. The denial that evil is a substance should not be confused with the denial that evil is real. Very different, but also enduring, is the therapeutic view of evil. Here the emphasis is primarily on natural evil, which is seen to be conducive to the development and strengthening of individuals and the race. Thus John Hick calls this mortal existence "a vale of soul-making."

Both of these positions make use, in their own ways, of the Free-Will Defense, which has figured prominently in recent philosophical discussions: If individuals are to be genuinely capable of doing what is right, they must also be capable of doing what is wrong. That is, human free will is a logically necessary limitation of God's power if moral creatures are to exist.

In contrast to those theists who attempt to reconcile evil with God, there are those atheists who simply, as it were, abandon the world to evil. God is dead, and the world is ultimately irrational. Camus provides one possible stance: We can at least recover something of human dignity by defying the irrational forces that will, finally "do us in." But theists want to know why this belief in the world as ultimately irrational is, philosophically, any less distasteful and problematic than their own belief in God.

BASIC IDEAS

- Natural evil and moral evil
- The problem of evil
- Theodicy
- Hume's statement of the problem
- Some standard solutions
  A limited God
  An inscrutable God
  The goodness of the whole
  The logical impossibility of a perfect world
  Evil as the necessary by-product of nature
- Evil as a privation of goodness
- The Free-Will Defense: for and against
- Evil as therapy
- Soul-making versus soul-breaking
- Evil as irrational
- Nihilism
- Anthropodicy
- The dignity of defiance

TEST YOURSELF

1. True or false: Alvin Plantinga believes that God could make a world in which everyone would always freely choose the good.

2. Why, according to some philosophers, is a perfect world logically impossible?

3. Mill solved the problem of evil simply by denying that God is_____.

4. Who is the source of the following? ". . . so long as a being is in process of corruption, there is in it some good of which it is being deprived."

5. Albert Camus taught that in the face of evil one ought to (a) commit suicide, (b) revolt, (c) resign oneself, (d) philosophize about it.

6. How did the ancient Christian writer Irenaeus figure in the discussion in this chapter?

7. St. Augustine's theory of evil as the absence of goodness is based on _____'s metaphysics.

8. What has Camus' novel *The Plague* to do with the problem of evil?

9. What would St. Augustine reply to the charge that his denial of evil as a substance renders evil *unreal*?

10. True or false: John Hick advocates *both* the therapy theory of evil *and* the Free-Will Defense.

- Do you think that the standard solutions to the problem of evil tend to trivialize the problem, or do any of them have real merit?

- Can you explain how St. Augustine's position on evil has its roots in a particular metaphysical view? By contrast, how would you characterize the metaphysical perspective that underlies Camus' position?

- Is it possible that what one feels about the problem of evil depends largely on one's prior beliefs on the existence of God? Isn't it likely that a theist will find a solution to the problem? Isn't it likely that an atheist will see it as disproving God's existence? What side of the fence are you on concerning the question of God's existence, and what difference does it make in your own view of the problem of evil?

- The Free-Will Defense always figures strongly in discussions about the problem of evil. Can you argue the Free-Will Defense back and forth? What do *you* make of this maneuver?

FOR FURTHER READING

John Cruickshank. *Albert Camus and the Literature of Revolt*. Oxford: Oxford University Press, 1959. A lucid treatment of Camus' idea of revolt in relation to his life, politics, and literature, and prefaced by a summarized and highly instructive "tribute" to Camus.

Brian Davies. *An Introduction to the Philosophy of Religion*. New York: Oxford University Press, 1982. Ch. 3. A brief, student-oriented chapter, raising relevant issues and concluding that evil is not a decisive evidence against God.

Austin Farrer. *Love Almighty and Ills Unlimited*. New York: Doubleday, 1961. A treatment of evil along specifically Augustinian lines, by a well-known philosopher.

Antony Flew. *Hume's Philosophy of Belief: A Study of His First Inquiry*. London: Routledge & Kegan Paul, 1961. Ch. 9. A thorough discussion of Hume's critical position on "the religious hypothesis."

Etienne Gilson. *The Christian Philosophy of St. Augustine*. Tr. L. E. M. Lynch. New York: Random House, 1960. Part II, sec. 3, and *passim*. A brief but helpful elucidation of Augustine's privation theory of evil, by a renowned medieval scholar.

Walter Kaufmann. *The Faith of a Heretic*. New York: McGraw-Hill, 1959. A lively rejection of the attempt to resolve the problem of evil from a biblical standpoint.

C. S. Lewis. *The Problem of Pain*. New York: Macmillan, 1962. A lucid and popular treatment of the problem of suffering (including animal suffering) by a foremost Christian apologist.

J. L. Mackie. *The Miracle of Theism: Arguments for and against the Existence of God*. Oxford: Clarendon Press, 1982. Ch. 9. Hefty discussions of standard and continuing issues pertaining to the problem of evil (survey of solutions, Free-Will Defense, divine omnipotence, etc.), with generally negative conclusions.

Ed. L. Miller. *God and Reason: An Invitation to Philosophical Theology.* Englewood Cliffs, NJ: Prentice-Hall, 1995. Ch. 8. A discussion, for beginners, of the problem of evil, with special reference to the Augustinian position.

Michael Peterson. *Evil and the Christian God.* Grand Rapids, MI: Baker, 1982. An Evangelical's attempt to reconcile evil with the God of the Bible and of classical theism, with special reference to the argument from gratuitous evil.

Michael Peterson et al. *Reason and Religious Belief: An Introduction to the Philosophy of Religion.* New York: Oxford University Press, 1991. Ch. 6. An introductory but sophisticated treatment of the problem of evil, reflecting current and influential options.

Nelson Pike (ed.). *God and Evil: Readings on the Theological Problem of Evil.* Englewood Cliffs, NJ: Prentice-Hall, 1964. A much-used collection of seven enduring statements, traditional and contemporary.

Alvin Plantinga. *God and Other Minds: A Study of the Rational Justification of Belief in God.* Ithaca, NY: Cornell University Press, 1967. Chs. 5–6 and 7, Part II. A sometimes technical discussion of God and evil, emphasizing recent debates concerning, for example, the Free-Will Defense and problems of divine omnipotence.

James F. Ross. *Philosophical Theology.* Indianapolis: Bobbs-Merrill, 1969. Chs. 5–6. An approach to the problem of evil along Thomistic-analytic lines.

Richard Swinburne. *The Existence of God.* Oxford: Clarendon Press, 1979. Ch. 11. A clear account of relevant issues (traditional approaches, Free-Will Defense, quantity of evil, etc.) rejecting evil as evidence against God.

R. A. Tsanoff. *The Nature of Evil.* New York: Macmillan, 1931. A complete history of the philosophical problem of evil and proposed solutions.

*In addition, see the relevant articles (e.g., "Evil, the Problems of") in *Routledge Encyclopedia of Philosophy,* ed. Edward Craig (London: Routledge, 1998), and *Stanford Encyclopedia of Philosophy,* http://plato.stanford.edu.

PART FOUR

THE QUESTION OF MORALITY

As was explained in Chapter 1, value-theory raises the question of value in general. The value of filets mignons, human deeds, works of art, political ideologies—all values are the concern of value-theory. It is not possible to consider all spheres of value, but it would seem necessary to consider at least two of them. In this part o f our book we will examine *ethical* or *moral values*, those values that define personal decisions and actions as good or evil, moral or immoral. In the final part we will look at *social* and *political values*, the values that determine the principles and institutions of our life together in society and the state.

Talk of moral and political values probably brings immediately to mind all sorts of exciting and dramatic issues, such as abortion, capital punishment, animal rights, feminism, the environment, war, sex, politics, minority rights, genetic engineering, and euthanasia. And rightfully so. All such issues presuppose, involve, and imply many kinds of values. But while it is expected, also rightfully, that value-theory must in the end illuminate such problems, it is usually not with these problems that value-theory directly concerns itself. More specifically, as a theoretical endeavor, moral philosophy or ethics is concerned with the clarification of fundamental ethical concepts, the elucidation of principles, and the critical discussion of positions and perspectives. It should be apparent that these tasks are, after all, much more important than the excited arguments about specific issues (such as those mentioned above), which all too often proceed without due regard for more fundamental questions. In the case of ethics, such questions are:

- What is moral goodness?
- Is morality relative or absolute?
- Are all moral values derived from an ultimate value?
- What are the epistemological bases of the ethical theories?
- Is there a distinction between what *is* and what *ought* to be?
- Does moral responsibility require free will?
- What is the relation between the private and the public good?

The truth is, of course, that even with its theoretical concerns, the philosophical question of morality stands more obviously related to concrete situations and practical questions than do the other fields of philosophy. And it is, therefore, here, with the question of morality (and again in Part Five, with the question of society), that philosophical activity will seem to many to be most related to the question of *living*.

CHALLENGES TO MORALITY

B efore we consider some of the more important ways philosophers have answered the question of morality, we must consider the prior question: Is morality, or at least traditional morality, even possible? Some have, indeed, maintained for various reasons that morality, as it is usually conceived, is *not* possible. *First,* we have the relativists or subjectivists, who argue that morality is a matter of individual judgment and that there are no common or universal moral obligations. *Second,* we must confront the determinist, who denies free will and asks, "If all things, including our choices, are completely predetermined, then how can there be any basis for moral responsibility?" *Third,* the psychological egoists claim that all actions are inevitably motivated by self-interest, and thus the unselfish acts of traditional morality are impossible. *Finally,* we have to reckon with the existentialists, who locate the basis of morality in evolving human nature itself.

THE CHALLENGE OF RELATIVISM

Probably the most serious challenge to morality is posed by *ethical relativism*. We have already encountered the idea of ethical relativism in the person of Protagoras. In fact, he provided this view with a motto for all time when he said that "a man is the measure of all things." Though Protagoras himself did not limit his statement to moral claims, it was natural that it was in the realm of morality that it was most obviously applied.

"A man is the measure of all things"

341

ETHICAL RELATIVISM

Ethical relativism, or ethical subjectivism, denies any absolute or objective moral values that are common to all, and affirms, rather, that the individual (a person, community, society, etc.) is the source and criterion of moral judgments.

Ethical relativism holds that the criterion of the truth or falsity of moral claims is the *individual*—the individual's perceptions, opinions, experiences, inclinations, and desires. This sort of relativism can take different forms, depending on what is meant by "individual." It might make ethical truth relative to the individual person, or the individual society, or community, or nation, or culture, or even the whole human race. But *any* form of ethical relativism denies that there are common or universal or *objective* moral values. It insists, rather, that moral values are private, individual, or *subjective.* Hence, ethical relativism versus ethical absolutism may be expressed also as ethical subjectivism versus ethical objectivism. However it is expressed, the issue is the same: What is the source or foundation of moral values and ideals? Are ethical values relative and subjective, or absolute and objective? Are they dependent upon the individual, or do moral values and ideals exist irrespective and independent of the individual? Is morality a matter of "different strokes for different folks"?

For those who embrace ethical relativism, more often than not it is the particular or individual *culture* that is said to define morality. We have encountered an instance of this already in B. F. Skinner's *Beyond Freedom and Dignity:*

> What a given group of people calls good is a fact; it is what members of the group find reinforcing as the result of their genetic endowment and the natural and social contingencies to which they have been exposed. Each culture has its own set of goods, and what is good in one culture may not be good in another. To recognize this is to take the position of "cultural relativism." What is good for the Trobriand Islander is good for the Trobriand Islander, and that is that. Anthropologists have often emphasized relativism as a tolerant alternative to missionary zeal in converting all cultures to a single set of ethical, governmental, religious, or economic values.[1]

One such anthropologist was Ruth Benedict, author of the much-read *Patterns of Culture.* In her essay "Anthropology and the Abnormal," she, like Skinner, equates cultural relativism and ethical relativism:

> Every society, beginning with some slight inclination in one direction or another, carries its preference farther and farther, integrating itself more and more completely

Are moral values relative or absolute? Subjective or objective?

Cultural relativism

---

[1] B. F. Skinner, *Beyond Freedom and Dignity* (Indianapolis, IN: Hackett, 2002), p. 128.

upon its chosen basis, and discarding those types of behavior that are uncongenial. Most of those organizations of personality that seem to us most incontrovertibly abnormal have been used by different civilizations in the very foundations of their institutional life. Conversely the most valued traits of our normal individuals have been looked on in differently organized cultures as aberrant. Normality, in short, within a very wide range, is culturally defined. It is primarily a term for the socially elaborated segment of human behavior in any culture; and abnormality, a term for the segment that that particular civilization does not use. The very eyes with which we see the problem are conditioned by the long traditional habits of our own society.

It is a point that has been made more often in relation to ethics than in relation to psychiatry. We do not any longer make the mistake of deriving the morality of our own locality and decade directly from the inevitable constitution of human nature. We do not elevate it to the dignity of a first principle. We recognize that morality differs in every society, and is a convenient term for socially approved habits. Mankind has always preferred to say, "It is morally good," rather than "It is habitual," and the fact of this preference is matter enough for a critical science of ethics. But historically the two phrases are synonymous.

The concept of the normal is properly a variant of the concept of the good. It is that which society has approved. A normal action is one which falls well within the limits of expected behavior for a particular society. Its variability among different peoples is essentially a function of the variability of the behavior patterns that different societies have created for themselves, and can never be wholly divorced from a consideration of culturally institutionalized types of behavior.

Each culture is a more or less elaborate working-out of the potentialities of the segment it has chosen. In so far as a civilization is well integrated and consistent within itself, it will tend to carry farther and farther, according to its nature, its initial impulse toward a particular type of action, and from the point of view of any other culture those elaborations will induce more and more extreme and aberrant traits.

Each of these traits, in proportion as it reinforces the chosen behavior patterns of that culture, is for that culture normal. Those individuals to whom it is congenial either congenitally, or as the result of childhood sets, are accorded prestige in that culture, and are not visited with the social contempt or disapproval which their traits would call down upon them in a society that was differently organized. On the other hand, those individuals whose characteristics are not congenial to the selected type of human behavior in that community are the deviants, no matter how valued their personality traits may be in a contrasted civilization.[2]

Why would one be an ethical relativist? Why would one ever assert with Protagoras that in matters of morality, "a man is the measure of all things"? Well, there is one gigantic but two-sided argument that relativists give over and over again. And, in fact, it is the argument that Protagoras himself gave. The argument is, first, that ethical views, opinions, and exhortations are largely or even completely conditioned by our circumstances. Obviously,

One big argument
for ethical relativism

---

[2]Ruth Benedict, "Anthropology and the Abnormal," *Journal of General Psychology* 10 (1934), pp. 72–74.

whether you think that X is right and Y is wrong is very much dependent upon—relative to—when and where you were born, your upbringing, your education, your religious instruction, and maybe even your skin color and your height. Do you really think that you would hold the same moral opinions if your fundamental circumstances had been radically different? Second, and aside from our circumstances, relativists usually take very seriously the differences, disputes, and downright confusion that reign everywhere in the area of morality.

When both of these lines of observations are put together they suggest strongly (maybe decisively) to some that there *are* no common or universal or objective values, and that morality is *relative*.

Probably the most powerful (and most popular) version of this argument for relativism points to the varying moral beliefs of different cultures. While many cultures think that eating dog meat is a delicacy, Americans are horrified by the practice and decry it as immoral. Or consider that some groups see nothing wrong with infanticide whereas most cultures view it as immoral. This might be called the *cultural differences argument* and can be expressed as follows:

1. Different cultures have different moral codes.
2. Therefore, there is no objective truth in morality. Right and wrong are only matters of opinion, and opinions vary from culture to culture.[3]

Such a position is not without its problems. For one thing, does not the argument for ethical relativism misfire? Surely it does not follow from the fact that one's moral opinions are conditioned or learned that they are therefore merely subjectively or relatively true. We have learned all sorts of things that, nonetheless, we believe to be true, and true for *everyone*: In fourteen hundred and ninety-two Columbus sailed the ocean blue; 2 + 2 = 4; it is wrong to beat your spouse, starve your children, and torture your pets; and so on. And how do disagreements about morality destroy its objectivity? We may disagree also about the nature of the universe, but we would hardly conclude from that that the universe *has* no nature! On the contrary, what is the point of disagreeing at all, unless we believe there is some real *truth* involved? It is important, then, to distinguish between our *opinions* of morality and *morality itself*. Certainly our opinions about morality differ, and certainly they are conditioned by and relative to all sorts of things. But in no other sphere would we so simple-mindedly confuse our opinions of the truth with the truth itself. Why here, where the implications are far more consequential?

Furthermore, if the individual is the basis of moral truth, then none of us could ever be mistaken in our moral opinions, for whatever we believe must be true. Or, in the larger interpretation of "individual," such as an individual group, morality would reduce to what happened to be believed

Many arguments against ethical relativism

---

[3]This specific formulation of the argument comes from James Rachels, *The Elements of Moral Philosophy*, 2d ed. (New York: McGraw-Hill, 1993).

THE GOLDEN RULE:
A UNIVERSAL MORAL PRINCIPLE?

"What you do not want done to yourself, do not do to others."

—Confucius (SIXTH CENTURY B.C.)

"Hurt not others with that which pains yourself."

—Buddha (FIFTH CENTURY B.C.)

"In happiness and suffering, in joy and grief, we should regard all creatures as we regard our own self, and should therefore refrain from inflicting upon others such injury as would appear undesirable to us if inflicted upon ourselves."

—Jainism (FIFTH CENTURY B.C.)

"Do not do to others all that which is not well for oneself."

—Zoroastrianism (FIFTH CENTURY B.C.)

"May I do to others as I would that they should do to me."

—Plato (FOURTH CENTURY B.C.)

"Do nothing to others which if done to you would cause you pain."

—Hinduism (THIRD CENTURY B.C.)

"What is hateful to yourself, do not do to your fellow man."

—Hillel (FIRST CENTURY B.C.)

"Whatsoever you would that men should do to you, do you even so to them."

—Jesus of Nazareth (FIRST CENTURY A.D.)

"Treat others as you would be treated yourself."

—Sikhism (SIXTEENTH CENTURY A.D.)

by the largest number of people. Both of these seem to many to be necessary but absurd implications of the relativist or subjectivist position.

Some have even charged that ethical relativism not only misfires but *backfires* inasmuch as it involves a sort of *practical contradiction*. It is the contradiction between saying one thing and living another. You may know someone who *claims* to be an ethical relativist, but do you know anyone who *lives* as one? Do we not all, in one way or another, impose our ideas of morality on others? Do we not hold others responsible for their actions? Do we not judge others as morally wrong or reprehensible? Do we not vote, crusade for causes, and make sacrifices for various ideals? But clearly all such actions are meaningful only on the assumption of an *objective* and *common* morality. In a word, this objection charges that there is really no such thing as a consistent subjectivist.

Is ethical relativism
practically
contradictory?

ETHICAL ABSOLUTISM

Ethical absolutism, or ethical objectivism, affirms that moral values are independent of individual opinions and ascribes to them an abiding and fixed reality common to all.

It should be noted, finally, that *if* you accept the above criticisms of ethical relativism, then you *must* be an ethical objectivist or absolutist. For either ethical relativism is true or ethical absolutism is true; there is no third alternative. If ethical relativism is false, then ethical absolutism must be true. Or, at least, so it seems to many. How does it seem to you?

THE CHALLENGE OF DETERMINISM

Another difficulty for morality is posed by the *determinist*. In fact, some would say that determinism renders morality (as most of us understand the word) impossible. We saw in an earlier discussion (in Chapter 6) that determinism is the view that all things are causally conditioned such that they could not be otherwise. We also considered some of the problematical implications of this view, though we must now consider more adequately its implications for morality.

What are these implications? If it is true that all things are causally determined, then this must apply also to our willing and choosing. And this means the *denial of free will*. And this means the *end of moral responsibility*. At least according to many. For is it not clear, they would insist, that moral responsibility *presupposes free will*? What sense is there in praise and blame and holding individuals accountable if one could not have done otherwise? If one does not choose and act *freely*? Is it not always relevant, when trying to establish blame or guilt or responsibility on the part of someone, to ascertain whether that person was forced, drugged, or suffering from some compulsion? Thus free will has seemed to many to be a condition for responsible, moral action.

William James explains the moral problem with the determinist position in a slightly different way in his essay "The Dilemma of Determinism." James focuses on the existence of "judgments of regret" after we have committed certain actions that we think are wrong. In a deterministic world, however, such judgments are impossible, as James explains:

> When murders and treacheries cease to be sins, regrets are theoretic absurdities and errors. The theoretic and the active life thus play a kind of see-saw with each other on the ground of evil. The rise of either sends the other down. Murder

". . . it is certain that if there is no free will there can be no morality."

—W. T. Stace

and treachery cannot be good without regret being bad; regret cannot be good without treachery and murder being bad. Both, however [on the deterministic model], are supposed to have been foredoomed; so something must be fatally unreasonable, absurd, and wrong in the world. It must be a place of which either sin or error forms a necessary part. From this dilemma there seems at first sight no escape. Are we then so soon to fall back into the pessimism from which we thought we had emerged? And is there no possible way by which we may, with good intellectual consciences, call the cruelties and treacheries, the reluctance and the regrets, *all* good together?[4]

Your decision between determinism, or the belief that everything, including your will, is causally determined, and indeterminism, the belief that some things, and therefore possibly the will, are not determined, may be a crucial one. And you cannot have it both ways—either determinism or indeterminism.

Determinism or indeterminism?

But we must not move too fast here. Determinism itself must be viewed in two lights: *hard*-determinism and *soft*-determinism.

The hard-determinist believes not only that all things are determined, but that they are determined ultimately by purely *external* factors, factors outside yourself and over which you have no control. Why did you choose X? *Ultimately* because of things like the circumstances of your birth, upbringing, education, environment, genetic structure—in a word because of everything that has contributed in any way to the shaping and placing of your person and those of all of your ancestors. To say it another way, you chose X because_____: Fill in here the uncountable causes that, extending as it were from the infinite past, converge at this moment on the movement of your will in favor of X.

Hard-determinism. . .

Is hard-determinism compatible with morality? According to the hard-determinists themselves, the answer is both Yes and No. On the yes side, the hard-determinist, no less than anyone else, decries murder, theft, and the torturing of starving children. The fact that people have no control over their actions, whether good or evil, has no bearing on those actions being, nevertheless, good or evil. The desire to torture starving children, like cancer, is an evil to be recognized as such and to be dealt with—as you would deal with cancer. Now you do not punish a cancer; you try to *treat* it and *heal* it. (Echoes of Skinner?) But this brings us to the no side of the answer. If morality implies the possibility of praise, blame, and punishment, then the hard-determinist

. . . and morality

---

[4]William James, "The Dilemma of Determinism," in *The Will to Believe and Other Essays in Popular Philosophy* (Cambridge, MA.: University Press, 1896), pp. 163–164.

Soft-determinism. . .

can scarcely accommodate morality. Certainly there is little room for praise, blame, and punishment in a view of things according to which no one is responsible for his or her condition in general, which means also his or her moral condition in specific. One is not *responsible,* period.

It is precisely to the issue of *responsibility* that *soft*-determinism speaks. The soft-determinist is, of course, a determinist, and holds, like the hard-determinist, that because of antecedent causes our choices could not be otherwise. But in contrast to the hard-determinist, the soft-determinist shifts our whole attention to the causes that lie *within* the individual. Our actions and choices *are* determined—by our desires, inclinations, attitudes, or, in a word, our *character.*

. . . and morality

In this way, the soft-determinists see determinism not only as compatible with morality but as *necessary* for morality. For, they say, your choices or actions can be judged moral or immoral, or you can be held accountable for them, only if they actually reflect your intentions, desires, attitudes, and so on. Would you hold someone responsible for an action that did not really spring from his or her character? Would you hold me morally accountable for hitting you in the face if it was the result of a sudden and uncontrollable muscle spasm? If, however, my hitting you in the face was the result of (or was *caused by*) my attitude toward you and my intention to cause you pain, isn't that a quite different situation? a situation in which I am *responsible* for my action? a *moral* situation? How then can there be moral behavior and moral judgment without determinism—character-determinism or *self*-determinism, as the position is also called?

David Hume provides a good statement of how praise and blame are possible only if the deeds that are praised or blamed are rooted in, or

---

The famous attorney Clarence Darrow to the prisoners of the Cook County Jail:

There is no such thing as a crime as the word is generally understood. I do not believe there is any sort of distinction between the real moral conditions of the people in and out of jail. One is just as good as the other. The people here can no more help being here than the people outside can avoid being outside. I do not believe that people are in jail because they deserve to be. They are in jail simply because they cannot avoid it on account of circumstances which are entirely beyond their control and for which they are in no way responsible. . . . There are people who think that everything in this world is an accident. But really there is no such thing as an accident. . . . There are a great many people here who have done some of these things (murder, theft, etc.) who really do not know themselves why they did them. It looked to you at the time as if you had a chance to do them or not, as you saw fit; but still, after all you had no choice. . . . If you look at the question deeply enough and carefully enough you will see that there were circumstances that drove you to do exactly the thing which you did. You could not help it any more than we outside can help taking the positions that we take.

caused by, the doer's character. From *An Enquiry Concerning Human Understanding*:

The only proper object of hatred or vengeance is a person or creature, endowed with thought and consciousness; and when any criminal or injurious actions excite that passion, it is only by their relation to the person, or connexion with him. Actions are, by their very nature, temporary and perishing; and where they proceed not from some *cause* in the character and disposition of the person who performed them, they can neither redound to his honour, if good; nor infamy, if evil. The actions themselves may be blameable; they may be contrary to all the rules of morality and religion: But the person is not answerable for them; and as they proceed from nothing in him that is durable and constant, and leave nothing of that nature behind them, it is impossible he can, upon their account, become the object of punishment or vengeance. According to the principle, therefore, which denies necessity, and consequently causes, a man is as pure and untainted, after having committed the most horrid crime, as at the first moment of his birth, nor is his character anywise concerned in his actions, since they are not derived from it, and the wickedness of the one can never be used as a proof of the depravity of the other.

Men are not blamed for such actions as they perform ignorantly and casually, whatever may be the consequences. Why? but because the principles of these actions are only momentary, and terminate in them alone. Men are less blamed for such actions as they perform hastily and unpremeditately than for such as proceed from deliberation. For what reason? but because a hasty temper, though a constant cause or principle in the mind, operates only by intervals, and infects not the whole character. Again, repentance wipes off every crime, if attended with a reformation of life and manners. How is this to be accounted for? but by asserting that actions render a person criminal merely as they are proofs of criminal principles in the mind; and when, by an alteration of these principles, they cease to be just proofs, they likewise cease to be criminal. But, except upon

THE PROBLEM OF FREE WILL AND DETERMINISM

Determinism

The view that all things, including the will, are causally determined.

(a) *Hard-determinism*
The will is determined ultimately by exterior factors beyond the responsibility of the individual.

(b) *Soft-determinism*
The will is determined by the character of the individual, and thus individuals are responsible for their choices.

Indeterminism

The view that some things, and therefore possibly the will, are free of causal determination.

the doctrine of necessity, they never were just proofs, and consequently never were criminal.

It will be equally easy to prove, and from the same arguments, that *liberty* . . . is also essential to morality, and that no human actions, where it is wanting, are susceptible of any moral qualities, or can be the objects either of approbation or dislike. For as actions are objects of our moral sentiment, so far only as they are indications of the internal character, passions, and affections; it is impossible that they can give rise either to praise or blame, where they proceed not from these principles, but are derived altogether from external violence.[5]

Does
soft-determinism
reduce to
hard-determinism?

But the indeterminists, or free-willists, are still unsatisfied. They raise an obvious question: It may be that my choice or action is determined by my own character, but how did I acquire this character—these particular attitudes, inclinations, desires, likes, and dislikes? Is not my character ultimately determined, again, by factors outside me, antecedent to me, and quite beyond my control? Does not soft-determinism have to give way, finally, to hard-determinism with its denial of moral responsibility? As far as *responsibility* goes, is there really any final difference between soft- and hard-determinism? A clearer reduction of soft-determinism to hard-determinism could hardly be found than that of Baron D'Holbach (1723–1789), an atheistic and mechanistic materialist. In the following, from *The System of Nature*, Holbach applies his mechanistic principle specifically to the question of morality, and concludes that all of our moral dispositions, no less than anything else about us, reduce, finally, to necessary determinations.

The *ambitious man* cries out: you will have me resist passions; but have they not unceasingly repeated to me that rank, honours, power, are the most desirable advantages in life? Have I not seen my fellow citizens envy them, the nobles of my country sacrifice every thing to obtain them? In the society in which I live, am I not obliged to feel, that if I am deprived of these advantages, I must expect to anguish in contempt; to cringe under the rod of oppression?

The *miser* says: you forbid me to love money, to seek after the means of acquiring it: alas! does not every thing tell me that, in this world, money is the greatest blessing; that it is amply sufficient to render me happy? In the country I inhabit, do I not see all my fellow citizens covetous of riches? but do I not also witness that they are little scrupulous in the means of obtaining wealth? As soon as they are enriched by the means which you censure, are they not cherished, considered and respected? By what authority, then, do you defend me from amassing treasure? What right have you to prevent my using means, which, although you call them sordid and criminal, I see approved by the sovereign? Will you have me renounce my happiness?

The *voluptuary* argues: you pretend that I should resist my desires; but was I the maker of my own temperament, which unceasingly invites me to pleasure? You call my pleasures disgraceful; but in the country in which I live, do I not witness the most dissipated men enjoying the most distinguished rank? Do I not behold that no one is ashamed of adultery but the husband it has outraged? Do

---

[5]David Hume, *An Enquiry Concerning Human Understanding,* in *Hume's Enquiries,* ed. L. A. Selby-Bigge, 2d ed. (Oxford: Clarendon Press, 1902), pp. 98–99.

not I see men making trophies of their debaucheries, boasting of their libertinism, rewarded with applause?

The *choleric man* vociferates: you advise me to put a curb on my passions, and to resist the desire of avenging myself: but can I conquer my nature? Can I alter the received opinions of the world? Shall I not be forever disgraced, infallibly dishonoured in society, if I do not wash out in the blood of my fellow creatures the injuries I have received?

The *zealous enthusiast* exclaims: you recommend me mildness; you advise me to be tolerant; to be indulgent to the opinions of my fellow men; but is not my temperament violent? Do I not ardently love my God? Do they not assure me, that zeal is pleasing to him; that sanguinary inhuman persecutors have been his friends? As I wish to render myself acceptable in his sight, I therefore adopt the same means.

In short, the actions of man are never free; they are always the necessary consequence of his temperament, of the received ideas, and of the notions, either true or false, which he has formed to himself of happiness; of his opinions, strengthened by example, by education, and by daily experience. . . .

If he understood the play of his organs, if he were able to recall to himself all the impulsions they have received, all the modifications they have undergone, all the effects they have produced, he would perceive that all his actions are submitted to that *fatality,* which regulates his own particular system, as it does the entire system of the universe: no one effect in him, any more than in nature, produces itself by *chance;* this, as has been before proved, is word void of sense. All that passes in him; all that is done by him; as well as all that happens in nature, or that is attributed to her, is derived from necessary causes, which act according to necessary laws, and which produce necessary effects, from whence necessarily flow others.

Fatality, is the eternal, the immutable, the necessary order, established in nature; or the indispensable connexion of causes that act, with the effects they operate.[6]

The indeterminist agrees with this but draws the opposite conclusion: not that there is no basis for praise, blame, responsibility, and virtuous conduct, but that determinism must be false! That is, the indeterminist can simply turn the tables: If someone says that since our wills are determined, there can be no morality, the indeterminist may answer that inasmuch as morality is a fact, our wills must *not* be determined! And, of course, the indeterminists have it in their favor that, as a matter of fact, we *do*—all of us, always, and unavoidably—live our lives on the assumption that there is free will and that people are *responsible.* Thus, according to the indeterminists, the determinists are a little like the relativists, who, as we saw in the last section, might *claim* their position to be true, but cannot *live* as if it were true. In fact, determinists turn out so much to be free-willists that W. T. Stace has concluded that the determinism–free-will problem can hardly be a real problem at all; rather, it must simply involve a misunderstanding in our philosophical language:

Morality as a fact of life

It is to be observed that those learned professors of philosophy or psychology who deny the existence of free will do so only in their professional moments and in their studies and lecture rooms. For when it comes to doing anything practical, even of

[6]Baron D'Holbach, *The System of Nature,* tr. H. D. Robinson (Boston: Mendum, 1869), pp. 94–95, 102.

WILLIAM JAMES ON "CHANCE"

One of the objections to indeterminism is that it leaves us with a world of pure chance. As William James points out, however, the idea of *chance* may not pose the threat that is often feared.

The stronghold of the deterministic sentiment is the antipathy to the idea of chance. As soon as we begin to talk indeterminism to our friends, we find a number of them shaking their heads. This notion of alternative possibility, they say, this admission that any one of several things may come to pass, is, after all, only a roundabout name for chance; and chance is something the notion of which no sane mind can for an instant tolerate in the world. What is it, they ask, but barefaced crazy unreason, the negation of intelligibility and law? And if the slightest particle of it exist anywhere, what is to prevent the whole fabric from falling together, the stars from going out, and chaos from recommencing her topsy-turvy reign?

Remarks of this sort about chance will put an end to discussion as quickly as anything one can find. I have already told you that "chance" was a word I wished to keep and use. Let us then examine exactly what it means, and see whether it ought to be such a terrible bugbear to us. I fancy that squeezing the thistle boldly will rob it of its sting.

The sting of the word "chance" seems to lie in the assumption that it means something positive, and that if anything happens by chance, it must needs be something of an intrinsically irrational and preposterous sort. Now chance means nothing of the kind. It is a purely negative and relative term, giving us no information about that of which it is predicated, except that it happens to be disconnected with something else—not controlled, secured, or necessitated by other things in advance of its own actual presence.

As this point is the most subtle one of the whole lecture, and at the same time the point on which all the rest hinges I beg you to pay particular attention to it. What I say is that it tells us nothing about what a thing may be in itself to call it "chance." It may be a bad thing, it may be a good thing. It may be lucidity, transparency, fitness incarnate, matching the whole system of other things, when it has once befallen, in an unimaginable perfect way. All you mean by calling it "chance" is that this is not guaranteed, that it may also fall out otherwise, for the system of other things has no positive hold on the

(continued on next page)

the most trivial kind, they invariably behave as if they and others were free. They inquire from you at dinner whether you will choose this dish or that dish. They will ask a child why he told a lie, and will punish him for not having chosen the way of truthfulness. All of which is inconsistent with a disbelief in free will. This should cause us to suspect that the problem is not a real one; and this, I believe, is the case. The dispute is merely verbal, and is due to nothing but a confusion about the meanings of words. It is what is now fashionably called a semantic problem.[7]

---

[7]W. T. Stace, *Religion and the Modern Mind* (Philadelphia: Lippincott, 1952), pp. 279–280.

chance-thing. Its origin is in a certain fashion negative: it escapes, and says, Hands off! coming, when it comes as a free gift, or not at all. . . .

Nevertheless, many persons talk as if the minutest dose of disconnectedness of one part with another, the smallest modicum of independence, the faintest tremor of ambiguity about the future, for example, would ruin everything, and turn this goodly universe into a sort of insane sand-heap or nulliverse—no universe at all. Since future human volitions are as a matter of fact the only ambiguous things we are tempted to believe in, let us stop for a moment to make ourselves sure whether their independent and accidental character need be fraught with such direful consequences to the universe as that.

What is meant by saying that my choice of which way to walk home after the lecture is ambiguous and a matter of chance as far as the present moment is concerned? It means that both Divinity Avenue and Oxford Street are called, but that only one, and that *either* one, shall be chosen. Now, I ask you seriously to suppose that this ambiguity of my choice is real; and then to make the impossible hypothesis that the choice is made twice over, and each time falls on a different street. In other words, imagine that I first walk through Divinity Avenue, and then imagine that the powers governing the universe annihilate ten minutes of time with all that it contained, and set me back at the door of this hall just as I was before the choice was made. Imagine then that, everything else being the same, I now make a different choice and traverse Oxford Street. You, as passive spectators, look on and see the two alternative universes—one of them with me walking through Divinity Avenue in it, the other with the same me walking through Oxford Street. Now, if you are determinists you believe one of these universes to have been from eternity impossible: you believe it to have been impossible because of the intrinsic irrationality or accidentality somewhere involved in it. But looking outwardly at these universes, can you say which is the impossible and accidental one, and which the rational and necessary one? I doubt if the most iron-clad determinist among you could have the slightest glimmer of light on this point. In other words, either universe *after the fact* and once there would, to our means of observation and understanding, appear just as rational as the other. . . .

But what a hollow outcry, then, is this against a chance which, if it were present to us, we could by no character whatever distinguish from a rational necessity! I have taken the most trivial of examples, but no possible example could lead to any different result.*

---

*William James, "The Dilemma of Determinism," in *The Will to Believe and Other Essays in Popular Philosophy* (Cambridge, MA: University Press, 1896), pp. 153–157.

It must be admitted, though, that the indeterminists are in an awkward spot too. They deny determinism as being incompatible with morality. But what do they replace it with? Actions and choices that are *un*caused? But this would seem to make our actions and choices utterly spontaneous, capricious, irrational, and arbitrary. And certainly this is just as incompatible with morality and responsibility as is determinism. Something is beyond one's control, and therefore not an object of praise or blame, as much whether it happened by pure chance as whether it was completely necessitated. But what, then, lies in this mysterious zone between pure chance and pure necessity? What might the indeterminist or free-willist *mean* by "uncaused" choices or "free" will? Some indeterminists or free-willists would withdraw at this point with a quiet, "I really don't know. But there must be some such. For it is certainly a bigger problem to reject morality than not to have a clear and coherent idea of free will. Take your choice. *But do you really have one?*"

Others, of a somewhat more analytic strain, have sought for clarification of our terms. We have seen that the whole determinism–free-will controversy is bound up with talk about causality, the principle that every event must have a cause. But is an act of the will really an "act" in any obvious or clear sense? And is a decision really an "event"? It has been suggested, not without merit, that maybe the language in which the whole problem has been posed is inappropriate from the start. Has it been something like a category mistake again? In any event, William K. Frankena's exhortation is well taken:

> . . . I think that moral philosophers cannot insist too much on the importance of actual knowledge and conceptual clarity for the solution of moral and social problems. The two besetting sins in our prevailing habits of ethical thinking are our ready acquiescence in unclarity and our complacence in ignorance—the very sins that Socrates died combatting over two thousand years ago.[8]

THE CHALLENGE OF PSYCHOLOGICAL EGOISM

A third challenge to morality comes from *psychological egoism*. The psychological egoist claims that all actions are inevitably motivated by self-interest. Regardless of appearances to the contrary, we are all selfish. When I stop to help an old lady cross the street, it might appear that I am being unselfish, but not so, says the psychological egoist. There is some selfish motive lurking beneath the surface that is the real motivation. Perhaps I want others to think highly of me or maybe I hope that she'll reward me with money.

Selfish motives

In its strongest form, psychological egoism claims that all of us, all the time, with all of our actions are pursuing nothing but our own self-interest. And we cannot do otherwise.

This last statement—"we cannot do otherwise"—is really the key; it helps us to understand both the theory and how it poses a challenge to morality. It shows, first, that this is a psychological theory, a claim about human nature rather than a theory of morality. Psychological egoism makes a claim about what we can (and cannot) do, not what we should

---

[8]William K. Frankena, *Ethics*, 2d ed. (Englewood Cliffs, NJ: Prentice-Hall, 1973), p. 13.

> When someone says, "Everything is determined by antecedent causes and could not have been otherwise," is that statement *itself* determined? Do you usually pay much attention to utterances that could not have been different, such as that of someone acting out a posthypnotic suggestion?

(and should not) do. As a result, it is really another form of determinism claiming that the selfishness of human behavior is determined.

The way that psychological egoism poses a challenge to morality is summed up best in the phrase "ought implies can." Immanuel Kant argued that it makes no sense to say that a person has a duty to do something—she *ought* to do it—unless the person is capable of committing the action—she *can* do it. In other words, you cannot be morally obligated to do X if it is impossible for you to do X. Thus to say that one ought to be unselfish implies that one is capable of acting on motives other than self-interest. But it is precisely this last statement that psychological egoism denies.

"Ought implies can"

While few philosophers defend psychological egoism in a direct way, it is a common view and one that requires a response. David Hume described psychological egoism as the principle of "self-love," claiming that it has been "much insisted on by philosophers, and has been the foundation of many a system."[9]

All psychological egoists acknowledge that people appear to be concerned for others, but are they really? Or is it just a façade hiding a deeper selfishness? Though not an egoist himself, Hume expresses the alleged hidden selfishness beautifully.

> . . . whatever affection one may feel, or imagine he feels for others, no passion is, or can be, disinterested; the most generous friendship, however sincere, is a modification of self-love; and even unknown to ourselves, we seek only our own gratification, while we appear the most deeply engaged in schemes for the liberty and happiness of mankind.[10]

---

[9]David Hume, *An Enquiry Concerning the Principles of Morals,* ed. J. B. Schneewind (Indianapolis: Hackett, 1983), p. 89.

[10]Ibid.

OUGHT IMPLIES CAN

To say that you ought (morally) to do something implies that it must be possible for you to do it (i.e., you can do it). In other words, you cannot be morally obligated to do something it is literally impossible for you to do.

PSYCHOLOGICAL EGOISM

The theory of human nature asserting that all actions are motivated exclusively by self-interest.

The most common response to psychological egoism—you've perhaps already started to do this in your own mind—is to point to certain actions as clear counterexamples. The fireman running into the burning building, the soldier who jumps on a grenade to save his friends, the mother who sacrifices everything for her children—aren't these obvious examples of unselfishness? Don't they clearly show that some actions are motivated by something other than self-interest?

Not for the psychological egoist they don't. These actions may seem to be altruistic, they say, but if we truly understood the motives, we'd see the selfishness deep inside. Consider the following story attributed to Abraham Lincoln, where he defends the psychological egoist view.

Mr. Lincoln once remarked to a fellow-passenger on an old-time mud coach that all men were prompted by selfishness in doing good. His fellow-passenger was antagonizing this position when they were passing over a corduroy bridge that spanned a slough. As they crossed this bridge they espied an old razor-backed sow on the bank making a terrible noise because her pigs had got into the slough and were in danger of drowning. As the old coach began to climb the hill, Mr. Lincoln called out, "Driver, can't you stop just a moment?" Then Mr. Lincoln jumped out, ran back, and lifted the little pigs out of the mud and water and placed them on the bank. When he returned, his companion remarked: "Now, Abe, where does selfishness come in on this little episode?" "Why, bless your soul, Ed, that was the very essence of selfishness. I should have had no peace of mind all day had I gone on and left that suffering old sow worrying over those pigs. I did it to get peace of mind, don't you see?"[11]

Lincoln's strategy here is to reinterpret the motives that appear on the surface. It appears to be an unselfish act until we reinterpret the motives in a selfish direction. This is a common strategy for psychological egoists, and it demonstrates why this is such a difficult challenge. For any counter-example you provide, someone can reinterpret the motives in an egoistic direction. And since motives are private—we cannot independently know what motivates the actions of another—there is no way to refute the psychological egoist theory.

---

[11]Quoted from the *Springfield* (Illinois) *Monitor* by F. C. Sharp in his *Ethics* (New York: Appleton-Century, 1928), p. 75.

"Of the voluntary actions of every man, the object is some good to himself."

—Hobbes

Thomas Hobbes used this strategy of reinterpreting motives in dissecting supposedly unselfish feelings such as pity and benevolence. Take, for example, what he says about charity:

> There can be no greater argument to a man, of his own power, than to find himself able not only to accomplish his own desires, but also to assist other men in theirs: and this is that conception wherein consisteth *charity*.[12]

Although psychological egoism is a powerful challenge to morality, it has drawn equally strong responses. Here we will limit our discussion to three of the most common objections.

First, one of the most common defenses of psychological egoism involves some confusion that obscures an important distinction relating to motives. It's often said that people are simply "doing what they want to do" and thus acting selfishly. But this is a mistake. To say that one "wants" to do something is ambiguous and does not necessarily support psychological

Some objections

---

[12]Thomas Hobbes, *On Human Nature* in *Body, Man, and Citizen*, ed. Richard S. Peters (New York: Collier, 1962).

PLATO'S RING OF GYGES

In *The Republic*, Plato provides a thought experiment that seems to support psychological egoism.* He tells the story of a magical ring—the Ring of Gyges—that makes the wearer invisible when turned a certain way. In the story, the one who finds the ring uses it to commit adultery and injustice. The moral of the story is that once freed from the threat of being caught, people will take whatever actions fit their self-interest with no thought for justice or morality. Thus humans are inherently selfish and act morally or consider the interests of others only because they fear the consequences of doing otherwise.

What would you do if you had such a ring? How do you think others would act if they could become invisible and be free from any consequences of their actions? Does the Ring of Gyges shed any light on the challenge of psychological egoism?

---

*Plato is not defending psychological egoism but simply expressing what he claims is a commonly held view to which he must respond in investigating the concept of justice. The story is found at the beginning of Book II of *The Republic*.

egoism. When we say that a person "does what she wants to do" this is not at all equivalent to the claim that she is acting selfishly. The first is a claim about the *source* of the motivation—it is hers—the second describes the *content*—it is selfish or unselfish. It is the latter claim that the psychological egoist must defend, and asserting that people always do what they want to do is no help.

Second, and more important, is there not a difference—a big difference—between saying that an act is *motivated* out of self-interest and saying that it is *attended* by self-interest? One may derive self-satisfaction, and rightfully so, from rescuing a drowning child from an icy river. But should we not distinguish this self-gratifying aspect of the act from the *motivation* of the act? The psychological egoist must claim not only that this good feeling exists, but also that it is the *sole motivation* for the act.

Finally, we must return to the matter of reinterpreting motives. As we said earlier, this strategy is irrefutable because of the private nature of motives. But this turns out to be an Achilles' heel of psychological egoism. If the theory is irrefutable, if it is impossible to show that it is false, then what meaning does it have? If nothing can count as evidence against the theory, then likewise nothing is evidence for it. We are left with an empty statement of intention rather than a claim about the world. The psychological egoist is announcing his intentions to interpret all motives as selfish. But there is no reason the rest of us must follow suit, especially in light of the implications of psychological egoism for morality.

THE CHALLENGE OF EXISTENTIALISM

Our final challenge to morality—*existentialism*—is a bit different from the others. It is not so much a challenge to *all* morality as it is a challenge to *traditional* morality, the rules and ways of thinking that we normally associate with right and wrong. This is especially true for anyone who associates morality with religious texts or rules—such as the Ten Commandments—or any sort of transcendent values. Existentialism is a clear challenge to these traditions, as we will soon discover.

We have already encountered the philosophy known as existentialism, and Albert Camus was cited in Chapter 13 as responding in an existentialist way to the problem of evil. It is difficult to say just what existentialism is, because the existentialists are so varied in their points of view. But that they represent, in different ways, challenges to traditional morality is evident.

For example, the Danish philosopher Søren Kierkegaard (1813–1855) taught the "teleological suspension of the ethical," according to which the individual is enabled to transcend ordinary ethical norms and receive his or her commandments immediately from God. The German Friedrich Nietzsche (1844–1900) rejected Christianity as involving a "slave-morality" and called for a "transvaluation of values" according to which "the will to power" as the basic principle of life will lead to the development of a higher type of humanity. Surely the best-known existentialist is the contemporary French writer and philosopher Jean-Paul Sartre (1905–1980). In addition to authoring works with ponderous titles such as *Being and Nothingness*, he wrote an essay entitled, simply, "Existentialism." This little work is often regarded as the best introduction to existentialism, and certainly it represents yet another existentialist's challenge to traditional morality.

According to Sartre, existentialism turns on its head any philosophy (think especially of Plato) that teaches that everything is what it is by virtue of a transcendent essence: *Essence precedes existence*. No, says Sartre. We begin with the *individual,* the concretely existing human being, the subject. The central tenet of existentialism, in any of its forms, is that *existence precedes essence.* What is first given is the existence of a particular person; only *after* that does the essence appear. Or, to say it another way, *subjectivity must be the starting point*. However, in its atheistic form, which Sartre himself espouses, existentialism finds nothing outside, above, or beyond the individual to which the individual can leap for its essence, definition, or meaning. God is dead, all objective and transcendent values have disappeared with him, and the individual is alone. This is the meaning of Sartre's famous pronouncement that we are "condemned to be free." Here, to be "free" means to be unconditioned by any moral law or eternal values.

What then do we do? Answer: We must accept the full burden of our freedom, and through our choices and commitments contribute to the

"Existence precedes essence"

We are "condemned to be free"

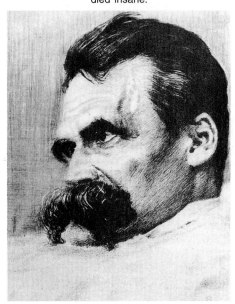

Friedrich Nietzsche was a classical philologist turned philosopher. Among his many works is one with the revealing title *Beyond Good and Evil*. His ideas about the "will to power" and the *Übermensch* ("superman") were later misappropriated by the Nazi party. Nietzsche died insane.

HUMANISM

As is evident from the word itself, humanism is the exaltation of humanity as the source and criterion of all value and meaning.

evolving essence of humanity. What we choose for ourselves, that we become. And what we become, that we contribute to the definition or essence of humanity, for each of us is part of humanity. If, then, we care about the essence of humanity—what it is and will become—we must have a care about our own individual commitments. This sense of aloneness and personal responsibility is the source of the emphasis by Sartre and other existentialists on the anxiety, dread, and despair of the "conscious" individual, the individual who knows the score.

You may be tempted to see here just another version of relativism, but there is a difference. In its crassest form, relativism denies that any value or idea is any better than another. Clearly Sartre is not saying this. It is true that there is no divine or transcendent foundation of values, and that is precisely why Sartre shifts the responsibility to individuals. Human beings in their freedom (in Sartre's existentialist sense) are themselves the basis of values, and in this sense values are real—evolving, developing, on the move, but *real*. In place of God or a transcendent source of values, ideals, meaning, and the like, this philosophy is truly *humanistic,* in that humanity stands center stage as the criterion of all meaning and value. It is important to see how this differs from the sort of relativism or subjectivism we considered earlier. That philosophy denied any objective or common values, locating them instead in *individuals*. This philosophy, on the other hand, affirms objective values, but locates them in *humanity*. The difference between subjectivism and humanism is caught by the two claims

Humanism

- A man is the measure of all things.
- Man is the measure of all things.

In the following, from his essay "Existentialism," Sartre explains the general nature of this philosophy and the moral implications of his version of it.

What is meant by the term "existentialism"?

Most people who use the word would be rather embarrassed if they had to explain it, since, now that the word is all the rage, even the work of a musician or painter is being called existentialist. A gossip columnist in *Clartés* signs himself *The Existentialist,* so that by this time the word has been so stretched and has taken on so broad a meaning, that it no longer means anything at all. It seems that for want of an advance-guard doctrine analogous to surrealism, the kind of people who are eager for scandal and flurry turn to this philosophy which in other respects does not at all serve their purposes in this sphere.

Actually, it is the least scandalous, the most austere of doctrines. It is intended strictly for specialists and philosophers. Yet it can be defined easily. What complicates matters is that there are two kinds of existentialist; first, those who are Christian, among whom I would include Jaspers and Gabriel Marcel, both Catholic; and on the other hand the atheistic existentialists, among whom I class Heidegger, and then the French existentialists and myself. What they have in common is that they think that existence precedes essence, or, if you prefer, that subjectivity must be the starting point.

Just what does that mean? Let us consider some object that is manufactured, for example, a book or a paper-cutter: here is an object which has been made by an artisan whose inspiration came from a concept. He referred to the concept of what a paper-cutter is and likewise to a known method of production, which is part of the concept, something which is, by and large, a routine. Thus, the paper-cutter is at once an object produced in a certain way and, on the other hand, one having a specific use; and one can not postulate a man who produces a paper-cutter but does not know what it is used for. Therefore, let us say that, for the paper-cutter, essence—that is, the ensemble of both the production routines and the properties which enable it to be both produced and defined—precedes existence. Thus, the presence of the paper-cutter or book in front of me is determined. Therefore, we have here a technical view of the world whereby it can be said that production precedes existence.

When we conceive God as the Creator, He is generally thought of as a superior sort of artisan. Whatever doctrine we may be considering, whether one like

The French writer and thinker Jean-Paul Sartre is probably the best-known existentialist. He was the author of numerous novels (including one entitled *Nausea*), plays, and political and philosophical works. A Marxist and atheist, Sartre locates the full responsibility for human meaning in the commitments and choices of individuals themselves.

that of Descartes or that of Leibnitz, we always grant that will more or less follows understanding or, at the very least, accompanies it, and that when God creates He knows exactly what He is creating. Thus, the concept of man in the mind of God is comparable to the concept of paper-cutter in the mind of the manufacturer, and, following certain techniques and a conception, God produces man, just as the artisan, following a definition and a technique, makes a paper-cutter. Thus, the individual man is the realization of a certain concept in the divine intelligence.

In the eighteenth century, the atheism of the *philosophes* discarded the idea of God, but not so much for the notion that essence precedes existence. To a certain extent, this idea is found everywhere; we find it in Diderot, in Voltaire, and even in Kant. Man has a human nature; this human nature, which is the concept of the human, is found in all men, which means that each man is a particular example of a universal concept, man. In Kant, the result of this universality is that the wild-man, the natural man, as well as the bourgeois, are circumscribed by the same definition and have the same basic qualities. Thus, here too the essence of man precedes the historical existence that we find in nature.

Atheistic existentialism, which I represent, is more coherent. It states that if God does not exist, there is at least one being in whom existence precedes essence, a being who exists before he can be defined by any concept, and that this being is man, or, as Heidegger says, human reality. What is meant here by saying that existence precedes essence? It means that, first of all, man exists, turns up, appears on the scene, and, only afterwards, defines himself. If man, as the existentialist conceives him, is indefinable, it is because at first he is nothing. Only afterward will he be something, and he himself will have made what he will be. Thus, there is no human nature, since there is no God to conceive it. Not only is man what he conceives himself to be, but he is also only what he wills himself to be after this thrust toward existence.

Man is nothing else but what he makes of himself. Such is the first principle of existentialism. It is also what is called subjectivity, the name we are labeled with when charges are brought against us. But what do we mean by this, if not that man has a greater dignity than a stone or table? For we mean that man first exists, that is, that man first of all is the being who hurls himself toward a future and who is conscious of imagining himself as being in the future. Man is at the start a plan which is aware of itself, rather than a patch of moss, a piece of garbage, or a cauliflower; nothing exists prior to this plan; there is nothing in heaven; man will be what he will have planned to be. Not what he will want to be. Because by the word "will" we generally mean a conscious decision, which is subsequent to what we have already made of ourselves. I may want to belong to a political party, write a book, get married; but all that is only a manifestation of an earlier, more spontaneous choice that is called "will." But if existence really does precede essence, man is responsible for what he is. Thus, existentialism's first move is to make every man aware of what he is and to make the full responsibility of his existence rest on him. And when we say that a man is responsible for himself, we do not only mean that he is responsible for his own individuality, but that he is responsible for all men.

The word subjectivism has two meanings, and our opponents play on the two. Subjectivism means, on the one hand, that an individual chooses and makes himself; and, on the other, that it is impossible for man to transcend human subjectivity. The second of these is the essential meaning of existentialism. When we say that man chooses his own self, we mean that every one of us does likewise; but we also mean by that that in making this choice he also chooses all men.

In fact, in creating the man that we want to be, there is not a single one of our acts which does not at the same time create an image of man as we think he ought to be. To choose to be this or that is to affirm at the same time the value of what we choose, because we can never choose evil. We always choose the good, and nothing can be good for us without being good for all.

If, on the other hand, existence precedes essence, and if we grant that we exist and fashion our image at one and the same time, the image is valid for everybody and for our whole age. Thus, our responsibility is much greater than we might have supposed, because it involves all mankind. If I am a workingman and choose to join a Christian trade-union rather than be a communist, and if by being a member I want to show that the best thing for man is resignation, that the kingdom of man is not of this world, I am not only involving my own case—I want to be resigned for everyone. As a result, my action has involved all humanity. To take a more individual matter, if I want to marry, to have children; even if this marriage depends solely on my own circumstances or passion or wish, I am involving all humanity in monogamy and not merely myself. Therefore, I am responsible for myself and for everyone else. I am creating a certain image of man of my own choosing. In choosing myself, I choose man.

This helps us understand what the actual content is of such rather grandiloquent words as anguish, forlornness, despair. As you will see, it's all quite simple. . . .

When we speak of forlornness, a term Heidegger was fond of, we mean only that God does not exist and that we have to face all the consequences of this. The existentialist is strongly opposed to a certain kind of secular ethics which would like to abolish God with the least possible expense. About 1880, some French teachers tried to set up a secular ethics which went something like this: God is a useless and costly hypothesis; we are discarding it; but, meanwhile, in order for there to be an ethics, a society, a civilization, it is essential that certain values be taken seriously and that they be considered as having an *a priori* existence. It must be obligatory, *a priori*, to be honest, not to lie, not to beat your wife, to have children, etc., etc. So we're going to try a little device which will make it possible to show that values exist all the same, inscribed in a heaven of ideas, though otherwise God does not exist. In other words—and this, I believe, is the tendency of everything called reformism in France—nothing will be changed if God does not exist. We shall find ourselves with the same norms of honesty, progress, and humanism, and we shall have made of God an outdated hypothesis which will peacefully die off by itself.

The existentialist, on the contrary, thinks it very distressing that God does not exist, because all possibility of finding values in a heaven of ideas disappears along with Him; there can no longer be an *a priori* Good, since there is no infinite and perfect consciousness to think it. Nowhere is it written that the Good exists, that we must be honest, that we must not lie; because the fact is we are on a plane where there are only men. Dostoievsky said, "If God didn't exist, everything would be possible." That is the very starting point of existentialism. Indeed, everything is permissible if God does not exist, and as a result man is forlorn, because neither within him nor without does he find anything to cling to. He can't start making excuses for himself.

If existence really does precede essence, there is no explaining things away by reference to a fixed and given human nature. In other words, there is no determinism, man is free, man is freedom. On the other hand, if God does not exist, we find no values or commands to turn to which legitimize our conduct. So, in the bright realm of values, we have no excuse behind us, nor justification before us. We are alone, with no excuses.

That is the idea I shall try to convey when I say that man is condemned to be free. Condemned, because he did not create himself, yet, in other respects is free; because, once thrown into the world, he is responsible for everything he does.[13]

Simone de Beauvoir[14] (1908–1986) was a colleague and companion of Sartre. She was a major contributor to the Sartrean strain of contemporary existentialism, but was in her own right an original philosopher and a founding contributor to a major social and intellectual movement—feminism. Certainly the most famous and influential of her works is the landmark book *The Second Sex*, first published in French in 1949 (two volumes). *A propos* of recent and continuing feminist concerns, the extract below displays an application of her ideas to a concrete situation.

"In itself"/"for itself"

Special attention should be given to the French expression *en soi*, which, along with *pour soi*, occurs often in Sartrean literature. In fact, they are fundamental to the whole perspective. *En soi* means, literally, "in itself," and in Sartrean contexts has reference to nonconscious being; this is contrasted with *pour soi*, literally, "for itself," which has reference to conscious being along with the taking of responsibility for one's choices. In respect of the situation of women specifically, de Beauvoir's thought is this. We

Simone de Beauvoir, who is often called the "mother of modern feminism," applied existentialist ideas to the situation of contemporary women.

[13]Jean-Paul Sartre, "Existentialism," tr. Bernard Frechtman, in *Existentialism and Human Emotions* (New York: Philosophical Library, 1957), pp. 12–18, 21–23.

[14]Pronounced *Bow-vwar'*.

FEMINIST ETHICS

As we have seen throughout the book, women have often been excluded from mainstream philosophy, a point made repeatedly by feminist thinkers. Ethics is certainly no exception. Feminist philosophers have written widely about the need for and shape of a specifically feminist ethics. In the following selection from Alison Jaggar, she lays out some "minimum conditions of adequacy" for any feminist ethics.

Feminist approaches to ethics are distinguished by their explicit commitment to rethinking ethics with a view to correcting whatever forms of male bias it may contain. Feminist ethics, as these approaches are often called collectively, seeks to identify and challenge all those ways, overt but more often and more perniciously covert, in which western ethics has excluded women or rationalized their subordination. Its goal is to offer both practical guides to action and theoretical understandings of the nature of morality that do not, overtly or covertly, subordinate the interests of any woman or group of women to the interests of any other individual or group.

While those who practice feminist ethics are united by a shared project, they diverge widely in their views as to how this project may be accomplished. These divergences result from a variety of philosophical differences, including differing conceptions of feminism itself, a perennially contested concept. The inevitability of such disagreement means that feminist ethics cannot be identified in terms of a specific range of topics, methods or orthodoxies. For example, it is a mistake, though one to which even some feminists occasionally have succumbed, to identify feminist ethics with any of the following: putting women's interests first; focusing exclusively on so-called women's issues;

(continued on next page)

need the other's "look" on us to know ourselves. But the other's "look" can also objectify us, in the sense of reducing us to *things,* stultifying our freedom to project our own possibilities, thus confining us to the state of *en-soi.* The "look" of the patriarchy (our male-dominated tradition) on women has projected her as an object (note the reference to "the brutish life of subjection to given conditions"), thus denying her own transcendence, or *pour-soi.* In *The Second Sex,* de Beauvoir is recalling women to their existence as free projections of possibilities—called here "transcendence." It should be apparent that in all of this we are still talking about what we earlier called "existential freedom."

. . . those who are condemned to stagnation are often pronounced happy on the pretext that happiness consists in being at rest. This notion we reject, for our perspective is that of existentialist ethics. Every subject plays his part as such specifically through exploits or projects that serve as a mode of transcendence; he achieves liberty only through a continual reaching out toward other liberties. There is no justification for present existence other than its expansion into an accepting women (or feminists) as moral experts or authorities; substituting "female" (or "feminine") for "male" (or "masculine") values; or extrapolating directly from women's experience.

Even though my initial characterization of feminist ethics is quite loose, it does suggest certain minimum conditions of adequacy for any approach to ethics that purports to be feminist.

1. Within the present social context, in which women remain systematically subordinated, a feminist approach to ethics must offer a guide to action that will tend to subvert rather than reinforce this subordination. Thus, such an approach must be practical, transitional and nonutopian, an extension of politics rather than a retreat from it. . . .

2. Since so much of women's struggle has been in the kitchen and the bedroom, as well as in the parliamentary chamber and on the factory floor, a second requirement for feminist ethics is that it should be equipped to handle moral issues in both the so-called public and private domains. It must be able to provide guidance on issues of intimate relations, such as affection and sexuality, which, until quite recently, were largely ignored by modern moral theory. . . .

3. Finally, feminist ethics must take the moral experience of all women seriously, though not, of course, uncritically. Though what is *feminist* will often turn out to be very different from what is *feminine,* a basic respect for women's moral experience is necessary to acknowledging women's capacities as moralists and to countering traditional stereotypes of women as less than full moral agents, as childlike or "natural."*

---

*Alison M. Jaggar, "Feminist Ethics: Some Issues for the Nineties," *Journal of Social Philosophy* 20, nos. 1–2 (Spring/Fall 1989).

indefinitely open future. Every time transcendence falls back into immanence, stagnation, there is a degradation of existence into the *"en-soi"*—the brutish life of subjection to given conditions—and of liberty into constraint and contingence. This downfall represents a moral fault if the subject consents to it; if it is inflicted upon him, it spells frustration and oppression. In both cases it is an absolute evil.

EXISTENTIALISM

The philosophy that emphasizes the existing individual, as opposed to abstractions or principles, as the point of departure for authentic philosophizing. Two existentialist slogans from Sartre:

- Existence precedes essence.
- Subjectivity must be the starting point.

Every individual concerned to justify his existence feels that his existence involves an undefined need to transcend himself, to engage in freely chosen projects.

Now, what peculiarly signalizes the situation of woman is that she—a free and autonomous being like all human creatures—nevertheless finds herself living in a world where men compel her to assume the status of the Other. They propose to stabilize her as object and to doom her to immanence since her transcendence is to be overshadowed and forever transcended by another ego (*conscience*) which is essential and sovereign. The drama of woman lies in this conflict between the fundamental aspirations of every subject (ego)—who always regards the self as the essential—and the compulsions of a situation in which she is the inessential. How can a human being in woman's situation attain fulfillment? What roads are open to her? Which are blocked? How can independence be recovered in a state of dependency? What circumstances limit woman's liberty and how can they be overcome? These are the fundamental questions on which I would fain throw some light. This means that I am interested in the fortunes of the individual as defined not in terms of happiness but in terms of liberty.[15]

We have already distinguished Sartre's humanistic existentialism from subjectivism. Nonetheless, Sartre's position has been attacked with criticisms similar to those we saw leveled against subjectivism. After all, if individual existence precedes the essence of humanity, and nothing at all precedes or conditions the individual's choices, then what is to prevent those choices from being purely arbitrary and, thus, the evolving essence of man as well? That is, if you don't begin with any meaning, how can you end with any?

A familiar objection

This is the point of one of Sartre's loudest critics, Gabriel Marcel (1889–1973), whom Sartre mentioned as a Christian existentialist in the above selection. (That Marcel is called an existentialist by Sartre himself, and yet attacked the very basis of Sartre's philosophy, reminds us of what a variety there is among existentialists.) Marcel represents the way in which one might be faithful to the existentialist thesis that subjectivity must be the starting point but, beginning with subjectivity or the concreteness of personal existence, might move to a theistic or transcendent basis of value and meaning. This, says Marcel, is exactly what we must do, for values are not chosen but *discovered*. They are *given*. They are *objective*. According to Marcel, the Sartrean approach bogs down in a hopeless contradiction: It claims that outside our own commitments there is no basis for moral choices, but then turns right around and insists that some choices are better than others. You cannot have it both ways, and you cannot give up (can you?) the view that some choices are better than others. We must, says Marcel, grant the *givenness* of values and meaning. And given by whom, except God? From Marcel's *The Philosophy of Existentialism:*

From [Sartre's] standpoint, values cannot be anything but the result of the initial choice made by each human being; in other words, they can never be "recognised" or "discovered." "My freedom," he states expressly, "is the unique foundation of

---

[15]Simone de Beauvoir, *The Second Sex,* tr. and ed. H. M. Parshley (New York: Vintage Books, 1952), pp. xxxiii–xxxiv.

values. And since I am the being by virtue of whom values exist, nothing—absolutely nothing—can justify me in adopting this or that value or scale of values. As the unique basis of the existence of values, I am totally unjustifiable. And my freedom is in anguish at finding that it is the baseless basis of values." Nothing could be more explicit; but the question is whether Sartre does not here go counter to the exigencies of that human reality which he claims, after all, not to invent but to reveal.

Not to deal exclusively in abstractions, let us take a concrete case. Sartre has announced that the third volume of his Les Chemins de la Liberté [The Ways of Freedom] is to be devoted to the praise of the heroes of Resistance. Now I ask you in the name of what principle, having first denied the existence of values or at least of their objective basis, can he establish any appreciable difference between those utterly misguided but undoubtedly courageous men who joined voluntarily the [Nazi] Anti-Bolshevik Legion, on the one hand, and the heroes of the Resistance movement, on the other? I can see no way of establishing this difference without admitting that causes have their intrinsic value and, consequently, that values are real. I have no doubt that Sartre's ingenuity will find a way out of this dilemma; in fact, he quite often uses the words "good" and "bad," but what can these words possibly mean in the context of his philosophy?

The truth is that, if I examine myself honestly and without reference to any preconceived body of ideas, I find that I do not "choose" my values at all, but that I *recognise* them and then posit my actions in accordance or in contradiction

Edvard Munch's *The Shriek* (1895) is sometimes
associated with the philosophy of existentialism
because of the emphasis in that philosophy
on the isolation and despair of the individual.

with these values, not, however, without being painfully aware of this contradiction. . . . It should perhaps be asked at this point if it is not Nietzsche who, with his theory of the creation of values, is responsible for the deathly principle of error which has crept into speculation on this subject. But although I am the last to underrate the objections to Nietzsche's doctrine, I am inclined to think that his view is less untenable than that of Sartre, for it escapes that depth of rationalism and materialism which is discernible, to me as to others, in the mind of the author of *L'Etre et le Néant* [*Being and Nothingness*].

I would suggest in conclusion that existentialism stands to-day at a parting of the ways: it is, in the last analysis, obliged either to deny or to transcend itself. It denies itself quite simply when it falls to the level of infra-dialectical materialism. It transcends itself, or it tends to transcend itself, when it opens itself out to the experience of the suprahuman, an experience which can hardly be ours in a genuine and lasting way this side of death, but of which the reality is attested by mystics, and of which the possibility is warranted by any philosophy which refuses to be immured in the postulate of absolute immanence or to subscribe in advance to the denial of the beyond and of the unique and veritable transcendence.[16]

CHAPTER 14 IN REVIEW

SUMMARY

In this chapter we have considered four basic questions that may be thought of as threatening or undermining the very idea of morality:

- Is morality purely relative?
- Are moral actions determined?
- Are all actions motivated by self-interest?
- Do values originate in human experience?

It has seemed to some that if the answer to any of these is Yes, then morality, at least in a more or less traditional sense, is rendered impossible from the very start.

The most serious challenge to morality comes from relativism: Values are purely relative, possessing no objective or absolute or *real* status beyond the individual's own notions. (Remember that "individual" may mean an individual person or an individual group.) The objectivist freely grants that, of course, our views or *opinions* about morality are largely relative (to circumstances of birth, upbringing, education, etc.), but that morality *itself* is the unconditioned reality that lies behind and makes ultimate sense of our moral quests and even our moral disputes.

Another threat is posed by the determinist, who says that since everything is predetermined, so are our own moral choices and decisions. The soft-determinist seeks to soften this blow with the explanation that our choices are determined, but by our own character, and that that is exactly

---

[16]Gabriel Marcel, *The Philosophy of Existentialism,* tr. Manya Harari (New York: Philosophical Library, 1956), pp. 86–88.

why we are responsible for them. It is important to ask whether this does not lead right back to hard-determinism, inasmuch as our character has been shaped largely beyond our own control (or has it?). In any event, the free-willist is often fond of turning the whole challenge on its head: Since morality is a nonnegotiable fact of our experience, and since it is unintelligible apart from free will, the will must be (in whatever obscure way) free.

Psychological egoism was the third challenge we considered. All actions are motivated solely by self-interest, according to the psychological egoist, so traditional morality is impossible. This theory of human nature poses a challenge similar to determinism since it denies the very possibility of being moral. One strategy the psychological egoist employs is reinterpreting motives, explaining supposedly selfless actions by the agent's desire for glory or self-satisfaction. Critics charge that such reinterpretation renders the theory meaningless and point to the difference between the source and content of motivations.

Finally, we considered the challenge delivered by existentialism. Here we have looked specifically at the perspective of Jean-Paul Sartre. Sartre summarizes all existential philosophies as teaching that existence precedes essence. According to Sartre's own atheistic view, there is no value, meaning, or definition of humanity apart from that which human beings themselves inject into the picture. Here, "Man is the measure of all things," and it *matters* what we choose and what we thereby make of humanity. On the other hand, this is just what bothers the critics: How *can* it matter if there is no justification *outside* us for our acts and commitments?

It *is* interesting, isn't it, that although none of these challenges is particularly new, the actual give-and-take world of morality goes right on as if nothing happened? Does morality ever actually succumb to any of these (largely theoretical) challenges?

BASIC IDEAS

- Relativism or subjectivism
- Absolutism or objectivism
- Cultural relativism
- Relativism as impractical
- Determinism
- Hard-determinism
- Soft-determinism (self-determinism)
- Indeterminism
- The obscurity of "free will"
- Determinism as impractical
- Psychological egoism
- Ought implies can
- Strategy of reinterpreting motives
- Plato's Ring of Gyges
- Source versus content of motivation

- Sartre: existentialism
  Existence precedes essence
  Subjectivity
  Freedom as the basis of values
- "In itself"/"for itself"
- Marcel's critique of Sartre

TEST YOURSELF

1. What is the big argument for ethical relativism?
2. In what way is ethical relativism said to "backfire"?
3. What did David Hume contribute to the discussion of free will versus determinism?
4. Characterize the general philosophical outlook of Simone de Beauvoir.
5. Recalling the discussion of B. F. Skinner in Chapter 6, is the following true or false? Hard-behaviorists are also hard-determinists.
6. Gabriel Marcel was (a) a modern proponent of ethical relativism, (b) a critic of Sartre's idea of freedom, (c) an emotivist, (d) a critic of determinism.
7. Why is determinism a challenge to traditional morality?
8. What is the meaning of Sartre's statement that "man is condemned to be free"?

QUESTIONS FOR REFLECTION

- Do you believe that the determinist's challenge to traditional morality is successful? If so, your problem is to give a coherent account of morality that can accommodate at the same time the denial of free will. If you don't think the challenge is successful, your problem is to give a coherent account of free will itself: It's easy to say what it isn't, but what *is* it? Is it necessary, for the sake of morality, simply to postulate an unknown something? Would that be so bad?
- Can you give a good account of the difference between Sartre's idea of freedom and the idea of freedom involved in the debate between free will and determinism?

FOR FURTHER READING

Hazel Barnes. *Sartre.* London: Quarlet Books, 1973. A compact introduction to the philosophical-literary contribution of Sartre, by a leading authority.

Simon Blackburn. *Being Good: A Short Introduction to Ethics.* Oxford: Oxford University Press, 2001. A short but very insightful introduction to the history of ethics and the process of moral deliberation.

Richard B. Brandt. *Ethical Theory: The Problems of Normative and Critical Ethics.* Englewood Cliffs, NJ: Prentice-Hall, 1959. Chs. 9, 11, and 20. Textbook discussions of emotivism, relativism, and determinism.

Frederick Copleston. *Contemporary Philosophy: Studies of Logical Positivism and Existentialism.* Paramus, NJ: Newman Press, 1956. Extended readable discussions of these two dominating philosophical perspectives, by a noted historian of philosophy.

Frederick Copleston. *A History of Philosophy.* Baltimore: Newman Press, 1946–1974. IX, Chs. 16–17. An overview of Sartre's existentialist philosophy with special reference to freedom as the basis of value.

Gerald Dworkin (ed.). *Determinism, Free Will, and Moral Responsibility.* Englewood Cliffs, NJ: Prentice-Hall, 1970. A collection of twelve essays, traditional and contemporary, on various aspects of the free-will/moral responsibility issue.

A. C. Ewing. *Ethics.* New York: Free Press, 1953. Chs. 7–8. Beginning but insightful treatments of various forms of subjectivism and the problems of morality and free will.

Joel Feinberg. "Psychological Egoism." In *Reason and Responsibility: Readings in Some Basic Problems in Philosophy,* ed. Joel Feinberg. Ninth ed. Belmont, CA: Wadsworth, 1996. A clear explanation of psychological egoism and convincing refutation.

Jonathan Glover. *Responsibility.* London: Routledge & Kegan Paul, 1970. A full discussion of the problem of free will and moral responsibility, with special reference to the criminal responsibility of the mentally ill.

John Macquarrie. *Existentialism.* New York: World, 1972. An excellent introduction to existentialist philosophy, with numerous references to Sartre.

Richard Norman. *The Moral Philosophers: An Introduction to Ethics.* Oxford: Oxford University Press, 1983. A chronological survey of the major historical figures in Western philosophical ethics.

James Rachels. *Elements of Moral Philosophy.* Second ed. New York: McGraw-Hill, 1986. One of the very best short introductions to ethics.

Peter Singer (ed.). *A Companion to Ethics.* Malden, MA: Blackwell, 1991. A comprehensive collection of articles on all major topics in ethics.

Paul Taylor (ed.). *Problems of Moral Philosophy: An Introduction to Ethics.* Belmont, CA: Dickenson, 1967. Chs. 2 and 6. Traditional and contemporary readings on relativism and moral responsibility in relation to free will.

Mark Timmons. *Moral Theory: An Introduction.* Lanham, MD: Rowman & Littlefield, 2002. A systematic review of major moral theories, both historical and contemporary.

W. H. Werkmeister. *Theories of Ethics: A Study in Moral Obligation.* Lincoln, NE: Johnsen, 1961. Chs. 1–2. A closely documented account and critique of the two main forms of emotivism.

Bernard Williams. *Morality: An Introduction to Ethics.* Cambridge: Cambridge University Press, 1972. An intelligent and concise discussion of relativism and amoralism.

*In addition, see the relevant articles ("Ethical Relativism," "Determinism," "Sarte, Jean-Paul," etc.) in *Routledge Encyclopedia of Philosophy,* ed. Edward Craig (London: Routledge, 1998), and *Stanford Encyclopedia of Philosophy,* http://plato.stanford.edu.

UTILITARIANISM

I
f, in spite of the countercriticisms, you find that any of the foregoing challenges to morality is successful, then you will have to face up to the question whether there can be any genuine, or at least traditional, morality at all. On the other hand, if you believe, say, that moral truths have an objective basis and that individuals are morally responsible, then we had best get on with the task of considering the various and sometimes radically different views of morality.

THE QUESTION OF CONSEQUENCES

That theories of morality may go in very different directions becomes apparent when we raise the question: Do the consequences of our actions matter? Obviously, they matter in *some* sense. When you vote, pull the trigger of a gun, feed the starving, bail out of an airplane, study for an exam, or perform an infinite number of other actions, the action is done *for the sake of something*. But do the consequences of our actions matter *morally*? That is, can our actions be judged moral or immoral on the basis of their consequences?

It will seem to many of you that the answer is obviously Yes. And a great many philosophers will agree with you. This type of ethical theory is called a *teleological* or *consequentialist* theory. We saw in an earlier chapter that teleology is the belief in purposes, ends, or goals in the universe. As you might guess, then, a teleological theory of morality is one that stresses the consequences of actions, and even makes the consequences of actions the criterion,

Do consequences matter?

Teleological and deontological theories of morality

373

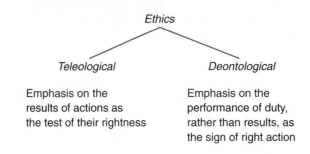

or test, of their rightness. An action is judged right or wrong, moral or immoral, depending on what happens as a result of it, its "payoff." Quite different from this type of ethical theory—in fact, directly opposed to it—is the *deontological* type. An important clue as to what this means lies in the Greek word from which it comes: *deō*, "to bind." On the deontological view, the will is bound to *duty*. That is, what makes an action right or wrong is the actor's conformity to his or her duty. And what the actor's duty is has nothing to do with what might or might not happen as a result of the action.

Later, in Chapter 16, we will consider the most influential deontological theory of morality. But first we will look at the most important teleological theory: utilitarianism.

WHAT IS UTILITARIANISM?

For many people, utilitarianism is just an eminently commonsensical philosophy. What is more natural, when confronted with a moral dilemma, than to ask something like: "What should I do to bring about the most happiness to the most people?" Whenever this has been your criterion of behavior, you have been a practicing *utilitarian*.

The actual application of the utilitarian criterion is, however, often a difficult and sometimes a dramatic affair. Consider this true scene:

> He saw a lifeboat sitting about three hundred yards off. It was a small craft, manned by half a dozen sailors. They were scanning the ship carefully.
>
> "Help!" Hudson cried out, "Help me. Over here."
>
> A flashlight winked. Its beam played along the stern of the *Andrea Doria*. Guided by Hudson's screams, the light focused on the desperate sailor clinging to the net.
>
> "Help me!" Hudson yelled again. "Quickly. Hurry."
>
> Hudson waited for the men to clasp their oars. He fought against the swift current, energized now by the sight of his rescuers.
>
> But the lifeboat did not move.
>
> "Help!" Hudson called once more. "Hurry. Please!"
>
> Still the lifeboat lay quietly in the water. The flashlight again blinked in Hudson's eyes. They saw him. They heard him. Why would they not come? *My God!* Hudson realized, *the ship is going down . . . now!* In his merchant marine training Hudson had been taught that a lifeboat must sit off at least three hundred yards to avoid being pulled under by a sinking ship. That was where the lifeboat lay. . . .

He lay silent for a time, riding the swells, waiting for the end. An orange globe of sun rose behind him, the fresh beginning of the day mocking the tragedy it revealed. The *Andrea Doria* lay more horizontal than vertical. Deck chairs, suitcases, random bits of clothing, and splintered wood swayed in the waves. Hudson climbed one notch higher on the net as it slowly sank lower into the sea.

His will returned. "Help!" he screamed. "Please come get me. You can't let me die."

He could see the men watching him from the lifeboat. But they did not reach for their oars.

The desperate man resorted to cursing once more. Then he prayed, not to God but to the men in the lifeboat. He cried. He begged.[1]

It's a simple problem: Should the lives of several be jeopardized in order possibly to save one more? Is it *really* a simple problem?

We can get at the real nature of utilitarianism in three stages. *First*, at the heart of utilitarianism lies the Principle of Utility. The word "utility" simply means "usefulness," but the utilitarians employ it to mean that which promoted the greatest balance of good over evil. Thus utilitarianism is

The Principle of Utility

1. The doctrine that we ought to act so as to promote the greatest balance of good over evil.

But there must be more, for we have not yet been told what the good *is*. In fact, *second*, utilitarianism has always gone hand in hand with hedonism, which certainly does specify the nature of the good. Hedonism is the doctrine that *pleasure* is the highest good and that production of pleasure is the criterion of right action. Thus, utilitarianism is

Utilitarianism as hedonism

2. The doctrine that we ought to act so as to promote the greatest balance of pleasure over pain.

But there is more, for we have not yet been told *whose* pleasure is to be maximized. In fact, *third*, utilitarianism (as the word is usually used) has always gone hand in hand specifically with *social* hedonism, the theory that we should promote the good of society or the pleasure of all people. Thus utilitarianism is not motivated out of *self*-interest but out of an interest for the greatest possible number of persons and aims at *their* satisfaction. Utilitarianism relies on the Benevolence Principle: Happiness is to be distributed as widely and as equally as possible among all people. Thus, utilitarianism is, finally,

Utilitarianism as social hedonism

The Benevolence Principle

[1]William Hoffer, *Saved! The Story of the "Andrea Doria"—The Greatest Sea Rescue in History* (New York: Summit Books, 1979), pp. 180–182.

Hedonism + Benevolence principle = Social hedonism or utilitarianism

UTILITARIANISM

The ethical doctrine that an action is right if, and only if, it promotes the greatest happiness for the greatest number of people.

3. The doctrine that we ought to act so as to promote the greatest happiness for the greatest number.

Utilitarianism is, obviously, a political perspective as well as a philosophical one. As a democratic point of view it has often been, over the years, the basis of legislative and judicial advances, social reforms, welfare movements, and egalitarian ideals. Not surprisingly, then, the most famous of the utilitarian philosophers have also usually been deeply involved in social and political issues—on the liberal side, naturally.

Utilitarianism: A political and philosophical view

BENTHAM'S VERSION: QUANTITY OVER QUALITY

Historically, social utilitarianism is identified with the English philosophers Jeremy Bentham and John Stuart Mill. (We realize that we are dealing here with remarkable men when we learn that Bentham was studying Latin when he was eight, and Mill was studying Greek at three!) These two thinkers, however, represent two different forms of utilitarianism, though the difference reduces to a matter of emphasis: in the one case an emphasis on *quantity* of happiness, and in the other an emphasis on *quality* of happiness.

The founder of modern utilitarianism was Jeremy Bentham (1748–1832). For Bentham, the process of making moral decisions is really quite simple. All you do is this: First, consider the various courses of action open to you; then, taking into account all the persons affected, and counting yourself as only one of them, calculate the pleasures and pains involved; then, choose the course of action that will result in the greatest balance of pleasure over pain.

As already indicated, when Bentham presses for the greatest balance of pleasure over pain, his idea of pleasure is a purely quantitative one. The *greatest* pleasure for the greatest number means for Bentham the *most* pleasure. That Bentham's really is a purely quantitative notion of pleasure is apparent from his well-known statement:

The greatest means the best

> Prejudice apart, the game of push-pin is of equal value with the arts and sciences of music and poetry. If the game of push-pin furnish more pleasure, it is more valuable than either.[2]

---

[2]Jeremy Bentham, *The Rationale of Reward,* in *The Works of Jeremy Bentham* (Edinburgh: Tait, 1838–43), II, i, 253.

Jeremy Bentham (shown here as a youth), a utilitarian philosopher who stressed the quantity over the quality of happiness

How do we determine the *most* pleasure? The idea of calculating pleasures and pains was formulated most explicitly in Bentham's idea of a *hedonic calculus*. According to Bentham, in attempting to calculate a pleasure, we must, as it were, measure or weigh it in seven ways, taking into account its

The hedonic calculus

1. *Intensity,* or how strong it is.
2. *Duration,* how long it will last.
3. *Certainty,* how likely it is to occur.
4. *Propinquity,* how near at hand it is.
5. *Fecundity,* its ability to produce still further pleasures.
6. *Purity,* its freedom from ensuing pains.
7. *Extent,* the number of people affected by it.

Bentham suggested the following verse as a prod to "lodging more effectively, in the memory, these points, on which the whole fabric of morals and legislation may be seen to rest":

> Intense, long, certain, speedy, fruitful, pure—
> Such marks in pleasures and in pains endure.
> Such pleasures seek, if private be thy end:
> If it be public, wide let them extend.
> Such pains avoid, whichever be thy view:
> If pains must come, let them extend to few.[3]

---

[3]Jeremy Bentham, *An Introduction to the Principles of Morals and Legislation,* ed. J. H. Burns and H. L. A. Hart (London: Athlone, 1970), p. 38.

BENTHAM ON ANIMAL RIGHTS

"The day may come when the rest of the animal creation may acquire those rights which never could have been witholden from them but by the hand of tyranny. The French have already discovered that the blackness of the skin is no reason why a human being should be abandoned without redress to the caprice of a tormentor. It may one day come to be recognized that the number of the legs, the villoscity of the skin, or the termination of the os sacrum, are reasons equally insufficient for abandoning a sensitive being to the same fate. What else is it that should trace the insuperable line? Is it the faculty of reason, or perhaps the faculty of discourse? But a full grown horse or dog is beyond comparison a more rational, as well as a more conversable animal, than an infant of a day, or a week, or even a month, old. But suppose they were otherwise, what would it avail? The question is not, Can they reason? nor Can they *talk*? but, *Can they suffer*?"

Jeremy Bentham, *Introduction to the Principles of Morals and Legislation* (Oxford: Clarendon Press, 1907), Ch. XVII.

By applying these seven criteria—someone has likened them to a moral thermometer—we ought to be able to grind out, like a machine, what course of action would deliver the most pleasure. Bentham himself speaks of "summing up all the values of all the pleasures." Not that we always would, could, or should indulge in this kind of precise hedonistic arithmetic. On the other hand, do not all of us in fact employ some such method, however roughly, every time we consider and weigh the pleasurable and painful consequences of a projected act?

A further note: Bentham realized that there is a difference between *knowing* what we ought to do and *doing* it. This is especially true in those situations where the happiness of others means self-sacrifice and pain for *you*. (To use our earlier term, Bentham was a psychological egoist.) Here Bentham's doctrine of the Four Sanctions is relevant: nature, law, opinion, and God. By "sanctions" Bentham means something like binding forces or threats, but it will do to think of these Four Sanctions as *motivations* for ethical behavior. If, in fact, we fail to do what we should, well, natural laws, civil laws, public or personal opinion, and God himself will make it unpleasant for us—in either this life or the next, or in both! Nature, law, opinion, and God "persuade" us to overcome our perverse inclinations and to act in accordance with social utility. Bentham also labeled the Four Sanctions as the physical, the political, the moral, and the religious. But he provided an example that, in any case, makes his meaning clear:

A man's good, or his person, are consumed by fire. If this happened to him by what is called an accident, it was a *calamity*; if by reason of his own imprudence (for instance, from his neglecting to put his candle out) it may be styled a punishment of the *physical* sanction; if it happened to him by the sentence of the political magistrate,

Bentham's Four
Sanctions

a punishment belonging to the *political* sanction; that is, what is commonly called a *punishment;* if for want of any assistance which his *neighbour* withheld from him out of some dislike to his *moral* character, a punishment of the *moral* sanction; if by an immediate act of *God's* displeasure, manifested on account of some *sin* committed by him or through any distraction of mind, occasioned by the dread of such displeasure, a punishment of the *religious* sanction.

As to such of the pleasures and pains belonging to the religious sanction, as regard a future life, of what kind these may be we cannot know. These lie not open to our observation.[4]

MILL'S VERSION: QUALITY OVER QUANTITY

Though Bentham was the founder of modern utilitarianism, his successor was certainly the most famous utilitarian of all: John Stuart Mill (1806–1873).

Mill's little volume with the simple title *Utilitarianism* is a classic of philosophical literature. Furthermore, a clearer expression of the philosophy of the greatest happiness for the greatest number could hardly be imagined. Consider his statement of its *hedonistic* nature:

> The creed which accepts as the foundation of morals "utility" or the "greatest happiness principle" holds that actions are right in proportion as they tend to promote happiness; wrong as they tend to produce the reverse of happiness. By happiness is intended pleasure and the absence of pain; by unhappiness, pain and the privation of pleasure. To give a clear view of the moral standard set up by the theory, much more requires to be said; in particular, what things it includes in the ideas of pain and pleasure, and to what extent this is left an open question. But these supplementary explanations do not affect the theory of life on which this theory of morality is grounded—namely, that pleasure and freedom from pain are the only things desirable as ends; and that all desirable things (which are as numerous in the utilitarian as in any other scheme) are desirable either for pleasure inherent in themselves or as means to the promotion of pleasure and the prevention of pain.[5]

And consider his statement of its *socialistic* nature:

> I must again repeat what the assailants of utilitarianism seldom have the justice to acknowledge, that the happiness which forms the utilitarian standard of what is right in conduct is not the agent's own happiness but that of all concerned. As between his own happiness and that of others, utilitarianism requires him to be as strictly impartial as a disinterested and benevolent spectator. In the golden rule of Jesus of Nazareth, we read the complete spirit of the ethics of utility. "To do as you would be done by," and "to love your neighbor as yourself," constitute the ideal perfection of utilitarian morality. As the means of making the nearest approach to this ideal, utility would enjoin, first, that laws and social arrangements should place the happiness or (as, speaking practically, it may be called) the interest of

---

[4]Ibid., p. 36.

[5]John Stuart Mill, *Utilitarianism,* ed. Oskar Piest (Indianapolis: Bobbs-Merrill, 1957), pp. 10–11.

ACT-UTILITARIANISM/RULE-UTILITARIANISM

Some philosophers these days are fond of distinguishing between *act-utilitarianism* and *rule-utilitarianism*. An obvious clue to what this distinction implies is contained in the words "act" and "rule." When you hear or see the word "act" you think immediately of something particular: a *particular* deed done in *this* situation. On the other hand, the word "rule" brings to mind something general: *types* of deeds to be done in *every* situation. For the act-utilitarian the question is, What particular action should be done in this situation to bring about the greatest happiness for the greatest number? For the rule-utilitarian the question is, What rule should be followed in this situation to bring about the greatest happiness for the greatest number?

A concrete example may help. The Gestapo is pounding on the door demanding to know whether Jews are hidden in the attic. We know that Jews *are* hidden in the attic, and we also know their fate—and maybe ours too—if this should be found out. The question is whether or not to tell the truth. Act-utilitarians will ask themselves, What *particular action* in this situation will produce the greatest happiness for the greatest number? And they may well decide to lie in order to save the Jews and thwart the Gestapo's evil intent. Rule-utilitarians, on the other hand, will ask, What *general rule* applied here will produce the greatest happiness for the greatest number? And they might well decide to tell the truth, persuaded that in spite of the unfortunate consequences in this particular situation, truthfulness on the whole or *generally* makes for the greatest happiness.

In the case of the classic utilitarians, such as Bentham and Mill, philosophers are not agreed whether they were act- or rule-utilitarians. This may show that the distinction, though useful in theory, is difficult to apply in practice, at least in an either/or manner. Mill, in fact, seems to have espoused both act- and rule-utilitarianism, though at different levels, which, after all, is probably a rather commonsensical position. We cannot live without rules of conduct, and such rules have been distilled through the experience and wisdom of the ages—they should probably be honored as making for the greatest happiness for the greatest number. On the other hand, some situations are so singular and exceptional (or at least may seem to be at the time) as not to fall into any general category or under any general rule. In such situations we may be forced to act on the basis of what we see dictated *there* as fostering the greatest happiness—though, admittedly, threats and the brandishing of guns, and passionate embraces in the backseat of a car may not make for the most objective moral judgments.

Some philosophers have also questioned whether rule-utilitarianism is truly a viable position. Their doubts are probably best understood with a simple question. If a person follows a rule in spite of the fact that breaking the rule would lead to better consequences, then how does the rule maximize utility? As we will see in the next chapter, following rules in spite of their consequences is a key element of deontological moral theories.

every individual as nearly as possible in harmony with the interest of the whole; and, secondly, that education and opinion, which have so vast a power over human character, should so use that power as to establish in the mind of every individual an indissoluble association between his own happiness and the good of the whole, especially between his own happiness and the practice of such modes of conduct, negative and positive, as regard for the universal happiness prescribes; so that not only he may be unable to conceive the possibility of happiness to himself, consistently with conduct opposed to the general good, but also that a direct impulse to promote the general good may be in every individual one of the habitual motives of action, and the sentiments connected therewith may fill a large and prominent place in every human being's sentient existence.[6]

Bentham and Mill stand together on the Principle of Utility as augmented by the Principle of Benevolence: Actions are right actions if, and only if, they produce pleasure or happiness or satisfaction of needs, and this pleasure or happiness or satisfaction is to be distributed among as many people as possible. With Bentham, Mill agreed also that the basic principles of social utilitarianism cannot be proved, at least not in the usual sense:

Can the principles of social utilitarianism be proved?

. . . questions of ultimate ends do not admit of proof, in the ordinary acceptation of the term. To be incapable of proof by reasoning is common to all first principles, to the first premise of our knowledge, as well as to those of our conduct.[7]

In another sense, though, there *is* a proof:

The only proof capable of being given that an object is visible is that people actually see it. The only proof that a sound is audible is that people hear it; and so of the other sources of our experience. In like manner, I apprehend, the sole evidence it is possible to produce that anything is desirable is that people do actually desire it.[8]

On the basis of the above quotation, some readers might think that Mill lapses after all into ethical subjectivism: If someone did *not* desire happiness, wouldn't this mean that for him, at least, happiness is not desirable? It should be clear that Mill would answer with another question: If someone did not see an object, would it mean that the object is invisible? Goodness is experienced as happiness, but it hardly follows that goodness has no objective reality apart from the experience of it. Emphatically, Mill, as well as Bentham and all other hedonists, is an objectivist in ethics. The real problem in the above quotation lies elsewhere, as we will see.

Where Mill really split with Bentham was over Bentham's purely *quantitative* view of pleasure. Without denying that quantity is a consideration in the calculation of pleasure, Mill believed that it is not as important as the consideration of *quality*.

The greatest means the best

---

[6]Ibid., pp. 22–23.

[7]Ibid., p. 44.

[8]Ibid., pp. 44–45.

Now such a theory of life excites in many minds, and among them in some of the most estimable in feeling and purpose, inveterate dislike. To suppose that life has (as they express it) no higher end than pleasure—no better and nobler object of desire and pursuit—they designate as utterly mean and groveling, as a doctrine worthy only of swine, to whom the followers of Epicurus were, at a very early period, contemptuously likened; and modern holders of the doctrine are occasionally made the subject of equally polite comparisons by its German, French, and English assailants.

When thus attacked, the Epicureans have always answered that it is not they, but their accusers, who represent human nature in a degrading light, since the accusation supposes human beings to be capable of no pleasures except those of which swine are capable. If this supposition were true, the charge could not be gainsaid, but would then be no longer an imputation; for if the sources of pleasure were precisely the same to human beings and to swine, the rule of life which is good enough for the one would be good enough for the other. The comparison of the Epicurean life to that of beasts is felt as degrading, precisely because a beast's pleasures do not satisfy a human being's conceptions of happiness. Human beings have faculties more elevated than the animal appetites and, when once made conscious of them, do not regard anything as happiness which does not include their gratification. I do not, indeed, consider the Epicureans to have been by any means faultless in drawing out their scheme of consequences from the utilitarian principle. To do this in any sufficient manner, many Stoic, as well as Christian, elements require to be included. But there is no known Epicurean theory of life which does not assign to the pleasures of the intellect, of the feelings and imagination, and of the moral sentiments a much higher value as pleasures than to those of mere sensation. It must be admitted, however, that utilitarian writers in general have placed the superiority of mental over bodily pleasures chiefly in the greater permanency, safety, uncostliness, etc., of the former—that is, in their circumstantial advantages rather than in their intrinsic nature. And on all these points utilitarians have fully proved their case; but they might have taken the other and, as it may be called, higher ground with entire consistency. It is quite compatible with the principle of utility to recognize the fact that some kinds of pleasure are more desirable and more valuable than others. It would be absurd that, while in estimating all other things quality is considered as well as quantity, the estimation of pleasure should be supposed to depend on quantity alone.[9]

For Mill, as for most, it hardly needs arguing that although push-pin may be more fun than poetry, it yields an inferior happiness. And can the joy of sex really compare with the joy of the intellect? (The answer is No.) Or to use Mill's language, wouldn't you rather be a dissatisfied human than a satisfied pig, or a dissatisfied Socrates than a satisfied fool? For Mill, as for Bentham, the action is to be pursued that makes for the greatest happiness for the greatest number. But whereas for Bentham "greatest" meant most, for Mill it meant best.

Who says which pleasures are the best?

Granted that two pleasures may differ in quality, who is to say which is the best? Mill answers that the decision must rest with those who have experienced both.

---

[9]Ibid., pp. 11–12.

JOHN STUART MILL

John Stuart Mill was born in London in 1806. Although he never attended school, his education was among the most remarkable ever. He was instructed entirely by his father, James Mill, who had him learning Greek at the age of three and Latin at eight. By the time he was fourteen he had read most of the Greek and Latin classics (in the original languages) and had become expert in widely differing fields, such as history and mathematics. His social and political liberalism had also been shaped at an early age under the influence of his father and his father's associate, Jeremy Bentham. Regarding his reading of Bentham,

(*continued on next page*)

If I am asked what I mean by difference of quality in pleasures, or what makes one pleasure more valuable than another, merely as a pleasure, except its being greater in amount, there is but one possible answer. Of two pleasures, if there be one to which all or almost all who have experience of both give a decided preference, irrespective of any feeling of moral obligation to prefer it, that is the more desirable pleasure. If one of the two is, by those who are competently acquainted with both, placed so far above the other that they prefer it, even though knowing it to be attended with a greater amount of discontent, and would not resign it for any quantity of the other pleasure which their nature is capable of, we are justified in ascribing to the preferred enjoyment a superiority in quality so far outweighing quantity as to render it, in comparison, of small account.[10]

---

[10]Ibid., p. 12.

Mill said: ". . . the feeling rushed upon me, that all previous moralists were super-seded, and that here indeed was the commencement of a new era of thought."

In 1823, Mill became a clerk for the East India Company, where his father was also employed. He remained with the company until 1858, eventually advancing to a high position. In 1826, Mill fell into a deep depression, which, in his autobi-ography, he likened to the lines of Coleridge:

A grief without a pang, void, dark and drear,
A drowsy, stifled, unimpassioned grief,
Which finds no natural outlet or relief
In word, or sigh, or tear.

After many months he rallied from this depression, aided by his own insight, "Ask yourself whether you are happy, and you will cease to be so," and by the poetry of Wordsworth.

The woman in Mill's life was Mrs. Harriet Taylor, whom he met when he was 25. They sustained a Platonic relationship for twenty years. Three years after her hus-band's death, Mill married her, and when, in 1858 while they were touring France together, she herself died, Mill bought a house in Avignon in order to be near her grave. Mill called her "the most admirable person I have ever known," and referred to his relation to her as "the honor and chief blessing of my existence." He also attributed to her much of the inspiration and content of his writings.

Although Mill never held an academic position, over many years he frequently contributed articles to journals and magazines and produced many volumes. His philosophical magnum opus was the *System of Logic,* published in 1843. A great champion of liberal causes and representative government, Mill was encouraged in 1865 to stand for election to Parliament. He refused to campaign, contribute to expenses, or defend his views, and *won.* He was defeated in the next election, 1868, and thereupon spent his time either in London or in Avignon, something of a recluse, and cared for by his wife's daughter, Helen. After a brief illness, he died in 1873.

Some of Mill's more important works are *System of Logic, Utilitarianism, Subjec-tion of Women, Principles of Political Economy, On Liberty, Utility of Religion,* and *Autobiography.*

And those who have experienced both invariably opt for the higher or more qualitative pleasures.

Now it is an unquestionable fact that those who are equally acquainted with and equally capable of appreciating and enjoying both do give a most marked preference to the manner of existence which employs their higher faculties. Few human creatures would consent to be changed into any of the lower animals for a promise of the fullest allowance of a beast's pleasures; no intelligent human being would consent to be a fool, no instructed person would be an ignoramus, no person of feeling and conscience would be selfish and base, even though they should be persuaded that the fool, the dunce, or the rascal is better satisfied with his lot than they are with theirs. They would not resign what they possess more than he for the most complete satisfaction of all the desires which they have in common with him. If they ever fancy they would, it is only in cases of unhappiness

PLEASURE: QUANTITY OR QUALITY?

- *Bentham:* "If the game of push-pin furnish more pleasure, it is more valuable."
- *Mill:* "It is better to be a human being dissatisfied than a pig satisfied."

so extreme that to escape from it they would exchange their lot for almost any other, however undesirable in their own eyes. A being of higher faculties requires more to make him happy, is capable probably of more acute suffering, and certainly accessible to it at more points, than one of an inferior type; but in spite of these liabilities, he can never really wish to sink into what he feels to be a lower grade of existence. . . . It is better to be a human being dissatisfied than a pig satisfied; better to be Socrates dissatisfied than a fool satisfied. And if the fool, or the pig, are of a different opinion, it is because they only know their own side of the question. The other party to the comparison knows both sides.[11]

Presumably, however, Mill is not inviting us to sample all possible pleasures! Mill also differed somewhat with Bentham on the matter of moral sanctions. He did not deny Bentham's "external" sanctions of nature, law, opinion, and God—motivations *outside ourselves* for certain behavior. Indeed, he claimed that there is no reason why, for example, "hope of favor and the fear of displeasure from our fellow creatures or from the Ruler of the universe," and any other motivations for moral behavior, should not buttress utilitarian action as well as other kinds of action. He adds, however, an "internal" sanction, a motivation *inside ourselves* to behave in certain ways. Mill calls this "a subjective feeling in our own minds" but it might just as easily be called *conscience*. He also calls it the "ultimate" sanction or motivation of all moral behavior.

Mill's internal sanction: conscience

The ultimate sanction, therefore, of all morality (external motives apart) being a subjective feeling in our own minds, I see nothing embarrassing to those whose standard is utility in the question, What is the sanction of that particular standard? We may answer, the same as of all other moral standards—the conscientious feelings of mankind. Undoubtedly this sanction has no binding efficacy on those who do not possess the feelings it appeals to; but neither will these persons be more obedient to any other moral principle than to the utilitarian one. On them morality of any kind has no hold but through the external sanctions. Meanwhile the feelings exist, a fact in human nature, the reality of which, and the great power with which they are capable of acting on those in whom they have been duly cultivated, are proved by experience. No reason has ever been shown why they may not be cultivated to as great intensity in connection with the utilitarian as with any other rule of morals.[12]

[11]Ibid., pp. 12–14.
[12]Ibid., p. 37.

MORAL SANCTIONS: EXTERNAL AND INTERNAL

- *External sanctions:* Motivations or coercions for moral behavior that derive from outside ourselves, such as respect for the natural order, fear of civil punishment, fear of social disapproval, and fear of God's judgment.

- *Internal sanctions:* Motivations or coercions for moral behavior that lie within ourselves, such as conscience.

Where does this internal sanction, this "feeling in our own minds," come from? Even though Mill has just spoken of it as a fact of human nature, he believes that it is not innate, but acquired and cultivated. On the other hand, this makes it no less natural. As he himself says, we also speak, reason, build cities, and cultivate the ground—activities natural to humans but certainly acquired.

Motives and intentions

In discussions of morality, the distinction between *what actually results* from one's actions and *why one did it* is often and rightly raised. In the first edition of *Utilitarianism* Mill took a fairly stark position: The moral rightness of an action is independent of the motive behind it. He was severely criticized for this, and in the second edition he added a footnote defending and further explaining himself.

He who saves a fellow creature from drowning does what is morally right, whether his motive be duty or the hope of being paid for his trouble; he who betrays the friend that trusts him is guilty of a crime, even if his object be to serve another friend to whom he is under greater obligations.*

*An opponent whose intellectual and moral fairness it is a pleasure to acknowledge (the Rev. J. Llewellyn Davies), has objected to this passage, saying,

THE FIRST PARAGRAPH IN MILL'S *SUBJECTION OF WOMEN:*

"The object of this Essay is to explain as clearly as I am able, the grounds of an opinion which I have held from the very earliest period when I had formed any opinions at all on social or political matters, and which, instead of being weakened or modified, has been constantly growing stronger by the progress of reflection and the experience of life: That the principle which regulates the existing social relations between the two sexes—the legal subordination of one sex to the other—is wrong in itself, and now one of the chief hindrances to human improvement; and that it ought to be replaced by a principle of perfect equality, admitting no power or privilege on the one side, nor disability on the other."

Mill was a great champion of what in his day were radical causes, including women's rights and the abolition of child labor and slavery. This cartoon (published in *Punch*, March 30, 1867) suggests that Mill's work on logic leads to women's liberation.

"Mill's Logic, or Franchise for Females"

"Surely the rightness or wrongness of saving a man from drowning does depend very much upon the motive with which it is done. Suppose that a tyrant, when his enemy jumped into the sea to escape from him, saved him from drowning simply in order that he might inflict upon him more exquisite tortures, would it tend to clearness to speak of that rescue as 'a morally right action'? Or suppose again, according to one of the stock illustrations of ethical inquiries, that a man betrayed a trust received from a friend, because the discharge of it would fatally injure that friend himself or someone belonging to him, would utilitarianism compel one to call the betrayal 'a crime' as much as if it had been done from the meanest motive?"

I submit that he who saves another from drowning in order to kill him by torture afterwards does not differ only in motive from him who does the same thing for duty or benevolence; the act itself is different. The rescue of the man is, in the case supposed, only the necessary first step of an act far more atrocious than leaving him to drown would have been. Had Mr. Davies said, "The rightness or wrongness of saving a man from drowning does depend very much"—not upon the motive, but—"upon the *intention*," no utilitarian would have differed from him. Dr. Davies, by an oversight too common not to be quite venial, has in this case confounded the very different ideas of Motive and Intention. There is no point which utilitarian thinkers (and Bentham pre-eminently) have taken more pains to illustrate than this. The morality of the action depends entirely upon the intention—that is, upon what the agent *wills* to do. But the motive, that is, the feeling which makes him will so to do, if it makes no difference in the act, makes none in the morality: though it makes a great difference in our moral estimation of the agent, especially if it indicates a good or a bad habitual *disposition*—a bent of character from which useful, or from which hurtful actions are likely to arise.[13]

Is Mill playing with words? squirming out of a legitimate criticism? Or is his distinction between *motives* and *intentions* valid and important?

SOME OBJECTIONS

Some obvious complaints

We mention here some of the objections made against utilitarianism specifically, and in the next section some objections to hedonism in all of its forms.

In *Utilitarianism*, Mill himself answers a whole string of rather obvious charges against utilitarianism. For example: Utilitarianism is a pig-philosophy that encourages the pursuit of base pleasures; it is a godless philosophy that establishes a criterion of morality independent of the question of God's will; it is such a "calculating" philosophy as to chill our human feelings for one another; it focuses attention on the consequences of actions to the exclusion of their motives; it asks us to do the impossible—namely, to anticipate endless chains of consequences from our actions. If you can't see how Mill would have answered such charges, the second chapter of *Utilitarianism* makes good philosophical reading.

But some other problems may be mentioned.

Social hedonism versus altruism

First, it should be evident that utilitarianism sidesteps *to some degree* the charge that it is egoistic. On the other hand, neither is it purely altruistic, focusing exclusively on the interests of others. Though it tells us to distribute happiness among as many people as possible, it also tells us never to forget that each of us is *one* of those people. Whether or not this is a problem depends on how strenuously you take the ideal of altruism. Perhaps social hedonism goes far enough in its concern for the interests of others. But maybe not. Did Jesus, Socrates, or St. Francis count himself even as *one*?

---

[13]Ibid., p. 24.

How might a utilitarian reason about the rightness or wrongness of

- Capital punishment?
- Abortion?
- War?
- Minority rights?
- Euthanasia?
- Genetic engineering?

Second, we have seen that all forms of hedonism, but especially Bentham's, employ some type of hedonic calculus, or computation of pleasures. Now this may look good on paper, but how practical is it? Is it really possible to measure and compare, say, the *intensity* of different pleasures in different people? Or even the same pleasure in the same person? Try it. Further, the hedonic calculus is geared to produce certain sorts of results. But though we *may* be able to foresee *some* of the consequences of our actions, who can really foresee all of them, to say nothing of the consequences of the consequences, and so on? We may grant that in certain very general cases the implications of our actions are fairly obvious, but even if we were utilitarians it is not in *these* situations that we would look for moral guidance, is it? It's when we *aren't* clear about the consequences that we need help.

Third, social hedonism results in some rather awkward puzzles. For example, we are told to act so as to promote the greatest happiness for the greatest number. But is not ten parts of happiness distributed over two people—five parts of happiness each—as much the greatest happiness for the greatest number as ten parts of happiness distributed evenly to ten people? It may be answered that this is where the *Justice Principle* comes in with the idea that happiness is to be spread over as many people as possible. But then we have to ask constantly, Who has how much pleasure? And, as one philosopher has observed, is it really meaningful to say that person A is three-and-a-half times as happy as person B? And in any event, would you be willing to dispatch someone to burn in hell forever even if you could thereby secure the eternal happiness of *every other person in the world*? Clearly, the utilitarian's numbers game is a difficult one to play.

Fourth, it is often objected that utilitarianism (or, for that matter, hedonism in general) is incompatible with the standards of morality that we actually employ. We recognize, for example, the *intrinsic* rightness (that is, rightness for its own sake and apart from its consequences) of acting fairly, telling the truth, and keeping promises. Could you break a promise *without batting an eye*, even if you knew it would promote happiness in general? And what about the possible conflict between the claims of utility and the claims of *justice*? Would you be willing to frame an innocent person if

> Is the hedonic calculus workable?

> Some embarrassing puzzles

> Are there more basic ideals than happiness?

FACTUAL JUDGMENTS AND VALUE JUDGMENTS

- A *factual judgment* is a judgment that describes some empirical state of affairs. Examples: "In fourteen hundred and ninety-two Columbus sailed the ocean blue," "Water freezes at 32 degrees Fahrenheit," and "Everyone seeks pleasure."

- A *value judgment* is a judgment that evaluates something or judges its worth. Examples: "Two heads are better than one," "Honesty is the best policy," and "Pleasure is the highest good."

WHAT'S WRONG WITH THIS PICTURE?

In the following scenario, Bernard Williams throws into clear relief what—in an admittedly bizarre situation—would be expected of Jim if he were a consistent utilitarian. At the same time, it will be clear to many that what is required on utilitarian grounds is utterly unacceptable. Or is it? What would you do if you were Jim?

Jim finds himself in the central square of a small South American town. Tied up against the wall are a row of twenty Indians, most terrified, a few defiant, in front of them several armed men in uniform. A heavy man in a sweat-stained khaki shirt turns out to be the captain in charge and, after a good deal of questioning of Jim which establishes that he got there by accident while on a botanical expedition, explains that the Indians are a random group of the inhabitants who, after recent acts of protest against the government, are just about to be killed to remind other possible protestors of the advantages of not protesting. However, since Jim is an honoured visitor from another land, the captain is happy to offer him a guest's privilege of killing one of the Indians himself. If Jim accepts, then as a special mark of the occasion, the other Indians will be let off. Of course, if Jim refuses, then there is no special occasion, and Pedro here will do what he was about to do when Jim arrived, and kill them all. Jim, with some desperate recollection of schoolboy fiction, wonders whether if he got hold of a gun, he could hold the captain, Pedro and the rest of the soldiers to threat, but it is quite clear from the set-up that nothing of that kind is going to work: any attempt at that sort of thing will mean that all the Indians will be killed, and himself. The men against the wall, and the other villagers, understand the situation, and are obviously begging him to accept. What should he do?*

*Bernard Williams, "A Critique of Utilitarianism," in J. J. C. Smart and Bernard Williams, *Utilitarianism: For and Against* (Cambridge: Cambridge University Press, 1973), pp. 98f.

doing so would maximize utility? If a utilitarian argument in favor of reinstating slavery succeeded in showing that the greatest happiness of the greatest number would be thus served, would we feel obligated to do so? Surely we do not really believe that it is right to pursue pleasure and happiness, even of the greatest number, *no matter what*. In the end, our pursuit of the general welfare appears to be conditioned by other and even more basic ideals.

Finally, *fifth*, utilitarianism faces a criticism because it is a *naturalistic* ethic—it takes its clue from nature, or from what *is*. In the case of utilitarianism, it is an appeal to *human* nature, and move specifically to the natural human desire for *pleasure*. Consider Bentham's claim that

Nature has placed mankind under the governance of two sovereign masters, pain and pleasure. It is for them alone to point out what we ought to do.[14]

[14]Bentham, *An Introduction to the Principles of Morals and Legislation*, p. 11.

It is often pointed out that the following statement by Mill (in *Utilitarianism*) involves a simple logical fallacy. What is it?

". . . each person's happiness is a good to that person, and the general happiness, therefore, a good to the aggregate of all persons."

UTILITARIANISM AND THE MORALITY OF MURDER

Utilitarianism tells us that the right action is the one that creates the greatest happiness for the greatest number of people. But what about situations where this requires killing another person? Is this still what utilitarianism requires? The philosopher Tom Regan uses the following story about his Aunt Bea to illustrate a powerful objection to the utilitarian approach to ethics.

My Aunt Bea is old, inactive, a cranky, sour person, though not physically ill. She prefers to go on living. She is also rather rich. I could make a fortune if I could get my hands on her money, money she intends to give me in any event, after she dies, but which she refuses to give me now. In order to avoid a huge tax bite, I plan to donate a handsome sum of my profits to a local children's hospital. Many, many children will benefit from my generosity, and much joy will be brought to their parents, relatives, and friends. If I don't get the money rather soon, all these ambitions will come to naught. The once-in-a-lifetime-opportunity to make a real killing will be gone. Why, then, not really kill my Aunt Bea? Oh, of course I *might* get caught. But I'm no fool and, besides, her doctor can be counted on to cooperate (he has an eye for the same investment and I happen to know a good deal about his shady past). The deed can be done . . . professionally, shall we say. There is *very* little chance of getting caught. And as for my conscience being guilt ridden, I am a resourceful sort of fellow and will take more than sufficient comfort—as I lie on the beach at Acapulco—in contemplating the joy and health I have brought to so many others.

Suppose Aunt Bea is killed and the rest of the story comes out as told. Would I have done anything wrong? Anything immoral? One would have thought that I had. But not according to utilitarianism. Since what I did brought about the best balance of totaled satisfaction over frustration for all those affected by the outcome, what I did was not wrong. Indeed, in killing Aunt Bea the physician and I did what duty required.

This same kind of argument can be repeated in all sorts of cases, illustrating time after time, how the utilitarian's position leads to results that impartial people find morally callous. It is wrong to kill my Aunt Bea in the name of bringing about the best results for others. A good end does not justify an evil means. Any adequate moral theory will have to explain why this is so. Utilitarianism fails in this respect and so cannot be the theory we seek.*

---

*Tom Regan, "The Radical Egalitarian Case for Animal Rights," in *In Defense of Animals*, ed. Peter Singer (Oxford: Basil Blackwell, 1985).

And Mill's claim that

> The only proof capable of being given that an object is visible is that people actually see it. . . . In like manner, I apprehend, the sole evidence it is possible to produce that anything is desirable is that people do actually desire it. . . . If the opinion which I have now stated is psychologically true—if human nature is so constituted as to desire nothing which is not either a part of happiness or a means of happiness—we can have no other proof, and we require no other, that these are the only things desirable.[15]

The objection to naturalistic ethics, often called the Naturalistic Fallacy, is often posed in the form of a question: Can an *ought* be derived from an *is*? Stated otherwise, it is the mistake of equating a *factual* judgment with a *value* judgment. These utilitarian thinkers clearly try to derive an *ought* from an *is*. Look at the two quotations above. Don't *factual* judgments seem to be mixed up with *value* judgments? What have our "natural masters," pain and pleasure, got to do with "what we ought to do"? And although what is psychologically true might have something to do with what is actually desired, what has it got to do with what is *desirable*, or *worthy* of desire, or *right*? This is exactly how G. E. Moore attacked this very passage in Mill.

> Well, the fallacy in this step is so obvious, that it is quite wonderful how Mill failed to see it. The fact is that "desirable" does not mean "able to be desired" as "visible" means "able to be seen." The desirable means simply what ought to be desired or deserves to be desired; just as the detestable means not what can be but what ought to be detested and the damnable what deserves to be damned. Mill has, then, smuggled in, under cover of the word "desirable," the very notion about which he ought to be quite clear. "Desirable" does indeed mean "what it is good to desire"; but when this is understood it is no longer plausible to say that our only test of *that,* is what is actually desired. Is it merely a tautology when the Prayer Book talks of *good* desires? Are not *bad* desires also possible?[16]

And philosophers have been attacking Mill in the same way ever since.

CHAPTER 15 IN REVIEW

SUMMARY

One major way of distinguishing between moral philosophies is to raise the question of consequences. Utilitarianism is a teleological ethic, emphasizing the consequences of actions as the criteria of their moral worth. Also, it identifies pleasure or happiness as the specific consequence to be attained. It is crucial to note, however, that it's not the pleasure or happiness of the individual but that of society: the greatest happiness for the greatest number.

---

[15]Mill, *Utilitarianism*, pp. 44, 48–49.

[16]George Edward Moore, *Principia Ethica* (Cambridge: Cambridge University Press, 1903), p. 67.

Bentham and Mill are, historically, the best representatives of the utilitarian position. Bentham pressed for a quantitative interpretation of the "greatest" happiness and propounded a hedonic calculus to assist in its determination. Mill pressed for a qualitative interpretation of the "greatest" happiness and urged that it is only the widely experienced individual who is in a position to extol the superiority of the qualitative pleasures—for example, the pleasures of the mind.

Although utilitarianism escapes the charge of egoism, it is subject to many of the complaints leveled against any hedonistic philosophy. Most notably, utilitarianism is, finally, in some sense a naturalistic ethic, finding its basis in what individuals actually, and naturally, desire and strive for. As such it is an obvious target for critics who distinguish *ought* from *is.*

BASIC IDEAS

- Consequences and morality
- Teleological and deontological theories of morality
- The Principle of Utility
- The Benevolence Principle
- Utilitarianism as social hedonism
- Utilitarianism as a political position
- Bentham's version of utilitarianism
- The hedonic calculus: seven criteria of the greatest pleasure
- Bentham's Four Sanctions
  Nature
  Civil law
  Opinion
  God
- Mill's version of utilitarianism
- The Principle of Utility as unprovable . . .
- . . . and provable
- Mill's criterion of the best pleasures
- Mill's internal sanction
- Mill on the difference between motives and intentions
- The Justice Principle
- The Naturalistic Fallacy

TEST YOURSELF

1. What is the basic difference between teleological and deontological theories of moralism?
2. Benevolence Principle + Hedonism = ? What is the Benevolence Principle and how does it relate to hedonism?
3. Who formulated a sevenfold hedonic calculus in order to measure the quantity of pleasure?

4. According to Mill, what is the only proof that anything is desirable?

5. Who said it? "If the game of push-pin furnish more pleasure, it is more valuable."

6. The big difference between Bentham's and Mill's versions of utilitarianism concerns _____ versus _____.

7. Exactly why is utilitarianism a *naturalistic* ethics?

8. What was G. E. Moore's objection to utilitarianism?

9. According to Mill, which of the following are relevant for the determination of a moral act? (a) number of people involved, (b) production of happiness, (c) quality of pleasure involved, (d) external sanctions.

QUESTIONS FOR REFLECTION

• What do you think of Mill's justification of utilitarianism? What about the Naturalistic Fallacy? Are there values to which even the greatest happiness for the greatest number might be sacrificed? What is to say that the greatest happiness for the whole human race is the highest good? If the whole human race were suddenly to disappear, by virtue of what could it *then* be said: "That's too bad"?

• Here we have encountered the distinction between "higher" and "lower" pleasures. What do you make of Mill's evidence for the qualitative superiority of the higher pleasures? Would *you* rather be an unsatisfied Socrates than a satisfied pig? Why?

• Are you a utilitarian? Any form of utilitarianism asserts that the morality of any action is determined by the (intended) consequences. Is that *your* belief?

FOR FURTHER READING

Michael D. Bayles (ed.). *Contemporary Utilitarianism*. Garden City, NY: Anchor Books, 1968. A collection of ten essays, evaluating utilitarianism from the standpoint of contemporary issues and perspectives.

Richard B. Brandt. *Ethical Theory: The Problems of Normative and Critical Ethics*. Englewood Cliffs, NJ: Prentice-Hall, 1959. Ch. 15. A discussion of "Moral Obligation and General Welfare," with special treatment of act- and rule-utilitarianism.

Frederick Copleston. *A History of Philosophy*. Baltimore: Newman Press, 1946–1974. VIII, Chs. 1–2. Chapters on "The Utilitarian Movement," with special treatment of Bentham's and Mill's ethical doctrines, by a noted historian of philosophy.

A. C. Ewing. *Ethics*. New York: Free Press, 1953. Ch. 3. An introductory and unsympathetic treatment of "The Pursuit of General Happiness."

W. D. Hudson (ed.). *The Is-Ought Question: A Collection of Papers on the Central Problem in Moral Philosophy*. London: Macmillan, 1969. Twenty-two essays by well-known thinkers on all aspects of the is-ought relation, with a helpful introduction by the editor.

Philip Blair Rice. *On the Knowledge of Good and Evil.* New York: Random House, 1955. Ch. 5. A chapter on Moore's criticism of Mill (Naturalistic Fallacy), somewhat sympathetic to the naturalist stance.

Henry Sidgwick. *The Method of Ethics.* London: Macmillan, 1907. An old but enduring sophisticated and systematic defense of a version of utilitarianism.

J. J. C. Smart and Bernard Williams. *Utilitarianism: For and Against.* Cambridge: Cambridge University Press, 1973. A defense by Smart and an especially compelling critique by Williams of act-utilitarianism.

W. H. Werkmeister. *Theories of Ethics: A Study in Moral Obligation.* Lincoln, NE: Johnsen, 1961. Ch. 5. A closely documented critical account of "universalistic hedonism," concentrating on Bentham's and Mill's versions.

*In addition, see the relevant articles ("Utilitarianism," "Mill, John Stuart," etc.) in *Routledge Encyclopedia of Philosophy*, ed. Edward Craig (London: Routledge, 1998), and *Stanford Encyclopedia of Philosophy*, http://plato .stanford.edu.

THE ROLE OF DUTY

Even aside from the objections mentioned, it has been charged that there is something basically wrong with utilitarianism. Something important has been left out. Aren't some things just right or wrong *no matter what*? Isn't there such a thing as unconditional obligation? *duty*? To be sure, it is precisely in its exaltation of *duty*, pure and simple, as the foundation of moral actions, that the theory in the present chapter is radically different.

MORALITY AS UNCONDITIONAL

First, we must remind ourselves of the important distinction between *teleological* and *deontological* ethics. We saw at the beginning of Chapter 15 that a teleological theory of morality is one that emphasizes the intended consequences or results of actions as the criteria of their rightness. And we considered the best example of this sort of ethical theory: utilitarianism, where the criterion of right action was the promotion of the general welfare. But however it may conceive the "good results," any teleological theory says, "Such-and-such is the right action because it produces such-and-such results." A theory like this is clear, straightforward, and commonsensical.

How odd it might sound, therefore, for someone to say, "The consequences or results of your actions have nothing at all to do with their rightness or wrongness!" This is a *deontological* conception of morality. You will recall that

The irrelevance of consequences

a deontological theory is one that sets up as the criterion of moral behavior not what might or might not happen—or be intended to happen—as a result of one's actions, but rather the intent to perform one's *duty* through a certain action.

This was exactly the thesis of Immanuel Kant, who, by the way, didn't think it a bit odd. In fact, he regarded it as the only *possible* way to conceive of genuine moral behavior. Why? Kant's answer is found, for the most part, in his *Foundations of the Metaphysics of Morals.* It is a small book, but, as the Kant scholar H. J. Paton says, "one of the small books which are truly great: it has exercised on human thought an influence almost ludicrously dispro-portionate to its size."[1]

For Kant, morality is a matter of *ought,* or *obligation.* Doesn't any moral theory tell us what we *ought* to do? This is not the problem. The problem is that a distinction is not usually drawn between the conditional *ought* and the *un*conditional *ought.* A conditional *ought* says, "You ought to do X if you want something-or-other to happen." The *ought* is conditioned by something-or-other. But the unconditional *ought* says, "You ought to do X, period." For Kant, only the unconditional *ought* is the *moral* ought. Why? Because, as we all recognize—don't we?—morality must be *neces-sary* and *universal;* that is, it must be absolutely binding, and absolutely binding on everyone alike: Whoever you are, whatever your situation, you ought to do X. But the conditional *ought* involves "ifs" and "in order thats" and therefore gets mixed up with all sorts of particular circum-stances, changing desires, personal inclinations, and so on. Any "moral-ity" (Kant would put it in quotation marks) founded on the conditional *ought* ("Do X if . . ." or "Do X, in order that . . .") will therefore be relative and particular rather than necessary and universal—but then it is not real morality, is it?

This is not to say that in deciding what we ought to do—how to fulfill our duty—we should never take the consequences of our actions into account. Often it is necessary to consider the results of an action in order to perceive whether it is our duty. But it is out of *duty* that we should act, not for the sake of the consequences. Stay with this until it is clear to you, or maybe consider an example. We borrow the following from yet another Kant scholar, Lewis White Beck.

> Imagine two soldiers who volunteer for a dangerous mission; because they see a task they ought to undertake, they voluntarily assume the responsibility for it. Certainly their act will have consequences; equally certain is the fact that they desire certain consequences for their act. The most careful consideration of these consequences, calculation as to how to achieve some desirable consequences and avoid others less desirable, and an ardent desire to attain the goal do not in the least detract from the morality of the men's action if they are indeed acting on the

[1]H. J. Paton, in the Preface to his translation of Immanuel Kant, *Foundations of the Metaphysics of Morals,* published as *Kant's Groundwork of the Metaphysics of Morals* (New York: Harper & Row, 1964), p. 8.

conviction that it is their duty to do these acts; their concern with the consequences may be an essential part of their conduct, necessary for the fulfillment of the obligation they have placed upon themselves. Now imagine that one of the men is killed before reaching his destination, while the other is successful; what moral judgment do we pass upon them? So far as we judge that their motives were equally good (and of course, as Kant repeatedly says, we cannot be sure what anyone's motives really are), we judge them in the same way. Their acts are judged to be equally moral, in spite of the fact that one succeeded and the other failed. Each did his "best," and what he earnestly attempted and the motives which led him to do what he did are the proper objects of moral judgment; what he accomplishes lies to a large extent beyond his control.[2]

Do you see that even with its possible interest in consequences this position is quite unlike, say, utilitarianism? There the question was, Did you act for the sake of promoting the general welfare? But here the question is, Aside from what you accomplish or even tried to accomplish, did you act out of duty?

But back to the main point. Another way Kant expresses his rejection of *conditioned* morality is by his rejection of any and all *naturalistic* ethics. As we explained earlier, a naturalistic ethics is one that bases its *ought* in some way on nature, say by an appeal to the physical world, or to psychology, or to human nature, or to history. But such an ethics would be based on what *happens* to be, or *might* be, or *could* be, whereas genuine morality is, again, a matter of *necessity* and *universality*. Do you see that happiness, for example, must for Kant be an impossible basis for moral laws?

This section is entitled "Morality as Unconditional." Is it clear that for Kant morality is not conditioned by (that is, not defined by, not bound by, not relative to, not based on) anything outside the morality of the act itself? Is it clear how, for Kant, the introduction of the empirical categories of consequences and nature not only clouds but absolutely distorts the idea of morality?

In the following, from the *Foundations of the Metaphysics of Morals*, Kant emphasizes with a vengeance the absolute necessity of separating genuine morality from all empirical considerations, and the necessity, instead, of deriving it *a priori* from pure reason. (By "anthropology," Kant means what can be known empirically about human nature.)

The irrelevance of nature

---

[2]Lewis White Beck, in the Preface to his translation of Immanuel Kant, *Foundations of the Metaphysics of Morals* (Indianapolis: Bobbs-Merrill, 1959), p. ix.

Kant objects to:

• Any teleological conception of moral action.

• Any naturalistic basis of moral action.

Moses with the Ten Commandments. These divine imperatives are a classic
example of the deontological approach that has shaped Western morality.

Since my purpose here is directed to moral philosophy, I narrow the proposed
question to this: Is it not the utmost necessity to construct a pure moral philosophy
which is completely freed from everything which may be only empirical and thus
belong to anthropology? That there must be such a philosophy is self-evident from
the common idea of duty and moral laws. Everyone must admit that a law, if it
is to hold morally, i.e., as a ground of obligation, must imply absolute necessity;
he must admit that the command, "Thou shalt not lie," does not apply to men
only, as if other rational beings had no need to observe it. The same is true for
all other moral laws properly so called. He must concede that the ground of
obligation here must not be sought in the nature of man or in the circumstances
in which he is placed, but sought a priori solely in the concepts of pure reason,
and that every other precept which rests on principles of mere experience, even

IMMANUEL KANT

The historian of philosophy Frederick Copleston has described Kant's life as "singularly uneventful and devoid of dramatic incident."

Immanuel Kant was born in 1724 in Königsberg, East Prussia (now Russia), on the Baltic Sea. Kant's father, who immigrated from Scotland (and changed the family name from Cant to Kant), was a saddler. The family was large, poor, and religious. They were Pietists (something like Prussian Puritans), and the continuous round of prayers, religious instruction, and observances is no doubt why Kant in his adult years never attended public worship except on extraordinary occasions. On the other hand, he embraced to the end the ethical principles of his early religious upbringing.

In 1740, he entered the University of Königsberg, where he drank in a broad survey of many fields: metaphysics, physics, algebra, geometry, psychology, astronomy, and logic. At the conclusion of his studies he earned a sparse livelihood by becoming a tutor to the Prussian gentry. It was during this time that he was introduced to high society, though he soon withdrew into the ivory tower of academic life. In 1755, he took what we would call a doctoral degree and became a lecturer at the university. In 1770, he was made professor. He taught and published first in science, anticipating Laplace's nebular hypothesis concerning the origin of the universe and Darwin's theory of evolution. But he turned gradually to metaphysics. Kant's lectures were said to be lively and even humorous—though one would never guess this from most of his writings.

(*continued on next page*)

In 1781, at the ripe age of 57, he published the monumental *Critique of Pure Reason*. This was followed by the *Critique of Practical Reason* and the *Critique of Judgment*. According to the German writer Herder, Kant spoke "the profoundest language that ever came from the lips of man." Profound perhaps, but perhaps also the most exasperating. He gave the manuscript of his first *Critique* to a colleague, Marcus Herz. Herz returned it half-read, with the explanation, "If I finish it, I am afraid I shall go mad!"

Kant lectured at the university for over forty years. In all this time he never traveled more than 60 miles from Königsberg, and for forty years did not spend so much as a single night outside that city. Kant was a small man (about five feet tall), extremely frail, and somewhat distorted in his frame. He was meticulous about his health, verging on the neurotic. His daily routine was extremely fixed, beginning every morning at 4:55. It is reported that his daily walk was so regular that he strolled for exactly one hour, eight times up and down the Linden Allee (which came to be nicknamed "The Philosopher's Walk"), and so punctual that the townspeople set their clocks by it. He never married and was, in fact, something of a misogynist. He died in senile dementia on February 12, 1804.

Kant's most important philosophical works include *Critique of Pure Reason, Critique of Practical Reason, Critique of Judgment, Prolegomena to any Future Metaphysics, Foundations of the Metaphysics of Morals, Metaphysical First Principles of Natural Science, Religion within the Bounds of Reason Alone,* and *On Perpetual Peace.*

a precept which is in certain respects universal, so far as it leans in the least on empirical grounds (perhaps only in regard to the motive involved), may be called a practical rule but never a moral law. . . .

But a completely isolated metaphysics of morals, mixed with no anthropology, no theology, no physics or hyperphysics, and even less with occult qualities (which might be called hypophysical), is not only an indispensable substrate of all theoretically sound and definite knowledge of duties; it is also a desideratum of the highest importance to the actual fulfillment of its precepts. For the pure conception of duty and of the moral law generally, with no admixture of empirical inducements, has an influence on the human heart so much more powerful than all other incentives which may be derived from the empirical field that reason, in the consciousness of its dignity, despises them and gradually becomes master over them. It has this influence only through reason, which thereby first realizes that it can of itself be practical. A mixed theory of morals which is put together both from incentives of feelings and inclinations and from rational concepts must, on the other hand, make the mind vacillate between motives which cannot be brought under any principle and which can lead only accidentally to the good and often to the bad.

From what has been said it is clear that all moral concepts have their seat and origin entirely a priori in reason. This is just as much the case in the most ordinary reason as in reason which is speculative to the highest degree. It is obvious that they cannot be abstracted from any empirical and hence merely contingent cognitions. In the purity of their origin lies their worthiness to serve us as supreme practical principles, and to the extent that something empirical is added to them

> "We can judge the heart of a man by his treatment of animals."
>
> —Kant

just this much is subtracted from their genuine influence and from the unqualified worth of actions.[3]

THE GOOD WILL

In this way, Kant eliminates from the start the least suggestion that morality can be based on our natural states and inclinations. He does not begrudge us, say, pleasure and happiness, but wants us to see that such "gifts of nature" cannot be the *foundation* of morality as rationally conceived.

Consider, for example, what we might call the innate gifts of intelligence, wit, and courage, or the accidental gifts of power, wealth, and honor. Does it take any great insight to see that these are not *absolute* goods? that they have no *intrinsic* or *unconditional* value? To see that this is so, just notice how any one of them could be corrupted or turned into an evil. Well, then, is there anything more basic than these that is absolutely and unconditionally good? Kant says Yes. And it is, in fact, the very thing that these other things depend on for their goodness, and without which they would become corrupted and turned into evil. What is this absolute good, the necessary and sufficient condition for all right action, the foundation of rational morality? The *good will*.

One of the most quoted passages in all philosophical literature is the opening sentence of the first section of the *Foundations:*

The good will as the basis for morality

> Nothing in the world—indeed nothing even beyond the world—can possibly be conceived which could be called good without qualification except a *good will.*

Kant goes on immediately to show how the good will underlies any possible goodness of our natural gifts:

> Intelligence, wit, judgment, and the other talents of the mind, however they may be named, or courage, resoluteness, and perseverance as qualities of temperament, are doubtless in many respects good and desirable. But they can become extremely bad and harmful if the will, which is to make use of these gifts of nature and which in its special constitution is called character, is not good. It is the same with the gifts of fortune. Power, riches, honor, even health, general well-being, and the contentment with one's condition which is called happiness, make for pride and even arrogance if there is not a good will to correct their influence on the mind and on its principles of action so as to make it universally comfortable to its end. It need hardly be mentioned that the sight of a being adorned with no feature of a pure

---

[3]Kant, *Foundations of the Metaphysics of Morals,* pp. 5, 27–28.

and good will, yet enjoying uninterrupted prosperity, can never give pleasure to a rational impartial observer. Thus the good will seems to constitute the indispensable condition even of worthiness to be happy.

Some qualities seem to be conducive to this good will and can facilitate its action, but, in spite of that, they have no intrinsic unconditional worth. They rather presuppose a good will, which limits the high esteem which one otherwise rightly has for them and prevents their being held to be absolutely good. Moderation in emotions and passions, self-control, and calm deliberation not only are good in many respects but even seem to constitute a part of the inner worth of the person. But however unconditionally they were esteemed by the ancients, they are far from being good without qualification. For without the principle of a good will they can become extremely bad, and the coolness of a villain makes him not only far more dangerous but also more directly abominable in our eyes than he would have seemed without it.

The good will is not good because of what it effects or accomplishes or because of its adequacy to achieve some proposed end; it is good only because of its willing, i.e., it is good of itself. And, regarded for itself, it is to be esteemed incomparably higher than anything which could be brought about by it in favor of any inclination or even of the sum total of all inclinations. Even if it should happen that, by a particularly unfortunate fate or by the niggardly provision of a stepmotherly nature, this will should be wholly lacking in power to accomplish its purpose, and if even the greatest effort should not avail it to achieve anything of its end, and if there remained only the good will (not as a mere wish but as the summoning of all the means in our power), it would sparkle like a jewel in its own right, as something that had its full worth in itself. Usefulness or fruitlessness can neither diminish nor augment this worth. Its usefulness would be only its setting, as it were, so as to enable us to handle it more conveniently in commerce or to attract the attention of those who are not yet connoisseurs, but not to recommend it to those who are experts or to determine its worth.[4]

What is a good will?

Pore over the above paragraphs until they are digested. Still, even though Kant here uses the phrase "good will" repeatedly, he does not say exactly what it means. If we somehow miss this, then we miss the whole point. For Kant a good will, or a *pure* will, is an intention to act in accordance with moral *law*, and moral law is what it is no matter what anything else is. To act out of a good will is, then, to do X because it is *right* to do X, and for no other reason. This would be *rational* morality.

An important note: Kant stresses the difference between acting "out of" duty and acting "in accordance with" duty. Obviously, we may do something that just happens to accord with what our duty is, but this would

---

[4]Ibid., pp. 9–10.

"Nothing in the world—indeed nothing even beyond the world—can possibly be conceived which could be called good without qualification except a *good will*."

—Kant

hardly make the action moral. In order to be really moral, our action must be done *out* of duty—that is, with a good will or with respect for the moral law. This may seem odd at first, but consider an example that Kant used. What should we say about a shopkeeper who is always honest with customers and never cheats them? Is he acting morally? Of course not, Kant says, because he is merely acting in self-interest to avoid losing business.

KANT'S CATEGORICAL IMPERATIVE

At this point Kant presents us with one of the most famous and important concepts in the history of ethics: the *Categorical Imperative*.

For Kant, the Categorical Imperative is the fundamental principle of morality. More accurately, it is a criterion or *test* by which we can make sure our actions are moral—that is, that they are motivated by a good will or performed out of duty. As Kant states it in its most general form, the Categorical Imperative is this:

The Categorical Imperative stated

> Act only according to that maxim by which you can at the same time will that it should become a universal law.[5]

That is to say, when you are about to do X, ask yourself whether it is possible to will that everyone else act in the same way. If the answer is Yes, then, says Kant, you may be assured that you are acting out of duty or with a good will. Why is this? We will explain in a moment exactly how the Categorical Imperative is a test of right action.

Sometimes the Categorical Imperative is referred to, for short, as the *Principle of Universalizibility*, since it asks us whether we can "universalize" our actions—that is, whether we could demand that everyone else in similar circumstances act in accordance with the same rule as we would. But we must not miss the significance of Kant's own—and more ponderous—expression. What is an *imperative*? It is a *command*. As a command, the Categorical Imperative addresses and constrains our will, which it recognizes might not always (and often enough doesn't!) gladly pursue what it ought. As a command, the Categorical Imperative reckons with our natural perversity; in fact, Kant believed, in his own way, in the traditional Christian doctrine of original sin. But why is this imperative called, further, *categorical*? Here we encounter again the distinction between doing something as a means of *achieving some end* and doing something simply because it's *right*. Kant says that all imperatives are either hypothetical or categorical. A *hypothetical* imperative would command you to do X if you wanted Y (notice the hypothetical form of the statement, "if . . . then"). But a *categorical* imperative would command you to do X inasmuch as X is intrinsically right—that is, right in and of itself, aside from any other considerations—no "ifs," no conditions, no strings attached.

What is an imperative?

Hypothetical and categorical imperatives

---

[5]Ibid., p. 39.

Kant himself clearly draws the distinction between hypothetical and categorical imperatives:

> All imperatives command either hypothetically or categorically. The former present the practical necessity of a possible action as a means to achieving something else which one desires (or which one may possibly desire). The categorical imperative would be one which presented an action as of itself objectively necessary, without regard to any other end.[6]

And Kant leaves no doubt as to which of these alone can have any bearing on morality, and why:

> . . . there is one imperative which directly commands a certain conduct without making its condition some purpose to be reached by it. This imperative is categorical. It concerns not the material of the action and its intended result but the form and the principle from which it results. What is essentially good in it consists in the intention, the result being what it may. This imperative may be called the imperative of morality.[7]

It is important to grasp this. A hypothetical imperative is *conditional on* ("if") or *subject to* things, circumstances, goals, and desires; and these, of course, change all the time, are relative to the individual, and so on. But a categorical imperative is *unconditional* (no "ifs") and *independent of* any things, circumstances, goals, or desires. It is for this reason that only a *categorical* imperative can be a *universal* and *binding* law—that is, a *moral* law, valid for all rational beings at all times.

THE TEST OF MORAL ACTIONS

Understandably, the Categorical Imperative, as the fundamental principle of morality, may leave you cold. To be sure, there is no talk here about exciting things like lying, stealing, and committing adultery. Instead, we are confronted by rather abstract talk about maxims and laws, without any particular *content*. It is true. Kant told us above—not in so many words, but at least in these *exact* words—that his Categorical Imperative, the foundation of rational morality, is concerned not with the *matter* but with the *form* of morality. On the other hand, its concern for the *form* is precisely for the sake of getting the *matter* right. Let's try to say this in several ways. The Categorical Imperative

Kant's "formalism"

- Isn't concerned with *what* you do but *how* you do it, since if the *how* is right the *what* will be right.
- Doesn't address specific moral issues but the nature of morality *itself*.
- Doesn't prescribe the rightness or wrongness of *particular* actions but what makes *any* action right or wrong.

---

[6]Ibid., p. 31.
[7]Ibid., p. 33.

THE MURDERER AT THE DOOR

For Kant, consequences are irrelevant to morality, *no matter what*! Probably the most famous example of the strictness of Kant's stance comes with the case of the murderer at the door. Imagine that your friend is hiding in your house and someone comes to the door looking to murder her. Would it be morally acceptable to lie about the whereabouts of your friend? While most of us would almost certainly say, Yes, Kant is firm. Even to the murderer at the door, you must always tell the truth.

If by telling a lie you have in fact hindered someone who was even now planning a murder, then you are legally responsible for all the consequences that might result therefrom. But if you have adhered strictly to the truth, then public justice cannot lay a hand on you, whatever the unforeseen consequence might be. It is indeed possible that after you have honestly answered Yes to the murderer's question as to whether the intended victim is in the house, the latter went out unobserved and thus eluded the murderer, so that the deed would not have come about. However, if you told a lie and said that the intended victim was not in the house, and he has actually (though unbeknownst to you) gone out, with the result that by so doing he has been met by the murderer and thus the deed has been perpetrated, then in this case you may be justly accused as having caused his death. For if you had told the truth as best you knew it, then the murderer might perhaps have been caught by neighbors who came running while he was searching the house for his intended victim, and thus the deed might have been prevented. Therefore, whoever tells a lie, regardless of how good his intentions may be, must answer for the consequences resulting therefrom even before a civil tribunal and must pay the penalty for them, regardless of how unforeseen those consequences may be. This is because truthfulness is a duty that must be regarded as the basis of all duties founded on contract, and the laws of such duties would be rendered uncertain and useless if even the slightest exception to them were admitted.

To be truthful (honest) in all declarations is, therefore, a sacred and unconditionally commanding law of reason that admits of no expediency whatsoever.*

---

*Immanuel Kant, "On a Supposed Right to Lie because of Philanthropic Concerns," supplement to *Grounding for the Metaphysics of Morals*, tr. James W. Ellington (Indianapolis: Hackett, 1993 [1785]), p. 65.

But, of course, this is largely true of any theory of morality. All right, then, we may state it even more strongly. According to Kant, when we seek to make a moral judgment about a possible course of action, what we primarily need to take into account has nothing to do with pleasure, pain, joy, welfare, happiness, Jews hiding in the attic, threats, or the brandishing of guns. Rather, it has to do with—what must seem exceedingly dull and formal by comparison—the possibility of a *contradiction in our action*.

And this brings us back to the way in which the Categorical Imperative is a *test* of moral actions. When embarking on a certain course of action, I must

The Categorical Imperative as a test of moral action

Some examples

ask: Does the universalizing of the principle of my action result in a contradiction? If so, the action fails the test and must be rejected as immoral. But it is important to see what is meant here by "contradiction." It is not a *logical* contradiction as often as a *practical* one. It might help to think of the latter sort of self-contradictory action as a *self-stultifying* or *self-defeating* one.

Kant himself provides some concrete examples of how the application of the Categorical Imperative might result in contradiction and backfire:

> 1. A man who is reduced to despair by a series of evils feels a weariness with life but is still in possession of his reason sufficiently to ask whether it would not be contrary to his duty to himself to take his own life. Now he asks whether the maxim of his action could become a universal law of nature. His maxim, however, is: For love of myself, I make it my principle to shorten my life when by a longer duration it threatens more evil than satisfaction. But it is questionable whether this principle of self-love could become a universal law of nature. One immediately sees a contradiction in a system of nature whose law would be to destroy life by the feeling whose special office is to impel the improvement of life. In this case it would not exist as nature; hence that maxim cannot obtain as a law of nature, and thus it wholly contradicts the supreme principle of all duty.

> 2. Another man finds himself forced by need to borrow money. He well knows that he will not be able to repay it, but he also sees that nothing will be loaned him if he does not firmly promise to repay it at a certain time. He desires to make such a promise, but he has enough conscience to ask himself whether it is not improper and opposed to duty to relieve his distress in such a way. Now, assuming he does decide to do so, the maxim of his action would be as follows: When I believe myself to be in need of money, I will borrow money and promise to repay it, although I know I shall never do so. Now this principle of self-love or of his own benefit may very well be compatible with his whole future welfare, but the question is whether it is right. He changes the pretension of self-love into a universal law and then puts the question: How would it be if my maxim became a universal law? He immediately sees that it could never hold as a universal law of nature and be consistent with itself; rather it must necessarily contradict itself. For the universality of a law which says that anyone who believes himself to be in need could promise what he pleased with the intention of not fulfilling it would make the promise itself and the end to be accomplished by it impossible; no one would believe what was promised to him but would only laugh at any such assertion as vain pretense.

THE CATEGORICAL IMPERATIVE

- It is an *imperative* because it *commands* you to do something.
- It is *categorical* because it commands you to do something *unconditionally*—that is, without regard to consequences or personal desires.

What the Categorical Imperative unconditionally commands is that in situation X you act in such a way as you could will everyone in situation X to act. If you can do that, then you stand a chance of acting from *duty* or out of a concern for what is right.

3. A third finds in himself a talent which could, by means of some cultivation, make him in many respects a useful man. But he finds himself in comfortable circumstances and prefers indulgence in pleasure to troubling himself with broadening and improving his fortunate natural gifts. Now, however, let him ask whether his maxim of neglecting his gifts, besides agreeing with his propensity to idle amusement, agrees also with what is called duty. He sees that a system of nature could indeed exist in accordance with such a law, even though man (like the inhabitants of the South Sea Islands) should let his talents rust and resolve to devote his life merely to idleness, indulgence, and propagation—in a word, to pleasure. But he cannot possibly will that this should become a universal law of nature or that it should be implanted in us by a natural instinct. For, as a rational being, he necessarily wills that all his faculties should be developed, inasmuch as they are given to him for all sorts of possible purposes.

4. A fourth man, for whom things are going well, sees that others (whom he could help) have to struggle with great hardships, and he asks, "What concern of mine is it? Let each one be as happy as heaven wills, or as he can make himself; I will not take anything from him or even envy him; but to his welfare or to his assistance in time of need I have no desire to contribute." If such a way of thinking were a universal law of nature, certainly the human race could exist, and without doubt even better than in a state where everyone talks of sympathy and good will, or even exerts himself occasionally to practice them while, on the other hand, he cheats

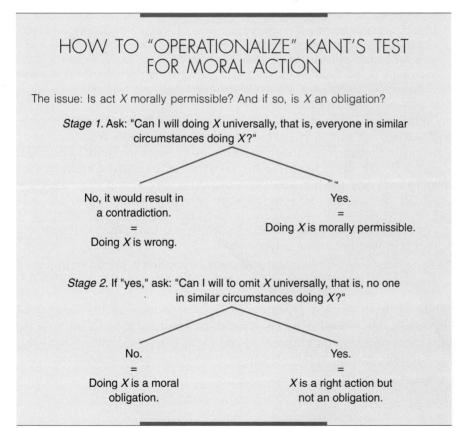

HOW TO "OPERATIONALIZE" KANT'S TEST FOR MORAL ACTION

The issue: Is act X morally permissible? And if so, is X an obligation?

Stage 1. Ask: "Can I will doing X universally, that is, everyone in similar circumstances doing X?"

No, it would result in a contradiction.

=

Doing X is wrong.

Yes.

=

Doing X is morally permissible.

Stage 2. If "yes," ask: "Can I will to omit X universally, that is, no one in similar circumstances doing X?"

No.

=

Doing X is a moral obligation.

Yes.

=

X is a right action but not an obligation.

How might a Kantian reason about the rightness or wrongness of

- Capital punishment?
- Women's rights?
- Racial discrimination?
- War?
- The CIA?
- Abortion?

when he can and betrays or otherwise violates the rights of man. Now although it is possible that a universal law of nature according to that maxim could exist, it is nevertheless impossible to will that such a principle should hold everywhere as a law of nature. For a will which resolved this would conflict with itself, since instances can often arise in which he would need the love and sympathy of others, and in which he would have robbed himself, by such a law of nature springing from his own will, of all hope of the aid he desires.

The foregoing are a few of the many actual duties, or at least of duties we hold to be actual, whose derivation from the one stated principle is clear. We must be able to will that a maxim of our action become a universal law; this is the canon of the moral estimation of our action generally. Some actions are of such a nature that their maxim cannot even be *thought* as a universal law of nature without contradiction, far from it being possible that one could will that it should be such. In others this internal impossibility is not found, though it is still impossible to *will* that their maxim should be raised to the universality of a law of nature, because such a will would contradict itself.[8]

To this point we have spoken in the singular of the Categorical Imperative. Actually, it should be added, Kant provided several formulations of Categorical Imperatives, though these are really best thought of as different versions of the same fundamental principle of morality. Certainly they overlap with one another, and they suggest important and differing ways in which the fundamental principle may be viewed and applied.[9]

Two versions
of the Categorical
Imperative

1. Act only according to that maxim by which you can at the same time will that it should become a universal law.
2. Act so that you treat humanity, whether in your own person or in that of another, always as an end and never as a means only.

While we have focused primarily on the first version of the Categorical Imperative, the second is no less important. Here the focus is on how we treat others and aims for universal respect for all persons. Martin Luther King, Jr., explicitly referred to this version in denouncing racial segregation.

---

[8]Ibid., pp. 39–42.
[9]Ibid., pp. 39, 52.

MARTIN LUTHER KING, JR., ON THE CATEGORICAL IMPERATIVE

"There must be a recognition of the sacredness of human personality. Deeply rooted in our political and religious heritage is the conviction that every man is an heir to a legacy of dignity and worth. . . .

"Segregation stands diametrically opposed to the principle of sacredness of human personality. It debases personality. Immanuel Kant said in one formulation of the *Categorical Imperative* that 'all men must be treated as *ends* and never as mere *means*.' The tragedy of segregation is that it treats men as means rather than ends, and thereby reduces them to things rather than persons. . . .

"But man is not a thing. He must be dealt with, not as an 'animated tool,' but as a person sacred in himself. To do otherwise is to depersonalize the potential person and desecrate what he is."

Martin Luther King, Jr., "The Ethical Demands of Integration," in *A Testament of Hope: The Essential Writings and Speeches of Martin Luther King, Jr.,* ed. James Melvin Washington (San Francisco: Harper & Row, 1986), pp. 118–119.

SOME OBJECTIONS

The first objection might, rather naturally, focus on the moral law itself. Kant assumes throughout that there is a moral law, a sort of moral rhyme and reason to things, a "moral law within" that is just as given as the starry heavens above, and that we can be in harmony with it by obeying the Categorical Imperative. But what if someone were to throw up his or her hands and exclaim, "There is no undergirding and overarching morality— it's all up for grabs!"? Does it not behoove Kant (and most other moral philosophers, as well) to *show* that there is some objective morality that moral philosophy reasons about? How this might be done has been considered in several places already. Do you recall the arguments against nihilism, emotivism, and subjectivism?

Is there a moral law?

Again, if Kant is clear about anything, it is that morality can in no way be based on anything empirical or natural. But why can't one, for instance a *naturalist,* simply turn the tables and say that morality *must* be based on nature—that is, defend naturalistic ethics? You will recall that this was precisely Mill's position, and Mill *followed* Kant, not hesitating to thumb his nose, as it were, at Kant's *a priorism.* Can ethical naturalism be so obviously wrongheaded as Kant made it out to be? But this brings us back to the problems with metaphysical and ethical naturalism themselves.

Back to naturalistic ethics?

Closely related, it has been charged that whatever Kant may have *intended,* his radical distinction between the moral world and the natural

A FEMINIST ALTERNATIVE: THE ETHICS OF CARE

One important response to Kant has come from feminist philosophers. They have argued that traditional moral theories are inadequate because of their exclusive focus on rationality (which is typically associated with masculinity). In particular deontological theories such as Kant's don't adequately account for the moral experience of most women. Feminists claim that rather than thinking of ethics in terms of autonomous individuals and abstract principles, women think of morality in terms of interpersonal relationships and connections. According to this theory, which has been labeled the "ethics of care," moral value resides in maintaining and nurturing caring relationships.

The ethics of care has its roots in the research of Harvard psychologist Carol Gilligan. Gilligan argued against the theory of moral development created by Lawrence Kohlberg, a prominent moral psychologist. From his research, Kohlberg had concluded that people go through different stages in their moral decision making. The highest stage, according to Kohlberg's theory, is very similar to Kant's version of moral reasoning. Women, however, almost never reached this highest stage and tended to get "stuck" at a lower level where moral decisions are based on norms from family and society.

Gilligan rejected the implications of Kohlberg's research that women are morally inferior to men. Her book, *In a Different Voice,* claimed that in their moral decision making women use a type of moral reasoning that is equally mature, but different from men's. Gilligan's research, using primarily women as subjects, led her to conclude that women tend to see ethics in terms of maintaining relationships and personal moral responsibility rather than abstract principles of right and wrong. Men tend to see a moral dilemma as a problem with a right or wrong answer, women

(*continued on next page*)

Downplaying the values of nature

world may have the *effect* of rendering us morally neutral toward nature. That is, it has the effect of stripping nature of its values and downplaying any moral responsibility we may have toward it. This is an especially big criticism in our day when philosophers have been quickened to the issues of environmental ethics and animal rights.

The treatment of nonhuman animals provides a clear example. While Kant argued that we should not be cruel to animals, the reason for this is revealing: Kant had no concern for the animals themselves—since they are not rational beings, they deserve no direct consideration, he argued. He worried, however, that cruelty toward animals could lead to cruelty toward our fellow humans. Thus Kant's is an entirely anthropocentric (human-centered) ethics that includes no obligations to nature.

Faculty psychology?

Another question: Does Kant's theory of morality presuppose a "faculty psychology"? Faculty psychology is the view that divides the person's inner life into distinct and different faculties with their own respective functions and powers. In Kant's theory, desires and inclinations are distinct from and subservient to the will, and the will is something different from

commonly understand such a dilemma as an interpersonal conflict that needs resolution.

In this excerpt from her book, *Speaking from the Heart,* Rita Manning expands upon this approach to ethics:

> An ethic of caring, as I shall defend it, includes two elements. First is a disposition to care. This is a willingness to receive others, a willingness to give the lucid attention required to appropriately fill the needs of others. In this sense, an ethic of care is contextual; my actions must be guided by this lucid attention. . . .
>
> This disposition to care assumes a commitment to an ideal of caring; the ethically preferred world is one in which creatures are caring and cared for. Its institutions support and sustain caring while simultaneously reducing the need for care by eliminating the poverty, despair, and indifference that create a need for care.
>
> Second, in addition to being sensitive to one's place in the world and to one's general obligation to be a caring person, one is also obligated to care for. (I am following Noddings in using "care for" to indicate caring as expressed in action.) In the paradigm case, caring for involves acting in some appropriate way to respond to the needs of persons and animals, but can also be extended to responding to the needs of communities, values, or objects. . . .
>
> I have often wondered if taking a class in moral philosophy was the best way for students to become sensitive to moral concerns. It seemed to me that a better way would be to have students work in soup kitchens or shelters for the homeless.*

---

*Rita Manning, *Speaking from the Heart* (Lanham, MD: Rowman & Littlefield Publishers, 1992).

and subservient to reason. It is a good question whether the activities of our inner lives can be split apart in this way.

Also, it may be objected to Kant's "universalizing" that every law has some exceptions. But a misunderstanding may be involved here. Kant never gave us any universal laws of action, but universal *maxims* of action. The emphasis is not on the *what* but the *how.* In spite of his own (unfortunate?) example of having to tell the truth irrespective of the consequences, his real point is that whether we tell the truth or not, we must act out of a good will or duty and no exceptions to *that*!

Finally, we come to the problem that you may feel more strongly, and that is probably because it is a more *practical* problem. The strict deontologist has told us, perhaps more times than we care to hear, that consequences (or at least the values of various consequences) are irrelevant for moral decision and action. Is this really practical advice? Who of us, knowing full well that, say, telling a lie would result in cruel and innocent suffering, would or could ignore this consequence? And is it not the case that sometimes we *should* wake up in the middle of the night worrying about the

The problem
of exceptions

Can consequences
be ignored?

consequences of some act or other committed the day before? When the chips are down, in a concrete existential situation, Kant's "formalism" might be too formal for its own good. Man does not live by bare principles alone. Does Kant demand of us that we be more rational than we can possibly be, or even should be?

CHAPTER 16 IN REVIEW

SUMMARY

In Chapter 15 we discussed an ethical theory that is both (1) teleological and (2) naturalistic. In this chapter, we have discussed an ethical perspective that is diametrically opposite in both of these respects.

As we have seen, the best example of such a perspective is found in the moral philosophy of Kant, who emphasized that if morality is to be truly necessary and universal, it cannot be based on accidental and fluctuating *empirical* considerations. That is why the consequences of actions are irrelevant for the morality or immorality of an action, as are considerations such as history, human nature, and the like. In the place of any teleological or naturalistic conception of morality, Kant substitutes a completely *a priori* conception: Morality must have a purely *rational* basis. This *a priori* or rational basis of morality is underscored by Kant's well-known pronouncement that only a good will is unconditionally good. That is, it is good in itself. On the other hand, it is a condition for all moral behavior: Without good will anything else, such as power or wealth, would be quickly abused or misappropriated.

What, more exactly, is the good or pure will? It is the intention to act in accordance with moral law, or to act only out of respect for what is right and not for any other reason. Kant formalizes this principle of all morality in the Categorical Imperative: "Act only according to that maxim by which you can at the same time will that it should become a universal law." The ability to universalize (apply to everyone) the rule by which we act in a given situation is a sufficient guarantee of the morality of our action, or that it is being done out of respect for the moral law alone.

As always, this philosophical position too is subject to many criticisms. One of the most common is that it is characterized by a certain abstractness or remoteness. To be sure, it may be difficult to bring to bear a rather lifeless and formal principle like the Categorical Imperative on the concrete and often vivid moral dilemmas we are frequently confronted by. On the other hand, that is just Kant's concern. Do we too easily and quickly decide these issues by obvious and immediate considerations that actually blind us to the real and *rational* basis of moral action?

BASIC IDEAS

- Deontological ethics
- The conditional versus the unconditional *ought*
- Kant's rejection of teleological ethics

- Kant's rejection of naturalistic ethics
- The good will as the basis for morality
- The Categorical Imperative
- Hypothetical versus categorical imperatives
- Kant's "formalism"
- The Categorical Imperative as a test for moral action
- Two versions of the Categorical Imperative
- Ethics of care

TEST YOURSELF

1. True or false: Kant's is a teleological ethics.
2. Which of the following is most relevant for Kant's theory of morality? (a) the well-being of society, (b) consequences of actions, (c) duty, (d) hypothetical imperatives.
3. What do nature, history, sociology, anthropology, or, in a word, *empirical* factors have to do with morality as Kant conceives it?
4. For Kant, the only truly good thing is a _____.
5. Why is Kant's basic principle of morality called the "Categorical Imperative"?
6. A moral proposition of the form "If you want X, then you should do Y" is called a _____ imperative. Why?
7. True or false: The Categorical Imperative isn't concerned with *what* you do but *how* you do it.
8. How is the Categorical Imperative a test for moral actions?

QUESTIONS FOR REFLECTION

- What do you think of the effort to establish morality on a purely *a priori* foundation? Do you believe in an objective moral law? Can such a law be dependent on or conditioned by *a posteriori* factors? What *is* its relation to the natural world?
- It is not quite right, is it, to say that for Kant the consideration of consequences is *utterly* irrelevant for the determination of a moral act. Can you explain *both* sides of Kant's view of consequences?

FOR FURTHER READING

C. D. Broad. *Five Types of Ethical Theory*. London: Routledge & Kegan Paul, 1930. Ch. 5. An exposition and critique of Kant's moral philosophy, from an old but standard work by a well-known philosopher.

Frederick Copleston. *A History of Philosophy*. Baltimore: Newman Press, 1946–1974. VI, Ch. 14. A clear and authoritative account of the essential points in Kant's moral philosophy.

A. C. Ewing. *Ethics*. New York: Free Press, 1953. Ch. 4. A beginner-oriented chapter on the "Duty for Duty's Sake," a summary and (negative) evaluation of Kant's ethics.

William K. Frankena. *Ethics*. Second ed. Englewood Cliffs, NJ: Prentice-Hall, 1973. Ch. 2. An elementary discussion of egoistic and deontological theories, with some specific treatment of Kant's ethics.

Carol Gilligan. *In a Different Voice: Psychological Theory and Women's Development*. Cambridge, MA: Harvard University Press, 1993. A feminist classic showing the differences in moral development between boys and girls.

Justus Hartnack. *Immanuel Kant: An Explanation of His Theory of Knowledge and Moral Philosophy*. Atlantic Highlands, NJ: Humanities Press, 1974. Ch. 3. A brief, clear account of Kant's ethical perspective in relation to his philosophy of religion.

Stephen Körner. *Kant*. Baltimore: Penguin Books, 1955. Ch. 6. A chapter on Kant's moral philosophy, from a standard work on Kant.

Ned Noddings. *Caring: A Feminine Approach to Ethics and Moral Education*. Berkeley: University of California Press, 1986. A clear exposition of the ethics of care by a leading proponent.

H. J. Paton. *The Categorical Imperative: A Study in Kant's Moral Philosophy*. London: Hutchinson, 1946. A complete and authoritative treatment of Kant's moral philosophy, by a foremost Kant scholar.

W. D. Ross. *Kant's Ethical Theory*. London: Oxford University Press, 1954. A full-scale study of Kant's ethical theory.

W. H. Werkmeister. *Theories of Ethics: A Study in Moral Obligation*. Lincoln, NE: Johnsen, 1961. Chs. 8–9. Closely documented and critical studies of the deontological ethics of Kant and some recent revisions of Kantianism.

Robert Paul Wolff (ed.). *Kant: A Collection of Critical Essays*. Garden City, NY: Anchor Books, 1967. Advanced discussions of aspects of Kant's philosophy, including his moral philosophy.

Robert Paul Wolff (ed.). *Kant's Foundations of the Metaphysics of Morals, with Critical Essays*. Indianapolis: Bobbs-Merrill, 1969. A translation of Kant's most important moral work, with worthwhile studies of special issues by nine Kantian scholars.

*In addition, see the relevant articles ("Deontological Ethics," "Kant, Immanuel," etc.) in *Routledge Encyclopedia of Philosophy*, ed. Edward Craig (London: Routledge, 1998), and *Stanford Encyclopedia of Philosophy*, http://plato.stanford.edu.

VIRTUE

We have now seen two different theories of morality: utilitarianism and Kant's ethics of duty. Although these approaches to morality are different, they both share one common feature: They focus on actions. Each theory gives us rules to determine which actions are right and which wrong, and guidance on what actions we should take and which we shouldn't. Utilitarianism, for example, tells us that the right action is the one that results in "the greatest good for the greatest number of people." Kant, on the other hand, argues that we must follow the Categorical Imperative in judging actions. In this last chapter on morality, we will look at a new approach. Actually, it's a very old theory of morality dating back over 2,000 years to the writings of Aristotle.

CHARACTER AND ACTION

Are actions the right focus for morality? That simple question is at the heart of virtue ethics, the traditional approach to ethics favored by Aristotle that has experienced renewed interest recently. Instead of looking at actions, virtue theory focuses on the *actor*, the person who is acting and particularly the character of this person. Virtues are traits of character that manifest themselves in action, but it's the traits themselves that most interest virtue theorists. These traits, they claim, tell us about the whole person, not just individual actions, and this is where we must look for a more complete understanding of morality.

Actor versus actions

417

Different theories
ask different
questions

One way to illustrate the differences between moral theories is to look at the questions they ask. Often the questions asked, even more than the answers given, point to the key differences. Utilitarians and deontologists both ask similar questions: What separates right and wrong actions? What rules should guide behavior? How do we determine the correct answer to individual moral dilemmas? But virtue ethicists are uncomfortable with these questions. Instead of asking, Is this the right thing to do?, they focus on other questions such as: What is a good person? What is the good of human life? What traits of character will lead to a good life? How do we acquire and cultivate these traits? Even when pushed for an answer on a specific action, they still differ in approach. They ask, What would a virtuous person do in this situation? Or how will the varying options affect one's character? None of these questions relate directly to actions. Instead they point to people, to whole people, that is, and the traits that make us who we are. To fully understand this different approach it's best to start from the beginning with Aristotle.

ARISTOTLE ON HAPPINESS AND VIRTUE

Of course Aristotle is not new to us: We encountered his critique of Plato and unique theory of the Forms in Chapter 3; and we explored his empiricism in Chapter 9. Aristotle is one of the philosophical giants who left his mark on nearly all areas of philosophy. But perhaps Aristotle's greatest philosophical work is his *Nicomachean Ethics*, where he lays out his theory of the virtues. Aristotle doesn't, however, start with the virtues. Instead he starts by talking about the good:

Everything aims
at the good

> Every art and every inquiry, and similarly every action and pursuit, is said to aim at some good; and for this reason the good has rightly been declared to be that at which all things aim.

These famous beginning lines set the tone for Aristotle's approach to morality, and it's important to make sure that we understand what he is saying and how it applies to ethics. If all things aim at some good, then what is the good for human beings? Aristotle's answer: *eudaimonia*, a Greek word variously translated as happiness or well-being. *Eudaimonia*/happiness is the highest good because it is complete and self-sufficient; we seek it for its own sake, not as a means to some other end. But Aristotle's idea of happiness might be different from yours, as you can see in this passage from Book I of the *Nicomachean Ethics*:

Eudaimonia =
happiness

> What is always chosen as an end in itself and never as a means to something else is called final in an unqualified sense. This description seems to apply to happiness above all else: for we always choose happiness as an end in itself and never for the sake of something else. Honor, pleasure, intelligence, and all virtue we choose partly for themselves—for we would choose each of them even if no

> "The concepts of obligation and duty—*moral* obligation and *moral* duty, that is to say—and of what is *morally* right and wrong ought to be jettisoned."
>
> —G. E. M. Anscombe

further advantage would accrue from them—but we also choose them partly for the sake of happiness, because we assume that it is through them that we will be happy. On the other hand, no one chooses happiness for the sake of honor, pleasure, and the like, nor as a means to anything at all. . . .

We see then that happiness is something final and self-sufficient and the end of our actions.

To call happiness the highest good is perhaps a little trite, and a clearer account of what it is, is still required. Perhaps this is best done by first ascertaining the proper function of man. For just as the goodness and performance of a flute player, a sculptor, or any kind of expert, and generally of anyone who fulfills some function or performs some action, are thought to reside in his proper function, so the goodness and performance of man would seem to reside in whatever is his proper function. Is it then possible that while a carpenter and a shoemaker have their own proper functions and spheres of action, man as man has none, but was left by nature a good-for-nothing without a function? Should we not assume that just as the eye, the hand, the foot, and in general each part of the body clearly has its own proper function, so man too has some function over and above the functions of his parts? What can this function possibly be? Simply living? He shares that even with plants, but we are now looking for something peculiar to man. Accordingly, the life of nutrition and growth must be excluded. Next in line there is a life of sense perception. But this, too, man has in common with the horse, the ox, and every animal. There remains then an active life of the rational element. The rational element has two parts: one is rational in that it obeys the rule of reason, the other in that it possesses and conceives rational rules. Since the expression "life of the rational element" also can be used in two senses, we must make it clear that we mean a life determined by the activity, as opposed to the mere possession, of the rational element. For the activity, it seems, has a greater claim to be the function of man.

The proper function of man, then, consists in an activity of the soul in conformity with a rational principle or, at least, not without it. In speaking of the proper function of a given individual we mean that it is the same in kind as the function of an individual who sets high standards for himself: the proper function of a harpist, for example, is the same as the function of a harpist who has set high standards for himself. The same applies to any and every group of individuals: the full attainment of excellence must be added to the mere function. In other words,

> "The good of man is an activity of the soul in conformity with virtue."
>
> —Aristotle

ARISTOTLE

Aristotle was born in 384 B.C. in Stagirus in the Greek Colony of Macedon. His father, Nicomachus, was the Macedonian court physician. His father died when Aristotle was 17, and he was sent to Athens to finish his studies. There, Aristotle joined Plato's Academy, where he studied and listened to Plato's lectures for 20 years.

At Plato's death in 347 B.C., Aristotle left Athens for Assos and the court of his friend, Hermeas, ruler of Assos and Atarneus. There he married the king's niece Pythias, and they had a daughter together. After the Persians killed Hermeas, Aristotle left, first for Lesbos and then to Mytilene in Macedon. There he joined the court of Phillip, the king of Macedon, to tutor his son, Alexander, who would go on to become Alexander the Great. At his father's death, Alexander took the throne and Aristotle left Macedon for Athens. There he founded his own school called the Lyceum, where he taught for 13 years.

After the death of his wife Pythias, Aristotle married a woman named Herphyllis, and they had a son together, Nicomachus. Aristotle's great work the *Nicomachean Ethics* is named after his son. The death of Alexander the Great sparked a revolt against anything Macedonian. Aristotle, having close ties to the Macedonian court, was falsely accused of impiety. To escape execution Aristotle fled, "lest the Athenians sin twice against philosophy," a reference to the execution of Socrates in Athens. Aristotle fled to Chalcis, where he died in 322 B.C. at the age of 62.

Aristotle wrote on many topics including politics, poetry, physics, astronomy, biology, and philosophy. He was an incredibly prolific writer—the English translations of Aristotle's existing works fill nearly 2,500 pages. This is, however, only a portion of Aristotle's writing, since many manuscripts have been lost. The books that survive today are generally considered to be his lectures, not writings intended for publication.

the function of the harpist is to play the harp; the function of the harpist who has high standards is to play it well. On these assumptions, if we take the proper function of man to be a certain kind of life, and if this kind of life is an activity of the soul and consists in actions performed in conjunction with the rational element, and if a man of high standards is he who performs these actions well and properly, and if a function is well performed when it is performed in accordance with the excellence appropriate to it; we reach the conclusion that the good of man is an activity of the soul in conformity with excellence or virtue, and if there are several virtues, in conformity with the best and most complete.

But we must add "in a complete life." For one swallow does not make a spring, nor does one sunny day; similarly, one day or a short time does not make a man blessed and happy.[1]

Here Aristotle clearly shows the *teleological* basis of his theory. A *telos* is the end or purpose of a thing. So the telos of a knife is to cut and the telos of a pen is to write. But what is the telos of a human being? What is the function or end or purpose of people? This is clearly not an easy question, but it's essential to the Aristotelian picture. What is it that people do uniquely, that no other creature or thing does? Clearly growth, reproduction, movement, and other activities we share with other living creatures are not the answer. We think and reason—that's what we do that other creatures do not.

So using our reason is the function of humans and acting in accord with virtue is the highest good. But what is a virtue? It's a character trait that we show through our actions. We're all familiar with traits such as honesty, generosity, and the like and these are exactly the virtues that Aristotle had in mind as well.

Let's take a moment to recap Aristotle's argument before talking more specifically about the virtues. Happiness or well-being is the highest good for humans. But happiness is not a mood or emotion for Aristotle, it's much more than that. We can be happy only if we fulfill our basic purpose or function. Humans, that is, must fulfill our *telos*; we must act as humans are supposed to act. The one thing that separates humans from other living things, Aristotle says, is reason. So humans will be happy only if we act according to reason. This use of reason is a virtue. Thus happiness requires that we develop our virtues. How do we develop virtues? In a word, habit, as Aristotle explains:

Virtue, as we have seen, consists of two kinds, intellectual virtue and moral virtue. Intellectual virtue, or excellence, owes its origin and development chiefly to teaching, and for that reason requires experience and time. Moral virtue, on the other hand, is formed by habit, *ethos*, and its name, *ethike*, is therefore derived, by a slight variation, from *ethos*. This shows, too, that none of the moral virtues is implanted in us by nature, for nothing which exists by nature can be changed by habit. For example, it is impossible for a stone, which has a natural downward movement, to become habituated to moving upward, even if one should try ten thousand times to inculcate the habit by throwing it in the air; nor can fire be

A teleological theory

telos = end/purpose

Happiness requires
virtue

[1]Aristotle, *Nicomachean Ethics*, 1097b–1098a, tr. Martin Ostwald (Indianapolis: Bobbs Merrill, 1962), pp. 15–18.

made to move downward, nor can the direction of any nature-given tendency be changed by habituation. Thus, the virtues are implanted in us neither by nature nor contrary to nature: we are by nature equipped with the ability to receive them, and habit brings this ability to completion and fulfillment.

Furthermore, of all the qualities with which we are endowed by nature, we are provided with the capacity first, and display the activity afterward. That this is true is shown by the senses: it is not by frequent seeing or frequent hearing that we acquired our senses, but on the contrary we first possess and then use them; we do not acquire them by use. The virtues, on the other hand, we acquire by first having put them into action, and the same is also true of the arts. For the things which we have to learn before we can do them we learn by doing: men become builders by building houses, and harpists by playing the harp. Similarly, we become just by the practice of just actions, self-controlled by exercising self-control, and courageous by performing acts of courage. . . .

In a word, characteristics develop from corresponding activities. For that reason, we must see to it that our activities are of a certain kind, since any variations in them will be reflected in our characteristics. Hence it is no small matter whether one habit or another is inculcated in us from early childhood; on the contrary, it makes a considerable difference, or, rather, all the difference.[2]

There is one more piece of the puzzle that we must fill in before moving on to talk about specific virtues. We know that humans should strive for virtue, that virtues are character traits, and that they are acquired through habit. But we won't really understand Aristotelian virtue theory until we recognize that virtues are means. At first this might sound strange: Virtues are good things, and isn't meanness the opposite of goodness? A *mean* in this case is a middle or, better yet, a midpoint between two poles or extreme positions. We might say that lukewarm is midway between hot and cold, so it would be a mean.

Virtues as means
between excess and
deficiency

Aristotle believed that all moral virtues are means because with any trait it's possible to have either an excess or a deficiency, and either will lead to a vice. Take, for instance, the case of giving money to others, what we often call charity. It's possible, Aristotle says, to go wrong in two different directions: to give either too much or too little. The excess we call being prodigal, and this is a vice to be wasteful or recklessly extravagant in giving money to others. On the other hand, far more people give little or nothing, and this too is a vice that we might call stinginess. The virtue is the mean between these extremes. The virtuous person is generous in giving her money, but not wasteful; she finds the midpoint and gives the right amount to the right people at the right time.

Likewise with all moral virtues—they are means between extremes. As always, it is best to let the philosophers speak for themselves:

Thus we see that an expert in any field avoids excess and deficiency, but seeks the median and chooses it—not the median of the object but the median relative to us.

If this, then, is the way in which every science perfects its work, by looking to the median and by bringing its work up to that point—and this is the reason why

---

[2]Aristotle, *Nicomachean Ethics*, 1103a 12–1103b 25, pp. 33–35.

VIRTUE

A good trait of character, manifested in habitual action.

it is usually said of a successful piece of work that it is impossible to detract from it or to add to it, the implication being that excess and deficiency destroy success while the mean safeguards it (good craftsmen, we say, look toward this standard in the performance of their work)—and if virtue, like nature, is more precise and better than any art, we must conclude that virtue aims at the median. I am referring to moral virtue: for it is moral virtue that is concerned with emotions and actions, and it is in emotions and actions that excess, deficiency, and the median are found. Thus we can experience fear, confidence, desire, anger, pity, and generally any kind of pleasure and pain either too much or too little, and in either case not properly. But to experience all this at the right time, toward the right objects, toward the right people, for the right reason, and in the right manner—that is the median and the best course, the course that is a mark of virtue.

Similarly, excess, deficiency, and the median can also be found in actions. Now virtue is concerned with emotions and actions; and in emotions and actions excess and deficiency miss the mark, whereas the median is praised and constitutes success. But both praise and success are signs of virtue or excellence. Consequently, virtue is a mean in the sense that it aims at the median. This is corroborated by the fact that there are many ways of going wrong, but only one way which is right—for evil belongs to the indeterminate, as the Pythagoreans imagined, but good to the determinate. This, by the way, is also the reason why the one is easy and the other hard: it is easy to miss the target but hard to hit it. Here, then, is an additional proof that excess and deficiency characterize vice, while the mean characterizes virtue: for "bad men have many ways, good men but one."

We may thus conclude that virtue or excellence is a characteristic involving choice, and that it consists in observing the mean relative to us, a mean which is defined by a rational principle, such as a man of practical wisdom would use to determine it. It is the mean by reference to two vices: the one of excess and the other of deficiency. It is, moreover, a mean because some vices exceed and others fall short of what is required in emotion and in action, whereas virtue finds and chooses the median. Hence, in respect of its essence and the definition of its essential nature virtue is a mean, but in regard to goodness and excellence it is an extreme.[3]

---

[3]Ibid., 1106b 5–1107a 8, pp. 42–44.

VIRTUE AS MEAN BETWEEN EXTREMES

Aristotle claims that all moral virtues are a midpoint or mean between excess and deficiency, both of which are vices. For example, courage is the mean between foolhardiness and cowardice.

By now you should have the basics of the virtue approach to morality. But understanding the general shape of virtue ethics is only half the picture. And probably the least important half. What we need to round things out is more details on specific virtues. What exactly does it mean to show tolerance, compassion, loyalty, or generosity? What did Aristotle mean by courage, temperance, and the like? Obviously, there are many, many virtues and it would be an impossibly large task to discuss them all. So here we'll tackle only a few, mostly traditional ones, but one with a new twist.

Courage

Courage is the first virtue Aristotle discusses in the *Nicomachean Ethics* and thus it is a good place for us to start as well. Courage is the virtue prescribing the proper attitude toward danger or fear, and like all virtues it is a mean between extremes. An excess of fear is cowardice—the cowardly person shrinks from any challenge and hides from all danger. At the opposite extreme, the foolhardy person displays a deficient amount of fear, rushing forward blindly (and foolishly) in the face of danger. To have courage is to find the mean between these vices.

We often think of courage as a military virtue for obvious reasons—clearly soldiers need courage when facing danger in battle. But courage goes far beyond war and is important to all of us. We all face danger and must strive for the right response, the proper balance of our fear. The courageous student is willing to report cheating on an exam in spite of her fears about what others will say. And it takes courage to stand up for one's beliefs when most others disagree.

Temperance

Temperance was a crucial Aristotelian virtue, but it's one that most of us rarely consider. It's the virtue associated with pleasures and pains, but particularly bodily pleasures such as eating, drinking, and sex. These appetites are, as Aristotle notes, "shared with the other animals," and missing the mean nearly always involves excess. The glutton eats too much, the drunkard drinks too much, both showing intemperance in their excessive behavior. But, as Aristotle notes, people who are deficient in pleasures and enjoy them too little are very rare. We don't really even have a name for such a trait, though we may call them insensitive.

Honesty

Honesty is undoubtedly one of the most commonly discussed virtues. But what exactly does it mean to be an honest person? Clearly there's more to it than always telling the truth, for that's no different than Kant's approach based on the moral law. No, the virtue approach to truth-telling involves both more and less than the injunction to always tell the truth. Consider a case where I am intending to lie, but accidentally tell the truth because of my ignorance. Does this show that I am an honest person? Of course not. I'm a liar who made a mistake. Aristotle is clear that it's not enough for virtue simply to commit a good act. In addition, one must act for the right reasons and from the proper state. The virtuous person must know that she is acting virtuously, must decide on the action for its own sake, and must act from a "firm and unchanging state." The honest person not only tells the truth, but does so as a matter of intention and habit.

This is a crucial point in understanding virtues. It's not simply the fact that the virtuous person "does the right thing." No, virtues involve a more holistic understanding of the person—his intentions, thoughts, and attitudes. This comes out clearly in looking at one's attitude toward others—human and nonhuman alike—that is, in the matter of humility.

Humility is commonly touted as a virtue. But, interestingly, Aristotle considered it to be a vice. He saw it as important that people take pride in their accomplishments and not be modest regarding achievement. Aristotle considered it to be a deficiency when someone was humble. But especially in modern times, humility is seen as a mean between arrogance and low self-esteem. To be humble is the mark, we say, of a fine character, one who recognizes his place in society.

A lack of humility is also seen by many as the cause not only of individual arrogance, but also of human destruction of other cultures, species, and ecosystems. The environmental philosopher Thomas Hill, Jr., argues that "destroyers of the environment lack an appreciation of their place in the universe":

So construed, the argument appeals to the common idea that awareness of nature typically has, and should have, a humbling effect. The Alps, a storm at sea, the Grand Canyon, towering redwoods, and "the starry heavens above" move many a person to remark on the comparative insignificance of our daily concerns and even of our species, and this is generally taken to be a quite fitting response. What seems to be missing, then, in those who understand nature but remain unmoved is a proper humility. Absence of proper humility is not the same as selfishness or egoism, for one can be devoted to self-interest while still viewing one's own pleasures and projects as trivial and unimportant. And one can have an exaggerated view of one's own importance while grandly sacrificing for those one views as inferior. Nor is the lack of humility identical with belief that one has power and influence, for a person can be quite puffed up about himself while believing that the foolish world will never acknowledge him. The humility we miss seems not so much a belief about one's relative effectiveness and recognition as an attitude which measures the importance of things independently of their relation to oneself or to some narrow group with which one identifies. A paradigm of a person who lacks humility is the self-important emperor who grants status to his family because it is *his,* to his subordinates because *he* appointed them, and to his country because *he* chooses to glorify it. Less extreme but still lacking proper humility is the elitist who counts events significant solely in proportion to how they affect his class. The suspicion about those who would destroy the environment, then, is that what they count important is too narrowly confined insofar as it encompasses only what affects beings who, like us, are capable of feeling.[4]

As Hill argues, the virtue of humility involves seeing one's proper place and one's true worth. What is interesting here is that the virtue of humility applies not simply to individuals but also to whole cultures and even our

---

[4]Thomas E. Hill, Jr., "Ideals of Human Excellence and Preserving the Natural Environment," *Environmental Ethics* 5 (1983).

A FEW MORAL VIRTUES

Courage	Justice
Temperance	Humility
Generosity	Tolerance
Magnificence	Loyalty
Magnanimity	Compassion
Mildness	Civility
Friendliness	Moderation
Honesty	Self-discipline
Wit	Tactfulness
Prudence	Thoughtfulness

Humility = seeing
one's proper place

species. Humility helps us to see that we are not the center of the universe but are just one species among many. Such an attitude, if widely adopted, would have dramatic effects on human actions. It would clearly prevent any logging or mining, for example, that would push other species toward extinction or permanently harm natural areas. Similarly, the person who believes that his culture is superior to all others lacks proper humility, and correcting this lack would go a long ways to remedying the lingering effects of imperialism and cultural insensitivity. One strength of virtue theory is its ability to extend beyond individual actions to these larger dimensions of morality.

OBJECTIONS

In spite of its growing popularity, virtue ethics still has its problems. Most critics focus on two points. First, they claim that the virtue approach does not help in resolving moral dilemmas or mediating between conflicting values. Second, critics charge that virtue ethics is an incomplete theory. Let's consider each argument a bit more closely.

The virtues and
moral dilemmas

One of the attractions of virtue theory is that it shifts attention away from moral conflicts and toward the neglected area of character. But does the pendulum swing too far? Does virtue theory end up ignoring action and the tough questions of moral dilemmas? Undeniably, ethics involves the question What should I do?, and one major objection to virtue ethics is that it's not helpful in answering this question. Knowing that courage, honesty, and humility are important to the good life is little help when a teenage girl is trying to decide whether or not to abort an unplanned pregnancy. Nor does virtue seem helpful when a doctor is considering whether or not to assist a terminally ill patient in committing suicide. In these cases and others like them, the individuals want to know what to do, which action they should take, what is the morally right path. It's just not obvious, according to the critics, that virtue ethics can tell us how a person should act or how to decide what to do in these cases. The claim that we should act virtuously seems like little help in the face of a difficult and pressing decision. Furthermore, what do we do when we seen to have conflicting virtues? For example, sometimes the virtues of honesty and compassion pull in opposite directions. If I hear students complaining about another class, honesty pushes me to confront the teacher, but compassion will prevent me from telling it like it is. Does virtue theory show us how to resolve these conflicts?

This leads directly to the second objection that virtue, while important, is an incomplete theory. The charge here is that we need to look more closely at what lies beneath the individual virtues. Why should one be courageous or honest or humble? Isn't the ultimate answer going to rely on other concepts or ideas of the good? Isn't it here, in the reasons that support virtues, that more work needs to be done?

Virtue theory
as incomplete

There are, of course, responses to these objections, and the debate continues as more and more philosophers look back to Aristotle for guidance. But there is one more tradition we must consider, which again draws its inspiration from Aristotle.

IS THERE A NATURAL LAW?

One of Aristotle's most important contributions was his insistence on *natural law* as the foundation of our social, political, and ethical structures and institutions. Already in his *Ethics* Aristotle distinguished between conventional law, or law that is established by general agreement, and natural law, which is derived directly from the natural order of the world and from built-in tendencies of human nature. Here, too, is an example of the close connection between the question of reality and the question of value. Aristotle's idea of natural law is part and parcel of his metaphysical view (as you know it from Chapter 3) of objective and fixed essences that define the rationality and orderedness, or *lawfulness,* of things. As with all other fundamental principles, the fundamental principles of our social and ethical life are discoverable in the very *nature* of things. The basic principles of social existence and institutions are not, therefore, "up for grabs"; rather, they are up for rational discovery, expression, and application.

Aristotle
on natural law

In the following paragraphs from *Politics,* Aristotle emphasizes that social organization is derived from nature—that is, from the essential order of things. Notice also that the state, "a creation of nature," is prior to the individual and necessary for the cultivation of human virtue.

"To act in conformity with virtue is nothing but acting, living, and preserving our being as reason directs."

—Spinoza

NATURAL LAW

General and universal rules of conduct, both personal and social, derived rationally from nature.

Hence it is evident that the state is a creation of nature, and that man is by nature a political animal. And he who by nature and not by mere accident is without a state, is either a bad man or above humanity; he is like the

Tribeless; lawless, heartless one

whom Homer denounces—the natural outcast is forthwith a lover of war; he may be compared to an isolated piece at draughts.

Now, that man is more of a political animal than bees or any other gregarious animals is evident. Nature, as we often say, makes nothing in vain, and man is the only animal whom she has endowed with the gift of speech. And whereas mere voice is but an indication of pleasure or pain, and is therefore found in other animals (for their nature attains to the perception of pleasure and pain and the intimation of them to one another, and no further), the power of speech is intended to set forth the expedient and inexpedient, and therefore likewise the just and the unjust. And it is a characteristic of man that he alone has any sense of good and evil, of just and unjust, and the like, and the association of living beings who have this sense makes a family and a state.

Further, the state is by nature clearly prior to the family and to the individual, since the whole is of necessity prior to the part; for example, if the whole body be destroyed, there will be no foot or hand, except in an equivocal sense, as we might speak of a stone hand; for when destroyed the hand will be no better than that. But things are defined by their working and power, and we ought not to say that they are the same when they no longer have their proper quality, but only that they have the same name. The proof that the state is a creation of nature and prior to the individual is that the individual, when isolated, is not self-sufficing; and therefore he is like a part in relation to the whole. But he who is unable to live in society, or who has no need because he is sufficient for himself, must be either a beast or a god: he is no part of a state. A social instinct is implanted in all men by nature, and yet he who first founded the state was the greatest of benefactors. For man, when perfected, is the best of animals, but, when separated from law and justice, he is the worst of all; since armed injustice is the more dangerous, and he is equipped at birth with arms, meant to be used by intelligence and virtue, which he may use for the worst ends. Wherefore, if he have not virtue, he is the most unholy and the most savage of animals, and the most full of lust and gluttony. But justice is the bond of men in states, for the administration of justice, which is the determination of what is just, is the principle of order in political society.[5]

[5]Aristotle, *Politics*, 1253a–b, tr. Benjamin Jowett, in *Basic Works of Aristotle*, ed. Richard McKeon (New York: Random House, 1941).

ST. THOMAS: FOUR KINDS OF LAW

- *Eternal law:* God's unalterable rule over all things.
- *Natural law:* Universal rules of conduct known from human nature.
- *Human law:* Statutes and legislation contrived by humans.
- *Divine law:* Specially revealed will of God for humanity's supernatural or religious end.

It has been seen already how St. Thomas took over much of Aristotle's philosophy and transformed it in a Christian light. Certainly this happened in the case of Aristotle's idea of natural law, and St. Thomas' Christianized version has become one of its most forceful expressions. Actually, St. Thomas distinguished *four* kinds of law, and it is necessary to spell out all of them if we are to appreciate the character and role of natural law in specific. (1) *Eternal law* is the governance of all things by the divine reason and, by virtue of its foundation in God himself, is unalterable and eternal. (2) *Natural law* refers to the eternal law as it is revealed specifically in human nature and known by human reason, which is an offspring of the divine reason; it provides direction for humanity's natural end—that is, its purpose in *this* world. (3) *Human law* refers to specific statutes and legislation contrived by humans in an attempt to express and apply the natural law to concrete and practical situations. (4) *Divine law* provides the direction for humanity's supernatural end—that is, its purpose for God and *eternity*—and is known only through divine grace and special revelation rather than through reason.

In St. Thomas' thinking, all of these are inseparably related to one another. Not to play down any of them, clearly the second and third hold the most relevance for our present discussion. Eternal law is an interesting metaphysical idea; divine law is an interesting religious or theological idea; but natural law and human law bear directly on ethical and political issues. In the following, from *Summa Theologiae,* St. Thomas comments especially on these:

> . . . law, being a rule and measure, can be in a person in two ways: in one way, as in him that rules and measures; in another way, as in that which is ruled and measured, since a thing is ruled and measured in so far as it partakes of the rule or measure. Therefore, since all things subject to divine providence are ruled and measured by the eternal law, as was stated above, it is evident that all things partake in some way in the eternal law, in so far as, namely, from its being imprinted on them, they derive their respective inclinations to their proper acts and ends. Now among all others, the rational creature is subject to divine providence in a more excellent way, in so far as it itself partakes of a share of providence, by being provident both for itself and for others. Therefore it has a share of the eternal reason, whereby it has a natural inclination to its proper act and end; and this participation of the eternal law in the rational creature is called the natural law. Hence the Psalmist, after saying (*Ps. iv. 6*): "Offer up the

St. Thomas: four kinds of law

St. Thomas Aquinas, not surprisingly, believed
that all law is rooted in God.

sacrifice of justice," as though someone asked what the works of justice are, adds: "Many say, Who showeth us good things?" in answer to which question he says: "The light of Thy countenance, O Lord, is signed upon us." He thus implies that the light of natural reason, whereby we discern what is good and what is evil, which is the function of the natural law, is nothing else than an imprint on us of the divine light. It is therefore evident that the natural law is nothing else than the rational creature's participation of the eternal law.

. . . a law is a dictate of the practical reason. Now it is to be observed that the same procedure takes place in the practical and in the speculative reason, for each proceeds from principles to conclusions, as was stated above. Accordingly, we conclude that, just as in the speculative reason, from naturally known indemonstrable principles we draw the conclusions of the various sciences, the knowledge of which is not imparted to us by nature, but acquired by the efforts of reason, so too it is that from the precepts of the natural law, as from common and indemonstrable principles, the human reason needs to proceed to the more particular determination of certain matters. These particular determinations, devised by human reason, are called human laws, provided that the other essential conditions of law be observed, as was stated above. Therefore Tully says in his *Rhetoric* that "justice has its source in nature; thence certain things came into custom by reason of their utility; afterwards these things which emanated from nature, and were approved by custom, were sanctioned by fear and reverence for the law."[6]

---

[6]St. Thomas Aquinas, *Summa Theologiae,* Pts. I–II, Qu. 91, Arts. 2–3, in *Basic Writings of St. Thomas Aquinas,* ed. Anton C. Pegis (Indianapolis, IN: Hackett, 1997), II.

> ". . . the light of natural reason, whereby we discern what is good and what is evil, which is the function of the natural law, is nothing else than an imprint on us of the divine light."
>
> —St. Thomas

It is important to see that although St. Thomas' doctrine of natural law was all wrapped up in a Christian view of reality, one does not have to be a Christian to believe in natural law: St. Thomas was, but Aristotle wasn't. What *is* required, however, is at least a *general* view of reality (which Aristotle and St. Thomas did in fact share) such that value in general, and moral and political values in specific, are seen as built right into the world and human nature from the start, and can be, as we said before, rationally discovered, expressed, and applied. Thus, while this does not presuppose a Christian perspective, it is no accident that the idea of natural law has been propounded mainly by thinkers of a religious or theistic bent. For such people believe, for one reason or another, that the universe is rational, that there is a rhyme and reason to things, and that values have an objective and abiding foundation.

Values in the world

To sum up, a morality based on natural law requires three things: first, a view of reality as a rational order with values built right into the world, including into human nature; second, an interpretation of the laws of nature such that they express not only what *is* the case, but also what *ought* to be; and finally, an understanding of moral judgments as "dictates of reason." Human reason is what allows us to discover natural laws and helps us to discern the right course of action. No one was more adamant about this point than St. Thomas, who argued that following reason and being a Christian were one and the same.

Moral judgments are "dictates of reason"

As with all theories we've studied, natural law has its difficulties. Here we will limit ourselves to two. First, many critics reject the metaphysical view on which natural law rests as inconsistent with the findings of modern science. Especially since Darwin, the idea that nature has values and purposes and functions in an orderly way has been under attack. Rather, critics say, things just happen more or less randomly. There is no plan or order to the workings of nature, it is simply the blind actions of the individual players. This is a serious charge since without a rational world natural law is lost.

Objections to natural law

> "To disparage the dictate of reason is equivalent to condemning the command of God."
>
> —St. Thomas Aquinas

A second criticism looks to the now familiar Naturalistic Fallacy. Nowhere is the move from *is* to *ought* more direct than in natural law with its claims that the natural functions of organisms define morality. If Hume is correct that you cannot derive values from facts, critics charge, then clearly we cannot find our moral guidance in the laws of nature. But as always we must be careful not to move too quickly here, especially with someone like Aristotle. As we saw earlier, what virtue means for Aristotle is simply performing our human function well. With this view the very distinction between facts and values has disappeared and with it the Naturalistic Fallacy. The critic, of course, has a response, but the time has come for us to move on to the question of society.

CHAPTER 17 IN REVIEW

SUMMARY

In this final chapter on the question of morality we took a turn away from actions and toward the character of the people acting. Virtue theory insists that morality is not a matter of rules and principles, but rather traits of character.

Aristotle's teleology is the foundation of the virtues. He argues that the purpose or good of humans is the use of reason to live a good life. Thus happiness is the ultimate good for humans, the one thing that we seek exclusively for its own sake and not as a means to other goods. The key to this happiness, for Aristotle, is virtue, established traits of character that manifest themselves in action. These virtues are means between the vices of excess and deficiency. The virtue approach has been criticized for ignoring tough moral choices and for its incompleteness.

We have already seen more than once how the Christian philosopher St. Thomas Aquinas was influenced by Aristotle, and this connection shows up again in their ethical and political ideas. Specifically, the important notion of natural law has deep roots in the Aristotelian-Thomistic tradition. Aristotle had already distinguished between conventional law (established by agreement) and natural law (rationally apprehended from nature), and St. Thomas elaborated the fourfold distinction: eternal law, natural law, human law, and divine law. According to St. Thomas, God is the foundation of all spheres of law, including natural law, which can be known rationally and which expresses the will of God for human beings in this world, and which is imperfectly expressed in human law, or legislation for our practical and social life together.

BASIC IDEAS

- Character versus action
- Aristotle on the good for humans
- Teleology
- Happiness

- Virtue
- A mean between extremes
- Some virtues:
    Courage
    Temperance
    Honesty
    Humility
- Natural law
- Aristotle: the human being as a "political animal"
- St. Thomas' four kinds of law:
    Eternal law
    Natural law
    Human law
    Divine law

TEST YOURSELF

1. What does Aristotle say is the function of human beings?
2. Courage is a mean between what two vices?
3. True or false: St. Thomas believed that natural law is the highest type of law.
4. How might it be claimed that Aristotle's doctrine of natural law is part and parcel of his metaphysics?
5. Who said it? ". . . the natural is nothing else than the rational creature's participation of the eternal law."

QUESTIONS FOR REFLECTION

- Virtue theory focuses on character rather than action, but obviously both are important. Can you think of ways to combine the insights from differing approaches to morality? What do you see as the most important elements of each theory, and how might we preserve the truth in each?
- What is the importance of the idea of natural law? How is it at once a metaphysical, epistemological, ethical, and social-political concept? Do you believe in it?

FOR FURTHER READING

Frederick Copleston. *A History of Philosophy.* Baltimore: Newman Press, 1946–1974. I, Ch. 31. A clear, succinct account of Aristotelian ethics including his concept of virtue, from a standard work.

Philippa Foot. *Virtues and Vices and Other Essays in Moral Philosophy.* Berkeley: University of California Press, 1978. A collection of essays by one of the philosophers who brought virtue theory back to the mainstream.

Etienne Gilson. *The Christian Philosophy of St. Thomas Aquinas.* Tr. L. K. Shook. New York: Random House, 1956. Part III, Ch. 1, sect. 4. A short account of St. Thomas' conception of law (eternal, natural, human), by a foremost Thomist authority.

Alasdair MacIntyre. *After Virtue: A Study in Moral Theory.* South Bend, IN: University of Notre Dame Press, 1981. One of the most important contemporary defenses of the virtue tradition.

D. J. O'Connor. *Aquinas and Natural Law.* London: Macmillan, 1968. A good introductory account of the theory of natural law.

James Rachels. *The Elements of Moral Philosophy.* Second ed. New York: McGraw-Hill, 1993. Chs. 4 and 12 on natural law and virtue. This little book is an excellent introduction to ethics.

Daniel Statman. *Virtue Ethics: A Critical Reader.* Washington, DC: Georgetown University Press, 1997. A collection of important essays on virtue ethics with a clear, systematic introduction to this approach.

J. O. Urmson. *Aristotle's Ethics.* Oxford: Basil Blackwell, 1988. The best short introduction to the ethical thinking and writings of Aristotle.

*In addition, see the relevant articles ("Aristotle," "Virtue," "Natural Law," etc.) in *Routledge Encyclopedia of Philosophy,* ed. Edward Craig (London: Routledge, 1998), and *Stanford Encyclopedia of Philosophy,* http://plato.stanford.edu.

PART FIVE

THE QUESTION
OF SOCIETY

It is a fine line—if any exists at all—between the question of moral values and the question of social and political values. Does not any ethical theory hold immediate implications for the larger context of the community or state? Can you imagine yourself in pursuit of your own good in complete independence of your social context? in complete indifference to it? Do not such issues as fairness, justice, freedom, and rights force themselves into the picture at some point? Consider the following list of sample issues:

- Civil disobedience
- Welfare
- Nuclear armament
- Women's rights
- Eugenics
- Racial discrimination
- Labor unions
- Pornography
- Abortion

Are these ethical issues? Are they social and political issues? Are they not clearly *both* ethical *and* social-political issues? Look at each one until you can say exactly how it involves and poses both an ethical and a social-political problem.

Another point: Social and political philosophy may appear to overlap at times with the social sciences, such as sociology and political science, but its task is really a different one. The social-political philosopher is not concerned with descriptive or empirical questions (we might call these "surface" questions), but with *normative* questions, or questions of *value:* What *is* the public good? How *should* it be implemented? What is the *basis* for talk of rights and justice?

LIBERTY

t is hardly possible to examine all of even the most relevant social-political theories. To be sure, in the next chapter we will look fairly carefully at democracy and the issues and perspectives that bear most importantly on our own contemporary situation. Following that we will raise the more general but fundamental idea of justice. For the moment, though, we will look at liberalism, not only because of intrinsic interest but also because of the way it sets the stage for subsequent developments.

THE LIBERAL PERSPECTIVE: LOCKE

When you see the word "liberal" you may think of something leftish or socialistic—something opposite to "conservative." In our present context, however, the word refers to a general social-political theory that, indeed, underlies our *whole* social and political system, including *both* liberals and conservatives. We might better call it *classical* liberalism. The heart of liberalism in this sense is evident from the word itself. "Liberalism" comes from the Latin *libertas,* "liberty" or "freedom." It insists on the freedom of the individual: both freedom *from* undue external and governmental controls, and freedom *to* pursue individual interests. Can you identify examples of *freedoms from* and *freedoms to,* in the first ten amendments to the U.S. Constitution? (They were ratified on December 15, 1791.)

Classical liberalism: freedom

439

JOHN LOCKE

John Locke was born in 1632 in a small town near Bristol, England, lost his mother at an early age, and was raised on Puritan principles by a stern father. His childhood studies centered on grammar and languages (Greek, Latin, Hebrew, and Arabic) and were so harsh as to cause Locke later to condemn excessive discipline in schools. Out of these austere beginnings, in 1652 the twenty-year-old Locke entered Oxford University. In spite of a distaste for Scholastic philosophy, which he thought obscure and irrelevant, he received his BA in 1656, followed by his MA, and became a tutor at Oxford in Greek and Latin.

After his father's death in 1661, which resulted in a small inheritance, Locke fell under the spell of the new sciences, and his interest in experimental and empirical methods came alive. Indeed, he now chose for himself the medical profession, though, as it turned out, he never actually practiced—except for delivering a baby

(*continued on next page*)

Amendment I

Congress shall make no law respecting an establishment of religion, or prohibiting the free exercise thereof; or abridging the freedom of speech, or of the press; or the right of the people peaceably to assemble, and to petition the Government for a redress of grievances.

Amendment II

A well regulated Militia, being necessary to the security of a free State, the right of the people to keep and bear Arms, shall not be infringed.

and removing a tumor from someone's chest. He was sidetracked by Descartes, who seemed to provide an impressive alternative to the still-dominant Scholastic philosophy.

In 1667, a close association with Lord Ashley, later first earl of Shaftesbury, thrust Locke into many political affairs and offices. He participated, for example, in drafting the constitution of the Crown Colony of Carolina. Largely for reasons of health, he spent 1675–1679 in France, where he pursued further his interest in Descartes. Upon his return to England he found that the continuing struggle against the divine right of kings lay somewhat closer to home. His friend Shaftesbury was in deep trouble with King Charles II because of his promotion of the common class against the king and nobles: He was dispatched to the Tower of London, eventually tried for treason, and acquitted. And Locke's own position was none too certain either. It was guilt by association, and he too was now denounced as a traitor. He fled to Holland in 1683 and hid in the house of a physician friend. Here he continued work on his *Essay Concerning Human Understanding* and produced several other pieces. The revolutionary plot of 1688 to place William of Orange on the English throne was successful, with some help from Locke himself, and in February 1689 he returned to England, escort of the princess of Orange, the future Queen Mary.

Locke's two most influential books were published in 1690: the *Essay* and *Two Treatises of Civil Government;* the first is a classic of empiricist epistemology, and in the latter Locke attacked the divine right of kings and proposed his own liberal political theory. During this time he continued to be actively occupied with the affairs of state, his practical contributions being much in demand.

In 1691, the aging Locke settled permanently in Oates, at the home of his friends Lord and Lady Marsham, continuing with his writing and participating in the controversy surrounding his *The Reasonableness of Christianity,* published in 1695. During his last and failing years he turned to biblical studies and wrote commentaries on the epistles of St. Paul. He died on October 28, 1704, as Lady Marsham was reading to him from the Psalms. She wrote: "His death was like his life, truly pious, yet natural, easy and unaffected." He was a giant in the history of philosophy, having contributed a monumental work on epistemology and having been a decisive voice for individual freedom and religious tolerance.

His major works include *Essay Concerning Human Understanding, First Letter Concerning Toleration, Two Treatises of Civil Government, Some Thoughts Concerning Education,* and *The Reasonableness of Christianity.*

Amendment III

No Soldier shall, in time of peace be quartered in any house, without the consent of the Owner, nor in time of war, but in a manner to be prescribed by law.

Amendment IV

The right of the people to be secure in their persons, houses, papers, and effects, against unreasonable searches and seizures, shall not be violated, and no Warrants shall issue, but upon probable cause, supported by Oath or affirmation, and particularly describing the place to be searched, and the person or things to be seized.

Amendment V

No person shall be held to answer for a capital, or otherwise infamous crime, unless on a presentment or indictment of a Grand Jury, except in cases arising in the land or naval forces, or in the Militia, when in actual service in time of War or public danger; nor shall any person be subject for the same offence to be twice put in jeopardy of life or limb; nor shall be compelled in any Criminal Case to be a witness against himself, nor be deprived of life, liberty, or property, without due process of law; nor shall private property be taken for public use, without just compensation.

Amendment VI

In all criminal prosecutions the accused shall enjoy the right to a speedy and public trial, by an impartial jury of the State and district wherein the crime shall have been committed, which district shall have been previously ascertained by law, and to be informed of the nature and cause of the accusation; to be confronted with the witnesses against him; to have compulsory process for obtaining Witnesses in his favor, and to have the Assistance of Counsel for his defence.

Amendment VII

In suits at common law, where the value of controversy shall exceed twenty dollars, the right of trial by jury shall be preserved, and no fact tried by a jury, shall be otherwise re-examined in any Court of the United States, than according to the rules of the common law.

Amendment VIII

Excessive bail shall not be required, nor excessive fines imposed, nor cruel and unusual punishments inflicted.

Amendment IX

The enumeration in the Constitution, of certain rights, shall not be construed to deny or disparage others retained by the people.

Amendment X

The powers not delegated to the United States by the Constitution, nor prohibited by it to the States, are reserved to the States respectively, or to the people.[1]

Classical liberalism may also be called *individualism,* inasmuch as it affirms the individual over the state, which is seen not as the master but as the servant of the individual, and as the guarantor of the individual's interests and rights.

The primary moving force of the classical liberal perspective was the English philosopher John Locke, who, as we saw in Chapter 9, was also one of the founders of modern empiricism. Several ideas are basic to an understanding of Locke's social-political theory.

---

[1]William MacDonald (ed.), *Documentary Source Book of American History, 1606–1926,* 3rd ed. (New York: Burt Franklin, 1926), pp. 229–230 (slightly edited).

CLASSICAL LIBERALISM

The social-political theory that stresses freedom from undue governmental interference and views the state as the guarantor of the basic liberties and rights of
the individual.

First, like many who preceded him, Locke believed that all private and
public good is based on the *natural law* that immediately displays fundamental rights and liberties. As with St. Thomas, the real foundation of
the natural law is God. And, as with St. Thomas, this natural and divine
law is "plain and intelligible to all rational creatures"—at least to as
many who will take the time and trouble. (Locke's idea of natural law
was no more a contradiction to his empiricism than was St. Thomas' idea
a contradiction to *his* empiricism. Knowledge, natural law, and all other
ideas as well result from reflection on experience.) Both of these ideas—
namely, that God is the objective source of natural law, and that this law
can be discovered rationally—are clear in the following lines from the
Essay Concerning Human Understanding:

> The idea of a Supreme Being, infinite in power, goodness, and wisdom, whose
> workmanship we are, and on whom we depend; and the idea of ourselves, as
> understanding, rational beings, being such as are clear in us, would, I suppose,
> if duly considered and pursued, afford such foundations of our duty and rules of
> action as might place *morality amongst the sciences capable of demonstration:*
> wherein I doubt not, but from self-evident propositions, by necessary consequences,
> as incontestable as those in mathematics, the measures of right and wrong might
> be made out, to any one that will apply himself with the same indifferency and
> attention to the one as he does to the other of those sciences.[2]

Next is Locke's idea of the *state of nature.* Others before him had stressed
the state of nature as the only adequate starting point for the development
of a system of social and political life. For we must seek to understand what
the human situation *really* is, before this becomes possibly confused or distorted by the imposition of the rules and regulations of civil government.
For example, it was very important for Locke, in his time, to question and
challenge the prevailing notion of the divine right of kings—that monarchs
are established by God, and that all others are, therefore, by nature subservient to them. Locke asks whether this is justified by an analysis of humanity in its *natural* state. And he answers with a resounding No! The natural
state is governed by natural law, and natural law legislates *freedom, equality,*
and therefore *inherent rights for all.*

Natural law, again

The "state of nature"

---

[2]John Locke, *Essay Concerning Human Understanding,* IV, 3, 18, ed. A. S. Pringle-Pattison (Oxford:
Clarendon Press, 1924).

The *state of nature* has a law of nature to govern it, which obliges everyone: and reason, which is that law, teaches all mankind, who will but consult it, that, being all *equal and independent,* no one ought to harm another in his life, health, liberty or possessions.[3]

Such a conclusion may not seem so striking today. But that only shows how deeply influenced our own values are by Locke's ideas, which, in his time, were certainly striking enough. It was a question of the *divine right of royalty* and the *divine royalty of right.*

The theoretical state of nature is, thus, very important. But it is only theoretical. In spite of its advantages of freedom and equality, we do not, nor can we, actually live in such a state, at least not for long. In the selection below, Locke tells us why. For one thing, most people do not pay sufficient attention to the rational dictates of natural law, and even if they did, their selfish concerns would prevent an unbiased application of it. Second, in such a state there would be no way of judging or arbitrating between the differences that would inevitably arise. And even so, third, no such judgment would have backing or authority so that it could be meaningfully enforced. Locke mentions these specific problems, but you can easily imagine others that would make life in a state of nature impossible from a practical standpoint. The conclusion: Men are quickly driven into society.

The social contract

Enter the idea of the *social contract.* As you know, any contract involves giving up something and getting something in return. A *social* contract is an agreement between members of a society according to which each forfeits certain rights and privileges in order to preserve others. Thus I see that it is much to my advantage to submit myself to government, to obey laws, and so on, if thereby I can secure my fundamental freedoms and rights, and *especially* if I, as one of the contractors, have a say, either directly (pure democracy) or indirectly (as in representative democracy), in the character of that government, its law, and the like.

[3]John Locke, *Second Treatise of Government,* 6, ed. C. B. Macpherson (Indianapolis: Hackett, 1980).

LOCKE'S FOURFOLD BASIS OF CLASSICAL LIBERALISM

- *Natural law:* The rationally knowable morality that is founded in God's will for his creatures.

- *State of nature:* The human condition of natural freedoms and rights prior to the imposition of social organization and regulation.

- *Social contract:* The agreement among a group of people to establish social organizations and regulations for the preservation of basic freedoms and rights.

- *Tacit consent:* The consent to and support of social organizations and regulations by virtue of an individual's continued participation in them.

It is important to see that the order of (1) state of nature and (2) social contract is a *logical* rather than a *historical* order. How many of us have ever actually lived in a state of nature? Do we not, rather, just find ourselves already members of some social system? No matter. That does not undermine the idea of the social contract, for as long as we remain in such a system (however we got there) we give *tacit consent*, says Locke, to that system. That is, the social contract is not necessarily something that is drawn up "once upon a time," but rather all the time: By their participation in the system, the members *continually* consent to, agree to, and support the contract.

"Tacit consent"

Of the Beginning of Political Societies

Men being, as has been said, by nature, all free, equal, and independent, no one can be put out of this estate, and subjected to the political power of another, without his own consent. The only way whereby any one divests himself of his natural liberty, and puts on the *bonds of civil society,* is by agreeing with other men to join and unite into a community for their comfortable, safe, and peaceable living one amongst another, in a secure enjoyment of their properties, and a greater security against any, that are not of it. This any number of men may do, because it injures not the freedom of the rest; they are left as they were in the liberty of the state of nature. When any number of men have so *consented to make one community or government,* they are thereby presently incorporated, and make *one body politic,* wherein the *majority* have a right to act and conclude the rest.

For when any number of men have, by the consent of every individual, made a *community,* they have thereby made that *community* one body, with a power to act as one body, which is only by the will and determination of the *majority:* for that which acts any community, being only the consent of the individuals of it, and it being necessary to that which is one body to move one way; it is necessary the body should move that way whither the greater force carries it, which is the *consent of the majority:* or else it is impossible it should act or continue one body, *one community,* which the consent of every individual that united into it, agreed that it should; and so everyone is bound by that consent to be concluded by the *majority.* And therefore we see, that in assemblies, impowered to act by positive laws, where no number is set by that positive law which impowers them, the *act of the majority* passes for the act of the whole, and of course determines, as having, by the law of nature and reason, the power of the whole.

And thus every man, by consenting with others to make one body politic under one government, puts himself under an obligation, to every one of that society, to submit to the determination of the *majority,* and to be concluded by it; or else this *original compact,* whereby he with others incorporates into *one society,* would signify nothing, and be no compact, if he be left free, and under no other ties than he was in before in the state of nature. For what appearance would there be of any compact? What new engagement if he were no farther tied by any decrees of the society, than he himself thought fit, and did actually consent to? This would be still as great a liberty, as he himself had before his compact, or anyone else in the state of nature hath, who may submit himself, and consent to any acts of it if he thinks fit.

For if *the consent of the majority* shall not, in reason, be received as *the act of the whole,* and conclude every individual; nothing but the consent of every individual can make anything to be the act of the whole: but such a consent is next to impossible ever to be had if we consider the infirmities of health, and avocations of business, which in a number, though much less than that of a common-wealth, will necessarily keep many away from the public assembly. To which if we add the variety of opinions, and contrariety of interests, which unavoidably happen in all collections of men, the coming into society be upon such terms it will be only like *Cato's* coming into the theater, only to go out again. Such a constitution as this would make the mighty *Leviathan* of a shorter duration, than the feeblest creatures, and not let it outlast the day it was born in: which cannot be supposed, till we can think, that rational creatures should desire and constitute societies only to be dissolved: for where the *majority* cannot conclude the rest, there they cannot act as one body, and consequently will be immediately dissolved again.

Whosoever therefore out of a state of nature unite into a *community* must be understood to give up all the power, necessary to the ends for which they unite into society, to the *majority* of the community, unless they expressly agreed in any number greater than the majority. And this is done by barely agreeing to *unite into one political society,* which is *all the compact* that is, or needs be, between the individuals, that enter into, or make up a *common-wealth*. And thus that, which begins and actually *constitutes any political society,* is nothing but the consent of any number of freemen capable of a majority to unite and incorporate into such a society. And this is that, and that only, which did, or could give beginning to any *lawful government* in the world.

Of the Ends of Political Society and Government

If man in the state of nature be so free, as has been said; if he be absolute lord of his own person and possessions, equal to the greatest, and subject to no body, why will he part with his freedom? why will he give up his empire, and subject himself to the dominion and control of any other power? To which it is obvious to answer, that though in the state of nature he hath such a right, yet the enjoyment of it is very uncertain, and constantly exposed to the invasions of others: for all being kings as much as he, every man his equal, and the greater part no strict observers of equity and justice, the enjoyment of the property he has in this state is very unsafe, very unsecure. This makes him willing to quit a condition, which, however free, is full of fears and continual dangers: and it is not without reason, that he seeks out, and is willing to join in society with others, who are already united, or have a mind to unite, for the mutual *preservation* of their lives, liberties and estates, which I call by the general name, *property*.

The great and *chief end,* therefore, of men's uniting into common-wealths, and putting themselves under government, *is the preservation of their property*. To which in the state of nature there are many things wanting.

First, There wants an *established,* settled, known *law,* received and allowed by common consent to be the standard of right and wrong, and the common measure to decide all controversies between them: for though the law of nature be plain and intelligible to all rational creatures; yet men being biased by their interest, as well as ignorant for want of study of it, are not apt to allow of it as a law binding to them in the application of it to their particular cases.

Secondly, In the state of nature there wants a *known and indifferent judge,* with authority to determine all differences according to the established law: for everyone in that state being both judge and executioner of the law of nature, men being partial to themselves, passion and revenge is very apt to carry them too far, and with too much heat, in their own cases; as well as negligence, and unconcernedness, to make them remiss in other men's.

Thirdly, In the state of nature there often wants *power* to back and support the sentence when right, and to give it due *execution.* They who by any injustice offended, will seldom fail, where they are able, by force to make good their injustice; such resistance many times makes the punishment dangerous, and frequently destructive, to those who attempt it.

Thus mankind, notwithstanding all the privileges of the state of nature, being but in an ill condition, while they remain in it, are quickly driven into society. Hence it comes to pass, that we seldom find any number of men live any time together in this state. The inconveniences that they are therein exposed to, by the irregular and uncertain exercise of the power every man has of punishing the transgressions of others, make them take sanctuary under the established laws of government, and therein seek *the preservation of their property.* It is this makes them so willingly give up everyone his single power of punishing, to be exercised by such alone, as shall be appointed to it amongst them; and by such rules as the community, or those authorized by them to that purpose, shall agree on. And in this we have the original *right and rise of both the legislative and executive power,* as well as of the governments and societies themselves. . . .

But though men, when they enter into society, give up the equality, liberty, and executive power they had in the state of nature, into the hands of the society, to be so far disposed of by the legislative, as the good of the society shall require; yet it being only with an intention in everyone the better to preserve himself, his liberty and property; (for no rational creature can be supposed to change his condition with an intention to be worse) the power of the society, or *legislative* constituted

A page from Locke's *Concerning Education,*
published in 1695

Of EDUCATION.   223

to be made, and what weight they
out to have.

§. 177. *Rhetorick* and *Logick* being *Rhetorick.*
the Arts that in the ordinary method *Logick.*
ufually follow immediately after Grammar, it may perhaps be wondered that
I have faid fo little of them: The reafon is, becaufe of the little advantage
young People receive by them: For I
have feldom or never obferved any one
to get the Skill of reafoning well, or
fpeaking handfomly by ftudying thofe
Rules, which pretend to teach it: And
therefore I would have a young Gen-
tleman take a view of them in the
fhorteft Syftems could be found, without dwelling long on the contemplation and ftudy of thofe Formalities,
Right Reafoning is founded on fome-
thing elfe than the *Predicaments* and *Pre-
dicables,* and does not confift in talking
in *Mode* and *Figure* it felf. But 'tis be-
fides my prefent Bufinefs to enlarge upon this Speculation: To come therefore to what we have in hand; if you
would have your Son *Reafon well,* let
him read *Chillingworth;* and if you
would have him fpeak well, let him
be converfant in *Tully,* to give him
the

THE INTERNATIONAL DECLARATION
OF THE RIGHTS OF MAN*

The Institute of International Law, considering that the juridic conscience of the civilized world demands the recognition of the individual's rights exempted from all infringements on the part of the State;

That the Declarations of Rights inscribed in a great many constitutions and notably in the American and French constitutions of the end of the eighteenth century, enacted laws not only for the citizen, but for the human being;

That the Fourteenth Amendment to the Constitution of the United States declares that no State shall "deprive any person of life, liberty, or property without due process of the law, nor deny to any person within its jurisdiction the equal protection of the laws";

That the Supreme Court of the United States, in a unanimous decision, ruled that, by the terms of this amendment, it applied within the jurisdiction of the United States "to all persons without distinction of race, color or nationality, and that tho equal protection of the laws is a guarantee of the protection of equal laws";

That, moreover, a certain number of treaties explicitly provide for the recognition of the rights of man;

That it is all important to spread throughout the entire world the international recognition of the rights of man;

Proclaims:

ARTICLE I

It is the duty of every State to recognize for every individual the equal right to life, liberty and property and to accord to every one on its territory the full and complete protection of the law without distinction of nationality, sex, race, language or religion.

(continued on next page)

by them, can *never be supposed to extend farther than the common good;* but is obliged to secure everyone's property by providing against those three defects above-mentioned that made the state of nature so unsafe and uneasy. And so whoever has the legislative or supreme power of any common-wealth, is bound to govern by established *standing laws,* promulgated and known to the people, and not by extemporary decrees, by *indifferent* and upright judges, who are to decide controversies by those laws; and to employ the force of the community at home, *only in the execution of such laws,* or abroad to prevent or redress foreign injuries, and secure the community from inroads and invasion. And all this to be directed to no other *end,* but the *peace, safety,* and *public good* of the people.[4]

Locke: the spirit
behind the U.S.
Constitution

Much of this should have a familiar ring. It is not for nothing that Locke is called the spiritual father of the U.S. Constitution. Thomas Jefferson, who in 1776 drafted the Declaration of Independence, declared outright that his

---

[4]Ibid., pp. 95–99, 123–127, 131.

ARTICLE II

It is the duty of every State to recognize for every individual the right to the free exercise, both public and private, of every faith, religion or belief of which the practice is not incompatible with public policy and good morals.

ARTICLE III

It is the duty of every State to recognize the right of every individual to the free use of the language of his choice and for instruction in this language.

ARTICLE IV

No motive whatsoever based directly or indirectly on difference of sex, race, language or religion can authorize a State to refuse to any of its nationals private and public rights and especially the admission to institutions of public instruction and the exercise of different economic activities, professions and industries.

ARTICLE V

The equality already provided is not to be nominal but really effective and excludes all discrimination, direct or indirect.

ARTICLE VI

No State has the right to withdraw, except for reasons taken from its general legislation, its nationality from those who for reasons of sex, race, language or religion it might wish to deprive of the rights guaranteed by the preceding articles.

---

*A declaration published by the Institute of International Law during its session held in New York on October 12, 1929.

intent was that it should embody the social and political principles of Locke and like-minded theorists. Are not the ideas of natural law, social contract, and individual rights apparent in the very first lines of the Declaration of Independence? And is not the very language at times almost identical with what we read above in Locke?

When in the Course of human events, it becomes necessary for one people to dissolve the political bands which have connected them with another, and to assume among the Powers of the earth, the separate and equal station to which the Laws of Nature and of Nature's God entitle them, a decent respect to the opinions of mankind requires that they should declare the causes which impel them to the separation.

We hold these truths to be self-evident, that all men are created equal, that they are endowed by their Creator with certain unalienable Rights, that among these are Life, Liberty, and the pursuit of Happiness. That to secure these rights, Governments are instituted among Men, deriving their just powers from the consent of the governed. That whenever any Form of Government becomes destructive of these ends, it is the Right of the People to alter or to abolish it, and to institute new Government, laying its foundation on such principles and organizing its powers in such form, as to them shall seem most likely to effect their Safety and Happiness.[5]

LIBERALISM AND CAPITALISM

Classical liberalism means many different kinds of freedom. One of these is economic freedom, the freedom of the individual, either alone or (as with corporations) in union with others, to own the means of production (land, tools, factories, etc.) and to produce and sell goods for a profit. This is *capitalism*. That Locke himself saw this as a legitimate aspect of his liberal and individualistic

The right of property

vision is clear from the recurring references to "property" in the quotation from his *Second Treatise*, as in the inherent right of the individual "to preserve himself, his liberty and property" (compare the phrase from the Declaration of Independence, "Life, Liberty and the pursuit of Happiness"). One could argue, in fact, that Locke regarded the right of property as the *most important* of natural rights. Certainly he has already told us that it is primarily out of interest in personal property that people enter into social contracts in the first place: "The great and *chief end*, therefore, of men's uniting into common-wealths, and putting themselves under government, *is the preservation of their property.*"

However, it was after the time of Locke, during the period of the Industrial Revolution, that this *economic* implication of liberalism became most clearly focused. More specifically, it was the Scottish writer Adam Smith (1723–1790) who, in his *Inquiry into the Nature and Causes of the Wealth of Nations*, gave decisive expression to the rights of the individual in a free marketplace—that is, capitalism. Smith's watchword was *laissez faire*, French for "let it alone,"

"Hands-off" economy

and often rendered as "hands off!" But it must be stressed that Smith and the *laissez faire* economists were not advocating the principle of allow-the-individual-complete-liberty-in-commerce-and-let-the-rest-be-damned. They believed—and is not the idea still believed?—that a *laissez faire* approach to economics would provide the best for *everyone*. The mechanisms involved in supply and demand and free enterprise make for an efficient and satisfying

The "invisible hand" behind capitalism

arrangement for all concerned: owner, merchant, worker, consumer. So, even though Smith advocated a hands-off economy, he believed in an "invisible

---

[5]MacDonald, *Documentary Source Book of American History, 1606–1926*, p. 191 (slightly edited).

CAPITALISM

The economic theory that advocates that the means of production, and the actual production and exchange of goods and wealth, should be owned and implemented by private individuals or corporations, with a view toward profit.

The Scot Adam Smith was the author of *The Wealth of Nations*, the classical statement of the capitalist theory of economics. It was published in 1776.

hand," or the mechanisms we just spoke of, such that whatever the capitalist's own intention might be, the interest and good of a capitalist society as a whole would be promoted. This comes out well in the following paragraph from the *Wealth of Nations:*

> . . . the annual revenue of every society is always precisely equal to the exchangeable value of the whole annual produce of its industry, or rather is precisely the same thing with that exchangeable value. As every individual, therefore, endeavours as much as he can both to employ his capital in the support of domestic industry, and so to direct that industry that its produce may be of the greatest value; every individual necessarily labours to render the annual revenue of the society as great as he can. He generally, indeed, neither intends to promote the public interest, nor knows how much he is promoting it. By preferring the support of domestic to that of foreign industry, he intends only his own security; and by directing that industry in such a manner as its produce may be of the greatest value, he intends only his own gain, and he is in this, as in many other cases, led by an invisible hand to promote an end which was no part of his intention. Nor is it always the worse for the society that it was no part of it. By pursuing his own interest he frequently promotes that of the society more effectually than when he really intends to promote it. I have never known much good done by those who affected to trade for the public good. It is an affectation, indeed, not very common among merchants, and very few words need be employed in dissuading them from it.[6]

---

[6]Adam Smith, *An Inquiry into the Nature and Causes of the Wealth of Nations,* ed. Edwin Cannan (New York: Modern Library, 1937), p. 423.

LIBERTY AND UTILITY

We have already encountered the British philosopher John Stuart Mill in Chapter 15 on utilitarianism as an ethical theory. Mill's most famous work, *On Liberty*, provides an argument for liberalism but from a very different starting point than Locke's theory of natural rights. Mill's exploration of "the nature and limits of the power which can be legitimately exercised by society over the individual" is based purely on the consequences or utility of such a system as he explains:

> It is proper to state that I forego any advantage which could be derived to my argument from the idea of abstract right as a thing independent of utility. I regard utility as the ultimate appeal on all ethical questions; but it must be utility in the largest sense, grounded on the permanent interests of man as a progressive being. Those interests, I contend, authorize the subjection of individual spontaneity to external control only in respect to those actions of each which concern the interest of other people. If anyone does an act hurtful to others, there is a *prima facie* case for punishing him by law or, where legal penalties are not safely applicable, by general disapprobation.

Here we see not only Mill's grounding of his liberalism in utilitarianism but also his key distinction between those actions that affect others and those that are entirely personal, affecting no one but yourself. It is this latter category, self-regarding actions, that Mill describes as "the appropriate region of human liberty." Mill summarizes the point with his famous "harm principle."

> The object of this essay is to assert one very simple principle, as entitled to govern absolutely the dealings of society with the individual in the way of compulsion and control, whether the means used be physical force in the form of legal penalties or the moral coercion of public opinion. That principle is that the sole end for which mankind are warranted, individually or collectively, in interfering with the liberty of action of any of their number is self-protection. That the only purpose for which power can be rightfully exercised over any member of a civilized community, against his will, is to prevent harm to others. His own good, either physical or moral, is not a sufficient warrant. He cannot rightfully be compelled to do or forbear because it will be better for him to do so, because it will make him happier, because, in the opinions of others, to do so would be wise or even right. These are good reasons for remonstrating with him, or reasoning with him, or persuading him, or entreating him, but not for compelling him or visiting him with any evil in case he do otherwise. To justify that, the conduct from which it is desired to deter him must be calculated to produce evil to someone else. The only part of the conduct of anyone for which he is amenable to society is that which concerns others. In the part which merely concerns himself, his independence is, of right, absolute. Over himself, over his own body and mind, the individual is sovereign.

John Stuart Mill, *On Liberty,* ed. Elizabeth Rapaport (Indianapolis: Hackett, 1978), pp. 9, 10.

Is it relevant that the *Wealth of Nations* was published in 1776? For better or for worse, these ideas have had everything to do with the shaping of the American social-political-economic system. And now we are in a better position to appreciate how the words "liberal" and "conservative" are used in contemporary political discussion. Both liberals and conservatives embrace the twofold idea of classical liberalism: (1) individual rights and (2) the social responsibility of the state. The difference is that conservatives defend individual freedom against the encroachment of the state, whereas liberals stress the responsibility of the state to ensure individual rights.

But the real attack on the classical liberal perspective originates far to the left of the liberals. And this brings us to the radical alternative and challenge of *Marxism*.

A RADICAL RESPONSE: MARX

If the perspectives we are considering in this part of the book seek to address actual, practical, social, and political life, then Marxism takes the prize. Perhaps no philosophy has had more of a direct impact on the social and political existence of untold numbers of people than that introduced by the German thinker and social theorist Karl Marx (1818–1883). By its nature, the Marxist program presses for change—radical and revolutionary change.

It is often the case that we must look for the roots of a philosophy in some earlier philosophy. In some important ways, the roots of Marxism lie in the German idealist thinker G. W. F. Hegel[7] (1770–1831). Hegel's philosophy is an enormous intellectual monument, but a few basic points will suffice for the moment. First, Hegel was an objective idealist. You will recall from Chapter 5 that an objective idealist believes that reality is "idea-istic" or spiritual in nature, but that it exists objectively or independently of us, "out there." Hegel himself believed in this way that reality was *spirit,* but, second, that this spiritual reality is constantly on the move, changing, advancing, and actualizing the ultimate state that he called *Absolute Spirit,* otherwise represented as the complete consciousness and freedom of reality. Finally, the mechanism by which this historical-spiritual process is achieved is called *dialectic.* In this context, "dialectic" means the give-and-take between opposite states resulting in always-emerging higher unities. More technically, this process is represented as the *synthesis* (or unity) of *thesis* and *antithesis*

The influence of Hegel

Historical dialectic

---

[7]Rhymes with *bagel.*

"Philosophers have only interpreted the world in various ways; the point, however, is to change it."

—Marx

(opposite states), a process going on constantly in all spheres of existence, and where, at any moment, a synthesis of opposites becomes itself an opposite to be synthesized with another:

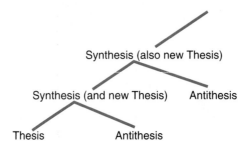

Synthesis (also new Thesis)

Synthesis (and new Thesis) Antithesis

Thesis Antithesis

What can this superspeculative and abstract conception have to do with the superpractical and down-to-earth concerns of Marxism? How does Hegel's process of the historical dialectic bear on Marx's political theory?

Marx took over the idea of the historical dialectic, but under the influence of another German philosopher, Feuerbach, gave it a materialistic twist. The result was *dialectical materialism*. This phrase was never used by Marx himself. Nevertheless, it serves well enough to suggest the character of the philosophical principles underlying his whole social and political program: Reality is matter, and its concrete expression and development are governed by the dialectic of history. But this is given a further twist when Marx focuses more specifically on matter as it reveals itself in economics, which, as you know, concerns money, but more accurately concerns the principles of production, distribution, and use of wealth and products. And now we are in a position to say what Marx's *real* concern was. It was to aid and abet the class warfare that is the social and economic expression of the historical dialectic: to achieve—even through revolutionary tactics— a classless society in which private ownership of the means of production (tools, factories, and so forth) would be abolished and wealth would be equitably distributed. This, of course, is *communism,* the social and economic and political expression of dialectical materialism.

So far, all ideas and theories. What really propelled Marx were two facts that stood in stark and dismal contradiction. First, Marx was a humanist.

*Marxism =
dialectical
materialism*

*Marxism and
communism*

MARXISM

- *Dialectical materialism:* The metaphysical view that reality is matter and motion, and evolves historically in accordance with the dialectical principle of the synthesis of opposite states.

- *Communism:* The economic theory that advocates the abolition of private ownership of the means of production and the revolutionary actualization of a classless society.

His exalted view of humanity included a belief in the innate goodness of persons, their perfectability, and their powers of self-realization. But, second, this is overpowered and thwarted by their actual social and economic condition. It must be remembered that Marx lived when the Industrial Revolution was playing right into the hands of capitalism. It was a time when increased and frantic production meant the enslavement of the working class (Marx called it the *proletariat*) to the owning class (the *bourgeoisie*); and it meant the degradation of the working class through, for instance, squalid working conditions, child labor, and a wage wholly determined by the owners. In a word—and this is a most important word in Marxism—it meant *alienation*.

"Alienation" means separation or estrangement. By alienation Marx intended considerably more than just the bitter estrangement of the workers from their capitalist superiors. In his *Economic and Philosophical Manuscripts* Marx explains the different kinds of alienation spawned by capitalist-controlled labor: Workers become alienated (1) from the objects they produce, (2) from themselves, (3) from their human nature, and (4) from their fellows. It is important to understand these four forms of alienation and to see exactly how labor, as Marx knew it, results in them. The following extract addresses specifically the way in which labor results in *self*-alienation.

> The worker becomes poorer the more wealth he produces and the more his production increases in power and extent. The worker becomes an ever cheaper commodity the more goods he creates. The *devaluation* of the human world increases in direct relation with the *increase in value* of the world of things. Labour does not only create goods; it also produces itself and the worker as a *commodity*, and indeed in the same proportion as it produces goods. . . .

Human possibilities versus economic repression

Alienation

What constitutes the alienation of labour? First, that the work is *external* to the worker, that it is not part of his nature; and that, consequently, he does not fulfil himself in his work but denies himself, has a feeling of misery rather than well-being, does not develop freely his mental and physical energies but is physically exhausted and mentally debased. The worker, therefore, feels himself at home only during his leisure time, whereas at work he feels homeless. His work is not voluntary but imposed, *forced labour.* It is not the satisfaction of a need, but only a *means* for satisfying other needs. Its alien character is clearly shown by the fact that as soon as there is no physical or other compulsion it is avoided like the plague. External labour, labour in which man alienates himself, is a labour of self-sacrifice, or mortification. Finally, the external character of work for the worker is shown by the fact that it is not his own work but work for someone else, that in work he does not belong to himself but to another person.

Just as in religion the spontaneous activity of human fantasy, of the human brain and heart, reacts independently as an alien activity of gods or devils upon the individual, so the activity of the worker is not his own spontaneous activity. It is another's activity and a loss of his own spontaneity.

We arrive at the result that man (the worker) feels himself to be freely active only in his animal functions—eating, drinking, and procreating, or at most also in his dwelling and in personal adornment—while in his human functions he is reduced to an animal. The animal becomes human and the human becomes animal.

Eating, drinking and procreating are of course also genuine human functions. But abstractly considered, apart from the environment of human activities, and turned into final and sole ends, they are animal functions.[8]

Marxism has undergone many changes, most notably through Marx's contemporary and compatriot Friedrich Engels and, later, the Russian revolutionary Vladimir Ilyich Lenin. But Marxism in any form begins with the contradiction Marx saw between a high estimation of the human being and the actual repressive and alienating conditions inflicted on the working classes, and it seeks, through varying levels of revolutionary force, to transcend the contradiction by means of communism. Its battle cry has been:

WORKERS OF THE WORLD UNITE!
YOU HAVE NOTHING TO LOSE BUT YOUR CHAINS!

[8]Karl Marx, *Early Writings,* tr. and ed. T. B. Bottomore (New York: McGraw-Hill, 1964), pp. 121–127.

A MESSAGE FROM MARTIN NIEMOELLER*

"First the Nazis went after the Jews, but I was not a Jew, so I did not object. Then they went after the Catholics, but I was not a Catholic, so I did not object. Then they went after the Trade-Unionists, but I was not a Trade-Unionist, so I did not object. Then they came after me, and there was no one left to object."

*A German pastor imprisoned in Dachau by the Nazis.

Out of this there eventually arose the communist revolution (led by Lenin) in Russia in 1917; the revolutions since then in China (Mao Tse-Tung) and Cuba (Castro); the Marxist agitations today in the Third World, such as Latin America; and labor unions and socialist programs everywhere.

SOME OBJECTIONS

We have now looked at the two dominant political-economic theories that competed in the twentieth century. Obviously, there are many objections to both theories, but here we limit our consideration to two major objections to each approach. Other objections and alternatives come out in the final two chapters.

For Marxism, we must start by first speaking to a *socioeconomic* point: Some believe that Marxists are too harsh in their rejection of all other social systems as incapable of introducing important social change. Certainly the situation now is different from what it was in Marx's own time. Has not even capitalism proved in some ways (never dreamed of by the early Marxists) to be self-correcting? To be capable of being governed by its own (though unending) dialectic of improvement? It is hardly necessary to be a Marxist to have a social conscience, to believe in and strive for the general welfare, to improve working conditions or to introduce child-labor laws, and to *change* things. Of course, it may be answered: "But your program of social change is too *slow*. We need radical change, and we need it now. Revolution is the only way!" But the idea of literal revolution, with its upheavals and probable bloodshed, is itself not unproblematic—unless you believe that the end justifies the means.

Second, a *moral* issue: It is frequently heard that Marxism is naive and over-optimistic in its own estimate of human nature: "Marxism is a wonderful theory. Too bad that it can't possibly work due to human nature." Is there any truth to the charge that the very repression of human values that Marxists so deplore in other forms of government reveals itself even more vividly in communist societies? Not to excuse other forms of government for their own failures, but what of Stalin's purges of the 1930s and 1950s? The communist ideal was pursued in the USSR for over sixty years. Where did it succeed in healing the alienation it so strongly denounces in other systems? Where did it outstrip competing systems with respect to human rights? Where did it maximize the self-actualization and full humanity that it claimed for its own citizens?

As a matter of fact, it would appear that the Marxist chickens came home to roost. Political-economic upheavals throughout Eastern Europe—beginning with Lech Walesa's Polish Solidarity movement and ending with the dismantling of the Berlin Wall and the fall of the Soviet Union—testify to the failure of Marxism in that part of the world. Some have even declared that Marxism is *dead*. Well, no. In other parts of the world entirely different cultural and economic circumstances still invite Marxism to make its case. And what will happen remains to be seen.

The socioeconomic question

The moral question

Returning to liberalism, we find that this seemingly victorious political theory is certainly not immune to objections. In fact, the debate over liberalism has been very heated in recent years, perhaps as a result of the difficulties with Marxism. Here we limit our discussion to a pair of closely related criticisms about individuals and community.

First, many object to liberalism for an excessive focus on individualism they believe is ultimately grounded in an untenable metaphysical conception of humans. For liberals, remember, the individual is supreme and the role of the state is to protect the conditions necessary for individuals to control their own lives as much as possible. Critics contend that humans are fundamentally social beings and thus our ties to others—friends, family, co-workers, and so on—are as important, or even more important, than our individual goals and interests. If this is true, if we are defined and guided as much by our relationships as by our individualism, then doesn't liberalism err by focusing so much on individuals as autonomous beings and ignoring social context?

A second objection builds off of this by pointing to the value of community as a shared value. Some critics look at the decline in community through the past several decades and blame liberal policies that focus on individuals. Is it surprising, they ask, that churches, schools, and other community groups have suffered when we have a political system that puts all the emphasis on individuals and their personal liberty? Instead, they argue, we need to recognize that community is a social value that can and will trump individual liberty in some cases. This is not to say that individual rights don't matter, only that the common good must also be considered in the mix.

In the next chapter we'll see how these liberal values play out in democracy, the political scheme most often associated with liberalism.

CHAPTER 18 IN REVIEW

SUMMARY

In this chapter we have looked at the two most important social-political perspectives that have developed in modern times, which compete yet today, and sometimes bitterly, for supremacy: liberalism and Marxism.

Liberalism is the ideology of freedom. We do not mean here some starry-eyed and romantic idea but the concrete freedom of the individual to pursue his or her interests, not only undeterred by undue governmental control, but also as *guaranteed* by government. In its most classical form this doctrine was expressed by Locke, who believed that both the private and public good are knowable from the natural law, which teaches plainly the equality and independence of each individual in his or her "natural state," unperturbed by civil government. Social life (or life together) requires, however, that individuals enter into a social contract or agreement to a degree of organization and regulation for the sake of the preservation of their freedoms.

One of the most basic of these freedoms, or "inalienable rights," is the pursuit of property, and this establishes the connection between liberalism and capitalism, the economic doctrine of the private ownership of the means of production and exchange of goods. The capitalistic ideals of private ownership and the free marketplace were most forcefully expressed by Adam Smith's economic slogan "hands off!" But this ideology, abetted by the Industrial Revolution, led in actual practice to exploitation, monopolies, a growing division between the "haves" and "have-nots," and the radical reaction of Marxism.

Marx was deeply influenced by Hegel's "dialectical" view of history, according to which history develops through the confrontation and synthesis of opposite states. Marx, interpreting this in a materialistic and economic way, called for a social revolution to bring about a more equitable distribution of wealth and the classless society, or communism. Only by means of this radical solution can the human alienation fostered by capitalism be healed.

BASIC IDEAS

- Liberalism
- The distinction between freedoms from and freedoms for
- Individualism
- The state of nature
- The social contract
- Tacit consent
- Capitalism
- *Laissez faire*
- "Invisible-hand" economy
- Hegelian dialectic
- Dialectical materialism
- Communism
- The Marxist concept of alienation
- Criticisms of Marxism/communism
  Socioeconomic
  Moral
- Criticisms of liberalism

TEST YOURSELF

1. Who wrote *Second Treatise of Government*?
2. In 1776, the United States was founded and the book entitled _____ was published. What was the connection between the two events?
3. Who was G. W. F. Hegel?
4. What is meant by saying that the order of (1) state of nature and (2) social contract is a *logical* rather than a *historical* order?
5. Marx taught that labor (according to the capitalist conception) alienates the worker from _____, from _____, from _____, and from _____.
6. Comment on Marxism as a theory of *reality*.
7. What is the relation of Marxism to communism?
8. True or false: Recalling the preceding chapter, communism has more in common with Mill's teaching than with Kant's.

QUESTIONS FOR REFLECTION

- In this book we have encountered several concepts of "freedom." Can you distinguish the freedom in the free-will–determinism debate, the freedom in Sartre's existential philosophy, and now the freedom involved in liberalism?

- The idea of natural law has appeared again in this chapter. Can you explain the exact connection of this idea with the rise of capitalism? What do *you* make of the notion of certain "inalienable" rights? Do these include the right of private property? Does this right sometimes involve an infringement of others' rights? Exploitation? Was Marx correct about the alienating power of capitalism?

- Capitalism and communism are economic theories of existence. What does this mean? Are such theories adequate to the totality of human experience? Does each of them leave out something important?

FOR FURTHER READING

Jean Baechler. *The Origins of Capitalism.* Tr. Barry Cooper. New York: St. Martin's Press, 1976. A useful discussion of the nature of capitalism and its historical development, with an opening chapter on Marxism.

Carl Cohen (ed.). *Communism, Fascism and Democracy.* New York: Random House, 1962. An anthology of statements that have contributed to the development of communist and democratic perspectives.

Gerald A. Cohen. *Karl Marx's Theory of History: A Defense.* Princeton, NJ: Princeton University Press, 1978. An analytic reconstruction and defense of an orthodox version of historical materialism.

Frederick Copleston. *A History of Philosophy.* Baltimore: Newman Press, 1946–1974. V, Chs. 7 and 19. Authoritative surveys of the political doctrines of Locke and Smith.

John Dunn. *Locke: A Very Short Introduction.* New York: Oxford University Press, 2003. An accessible entry to John Locke's life and philosophical ideas.

Joel Feinberg. *Social Philosophy.* Englewood Cliffs, NJ: Prentice-Hall, 1973. A student-oriented survey of the general issues.

Milton Friedman and Rose Friedman. *Free to Choose.* New York: Harcourt Brace Jovanovich, 1980. A defense of capitalism, for a popular reading audience, by a leading advocate of the capitalist system and his wife.

Robert E. Goodin and Philip Pettit (eds.). *A Companion to Contemporary Political Philosophy.* Malden, MA: Blackwell, 1993. A collection of essays by major thinkers about a wide range of issues in political philosophy.

J. W. Gough. *The Social Contract: A Critical Study of Its Development.* Oxford: Clarendon Press, 1936. A complete discussion of the concept of the social contract from ancient to modern times, including a good account of "Locke and the English Revolution."

Jean Hampton. *Political Philosophy.* Boulder, CO: Westview Press, 1997. A readable introduction to major topics in the field.

Michael Harrington. *The Twilight of Capitalism.* New York: Simon & Schuster, 1976. A critique of the capitalist system, by a well-known democratic socialist.

John Hoffman. *Marxism and the Theory of Praxis: A Critique of Some New Versions of Old Fallacies.* London: Lawrence & Wishart, 1975. A critical appraisal, with valuable historical information, of Marxism in its social implementation.

Will Kymlica. *Contemporary Political Philosophy.* Second ed. New York: Oxford University Press, 2001. Survey of recent work in political thought.

E. J. Lowe. *Locke,* The Routledge Philosophers. London: Routledge, 2005. Interpretation and analysis covering the full range of Locke's philosophical system.

Tibor Machan. *The Libertarian Reader.* Savage, MD: Rowman & Littlefield, 1982. A collection of 21 essays by contemporary philosophers, economists, political scientists, and the like in defense of libertarianism.

Douglas MacLean and Claudia Mills (eds.). *Liberalism Reconsidered.* Totowa, NJ: Rowman & Allanheld, 1983. A collection of studies evaluating various issues in liberalism: equality, rights, law, democracy, foreign policy, and so on.

Vincente Medina. *Social Contract Theory.* Savage, MD: Rowman & Littlefield, 1990. A critical exposition of the leading representatives of the "contractarian" tradition, such as Hobbes, Locke, Rousseau, Kant, and Rawls.

G. H. R. Parkinson (ed.). *Marx and Marxism.* Cambridge: Cambridge University Press, 1982. A collection of contemporary evaluations of issues involved in Marxism: the state, science, justice, revolution, metaphysics, and so on.

K. R. Popper. *The Open Society and Its Enemies.* Fourth ed. Princeton, NJ: Princeton University Press, 1963. II. A historical and philosophical account of the rise of Marxism and the aftermath.

Melvin Rader. *Marx's Interpretation of History.* New York: Oxford University Press, 1979. A helpful, general exposition, emphasizing Marx's humanistic concerns.

Michael J. Sandel (ed.). *Liberalism and Its Critics.* New York: New York University Press, 1984. A collection of major essays by liberal and communitarian thinkers.

Michael J. Sandel. *Liberalism and the Limits of Justice.* Second ed. Cambridge: Cambridge University Press, 1998. A leading liberal outlines his criticism of John Rawls.

Jules Steinberg. *Locke, Rousseau, and the Idea of Political Obligation.* Westport, CT: Greenwood Press, 1978. A critical examination of the consent theory of political obligation as employed in the liberal-democratic tradition, with specific treatment of Locke.

Leo Strauss and Joseph Cropsey (eds.). *History of Political Philosophy.* Third ed. Chicago: University of Chicago Press, 1987. A comprehensive collection of essays on all the major thinkers in Western political thought.

Richard Taylor. *Freedom, Anarchy, and the Law: An Introduction to Political Philosophy.* Second ed. Buffalo, NY: Prometheus Books, 1982. A beginning-level discussion of the central issues of political philosophy, written from a libertarian standpoint.

David Thomas. *The Routledge Philosophy Guidebook to Locke on Government.* London: Routledge, 1995. Approachable philosophical introduction to Locke's *Second Treatise.*

John Wild. *Plato's Modern Enemies and the Theory of Natural Law.* Chicago: University of Chicago Press, 1953. A treatment primarily of Plato's position, but with general discussion of natural law and in relation to contemporary thinking.

*In addition, see the relevant articles ("Social Contract," "Liberalism," "Marx, Karl," etc.) in *Routledge Encyclopedia of Philosophy,* ed. Edward Craig (London: Routledge, 1998), and *Stanford Encyclopedia of Philosophy,* http://plato.stanford.edu.

DEMOCRACY

In Chapter 18 we focused on individual liberty as a foundation for government or society. Here we turn our attention to the related questions of who governs and, more to the point, what provides legitimacy to a governing authority. Probably everyone is familiar with "Might makes right" as one statement of the view that authority comes from strength or perhaps military power. Dictators use this as their source of authority. Alternatively, the idea of the "divine right" of kings was very powerful at times in history as a way of indicating that God gives some people the right to rule. A third option, defended by Plato later in this chapter, is that superior intelligence is the basis for ruling. While all of these options merit consideration, democracy takes a different tack. It argues that the people, all citizens, have the ultimate authority and that the government is legitimate only when it has the support of the people. Let's take a closer look at this central idea in modern political thought.

GOVERNMENT BY THE PEOPLE

Everyone is familiar with democracy, but as philosophers we must dig deeper and ask, What do we really mean when we say that a society should be "democratic"? To start, let's distinguish, once again, between two different meanings. In the same way we noted in Chapter 18 that the liberalism that philosophers are concerned about is not the same as being liberal versus conservative, the democrats we'll read about here are not members of one political party. Both the Democratic and Republican parties in U.S. politics are committed to democracy (and to our country as a republic, for that matter); their differences lie elsewhere.

Where do we start then in exploring democracy? As we've seen throughout the book, one useful place to start is with the word itself, trying to understand its roots and meaning. "Democracy" comes from two Greek words, *demos* meaning "common people" and *kratos* meaning "rule." Thus democracy literally means rule by the people. We can see this quite clearly in the opening words of the Declaration of Independence, the 1776 document used to signal the intention of the original colonies to split from Britain and the reasons behind this split.

We hold these truths to be self-evident, that all men are created equal, that they are endowed by their Creator with certain unalienable Rights, that among these are Life, Liberty and the pursuit of Happiness.—That to secure these rights, Governments are instituted among Men, deriving their just powers from the consent of the governed,—That whenever any Form of Government becomes destructive of these ends, it is the Right of the People to alter or to abolish it, and to institute new Government, laying its foundation on such principles and organizing its powers in such form, as to them shall seem most likely to effect their Safety and Happiness.

It's worth taking the time to examine carefully some of the key language used by Thomas Jefferson, the chief author of the Declaration of Independence, in making the case for independence. He talks about equality and natural rights, familiar concepts from our study of John Locke in the preceding chapter. Jefferson had read Locke and was heavily influenced by his writings. We should also note that liberalism and democratic government often go hand in hand and the phrase "liberal democracy" is quite common.

No idea is more important in this document, and to the basic idea of democracy, than consent. Democracy is based on the consent, or agreement, of the people, and this is how the democratic society gains its legitimacy and power. As we will see, this really is the defining feature and core idea of democracy. The notion of consent, like everything in philosophy, is open to criticism and debate as we will see soon enough. But first we must look at how democracy comes out of the thinking of a key philosopher of the French enlightenment, Jean-Jacques Rousseau (1712–1778).

ROUSSEAU'S SOCIAL CONTRACT

To say that democracy is government "by the people" and derives its power from the agreement or consent of the people is a good start, but how does this work? Who are "the people"? To what do they agree? And how does that translate into government, law, and a stable society? These questions were foremost in the minds of European thinkers in the modern period, as we have seen with John Locke.

For Rousseau, like Locke, the central fact of human existence is freedom. Humans are fundamentally free, and this freedom forms the starting point, the foundation, for their relations with others and the formation of society.

In one of the most famous first lines in philosophy, Rousseau starts his landmark work, *The Social Contract*, with this seeming paradox:

> Man is born free, and everywhere he is in chains.

Chains? What chains? Obviously Rousseau doesn't mean that literally we all are chained up in slavery. Instead he is referring to the way that all of us have given up certain basic freedoms as part of our associations with others, our belonging to groups, and our membership in society. Isn't it obvious that we are constrained and limited in many ways by the rules and obligations of living in community with other people? Even in the "land of the free" there are many things I cannot do. For example, when I drive my car, my routes, my speed, and dozens of other things are ultimately controlled by government regulations and social norms. I face penalties, many of them quite severe, if I fail to follow the rules.

Rousseau rightly recognized that this is true of our lives more generally when we live in a country and under the rule of a government. He was not trying to overturn governments and plunge us into anarchy, but he was very interested in asking about the nature of these associations that limit our freedom. What makes some restrictions on our freedom troublesome and others perfectly legitimate? The answer, Rousseau thought, was fairly straightforward: consent. Legitimate restrictions on my freedom, and thus legitimate government, is that to which I agree. This is the foundation of the social contract, the main idea of Rousseau's democratic theory.

Restrictions on freedom

What is this social contract? It's an agreement between individuals to mutually limit their freedom in order to gain the benefits of community. Think about it. If you were given the choice between living in perfect freedom but isolation and fear, or agreeing to give up some freedom to gain the security and benefits of community, which would you choose? Rousseau argues that all rational people would opt for community. But not just any community. I wouldn't agree to a community where I was a slave. No, it's only some types of communal arrangements and certain restrictions on freedom that individuals would consent to. These communities and the corresponding rules and laws are those that are legitimate, according to Rousseau, because they have the consent of the governed.

The social contract

In the following passage from *The Social Contract*, Rousseau provides more details about the social contract and how it solves the problem of legitimate government:

> [4] "To find a form of association that will defend and protect the person and goods of each associate with the full common force, and by means of which each, uniting with all, nevertheless obey only himself and remain as free as before." This is the fundamental problem to which the social contract provides the solution.
>
> [5] The clauses of this contract are so completely determined by the nature of the act that the slightest modification would render them null and void; so that although they may never have been formally stated, they are everywhere the same, everywhere tacitly admitted and recognized; until, the social compact

having been violated, everyone is thereupon restored to his original rights and resumes his natural freedom while losing the conventional freedom for which he renounced it.

[6] These clauses, rightly understood, all come down to just one, namely the total alienation of each associate with all of his rights to the whole community: For, in the first place, since each gives himself entirely, the condition is equal for all, and since the condition is equal for all, no one has any interest in making it burdensome to the rest.

[7] Moreover, since the alienation is made without reservation, the union is as perfect as it can be, and no associate has anything further to claim: For if individuals were left some rights, then, since there would be no common superior who might adjudicate between them and the public, each, being judge in his own case on some issue, would soon claim to be so on all, the state of nature would subsist and the association necessarily become tyrannical or empty.

[8] Finally, each, by giving himself to all, gives himself to no one, and since there is no associate over whom one does not acquire the same right as one grants him over oneself, one gains the equivalent of all one loses, and more force to preserve what one has.

[9] If, then, one sets aside everything that is not of the essence of the social compact, one finds that it can be reduced to the following terms: *Each of us puts his person and his full power in common under the supreme direction of the general will; and in a body we receive each member as an indivisible part of the whole.*[1]

The general
will

The closing lines of this excerpt introduce another key concept from Rousseau's theory of democracy: the general will. The general will, Rousseau tells us, is what we consent to and what provides "supreme direction" in governing social life. While scholars debate Rousseau's precise meaning of the general will, the basic idea is quite simple. Just as each individual has certain things that he or she wants, so a community of people has its own goals as a community, which may or may not be identical to the will of any of its members. It may sound strange to say that a group of people has a will of its own, but think of any organization that you belong to. Let's say that you are a member of an orchestra. The will or goal of the orchestra is to play music well, even though on a particular day some of the individual musicians may be absent or distracted. Perhaps a violinist is home with the flu, and a trumpet player would rather be outside walking in the sunshine, and a clarinetist wants to end the rehearsal so he can have lunch, and so on. Indeed, perhaps no one really wants to be there. Yet the orchestra, as an orchestra, nevertheless has the goal of playing music well. Rousseau's idea is that for a political community to flourish, the individuals must subordinate their particular goals (or "private wills") to the good of the community (or the "general will"), just as for an orchestra to succeed, the musicians must concentrate and play well even when they don't feel like it.

---

[1]Jean-Jacques Rousseau, *The Social Contract and Other Later Political Writings,* ed. Victor Gourevitch (Cambridge: Cambridge University Press, 1997), pp. 49–50.

JEAN-JACQUES ROUSSEAU

Jean-Jacques Rousseau was born in Geneva in 1712. His mother died soon after his birth, and when he was a boy his father was expelled from the city for striking an army officer. Rousseau grew up in the care of an uncle who did not want to pay for his education, so even though he went on to become a famous philosopher, he had almost no formal schooling. In fact, he was so unhappy in Geneva that he ran away from home when he was sixteen. For many years he traveled as a vagabond through Italy and France, having many hilarious and sometimes sad adventures, which he later chronicled in his famous autobiography called *Confessions*. Eventually he settled in Paris, where he became friends with many leading figures of the radical intellectual movement known as the French Enlightenment.

Rousseau soon experienced one of the greatest literary and philosophical triumphs ever recorded. Within the space of twelve years he published four of the most important philosophical works of the Enlightenment: "Discourse on the Sciences and Arts" (1750), "Discourse on the Origin of Inequality" (1755), a treatise on education called *Emile* (1762), and his great work of political philosophy *The Social Contract* (1762). During this period he also composed a popular opera, *The Village Soothsayer*, as well as a novel, *Julie*, which some scholars have calculated to be the best-selling book of the eighteenth century. In the space of a decade, Rousseau went from being destitute and unknown to rivaling Voltaire as the most famous author in the French language.

The good times did not last, however. Rousseau soon found himself in trouble with the political and religious authorities. No one was surprised, because in *Emile* and *The Social Contract* he published scathing criticism of the society in which he lived. For example, he argued that people should make their own laws and elect their own leaders, even though France at the time was governed by a powerful hereditary monarchy. Furthermore, he denied the Christian idea of "original sin" and the validity of the church's sacraments as a means of earning salvation, in spite of the fact that the Catholic Church in France had the power to persecute dissenters. Chased by the police, Rousseau fled France, yet his views were so radical that he found himself unwelcome everywhere he tried to settle.

The last years of Rousseau's life were troubled. Although he was able to return to France, he continually feared arrest. Furthermore, many of the great thinkers of the Enlightenment turned on him because of his view that the arts and sciences corrupt morality. Thus, alienated by the conservatives in the government and church, as well as by the radical philosophers of the Enlightenment, he spent his last years as an outcast. Yet he continued to write, and during these final years he produced two of his most celebrated works, *Confessions* and *Reveries of a Solitary Walker*, the latter of which was left unfinished at his death in 1778. Although some of his ideas were unpopular at the time, he became celebrated again during the French Revolution, and he was one of the strongest influences on the next generation of philosophers, including Immanuel Kant.

As always, we need to let the philosopher speak for himself on the nature of the general will:

[1] From the preceding it follows that the general will is always upright and always tends to the public utility: but it does not follow from it that the people's deliberations are always equally upright. One always wants one's good, but one does not always see it: one can never corrupt the people, but one can often cause it to be mistaken, and only when it is, does it want what is bad.

[2] There is often a considerable difference between the will of all and the general will: the latter looks only to the common interest, the former looks to private interest, and is nothing but a sum of particular wills; but if, from these same wills, one takes away the pluses and the minuses which cancel each other out,* what is left as the sum of the differences is the general will.

[3] If, when an adequately informed people deliberates, the Citizens had no communication among themselves, the general will would always result from the large number of small differences, and the deliberation would always be good. But when factions arise, small associations at the expense of the large association, the will of each one of these associations becomes general in relation to its members and particular in relation to the State; there can then no longer be said to be as many voters as there are men, but only as many as there are associations. The differences become less numerous and yield a less general result. Finally, when one of these associations is so large that it prevails over all the rest, the result you have is no longer a sum of small differences, but one single difference; then there is no longer a general will, and the opinion that prevails is nothing but a private opinion.

[4] It is important, then, that in order to have the general will expressed well, there be no partial society in the State, and every Citizen state only his own opinion.† Such was the single sublime institution of the great Lycurgus. That if there are partial societies, their number must be multiplied, and inequality among them prevented, as was done by Solon, Numa, Servius. These are the only precautions that will ensure that the general will is always enlightened, and that the people make no mistakes.

*Each interest, says the M[arquis] d'A[rgenson], has different principles. The agreement between two individual interests is formed by opposition to a third party's interest. He might have added that the agreement between all interests is formed by opposition to each one's interest. If there were no different interests, the common interest would scarcely be sensible since it would never encounter obstacles: everything would run by itself, and politics would cease to be an art.

†"In truth, says Machiavelli, some divisions harm Republics, and some benefit them; harmful are those that are accompanied by factions and parties; beneficial are those that do not give rise to factions and parties. Therefore, since the founder of a Republic cannot prevent enmities, he must make the best provision possible against factions." Hist[ory], of Floren[ce], Bk. VII [ch. I].[2]

Note how Rousseau emphasizes the need for unity without factions among people or division of the society into smaller units. He believes—Do you think he's right?—that under the right conditions there is a consensus about the good for the whole community. This is not, we must be clear, to say that everyone will agree about what to do, but rather that an identifiable

[2]Ibid., pp. 59–60.

HOBBES ON HUMAN NATURE

In Chapter 6 we encountered the Englishman Thomas Hobbes as an example of a materialist philosopher. But Hobbes is probably best known for his political thinking. In fact, one short quote from his major work, *Leviathan,* is probably more widely recognized than its author. Hobbes' claim that life is "solitary, poor, nasty, brutish and short" is one of those catchy phrases that people love to quote.

For Hobbes, like all of us, his thinking about society was shaped by his view of human nature. Are humans naturally good, cooperative people? Or do we tend to be selfish, restrained from evil only by societal pressures and the threat of punishment? How we answer such questions plays a major role in what sort of social organization we favor, how much power we think government should have, and what is necessary for people to form a state.

Unlike Rousseau, who thought that altruism was possible, Hobbes saw humans as inherently selfish. This is why he described the state of nature as a state of war that pits "every man against every man."

This difference in opinion about human nature—Is altruism possible or not?—leads to radically different conclusions. Whereas Rousseau thinks citizens must obey only the laws to which they consent, Hobbes argues for an all-powerful sovereign whose authority is absolute. What is your view of human nature, and how does it shape your thinking about politics and the government?

"The life of man, solitary, poor, nasty, brutish, and short."

—Hobbes

direction that benefits society and its members can be discerned through the process of deliberation and voting. Then all individuals must agree to subordinate their personal desires and interests—their private wills—to the good of the whole—the general will.

Let's take a moment to recap before moving on to consider some objections to Rousseau in particular and democracy in general. Humans, according to Rousseau, have perfect freedom but they voluntarily give up much of that freedom when they live in community. What makes some laws—that is, restrictions on freedom—legitimate is that individuals agree to them in order to make their lives better. This agreement among individuals to live in community is what Rousseau calls the social contract, since individuals consent to a social arrangement. Ultimately it is the general will, or common good, that governs the social contract and to which individuals agree.

Of course almost everyone would agree that, for a community to flourish, its members must sometimes subordinate their own wishes to the needs of the whole. In other words, citizens should obey the law even when they don't want to. What is distinctive about Rousseau's theory, and about democratic theories in general, is the further claim that citizens are morally obligated to obey the laws only when they have been given a say in making the law. It is only the citizens' consent that gives the rulers the right to rule and that gives moral authority to the laws and government policies.

Let's move on to consider three of the many objections to democracy.

SOME OBJECTIONS

The problem of consent

Perhaps the most common objection to democracy is often called the problem of consent. If consent is the heart of democracy, it's also a central problem for democracy. What makes a democratic state legitimate is that the people consent, but how exactly do citizens give their consent? I certainly don't remember ever agreeing to the Constitution or the general structure of our government. How about you? The objection here is really quite simple and applies not only to Rousseau's social contract theory but also to most defenses of democracy. How can consent be the basis of democratic government when most citizens do not explicitly give their consent?

Implied consent

The most common response here is to appeal to some notion of implied or tacit consent. It's not that we explicitly agree to the social contract, but rather that our consent is assumed because of something we do, don't do, or the way we accept certain services. For example, some philosophers argue that accepting the benefits of society—police protection, public schools, postal service, and so on—effectively amounts to agreeing to the basic structure and rules of society. Similarly, you might say that anyone who votes in a public election is tacitly consenting to the rules of society. Finally, some have argued that we agree to be part of society simply by not leaving. I could, according to this argument, pick up and move if I wasn't willing to agree to the social contract of my democratic society. Since I don't leave, I am implying my consent.

But is it really clear that all citizens give their implied consent? Consider David Hume's response to the "love it or leave it" version of the implied consent argument:

> Can we seriously say that a poor peasant or artisan has a free choice to leave his country, when he knows no foreign language or manners, and lives from day to day, by the small wages he acquires? We may as well assert, that a man, by remaining in a vessel, freely consents to the dominion of the master; though he was carried on board while asleep, and must leap into the ocean, and perish, the moment he leaves her.[3]

Similar concerns can be raised about the other ways citizens supposedly give their consent. Voting seems great until we remember than more than half the citizens never vote in many democracies (including the United

---

[3]David Hume, *Essays Moral, Political, and Literary*, ed. Eugene F. Miller (Indianapolis, IN: Liberty Fund, 1985), p. 475.

States). How about accepting public services? Needless to say, most people aren't agreeing to anything when they mail a letter or pay a parking ticket. The basic problem remains: Without explicit agreements from all citizens it is difficult to see how consent can truly be the foundation of a legitimate society. One humorous way to sum up this objection is with the anonymous quotation: "Implied consent isn't worth the paper it isn't written on."

A second major objection to democracy relates to the majoritarian element of the theory. Democracy is rule by the people, but it's not *all* the people who rule, only the majority. It's an advantage—Isn't it?—that the majority rules in a democratic state. Well, it depends on whether or not you are in the majority and on what the majority decides. In Chapter 18 we saw how liberalism aims to protect the rights of all people, and fears about loss of basic rights and liberties motivate this worry about democracy.

What happens if the majority decides that rap music should be banned, but rap happens to be your favorite music? More generally, what rights do citizens have when they are in the minority? This concern about democracy is often referred to as the "tyranny of the majority." If there is no person or group above the body of citizens themselves, then there is no check against the majority if it wishes to exploit a minority. One sad example of this is slavery. Many of the world's monarchies outlawed slavery before the supposedly democratic United States did. Alexis de Tocqueville noted this very concern in his commentary, *Democracy in America*.

Tyranny of the majority

> In my opinion, the main evil of the present democratic institutions of the United States does not arise, as is often asserted in Europe, from their weakness, but from their irresistible strength. I am not so much alarmed at the excessive liberty which reigns in that country as at the inadequate securities which one finds there against tyranny. An individual or a party is wronged in the United States, to whom can he apply for redress? If to public opinion, public opinion constitutes the majority; if to the legislature, it represents the majority and implicitly obeys it; if to the executive power, it is appointed by the majority and serves as a passive tool in its hands. The public force consists of the majority under arms; the jury is the majority invested with the right of hearing judicial cases; and in certain states even the judges are elected by the majority. However iniquitous or absurd the measure of which you complain, you must submit to it as well as you can.[4]

One solution to the tyranny of the majority is to strengthen the multiple checks and balances in the U.S. Constitution to make it difficult for the majority to exercise its will. For example, although the people could in theory overturn the Thirteenth Amendment, which outlaws slavery, it would be very difficult to do so because of the multiple procedural hurdles along the way. Yet this is paradoxical because what are these hurdles except instruments for preventing the people from expressing their will? And isn't the will of the people exactly what democracy celebrates and counts on? One is left wondering whether the solution to the tyranny of the majority isn't simply the "tyranny of the minority."

[4]Alexis de Tocqueville, *Democracy in America*, tr. Arthur Goldhammer (New York: The Library of America, 2004), p. 290.

Perhaps the strongest objection to democracy is simply that an alternative arrangement is better. Winston Churchill famously commented: "Democracy is the worst form of government except all the others that have been tried." But certainly not everyone agrees. Plato, for one, thought democracy was one of the worst forms of government and instead favored rule by an elite. We began our study of philosophy with Plato, and we return to him here at the end.

PLATO'S PHILOSOPHER KINGS

We end with Plato for two reasons. First, he vividly represents an important alternative to democracy that we might call *elitism*, rule by a select few. Second, he is an excellent example of the way in which philosophers have conceived social-political issues not only as a necessary part of the philosophical enterprise but also as closely connected with other philosophical issues. It says something very important about Plato that his most famous work, and indeed possibly the most famous work in the history of philosophy, was called the *Republic*. It was a book about the *state*. Well, yes and no. At least it was a book that showed how social-political issues can be all bound up with other philosophical concerns, such as ethics, metaphysics, epistemology, and even art.

Plato's
Republic

We can be more specific. In Chapter 3 we provided some long quotations from the *Republic* for the sake of explaining Plato's theory of reality and knowledge. Do you recall Plato's Analogy of the Sun, the image of the Divided Line, and the Allegory of the Cave? Now we can say just what all of that had to do with the *state*. Plato certainly did have a particular (some would say peculiar) view of the state, and a view that had everything to do with his view of reality and knowledge.

Some degenerate
forms of
government

In the *Republic* Plato considered several political theories of his own time and rejected them. Whether or not we too reject them, it will do us no harm to review them. Moving from bad to worse, Plato first rejected *timocracy*, by which he meant the rule by those who are primarily motivated by ambition and honor. In such rulers, an inferior part of the soul, the spirited and emotional part, has gained dominance. He also rejected *oligarchy* or *plutocracy*, the rule by the rich. A preoccupation with wealth is even more base than a preoccupation with honor, and, moreover, the rule by the wealthy would inevitably bring about alienation and class warfare between "the haves" and "the have-nots." Next he rejected *democracy*, our interest here, as yet a further degeneration of government, though he meant by this word something different from what we today understand by it. For Plato, in a smallish city-state like Athens, democracy meant the actual and equal participation of every citizen in the affairs of state, rather than participation by representation. But this is to reduce government to the lowest common denominator—as Plato saw it, when we have majority rule we have *mob* rule. Finally, and worst of all, Plato rejects *despotism*, or *tyranny*, or *dictatorship*, the absolute rule of a single individual. Of course there may be such

Plato rejected:

- Timocracy
- Plutocracy
- Democracy
- Dictatorship

He advocated

- Aristocracy

But exactly what did Plato mean by these terms?

a thing as a "benevolent dictator" but, Plato believed, never for long. According to Lord Acton's famous saying, "All power corrupts; absolute power corrupts absolutely." Eventually, such a ruler will be ruled by the very worst in himself, resulting in gross injustice and loss of the personal liberty that government ought to ensure.

Well then, *what*? Plato's answer: *aristocracy.* Again, however, Plato did not mean by this term what is today usually meant. When we hear the word "aristocracy" we think of the nobility class, as in the expression "the landed aristocracy." But the word itself simply means "rule of the *best*," and that is exactly what Plato favored—the rule of the best. And who are the best? Those who are enlightened with regard to reality, truth, and goodness. And who are these? Why, *philosophers,* of course—those who have emerged from the darkness of the Cave and have beheld the Good. Plato himself calls this the central thesis of the *Republic:* "Philosophers must be kings."

"Philosophers must be kings"

In the following passages from the *Republic,* Plato, through the mouth of Socrates, announces this revolutionary social program and explains what it is that makes the philosopher the "best" and makes him or her (it could easily be a *her* for Plato) the most qualified to rule.

Unless either philosophers become kings in their countries or those who are now called kings and rulers come to be sufficiently inspired with a genuine desire for wisdom; unless, that is to say, political power and philosophy meet together, while the many natures who now go their several ways in the one or the other direction are forcibly debarred from doing so, there can be no rest from troubles, my dear Glaucon, for states, nor yet, as I believe, for all mankind; nor can this commonwealth which we have imagined ever till then see the light of day and grow to its full stature. This it was that I have so long hung back from saying; I knew what a paradox it would be, because it is hard to see that there is no other way of happiness either for the state or for the individual.

. . . Since the philosophers are those who can apprehend the eternal and unchanging, while those who cannot do so, but are lost in the mazes of multiplicity and change, are not philosophers, which of the two ought to be in control of a state?

I wonder what would be a reasonable solution.

To establish as Guardians whichever of the two appear competent to guard the laws and ways of life in society.

True.

Well, there can be no question whether a guardian who is to keep watch over anything needs to be keen-sighted or blind. And is not blindness precisely the condition of men who are entirely cut off from knowledge of any reality, and have in their soul no clear pattern of perfect truth, which they might study in every detail and constantly refer to, as a painter looks at his model, before they proceed to embody notions of justice, honour, and goodness in earthly institutions or, in their character of Guardians, to preserve such institutions as already exist?

Certainly such a condition is very like blindness.

Shall we, then, make such as these our Guardians in preference to men who, besides their knowledge of realities, are in no way inferior to them in experience and in every excellence of character?

It would be absurd not to choose the philosophers, whose knowledge is perhaps their greatest point of superiority, provided they do not lack those other qualifications.

What we have to explain, then, is how those qualifications can be combined in the same persons with philosophy.

Certainly.

The first thing, as we said at the onset, is to get a clear view of their inborn disposition. When we are satisfied on that head, I think we shall agree that such a combination of qualities is possible and that we need look no further for men fit to be in control of a commonwealth. One trait of the philosophic nature we may take as already granted: a constant passion for any knowledge that will reveal to them something of that reality which endures for ever and is not always passing into and out of existence. And, we may add, their desire is to know the whole of that reality; they will not willingly renounce any part of it as relatively small and insignificant, as we said before when we compared them to the lover and to the man who covets honour.

True.

Is there not another trait which the nature we are seeking cannot fail to possess—truthfulness, a love of truth and a hatred of falsehood that will not tolerate untruth in any form?

Yes, it is natural to expect that.

It is not merely natural, but entirely necessary that an instinctive passion for any object should extend to all that is closely akin to it; and there is nothing more closely akin to wisdom than truth. So the same nature cannot love wisdom and falsehood; the genuine lover of knowledge cannot fail, from his youth up, to strive after the whole of truth.

I perfectly agree.

Now we surely know that when a man's desires set strongly in one direction, in every other channel they flow more feebly, like a stream diverted into another bed. So when the current has set towards knowledge and all that goes with it, desire will abandon those pleasures of which the body is the instrument and be concerned only with the pleasure which the soul enjoys independently—if, that is to say, the love of wisdom is more than a mere pretence. Accordingly, such a one will be temperate and no lover of money; for he will be the last person to care about the things for the sake of which money is eagerly sought and lavishly spent.

That is true.

ARISTOTLE'S DEFENSE OF DEMOCRACY

Aristotle rejected the communistic and bizarre features of Plato's utopian state, as well as his intellectual elitism. Even though Aristotle himself believed, in his own way, in the rule of the best (not just anybody can occupy the highest offices), and even though he rejected *extreme* democracy (mob rule, again), he did believe, more commonsensically than Plato, that an adequate form of government must accommodate the rank and file of the citizenry with its collective experience and good sense, to say nothing of its greater stake in the political enterprise.

The principle that the multitude ought to be supreme rather than the few best is one that is maintained, and, though not free from difficulty, yet seems to contain an element of truth. For the many, of whom each individual is but an ordinary person, when they meet together may very likely be better than the few good, if regarded not individually but collectively, just as a feast to which many contribute is better than a dinner provided out of a single purse. For each individual among the many has a share of virtue and prudence, and when they meet together, they become in a manner one man, who has many feet, and hands, and sense; that is a figure of their mind and disposition. Hence the many are better judges than a single man of music and poetry; for some understand one part, and some another, and among them they understand the whole. There is a similar combination of qualities in good men, who differ from any individual of the many, as the beautiful are said to differ from those who are not beautiful, and works of art from realities, because in them the scattered elements are combined, although, if taken separately, the eye of one person or some other feature in another person would be fairer than in the picture. Whether this principle can apply to every democracy, and to all bodies of men, is not clear. Or rather, by heaven, in some cases it is impossible of application; for the argument would equally hold about brutes; and wherein, it will be asked, do some men differ from brutes? But there may be bodies of men about whom our statement is nevertheless true. And if so, the difficulty which has been already raised, and also another which is akin to it—viz. what power should be assigned to the mass of freemen and citizens, who are not rich and have no personal merit—are both solved. There is still a danger in allowing them to share the great offices of state, for their folly will lead them into error, and their dishonesty into crime. But there is a danger also in not letting them share, for a state in which many poor men are excluded from office will necessarily be full of enemies. The only way of escape is to assign to them some deliberative and judicial functions. For this reason Solon and certain other legislators give them the power of electing to offices, and of calling the magistrates to account, but they do not allow them to hold office singly. When they meet together their perceptions are quite good enough, and combined with the better class they are useful to the state (just as impure food when mixed with what is pure sometimes makes the entire mass more wholesome than a small quantity of the pure would be), but each individual, left to himself, forms an imperfect judgement.*

---

*Aristotle, *Politics,* 1281a–b, tr. Benjamin Jowett, in *Basic Works of Aristotle,* ed. Richard McKeon (New York: Random House, 1941).

Again, in seeking to distinguish the philosophic nature, you must not overlook the least touch of meanness. Nothing could be more contrary than pettiness to a mind constantly bent on grasping the whole of things, both divine and human.

Quite true.

And do you suppose that one who is so high-minded and whose thought can contemplate all time and all existence will count this life of man a matter of much concern?

No, he could not.

So for such a man death will have no terrors.

None.

A mean and cowardly nature, then, can have no part in the genuine pursuit of wisdom.

I think not.

And if a man is temperate and free from the love of money, meanness, pretentiousness, and cowardice, he will not be hard to deal with or dishonest. So, as another indication of the philosophic temper, you will observe whether, from youth up, he is fair-minded, gentle, and sociable.

Certainly.

Also you will not fail to notice whether he is quick or slow to learn. No one can be expected to take a reasonable delight in a task in which much painful effort makes little headway. And if he cannot retain what he learns his forgetfulness will leave no room in his head for knowledge; and so, having all his toil for nothing, he can only end by hating himself as well as his fruitless occupation. We must not, then, count a forgetful mind as competent to pursue wisdom; we must require a good memory.

By all means.

Further, there is in some natures a crudity and awkwardness that can only tend to a lack of measure and proportion; and there is a close affinity between proportion and truth. Hence, besides our other requirements, we shall look for a mind endowed with measure and grace, which will be instinctively drawn to see every reality in its true light.

Yes.

Well then, now that we have enumerated the qualities of a mind destined to take its full part in the apprehension of reality, have you any doubt about their being indispensable and all necessarily going together?

None whatever.

Then have you any fault to find with a pursuit which none can worthily follow who is not by nature quick to learn and to remember, magnanimous and gracious, the friend and kinsman of truth, justice, courage, temperance?

No; Momus himself could find no flaw in it.

Well then, when time and education have brought such characters as these to maturity, would you entrust the care of your commonwealth to anyone else?[5]

It is difficult to say just how seriously one is to take Plato's proposal, though it is known that he himself tried to implement such a philosopher-kingship in Syracuse. But taking it as seriously as we can, not everyone will be thrilled with the announcement that philosophers must rule over

[5]Plato, *The Republic*, 473C–E, 484B–487A, tr. Francis MacDonald Cornford (New York: Oxford University Press, 1941).

the rest. In the first place, not everyone shares a Platonic conception of reality, truth, and the like, and thus not everyone could agree with Plato as to just who the true philosophers are. Furthermore, any form of intellectual aristocracy would fail to gain the consent of a large segment of a society that is always suspicious of the "egghead" elite. You may have heard the pronouncement: "I would rather be governed by the first twenty names in the Boston telephone directory than all the professors at Harvard." Then, too, not everyone would like other features of Plato's social-political program. It is true that he was one of the earliest advocates of women's rights, but he also proposed a program of eugenics, arranged marriages, community of property and children, and censorship.

CHAPTER 19 IN REVIEW

SUMMARY

In this chapter we focused on the central idea of democracy, a concept that is extremely important to our contemporary political situation. The word *democracy*, we learned, means "rule by the people," and central to any theory of democracy is the idea of consent. According to democratic theory, it is the agreement or consent of the people that makes for a legitimate government or law. We can easily see the central role of consent in the founding documents of the United of States of America.

The French philosopher Jean-Jacques Rousseau was a pioneer in developing a theory of democracy. Rousseau took freedom as his starting point but argued that all people give up much of that freedom in order to live in society. While this giving up is crucial to the formation of a community, the real story is that it is only those freedoms that humans voluntarily give up that are legitimate government powers. Rousseau used this notion of our consent to restrictions as the basis of a social contract, the implied agreement that individuals have with one another to live together. The shared interests that bring people together are summed up in the general will, a phrase that describes the common good of all people, not just the interest of the few. Rousseau's theory, and democracy in general, are open to many objections. In this chapter we focused on two: the problem of consent and the tyranny of the majority. Democracy is based on consent, but do citizens actually agree to anything? Even if they do, isn't there a danger of the majority imposing their will on a minority? In the end, the best defense for democracy may be the pragmatic one that, despite its flaws, it is the best system we have.

You may recall at the beginning of Chapter 3 we said that Plato was the first *systematic* philosopher in the sense that he was the first to work out the implications of a fundamental philosophical principle for all major spheres of our experience. And we saw what his idea of Form meant for his theory of reality, his theory of knowledge, and even his theory of art. In this chapter we saw what it meant for his theory of the state. Plato's thesis that "philosophers must be kings" follows from his view that only philosophers are in touch with absolute truth and reality, and since this means that only they know what the absolute good is, philosophers alone are fit to rule over the rest of the people. Many will reject this aristocratic conception of government as elitist, as did Plato's student Aristotle. Aristotle shared Plato's fears about mob rule, but he opted nonetheless for a more democratic form of government that would reflect and represent the common interest as seen by the citizenry itself.

BASIC IDEAS

- Rousseau on freedom
- Consent
- Social contract
- General will
- Problem of consent
- Tyranny of the majority
- Elitism
- Plato: degenerate forms of government
    Timocracy
    Plutocracy
    Democracy
    Dictatorship
- Aristocracy
- Plato: why philosophers must be kings
- Aristotle's democracy

TEST YOURSELF

1. True or false: Plato rejected democracy, though he favored democracy over tyranny.
2. Both Plato and Aristotle desired the rule of the *best*. But how did they differ?
3. According to Plato, the best form of government is_____.
4. True or false: Rousseau argued for the divine right of kings.
5. The idea that government is based on the voluntary agreement of all citizens is called_____.
6. What is the problem of consent?

QUESTIONS FOR REFLECTION

- If elitism means rule by a select few, is there anything to be said in its favor? Does it matter *why* the elite are "select"? Would you not gladly submit yourself to the elite (best trained, etc.) in other fields, say, medicine or education? Or would you rather be governed by the first twenty names in the Boston phone book? What's to be said for and against *this* view?

- If majority rule is the key to democracy, how do you protect against the majority oppressing a minority? If we do this by limiting the power of the majority, is it still a democracy?

FOR FURTHER READING

Julia Annas. *An Introduction to Plato's "Republic."* Oxford: Clarendon Press, 1981. A clear and systematic exposition of a work that is central in the history of both philosophical and political thought.

Frederick Copleston. *A History of Philosophy.* Baltimore: Newman Press, 1946–1974. I, Chs. 24 and 32. Excellent accounts of the social-political doctrines of Plato and Aristotle.

Edwin Curley. "Introduction to Hobbes' *Leviathan*" in *Leviathan.* Indianapolis: Hackett, 1994. A very accessible and clear explanation of the main ideas in Hobbes' greatest work, with special attention given to correcting common misinterpretations.

Robert A. Dahl. *Democracy and Its Critics.* New Haven, CT: Yale University Press, 1989. Influential survey of major problems in democratic theory.

Nicholas Dent. *Rousseau,* The Routledge Philosophers. London: Routledge, 2005. Comprehensive and sympathetic survey of Rousseau's life and works.

David Gauthier. *The Logic of Leviathan.* Oxford: Oxford University Press, 1969.

G. M. A. Grube. *Plato's Thought.* London: Methuen, 1935. Ch. 3. A lucid discussion of Plato's doctrine of "statecraft," from a standard work.

David Held. *Models of Democracy.* Cambridge: Polity Press, 2006. Carefully analyzes types of democracies and associated problems.

G. E. R. Lloyd. *Aristotle: The Growth and Structure of His Thought.* Cambridge: Cambridge University Press, 1968. Ch. 11. A readable overview of Aristotle's political ideas, with frequent references to his texts.

Roger D. Masters. *The Political Philosophy of Rousseau.* Princeton, NJ: Princeton University Press, 1968. Classic study of Rousseau's political thought with emphasis on the social contract.

David Ross. *Aristotle.* Fifth ed. London: Methuen, 1949. Ch. 8. A chapter on Aristotle's politics, neatly divided into specific topics, from a standard work.

Ian Shapiro. *The State of Democratic Theory.* Princeton, NJ: Princeton University Press, 2003. Analysis of recent trends in the philosophical analysis of democracy.

Gregory Vlastos (ed.). *Plato: A Collection of Critical Essays.* II. Garden City, NY: Anchor Books, 1971. An anthology of advanced studies including several on Plato's political ideas.

John Wild. *Plato's Modern Enemies and the Theory of Natural Law.* Chicago: University of Chicago Press, 1953. A full-scale study, defending Plato's political theory from modern misrepresentations and misunderstandings, and developing it (especially as a natural law philosophy) in its historical context.

Robert Wokler. *Rousseau: A Very Short Introduction*. New York: Oxford University Press, 2001. Engaging and brief overview of his philosophical ideas.

*In addition, see the relevant articles ("Rousseau," "Plato," "Democracy," etc.) in *Routledge Encyclopedia of Philosophy*, ed. Edward Craig (London: Routledge, 1998), and *Stanford Encyclopedia of Philosophy*, http://plato.stanford.edu.

JUSTICE

t is appropriate that we conclude with some comment on what is probably the most basic idea of social and political philosophy: the idea of *justice*. If only we could be clear about justice, how much easier would our task be! But getting clear on justice may be more difficult than you think. Upon reflection, does your own idea of justice turn out to be some vague notion involving equality or fairness? But what constitutes equality or fairness? Does it involve the distribution of goods? But how much, to whom, and on what basis? Does it involve worthiness? But what is the basis of worthiness— talent, power, productivity? Does it involve social responsibility? But how is this to be measured?

THE PROBLEM

To be sure, various ideas of justice have already made their appearance, explicitly or implicitly, in the moral and social-political theories we have been discussing. Think of Plato's identification of justice with the rule of reason both in the individual and in the state; or Mill's utilitarian idea of a distribution of goods that would result in the greatest happiness of the greatest number; or Marx's definition: From each according to his ability, to each according to his need. The problem is obviously a very big one. Our purpose in this chapter is to focus on only a few, but very important, recent contributions to the discussion.

In his provocative book *After Virtue*, Alasdair MacIntyre sets forth the problem in one of the forms readily familiar to Americans:

> A, who may own a store or be a police officer or a construction worker, has struggled to save enough from his earnings to buy a small house, to send his children to the local college, to pay for some special type of medical care for his parents. He now finds all of his projects threatened by rising taxes. He regards this threat to his projects as *unjust;* he claims to have a right to what he has earned and that nobody else has a right to take away what he acquired legitimately and to which he has a just title. He intends to vote for candidates for political office who will defend his property, his projects *and* his conception of justice.
>
> B, who may be a member of one of the liberal professions, or a social worker, or someone with inherited wealth, is impressed with the arbitrariness of the inequalities in the distribution of wealth, income and opportunity. He is, if anything, even more impressed with the inability of the poor and the deprived to do very much about their own condition as a result of inequalities in the distribution of power. He regards both these types of inequality as *unjust* and as constantly engendering further injustice. He believes more generally that all inequality stands in need of justification and that the only possible justification for inequality is to improve the condition of the poor and the deprived—by, for example, fostering economic growth. He draws the conclusion that in present circumstances redistributive taxation which will finance welfare and the social sciences is what justice demands. He intends to vote for candidates for political office who will defend redistributive taxation *and* his conception of justice. . . .
>
> The logical incompatibility is not difficult to identify. A holds that principles of just acquisition and entitlement set limits to redistributive possibilities. If the outcome of the application of the principles of just acquisition and entitlement is gross inequality, the toleration of such inequality is a price that has to be paid for justice. B holds that principles of just distribution set limits to legitimate acquisition and entitlement. If the outcome of the application of the principles of just distribution is interference—by means of taxation or such devices as eminent domain—with what has up till now been regarded in this social order as legitimate acquisition and entitlement, the toleration of such interference is a price that has to be paid for justice. We may note in passing—it will not be unimportant later—that in the case of both A's principle and B's principle the price for one person or group of persons receiving justice is always paid by someone else. Thus different identifiable social groups have an interest in the acceptance of one of the principles and the rejection of the other. Neither principle is socially or politically neutral.[1]

Now there are two radically different ways in which the conflict between A and B may be resolved, and these involve, of course, two radically different views of justice. In recent years, these two different views have received forceful and influential expression in John Rawls, whose major work, *A Theory of Justice,* argues in favor of B's position, and Robert Nozick, whose major work, *Anarchy, State, and Utopia,* argues in favor of A's position. We will look first at Rawls, then Nozick, and turn finally to a feminist notion of justice that seeks to advance the discussion in still a different direction.

[1]Alasdair MacIntyre, *After Virtue: A Study in Moral Theory* (Notre Dame, IN: University of Notre Dame Press, 1981), pp. 227–229.

"Justice is the first virtue of social systems, as truth is of systems of thought."

—Rawls

RAWLS: JUSTICE AS FAIRNESS

In his books *Justice as Fairness* and *A Theory of Justice,* as well as in other writings, Rawls has propounded a theory of justice that has proven to be extremely important. Some have even spoken of the "Rawlsmania" that has seized recent discussions.

The attempt to combine both (1) the *libertarian* view of justice as consisting in personal liberty and (2) the *socialist* view of justice as consisting in the social equality is called (3) the *liberal* view of justice. Clearly, Rawls stands in the liberal tradition. He believes that it is not necessary to stall forever between the ideals of individual liberty on the one hand and a more equitable distribution of goods on the other: He attempts to develop a concept of justice that would unite the virtues of both the libertarian and the egalitarian or socialist perspectives. The liberal view of justice can, however, take two different forms. These are (1) the *contractual* (think of Locke), which involves an agreement between persons who willingly delimit certain of their freedoms in exchange for greater equality, say, equality of wealth, opportunity, and the like, and (2) the *utilitarian* (think of Mill), which involves the adoption of rules that would promote the maximization of happiness. That Rawls espouses the contractual version of the liberal view of justice we shall now see.

In the first reading below, Rawls expresses the heart of his theory in his own words, but we may summarize the main points. Reminiscent of the old-line social-contractors, Rawls starts out with his idea of *the original position* (Locke called it the state of nature), emphasizing that this is a purely

The liberal view of justice

"The original position"

THREE VIEWS OF JUSTICE

Libertarian	*Socialist*	*Liberal*
Personal liberty is the highest social ideal.	Equity of persons is the highest social ideal.	A combination of liberty and equality is the highest social ideal.
		(a) *Contractual:* Trades off equality for greater welfare.
		(b) *Utilitarian:* Accepts any kind of inequality if it maximizes happiness.

hypothetical or imaginary situation. In order to ensure that whatever principle of justice we adopt is really fair to all concerned (hence his idea of "justice as fairness") we must try to imagine ourselves as stripped of all factors that could possibly prejudice us in favor of one principle rather than another. Obviously, if you are the president of Consolidated Steel, or a Wall Street tycoon, or a shipping magnate, your interests will tempt you in a different direction than if you are a Chicano migrant worker. It is as difficult as it is necessary to adopt what Rawls calls a *veil of ignorance,* a veil that will cover up, for the moment at least, what we very well know about our own vested interests but need to *forget* if our principle is to be born in a climate of objectivity—everybody in the same boat, everybody standing to lose or gain the same things. The participants naturally will not be a party to any principle that, when the veil is lifted, might mean a loss of their fair share of the pie. On the other hand, neither will they be a party to any principle that might grant them *more* than a fair share, since there is no guarantee that when the veil is lifted they will be on the receiving end. These social-contractors will all therefore favor a principle that will result in at least, but not more than, a fair share for all. Approaching the matter in this way, we have a basis for discussing and formulating a principle of justice in an impartial way, one that is not tilted in the direction of any special interests.

In all of this Rawls presupposes a degree of *rationality* on the part of the social-contractors. The whole enterprise will be doomed from the start without an intuitive sense of fairness, without goodwill, and without an honesty and realism about what agreements can actually be honored and kept.

The "veil of ignorance"

Rationality

The Main Idea of the Theory of Justice

My aim is to present a conception of justice which generalizes and carries to a higher level of abstraction the familiar theory of the social contract as found, say, in Locke, Rousseau, and Kant. In order to do this we are not to think of the original contract as one to enter a particular society or to set up a particular form of government. Rather, the guiding idea is that the principles of justice for the basic structure of society are the object of the original agreement. They are the principles that free and rational persons concerned to further their own interests would accept in an initial position of equality as defining the fundamental terms of their association. These principles are to regulate all further agreements; they specify the kinds of social cooperation that can be entered into and the forms of government that can be established. This way of regarding the principles of justice I shall call justice as fairness.

Thus we are to imagine that those who engage in social cooperation choose together, in one joint act, the principles which are to assign basic rights and duties and to determine the division of social benefits. Men are to decide in advance how they are to regulate their claims against one another and what is to be the foundation charter of their society. Just as each person must decide by rational reflection what constitutes his good, that is, the system of ends which it is rational for him to pursue, so a group of persons must decide once and for all what is to count among them as just and unjust. The choice which rational men would make in this hypothetical situation of equal liberty, assuming for the present that this choice problem has a solution, determines the principles of justice.

In justice as fairness the original position of equality corresponds to the state of nature in the traditional theory of the social contract. This original position is not, of course, thought of as an actual historical state of affairs, much less as a primitive condition of culture. It is understood as a purely hypothetical situation characterized so as to lead to a certain conception of justice. . . .

The Veil of Ignorance

The idea of the original position is to set up a fair procedure so that any principles agreed to will be just. The aim is to use the notion of pure procedural justice as a basis of theory. Somehow we must nullify the effects of specific contingencies which put men at odds and tempt them to exploit social and natural circumstances to their own advantage. Now in order to do this I assume that the parties are situated behind a veil of ignorance. They do not know how the various alternatives will affect their own particular case and they are obliged to evaluate principles solely on the basis of general considerations.

It is assumed, then, that the parties do not know certain kinds of particular facts. First of all, no one knows his place in society, his class position or social status; nor does he know his fortune in the distribution of natural assets and abilities, his intelligence and strength, and the like. Nor, again, does anyone know his conception of the good, the particulars of his rational plan of life, or even the special features of his psychology such as his aversion to risk or liability to optimism or pessimism. More than this, I assume that the parties do not know the particular circumstances of their own society. That is, they do not know its economic or political situation, or the level of civilization and culture it has been able to achieve. The persons in the original position have no information as to which generation they belong. These broader restrictions on knowledge are appropriate in part because questions of social justice arise between generations as well as within them, for example, the question of the appropriate rate of capital saving and of the conservation of natural resources and the environment of nature. There is also, theoretically anyway, the question of a reasonable genetic policy. In these cases too, in order to carry through the idea of the original position, the parties must not know the contingencies that set them in opposition. They must choose principles the consequences of which they are prepared to live with whatever generation they turn out to belong to. . . .

Thus there follows the very important consequence that the parties have no basis for bargaining in the usual sense. No one knows his situation in society nor his natural assets, and therefore no one is in a position to tailor principles to his advantage. We might imagine that one of the contractees threatens to hold out unless the others agree to principles favorable to him. But how does he know which principles are especially in his interests? The same holds for the formation of coalitions: if a group were to decide to band together to the disadvantage of the others, they would not know how to favor themselves in the choice of principles. Even if they could get everyone to agree to their proposal, they would have no assurance that it was to their advantage, since they cannot identify themselves either by name or description. . . .

The restrictions on particular information in the original position are, then, of fundamental importance. Without them we would not be able to work out any definite theory of justice at all. We would have to be content with a vague formula stating that justice is what would be agreed to without being able to say much, if anything, about the substance of the agreement itself. The formal constraints of the concept of right, those applying to principles directly, are not sufficient for our purpose. The veil of ignorance makes possible a unanimous choice of a particular conception of justice. Without these limitations on knowledge the bargaining problem of the original position would be hopelessly complicated. Even if theoretically a solution were to exist, we would not, at present anyway, be able to determine it. . . .

The Rationality of the Parties

. . . There is one further assumption to guarantee strict compliance. The parties are presumed to be capable of a sense of justice and this fact is public knowledge among them. This condition is to insure the integrity of the agreement made in the original position. It does not mean that in their deliberations the parties apply some particular conception of justice, for this would defeat the point of the motivation assumption. Rather, it means that the parties can rely on each other to understand and to act in accordance with whatever principles are finally agreed to. Once principles are acknowledged the parties can depend on one another to conform to them. In reaching an agreement, then, they know that their undertaking is not in vain; their capacity for a sense of justice insures that the principles chosen will be respected. It is essential to observe, however, that this assumption still permits the consideration of men's capacity to act on the various conceptions of justice. The general facts of human psychology and the principles of moral learning are relevant matters for the parties to examine. If a conception of justice is unlikely to generate its own support, or lacks stability, this fact must not be overlooked. For then a different conception of justice might be preferred. The assumption only says that the parties have a capacity for justice in a purely formal sense: taking everything relevant into account, including the general facts of moral psychology, the parties will adhere to the principles eventually chosen. They are rational in that they will not enter into agreements they know they cannot keep, or can do so only with great difficulty. Along with other considerations, they count the strains of commitment. Thus in assessing conceptions of justice the persons in the original position are to assume that the one they adopt will be strictly complied with. The consequences of their agreement are to be worked out on this basis.[2]

The stage thus set, Rawls introduces his principle of justice, which is actually *two* principles. The first attempts to accommodate the libertarian ideal of individual freedoms and rights, and is directed to that part of the social structure that establishes such liberties: "Each person is to have an equal right to the most extensive basic liberty compatible with a similar liberty for others." This is called the Principle of Equal Basic Liberty for All. The second principle of justice is directed rather to the economic facts of social life and is more complicated. It attempts to accommodate the egalitarian ideal of an equitable distribution of wealth while accommodating at the same time a reasonable *in*equitable distribution. It accomplishes this by insisting that such inequities result in an advantage for all and, most notably, for the *least* advantaged. Is it not to your advantage that your dentist earns more than you do, if as a result you receive better dental care? Thus, the second principle of justice: "Social and economic inequalities are to be arranged so that they are both (a) reasonably expected to be to everyone's

The Principle
of Equal Basic
Liberty for All

---

[2]John Rawls, *A Theory of Justice* (Cambridge, MA: Harvard University Press, 1971), pp. 11–12, 136–137, 139–140, 145.

advantage, and (b) attached to positions and offices open to all." This is called the Difference Principle.

As Rawls states, each of these principles embodies in different ways a more general idea, the General Conception of Justice: "All social values—liberty and opportunity, income and wealth, and the bases of self-respect—are to be distributed equally unless an unequal distribution of any, or all, of these values is to everyone's advantage."

Two Principles of Justice

I shall now state in a provisional form the two principles of justice that I believe would be chosen in the original position. . . .

The first statement of the two principles reads as follows.

First: each person is to have an equal right to the most extensive basic liberty compatible with a similar liberty for others.

Second: social and economic inequalities are to be arranged so that they are both (a) reasonably expected to be to everyone's advantage, and (b) attached to positions and offices open to all. . . .

By way of general comment, these principles primarily apply, as I have said, to the basic structure of society. They are to govern the assignment of rights and duties and to regulate the distribution of social and economic advantages. As their formulation suggests, these principles presuppose that the social structure can be divided into two more or less distinct parts, the first principle applying to the one, the second to the other. They distinguish between those aspects of the social system that define and secure the equal liberties of citizenship and those that specify and establish social and economic inequalities. The basic liberties of citizens are, roughly speaking, political liberty (the right to vote and to be eligible for public office) together with freedom of speech and assembly; liberty of conscience and freedom of thought; freedom of the person along with the right to hold (personal) property; and freedom from arbitrary arrest and seizure as defined by the concept of the rule of law. These liberties are all required to be equal by the first principle, since citizens of a just society are to have the same basic rights.

The second principle applies, in the first approximation to the distribution of income and wealth and to the design of organizations that make use of differences in authority and responsibility, or chains of command. While the distribution of wealth and income need not be equal, it must be to everyone's advantage, and at the same time, positions of authority and offices of command must be accessible to all. One applies the second principle by holding positions open, and then, subject to this constraint, arranges social and economic inequalities so that everyone benefits.

These principles are to be arranged in a serial order with the first principle prior to the second. This ordering means that a departure from the institutions of equal liberty required by the first principle cannot be justified by, or compensated for, by greater social and economic advantages. The distribution of wealth and income, and the hierarchies of authority, must be consistent with both the liberties of equal citizenship and equality of opportunity.

. . . For the present, it should be observed that the two principles (and this holds for all formulations) are a special case of a more general conception of justice that can be expressed as follows.

All social values—liberty and opportunity, income and wealth, and the bases of self-respect—are to be distributed equally unless an unequal distribution of any, or all, of these values is to everyone's advantage.

Injustice, then, is simply inequalities that are not to the benefit of all. Of course, this conception is extremely vague and requires interpretation.

As a first step, suppose that the basic structure of society distributes certain primary goods, that is, things that every rational man is presumed to want. These goods normally have a use whatever a person's rational plan of life. For simplicity, assume that the chief primary goods at the disposition of society are rights and liberties, powers and opportunities, income and wealth. . . . These are the social primary goods. Other primary goods such as health and vigor, intelligence and imagination, are natural goods; although their possession is influenced by the basic structure, they are not so directly under its control. Imagine, then, a hypothetical initial arrangement in which all the social primary goods are equally distributed: everyone has similar rights and duties, and income and wealth are evenly shared. This state of affairs provides a benchmark for judging improvements. If certain inequalities of wealth and organizational powers would make everyone better off than in this hypothetical starting situation, then they accord with the general conception.

Now it is possible, at least theoretically, that by giving up some of their fundamental liberties men are sufficiently compensated by the resulting social and economic gains. The general conception of justice imposes no restrictions on what sort of inequalities are permissible; it only requires that everyone's position be improved. We need not suppose anything so drastic as consenting to a condition of slavery. Imagine instead that men forego certain political rights when the economic returns are significant and their capacity to influence the course of policy by the exercise of these rights would be marginal in any case. It is this kind of exchange which the two principles as stated rule out; being arranged in serial order they do not permit exchanges between basic liberties and economic and social gains. The serial ordering of principles expresses an underlying preference among primary social goods. When this preference is rational so likewise is the choice of these principles in this order.[3]

It should be clear by now that Rawls has attempted to provide rational grounds in support of B's position as represented by MacIntyre at the beginning of our chapter: He has argued, as it might be put generally, for a *principle of equality with respect to needs.* That in the eyes of many he has succeeded at least in something is evident from the way his work has been hailed as a monumental contribution to social philosophy. But it has at the same time provoked considerable criticism. One of his most effective adversaries is Robert Nozick, who, as we will see in the next section, represents an altogether different perspective on justice and argues just as strongly in support of A's position. In the meantime, however, we may consider some specific criticisms leveled against Rawls.

Much of the controversy has centered on Rawls' proposal of the veil of ignorance. For example, can we so easily draw the conclusion Rawls wants us to from a premise we know to be false? If we were really operating behind a veil of ignorance, that would be one thing. But, as it is, could one really "think away" his or her wealth, beauty, talent, and general advantage, for the sake of a principle that might immediately nullify them? The

---

[3]Ibid., pp. 60–63.

RAWLS' TWO PRINCIPLES OF JUSTICE

- *The Principle of Equal Basic Liberty for All:* Each person is to have an equal right to the most extensive basic liberty compatible with a similar liberty for others.

- *The Difference Principle:* Social and economic inequalities are to be arranged so that they are both (a) reasonably expected to be to everyone's advantage, and (b) attached to positions and offices open to all.

RAWLS' GENERAL CONCEPTION OF JUSTICE

According to Rawls, his two principles of justice are particular expressions of a more general conception:

- All social values are to be distributed equally unless an unequal distribution of any, or all, of these values is to everyone's advantage.

theory is, says the critic, very nice but very abstract and hypothetical by comparison to the situation in which people actually find themselves—especially if they are, as Rawls hopes them to be, *rationally self-interested.* Someone has suggested, for example, that if you own a painting you know to be worth $5,000, you would not sell it for $100 simply because you might if you *didn't* know it was worth $5,000! Again, there is a big difference between signing a contract and *imagining* that you have signed a contract. When the chips are down, hypothetical or *imaginary* contracts can't be expected to enforce anything. Must not the implementability of Rawls' view depend on some deeper moral principle?

<aside>Is the veil of ignorance too hypothetical?</aside>

Similarly, it has been seen that Rawls' theory depends for its life on our desire in the state of ignorance (if we *could* cultivate such a state) to "minimize the risk" of things turning out to our disadvantage in the actual world. This, says Rawls, would be a *rational* approach. But why is it any more *rational* to take the road of minimizing the risk than that of maximizing the gain? To be sure, if it meant turning up penniless, diseased, ugly, and outcast, then understandably one would take the minimizing road. But that is *not* usually the choice, and one might *reasonably* gamble a so-so condition for a little more advantage—wouldn't one?

<aside>Why not maximize the gain?</aside>

Further, it has been objected that, contrary to Rawls' insistence, his principles might run exactly opposite to our deepest intuitions about morality, equality, society, and the like. This point (along with several others) is forcefully made by William R. Marty:

<aside>Does Rawls' theory contradict our moral sensibilities?</aside>

> . . . two men are shipwrecked on an island. One works hard. He plows the ground, plants seed, weeds his field, chases the birds away, waters the crop through the heat and dryness of summer, builds a shed to store the grain through the blizzards of winter, builds himself a cabin to survive the cold, and then harvests the crop. The other man, by happenstance formerly a hit man, acts differently. Through the

hot summer he sits in the shade of the tree, swims in the pleasant lagoon, and lives idly off the fat of the land for the living is easy, and besides, when winter comes, he plans to knock the other man on the head while he sleeps and take his grain, his shed, and his shelter. This man neither makes a crop, thereby earning his keep, nor has he the good in his heart.

Now to whom, in this hypothetical situation, does that store of grain rightly belong? Our intuitive sense is clear. It belongs to the one who by his planning, effort, and sacrifice produced it, not to the one who sat by in deliberate and malicious idleness in anticipation of gaining the grain without effort except for one foul deed. In this case, all the grain clearly belongs to the one, and none to the other. But, apply the Rawlsian technique for locating the just distribution: Take the two men from the island, strip them of any knowledge of how or by whom the grain was produced (put them, that is, behind the Veil of Ignorance), and let them then, on the basis of rational calculation of self-interest, divide the grain, and how will they divide it? They will divide it equally for, as Rawls asks us, why should either accept less than half and why should either give up more than half?. . .

The Rawlsian method certainly provides a shrewd strategy about how to get the pie cut equally, but is the result justice? That would depend on whether justice requires, in all cases, or in particular cases, an equal division. But in some cases, as the preceding example illustrates, justice clearly does not require or even allow an equal division. Rawls's distribution is faulty because it divorces distribution from a number of things that can legitimately give a claim to a particular share of a distribution. Thus allocation, à la Rawls, divorces distribution from contribution (who bought or brought the pie makings?), effort (who baked it?), risk (what if there are a number of pies from which to choose the one to divide, but one is booby-trapped so that it will explode and kill the slicer?), need (what if some among whom the pie is to be divided are fat and well-fed, but others are malnourished or starving?), skill or excellence (what if two come to the party, each bringing a pie, but one is a good cook and the other is not, how then should the pies be divided?), or responsibility and performance (again two cooks, but one exercises care to be clean and use sanitary ingredients while the other, sloppy in habits and careless in cooking, is likely to have a pie that will make people ill?). None of these—contribution, effort, risk, need, skill, excellence, responsibility, and performance—is dealt with adequately by the Rawlsian scheme, except perhaps need, and need only if an equal distribution will meet the needs of all, which of course it won't—consider the medical problems of people requiring a clotting factor for their blood or a kidney machine. Either requires more expense than the average income share of even the richest society on earth, hence in these cases an equal division would be a fatal division. . . .

In particular, the Rawlsian structure fails because the same Veil of Ignorance that was designed to hide from those in the Original Position their place in the society-to-be in order to prevent them from rationalizing their self-interest and calling it justice, also hides from them all the particular details that they must know if they are to know what a just distribution is. Thus it hides from them who produced the grain on that island and who did not, which makes it impossible for them to know who earned that grain and who did not, and it hides from them all information about individual efforts or lack of effort, about individual contributions or lack thereof, about handicaps, choices, needs, duties fulfilled, or responsibilities not met. It hides from them, in other words, precisely what they must know to distribute justly, unless just distribution among individuals has absolutely nothing to do with what those individuals choose or do or leave undone, and that is a patent absurdity that would make the whole concept of a just or unjust distribution meaningless. Consequently, the Rawlsian scheme does not lead those in the Original Position (or us) to justice unless that hit man deserves as much as the hard worker. Analytically, the scheme cannot lead those in the Original Position to justice because it blinds them to all the individual actions and choices that are the foundation of a just distribution. Analogically, Rawls has given us Justice blindfolded to make her impartial, but he has deprived her of the scales by which alone she can tell what justice among individuals requires. . . .

The Rawlsian method for finding justice fails because its structure presupposes, without proving, that an equal division is a fair division; because that same structure makes us indifferent to whether justice is done; and because, even if we cared, it hides from us all knowledge of the particular facts on which claims to a particular share must rest. The Rawlsian strategy makes it to our self-interest to choose a division contrary to our deepest intuitions of justice, and contrary to previous teachings of justice. It can and does defend outrageously unjust divisions. It simply fails as a serious means of locating justice.[4]

NOZICK: JUSTICE AS ENTITLEMENT

As we said above, however, it is necessary to consider the possibility that Rawls' whole enterprise is fundamentally misguided and that the true nature of justice is to be sought along altogether different lines. Robert Nozick takes this stance and argues that the truth of the matter lies not in B's position but A's. He argues, that is, not for a *principle of equality with respect to needs,* but rather a *principle of equality with respect to entitlement.*

With Nozick, as with Rawls, we are back to Locke and to talk about the state of nature and the social contract, but now with a renewed emphasis on individual rights and a decided turn in the direction of libertarianism. (Nozick himself confesses that when he started out he was repelled by libertarian views, but slowly became convinced of such views on unthwartable rational grounds.) The two most obvious features of Nozick's theory are his emphasis on the *minimal state* and his conception of *justice as entitlement.*

We begin with his emphasis on the minimal state. The tone of Nozick's whole enterprise is sounded in the very opening lines of the preface to his *Anarchy, State, and Utopia:*

The minimal state

> Individuals have rights, and there are things no person or group may do to them (without violating their rights). So strong and far-reaching are these rights that they raise the question of what, if anything, the state and its officials may do. How much room do individual rights leave for the state? . . .
>
> Our main conclusions about the state are that a minimal state, limited to the narrow functions of protection against force, theft, fraud, enforcement of contracts, and so on, is justified; that any more extensive state will violate persons' rights not to be forced to do certain things, and is unjustified; and that the minimal state is inspiring as well as right. Two noteworthy implications are that the state may not

[4]William R. Marty, "Rawls and the Harried Mother," *Interpretation* 9 (1981), pp. 387–389, 393–395.

use its coercive apparatus for the purpose of getting some citizens to aid others, or in order to prohibit activities to people for their own good or protection.[5]

Nozick otherwise labels his minimal state with the more descriptive expression "night-watchman state." What does this mean? It means that the proper function of the state is like that of a night watchman whose task it is to prowl about for the purpose of protecting the goods of those who have hired him. In the case of the state—the minimal state—its purpose is, and is *only*, to protect the rights and properties of its citizens, to enforce contracts, and the like. Anything beyond this would be itself an infringement on individual rights. So, there are many things that the state *cannot* do: It can't tell you what you may or may not do with your own body; it can't make you pay taxes to support food stamps, or, for that matter, any welfare programs; it can't dictate what you may read, see, smoke, or snort; it can't make you pay a portion of your income for social security; it can't tell you whom to hire or fire; it can't tell you to whom you may or may not rent your apartment or sell your home; and so on.

But what is the justification of this conception of the state? Well, the answer lies in the very opening words of the above quotation: "Individuals have rights."

Nozick follows the traditional Lockean idea that, in the state of nature, we find ourselves endowed with certain inalienable rights. And, like Locke, he believes (though he does not seek to demonstrate) that these rights are *inherent*. On the other hand, whereas some of these rights are nontransferable, such as life, liberty, and the pursuit of property, others are transferable, such as those rights we participants in the social contract voluntarily transfer to the state in order to guarantee the preservation of the more basic ones. One of the more basic ones, as we just said, is the right of the pursuit of private property or goods. And this brings us to Nozick's idea of justice as entitlement.

The entitlement theory

In a word, the entitlement theory is this: People are entitled to the property they have acquired legitimately, and they are entitled to dispose of it any way they want as long as this does not infringe on the rights of others. More specifically, three issues underlie this view. The first concerns the original *acquisition* of holdings—that is, the coming to be owned or the appropriation by someone of some previously unowned or unappropriated something. If such a something is appropriated when there is enough of that something left over for everyone else, then such an acquisition is legitimate. This Nozick calls the Principle of Justice in Acquisition. The second issue concerns the *transfer* of holdings—that is, the process by which a holding is acquired from someone who previously held it. When something is held by an act of legitimate transfer from someone who acquired it by a just, original acquisition, then such a holding is legitimate. This Nozick calls the Principle of Justice in Transfer. The third issue concerns the unfortunate fact that not all holdings are legitimate—that is, not all holdings have been

The Principle of Justice in Acquisition

The Principle of Justice in Transfer

---

[5]Robert Nozick, *Anarchy, State, and Utopia* (New York: Basic Books, 1974), p. ix.

NOZICK'S THREE PRINCIPLES OF JUSTICE IN HOLDINGS

- *The Principle of Justice in Acquisition:* An acquisition of something is just if the something is previously unowned and the acquisition leaves enough to meet the needs of others.
- *The Principle of Justice in Transfer:* A holding is just if it has been acquired through a legitimate transfer from someone who has acquired it through a legitimate transfer or through original acquisition.
- *The Principle of the Rectification of Injustice in Holdings:* An honest attempt must be made to identify the sources of illegitimate holdings and to compensate the victims.

acquired either by a just act of original acquisition or by a just act of transfer: Just think of the holdings that have been acquired through fraud, intimidation, theft, and exploitation. Thus we need a principle by which to set right the illegitimate and unjust intrusions into the practice of justice in holdings. For Nozick this amounts to a kind of commonsensical attempt to determine at what point the unjust intrusion occurred and to recompense the subsequent victims for the violation of their holding rights. This Nozick calls the Principle of the Rectification of Injustice in Holdings.

These points are expressed in Nozick's own idiom in the following extract from his *Anarchy, State, and Utopia:*

> If the world were wholly just, the following inductive definition would exhaustively cover the subject of justice in holdings.
>
> 1. A person who acquires a holding in accordance with the principles of justice in acquisition is entitled to that holding.
> 2. A person who acquires a holding in accordance with the principles of justice in transfer, from someone else entitled to the holding, is entitled to the holding.
> 3. No one is entitled to a holding except by (repeated) applications of 1 and 2.
>
> The complete principles of distributive justice would say simply that a distribution is just if everyone is entitled to the holdings they possess under the distribution.
>
> A distribution is just if it arises from another just distribution by legitimate means. The legitimate means of moving from one distribution to another are specified by the principles of justice in transfer. The legitimate first "moves" are specified by the principle of justice in acquisition. Whatever arises from a just situation by just steps is itself just. The means of change specified by the principles of justice in transfer preserve justice. As correct rules of inference are truth-preserving, and any conclusion deduced via repeated application of such rules from only true premises is itself true, so the means of transition from one situation to another specified by the principle of justice in transfer are justice-preserving, and any situation actually arising from repeated transitions in accordance with the principle from a just situation is itself just. The parallel between justice-preserving

The Principle of the Rectification of Injustice in Holdings transformations and truth-preserving transformations illuminates where it fails as well as where it holds. That a conclusion could have been deduced by truth-preserving means from premises that are true suffices to show its truth. That from a just situation a situation *could* have arisen via justice-preserving means does *not* suffice to show its justice. The fact that a thief's victims voluntarily *could* have presented him with gifts does not entitle the thief to his ill-gotten gains. Justice in holdings is historical; it depends upon what actually has happened. We shall return to this point later.

Not all actual situations are generated in accordance with the two principles of justice in holdings: the principle of justice in acquisition and the principle of justice in transfer. Some people steal from others, or defraud them, or enslave them, seizing their product and preventing them from living as they choose, or forcibly exclude others from competing in exchanges. None of these are permissible modes of transition from one situation to another. And some persons acquire holdings by means not sanctioned by the principles of justice in acquisition. The existence of past injustice (previous violations of the first two principles of justice in holdings) raises the third major topic under justice in holdings: the rectification of injustice in holdings. If past injustice has shaped present holdings in various ways, some identifiable and some not, what now, if anything, ought to be done to rectify these injustices? What obligations do the performers of injustice have toward those whose position is worse than it would have been had the injustice not been done? Or, than it would have been had compensation been paid promptly? How, if at all, do things change if the beneficiaries and those made worse off are not the direct parties in the act of injustice, but, for example, their descendants? Is an injustice done to someone whose holding was itself based upon an unrectified injustice? How far back must one go in wiping clean the historical slate of injustices? What may victims of injustice permissibly do in order to rectify the injustices being done to them, including the many injustices done by persons acting through their government? I do not know of a thorough or theoretically sophisticated treatment of such issues. Idealizing greatly, let us suppose theoretical investigation will produce a principle of rectification. This principle uses historical information about previous situations and injustices done in them (as defined by the first two principles of justice and rights against interference), and information about the actual course of events that flowed from these injustices, until the present, and it yields a description (or descriptions) of holdings in the society. The principle of rectification presumably will make use of its best estimate of subjunctive information about what would have occurred (or a probability distribution over what might have occurred, using the expected value) if the injustice had not taken place. If the actual description of holdings turns out not to be one of the descriptions yielded by the principle, then one of the descriptions yielded must be realized.

The general outlines of the theory of justice in holdings are that the holdings of a person are just if he is entitled to them by the principles of justice in acquisition and transfer, or by the principle of rectification of injustice (as specified by the first two principles). If each person's holdings are just, then the total set (distribution) of holdings is just.[6]

But how does all of this apply to the concrete, practical problem before us in this chapter? What is the real payoff, as it were, with respect to the problem of a just distribution of goods? The answer is given in the above

[6]Ibid., pp. 151–153.

THE COMPLETE PRINCIPLE
OF DISTRIBUTIVE JUSTICE

A distribution is just if everyone is entitled to the holdings they possess under the distribution.

quotation in the unambiguous assertion that ". . . the complete principle of distributive justice would say simply that a distribution is just if everyone is entitled to the holdings they possess under the distribution." Again, the controlling idea is *entitlement*. We saw that for Rawls the key idea with respect to the question of the just distribution of goods is *fairness*. For Nozick it is *entitlement*. Thus, according to Nozick, the nonvoluntary redistribution of income or goods to achieve, as he calls it, "equality of material condition" is impermissible. It is impermissible because a state that forces or coerces some to contribute to the welfare of others violates the rights of those who are forced. If this statement seems to be weak, consider Nozick's claim that

> your being forced to contribute to another's welfare violates your rights, whereas someone else's not providing you with things you need greatly, including things essential to the protection of your rights, does not *itself* violate your rights, even though it avoids making it more difficult for someone else to violate them.[7]

Just as Nozick's position is a response to Rawls', so does Rawls' position pose the most obvious question to Nozick's: *But is it fair?* Here we will not rehearse the ins and outs of Rawls' approach all over again; we only remind ourselves of the deep differences between the sensibilities and intuitions of A and B, with whom we began our discussion, or between Nozick and Rawls, who represent more philosophically and argumentatively A and B. Suffice it to say that those fundamental differences revolve around the questions, as posed in biblical language, "Am I my brother's keeper?" and if so, to what degree does my brother have a claim on what I have acquired, earned, or produced? Of course, it must be remembered that what is in

The complete principle of distributive Justice

But is it *fair?*

[7]Ibid., p. 30.

"All who are not lunatics are agreed about certain things: that it is better to be alive than dead, better to be adequately fed than starved, better to be free than a slave."

—Bertrand Russell

view here are structures and principles of the social and political order: Being either a Rawlsian or Nozickian does not prevent you from selling what you have and giving to the poor, but it *does* dictate what you think you can legitimately be *compelled* to do. In this case, what do you perceive to be the key terms—*fairness* or *entitlement*?

Related to the Is it fair? question is the following consideration. According to Nozick, the *have-nots* are put out with the *haves* not only because they think that the wealth of the *haves* is not deserved but also because it *is* deserved and earned—that is, a matter of resentment against the deserving rich. But surely this flies in the face of a most obvious fact. It is not clear to all that the richest are the hardest working, the most talented, or superior in character—in a word, the most deserving. Are the rich not, in many instances at least, the laziest, the most exploitive, and the least deserving? So is it really just a matter of the poor being *jealous* of the rich? Do the poor not have a legitimate complaint about a social structure wherein the wealth is sometimes distributed with little regard to what a person deserves? Of course, this simply challenges immediately the adequacy of *entitlement* as a determinant of justice.

Do natural rights need to be defined?

One of the most frequent complaints against Nozick concerns his emphasis on natural rights. To be sure, fundamental to Nozick's whole position is his appeal to the Lockean doctrine of such rights. But nowhere does one find a sustained defense of this doctrine. Any social-political ideology that begins with an appeal to intuited or self-evident principles is already vulnerable precisely at that point. Locke's very point of departure was in this way a weak one, and so is Nozick's. Even so, there are other conceptions of natural rights, and other social-political theories derived therefrom. After all, doesn't Rawls, too, rely heavily on the idea of natural rights?

Does Nozick's theory contradict our moral sensibilities?

Finally, when we suggested earlier some possible criticisms of Rawls, it was asked whether his position doesn't offend our moral sensibilities. But now the same may be asked of Nozick. For example:

> It is an extraordinary but apparent consequence of this view that for a government to tax each of its able-bodied citizens five dollars a year to support cripples and orphans would violate the rights of the able-bodied, and would be morally impermissible, whereas to refrain from taxation even if it meant allowing the cripples and orphans to starve to death would be morally required governmental policy.[8]

Of course Nozick would hope that without taxation (God forbid!) such unfortunate situations could be remedied through voluntary contributions, but in the end the rights of the entitled must be upheld—the chips will just have to fall where they fall. On the other hand, Nozick does grant the possibility that the moral "side of constraints" of his theory might have to be set aside in order to avert a "catastrophic moral horror." But apart from this possible internal contradiction (Do the legitimately entitled have

[8]Samuel Sheffler, "Natural Rights, Equality, and the Minimal State," *Canadian Journal of Philosophy* (March 1976), p. 62.

inviolable rights or not?), the author just quoted asks how many cripples and orphans would have to die to constitute such a horror. Until that question is answered, the Nozickian concession to a catastrophic moral horror is meaningless.

MACINTYRE: JUSTICE AS VIRTUE

Both the Rawlsian and Nozickian accounts of justice have been challenged by Alasdair MacIntyre in his much-acclaimed *After Virtue,* on the grounds that they both *leave out something crucial:*

> . . . there is . . . an element in the position of both A and B which neither Rawls's account nor Nozick's captures, an element which survives from that older, classical tradition in which the virtues were central.[9]

From the reference to "that older, classical tradition" we leapfrog a long way backward in philosophical history, and from the reference to "the virtues," we know that MacIntyre's conception of justice is going to have something to do with individual character or worth.

More specifically, MacIntyre plays up on the idea of *desert*—how *deserving* a person is—as the crucial component of justice, and the one that is missing in both Rawlsian and Nozickian theories. If we return to our old friends A and B, we see that desert plays a central role in their positions: The hard-working A, it will be recalled, certainly saw himself as *deserving* of what he has earned, and B emphasized that the poverty of the disadvantaged is an undeserved plight. But this idea of desert is exactly what neither Rawls nor Nozick accommodates. MacIntyre explains why:

> Neither Rawls's account nor Nozick's allows this central place, or indeed any kind of place, for desert in claims about justice and injustice. Rawls. . . allows that common sense views of justice connect it with desert, but argues first that we do not know what anyone deserves until we have already formulated the rules of justice (and hence we cannot base our understanding of justice upon desert), and secondly that when we have formulated the rules of justice it turns out that it is not desert that is in question anyway, but only legitimate expectations. He also argues that to attempt to apply notions of desert would be impracticable.
>
> Nozick is less explicit, but his scheme of justice being based exclusively on entitlements can allow no place for desert. He does at one point discuss the possibility of a principle for the rectification of injustice, but what he writes on that point is so tentative and cryptic that it affords no guidance for amending his general viewpoint. It is in any case clear that for both Nozick and Rawls a society is composed of individuals, each with his or her own interest, who then have to come together and formulate common rules of life. In Nozick's case there is the additional negative constraint of a set of basic rights. In Rawls's case the only constraints are those that a prudent rationality would impose. Individuals are thus in both accounts primary and society secondary, and the identification of

---

[9]MacIntyre, *After Virtue,* p. 231.

individual interests is prior to, and independent of, the construction of any moral or social bonds between them. But . . . the notion of desert is at home only in the context of a community whose primary bond is a shared understanding both of the good for man and of the good of that community and where individuals identify their primary interests with reference to those goods. Rawls explicitly makes it a presupposition of his view that we must expect to disagree with others about what the good life for man is and must therefore exclude any understanding of it that we may have from our formulation of the principles of justice. Only those goods in which everyone, whatever their view of the good life, takes an interest are to be admitted to consideration. In Nozick's argument too, the concept of community required for the notion of desert to have application is simply absent.

. . . Rawls and Nozick articulate with great power a shared view which envisages entry into social life as—at least ideally—the voluntary act of at least potentially rational individuals with prior interests who have to ask the question "What kind of social contract with others is it reasonable for me to enter into?" Not surprisingly it is a consequence of this that their views exclude any account of human community in which the notion of desert in relation to contributions to the common tasks of that community in pursuing shared goods could provide the basis for judgments about virtue and injustice.[10]

The community versus the individual

Among other things, and most important, MacIntyre here charges that for both Rawls and Nozick the interests of the individual are emphasized first and over against that of the community. It is the absence of the idea of community in Rawls and Nozick that accounts for their failure to accommodate in their theories the idea of *desert*. For, as MacIntyre just told us, "the notion of desert is at home only in the context of a community whose primary bond is a shared understanding both of the good for man and of the good of that community and where individuals identify their primary interests with reference to those goods." That is, the idea of desert—people getting what they deserve—makes sense only when it is appreciated that "we're all in this together," and that some do better than others in the pursuit and maintenance of the common, shared goods.

The relevance of the past

A second way Rawls and Nozick rule out desert, says MacIntyre, is by excluding the past on which someone might otherwise base a claim to desert. In the case of Rawls, it will be recalled, it is irrelevant how the needy got into their present situation of need; all that matters is that right now a just pattern of distribution be enacted. If so, it is pointless for the needy to appeal to any past facts that might make them more deserving of a share of the distribution than others. For Nozick, to be sure, it is the present pattern of distribution that is irrelevant, since only what has been legitimately acquired in the past is relevant; but by making legitimate entitlements the *only* criterion for distribution, he fosters, as MacIntyre calls it, a "mythology about the past" that excludes certain other relevant factors and factors that bear upon desert. For, as MacIntyre explains in the following, if we go back far enough in the past, many legitimate acquisitions dissolve more and more into obviously *il*legitimate acquisitions.

---

[10]Ibid., pp. 232–233.

CRITERIA FOR DISTRIBUTIVE JUSTICE?

In his book *Social Philosophy*, Joel Feinberg argues that

> Differences in a given respect are *relevant* for the aims of distributive justice
> . . . only if they are differences for which their possessors can be held respon-
> sible; properties can be the grounds of just discrimination between persons
> only if those persons had a *fair opportunity* to acquire or avoid them.*

He then identifies and evaluates five possible criteria, under the "fair opportunity"
requirement, by which a distribution of goods may be called just:

- Equality (all people are at least human beings).
- Need (some people have greater needs than others).
- Merit (some people display greater merit—think of distinguished achievements—
  than others).
- Contribution (some people contribute more to the social wealth than others).
- Effort (some people are more hardworking than others).

What are the *pros* and *cons* for each of these criteria? Do they exhaust the possibilities? Can more than one of them be applied at the same time?

---

*Joel Feinberg, *Social Philosophy* (Englewood Cliffs, NJ: Prentice-Hall, 1973), p. 108.

... central to Nozick's account is the thesis that all legitimate entitlements can be
traced to legitimate acts of original acquisition. But, if that is so, there are in
fact very few, and in some large areas of the world *no*, legitimate entitlements.
The property-owners of the modern world are not the legitimate heirs of Lockean
individuals who performed quasi-Lockean ("quasi" to allow for Nozick's emenda-
tions of Locke) acts of original acquisition; they are the inheritors of those who,
for example, stole, and used violence to steal the common lands of England from
the common people, vast tracts of North America from the American Indian, much
of Ireland from the Irish, and Prussia from the original non-German Prussians. This
is the historical reality ideologically concealed behind any Lockean thesis.[11]

In fairness to Nozick it will be recalled that he does sponsor the Principle
of the Rectification of Injustice in Holdings, which was intended to redress
such injustices as MacIntyre here speaks of. On the other hand, we saw also
that MacIntyre (quotation on p. 497) judges Nozick's principle to be so
"tentative and cryptic" as to provide no real help.

Thus far our discussion of MacIntyre has been an essentially negative
one—we have spelled out his central objections to the Rawlsian and Nozickian approaches to justice. We must now spell out more clearly what
MacIntyre intends to *replace* these with. The key word, as we have seen, is

---

[11]Ibid., p. 234.

"Justice is the virtue of rewarding desert and of repairing failures in rewarding desert within an already constituted community. . . ."

—Alasdair MacIntyre

desert: Both A and B, in spite of their differences, appeal to desert, and this, says MacIntyre, "exhibits an adherence to an older, more traditional, more Aristotelian and Christian view of justice."[12] This older tradition is also called *the tradition of the virtues,* which we studied in Chapter 17.

The tradition
of the virtues

Now, what has this to do with existence at the social level? It will be recalled that for Aristotle (and now for MacIntyre too) man is a *politikon zoon,* a "political animal." It is no surprise, therefore, that the virtues play a role not only in the life of the individual but also in social life. The *polis,* or social community, is, after all, formed for the realization of a common good and, as in the individual, the virtues are conducive to the good, but now the *common* good or well-being of the community. This of course makes for the possibility of praise and blame for virtues and vices, those qualities or practices that further or hinder the community's shared vision of the common good. Now the application of law, intended to regulate behavior conducive to the common good, requires the virtue of justice, which is the rewarding of desert (that idea again) and which, as a virtue, involves judgment or insight *kata to orthon logon,* "in accordance with right reason."

Virtues and
the community

This, then, is broadly both Aristotle's and MacIntyre's approach to social justice, and it should be apparent that it is, both in spirit and in substance, quite different from the contemporary approaches (think of both Rawls and Nozick) that stress *individual* rights and needs.

[The] notion of the political community as a common project is alien to the modern liberal individualist world. This is how we sometimes at least think of schools, hospitals or philanthropic organizations, but we have no conception of such a form of community concerned, as Aristotle says the *polis* is concerned, with the whole of life, not with this or that good, but with man's good as such.[13]

Rawls and Nozick
versus MacIntyre

In spite of their differences, both Rawls' and Nozick's conceptions of justice are emphatically rooted in the Lockean tradition of individual rights. Whether justice is conceived as fairness (Rawls) or entitlement (Nozick), the orientation of their theories is to the individual—his or her needs and rights—and to some sort of social contract that secures those rights. With MacIntyre it is quite different. Our view is lifted from the individual and focused on the larger community and the shared, common good to which the individual participants in that community contribute through their

---

[12]Ibid.
[13]Ibid., p. 146.

virtuous activity. This latter, and more classical, view is much less compart-mentalized and more holistic than the former: In an authentic concept of justice there is much more to be taken into account than individuals, their needs, and their rights.

Though written before MacIntyre's *After Virtue,* Joel Feinberg's critique of the merit criterion of distributive justice is certainly relevant for the justice-as-virtue position. Feinberg raises four questions: Should a person be rewarded for what he or she *is* rather than *does*? Is it practical to try to "police" moral defects in persons? Is it appropriate to reward virtuous activity with economic prizes? Would such rewards provide an inappropri-ate incentive for virtuous activity, which, by its nature, should be otherwise motivated?

Some questions for MacIntyre

Those who would propose rewarding personal *virtues* with a larger than average share of the economic pie, and punishing defects of character with a smaller than average share, advocate assigning to the economic system a task normally done (if it is done at all) by noneconomic institutions. What they propose, in effect, is that we use retributive criteria of distributive justice. Our criminal law, for a variety of good reasons, does not purport to punish people for what they are, but only for what they do. A man can be as arrogant, rude, selfish, cruel, insensitive, irresponsible, cowardly, lazy, or disloyal as he wishes; unless he *does* something prohibited by the criminal law, he will not be made to suffer legal punishment. At least one of the legal system's reasons for refusing to penalize

RAWLS AND NOZICK VERSUS MACINTYRE

Justice as fairness   Justice as entitlement

Justice as virtue

The Lockean tradition

The Aristotelian tradition

The individual is endowed with personal rights.

The individual is a political animal.

Participation in the social contract as security of personal rights.

Virtuous participation in the shared vision of the common good.

character flaws as such would also explain why such defects should not be listed as relevant differences in a material principle of distributive justice. The apparatus for detecting such flaws (a "moral police"?) would be enormously cumbersome and impractical, and its methods so uncertain and fallible that none of us could feel safe in entrusting the determination of our material allotments to it. We could, of course, give roughly equal shares to all except those few who have *outstanding virtues*—gentleness, kindness, courage, diligence, reliability, warmth, charm, considerateness, generosity. Perhaps these are traits that deserve to be rewarded, but it is doubtful that larger economic allotments are the appropriate vehicles of rewarding. As Benn and Peters remind us, "there are some sorts of 'worth' for which rewards in terms of income seem inappropriate. Great courage in battle is recognized by medals, not by increased pay." Indeed, there is something repugnant, as Socrates and the Stoics insisted, in paying a man to be virtuous. Moreover, the rewards would offer a pecuniary motive for certain forms of excellence that require motives of a different kind, and would thus tend to be self-defeating.[14]

OKIN: JUSTICE, GENDER, AND THE FAMILY

A feminist critique

Throughout this book we've seen how feminists often take a different approach to major philosophical issues and debates. The question of justice is no exception. Feminists have criticized all of the theories of justice we've considered so far for focusing too much on men and ignoring the unique experiences and concerns of women. Earlier we saw feminist alternatives to traditional morality such as the ethics of care. Here we look at how one feminist, Susan Moller Okin, takes justice in a new direction.

Traditionally, nearly all theories of justice have ignored certain realms of human life, most notably the family. Justice has been seen as a matter for the courtroom, the capital, and the relations between citizens, but not something that is relevant to the kitchen or bedroom or family matters. This is definitely not a coincidence, feminists say, since most philosophers who write about justice are men while the home and family have tended to be primarily the female realm.

Feminists argue that this must change, that we must begin to see the relevance of justice to these traditionally private realms. But how do we make this change? More importantly, where do we begin? At least one prominent feminist thinker suggests that we begin by taking a closer look at justice within the family and by cultivating an increased awareness of the effects of gender in our society.

Gender

In *Justice, Gender, and the Family*, Susan Moller Okin argues that the main problem with theories of justice is that they ignore gender. When Okin and other feminists use the term "gender," they don't mean simply sex or the biological differences between males and females. These differences are normal, healthy, and undeniable. No, "gender" is a politically charged term used by feminists to represent the inequality in our society and its

[14]Joel Feinberg, *Social Philosophy* (Englewood Cliffs, NJ: Prentice-Hall, 1973), p. 113.

treatment of women. Okin defines gender as "the deeply entrenched insti-tutionalization of sexual difference,"[15] a difference that is not real but socially constructed.

Why is it that in all this discussion of justice women tend to be ignored? Okin argues that a peculiar double standard regarding the family is at least part of the story.

How can theories of justice that are ostensibly about people in general neglect women, gender, and all the inequalities between the sexes? One reason is that most theorists *assume,* though they do not discuss, the traditional, gender-structured family. . . .

In the past, political theorists often used to distinguish clearly between "pri-vate" domestic life and the "public" life of politics and the marketplace, claiming explicitly that the two spheres operated in accordance with different principles. They separated out the family from what they deemed the subject matter of politics, and they made closely related, explicit claims about the nature of women and the appropriateness of excluding them from civil and political life. Men, the subjects of the theories, were able to make the transition back and forth from domestic to public life with ease, largely because of the functions performed by women in the family. When we turn to contemporary theories of justice, superficial appearances can easily lead to the impression that they are inclusive of women. In fact, they continue the same "separate spheres" tradition, by ignoring the family, its division of labor, and the related economic dependency and restricted opportunities of most women. The judgment that the family is "nonpolitical" is implicit in the fact that it is simply not discussed in most works of political theory today. In one way or another, almost all current theorists continue to assume that the "individual" who is the basic subject of their theories is the male head of a fairly traditional household. Thus the application of principles of justice to relations between the sexes, or within the household, is frequently, though tacitly, ruled out from the start. In the most influential of all twentieth-century theories of justice, that of John Rawls, family life is not only assumed, but is assumed to be just—and yet the prevalent gendered division of labor within the family is neglected, along with the associated distribution of power, responsibility, and privilege.

Moreover, this stance is typical of contemporary theories of justice. . . .

What is the basis of my claim that the family, while neglected, is *assumed* by theorists of justice? One obvious indication is that they take mature, inde-pendent human beings as the subjects of their theories without any mention of how they got to be that way. We know, of course, that human beings develop and mature only as a result of a great deal of attention and hard work, by far the greater part of it done by women. But when theorists of justice talk about "work," they mean paid work performed in the marketplace. They must be assuming that women, in the gender-structured family, continue to do their unpaid work of nurturing and socializing the young and providing a haven of intimate relations—otherwise there would be no moral subjects for them to theorize about. But these activities apparently take place outside the scope of their theories. Typically, the family itself is not examined in the light of whatever standard of justice the theorist arrives at.

---

[15]Susan Moller Okin, *Justice, Gender, and the Family* (New York: Basic Books, 1989), p. 6.

The continued neglect of the family by theorists of justice flies in the face of a great deal of persuasive feminist argument. Scholars have clearly revealed the interconnections between the gender structure inside and outside the family and the extent to which the personal is political. They have shown that the assignment of primary parenting to women is crucial, both in forming the gendered identities of men and women and in influencing their respective choices and opportunities in life. Yet, so far, the simultaneous assumption and neglect of the family has allowed the impact of these arguments to go unnoticed in major theories of justice.[16]

Okin provides a powerful critique and a persuasive one: Theorists both ignore and assume the traditional, gendered family. As feminists have shown, male bias pervades many areas of our society, so why should we think that justice would be an exception? But critique is only half the equation; we also need a remedy or at least a proposal for change. We need to know what a feminist theory of justice would look like. For Okin, the key lies in striving for what she calls "humanist justice," which must include justice in the family. The way to achieve humanist justice, Okin argues, is through eliminating gender and establishing true equality among all people.

Humanist justice

I have suggested that, for very important reasons, the family *needs* to be a just institution, and have shown that contemporary theories of justice neglect women and ignore gender. How can we address this injustice?

This is a complex question. It is particularly so because we place great value on our freedom to live different kinds of lives, there is no current consensus on many aspects of gender, and we have good reason to suspect that many of our beliefs about sexual difference and appropriate sex roles are heavily influenced by the very fact that we grew up in a gender-structured society. All of us have been affected, in our very psychological structures, by the fact of gender in our personal pasts, just as our society has been deeply affected by its strong influence in our collective past. Because of the lack of shared meanings about gender, it constitutes a particularly hard case for those who care deeply about both personal freedom and social justice. The way we divide the labor and responsibilities in our personal lives seems to be one of those things that people should be free to work out for themselves, but because of its vast repercussions it belongs clearly within the scope of things that must be governed by principles of justice. Which is to say, in the language of political and moral theory, that it belongs both to the sphere of "the good" and to that of "the right."

Any just and fair solution to the urgent problem of women's and children's vulnerability must encourage and facilitate the equal sharing by men and women of paid and unpaid work, of productive and reproductive labor. We must work

[16]Ibid., pp. 8–9.

"Family life as typically practiced in our society is not just, either to women or to children. Moreover, it is not conducive to the rearing of citizens with a strong sense of justice."

—Susan Moller Okin

toward a future in which all will be likely to choose this mode of life. A just future would be one without gender. In its social structures and practices, one's sex would have no more relevance than one's eye color or the length of one's toes. No assumptions would be made about "male" and "female" roles; childbearing would be so conceptually separated from child rearing and other family responsibilities that it would be a cause for surprise, and no little concern, if men and women were not equally responsible for domestic life or if children were to spend much more time with one parent than the other. It would be a future in which men and women participated in more or less equal numbers in every sphere of life, from infant care to different kinds of paid work to high-level politics. Thus it would no longer be the case that having no experience of raising children would be the practical prerequisite for attaining positions of the greatest social influence. Decisions about abortion and rape, about divorce settlements and sexual harassment, or about any other crucial social issues would not be made, as they often are now, by legislatures and benches of judges overwhelmingly populated by men whose power is in large part due to their advantaged position in the gender structure. If we are to be at all true to our democratic ideals, moving away from gender is essential.[17]

CHAPTER 20 IN REVIEW

SUMMARY

In this chapter we have focused on the idea of justice as being in some way fundamental to all social-political philosophy. And we have presented four important and contemporary attempts to explicate this central concept and apply it to the realities of the social-political world.

The first of these theories of justice, that of Rawls, tries to combine the ideals of libertarianism with those of egalitarianism, and to provide principles that would assure the implementation of justice conceived as fairness. Echoing somewhat the old ideas of the state of nature and the social contract, Rawls has argued that it should be possible to bracket out our individual interests and advantages (the veil of ignorance) long enough to perceive what would be fair and advantageous to all. More specifically, in this original position we should be guided by Rawls' two principles of justice: (1) the Principle of Equal Basic Liberty for All and (2) the Difference Principle. The first of these establishes equal liberty, and the second fosters equal income and social position. These are geared to reducing inequities: Differences in wealth and position would be fostered only when such differences would contribute to the advantage of all.

If Rawls argues generally for a principle of equality with respect to *needs*, Nozick argues for a principle of equality with respect to *entitlement*. Here too we encounter an echo of Locke but with a libertarian emphasis on individual rights. This is reflected in Nozick's conception of the minimal or "night-watchman" state, the role of which is solely to protect individual rights, and his conception of justice as entitlement. This latter may be unpacked in terms of Nozick's three principles of justice in holdings: (1) the Principle

---

[17]Ibid., pp. 170–172.

of Justice in Acquisition, (2) the Principle of Justice in Transfer, and (3) the Principle of the Rectification of Injustice in Holdings. These principles guarantee the legitimacy of the original acquisition of property through transfer of legitimately acquired property, and an attempt to rectify violations of the first two principles. With respect to the distribution of goods, Nozick's proposition is clear from his complete principle of distributive justice, which identifies a just distribution as one in which each individual is entitled to his or her holdings.

Both Rawls' and Nozick's theories of justice have been subjected to various criticisms, but they are rejected by MacIntyre on the grounds that they fail to accommodate the idea of desert, which in turn is bound up with MacIntyre's conception of justice as *virtue*. With this MacIntyre argues for a return to an older, classical tradition, represented best by Aristotle, the tradition of the virtues, where virtue is understood as activity conducive to well-being. Here (and in contrast to Rawls, Nozick, and the Lockean tradition) the emphasis is shifted from the rights of the individual to the good of the individual and, in the larger picture, to the common good of the community in which the individual is necessarily a part. The individual's virtuous (or not) and deserving (or not) contribution to this shared vision is the basis for a notion of justice as virtue: Justice is the rewarding of the virtuous activity that enhances the common good of man, the "social animal."

Feminists criticize all of these theories of justice for privileging male experience and ignoring gender bias and the family. Susan Moller Okin argues that we must deal with the deeply entrenched effects of gender in society before justice is even possible. We also need to extend the reach of justice beyond the public realm and into the family. Justice in the gender-structured family is necessary, Okin claims, for justice in society as a whole.

BASIC IDEAS

- Three views of justice
- "The original position"
- The "veil of ignorance"
- Rawls' two principles of justice:
    The Principle of Equal Basic Liberty for All
    The Difference Principle
- Rawls' general conception of justice
- Rawls' theory of justice as a synthesis of libertarian and egalitarian perspectives
- The minimal or "night-watchman" state
- Justice as entitlement
- Nozick's three principles of justice in holdings:
    The Principle of Justice in Acquisition
    The Principle of Justice in Transfer
    The Principle of the Rectification of Injustice in Holdings
- Nozick's complete principle of distributive justice

- MacIntyre's emphasis on desert
- Individual rights versus the good of the community
- The relevance of the past for a just distribution
- Feinberg's questions for MacIntyre
- Okin's critique of traditional theories of justice
- Justice in the family
- Gender

TEST YOURSELF

1. True or false: Rawls' first principle of justice is intended to promote egalitarianism.
2. Nozick's is a theory of "justice as _____."
3. MacIntyre's theory of justice has most in common with (a) Locke, (b) Marx, (c) Aristotle, (d) the libertarians.
4. Why do some object to Rawls' idea of the veil of ignorance?
5. Recalling previous chapters, Rawls' idea of the original position has most in common with (a) Aristotle, (b) Locke, (c) St. Thomas, (d) Rousseau.
6. True or false: Nozick proposes no principle aimed at the rectification of injustice.
7. What is meant by the claim that MacIntyre's is a more "holistic" conception of justice than Rawls' or Nozick's?
8. What thinkers in this chapter champion a social contract as providing security for personal rights?

QUESTIONS FOR REFLECTION

- Does Rawls' theory of justice succeed in combining the best of the libertarian and egalitarian ideals? Why is such a distinction irrelevant for Nozick?
- What about the objection that Rawls' theory is very attractive in principle but has little hope of actual implementation? Does this objection apply also to Nozick and MacIntyre? Is *any* social-political ideal or principle free from this problem? Do you agree with the charge that the practice of any of these theories might fly in the face of your intuitions about morality?
- Do you agree with Okin that justice is relevant not only to public affairs but also to the private realm such as the family?
- How would *you* come to grips with the problem of justice? Do Rawls', Nozick's, MacIntyre's, or Okin's theories provide you with any insights and illumination?

FOR FURTHER READING

Kenneth Cauthen. *The Passion for Equality.* Savage, MD: Rowman & Littlefield, 1987. A historical survey of the concept of equality in America and a proposal in the light of the contributions of Rawls and Nozick.

Frederick Copleston. *A History of Philosophy.* Baltimore: Newman Press, 1946–1974. I, Ch. 31. A clear, succinct account of Aristotle's ethics, including his concept of virtue, from a standard work.

Norman Daniels (ed.). *Reading Rawls: Critical Studies of "A Theory of Justice."* New York: Basic Books, 1974. Fourteen essays representing and evaluating aspects of Rawls' theory, with a useful, summarizing introduction by the editor.

R. E. Ewin. *Liberty, Community and Justice.* Savage, MD: Rowman & Littlefield, 1987. An inquiry into the nature of individuals' liberty in relation to community, based on the work of Thomas Hobbes.

John Hospers. *Human Conduct: An Introduction to the Problem of Ethics.* New York: Harcourt, Brace & World, 1961. Ch. 9. A textbook discussion of justice, including its relation to the ideas of equality, reward, and punishment, by a well-known social-political philosopher.

Louis I. Katzner. *Man in Conflict: Traditions in Social and Political Thought.* Encino, CA: Dickenson, 1975. A student-oriented text on standard topics in social philosophy (freedom, social contract, forms of government), including a treatment specifically of justice with special reference to Rawls.

Kenneth Kipnis and Diana T. Meyers (eds.). *Economic Justice: Private Rights and Public Responsibilities.* Savage, MD: Rowman & Littlefield, 1985. Twenty philosophers and social theorists on the economically just society, in the context of the distributive justice versus property rights debate spawned by Rawls and Nozick.

Rex Martin. *Rawls and Rights.* Lawrence: University Press of Kansas, 1985. A complete appraisal of Rawls' theory of justice, with special treatment of his account of rights.

James W. Nickel. *Making Sense of Human Rights.* Berkeley: University of California Press, 1987. An account and defense of the idea of human rights that has come to play a large role in contemporary liberalism.

Kai Nielsen. *Equality and Liberty: A Defense of Radical Egalitarianism.* Totowa, NJ: Rowman & Allanheld, 1985. A hefty but lively plea for radical egalitarianism, with extended treatment and criticism of Rawls and Nozick.

Susan Moller Okin. *Justice, Gender, and the Family.* New York: Basic Books, 1989. Classic argument about the way liberalism discriminates against women.

Jeffrey Paul (ed.). *Reading Nozick: Essays on "Anarchy, State, and Utopia."* Totowa, NJ: Rowman & Littlefield, 1981. A large collection of studies that represent and criticize various aspects of Nozick's position, with an introduction that summarizes both Nozick and his critics.

Nicholas Rescher. *Distributive Justice.* Indianapolis: Bobbs-Merrill, 1966. An analysis of this single, important concept, from a utilitarian standpoint.

Michael Walzer. *Spheres of Justice.* New York: Basic Books, 1983. A wide-ranging and influential discussion of liberty and the good.

Robert Paul Wolff. *Understanding Rawls: A Reconstruction and Critique of "A Theory of Justice."* Princeton, NJ: Princeton University Press, 1977. A complete commentary and severe criticism of Rawls' theory.

*In addition, see the relevant articles ("Justice," "Rights," etc.) in *Routledge Encyclopedia of Philosophy,* ed. Edward Craig (London: Routledge, 1998), and *Stanford Encyclopedia of Philosophy,* http://plato.stanford.edu.

POSTSCRIPT

What a man knows at fifty that he did not know at twenty is, for the most part, incommunicable. The laws, the aphorisms, the generalizations, the universal truths, the parables and the old saws—all of the observations about life which can be communicated handily in ready, verbal packages—are as well known to a man at twenty who has been attentive as to a man at fifty. He has been told them all, he has read them all, and he has probably repeated them all before he graduates from college; but he has not lived them all.

What he knows at fifty that he did not know at twenty boils down to something like this: The knowledge he has acquired with age is not the knowledge of formulas, or forms of words, but of people, places, actions—a knowledge not gained by words but by touch, sight, sound, victories, failures, sleeplessness, devotion, love—the human experiences and emotions of this earth and of oneself and other men; and perhaps, too, a little faith, and a little reverence for things you cannot see.[1]

---

[1]Adlai E. Stevenson, *What I Think* (New York: Harper, 1956), p. 174.

A (SHORT) PHILOSOPHICAL DICTIONARY

The following entries are geared specifically to the present text, though the list is sufficiently comprehensive to assist any philosophy student. The decision to enter noun forms on some occasions and adjectival forms on others has not been arbitrary but determined by the way in which the terms tend to be used in the text. Of course, many of the terms included here are also (and perhaps otherwise) explained in the "running glossary" found throughout the book. When terms in the entries are themselves in some form separate entries, this is indicated, when appropriate, by the use of **boldface** type. "Ca." (abbreviation of Laatin, *circa*) = "approximately." When only one date is given, it is the presumed date at which the philosopher was most active.

> "Dictionaries are like watches. The best cannot be expected to go quite true, but the worst is better than none."
>
> —Samuel Johnson

A posteriori: In **epistemology,** pertaining to knowledge derived from, or posterior to, sense experience.

A priori: In **epistemology,** pertaining to knowledge acquired *independently* of, or prior to, sense experience.

Absolute: That which is independent of or unconditioned by anything outside itself.

Abstraction (abstract idea): A general idea, an idea from which particularizing features of existing things have been removed (e.g., "table," "dog," or "human") or that results when what a number of particular things have in common is abstracted (e.g., "redness" from various red things).

Accidental: In **metaphysics,** a feature or characteristic that does not belong necessarily to the nature of a thing.

Actuality: In **Scholastic** philosophy, the state of being something in reality as opposed to being something merely **potentially.**

Aesthetics: Philosophy of art, or philosophical reflection on the nature of art and of our experience of beauty.

Albert the Great (Albert Magnus): (ca. 1193–1280) Dominican priest and **Scholastic** philosopher of great breadth, who popularized much **Aristotelian** and Arabic philosophy and exerted a great influence on the philosophical development of **St. Thomas Aquinas.**

Alienation: In **Marxism,** the estrangement, induced by **capitalist** exploitation, of the worker from his or her product, self, human nature, and neighbors.

Altruism: The belief that everyone ought as much as possible to seek the good of others.

Ambrose, St.: (ca. 339–397) Bishop of Milan, staunch defender of Christian orthodoxy, who was largely responsible for **St. Augustine's** conversion.

Analogy, method of: In **logic,** a form of **inductive reasoning** in which a **conclusion** is drawn about some feature of one member of a class on the basis of a resemblance in some other respect to other members of the class.

Analogy of the Sun: **Plato's** comparison of the function of the sun in the visible world to the function of the **Good** in the **intelligible** world: As the sun illuminates sensible things with light and causes them to exist, so the Good irradiates the **Forms** with truth and causes them to exist.

Analytic philosophy: An emphasis in twentieth-century philosophy (largely British) on linguistic analysis, or the analysis of language, as a means of identifying the sources of, and resolving, philosophical problems. More generally, the emphasis on definition, logical scrutiny, conceptual coherence, marshaling of evidence, and so on.

Analytic proposition: A proposition that is true by definition, or **logically** necessary, as in "All triangles have three sides."

Anaxagoras: (ca. 475 B.C.) Pre-Socratic philosopher of the **Pluralist** tradition who identified reality with an infinite number of infinitely divisible "seeds," governed by Mind, and the first to claim that the sun and moon were not gods but earthlike bodies.

Anaximander: (ca. 575 B.C.) Pre-Socratic philosopher of the Ionian tradition who believed that reality originates from an indefinite mixture of opposing sensible qualities, the Boundless.

Anaximenes: (ca. 550 B.C.) Pre-Socratic philosopher of the Ionian tradition who taught that the ultimate reality is air, through rarefaction and condensation of which sensible things have arisen.

Anselm, St.: (1033–1109) Benedictine monk, eventually Archbishop of Canterbury, who advocated the rational defense of Christian ideas, and propounded the **Ontological Argument** for the existence of God.

Anthropomorphism: The representation of something nonhuman—for example, God—in the likeness of human beings.

Archetype: A model, pattern, or paradigm.

Argument: An attempt to show that some claim is true (the **conclusion**) by providing reasons for it (the **premises**).

Argumentum ad Hominem: "Appeal to the man"; an **informal fallacy** that irrelevantly attacks the person making a claim rather than attacking the claim itself (abusive form) or seeks to undermine a claim by calling attention to the (irrelevant) circumstances of the one making the claim.

Argumentum ad Ignorantiam: "Appeal to ignorance"; an **informal fallacy** that affirms the truth of something on the basis of the lack of evidence to the contrary.

Argumentum ad Populum: "Appeal to the crowd"; an **informal fallacy** that seeks to strengthen a claim by emotional appeal to the passions and prejudices of the listeners.

Aristocracy: As a theory of government, rule by the best or most noble, usually rule by the nobility class.

Aristotle: (383–321 B.C.) Greek thinker who wrote on all philosophical and many scientific topics, most notably **metaphysics, ethics,** and **logic,** and a **teleologist** who rejected **Plato's** separated **Forms** in favor of **immanent Forms**—the Form "Dog" is not an **essence** existing apart from individual dogs but rather inhering in each dog.

Atom: Literally, an "uncuttable," regarded by some premodern materialists as the ultimate building block of reality.

Attribute: Property or characteristic attributed to or predicated of something.

Augustine, St.: (354–430) Latin Church Father, Bishop of Hippo in North Africa, who adapted **Platonic** (more specifically, **Neo-Platonic**) philosophy to Christian theology.

Autonomous: The state of being self-controlling, **independent,** or free.

Beauvoir, Simone de: (1908–1986) French author and one of the leading founders of the contemporary feminist movement, who applied the principle of **existential** freedom to the oppressed woman.

Behaviorism: The school of psychology that, by defining psychological terms (e.g., pain) in terms of observable behavior (e.g., sobbing), claims that observable behavior is the proper object of psychological study.

Benedict, Ruth: (1887–1948) American cultural anthropologist (student of Margaret Mead) whose investigations and writings have emphasized the diversity of cultural behavior patterns, which is taken by many (including herself) as evidence for **cultural relativism.**

Benevolence Principle: Happiness is to be distributed as widely and as equally as possible among all people.

Bentham, Jeremy: (1748–1832) English **ethicist** and social philosopher, founder of modern **utilitarianism,** who emphasized a quantitative conception of the "greatest" pleasure in his definition of happiness.

Berkeley, George: (1685–1753) Anglican bishop and philosopher who theorized about the nature of vision, but, most notably, denied the existence of **matter** and propounded the most famous version of **subjective idealism.**

Big Bang theory: A **cosmological** model according to which the present hypothesized expanding universe has resulted from an explosion of concentrated matter about 15 billion years ago.

Bourgeoisie: In **Marxist** theory, the owning or propertied class, standing in opposition to the **proletariat** or nonpropertied working class.

Broad, C. D.: (1887–1971) English philosopher, contributor to many fields including, most notably, **epistemology, ethics,** philosophy of science, and psychical research.

Calvin, John: (1509–1564) French theologian and leader of the reformed (as opposed to **Lutheran**) branch of the Protestant Reformation.

Camus, Albert: (1913–1960) French playwright, novelist, essayist, resistance fighter, winner of the Nobel Prize for literature, and a foremost atheistic **existentialist** thinker.

Capital: Money, property, or goods having an exchange value, owned by an individual or firm.

Capitalism: The economic theory that advocates that the means of production, and the actual production and exchange of goods and wealth, should be owned and implemented by private individuals or corporations with a view toward profit.

Carneades: (ca. 150 B.C.) Leader of the "Academicians," a school of **skepticism** that developed out of **Plato's** Academy.

Categorical Imperative: In **Kant,** the principle of moral conduct: "Act only according to that maxim by which you can at the same time will that it should become a universal law"; more generally, a **moral** command with no "ifs" or "buts."

Categorical proposition: A proposition that affirms or denies that one class of things is included in another (e.g., "All U.S. presidents have been males").

Category mistake: The mistake of employing a concept within a conceptual system to which it is inappropriate (e.g., "I see the carburetor, battery, generator, pistons, etc., but where is the power?").

Causality, principle of: Everything that comes into being is caused, or comes into being by virtue of something outside itself.

Cave, Allegory of the: **Plato's** image whereby he likens the education and ascent of the soul to making one's way out of a darkened cave, which is initially mistaken for reality, into the upper world illuminated by the sun.

Chomsky, Noam: (b. 1928) American thinker who has argued on linguistic grounds (specifically on the basis of **generative grammar**) for the existence of **innate** intellectual structures.

Chōrismos: Greek for "separation" or "gap," applied by **Aristotle** in criticism of **Plato's** theory of **Forms** which represented them as **transcendent** and removed from (separated from) the things they are supposed to be the cause of.

Clarification Principle: The clarity of an idea, distinction, and the like is always more apparent after the idea has been clarified.

Cogito ergo sum: Latin expression employed by **Descartes** for the **indubitable** starting point of philosophizing: "I think, therefore I am."

Cognitive: Pertaining to the act or process of knowing.

Cognitive science: An interdisciplinary (psychology, philosophy, computer sciences, linguistics) exploration of the processes that underlie thinking, utilizing a computational (computerlike) model of mind.

Communism: In the **Marxist** variety, the economic-political theory that advocates the abolition of private ownership of the means of production and distribution, and the actualization of a classless society that practices the principle "From each according to one's ability; to each according to one's need."

Complete principle of distributive justice: A distribution is just if everyone is entitled to the holdings he or she possesses under the distribution.

Complex idea: An idea that combines several simple or unanalyzable ideas (e.g., "apple" is compounded out of "red," "sweet," etc.) or other complex ideas (e.g., "typewriter" is composed of keys, carriage, levers, etc.).

Conclusion: In an **argument,** the proposition that is supported by the **premises.**

Conditional proposition: See *Hypothetical proposition.*

Conditioned: See *Contingent.*

Confucius: (5th–6th century B.C.) Chinese sage, teacher of practical and ethical wisdom.

Consequentialism: See *Teleological ethics.*

Conservation of energy, principle of: The amount of energy in any closed system (and therefore the universe) remains constant; that is, it can be of itself neither created nor destroyed.

Consistency Principle: Any logically consistent proposition may be true, but no self-contradictory proposition can be true.

Contiguity: The state of one thing being in spatial contact with or touching another.

Contingent: The state of being dependent for existence on something else.

Copernicus, Nicholas: (1473–1543) Polish astronomer, advocate of the helio-centric model of the universe, which locates the sun in the center.

Copleston, Frederick C.: (b. 1907) English priest and defender of **theism** and **Thomism,** author of a standard, multivolume history of philosophy.

Corporeal: Pertaining to what exists as a physical body and is apprehensible by the senses.

Cosmological Argument: A **proof** for God's existence: God must exist as the ultimate cause of the **contingent,** physical universe; also called the First-Cause Argument.

Cosmology: Study of the origin, nature, and principles constituting the physical universe.

Cosmos: From the Greek *kosmos,* "ornament," eventually designating the world or universe.

Cratylus: (ca. 500 B.C.) Pre-Socratic thinker who maintained an extreme interpretation of **Heraclitus'** doctrine of flux.

Cultural relativism: The view that **morality** and other values are rooted in the experience, habits, and preferences of a culture.

Darwin, Charles: (1809–1882) English naturalist and most influential proponent of biological **evolution,** which held far-reaching philosophical implications.

Deculturalization Principle: It is necessary to distinguish the real substance of a philosophy, theory, and the like, from the particular cultural forms (e.g., cosmology) in which it is accidentally expressed.

Deductive reasoning: Reasoning in which the **conclusion** follows with logical necessity from the **premises.**

Deity: God, the divinity, the divine nature.

Democracy: Literally, rule by the people; government in which the power is vested in the body of citizens, either directly or through elected representatives.

Democritus: (ca. 425 B.C.) Pre-Socratic philosopher who identified reality with indivisible material particles (**atoms**) moving randomly in empty space.

Deontological ethics: The view that emphasizes the performance of duty, rather than results, as the sign of right action.

Descartes, René: (1596–1650) French philosopher, mathematician, and physicist, propounder of strict **rationalism** and **mind-matter dualism,** traditionally called the father of modern philosophy.

Design Argument: See *Teleological Argument.*

Despotism: See *Dictatorship.*

Determinism: The view that everything that comes into being is caused in such a way that it could not have been otherwise.

D'Holbach, Paul-Henri Thiry, Baron: (1723–1789) German atheist, **materialist, mechanist,** and relentless critic of organized religion, especially Catholicism.

Dialectical: Pertaining to, or of the nature of, reasoning, argumentation, give-and-take, and the like.

Dialectical materialism: The **metaphysical** view that reality is **matter** and motion and evolves historically in accordance with the **dialectical** principle of the synthesis of opposite states.

Dictatorship: Absolute rule by a single individual who, usually, has acquired power through unlawful means.

Diderot, Denis: (1713–1784) French deist, **materialist,** and finally pantheist, and contributor to the French Encyclopédie, a controversial, irreverent, multivolume compendium of French "philosophy."

Difference Principle: Social and economic inequalities are to be arranged so that they are both (a) reasonably expected to be to everyone's advantage, and (b) attached to positions and offices open to all.

Diogenes Laertius: (ca. 225) Author of *Lives of Eminent Philosophers,* the source of much knowledge about ancient philosophers.

Disjunctive proposition: A proposition that poses alternatives indicated by the words "either. . . or" (e.g., "Either the players' shirts are red or they are blue").

Disjunctive syllogism: A syllogism in which one premise is a disjunctive proposition (e.g., X or Y, not-X, therefore Y).

Dispositions (mental): **Ryle's** term for the observable data by which mind is best understood: capacities, proclivities, habits, and so on.

Distributive justice, complete principle of: A distribution is just if everyone is entitled to the holdings he or she possesses under the distribution.

Divided Line, the: **Plato's** image of a line bisected above and below to represent, on one side, his conception of degrees of being and, on the other, corresponding degrees of knowledge.

Divine law: God's salvific intention for his creatures, known through divine revelation.

Dostoievsky, Fyodor: (1821–1881) Russian novelist and thinker whose work has influenced and expressed strains of **existential** philosophy.

Double-aspect theory: In **Spinoza,** the view that there is only one reality, unknown to us except through its **attributes** of mind and matter, two of the infinite number of aspects of this one reality.

Dualism: **Metaphysically,** the view that reality consists ultimately of two fundamentally different entities.

Ducasse, C. J.: (1881–1969) American philosopher who contributed to and wrote on all fields of philosophy, including symbolic **logic** and the "wild facts" of ESP.

Economic determinism: The theory that all, or the most important, human action results necessarily from economic factors alone, such as income, prices, trade, or even the structure of the system itself.

Efficient cause: The agent through which something comes into being.

Egoism: Literally, "I-ism," the emphasis on the self as the ultimate reality, central concern, and the like (not to be confused with egotism, i.e., selfishness).

Egoistic hedonism: The doctrine that the pursuit and production of one's own pleasure are the highest good and the criterion of right action.

Eidological Argument: A proof for God that requires God as the cause of our idea of perfection.

Eleatic: Pertaining to the school of philosophy founded by **Parmenides** of Elea, in southern Italy.

Elitism: In political philosophy, rule by a select few.

Empedocles: (ca. 450 B.C.) Pre-Socratic philosopher of the **Pluralist** tradition who identified reality with the four elements (earth, water, air, fire), which he viewed as combining and separating under the influence of "Love" and "Strife" respectively.

Empiricism: The belief that knowledge about existing things is acquired through sense experience.

En soi: French, "in itself," used in **Sartrean existentialism** in reference to nonconscious being.

Engels, Friedrich: (1820–1895) German **socialist** thinker; friend, follower, and systematizer of **Marx.**

Environmental ethics: Application of principles of obligation or right action to issues of the environment, such as pollution, conservation, treatment of animals, and so on.

Epicharmus: (ca. 500 B.C.) Father of Greek comedy who wrote plays satirizing Pre-Socratic philosophers.

Epistemological dualism: The view that the act of knowing involves primarily two components: the mind that does the knowing and its ideas(s) that are known.

Epistemology: The study or theory of knowledge.

Equal Basic Liberty for All, Principle of: Each person is to have an equal right to the most extensive basic liberty compatible with a similar liberty for others.

Esse: Latin, "to be," and hence "being" or "act of being."

Esse est percipi: **Berkeley's** summary of expression of his **subjective idealism:** "To be is to be perceived."

Essence: The nature or "whatness" of something; that which makes something the kind of thing it is.

Eternal law: The unalterable governance of all things by the divine reason.

Ethical absolutism (Ethical objectivism): The view that **moral** values are independent of human opinion and have a common or universal application.

Ethical relativism (Ethical subjectivism): The denial of any **absolute** or **objective moral** values, and the affirmation of the individual (person, community, culture, etc.) as the source of **morality.**

Ethics: The theory of good and evil as applied to personal actions, decisions, and relations; **moral** values.

Ethics of care: Feminist approach to ethics emphasizing women's experience, especially the attitude and expression of caring.

Evidentialism: The thesis that belief in God is wrong if not based on rational evidence.

Evil, the problem of: See *Theodicy*.

Evolution, theory of: In biology, the theory advanced by Charles Darwin that present life forms have developed gradually from earlier, more primitive forms by means of natural selection, which eliminates maladapted forms while new forms are generated by spontaneous mutations.

Ex nihil nihil fit: Latin, **Scholastic** expression of the **principle of causality:** "From nothing, nothing comes."

Executive: In government, pertaining to the person or persons who carry out and enforce the laws, policies, and the like of the government.

"Existence precedes essence": A summary of the (especially atheistic) **existentialist** view that what the human being is, or human **essence,** is created by choices made by existing subjects.

Existential freedom: The denial that values are imposed on humans from without; human **autonomy** in the creation of values.

Existential meaning: The personal importance or relevance of an experience, idea, and so on.

Existential proposition: A proposition that affirms or denies the existence of something.

Existentialism: A nineteenth- and twentieth-century philosophical perspective that disdains **abstractions** and focuses on the concrete reality and freedom of the existing individual.

Extension: The property of occupying space.

External sanctions: In **Bentham,** motivations lying outside us (e.g., law, opinion, God) for behavior of a certain kind.

External world: The objects existing outside and **independently** of our minds.

Fabian socialism: A doctrine originating in 1884 in England, advocating a gradual and peaceful cultivation of **socialism.**

Factual judgment: A judgment that describes some **empirical** state of affairs.

Faculty: An agent or power by which the mind or soul knows and acts (e.g., memory, will, imagination).

Faculty psychology: An understanding of the mind that distinguishes its several differing capacities and their respectively different functions.

Fallacy: Mistake in reasoning, due to a failure in following the rules for the formal structure of valid arguments (**formal fallacy**) or carelessness regarding relevance and clarity of language (**informal fallacy**).

Fatalism: See *Determinism*.

Feinberg, Joel: (b. 1926) American philosopher, most noted for his contributions to legal and political philosophy, and especially his work on **moral** limits in the application of criminal law.

Feminism: Commitment to the abolition of male bias and domination in society.

Feuerbach, Ludwig: (1804–1872) German **naturalist** and atheist who interpreted God and religion as human projections upon the universe.

Final cause: The end or purpose of a thing.

First-Cause Argument: See *Cosmological Argument.*

Fletcher, Joseph: (b. 1905) American theologian and **ethicist** who popularized the notion of "**situation ethics.**"

Flew, Antony: (b. 1923) British **analytic** philosopher, **Hume** scholar, and antagonist of **theism** and Christianity.

Form: In **metaphysics,** the **essence,** nature, or "whatness" of a thing.

Form philosophy: Any philosophy that posits **Form** or **essence** as a central **metaphysical** category.

Formal cause: The **essence** or nature of a thing.

Formal fallacy: Mistake in reasoning due to failure in following the rules for the formal structure of **valid arguments.**

Formalism, ethical: A characterization of **Kant's** criterion of **moral** action, which stresses not the content of the action but the conformity of the will to **moral** principle.

Formalism, mathematical: The view that mathematical study is not about any real entities, either outside the mind (**logicism**) or inside the mind (**intuitionism**).

Forms, theory of the: The belief in **transcendent essences** that cause particular things, by "**participation**" or "**imitation,**" to have their general natures.

Fortuitous: Happening accidentally or by chance.

Foundationalism: The belief that all knowledge rests ultimately on fundamental truths that are themselves not subject to any proof and are the foundations of all other truths.

Francis of Assisi, St.: (1182–1226) Christian mystic, traditional example of **altruism,** founder of the Franciscan monastic order.

Frankena, William K.: (b. 1908) American **analytic** philosopher, best known for his contributions to **ethical** theory.

Free enterprise: See *Capitalism.*

Free-Will Defense: An attempted solution to the problem of **moral** evil: Human beings are endowed with free will by God as a condition for genuine **morality,** trust, love, and the like, though it also makes possible the introduction of **moral evil** into the world.

Freud, Sigmund: (1856–1939) German father of psychoanalysis, whose doctrine of the unconscious, and similar concepts, has greatly influenced some recent philosophers, such as **Sartre.**

Functionalism: The idea, especially applied to mind, that the nature of something is better understood in light of its function than what it is made of.

Galileo, Galilei: (1564–1642) Italian physicist and astronomer whose heliocentric model of the universe (following **Copernicus**) held far-reaching philosophical and religious consequences.

Gaunilon: (ca. 1075) Benedictine monk of Marmoutier, critic of **St. Anselm's Ontological Argument.**

Gender: Term used by feminists to represent the inequalities arising from the institutionalization of sexual difference.

Generalization, method of: A form of **inductive reasoning** in which a **conclusion** is drawn about some feature of all members of a class on the basis of repeated observation of that feature in particular instances.

Generative grammar: A hypothetical set of rules that will produce all, and only, the grammatical sentences of a language, usually associated with a particular school of linguistics dominated by **Chomsky.**

Genetic fallacy: An **informal fallacy** that directs attention to the origin or causes (sociological, psychological, etc.) of a belief rather than its **rational** foundation.

Geometrical method: A method for philosophizing modeled on geometrical procedures, most notably **intuition** and **deduction.**

Ghost in the Machine, the: **Ryle's** characterization of **Descartes'** influential idea that the physical body is inhabited by a spiritual **substance,** mind.

Good, the Form of the: In **Platonic** philosophy, a characterization of the **Form** of Forms, the ultimate principle of all Being and Knowledge.

Gorgias of Leontini: (ca. 525 B.C.) Extreme **skeptic** who denied the possibility of any knowledge of existing things.

Hanson, Norwood Russell: (1924–1967) Astronomer and physicist, who addressed issues in the philosophy of science and advanced a post-**quantum mechanics** analysis of matter.

Hard behaviorism: The form of **behaviorism** that extends itself beyond the task of describing behavior to the claim that there is no "inner person" beyond behavior.

Hard-determinism: The view that the will is **determined** ultimately by factors beyond the responsibility of the individual.

Hedonic calculus: The means of calculating the quantity of a pleasure by applying criteria such as intensity, extent, duration, and so on.

Hedonism: The **ethical** doctrine that pleasure is the highest good, and the production of pleasure is the criterion of right action.

Hegel, Georg Wilhelm Friedrich: (1770–1831) German **objective idealist** who viewed the world and history as unfolding by means of **historical dialectic** toward the synthesis of all opposites, an ultimate state he referred to as the Self-Consciousness of Absolute Spirit.

Heidegger, Martin: (1889–1976) German philosopher, a central figure in **existentialist** thought, who indicted contemporary persons for failing to address and assume responsibility for their nature as *Dasein*, sometimes rendered "being-in-the-world."

Heisenberg, Werner: (1901–1976) German physicist, pioneer in elementary particle theory, and propounder of the **uncertainty principle.**

Heraclitus: (ca. 500 B.C.) Pre-Socratic philosopher of the Ionian tradition who taught that fire is the ultimate reality, and that all things are in a state of flux governed by a divine, cosmic Law.

Herder, Johann Gottfried von: (1744–1803) German philosopher and poet, a **religious humanist** of undying faith in the natural and historical development of the human species.

Hick, John: (b. 1922) English philosopher of religion, advocate of the character-building or soul-making theory of evil (the experience of suffering is conducive to development, maturity, etc.) and **religious pluralism.**

Historical (Hegelian) dialectic: The mechanism by which history is thought to move toward its fulfillment, consisting of the continual and progressive resolution of one state (thesis) and its opposite state (antithesis) into a higher state (synthesis).

Historicism: The view that stresses the temporal and cultural conditionedness of one's perspectives, theories, and the like.

Hobbes, Thomas: (1588–1679) English thinker and writer who propounded **materialism** and a **social contract** theory of justice.

Human law: Legislation conceived by humans for the purpose of applying the **natural law** to specific situations.

Humanism: The view that human reality is the highest reality and value.

Hume, David: (1711–1776) Scottish philosopher whose defense of radical **empiricism** led to **skepticism** and **phenomenalism.**

Hume's fork: A way of representing **Hume's** doctrine that there is no middle ground between necessary truths whose basis lies in the **relations of ideas,** and **contingent** truths whose basis lies in some experience.

Huxley, Aldous: (1894–1963) English novelist and social critic.

Hylomorphic composition: Literally, **matter-form** composition, the view that all natural things require for their existence both passive "stuff" and active, determining **essence.**

Hypothetical proposition: A proposition in which the antecedent ("if . . .") conditions the consequent ("then . . .").

Idealism: In **metaphysics,** the theory that all reality consists of mind and its ideas.

Identical judgment: See *Analytic proposition.*

Identity, Law of: A thing is what it is; a true proposition is true.

Identity Thesis: The equation of mental states with brain states.

Imitation, metaphor of: A metaphor by which **Plato** attempted to elucidate the relation between sensible things and their **Forms:** Sensible things are mere imitations or copies of their ideal essences.

Immanence: The state of being within or **inherent** in something.

Immanent Forms: An expression of the **Aristotelian** claim, against **Plato's** doctrine of the *separated* **Forms,** that **Forms** are *in* the sensible things of which they are the **Forms.**

Immutability: The state of being immovable, not subject to change.

Incompatibilism: The belief that genuine free will is logically incompatible with **determinism.**

Indefinite Dyad: Literally, "Indefinite Two"; an ancient way of representing the indeterminate plurality, stuff, or **matter** that is molded, ordered, or determined by the One, which represents **essence** or definiteness.

Independence: In **metaphysics,** existence that is unconditioned by something outside itself.

Indeterminism: The view that some things, and therefore possibly the will, are free of **causal** determination.

Individualism: See *Liberalism, classical.*

Indubitable: That which is not susceptible to any doubt.

Inductive reasoning: Reasoning in which the **conclusion** follows with probability from the **premises.**

Ineffable: Inexpressible in language.

Inference: The connection by which the **conclusion** of an **argument** follows from the **premises.**

Infinite regress: A series of claims, explanations, elements, factors, and the like, dependent successively on one another without end.

Informal fallacy: Mistake in reasoning due to carelessness regarding relevance and clarity of language.

Inherent: Existing in something as an inseparable **quality.**

Innate ideas: The view that at least some ideas are inborn, present to the mind at birth.

Inscrutability: The state of being incomprehensible or beyond understanding.

Instinct: A pattern of behavior that is inborn, invariable, and unique to a particular species.

Intellectual consciousness: Awareness of pure (nonsensible) ideas in our minds.

Intelligible: Pertaining to, or being of the nature of, thought (as opposed to sense experience).

Intelligible species: A **Scholastic** way of referring to the general idea of something, **abstracted** from its particular instances of sensible things.

Intentionality: The fact, sometimes posed as a problem for physicalists, that mental states (such as beliefs, attitudes, etc.) are directed *toward* or are *about* something or *refer* to things other than themselves.

Interactionism: The view that **mind** and **matter,** in spite of their radical difference, stand in a reciprocal **causal** relation.

Internal sanction: In **Mill,** a motivation lying within us (e.g., feeling or conscience) for behavior of a certain kind.

Intrinsic: Belonging properly or naturally to a thing.

Intuition: The faculty by which truth is apprehended immediately, apart from sense experience or other ideas; in **Kant,** perceptual awareness of things.

Intuitionism: In **epistemology,** the view that we have direct awareness of at least some fundamental ideas about reality as universally and necessarily true.

Intuitionism, mathematical: The view that the objects of mathematical study are mind-created mental entities.

"Invisible hand": A way of representing how the interests of the **capitalist** society are promoted by mechanisms of supply and demand and **free enterprise,** aside from individual interests.

Irenaeus, St.: (ca. 130–ca. 202) Church Father and Bishop of Lyon, who wrote (in Greek and Latin) chiefly against early Christian heresies, and saw human suffering as a means of education and growth for the individual and for the race.

Irrational: Pertaining to what is incompatible or in tension with the principles of reason itself (strict sense), or with general experience, expectation, and the like (loose sense).

Jaggar, Alison: Contemporary, American philosopher writing on feminist ethics and social justice.

Jainism: A sixth-century ascetic **religion** and discipline (fourteen stages of perfection) founded in India in opposition to traditional Hinduism.

James, William: (1842–1910) American psychologist and philosopher who was a major contributor to **pragmatism** and was sympathetic to religious claims.

Jaspers, Karl: (1883–1969) German contributor to **existentialism** who stressed that awareness of the limitations, ambiguities, and anguish of human existence makes possible authentic philosophizing and, more specifically, the exercise of authentic human freedom.

Justice in Acquisition, Principle of: An acquisition of something is just if the something is previously unowned and the acquisition leaves enough to meet the needs of others.

Justice in Transfer, Principle of: A holding is just if it has been acquired through a legitimate transfer from someone who has acquired it through a legitimate transfer or through original acquisition.

Justice Principle: Happiness is to be distributed among as many people as possible.

Kant, Immanuel: (1724–1804) German thinker, most notably **epistemologist** who conceived **theoretical reasoning** to be **conditioned** by *a priori* categories, and **ethicist** who identified **morality** with duty and the good will.

Kierkegaard, Søren: (1813–1855) Danish Christian author and philosopher who stressed the individual's "**subjectivity**" or passionate commitment as the most important truth; often called the "father of modern **existentialism**."

La Mettrie, Julien Offray de: (1709–1751) French physician and thinker who propounded a strict **mechanistic** view of the universe, including animals and humans.

Laissez faire: French, "hands off," expressing the sort of economic policy in which the market is completely free of government control.

Laplace, Pierre Simon de: (1749–1827) French astronomer and mathematician who propounded a **mechanistic** view of the universe.

Legislative: Pertaining to the function (usually of an elected body) of making, changing, and repealing laws.

Leibniz, Gottfried Wilhelm: (1646–1716) German mathematician and **rationalist** philosopher who taught that reality is a harmonious whole, mathematically and **logically** governed, consisting of an infinite number of "**monads**" or spiritual **atoms.**

Lenin, Vladimir Ilyich: (1870–1924) **Marxist** leader of the Russian Revolution of 1917.

Leucippus: (ca. 450 B.C.) Pre-Socratic philosopher of the **Pluralist** tradition who identified reality with an infinite number of indivisible material particles *(atoms)* moving randomly in empty space.

Lewis, C. S.: (1898–1963) Oxford scholar of medieval literature and popular Christian apologist.

Liberalism, classical: The social-political theory that stresses freedom from undue governmental interference and views the state as the guarantor of the basic liberties and rights of the individual.

Libertarianism: The insistence on radical freedom with respect to both private interests and enterprise, and on a purely protective role of government.

Linguistic universals: Innate, fundamental features of structure and organization present in all languages.

Living option: An idea that, due to culture, environment, upbringing, and the like, is familiar and believable.

Locke, John: (1632–1704) English thinker, most notably **epistemologist** who inaugurated modern **empiricism,** and political philosopher who advocated **classical liberalism** along with a **social contract** theory.

Logic: The formulation and study of the principles of correct reasoning.

Logicism: The view that the objects of mathematical study are objective, extra-mental entities.

Lucian: (ca. 175) Roman author who parodied philosophical doctrines in his Sale of the Philosophers.

Lucretius: (ca. 60 B.C.) Roman poet, author of *The Nature of Things,* a poetic defense of **materialism.**

Luther, Martin: (1483–1546) German theologian, author, and Bible translator, traditionally regarded as the father of the Protestant Reformation.

MacIntyre, Alasdair: (b. 1929) British philosopher (now teaching in the United States) trained in the **analytic** tradition and presently advocating an **Aristotelian** and **Thomistic** theory of **ethics.**

Mackie, J. L.: (1917–1983) British **analytic** philosopher and critic of **theism.**

Malcolm, Norman: (1911–1990) American **analytic** philosopher who contributed much to the philosophy of mind and formulated an influential version of the **Ontological Argument.**

Malebranche, Nicholas de: (1638–1715) French Cartesian philosopher who attempted a solution to the **mind-body problem** by an appeal to **occasionalism.**

Manichaeism: A synthesis of Zoroastrian and Christian ideas effected by the Persian prophet Mani (died ca. 275), influential during the third to seventh centuries, characterized by a radical **dualism** of two principles, Good and Evil, conceived as ultimate realities locked in eternal struggle.

Marcel, Gabriel: (1889–1973) French Catholic **existentialist,** critic of **Sartre,** and advocate of **objective** values.

Marx, Karl: (1818–1883) German thinker and social theorist, the father of modern **dialectical materialism** and **communism.**

Material cause: The "stuff" something is made of.

Materialism: In **metaphysics,** the view that reality consists only of physical entities with their physical properties.

Matter: In **Aristotle** and **St. Thomas,** that out of which something is made and which is always potentially something different; in **Descartes,** a **substance** that is extended or occupies space; in modern philosophy, the **substance** that underlies and upholds **sensible** qualities.

Matters of fact: Ideas that are derived from specific experiences (e.g., "Water freezes at 32 degrees Fahrenheit") and thus bear upon and inform us about the world.

Mechanism: The view that conceives of the universe and everything in it as a machine—that is, as governed by a fixed and finite number of laws.

Medical materialism: A label contemptuously applied to attempts to undermine the religious and spiritual significance of religious experiences by attributing them to disorders of a psychological or even physiological nature.

Metaphysics: The study or theory of reality; sometimes used more narrowly to refer to **transcendent** reality—that is, reality that lies beyond the physical world and cannot therefore be grasped by means of the senses.

Mill, John Stuart: (1806–1873) English philosopher who contributed to many fields, most notably **ethics** and social philosophy; most famous **utilitarian** who emphasized the qualitative conception of "greatest" pleasure.

Mind: In **Descartes,** a thinking **substance,** that which underlies and upholds the various intellectual functions.

Mind-body problem: The difficulty of explaining the **causal** relation, supposing there is one, between the **mind** and the body when they are conceived as essentially different **substances.**

Mind-matter dualism: The view that all natural things reduce ultimately to two irreducible and essentially different **substances: mind** and **matter.**

Minimal state: A conception of the state that limits its function to the protection of its citizens' rights, properties, contracts, and the like.

Modified Sergeant Friday Principle: We should cultivate an awareness of what a philosopher has actually said: "Just the text, ma'am, just the text."

Monad: A basic **metaphysical** entity, the fundamental unit of some structure.

Monism: Metaphysically, the belief that reality is in some sense one, usually one in essence or nature.

Moore, G. E.: (1873–1958) English philosopher, one of the originators of the **analytic** tradition, an **ethical intuitionist** who coined the term "**Naturalistic Fallacy.**"

Moral Argument: **Proof** for God's existence: God must exist as the only adequate foundation of genuine (**objective**) **morality.**

Moral evil: The evil that springs from the human will, such as the Nazi death camps, the Stalin purges, the Manson murders, the Spanish Inquisition, and the Sand Creek Massacre.

Moral law: The **objective** and **absolute moral** principles that are imperfectly expressed in **ethical** codes, legislation, and the like.

Moral relativism: See *Ethical relativism.*

Morality: Belief in and conformity to principles of virtuous conduct.

Naive realism: The uncritical belief in an external world and in our ability to know it.

Natural evil: Evil or suffering that springs from natural causes, such as avalanches, droughts, the great San Francisco earthquake, and the Black Death.

Natural law: General and universal rules of conduct, both personal and social, derived from nature, which is conceived as rationally ordered.

Natural theology: The systematic pursuit of a knowledge of God by means of the natural intellect, unaided by **special revelation.**

Naturalism: In **metaphysics,** the view that only that exists which is, at least in principle, susceptible to scientific investigation.

Naturalistic ethics: Theories of **moral** obligations based on and derived from nature, including human nature.

Naturalistic Fallacy: Mistake of equating a *factual* **judgment** with a *value* **judgment,** or confusing a natural property (e.g., pleasure) with a non-natural property (e.g., good).

Neo-Platonism: A later and more mystical version of **Platonism,** most notably associated with the Greek philosopher **Plotinus** (ca. 200).

Newton, Sir Isaac: (1642–1727) English mathematician, physicist, and philosopher of a deistic character (God exists but is uninterested in his creation), and whose classical mechanics (cf. his laws of motion) greatly influenced subsequent philosophy.

Nietzsche, Friedrich: (1844–1900) German **existentialist** author and philosopher, severe critic of the "weak" values of traditional Christianity and advocate of the virtues of "the **will to power.**"

Nihilism: Literally, "nothingism"; generally, the rejection of any **transcendent** values or ultimate meaning.

Noetic: Pertaining to or conveying knowledge.

Nominalism: The doctrine that **Forms,** or **universals,** are merely names by which things possessing similar features are grouped together.

Non-Contradiction, Law of: Nothing can both be and not be at the same time and in the same respect.

Nonrational: Pertaining to what is other than or different from reason, such as authority, intuition, mystical experience, and the like.

Noumenal world: In **Kant,** the world of things as they are in themselves, as opposed to their appearances in sense experience.

Nozick, Robert: (b. 1938) American philosopher, most noted for his defense of **libertarianism,** and who views philosophy as a sort of humanistic art form in which many different positions may be legitimately embraced.

Objective idealism: The theory that things (ideas) exist **independently** of our perception of them.

Objectivism (moral): See *Ethical absolutism.*

Objectivity: In **metaphysics,** existence that is **independent** or unconditioned.

Occasionalism: The view that on the occasion of bodily stimuli or impressions God creates the appropriate idea and response in the mind, and vice versa.

Ockham, William of: (ca. 1285–1349) English **Scholastic** and **Franciscan,** one of if not *the* greatest philosopher of the fourteenth century, who advocated **nominalism** and otherwise argued against **St. Thomas'** theological **rationalism,** and is best known for "**Ockham's Razor,**" directed against the belief in the **objective** reality of **universals.**

Ockham's Razor: An expression for the ideal of **simplicity** or economy in explanation, attributed to the fourteenth-century Scholastic **William of Ockham:** *Entia non sunt multiplicanda praeter necessitatem* ("Entities are not to be multiplied without necessity").

Oligarchy: The rule by a few.

Omnibenevolence: The state, usually attributed to God, of possessing unlimited love or complete benevolence.

Omnipotence: The state, usually attributed to God, of possessing unlimited power.

Omniscience: The state, usually attributed to God, of possessing unlimited knowledge.

Ontological Argument: A **proof** for God's existence: God must exist inasmuch as the attribute of existence (or, in some forms, necessary existence) is part of his nature.

Original position: See *State of nature.*

Original sin: The traditional, orthodox Christian doctrine that the universal sinfulness of humans is traceable to Adam's initial sin.

Paley, William: (1743–1805) English philosopher, theologian, clergyman, and, most notably, proponent of the **Teleological Argument** and **"watch analogy."**

Parmenides: (ca. 475 B.C.) Pre-Socratic philosopher of the Italian tradition, founder of the **Eleatic** School, who taught that it is rationally necessary that reality be one and **immutable.**

Participation, metaphor of: A metaphor by which **Plato** attempted to elucidate the relation between **sensible** things and their **Forms: Sensible** things participate or "share" in their ideal **essences.**

Pascal, Blaise: (1623–1662) French mathematician and apologist for Christianity who argued for the necessity of **nonrational** grounds for belief, such as "the reasons of the heart."

Passivity of perception: The experience in which external, **sensible** realities impose themselves upon us, **independently** of our desire or will.

Pelagianism: Christian heresy, taught by Pelagius (early fifth century) and combated by **St. Augustine,** which denied **original sin** with its bondage of the will and stressed human capacity freely to do good.

Petitio Principii: "Begging of the question"; an **informal fallacy** that includes the **conclusion** of an **argument,** usually disguised, in one of its premises; also called circular reasoning.

Phantasm: In **Scholastic** terminology, the image, formed in the intellect, of a **sensible** thing.

Phenomenal world: In **Kant,** the world of things as they appear to us in sense experience, as opposed to how they are in themselves.

Phenomenalism: The view that we have no **rational** knowledge of anything, including the **mind,** beyond what is disclosed in the **phenomena** of perceptions.

Phenomenology: Philosophical perspective that emphasizes what is immediately disclosed in consciousness as the proper object of philosophical reflection.

Phenomenon: Literally, an appearance; usually, an object of sense experience.

Philodoxical: Pertaining to the love of (mere) opinions.

Philosophical theology: See *Natural theology.*

Philosophy: Literally, "the love of wisdom"; the attempt to give a **rational** and coherent account of the most fundamental issues, through an examination and manipulation of relevant concepts.

Physicalism: See *Identity Thesis.*

Place, U. T.: (b. 1924) English philosopher and psychologist, early advocate of the **Identity Thesis.**

Plantinga, Alvin: American philosopher of religion who has contributed much to current discussion of the **theistic** arguments (advocating a version of the **Ontological Argument**), the **problem of evil** (advocating a version of the **Free-Will Defense**), and religious **epistemology** (advocating "reformed epistemology" and "**properly basic beliefs**").

Plato: (427–347 B.C.) The first great systematic or synoptic philosopher whose work survives in real quantity, propounder of **transcendent Forms** (or **essences**) as the **absolute** realities, which are imperfectly mirrored by things in the **sensible** world and are known through the intellect alone.

Plotinus: (ca. 200) Greek philosopher, originator of **Neo-Platonism.**

Pluralism: The view that holds that ultimate reality consists of many things, and that usually emphasizes the disparateness or disconnectedness of things; in **Rorty,** the emphasis on the "theory-laden" or nonneutral character of positions or views.

Plutocracy: Rule by the wealthy.

Postmodernism: A contemporary interdisciplinary movement stressing the holistic, **pragmatic,** historically **relative,** and theory-laden character of judgments and knowledge.

Potentiality: In **Scholastic** philosophy, the **matter** in a thing by virtue of which it may be changed into something different.

Pour soi: French, "for itself," used in **Sartrean existentialism** in reference to conscious being.

Practical principle: In **Kant** and some other **moral** philosophers, truth or claim pertaining to **morality.**

Practical reason: In **Kant,** the reasoning faculty that is inspired by awareness of **moral** duties.

Praeparatio anthropologica: Latin, "preparation for humankind."

Pragmatism (pragmatic theory of truth): An American philosophy that identifies the meaning of concepts and the truth of propositions with their practical bearing, consequences, results, and so on.

Preestablished harmony: The view that bodily and physical states have been preordained by God to correspond at every point with appropriate mental states.

Preexistence: Usually of the soul; the doctrine of an existence prior to embodiment in this world.

Premises: Propositions stating the reasons or evidence that support or establish the **conclusion** within an **argument.**

Primary qualities: Those **sensible qualities** of a thing that exist **independently** of a perceiver (e.g., size, shape, motion).

Proletariat: In **Marxist** theory, the working class, standing in opposition to the **bourgeoisie,** the propertied class that owns the means of production.

Proof: See *Argument.*

Properly basic belief: A belief that is reasonable to accept, though without support from other propositions believed to be true.

Protagoras: (ca. 425 B.C.) A **Sophist** who taught the **subjectivity** or **relativity** of reality and truth.

Providence (divine): God's general direction over the world and of history; the realization of his purposes.

Psycholinguistics: The study of the mental processes underlying the acquisition, production, and comprehension of language.

Psychological egoism: The belief that everyone by nature seeks his or her self-interest.

Psychosomatic: Pertaining to the mind's ability to induce physiological states.

Pyrrho: (ca. 300 B.C.) **Skeptic** philosopher who emphasized the **relativity** of all reason, perception, and custom; founder of the ancient school called the **Skeptics.**

Pythagoras: (ca. 600 B.C.) Pre-Socratic philosopher of the Italian tradition who identified reality with number (i.e., numerical ratios, harmonies, etc.).

Quality, sensible: A feature or characteristic that is apprehended by the senses (e.g., color).

Quantum mechanics: The application of quantum theory (energy and other measurable attributes of **matter** are transmitted in discrete units or quanta) to the interaction of **matter** and energy and to the motions of **atomic** particles.

Quine, Willard V.: (b. 1908) American philosopher of an **empiricist** and **analytic** bent who has made major contributions to **logic** and the philosophy of language.

Raison d'être: French, "reason for being."

Rashdall, Hastings: (1858–1924) Anglican theologian, philosopher, and historian, known most notably for his contributions to **ethical** theory.

Rational theology: See *Natural theology.*

Rationalism: The affirmation of reason in general, with its interest in evidence, examination, and evaluation, as authoritative in all matters of belief and conduct (loose sense); the belief that at least some truths about reality are acquired **independently** of sense experience, through reason alone (strict sense).

Rawls, John: (b. 1921) American philosopher who has revived a **social contract** approach (that of **Locke, Rousseau,** and **Kant**) to political philosophy.

Realism: In **metaphysics,** the doctrine that **Forms,** or **essences,** possess **objective** reality.

Recollection, theory of: The theory that essential knowledge, or knowledge of ultimate truths, was acquired in a former existence and is recalled in the present life.

Rectification of Injustice in Holdings, Principle of the: An honest attempt must be made to identify the source of illegitimate holdings and to compensate the victims.

Reformed epistemology: An anti-**evidentialist** and **Calvinist** view, according to which belief in God is a **properly basic belief** requiring no **rational** justification.

Relations of ideas: In **Hume,** ideas such that, by virtue of their meanings and relations, one cannot be had without the other, as in the idea of a triangle and the idea of three sides; relations of ideas constitute the basis for **logically** necessary truths, but bear not at all on beliefs or reasoning concerning **matters of fact.**

Relativism: See *Ethical relativism.*

Relativity: In philosophy, the emphasis on the diversity (and thus non**absoluteness**) of reason, perceptions, customs, **morality,** and the like.

Relativity of perception: The inevitable variation in different persons' perceptions of **sensible qualities.**

Religion: Usually, a set of beliefs, related rituals, and **ethical** principles, centered on a conception of God, divine reality, or nature; more fundamentally, the commitment (involving belief and practice) to what is conceived to be highest in worth, power, reality, meaning, and so on.

Representative democracy: Rule by the people through their elected representative agents.

Representative perception: The view that our ideas represent or correspond to objects in the **external world.**

Representative theory of ideas: See *Representative perception.*

Revealed theology: Knowledge of God based on **special revelation,** as in divine self-disclosure in the Bible or by Jesus Christ.

Rorty, Richard: (b. 1931) American philosopher, associated with postmodernism, who exemplifies a **skeptical** stance toward traditional **epistemology** and who advocates a form of **historicism** and **pluralism.**

Rousseau, Jean-Jacques: (1712–1778) French author and social philosopher, best known for his idea of the "noble savage" in a **state of nature** and for his contributions to **social contract** theory.

Russell, Bertrand: (1872–1970) English philosopher, social critic, mathematician, and Nobel Prize winner, who was influential in the development of recent **analytic** philosophy.

Ryle, Gilbert: (1900–1976) English **analytic** philosopher who sought to clarify the "logical geography" of our knowledge of mind, and, most notably, to dispel the Cartesian myth of the **Ghost in the Machine** as resting on a **category mistake.**

Saecula saeculorum: Latin, "ages of the ages," usually rendered "world without end."

Sartre, Jean-Paul: (1905–1980) French author and philosopher, best-known proponent of **humanistic existentialism, Marxist** advocate of political causes, French resistance fighter in World War II, and winner of Nobel Prize for literature.

Scholasticism: The predominant system or method of theological and philosophical teaching during the Middle Ages, based largely on the Church Fathers and **Aristotle.**

Science: An organized body of knowledge about the natural (i.e., **sensible** or physical) world, together with a model that explains the world on naturalistic principles and that is in principle testable by observation or experiment.

Scientific method: The procedure by which **scientific** knowledge of the natural world is acquired: (a) hypothesis or theory building, (b) prediction of observable results, (c) experimental confirmation or falsification, (d) modification of the theory, if required.

Searle, John: (b. 1932) American philosopher of language, **cognitive scientist,** and **physicalist** who denies, however, that all aspects of the human mind are duplicable by machines.

Second Law of Thermodynamics: The physical principle that entropy, which is a measure of disorder, tends to increase with a result that energy (heat) is being uniformly distributed throughout space.

Secondary qualities: Those **sensible qualities** pertaining to a thing that depend for their existence and particular character on a perceiver and the perceiver's particular sense organs, brain, and related organs (e.g., color, taste, sound).

Second-order studies: Reflection on the history, nature, role, methodology, language, and the like of a discipline or inquiry.

Self-determinism: See *Soft-determinism.*

Self-intuition: The immediate awareness we have of our own selves, consciousness, mental states, and the like.

Sense datum: An object of sense experience as presented to the mind.

Sensible: In **epistemology,** the quality of being apprehensible by one or more of the five senses.

Sensory consciousness: Awareness of images produced in our minds through sense experience or **sensible** objects in the external world.

Simple idea: An idea that is unanalyzable into more basic ideas (e.g., red and anger).

Simplicity, principle of: One explanation is preferred over another by virtue of its employment of fewer and/or simpler factors.

Situation ethics: The view that **morally** right action is dictated not by general rules but by immediate circumstances.

Skepticism: A doubting or disbelieving state of mind (loose sense); the philosophical doctrine that absolute knowledge is unattainable (strict sense).

Skinner, B. F.: (1904–1990) American psychologist, most noted for his contributions to the theory and methodology of **behaviorism,** and who interpreted the person as a "repertoire of behavior" to be improved through technology.

Slave morality: **Nietzsche's** contemptuous term for traditional Christian **ethics,** with its "weak" virtues and incapacity to affirm life.

Smart, J. J. C.: (b. 1920) Australian **analytic** philosopher, **materialist** (advocate of the **Identity Thesis**) and defender of act-**utilitarianism.**

Smartness Principle: Always assume that the philosopher is smarter than you are—at least, for as long as possible.

Social contract: The agreement among a group of people to establish social organizations and regulations for the preservation of basic freedoms and rights.

Social hedonism: See *Utilitarianism.*

Socialism: The theory that advocates community ownership of land, **capital,** and means of production.

Socrates: (ca. 470–399 B.C.) Philosophical "gadfly" of Athens, who turned philosophical attention to definitions or the **essences** of things, and to **ethical** and political issues.

Socratic problem: The difficulty of identifying in the **Platonic** dialogues the authentic teachings of **Socrates.**

Soft behaviorism: The form of **behaviorism** that limits itself to the description of observable behavior.

Soft-determinism: The view that the will is determined by the character of the individual, and thus individuals are responsible for their choices.

Solipsism: The belief in the existence of one's mind alone, all other things being simply its perceptions.

Sophism: An argument possessing merely the appearance of forcefulness.

Sophist: Literally, "wiseman"; historically, an ancient Greek philosopher particularly adept in manipulative reasoning, sometimes accused of being a philosophical charlatan who "made the weaker argument appear to be the stronger, and the stronger argument to be the weaker."

Sophistical: Possessing the mere appearance of argumentative forcefulness.

Sound argument: A **deductive argument** that is **valid** and whose **premises** are true.

Sovereign: An individual authorized by the community to act on their behalf to guarantee safety.

Special creation: The view that the universe, including humans, was created immediately by God, all at once, in the form in which it now exists.

Special revelation: A self-disclosure on the part of God whereby he explicitly reveals himself in a book, person, event, and the like.

Species: A class of individuals possessing common characteristics or qualities.

Speculative philosophy: The attempt to raise and to answer the ultimate and most far-ranging questions and to make sense of reality and experience as a whole.

Speculative principle: A truth or claim pertaining to reality.

Spinoza, Benedict: (1632–1677) Dutch **monist** and pantheist, who conceived all reality to be God, an infinite **substance** possessing infinite **attributes,** two of which are known by us, **mind** and **matter,** which parallel one another inasmuch as they are two aspects of the same **substance.**

State of nature: The human condition of natural freedoms and rights prior to the imposition or development of social organizations and regulations.

Steady State theory: The **cosmological** model according to which hydrogen atoms are continually coming into existence to fill the emptiness created by receding galaxies, resulting in a universe that is always in the same state.

Stoicism: Greek philosophical movement beginning in about 300 B.C., emphasizing the divine, cosmic plan and resignation to its various allotments to individuals.

Subjective idealism: The theory that things (ideas) are dependent on perception for their existence.

Subjectivism: See *Ethical relativism.*

Subjectivity: In **existentialism,** the concretely existing individual as the point of departure for authentic philosophizing.

Substance: Literally, "that which underlies or upholds"; used in modern philosophy to signify the foundation that underlies **sensible qualities** or intellectual activities.

Substantial Form: A feature or characteristic that belongs necessarily to the nature of a thing.

Substratum: Literally, "that which lies under" (see *Substance*).

Supernaturalism: The belief in a reality beyond the natural (space and time) and (usually) upon which the natural is dependent for its existence.

Syllogism: A common form of **deductive argument** consisting of two **premises** and a **conclusion.**

Synthetic *a priori* proposition: A proposition in which the predicate adds something to the subject and the truth of which is known **independently** of sense experiences.

Synthetic proposition: A proposition that is not logically necessary, the predicate adding something to the subject.

Systematic doubt: The process in which anything susceptible to doubt *is* doubted in the interest of discovering something **indubitable.**

Systematic philosophy: A philosophy in which the central idea is worked out for and unifies a broad range of areas such as **metaphysics, ethics, cosmology,** and **aesthetics.**

Tabula rasa: Literally, "blank tablet"; used to express the **empiricist** idea that at birth the mind is empty, awaiting the input of sense experiences.

Tacit consent: The consent to and support of social organizations and regulations by virtue of an individual's continued participation in them.

Taylor, Richard: (b. 1919) American philosopher trained in the **analytic** tradition, and who has applied those techniques to existential questions.

Technology of behavior: The use of tools and techniques for the alteration and improvement of behavior.

Teleological Argument: A **proof** for God's existence: God, an intelligent being, must exist as the cause of the **teleology** (design, beauty, unity, harmony, etc.) of the physical universe; also called the Design Argument.

Teleological ethics: The view that emphasizes the results of actions as the test of their rightness.

Teleological suspension of the ethical: **Kierkegaard's** idea that in an immediate relation with God, universal **moral** principles, or norms, are transcended, and the individual acquires his or her injunction directly from God.

Teleology: The study of ends, goals, and purposes, often in relation to the physical universe.

Telos: Greek, end, goal, purpose.

Temporal: Pertaining to time.

Tennant, F. R.: (1866–1957) English **scientist,** philosopher, and theologian who propounded a "scientific" version of the **Teleological Argument** involving **theistic evolution.**

Teresa of Avila, St.: (1515–1582) Spanish mystic and reformer of the Carmelite religious order, author of several works on Christian spirituality.

Tertullian: (ca. 160–ca. 225) African Church Father whose writings (Latin) were germinal to the development of Christianity, and who is best known for his insistence on **special revelation** as against the deceptions of perverse pagan philosophies.

Thales: (ca. 600 B.C.) Pre-Socratic philosopher of the Ionian tradition who taught that water is the ultimate reality; traditionally called the first philosopher.

Theism: The belief in God; usually one God, transcendent, creator, and so on.

Theistic evolution: The belief that God uses natural **evolutionary** processes to bring about his desired effect.

Theodicy: From Greek, "justification of God"; the attempt to defend the traditional view of God's existence and nature against the seemingly incompatible existence of evil in the world.

Theology: The systematic pursuit of a knowledge of God.

Theoretical reason: In **Kant,** the reasoning faculty that employs and is limited by the *a priori* concepts of the understanding.

Third-Man Argument: A criticism of the doctrine of **Plato's** separated, tran-scendent **Forms** as leading to an **infinite regress** of explanatory **Forms.**

Thomas Aquinas, St.: (ca. 1225–1274) The most famous representative of **Scholasticism,** who drew largely upon the **metaphysics** and classical **empiricism** of **Aristotle** in constructing a complete Christian philosophy, including influential **proofs** for God's existence.

Thomistic: Pertaining to the philosophy of **St. Thomas Aquinas.**

Tillich, Paul: (1886–1965) German Protestant **theologian** who fled the Nazi regime to continue his work in the United States, and taught that the significance of Christianity lies with the **existential** power of its myths and symbols and that the "Ground of Being" is "above" the God of traditional **theism.**

Timocracy: Rule by the honorable, or at least honored.

Transcendence: Existence beyond, and thus unconditioned by, space and time.

Transcendental: In **Kant,** pertaining to knowledge or thinking that is con-ditioned by the mind's *a priori* concepts.

Transformational grammar: An early version of **Chomsky's generative grammar** that attempted to account for the underlying relatedness of certain types of sentences (e.g., active and passive) by proposing that all sentences have an underlying abstract grammatical representation, or deep structure, from which various structures are derived through a series of transformations.

Tyranny: See *Dictatorship.*

Uncertainty principle: It is not possible in principle to know beyond a degree of precision both the position and momentum (or any other pair of observables similarly related) of atomic and subatomic particles.

Universal idea: An idea that expresses the common nature or **essence** of things included in a class (e.g., table, dog, human).

Universalizability, Principle of: See *Categorical Imperative.*

Utilitarianism: The **ethical** doctrine that an action is right if, and only if, it promotes the greatest happiness for the greatest number of people.

Utility, Principle of: We are obligated to act so as to promote the greatest balance of good over evil.

Utopian: Pertaining to social or political ideals, as in the utopian or ideal society.

Validity: The conformity of a **deductive argument** to a proper **argument-**form such that if the **premises** are true, the **conclusion** must be true.

Value judgment: A judgment that evaluates something or judges its worth.

Value-theory: The study of value in all of its manifestations.

Veil of ignorance: A metaphor for the need temporarily to forget, as it were, our own vested interests with respect to considerations of justice.

Veridical: Corresponding to reality; true, genuine.

Virtue: An admirable trait of human character acquired through habit.

Virtue ethics: The theory that morality consists in striving to live a virtuous life, not following rules of right action.

Voltaire (François Marie Arouet): (1694–1778) French dramatist, historian, essayist, philosopher of a deist bent, opponent of religious evils, and contributor to the French *Encyclopédie,* a controversial, irreverent, multi-volume compendium of French "philosophy."

Watch analogy: An analogy introduced by **Paley** in evidence of God's existence: There must be a God who is to the universe as a watchmaker is to a watch.

Weil, Simone: (1909–1943) French philosopher, revolutionary activist, and mystic who died in England during World War II from self-imposed malnutrition.

Will to power: The central idea of **Nietzsche's ethics,** in which the "super-man" transcends traditional, conventional values, regarded as weak and life-denying, and celebrates creative and life-affirming values.

Xenophanes: (ca. 500 B.C.) Pre-Socratic philosopher in the Ionian tradition, who identified the underlying reality with earth and water, and advanced a **rational** and non-**anthropomorphic** conception of a single, supreme deity.

Zeno of Elea: (ca. 440 B.C.) Pre-Socratic philosopher who defended the thesis of his master, **Parmenides,** that reality must be one and **immutable,** by devising paradoxes that result from the claim that plurality and motion are real: Zeno's Paradoxes.

CREDITS

Text Credits

Definitions of "mechanism," "mechanist," and "mechanistic" from *Funk & Wagnalls Standard College Dictionary* by Funk and Wagnalls. Copyright © 1977 by Harper & Row, Publishers, Inc. Reprinted by permission of HarperCollins Publishers.

St. Thomas Aquinas: From *Summa Theologiae*, in *Basic Writings of Saint Thomas Aquinas*, Vols. 1 and 2, edited by Anton C. Pegis. Copyright © 1945 by Random House, Inc. Copyright renewed 1973 by Random House, Inc. Reprinted 1997 by Hackett Publishing Company, Inc. Reprinted by permission of Hackett Publishing Company, Inc. All rights reserved.

Aristotle: From *Nicomachean Ethics*, Martin Ostwald, translator, 1st Edition, © 1962. Reprinted by permission of Pearson Education, Inc., Upper Saddle River, NJ.

St. Augustine: From *Against the Academicians*, translated by Sister Mary Patricia Garvey (Milwaukee, WI: Marquette University Press, 1957). Reprinted by permission of Marquette University Press. From the book *The Enchiridion on Faith, Hope, and Love* by St. Augustine. Copyright © 1961 by Henry Regnery Publishing. All rights reserved. Reprinted by special permission of Regnery Publishing Inc., Washington, DC. From *On Free Choice of the Will*, translated by Anna S. Benjamin and L. H. Hackstaff, © 1964. Reprinted by permission of Pearson Education, Inc., Upper Saddle River, NJ.

Simone de Beauvoir: From *The Second Sex* by Simone de Beauvoir, translated by H. M. Parshley, copyright 1952 and renewed 1980 by Alfred A. Knopf, a division of Random House, Inc. Used by permission of Alfred A. Knopf, a division of Random House, Inc.

Lewis White Beck: From the Preface to his translation of Immanuel Kant, *Foundations of the Metaphysics of Morals*, 2nd Edition, © 1990. Reprinted by permission of Pearson Education, Inc., Upper Saddle River, NJ.

Ruth Benedict: From "Anthropology and the Abnormal," *The Journal of General Psychology*, vol. 10, no. 2 (1934), pp. 59–82. Reprinted with permission of the Helen Dwight Reid Educational Foundation. Published by Heldref Publications, 1319 Eighteenth St. NW, Washington, DC 20036-1802. Copyright © 1934.

Black Elk: Reprinted from *Black Elk Speaks: Being the Life Story of a Holy Man of the Oglala Sioux* by John G. Neihardt, by permission of the University of Nebraska Press. Copyright © 1932, 1959, 1972 by John G. Neihardt. Copyright © 1961 by the John G. Neihardt Trust. © 2000 by the University of Nebraska Press.

Albert Camus: From *The Myth of Sisyphus* by Albert Camus, translated by Justin O'Brien, copyright © 1955, copyright renewed 1983 by Alfred A. Knopf, a division of Random House, Inc. Used by permission of Alfred A. Knopf, a division of Random House, Inc.

Noam Chomsky: From *Aspects of the Theory of Syntax*. Copyright © 1965 by The Massachusetts Institute of Technology. Reprinted by permission of The MIT Press. From "Language and the Mind," in *Readings in Psychology Today* (Del Mar, CA: C.R.M. Books, 1969). Reprinted by permission of the author.

Paul M. Churchland: From *Matter and Consciousness: A Contemporary Introduction to the Philosophy of Mind*. © 1984 Massachusetts Institute of Technology. Reprinted by permission of The MIT Press.

Frederick Copleston: From *A History of Philosophy* by Frederick Copleston. Copyright 1946 by Frederick Copleston. Used with permission of Paulist Press. www.paulistpress.com.

William A. Dembski: From "The Intelligent Design Movement," *Cosmic Pursuit*, Spring 1998. Copyright © William A. Dembski. Reprinted by permission of the author.

René Descartes: From *Discourse on Method, Meditations on First Philosophy*, and *Rules for the Direction of the Mind*, in *The Philosophical Works of Descartes*, translated by Elizabeth S. Haldane and G. R. T. Ross (Cambridge: Cambridge University Press, 1911), I. Reprinted with the permission of Cambridge University Press.

Joel Feinberg: From *Social Philosophy* by Joel Feinberg, © 1973. Reprinted by permission of Pearson Education, Inc., Upper Saddle River, NJ.

Stanley J. Grenz: From "Star Trek and the Next Generation: Postmodernism and the Future of Evangelical Theology," *Crux*, vol. XXX, no. 1 (March 1994), pp. 24–32. Reprinted by permission of the author and the editors of *Crux*.

W. K. C. Guthrie: From *A History of Greek Philosophy*, vol. I. © Cambridge University Press 1962. Reprinted with the permission of Cambridge University Press.

Martin Heidegger: From *An Introduction to Metaphysics*, translated by Ralph Manheim. © 1959 by Yale University Press, Inc. Reprinted by permission of Yale University Press.

John Hick: From *Evil and the God of Love*, Revised Edition, by John Hick. Copyright © 1966, 1977 by John Hick. Reprinted by permission of the author.

Thomas E. Hill, Jr.: From "Ideals of Human Excellence and Preserving the Natural Environment," *Environmental Ethics*, vol. 5 (1983). Reprinted by permission of Thomas E. Hill, Jr.

William Hoffer: From *Saved! The Story of the "Andrea Doria"—The Greatest Sea Rescue in History*. Copyright © 1979 by William Hoffer. Reprinted by permission of William Morris Agency, LLC on behalf of the author.

Institute of International Law: "The International Declaration of the Rights of Man." A Declaration published by the Institute of International Law during its session held in New York on October 12, 1929. Reprinted by permission of the Institute of International Law.

Isaiah 55:8–9: From *New Revised Standard Version Bible*, copyright 1989, Division of Christian Education of the National Council of the Churches of Christ in the United States of America. Used by permission. All rights reserved.

Alison Jaggar: From "How Can Philosophy Be Feminist?" *American Philosophical Association Newsletter on Feminism and Philosophy* (April 1988), pp. 4, 6, 8. Reprinted by permission of the author. From "Love and Knowledge: Emotion in Feminist Epistemology," *Inquiry*, 32, no. 2 (June 1989), pp. 151–176. Reprinted with permission from Taylor & Francis, Oslo, Norway. From "Feminist Ethics: Some Issues for the Nineties," *Journal of Social Philosophy*, 20, nos. 1–2 (Spring/Fall 1989). Reprinted by permission of Blackwell Publishing Ltd.

Robert Jastrow: From *God and the Astronomers* by Robert Jastrow. New York: Warner Books, 1978. Reprinted by permission of the Carol Mann Agency, as agent for the author.

Job 38:1–11: From *New Revised Standard Version Bible*, copyright 1989, Division of Christian Education of the National Council of the Churches of Christ in the United States of America. Used by permission. All rights reserved.

Immanuel Kant: From *Prolegomena to Any Future Metaphysics*, translated by Lewis White Beck, © 1950. Reprinted by permission of Pearson Education, Inc., Upper Saddle River, NJ. From *Foundations of the Metaphysics of Morals*, 2nd Edition, translated by Lewis White Beck, © 1990. Reprinted by permission of Pearson Education, Inc., Upper Saddle River, NJ. From "On a Supposed Right to Lie Because of Philanthropic Concerns," supplement to *Grounding for the Metaphysics of Morals*, translated by James W. Ellington. Copyright © 1993 by Hackett Publishing Company, Inc. Reprinted by permission of Hackett Publishing Company, Inc. All rights reserved.

Martin Luther King, Jr.: From "The Ethical Demands of Integration." Reprinted by arrangement with The Heirs to the Estate of Martin Luther King Jr., c/o Writers House as agent for the proprietor, New York, NY. Copyright 1963 Martin Luther King Jr., copyright renewed 1991 Coretta Scott King.

Diogenes Laertius: Reprinted by permission of the publishers and the Trustees of the Loeb Classical Library from *Diogenes Laertius: Volume II*, Loeb Classical Library, Volume L 185, translated by R. D. Hicks, pp. 493–499, Cambridge, Mass.: Harvard University Press, copyright 1925 by the President and Fellows of Harvard College. The Loeb Classical Library® is a registered trademark of the President and Fellows of Harvard College.

Lucretius: From *The Nature of Things: A New Translation* by Lucretius, translated by Frank O. Copley. Copyright © 1977 by W. W. Norton & Company, Inc. Used by permission of W. W. Norton & Company, Inc.

Alasdair MacIntyre: From *After Virtue: A Study in Moral Theory.* © 1981 by the University of Notre Dame. Reprinted with permission of the University of Notre Dame Press.

Norman Malcolm: From "Anselm's Ontological Arguments," *The Philosophical Review*, Vol. LXIX, No. 1 (January 1960). Copyright 1960, Cornell University Press. All rights reserved. Used by permission of the publisher, Duke University Press.

Gabriel Marcel: From *The Philosophy of Existentialism*, translated by Manya Harari. Copyright © 1956 by Philosophical Library. Reprinted by permission of Philosophical Library, New York.

William R. Marty: From "Rawls and the Harried Mother," *Interpretation*, 9, nos. 2 and 3 (September 1981). Reprinted by permission of *Interpretation: A Journal of Political Philosophy*, Queen's College, The City University of New York.

Karl Marx: From *Early Writings*, translated and edited by T. B. Bottomore. Copyright © 1964 by The McGraw-Hill Companies, Inc. Reprinted with permission.

Robert Nozick: From *Anarchy, State, and Utopia* by Robert Nozick. Copyright © 1974 by Basic Books, Inc. Reprinted by permission of Basic Books, a member of Perseus Books Group.

Susan Moller Okin: From *Justice, Gender, and the Family* by Susan Moller Okin. Copyright © 1989 by Basic Books, Inc. Reprinted by permission of Basic Books, a member of Perseus Books Group.

Blaise Pascal: From *Pensées*, translated with an introduction by A. J. Krailsheimer (London: Penguin Classics, 1966), pp. 122–123. Copyright © A. J. Krailsheimer, 1966. Reproduced by permission of Penguin Books Ltd.

Alvin Plantinga: From "The Twin Pillars of Christian Scholarship," in *Seeking Understanding: The Stob Lectures, 1986–1998*. © 2001 Wm. B. Eerdmans Publishing Company, Grand Rapids, Michigan. Reprinted by permission of the publisher; all rights reserved. From *God, Freedom, and Evil*. © 1974 Wm. B. Eerdmans Publishing Company, Grand Rapids, Michigan. Reprinted by permission of the publisher; all rights reserved.

Plato: From *Apology* and *Phaedo* from *The Last Days of Socrates*, translated with an introduction by Hugh Tredennick (Harmondsworth, Middlesex: Penguin Classics, 1954), pp. 62–63, 71–72, 109–111, 111–112, 122–125, 159. Copyright © Hugh Tredennick, 1954. Reproduced by permission of Penguin Books Ltd. From "Euthyphro," reprinted from Lane Cooper (trans.), *Plato on the Trial and Death of Socrates: Euthyphro, Apology, Crito, Phaedo*. Copyright © 1941 by Lane Cooper. Copyright renewed 1968. Used by permission of the publisher, Cornell University Press. From *The Republic of Plato*, translated by Francis MacDonald Cornford (Oxford: Clarendon Press, 1941). By permission of Oxford University Press.

John Rawls: Reprinted by permission of the publisher from *A Theory of Justice* by John Rawls, pp. 11–12, 60–63, 136–137, 139–140, 145, Cambridge, Mass.: The Belknap Press of Harvard University Press, Copyright © 1971, 1999 by the President and Fellows of Harvard College.

Tom Regan: From "The Radical Egalitarian Case for Animal Rights," in *In Defense of Animals*, edited by Peter Singer (Oxford: Basil Blackwell, 1985). Reprinted by permission of Blackwell Publishing Ltd.

Richard Rorty: From *Philosophy and the Mirror of Nature*. © 1979 Princeton University Press. Reprinted by permission of Princeton University Press.

Jean-Jacques Rousseau: From *The Social Contract and Other Later Political Writings*, edited and translated by Victor Gourevitch. © Cambridge University Press 1997. Reprinted with the permission of Cambridge University Press.

Bertrand Russell and F. C. Copleston: From "The Existence of God: A Debate between Bertrand Russell and Father F. C. Copleston," from *Why I Am Not a Christian* by Bertrand Russell. © 1957 by George Allen & Unwin Ltd. Reproduced by permission of Taylor & Francis Books UK.

Gilbert Ryle: From *The Concept of Mind* (London: Hutchinson, 1949), pp. 11–12, 16. © 1949 by Gilbert Ryle. Reprinted by permission of Cengage Learning Services Limited, on behalf of Taylor & Francis Books (UK).

Jean-Paul Sartre: From "Existentialism," translated Bernard Frechtman. Copyright 1947 by The Philosophical Library, Inc. In Jean-Paul Sartre, *Existentialism and Human Emotions* (New York: Philosophical Library, 1957). Reprinted by permission of Philosophical Library, New York.

John Searle: Reprinted by permission of the publisher from *Minds, Brains, and Science* by John Searle, pp. 15–17, Cambridge, Mass.: Harvard University Press, Copyright © 1984 by John R. Searle.

B. F. Skinner: From *Beyond Freedom & Dignity*. Copyright © 1971 by B. F. Skinner. Reprinted 2002 by Hackett Publishing Company, Inc., by arrangement with the B. F. Skinner Foundation. Reprinted by permission of Hackett Publishing Company, Inc. All rights reserved.

J. J. C. Smart: From "Materialism," *Journal of Philosophy*, 22 (October 1963), pp. 651–653, 660. Reprinted by permission of Blackwell Publishing Ltd.

Adlai E. Stevenson: Excerpt from p. 174 from *What I Think* by Adlai E. Stevenson. Copyright 1954, © 1955, 1956 by R. Keith Kane, renewed © 1982, 1983, 1984 by Adlai Stevenson, Borden Stevenson, and John Fell Stevenson. Reprinted by permission of HarperCollins Publishers.

Richard Taylor: From *Metaphysics*, 2nd edition, by Richard Taylor, © 1974. Reprinted by permission of Pearson Education, Inc., Upper Saddle River, NJ.

F. R. Tennant: From *Philosophical Theology* (Cambridge: Cambridge University Press, 1930), II. Reprinted with the permission of Cambridge University Press.

Bernard Williams: From "A Critique of Utilitarianism," in J. J. C. Smart and Bernard Williams, *Utilitarianism: For and Against*. © Cambridge University Press 1973. Reprinted with the permission of Cambridge University Press.

Mark B. Woodhouse: From *A Preface to Philosophy*, 2nd edition, by Mark B. Woodhouse. © 1980. Reprinted with permission of Wadsworth, a division of Thomson Learning: www.thomsonrights.com. Fax 800-730-2215.

Photo Credits

P. 2, Hans Erni, Luzern, Switzerland. Pp. 6, 10, © Bettmann/Corbis. P. 18, © Culver Pictures. P. 36, M. C. Escher's "Waterfall" © 2007 Cordon Art B.V.-Baarn, Holland. All rights reserved. P. 41, The Vatican Museum, Vatican City. P. 59, © Culver Pictures. P. 75, © Alinari/Art Resource, NY. P. 85, © Bettmann/Corbis. P. 88, New York Public Library, Astor, Lenox, and Tilden Foundations. P. 112, © National Portrait Gallery, London. P. 118, M. C. Escher's "Fish and Boats" © 2007 Cordon Art B.V.-Baarn, Holland. All rights reserved. Pp. 135, 137, © National Portrait Gallery, London. P. 149, © Christopher S. Johnson/Stock Boston. P. 158, © Jian Chen/Art Resource, NY. P. 163, New York Public Library, Astor, Lenox, and Tilden Foundations. P. 172, Courtesy Richard Rorty. P. 189, Courtesy The Metropolitan Museum of Art, Catherine Lorillard Wolfe Collection, Wolfe Fund, 1931 (31.45). Photograph © 1995 The Metropolitan Museum of Art. P. 199, Courtesy Noam Chomsky. P. 219, New York Public Library, Astor, Lenox, and Tilden Foundations. P. 244, "Sky-watcher" by Susan Seddon Boulet, reproduced from her book *Shaman,* with permission from Pomegranate Artbooks, Petaluma, California, © Susan Seddon Boulet. P. 246, © 1966 Time, Inc./Time Life Pictures/Getty Images. P. 254, © Bettmann/Corbis. P. 261, © National Portrait Gallery, London. P. 263, New York Public Library, Astor, Lenox, and Tilden Foundations. P. 288, Religion News Service Photo. P. 300, © Culver Pictures. P. 317, © Scala/Art Resource, NY. P. 324, Photo courtesy The Claremont Courier. P. 330, © UPI/Bettmann/Corbis. P. 338, © Giraudon/Art Resource. P. 359, © AKG London. P. 361, © Culver Pictures. P. 364, © Gisele Freund/Photo Researchers, Inc. P. 368, Digital Image © The Museum of Modern Art/Licensed by Scala/Art Resource, NY. Pp. 377, 383, © National Portrait Gallery, London. Pp. 400, 401, © Culver Pictures. P. 420, © Réunion des Musées Nationaux/Art Resource, NY. P. 430, © Culver Pictures. P. 436, © The Museum of Modern Art/Licensed by Scala/Art Resource, NY. © 2007 Artists Rights Society (ARS), New York/ADAGP, Paris. P. 440, New York Public Library, Astor, Lenox, and Tilden Foundations. P. 451, The Hunterian Museum, University of Glasgow. P. 455, © AKG London.

INDEX

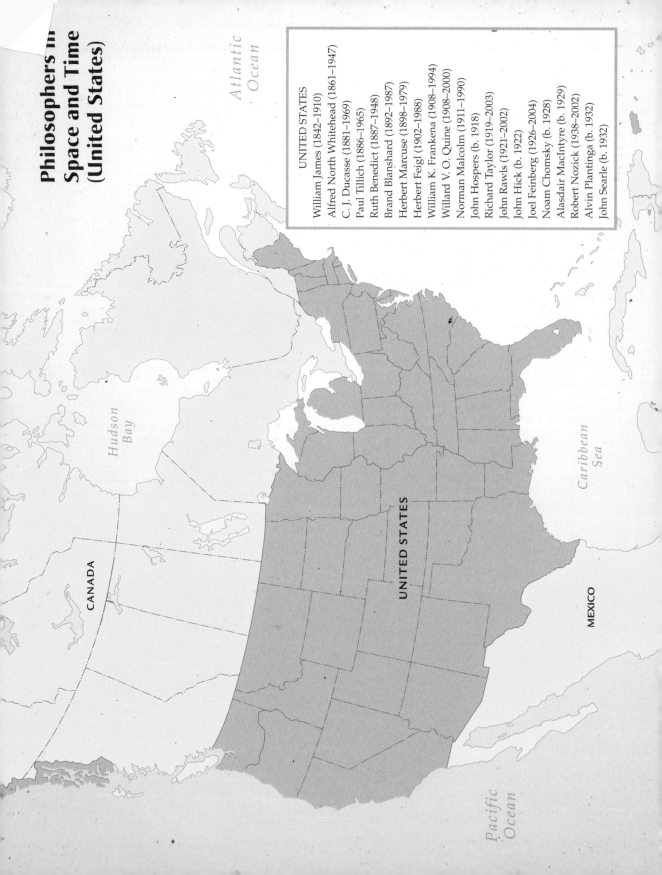

Philosophers in Space and Time (United States)

UNITED STATES

William James (1842–1910)
Alfred North Whitehead (1861–1947)
C. J. Ducasse (1881–1969)
Paul Tillich (1886–1965)
Ruth Benedict (1887–1948)
Brand Blanshard (1892–1987)
Herbert Marcuse (1898–1979)
Herbert Feigl (1902–1988)
William K. Frankena (1908–1994)
Willard V. O. Quine (1908–2000)
Norman Malcolm (1911–1990)
John Hospers (b. 1918)
Richard Taylor (1919–2003)
John Rawls (1921–2002)
John Hick (b. 1922)
Joel Feinberg (1926–2004)
Noam Chomsky (b. 1928)
Alasdair MacIntyre (b. 1929)
Robert Nozick (1938–2002)
Alvin Plantinga (b. 1932)
John Searle (b. 1932)

Atlantic Ocean

Hudson Bay

Caribbean Sea

CANADA

UNITED STATES

MEXICO

Pacific Ocean